EX LIBRIS

EDGAR BECKMAN

The Decline of Bismarck's European Order

Franco-Russian Relations, 1875-1890

"Si l'unité de l'Allemagne, que vous ne desirez sans doute pas plus que moi, venait à se faire, il faudrait encore pour la manier un homme capable d'exécuter ce que Napoléon lui même n'a pu exécuter et, si cet homme se rencontrait, si cette masse en armes devenait menaçante, ce serait notre affaire à vous et à moi."

The Tsar Nicholas I to the French Ambassador in Petersburg, 1849, as quoted by Alexis de Tocqueville in his *Souvenirs*.

The Decline of
Bismarck's European Order
Franco-Russian Relations, 1875-1890

BY GEORGE F. KENNAN

PRINCETON UNIVERSITY PRESS

Publication of this book has been aided by the Whitney Darrow Publication
Reserve Fund of Princeton University Press
This book has been composed in Linotype Times Roman

Clothbound editions of Princeton University Press books
are printed on acid-free paper, and binding materials are
chosen for strength and durability

Printed in the United States of America by Princeton
University Press, Princeton, New Jersey

CONTENTS

Contents

PLATES

AUTHOR'S NOTE

The number of those from whom I have received assistance and support in the preparation of this volume is so great that space does not permit me to mention them all.

My gratitude goes out, in the first instance, to the Institute for Advanced Study which, notwithstanding the retired status I have enjoyed ever since 1974, has continued to support my work in several ways, and not least by its incomparable atmosphere of understanding and consideration for all scholarly endeavor.

In this connection I must also record my debt to a whole series of research assistants, and particularly to Mrs. M. Yoma Ullman and to Mrs. Janet Rabinowitch, both mature scholars in their own right, whose enthusiastic approach to this subject, full of wit, imagination, and insight, would have been an inspiration to any historian.

Equally great is my debt to the faithful and long-suffering secretaries, Miss Janet Smith and Mrs. Constance M. Goodman, who have patiently typed, retyped, and typed again, endless pages of this treatise, sweetly concealing whatever thoughts they may have had about an author who could not do better than that in deciding what he wanted to say the first time.

For devoted help and gentle discipline in the final editing of the volume, I am greatly indebted to Mrs. Edith W. Kirsch, whose experience as a scholar and editor in the field of art history proved to be of no smaller value in relation to the history of diplomacy.

Among other individuals in the United States to whom I must record my debt, the following richly deserve this special mention:

First and foremost, my friend Charles Tacquey, diplomat, economist, and philosopher, for whose devoted interest and unselfish help on many occasions I have difficulty finding adequate words of appreciation; then,

Anna Mikhailovna Bourgina, of the Hoover Institution on War, Revolution and Peace, for her valuable and spontaneous assistance in uncovering some of the details of the early life of the elusive and mysterious Elie de Cyon; and

my friend and neighbor, Professor Fritz Stern, for his thoughtfulness and generosity in reproducing and making available to me letters from the Bleichröder correspondence as well as data from the Paris police files, again relating to Cyon; and

Professors Charles and Barbara Jelavich, of the University of Indiana, for their kindness in supplying me with materials on the Giers family.

I am greatly indebted to the Archive of Russian and East European History and Culture at Columbia University, to its long-time Curator, Mr. Lev F. Magerovsky, and to the living members of the Urusov family, for permission to examine the papers of the Russian diplomat, Prince L. P. Urusov.

In the case of Europe, my thanks must go out in the first instance to all those persons in France who so generously gave help with this inquiry, among others:

to my good friend M. Jean Laloy, at one time Directeur du service des Archives at the Quai d'Orsay, and to his deputy, M. Maurice Degros, for their kindness in making available to me the pertinent volumes of the French diplomatic correspondence;

to the Librarian of the French Foreign Office, M. Georges Dethan, and his excellent staff at the Library, whose hospitality and facilities I was permitted to enjoy while working on the French diplomatic documents, and to whom I am indebted for a long series of courtesies well beyond the call of official duty;

to the families-descendant of General Raoul Le Mouton de Bois-deffre, of General Félix Appert, and of Ambassador Paul de Laboulaye, all of whom went out of their way to make available to me such of their family papers as might shed light on the matters treated in this volume;

to Baron Guy de Rothschild, at the Banque Rothschild, for his help in guiding me to sources of information on French financial affairs of the 1880's;

to Messrs. Pierre André and Francis Ley (himself a diplomatic historian of distinction) at the Banque Worms, for their valuable assistance in uncovering the circumstances of the first French loans to Russia;

and to M. Pierre Caillet, then Conservateur en Chef at the Archives Nationales, who received me with great kindness at the outset of my work in Paris, helped me to find my way among what were then to me the mysteries of French archival collections, and even forgave me when, in a moment of true professorial absent-mindedness, I walked away with his hat.

In Copenhagen, I was received with much kindness, and my researches were importantly aided, by the National Archivist, Mr. J. Hvidtfeldt; by the Archivist of the Danish Foreign Office, Dr. Viggo Sjøqvist; and by the latter's successor in that position, Mr. Klaus W. H.

Kjølsen—to all of whom my special thanks go out for their interest and attention.

I was similarly favored, in Brussels, by the interest and assistance of the Grand Marshall of the Royal Court and former Director of the Royal Library, Dr. Herman Liebaers; of the Royal Archivist, M. Émile Vandewoude; and of Professor Jacques Willequet, Archivist of the Belgian Foreign Office—all of whom gave patient attention to my concerns and went out of their way to be helpful.

Baron Aufsess and Freiherr von Andrian-Werburg, at the Sächsisch-Coburgsche Hausarchiv in Coburg, were both helpful to me in my effort to run down the provenance of the "Ferdinand documents"; and I must acknowledge with special thanks their kindness in supplying me with microfilms of letters from the Coburg family papers.

Although the facilities extended to me in these instances did not go beyond those normally extended to scholars, I should like also to express my appreciation to the respective archivists of the Haus-, Hof-, und Staatsarchiv, in Vienna; of the Politisches Archiv of the German Foreign Office, in Bonn; of the Arkhiv Vneshnei Politiki Rossii (Archive of Foreign Policy of Russia) and the Rukopisny Otdel (Manuscript Division) of the Lenin Library, in Moscow, for the courtesies extended to me in those places.

I am satisfied that there is no system for the English transliteration of Russian terms which, if fully consistent, does not at times appear forced, and—conversely—that there is none which seems natural that is at all times consistent. I have, therefore, while basing myself on the old Department of State table on which I was brought up, not hesitated to introduce the "y" before the "e" wherever this seemed necessary to indicate the existence of two syllables rather than one (as in "Alekseyev" or "Griboyedov") or to indicate a strongly accentuated "yeh" sound in the Russian pronunciation (as in "Yegorov" or "vyedomosti"). In a very few instances (such as "Pyotr") "e" has been changed to an "o" to avoid what would otherwise have seemed an intolerable degree of violence to the Russian pronunciation.

Proper first names have been given the common anglicized spelling, if one existed, wherever they pertained to well-known people and were used alone or with only the last name (as, for example, "Alexander II" or "Paul Shuvalov"), but the direct transliteration from the Russian has been retained for the combined rendering of the given name, patronym, and last name in the Russian fashion (for example, "Pavel Petrovich Shuvalov"). In references to the authors and titles of Russian-language sources, however, I have followed the Library of Congress transliteration table, in order to facilitate access to these volumes by the reader who might wish to consult them. As a result, there will be slight variations in the spelling of some names, as between the text and the notes.

Where the names of Russian personages were of foreign origin, and where a common Western spelling existed, I have used the Western version ("Lamsdorf" or "Mohrenheim") rather than a direct transliteration from the Russian (which would have been "Lamzdorf" and "Morengeim"). I have done the same for names of cities and places; thus "Moscow" for "Moskva," "Archangel" for "Arkhangelsk," and "Caucasus" for "Kavkaz." Soft and hard signs have been omitted.

George F. Kennan

Princeton
October 1978

The Decline of Bismarck's European Order

Franco-Russian Relations, 1875-1890

INTRODUCTION: THE APPROACH

This study has its origin in a long-standing preoccupation with the First World War—as a phenomenon in history and as a factor in the life of our own time. It is a preoccupation dating back to a period when I was a young and rather lonely man, living in Germany and the Baltic states, and consuming (for boredom is the greatest of stimuli to intellectual curiosity) some of the great German and other war literature of the Weimar period: Remarque, Haček, Hemingway, Bulgakov, and others. The initial effect of this confrontation through the printed page with a reality—namely the holocaust of 1914-1918—which lay scarcely a decade in the past was to force me to ponder the immense apparent injustice which the recent war had represented. Why, I was obliged to ask, had some eight million men, most of them young and on the very threshold of the fruition of life, been obliged to renounce the privilege of leading out their lives, to abandon those lives in horror, agony, and hopelessness, whereas I, now no older than most of them were, was permitted, because I was born some four or five years later than they were, to live in comfort and safety, and to look forward to enjoying at least the opportunity for mature self-expression? This question had both religious and social connotations.

And this was just the beginning. With the passage of time, after years of residence in Communist Russia and Nazi Germany and with the phenomenon of the Second World War now before me, it was borne in upon me to what overwhelming extent the determining phenomena of the interwar period, Russian Communism and German Nazism, and indeed then the Second World War itself, were the products of that first great holocaust of 1914-1918: Nature's revenge, if you will, for the fearful abuse of the process of human life which that holocaust had represented, but a revenge inflicted, as seems to be Nature's way, on a later and innocent generation. And thus I came to see the First World War, as I think many reasonably thoughtful people have learned to see it, as *the* great seminal catastrophe of this century—the event which, more than any others, excepting only, perhaps the discovery of nuclear

3

weaponry and the development of the population-environmental crisis, lay at the heart of the failure and decline of this Western civilization.

Very well. But who could help, with all this in mind, being struck by the contrast between these apocalyptic results, on the one hand, and the accounts of the delirious euphoria of the crowds that milled around on the streets of the great European capitals at the outbreak of war in 1914, abandoning themselves to the pleasing delusion that in the pageantry of the moment—the blaring bands, the fluttering of flags, the fond fare-wells to departing reservists at the railway stations, the sense of a new national fellowship and solidarity—they were seeing the onset of some new and wonderful historical era, pregnant with pleasing self-sacrifice, adventure, valor, and glory? Were we not, it had to be asked, in the face of some monstrous miscalculation—some pervasive failure to read cor-rectly the outward indicators of one's own situation?

Of course, human ability to see into the future had always been lim-ited. But this twentieth century, we were brought up to believe, was an age of unprecedented enlightenment—the culmination of several dec-ades of spectacular scientific progress, marking the emergence, for the first time, of a civilization holding at its command all the manifold tools of modern science and a rich record of historical experience. In such a civilization there should have been, one might have thought, at least a reasonable measure of concordance between expectation and result— a reasonable ability to calculate the relationship between observable cause and conceivable effect. And yet, in the instance at hand, there was not. How to explain this? Must not the mature generation of 1914 have been the victim of certain massive misunderstandings, invisible, of course, to themselves but susceptible of identification today? And if so, should one not attempt to identify them? Where was it that all these people went wrong? Their problems of understanding were by definition different from those of later generations. The relevance of one to the other would never be complete. But was there not a possibility that if we could see *how* they went wrong, if we could identify the tendencies of mass psychology that led them thus astray, we might see where the dangers lay for ourselves in our attempt to come to terms with some of the great problems of public policy of our own day?

All this drew attention, once again, to the hackneyed subject of the origins of the First World War. It was a subject that had been extensively chewed over in the 1920's and 1930's by way of reaction to the war-guilt clause of the Treaty of Versailles, so much so that by the outbreak of the Second World War everyone was tired of it. But these earlier explorations had been inspired in large measure by the effort either to pin upon others the responsibility for the catastrophe or to deny it for one's self; and they had served, accordingly, primarily to cancel each other out. By the end of the 1930's, with the immediate trauma of the conflict now rapidly fading, it was clear to every thoughtful observer that the origins of the war lay on a plane far deeper in space than the policies and actions of any single government or group of governments, and deeper in time than the final weeks immediately preceding the outbreak of war in 1914.

The indications were, then, for a review of the history of the origins of the war. But here, another complication presented itself—one which was destined to baffle the historian increasingly as the century ran its course; and this was the overwhelming, indeed unmanageable, abundance of source material. With the passage of decades, new material was constantly being published, and enormous collections of documentary evidence, heretofore locked away in governmental archives, were now becoming accessible to scholars. Other historians—scholars with quieter lives, more erudite to begin with, and less burdened by involvement with the abundant vanities of the contemporary world— might attempt to stem this flood of new documentation and even to master it, intellectually. One or two did. These words are not meant to depreciate the value of what they accomplished. But their works, aside from unavoidably involving a high degree of generalization, tended to be of such dimensions that they surpassed the patience and curiosity of the lay reader and achieved their greatest value as works of reference rather than as ones of intellectual penetration. And it was clear that this sort of effort, in any case, was not for the likes of me.

I saw myself reduced, therefore (not just in this present study but in earlier historical efforts as well), to resort to a species of what might be called micro-history: to take, that is, a smaller sector of happenings rather than a larger one, and to look at it in high detail, as through some sort of historical microscope, with a view not to attempting to describe the totality of the relevant events, but rather to examining the texture of the process; not to recording all the significant things that happened but rather to showing how they were happening; above all to revealing by what motives and concepts men were driven, as they said and did the things that the record reveals. To the task at hand— the identification of those traits of the Victorian-Edwardian outlook that caused people to wander so blindly into the horrors of the First World War—this process would do, after all, as well as any other and possibly better than some.

Not the totality of the origins of the First World War but a small sector of them was, then, what was indicated. But why precisely the Franco-Russian relationship? And why as far back as the 1870's? Here, the answers were easier. First, because the Franco-Russian alliance of 1894 was without question one of the major components out of which the fateful situation of 1914 was constructed, and of particular importance as a factor causing what began as a Balkan quarrel to grow into a conflict involving most of western Europe. Secondly, for the simple reason that I had, for scholarly purposes, the languages essential to the study of this subject: English, French, German, and Russian— a mundane factor, if you will, but one which every scholar of diplomatic history has to take into account. But finally, and outstandingly, because nowhere was this euphoria, as mentioned above, more strikingly and abundantly present than in the case of France and Russia (one has only to recall the hysterical mass enthusiasm that attended the reciprocal fleet visits in the early 1890's); and nowhere was the contrast more dramatic between these exalted expectations and the utterly catastrophic results, for both parties, of the war to which the alliance helped to lead: for the Tsar's regime—total destruction, in an orgy of horror and civil bloodshed unprecedented in the modern age; for the French—a fearful sacrifice of young manhood, and only fifteen years later the spectre of Hitler at their borders, consequences in relation to which the loss of the many billions loaned by the small French investor to the Tsarist government pales into a deserved insignificance.

This study was undertaken then, with a view to examining the origins (and eventually, if time and strength should permit, the consequences) of the Franco-Russian alliance, and to seeing whether, out of the materials thus brought to light, there might not emerge something resembling an image of those habits of thought, those visions of self and of circumstance, those assumptions and readings of observable reality, which misled people into expecting, from this single international arrangement, results so dramatically different from those that actually occurred.

The present volume is intended to cover only the historical background, in the period 1875-1890, against which, in the early 1890's, the alliance was actually to be negotiated and concluded. For me, personally, even this segment of the entire story yields its conclusions; and they will be described at the close of this account. Whether they could not have been reached with less effort of research—whether the same conclusions could not have been arrived at on the basis of other secondary material already available—is a question I cannot answer. This was *my* way of going about the task. Every scholar has his own. I hope that the tale will serve, at the least, to refresh in the minds of people of this epoch the fading image of European diplomatic life and thought, as all this existed in decades now nearly a century in the past: a function the value of which exceeds that of mere entertainment, for in the people of that age we can see, not entirely but in larger degree than is generally supposed, ourselves.

The period of history dealt with here was one inaugurated, and to some extent shaped, by the great events of the years from 1864 to 1871: the unification of Germany; the exclusion of Austria from the special position she had previously occupied as a member of the community of German states; the defeat, humiliation, and isolation of France. These events constituted a decisive change in the political map of Europe. And for none of the European Powers was this change of greater significance—for none did it present more challenging problems of policy —than for the two immediate neighbors of the new united Germany to east and west: Russia and France.

In the past, France had been able to exploit, in the interests of her own security, the differences *among* the various German states. She was faced now, if she was to work her way out of the isolation in which the unhappy ending of the Franco-German War of 1870 had left her, with the necessity of looking for support outside Germany—support against the united Germany with whom, alone, she felt unable to cope. There were several places where such support could possibly be sought, but two of them were of special significance: one was Austria-Hungary; the other was Russia.

Austria-Hungary, for various reasons, was never a very likely partner. When that Power was theoretically available—in the years 1871 to 1879—France was not yet in a position to ally herself with anyone. When France began to become once more in serious degree *bündnis-fähig* (i.e., eligible as a possible partner in an alliance), Austria was already allied with Germany. Beyond this, the will was lacking on the Austrian side. There was, in Austria, no widespread spirit of revenge with relation to Germany comparable to that which existed in France. Austria had too many problems of her own, and too much need for German support in the solution of them, to be a suitable partner in an anti-German association. Nor was her military power such as to excite very extensively the interest of French strategists.

This left Russia: a country already known for its vast military manpower, and one whose policies, though for the moment not unfriendly to Germany, were still, as of the 1870's, not irrevocably committed. It was inevitable that France should look in this direction. The sense of humiliation and resentment flowing from the defeat of 1870 was profound and enduring. France was not accustomed to the experience of total defeat, in the modern manner. The desire for revenge permeated, in one way or another, almost the whole of French society. It would, as Bismarck believed, probably have existed, and this in scarcely smaller degree, even had the Germans not insisted on taking Alsace and Lorraine; but this loss of territory served as a convenient symbol and rallying-point for it. Equally profound was the belief that France would never be able to achieve this revenge by her own efforts alone: that to make this possible she would have to have an ally.

For these reasons, the thought of an alliance with Russia was never, through the entire period from 1871 to 1894, wholly absent from the minds of French political and military leaders. There never was a time when this possibility did not appear as the greatest hope, the highest ultimate objective, of French policy. There were moments when, for one reason or another, this or that French statesman would not be interested in pursuing this possibility as an immediate objective of policy, for early realization. But by and large, the logic of it was inexorable; and it may safely be said that to the extent crcumstances permitted—to the extent it was possible, that is, at any given time, to move in this direction without provoking preventive action on the part of the Germans or other undesirable consequences—the French were generally to be had for the enterprise. As one Russian diplomat put it to the French Russian specialist, Anatole Leroy-Beaulieu, in 1871:[1] "En prenant l'Alsace-Lorraine, Bismarck travaille pour nous. Strasbourg et Metz à l'Allemagne, c'est, pour la prochaine guerre, la France à notre dévotion." ("In taking Alsace-Lorraine, Bismarck is doing our work. Germany's possession of Strasburg and Metz means, for the next war, France at our service.")

For Russia, the situation was quite different. There was no exact counterpart, here, for the humiliation of 1870. Close family bonds united the Russian and German imperial houses. To the extent Russians were to persuade themselves, in the years to come, that they had an enemy to the west of them, it would be Austria-Hungary, not Germany, who would figure most prominently in this role. And then there was the ideological distaste experienced at the Russian court for the political personality of republican France—a distaste concentrated in the mentality of an absolute ruler who was himself the chief architect of Russian policy. This was a reaction which found no parallel in the mild, confused, and highly variable feelings with which French republican politicians viewed the institution of monarchy in Russia.

To be sure, there would be, at all times in the years following 1871, people of some influence in Russian society who would favor an alliance with France. Their voices would be at times weak, at other times strong. Public opinion, too, would fluctuate. But there would never be, on the part of responsible Russian statesmanship as a whole, anything resembling the degree of commitment to this prospect that existed in France. Russian policy makers, in contrast to the French ones, had a number of options. They could, of course, ally themselves with France; that was one possibility; but there were other ways they could survive. The question as to whether, or when, such an alliance would come into existence thus became a question as to whether or when circumstances would be such as to impel the Russians to opt for this alternative and to commit themselves to a common action with France.

Bismarck was, of course, at all times aware of this. He saw to it during the entire period of his responsibility for German policy, albeit with increasing difficulty as the years of the 1880's ran their course, that such a set of circumstances did not come into existence. In this he was effectively aided, down to 1887, by the passivity or lack of imagination that characterized the series of French politicians who bore (as a rule briefly and spasmodically) responsibility for the formulation of French policy. These included no one even remotely comparable in stature or in authority to the towering figure who, until 1890, faced them on the German side of the line. But eventually the circumstances in question did arise; and it is the purpose of the present work to describe the manner in which this came to pass.

To do this involved confrontation with a series of subsidiary problems to which, in the existing secondary literature, no fully satisfactory answers had been found. Were there really clandestine contacts, for example, running as far back as the early 1870's, between the French and Russian general staffs? Was the Tsar Alexander III justified in his suspicion that his ostensible allies, the Austrians and Germans, were secretly working against him in the Balkans and were really responsible for the successive discomfitures and reverses sustained in the 1880's by Russian policy in Bulgaria? This suspicion, after all, played a leading part in weaning him from his political and contractual relationship with the Germans and Austrians and placing him in a position where an alliance with France appeared as the only halfway-promising alternative. And did the Tsar wait for the lapse of his treaty relationship with Germany, in 1890, before moving towards this alliance with France, or were there really Russian approaches to the French along this line as early as 1879, and again in 1886?

To what extent, again, was the breakdown of Russia's relationship with the German and Austro-Hungarian courts the product of the activity of the civilian chauvinists in France and the Panslavs in Russia, or of the military hotheads on both sides? What value is one to attach to the extravagant claims of such shadowy figures as Élie de Cyon and

9

Jules Hansen to have been important promoters of the alliance? How did the French foreign minister, in 1887, come to feed into the Tsar's hands, under utmost secrecy, false documents designed to persuade the latter of the faithlessness of Bismarck? And was there a modicum of truth in the suggestions these documents were designed to convey, even if the documents themselves were spurious? To what extent, in other words, was the alliance the product of well-considered and compelling national interest on both sides, and to what extent the product of self-interest, prejudice, and intrigue?

I have felt obliged to satisfy myself as best I could about the answers to these and other such questions; and the reader, it seemed to me, had a right to see the evidence on which such conclusions were based. It is these considerations that have dictated, in large measure, the character of the book. But it is my hope that the work will serve, in addition to this severely scholarly purpose, to illuminate something of the diplomatic customs of the time, and to evoke that ineffable quality of atmosphere without which no era of history can be made real and plausible to those who have not themselves experienced it.

PROLOGUE: THE STRANGE EVENTS OF 1875

At the outset of the year 1875, Franco-German relations were, so far as anyone knew and so far as there was any reason to suppose, entirely peaceful. The end of the Franco-Prussian War of 1870-1871 now lay nearly four years in the past. The French had recently paid off—somewhat ahead of time, actually—the financial indemnity laid upon them by the terms of the peace settlement. They had also proceeded with unexpected vigor and effectiveness to restore the strength of their armed services. Despite the considerably smaller size of the French population, the size of their army was already approaching that of Germany. This, together with the open talk of *revanche* then current in certain sections of French opinion, was not unnaturally viewed with raised eyebrows in Germany, and especially by Bismarck himself. The French government of that time was generally regarded as one in which the monarchists had the dominant influence; and Bismarck suspected the monarchists, with their heavy Catholic support, of being the center of hostility to the newly created German Reich.

This was, however, in itself no reason for anxiety over the possibility of any early military complications. The restoration and modernization of the French army was far from complete. France's recovery from the war, generally, was only partly accomplished. Realistic people on both sides recognized that in these circumstances a French attack on Germany was quite out of the question, particularly in the absence of some powerful ally for France; and of this last there was then, and for long would continue to be, no sign.

As for the Germans, they had equally little incentive to make war on France at that juncture. They had just won a war against her. Their maximum territorial demands had been met with the acquisition of Alsace-Lorraine—met, in fact, in even greater degree than Bismarck himself had thought necessary or desirable. They had, therefore, no rational motive for wishing to launch a new attack on the recently defeated enemy; and Bismarck, as a man highly conscious of the fact that wars, if they were to serve any useful purpose, had to have con-

11

crete and realistic objectives, would have been the last to disregard this fact.

There were, to be sure, certain highly placed German military figures whose enthusiasm for martial exercises was such that they would no doubt happily have gone to war all over again, for purely professional reasons, then or at any other time, had they been permitted to do so. That some of these latter occasionally muttered thoughts about the desirability of attacking France while she was still weak, and thus putting an end to her effort of rearmament, may well be believed. But these were not the people who were in charge of Germany's destiny at that point; and there was no reason why anyone should have been deceived in this respect. Policy was firmly in the hands of Bismarck and the Kaiser; and neither of them had any desire to launch a new war, or any thought of doing so.

These circumstances notwithstanding, the spring of the year 1875 was marked by a war scare of major dimensions. By the beginning of April most of Europe had been persuaded that there was serious danger of an early outbreak of war between the two Powers. And then, in early May, just when this state of high apprehension had started to subside and people were beginning to recognize that there was no serious danger of war after all, there took place a visit to Berlin of the two senior Russian statesmen of the time—the Tsar, Alexander II, and his chancellor, Prince Gorchakov—from which visit there emerged a widespread impression (in the case of much of Russian and French opinion a lasting one) that the Germans had indeed intended to attack France, but that the Tsar had issued to them a warning of such force as to cause them to desist from this intention, thus preserving the peace of Europe.

These impressions were both wholly erroneous. There was no intention at any time on either side to initiate a war. Alexander II placed no credence in the reports of a German intention to attack France. Logically therefore, he could have given no warnings to his uncle the German Kaiser, and indeed gave none. When the whole affair was over he professed amazement, in fact, at discovering that he was held to have preserved the peace of Europe.

Yet the belief that the danger was real, and that only the Tsar's powerful word had prevented the Germans from attacking, endured in both France and Russia, became strongly rooted in the historiography of the period, and can be found reflected down to the present day in the secondary literature concerned therewith.

How are confusions of such gravity and such massivity to be explained? What circumstances could have given rise to them?

The details of this episode have been often recounted in secondary literature; and the publication of large portions of both the relevant French and the German documentation has provided a fairly extensive, and in general quite adequate, basis for retrospective judgment. The following discussion does not purport to be a new attempt at scholarly analysis of the great body of available material; but it will be useful to note those features of the episode that shed the most light on the answers to the questions just posed.

Let us first note, seriatim, what would seem to have been the initial major causes of the war scare:

1. The Germans, in February 1875, protested to the Belgian government over the failure of the Belgian authorities to suppress certain rather minor anti-German demonstrations in Belgium. The question was never of major importance. The dispute soon petered out in a trail of weary legalistic arguments. Yet the French foreign minister, the Duc Decazes, saw, or professed to see, in this incident a sign of German aggressiveness, alarming to France, and expressed this alarm in a number of his official documents.

2. The German authorities got wind of the fact that the French were attempting to purchase in Germany, through middlemen, some 10,000 horses of military quality. Bismarck thought this was a bit too much and imposed an embargo on the export of horses from Germany without special license. This got bruited about in the German press, a portion of which professed to see in the French desire to buy these horses a menacing intention on the French side to ready their forces for an early attack. The French press, for its part, professed to see in this exaggerated reaction further evidence that Germany was herself preparing to attack but was trying to throw the blame on France by demonstrating that the latter had aggressive intentions. The Duc Decazes took a similar view. Both of these interpretations were wholly without substance.

3. Scarcely a week after the German embargo on the horses, the French parliament passed a new army law, which provided, among other things, for an increase in the number of battalions per infantry regiment from three to four. The reform was a complicated one, scarcely to be understood by others than military specialists, and certainly not by the general public. It actually provided for no significant increase in manpower of the regular peacetime forces, and

could not, therefore, have been motivated by an intention to launch an early attack on Germany. The German government was correctly informed of all this by its military attaché in Paris, but some of the military leaders were reluctant to credit the attaché's opinion. The German press, too, took up the issue with more enthusiasm than discrimination, and professed to see in the new measure an intention to increase the French forces at once by 144,000 men. Again, the French were made suspicious by the airing of unjustified German suspicions, and saw this as a mask for aggressive designs on the German side. Such are the dialectics of exaggerated military fears.

4. In the ensuing days and weeks, the Duc Decazes sent out to the French envoys at the various leading European capitals a series of alarming messages, suggesting danger of an early German attack. These leaked both to the local diplomatic communities and to the press of the various countries and heightened the wave of alarm that was now spreading through Europe. They also had the unfortunate effect of evoking from some of the French representatives, as ministerial instructions are apt to do in all foreign services, despatches back to the Ministry, designed to reinforce the views (in this case, the fears) the minister had expressed.

A number of historians, reviewing the circumstances of this baffling false crisis, have come to the conclusion that the Duc Decazes, in spreading these alarming interpretations, was acting disingenuously, striving deliberately to create the impression of an acute danger where none existed, with a view to putting Bismarck in the wrong and arousing all of European opinion against him. To a certain extent this was true; but it was not the whole story. The writer of these lines, poking around among the tattered and crumbling pages of the Paris *Figaro* in the crowded storefront reading room of that publication on the Rue Montmartre in Paris, found in the issue for the 21st of May, 1887, some interesting memoirs of the amiable and honorable General Le Flô, who had been French Ambassador in Russia at the time of this incident. Le Flô, it seems, had spent the month of March 1875 on leave of absence in France. On the eve of his return to his post, in early April, he paid a call on French President Marshal MacMahon. He complained to the president that he was personally embarrassed by all this talk in France about the danger of a German attack: the Russians did not believe it; they could not understand the French jitters; he did not know how to defend the French position. "Ah," said the president, "it is evident that you are not fully informed." Whereupon he pulled out from his desk, and showed to the ambassador, a sheaf of documents, two of which were letters he had received from someone whom Le Flô later described only as "un des plus grands personnages de l'Europe, un prince." In the first of these letters, MacMahon was told: "You are going to be attacked in the spring." In the second, the interpretation was slightly altered: the war, it was said, had been postponed until September.

One contemporary observer, a man well connected in French military circles, alleged that the author of these two letters was the Prince of Wales; and indeed, this is highly plausible. It would appear that 1874 was the year when the future King Edward VII made Mac-Mahon's acquaintance. He had recently been visiting at the Danish court, a center for much of the anti-Bismarckian gossip then current in European royal circles. Even more recently he had attended the confirmation of the young German Prince William (the future Kaiser) and had visited on that occasion with the latter's mother (his own sister) and her husband. From these latter, both strongly anti-Bismarckian, he could well have picked up some of the irresponsible alarmist talk then current in German military circles.

Wherever the letters came from, it is clear that they made a deep impression on MacMahon and Decazes, as well as upon Le Flô himself, and influenced the further conduct of all three men with relation to the episode in question. The incident may stand, in fact, as evidence of the great and lasting mischief that can be done in international affairs by irresponsible and inaccurate gossip, when peddled under the seal of secrecy to persons in high position.

5. Bismarck, noting various evidences of this high state of alarm in the senior echelons of the French government, was puzzled but not wholly displeased by them. It would do the French no harm, he felt, to be made to realize that their talk of revenge and their busy program of rearmament were capable of producing dangerous reactions elsewhere.

This was no doubt the background, if not the cause, of the appearance in the German press, about that time, of a number of rather inflammatory polemic articles, the most famous of which was that which appeared on the 8th of April in the *Post*, entitled "Ist Krieg in Sicht?" ("Is war in sight?"). It was intimated in this article that while there was no proof that the French were planning to attack Germany, there was also no proof that they were not; and this was followed by elaborate speculation on the possibility of a French alliance, under the aegis of the Vatican, with Catholic Italy and Austria, directed against Germany—a vision very close to Bismarck's own unreasoning fears of hostile ultramontane influences.

Bismarck has often been charged with inspiring, if not dictating, this editorial. There is no adequate evidence that he did either. But there is also no reason to suppose that he regretted its appearance. It represented, in any case, the high point of uneasiness throughout Europe over the presumed danger of war.

With this, the series of alarming events came for a time to an end; reiterations of peaceful intent were exchanged on both sides; and by the middle of April the whole excitement had begun to decline. But at this point, the anxieties of the Duc Decazes were suddenly impelled to new levels of intensity by a further incident, no less trivial than the others but having to do this time, at least indirectly, with the Russians. It was a complicated one; and the description of it requires a deeper breath.

In the late winter of 1875, the German Ambassador in Petersburg, Prince Reuss, having hurt his foot, was obliged to go to western Europe for treatment. The Embassy was left in charge of a first secretary, Count Alvensleben. There was, just at that time, a minor difficulty between the German and Russian governments over the behavior of a Russian consular official in the Balkans towards his German colleague. Alvensleben had occasion to discuss the matter with the Russian chancellor, Prince Gorchakov. Gorchakov, old, vain, and pompous, was in the habit of lording it over junior diplomatic officials in Petersburg; and Alvensleben, intimidated no doubt by the chancellor's great prestige in contrast to his own humble rank, failed to hold his own in this discussion with sufficient vigor and firmness of speech to please his own high-powered master, Bismarck. (This was just the time when the tension between Bismarck and Gorchakov, arising largely from the latter's resentment of the former's now immense prestige, was beginning to reveal itself.) Bismarck decided, therefore, that it was necessary to strengthen the Petersburg Embassy, in Reuss' absence, with someone who would not be afraid to stand up to Gorchakov when the occasion required; and he detailed to Petersburg temporarily, for this purpose, a high-ranking German diplomat, Joseph Maria von Radowitz, who happened to be just then in Berlin between assignments.

Radowitz, the purpose of whose temporary assignment was no secret to the Russians, had, upon arriving in Petersburg, a polite and agreeable introductory talk with the Tsar (who was above these petty frictions), and then proceeded to call on Gorchakov. Radowitz's own official report of the conversation does not suggest that the interview was a particularly acrimonious one—certainly the usual rules of diplomatic courtesy were observed by both parties throughout. Gorchakov, however, appears to have been discontented either with the substance of the talk or with the mere fact and circumstances of Radowitz's appearance. His adverse reaction found its echo elsewhere; and Radowitz was very coldly received by the Petersburg bureaucracy and in court society. He remained only a short time in Russia. But his presence there gave rise to a rumor that the real reason he had come was to solicit Russian assistance, or at least Russian neutrality, for a German attack on France, offering as a *quid pro quo* certain concessions to Russia at the expense of the Turks.

There was, as documents now available confirm, not the slightest truth in this report. Nevertheless, the French Embassy at Petersburg took it up, believed it instantly, and passed it on as a confirmed fact to Paris, where it fell, as oil to the fire, on the excited sensibilities of the Duc Decazes. The same rumor, spread about in the Berlin diplomatic colony (by, among others, an unidentified "Russian lady"), reached the ears of the highly anti-Bismarckian and pro-Russian French Ambassador to Germany, the Viscount Gontaut-Biron. He, too, accepted it, then and forever more, as the gospel truth.

By the 21st of April Radowitz had completed his temporary mission in Petersburg and returned to Berlin. On the evening of that day, Gontaut-Biron encountered him at a dinner at the British Embassy. Well aware of the importance attached by his own foreign minister to the possible enlistment of Russian help in restraining the presumably warbent Germans, and misled by the rumors surrounding the recent Radowitz mission to Petersburg (which caused him to suppose Radowitz to be a much more important figure, and closer to Bismarck, than he really was), Gontaut-Biron drew the German guest aside after dinner and proceeded, with what must have been a passionate interest and intensity, to draw him out.

The conversation was at first unexceptional. The two men agreed that the war scare had abated. Each expressed pleasure and relief over this fact. Then, however, the talk fell, most unhappily, on Alsace-Lorraine; and Radowitz, who later freely admitted that he would have done better to fall silent at this point, permitted himself to be drawn out.

What was actually said, we shall never know for sure. Radowitz, to whom it seems not to have occurred at the moment that the talk might be of any great importance, later claimed that all he had tried to do was to explain to the ambassador that if the French persisted in their unwillingness to accept the loss of the two provinces, and if the talk of *revanche* continued and came to constitute a fixed objective of French policy, then there would be people in Germany (he evidently had mainly the military leaders in mind) who would someday begin to say: "If we see a French attack coming, would it not be better for us to choose the moment of conflict from the standpoint of our convenience, rather than permit the French to choose it?" Radowitz did not say this was his own view. Gontaut-Biron, however, chose to interpret it as a deliberate threat and rationalization of an early German attack, all the more important for being uttered by one who was allegedly an intimate of Bismarck, authorized to express the latter's views.

This was, of course, grist—of no poor quality—to Decazes's mill. Upon the receipt of Gontaut's long despatch reporting the conversation, he did not lose a moment's time. He sat right down and drafted a circular to the French Embassies in all the leading European posts, attaching to it Gontaut's despatch, somewhat distorting the meaning of that despatch to make Radowitz's remarks look even worse than Gontaut had made them look, and asking the various ambassadors to be guided by this material in their talks with the leaders of the governments to which they were accredited.

Curiously enough, in the penultimate paragraph of this document, the minister also gave it as his impression that in recent days there had been an improvement in the situation, and suggested that this was due to the wise and impelling advice given (to the Germans, presumably) by "le Cabinet de St. Pétersbourg." (This, although the Russians, to date, had said nothing at all to the Germans about the whole matter.) Attached to this material, as sent to Le Flô, was also a personal letter from the foreign minister which was even more inflammatory in language than the circular itself.

Le Flô had already had occasion, before receiving these materials, to speak to the Tsar about the French fears of a German attack. The Tsar, on that occasion, had expressed disbelief in the reality of these fears, saying in effect to the ambassador: "Relax. You have nothing to fear at this point. If there should ever be real danger of war, you would learn of it in good time, and from no one other than myself. I would be the first to tell you."

Now, Decazes, in his personal letter, took up this statement of the Tsar (which Le Flô had duly reported to Paris) and magnified it out of all relation to its original meaning, professing to see in it a limited assurance of Russian support in the event of a German attack. Yet even this failed fully to reassure him. The Tsar's intervention would be all right, he wrote, if it were exercised in time. "But," he went on,

> it is just because his will to maintain peace is well known in Berlin, it is because they know that he would energetically protest against any perverse designs, it is just because of all this that I cannot divest myself of the fear that those designs will be carefully hidden from him, and that one day they (the Germans) will make up their minds to confront him with an accomplished fact. I should have that fear no longer, and my security would be absolute, the day his Majesty would declare that he would look

18

on a surprise as on an insult, and *that he would not permit such an iniquity to pass.* One word like that would simply insure the peace of the world, and it would be worthy of Emperor Alexander to utter it. His Majesty has deigned to tell you that in the day of danger we would be warned, and warned by him. . . . But if he himself were not warned in time, his Majesty would be obliged to understand and to acknowledge that he also had been deceived and taken by surprise, and that, as it were, he had been made the involuntary accomplice of the trap laid for us, and I, moreover, wish to be certain that his Majesty would avenge what would practically constitute an insult to himself, and would shield with his sword those who trusted to his aid.[1]

Le Flô, on receiving these various documents, took them to Gorchakov. Instead of letting Le Flô describe them, Gorchakov insisted on reading them himself, and then prevailed upon the hesitant ambassador to let him take them and show them to the Tsar. This was done. Both the Tsar and Gorchakov should have recognized without difficulty, from the language of these communications, what the French foreign minister was attempting to do: namely, to extract, first, a promise of Russian military support in the event of another conflict with Germany; and secondly, on the basis of that guaranty, to induce the Russians to issue a warning to the Germans that they would have Russia to deal with if they got themselves into a conflict with the French. This was strong medicine; and the two Russian statesmen would have done well, if they did not want this interpretation to be put on their words, to make it clear to the French at that point that they did not believe in the reality of the fancied threat and were therefore not prepared to make any suggestions to the Germans about policy towards France in the existing circumstance.

This they failed to do. Aside from a mild observation by Gorchakov to the ambassador that the reference to Russia's drawing her sword was going a bit far (they did not anticipate, Gorchakov said, any need to be drawing swords; things would be settled without the need for such expedients), they contented themselves with reaffirming what the Tsar had said on the earlier occasion, namely, that if such a danger should ever arise, the French would learn of it from him. And with that they unwisely fell silent, leaving the ambassador to glow with excitement from the impression that he had committed the Russian monarch to something little short of an outright military alliance. "This," he reported triumphantly to his equally exalted Foreign Minister, "was a new and precious affirmation of an important promise which thus remains intact, and (constitutes) a major guaranty of our security."

Four days later, the Tsar and Gorchakov arrived in Berlin, en route to European watering places. While there, each saw his opposite number: the Tsar—his uncle, Kaiser William I; Gorchakov—the German chancellor, Bismarck.

The talk between the two Emperors could not have gone off more amicably. Neither seems fully to have understood the game that was now being played by the French foreign minister. They agreed that there was no reality behind the war scare. The Kaiser deplored the mischief-making by the press, to which he was inclined to attribute the whole confusion. The two monarchs parted on the best of terms, apparently unaware that anything of great importance was afoot.

Not so, the two chancellors. Bismarck was well aware, by this time, that the Russians were being pressed by the French to urge him to desist from an attack he had had no intention of launching; and he was far from pleased to find himself placed in this position. Just what was said in the course of the interview, we do not know. Gorchakov assured the French Ambassador, immediately afterwards, that there was no question of war; and he inquired delicately, once more, whether the French fears had not been slightly exaggerated—a query which appears to have made no impression on the ambassador or, when relayed to Paris, on his foreign minister. But Gorchakov said nothing to suggest that his interview with the German chancellor had been a tense or unpleasant one.

Bismarck, on the other hand, writing of the interview many years later, gave quite a different picture. According to this version, he overwhelmed his Russian colleague with bitter and sardonic reproaches over the whole comedy that he felt was being enacted. Why, he claimed to have asked, did Gorchakov have to come suddenly hopping onto his shoulders from behind with this absurd approach? Was this the behavior of a friend? What did the Russians want of him, anyway? Would Gorchakov like him to issue five-franc pieces with the inscription: "Gorchakov protège la France"? Or would Gorchakov prefer that he, Bismarck, build a theater in the German Embassy in Paris, where Gorchakov could appear, under a placard with this same slogan, attired as a guardian angel in a white robe?

Whether these words were actually uttered on the occasion in question or were the product of the fanciful memory of an aging man, there is no reason to doubt that they were accurately descriptive of Bismarck's outraged feelings of that moment, and that he unburdened himself of these feelings in one way or another. This being the case, the matter might have rested there if nothing more had been said. But following the visit each of the two Russian statesmen, Gorchakov and the Tsar, sent off confidential messages, each of which was leaked to the press, in each case in garbled form, and each of which tended, in its garbled form, to confirm precisely the thesis the French were concerned to establish.

Gorchakov's message was a circular telegram to the various Russian diplomatic missions, to the effect that "The Russian Emperor is leaving Berlin entirely convinced of the conciliatory disposition which prevails there and which assures the maintenance of peace." The message, slightly but significantly garbled so as to read "which now assures peace" (instead of "assures the maintenance of peace"),* promptly found its way into the press and was widely reproduced there. How was it to be understood? Did the "conciliatory disposition" come into existence in Berlin only after the Tsar's arrival there? And, if so, was it not precisely his visit, and his warning words to the Kaiser, that had made the difference?

The second statement was both more serious and more absurd. At the Tsar's request, Gorchakov addressed a telegram in the monarch's name to the latter's sister, the Queen of Württemberg, then at her place of residence in Baden. The message appears to have consisted of, or included, a statement to the effect that "J'emporte de Berlin assurances formelles de la paix." ("I bring from Berlin formal assurances of peace.") This, leaked by the Baden telegraph office to a local journalist, was reproduced by the latter as: "L'emporté de Berlin donne des assurances formelles de la paix." ("The frenzied one of Berlin gives formal assurances of peace.") This version, with its unheard-of insult to the Germans, came to the attention of the rest of the German press, and was the subject of angry German editorials. And it was, of course, also noted in France, with both amusement and delight.

With this, the tragicomical episode of the 1875 war scare and the supposed rescuing of France from German attack by Russian intervention came to an end. The French had won, hands down. On European opinion of the time, as well as on the subsequent historiography of the period, an indelible impression had been produced that while French fears might have been slightly exaggerated, there must have been some substance to them: there must have been, that is, some danger of a German preventative attack; but that this danger, whatever it amounted to, had been allayed by the strong minatory words of the Russian Tsar, warning the Germans that they would have Russia to deal with as well as France if they dared to touch the latter country. This was an instance in which French diplomacy, inspired by passion, determination, energy,

* This garble was understandable: the phrase "qui assurent maintien de la paix" became "qui assurent maintenant la paix." (A facsimile of the original telegram will be found in A. Z. Manfred, *Obrazovanie russko-frantsuzskogo soyuza* [Moscow: Nauka, 1975] at p. 98.)

21

imagination, and finesse, had prevailed with ease over the sleepy complacency of the Germans, not only creating thereby a brilliant political fiction but establishing it for decades to come in the historical record of the period.

The success of this manoeuvre cannot be laid, of course, exclusively to the diplomacy of the French. The Germans also had their share of the blame. Bismarck's emotional fixation about the dangers presented to Germany by Catholic Europe played into the hands of his detractors, as did his readiness to let the war scare take its course, believing that it would frighten the French into a more reasonable attitude. Even more to blame than the German chancellor himself was, of course, the jittery and belligerent German press.

The contribution made by the Russians is also not to be underrated. The Tsar and Gorchakov, while willing to assure the French Ambassador privately that they saw no evidence of any intention on the part of the Germans to attack France, at no time indicated this publicly. By failing to convey to the European public the true circumstances of their visit to Berlin, and by allowing the impression to be established that their talks with the Germans were the cause of the rapid decline of the danger of war, they played into the hands of the French and made possible the success of Decazes' entire operation. For this, Gorchakov, jealous of Bismarck and apparently not above indulging in a certain wicked enjoyment at the latter's discomfiture, was chiefly to blame; but the Tsar, too, by his reiteration of a cloudy and ambivalent statement, and by ignoring the fact that the French were only too obviously misinterpreting that statement, also made, consciously or otherwise, an important contribution of his own.

Nevertheless, the principal architect of the confusion was, of course, the Duc Decazes. To what extent this manoeuvre on his part was disingenuous, or to what extent he was acting in good faith under the influence of the misinformation given to MacMahon by the unidentified crowned head, and to what extent he really believed that the Russians had saved France by preventing a German attack: this, we shall presumably never know. Granting the human capacity for self-deception in the service of self-interest, the answer may well be: a bit of both. It must be conceded, in any case, that he played his cards with consummate skill and effectiveness.

———————

This episode, preceding by nearly twenty years the final conclusion of the alliance to the origins of which this volume is addressed, has been recounted at this point because of the profound and enduring influence it exerted, over all the ensuing twenty years, on French opinion and above all on French attitudes towards Russia. From this moment on, it would be the unshakable conviction of many millions of Frenchmen, including most French statesmen, that the key not only to France's security but also to the solution of her greatest international difficulties— the key to the expunging of the humiliation of the Franco-Prussian War, to the recovery of lost provinces, to the restoration of France's lost leadership in Europe and, along with that, of her pride, her self-confidence, and her belief in herself and her future—lay with Russia, and nowhere else. That this impression involved a wishful and unrealistic image of what Russia really was, of what could be reasonably expected of her, and of what it might do to her to become an instrument in the hands of a western European country, to be wielded for the settlement of quarrels other than her own.

All this was something that would not be demonstrated until the sad and terrible days of the autumn of 1917, when the Russian Empire, breaking up in chaos and horror (and not least as a result, of its effort to honor the Franco-Russian alliance), would fail not only France but the Western allies in general. Until that time, the illusion that Russia was the answer to France's problems would endure. Never for a moment would it be absent from the minds of French statesmen, French journalists, French patriots of every brand. Without it, the tale that follows —of the ways and stages by which both France and Russia felt their way towards a fateful military alliance—would be unintelligible.

Part I

THE BACKGROUND

Chapter One

RUSSIAN OPINION AND THE WAR WITH TURKEY

It would be idle, in considering the Russia of the 1870's, to speak of such a thing as "public opinion" in connection with international affairs. The mass of the Russian people, of whom the peasantry constituted some 80 percent, had no knowledge of the intricacies of high diplomacy and no means of arriving at judgments on questions of foreign policy. This did not, as a rule, enter into their concerns. At the other end of the spectrum stood, of course, the Tsar himself, who, being an autocrat and not a constitutional monarch, had, in theory at least, unlimited power to shape Russia's external relations according to his own judgments and desires.

Between these two extremes there was, however, in the late nineteenth century, a considerable body of people who had it in their power to exert, directly or indirectly, some degree of influence upon the reactions and decisions of the Tsar and his responsible ministers. These included persons of elevated social status at court (particularly members of the imperial family), higher officials of the governmental bureaucracy, senior clerical figures, prominent businessmen, members of the high command of army and navy, and, finally, leading editors, publicists, and writers. Since influence of this nature was a relative, constantly changing, and not easily identifiable quantity, it is impossible to say how numerous these people were. They probably numbered in the hundreds, scarcely in the thousands.

Among this influential element there was one important faction composed of people who were reasonably content with Russia's international position, who wanted to see peace preserved in her external relationships, and who favored, for this reason, the continued cultivation—even at the cost of a generally conciliatory and restrained foreign policy—of friendly and peaceful relations with Russia's two immediate western Great-Power neighbors: Germany and Austria-Hungary. The members of this faction, concentrated largely in the capital city of Petersburg, tended to be either people of conservative disposition or people of a certain international sophistication, or both. They included a few of the higher nobility; at least one grand duke (Mikhail Nikolaye-vich, brother of Tsar Alexander II, and married to a German princess); one or two cabinet ministers in fields other than foreign affairs; a handful of the ambassadors abroad; figures prominent in certain of the commercial circles (principally in Petersburg and the Baltic states); and, above all, the man who, from 1876 to April 1882, was deputy (and often "acting") foreign minister, and who thereafter was to be foreign minister in his own right through the entire reign of Alexander III: Nikolai Karlovich Giers, about whom more will be said below.

Opposed to this conservative, internationally minded, and generally Westernized faction that favored good relations with Germany and avoidance of conflict with the European Powers, there was one of contrary disposition, made up of several elements united by a spirit of active —sometimes exalted—nationalism, envious of Bismarck for the success he had enjoyed in the unification of Germany, eager to see Russian prestige elevated by exploits of similar magnitude and impressiveness, and inclined—all of them—to look to the southwest, to the Balkans and the Straits, as the theater for what they envisaged as a dramatic expansion of Russia's power and influence.

Prominent among these last—so much so that their designation was often taken as a species of code name for this entire body of Russian opinion—were the so-called Panslavs. These (not to be confused with the Slavophils, whose concerns were rather of a philosophic nature and whose attention was directed primarily to the internal Russian scene) were people who saw Russia as the natural protecting power for all the Slavic peoples of the Balkan and central European regions. They aspired to the liberation of these smaller Slavic peoples from the Austro-Hungarian and Turkish Empires in which they were then, almost without exception, included,* and to their inclusion, in one way or another, into the territorial confines, or the immediate sphere of influence, of Russia herself. They professed to regard Russia as the natural mother and protector for these peoples (of whom, in most instances, they knew very little); and they found in this rather patronizing attitude a rationali-zation for the purely nationalistic impulses which, one must be permitted to conclude, were at the real emotional source of their words and con-duct. It was, of course, inevitable that persons so inclined should see in the Turkish and Austro-Hungarian Empires the obstacles to the realiza-tion of their dreams, and should advocate policies that could not fail to impinge upon the interests of these two great neighbors.

* The Poles, of course, were an exception, in so far as they were divided among the Russian, German, and Austrian Empires.

Closely allied with the Panslavs and in part (but only in part) identical with them were those whose interest in the non-Russian peoples of the Balkans and eastern Europe had a religious, rather than a linguistic-nationalistic, origin. These people pictured Russia as the patron and protector—not of Slavic peoples as such or of Slavic peoples alone, but of all those peoples who belonged to, or were conceived as desiring to belong to, the Christian churches of the Eastern Rite. Since some of the Slavs (as for example the Czechs, Slovaks, and Croats) did not fit into this category, whereas certain of the non-Slavic peoples (the Greeks and Rumanians) did, the ambitions of these religiously oriented Russian imperialists had a focus only in part (in large part, to be sure) identical with that of the Panslavs.

A third element interested in an active Russian policy in the Balkans was made up of those higher officials, diplomatic and military, whose attention was absorbed by what they viewed as the struggle with the British for supremacy in the eastern Mediterranean, the Middle East, and Central Asia. To them, the most important question of Russian foreign policy was that of power, of decisive influence, at the Dardanelles and the Bosporus. This orientation was in some instances supported by strong Panslav sympathies, and sometimes even went hand in hand with activities along the Panslav line; but the two motivations were not to be confused. To the Panslavs, Austria-Hungary, as a Power already holding dominion over several Slavic peoples and as a leading competitor for dominant influence over those about to be liberated from Turkish rule, appeared as the principal adversary and potential military enemy. For the others, it was England that loomed largest in this capacity, though it was clear to them, too, that the Turks themselves were a vital factor in the equation, and that the Austrians, sitting as they did on the flank of Russian military lines of communication to the Straits region, would also in some way have to be coped with.

All three of these tendencies had powerful sources of support in Russian society and government. It is difficult to distinguish this support with relation to the particular tendency in question. Often the sympathies related to all three.

In the religious field there was the commanding figure of Konstantin Petrovich Pobyedonostsev, "Ober-Prokuror" of the Holy Synod (which, in the absence of a patriarch, administered the affairs of the Russian-Orthodox Church), tutor to successive crown princes, and generally considered to be one of the two or three most powerful men in Russia next to the Tsar himself. The Panslavs, on the other hand, had important support among the academic intellectuals as well as among sections of the clergy and the wealthy merchant class in Moscow and other cities of central and southern Russia, and even considerable support in high court circles.

All these tendencies were viewed with sympathy in the semi-independent Asiatic Department of the Foreign Office, whose field of competence included the Balkans and whose staff consisted almost exclusively of people who had had experience in that field. This department did not hesitate, over the years, to pursue policies at variance, to one degree or another, with that of what was called the "Chancery" (or sometimes the "Little Chancery"), where relations with the great western European Powers were conducted. It is worth noting that whereas the Asiatic Department was staffed, generally speaking, with people of pure Russian origin, usually Orthodox by religious affiliation and most often natives of the interior regions of Russia, the Chancery had, among its senior officials, a high percentage of German Balts and others of a Western orientation, for some of whom French was a more natural medium of personal and official discourse than Russian. The Chancery, in other words, was more cosmopolitan, less nationalistic, less interested in Balkan and oriental adventures; but it had full control, in the main, only over the formal diplomatic relations with the great Western Powers. The conduct of political intrigue on Russia's southwestern borders escaped its competence and its responsibility.

In the pursuit of its quasi-independent and often aggressive Balkan policies, the Asiatic Department made frequent use of the ostensibly private Panslav committees in the major cities (particularly Moscow, Odessa, and Petersburg) as channels for financing and conducting activities for which the Russian government was disinclined to acknowledge formal responsibility. Its contacts with the private Panslav circles were thus intimate, and often of a quasi-operational nature.

A number of the diplomatic and consular officials who served in those areas that were the concern of the Asiatic Department were strong sympathizers with one or the other of these nationalist and expansionist tendencies. Of these, the most prominent, active, and influential was the former head of the department and ambassador at Constantinople Count N. P. Ignatyev, a man whose stormy official career was to end, in the early 1880's, with a brief and unhappily terminating tour of service as minister of the interior. Imaginative, nimble, high-powered, and persuasive, Ignatyev, in his ideas and efforts of diplomacy, often ran rings around his slower colleagues, Russian and foreign, leaving them in a state of bewilderment which easily conduced to suspicion and gave him an international reputation, perhaps exaggerated, for slickness and mendacity. He was strongly anti-Austrian; and had he been given his head, Russia would no doubt have tried to go it alone in the Balkans and at the Straits, looking to daring and adroitness in diplomacy to make up for whatever other resources she might have lacked for the successful pursuit of such a course. Such was his resourcefulness that one feels he might well have pulled it all off, provided only that he could have avoided frightening the British and others into a renewal of the Crimean War. But he had rivals and enemies at home, and the ministers of war and foreign affairs normally stood between him and the Tsar; so his daring schemes tended to be watered down and delayed in execution, if they were not rejected outright. This robbed them, relying as they did on the boldness and dash of execution which Ignatyev, left to himself, would presumably have given them, of whatever success they might otherwise have had, and left him, only too often, sitting uncomfortably somewhere in the middle, saddled with a semi-responsibility for policies that he considered "too little and too late."

In the mid-1870's Ignatyev was, as ambassador in Constantinople, at the height of his success as a diplomatist. He was not to realize, as it turned out, the higher ambitions he no doubt entertained; but his striking figure, always arresting and always in motion, continued for many years to stand close to the center of Panslav tendencies and activities, and played its part, in this way, in the shaping of Russian policy towards all the other major European Powers, including France.

In his capacity as an outstanding inspirer and executor of Panslav-nationalist policies, Ignatyev was flanked by a considerable body of other diplomatic and consular officials whose careers proceeded under the aegis of the Asiatic Department and who served as its diplomatic or quasi-diplomatic representatives at the lesser Balkan and Levantine posts (mostly ones of a consular nature). Only nominally under control of the Petersburg "Chancery," these men often worked more intimately for the Ministry of the Interior (i.e., for the secret police establishment) or for the various Panslav committees than they did for the Foreign Office itself. This lent to the Russian diplomacy of the period a certain baffling ambivalence which was the source of much frustration to foreign diplomats; for it was hard to call the Russian foreign minister to account for activities over which he had relatively little control.

Of great importance—greater, possibly, even than that forthcoming from the Asiatic Department of the Foreign Office—was the support these Panslav and nationalistic tendencies enjoyed in military circles. Here, the most conspicuous role was played by certain officers who threw themselves as individuals into enthusiasms of this nature, in some instances even at the cost of their regular military careers. Outstanding among these were the two generals, Rostislav Andreyevich Fadyeyev (1824-1883) and Mikhail Grigoryevich Chernyayev (1864-1898). The

31

former, much the older of the two, was prominent as a writer and pamphleteer, and as a fiery proponent of a war with Austria. Chernyayev, popularly dubbed the "Lion of Tashkent" for his military successes as commander in Central Asia, even left the regular Russian military service for a time, as we shall see shortly, to lend his military experience to the Panslav cause. Of even greater prominence, after 1877, was another general who won immense popularity by his military exploits in Central Asia and then in the Russo-Turkish War, Mikhail Dmitriyevich Skobelev (1843-1882), a man who might well have become a political figure of much significance had he not died suddenly in 1882.

All these men lent glamor and enthusiasm to the nationalist cause in one way or another; but of equal if not greater importance in the formulation of Russian policy were those other military figures, less prominent in the public eye, who, while sympathizing with the tendencies in question, pursued their work quietly and inconspicuously in the offices of the general staff or the War Ministry or the leading provincial military commands. Some of these will be identified in other connections, below. Suffice it to note, here, that they had their own organ of publicity, the newspaper *Svyet*, and that they were often in closest touch with Panslav and other nationalistic figures outside the official establishment.

Finally, mention must be made of the two men most intimately responsible, in the 1870's, for the designing and the expressing of Russian foreign policy: the elderly chancellor and foreign minister of Alexander II, Prince Aleksandr Dimitriyevich Gorchakov (1798-1883), mentioned above, and the Tsar himself.

Gorchakov, who by the mid-1870's had already lived somewhat beyond his time, was by no means a whole-hearted enthusiast for the nationalistic tendencies just mentioned—most of his training and experience had been, after all, in western Europe; but he was obliged to recognize the power these tendencies exerted upon the Tsar and influential Russian opinion; and his resentful jealousy of Bismarck at this stage of his life often placed him in company with these essentially anti-German tendencies.

As for the Tsar, Alexander II, his was a somewhat enigmatic political personality, resembling in this respect that of his uncle, Alexander I. Whoever attempts to define his political attitudes ventures, inevitably, onto thin ice. Suffice it to say that while nothing ever shook his sense of loyalty to his other uncle, the first Kaiser of the newly established German Empire, or his admiration for the German army, he, too, was not insensitive to nationalistic opinion in the more influential echelons of Russian society. He became increasingly vulnerable, as the 1870's ran their course, to pressures from the nationalist side, not least in response to the Panslav tendencies of his mistress (and later morganatic wife) Princess Ekaterina Dolgorukaya, and her entourage. One sees in him, in the mid-1870's, a vacillating figure, torn between his German attachments, on the one hand, and his aversion for Austria and inability to resist Panslav pressures, on the other.

It must be noted, finally, that these nationalistic and essentially aggressive tendencies found strong support and expression in large sections of the Russian press. Outstanding in this respect were the journals put out by the great conservative editor, Mikhail Nikoforovich Katkov: the Moscow daily, *Moskovskie Vyedomosti*, the dean of all Russian secular newspapers and greatly influential in Petersburg as well as in Moscow, and its partner, the monthly *Russki Vyestnik*. The Panslav tendencies in particular were given passionate support by the last of the great Slavophil publicists, Ivan Sergeyevich Aksakov, in his journal *Rus*, also published in Moscow. In Petersburg, too, there were a number of papers which followed the nationalistic-Panslav line: notably the strongly conservative *Novoye Vremya*; the *Svyet*, with its military connections; the liberal but nonetheless panslavistically inclined *Novosti*; and the organ of the reactionary Ministry of Education, the *Sankt-Petersburgskie Vyedomosti*. Among them, these journals kept up, over the years, a running fire of criticism of the Foreign Office for its alleged excessive deference to western European opinion and its failure to give adequate support to anti-Austrian policies in the Balkans.

As the war scare proceeded, in the spring of 1875, there were just beginning those disorders and uprisings against the Turks in Herzegovina and other Balkan regions which were to lead, after many intervening vicissitudes, to the outbreak of the Russo-Turkish War, two years later.

The historian who feels a need to touch lightly and incidentally on the origins, the course, and the immediate consequences of this military conflict faces a forbidding task, for the complexities of the unstable and constantly changing diplomatic environment in which all this proceeded defy easy generalization. It took the late B. H. Sumner more than 550 pages, together with a number of documentary annexes, to summarize, in a work of outstanding scholarly and literary quality,[1] the main points of this story. But since there are few readers who will have, at a distance of one hundred years, much of this background in mind, the following is offered, with due apology for its inevitable inadequacy, as a reminder of the major outlines of what occurred.

The progressive disintegration, in the late nineteenth century, of the Turkish Empire in the Balkans created problems both for the Austrians and for the Russians. For the Austrians, these problems were much more immediate and more serious than for the Russians; for it was clear that the fate of the Slavic, or Slavic-speaking peoples now detaching themselves from Turkish control (the Montenegrins, Bosnians, Macedonians, Bulgarians, etc.) would have an important influence on the attitudes and aspirations of those of their fellow Slavs who were included in the Austro-Hungarian Empire. The new solutions to be found for the status of these emerging nationalities were thus a matter of vital interest to Vienna. For the Russians it was not a matter of *vital* interest, although the incorporation of any of these peoples into the Austro-Hungarian Empire, or even their close alliance with it, would of course, have had a significant effect on the balance of power in southeastern Europe, and one which Russian strategists would not have been able to ignore.

But this question naturally engaged the interest of the Panslav-nationalist circles in Russia in the most intimate way, for it concerned a region which they had marked out in their own dreams as the theater of Russia's future success and glory. They felt obliged to come to the assistance of the Balkan Slavs in their efforts to emancipate themselves from the rule of the Turks; but they had also to assure, if they could, that this emancipation should take place in a manner that would not bring the respective peoples under Austrian, rather than Russian, influence.

It might thus be said, by way of rough summary of the stakes which the two empires, the Austro-Hungarian and the Russian, had in the solution to these problems, that the Austrian interest was essentially of a defensive nature, consisting of the wish to see that the distintegration of the Turkish Empire did not lead to that of Vienna's own empire as well, whereas the Russian interest was essentially offensive, involving as it did the effort to extend a dominant Russian influence to a new region, primarily for the gratification of romantic-national aspirations.

When the Herzegovinian revolt against the Turks broke out, in 1875, the first Russian impulse was to internationalize the problem by supporting Austrian proposals for joint pressures on the Turks to meet the insurgents halfway with new programs of reform. This effort was unsuccessful. There was insufficient unity among the Great Powers, and even within the Russian establishment, to permit any successful action along this line. Nor were the Turks prepared to move very far in this direction.

Nevertheless, the Herzegovinian uprising would probably have failed and collapsed of its own weaknesses had it not been for the very extensive support given to the insurgents, partly by the Serbs and Montenegrins but outstandingly by the Panslav committees in Russia. This support, and the agitation accompanying it, were effective in inflaming local opinion, if not in assuring the military success of the rebellious elements. By mid-1875 half the Turkish Balkan Empire was in an uproar. The danger centered, inevitably, around Turkish relations with the already independent Serbia as an immediate neighbor and strong supporter of the insurgents; and in July 1876 war broke out between Turkey and Serbia.

All this, involving as it did not just the fate of the rebellious provinces but also of the brother-Slavs in Serbia, fanned the passions of the Russian Panslavs to a white heat. There were elaborate and excited fund-raising activities among the Russian public; a force of military volunteers was despatched to Serbia amid huge enthusiasm; General Chernyayev took leave from the Russian army and himself proceeded to Serbia to command, under highly confused arrangements, not just these volunteers but the entire Serbian armed forces.

The enterprise, as it turned out, was a military disaster. The Turks proved clearly superior to their opponents. By December 1876, their military superiority had been clearly established, and the Serbs were obliged to sue for an armistice.

Panslav opinion in Russia was by this time aroused to a fever pitch of anger and frustration; and the question naturally arose as to whether the Russian government should not now go to war against the Turks by way of support for the Slavic cause. On principle, there was no great reluctance to do this on the part of the Tsar and his leading advisers; they saw, in fact, no acceptable alternative. (Russian mobilization actually began well before the final Serbian collapse.) But there was danger that any unilateral Russian action would so arouse the fears and suspicions of the other great European Powers that Russia would find herself confronted in effect with a renewal of the relatively recent Crimean coalition against her, reinforced this time by the Austrians.

In order to avoid this, highly complex and confused negotiations were hastily put in hand with the other European Powers, but particularly with the Austrians, whose reaction was of vital importance. These latter negotiations were finally successful for immediate purposes, insofar as something resembling an agreement was arrived at with the Austrians, the essential feature of which was a grudging Russian consent (often known, though somewhat inaccurately, as the Reichstadt Agreement) to tolerate an Austrian occupation of Bosnia and Herzegovina, or portions thereof, against an assurance that Austria would not take advantage of Russia's military involvement with Turkey to move against her. In a rough and proximate way, this understanding served its purpose, insofar as Austrian restraint, if not neutrality, was assured for the duration of the struggle with Turkey; but because of the extreme unclarity of the terms in which it was embodied, and of the great secrecy which surrounded it then and for years to come, it was destined to be a source of much trouble in the future. It stands in the historical record as one more striking example of the danger of hasty and imprecise agreements among Great Powers on major questions of international relations.

Since it was clear that in a war against Turkey, Russian forces would be obliged not only to cross Rumania but to make it a veritable base of operations, a preliminary agreement had also to be concluded with the government of that country—an agreement which did not prevent the Russians from insisting successfully when the war was over, to the great embitterment of the Rumanians, on cession of the Rumanian province of Bessarabia to Russia, in return for the previously Turkish Dobrudja.

In April 1877 the Russians launched military operations against Turkey. These were attended by the usual massive confusion and bungling. The Russian advance in the direction of Constantinople was held up for months through the late summer and fall, by the heroic Turkish defense of a flanking position at Plevna, a position from which the Russians finally succeeded in dislodging the Turks only in December, and after the sacrifice of several tens of thousand men. After that the advance proceeded rapidly enough; and by the end of January the Russians had reached the Sea of Marmora, albeit at a point still some distance from Constantinople. Here their forward movement came to an end, however, partly because the Turks were now reduced to a point where they were willing to discuss the Russian terms; partly because the Russian forces were themselves exhausted and seriously decimated by disease; but partly also, and very importantly, because the British had now sent a fleet, together with a landing force, to the Sea of Marmora, and had made it plain that an attempt by the Russians to occupy Constantinople would meet with their opposition and countermeasures. This was a serious threat, because the British had the capability, if they wished to exert it, not only of cutting off Constantinople from Asiatic Turkey but of entering the Black Sea, interrupting the maritime supply lines serving the Russian forces on the peninsula, and in general reviving the threat the Russians had faced during the Crimean War.

In the face of all these complications Ignatyev, taking advantage of the exhaustion of the Turks, pressed upon the latter (to the high indignation of much of the rest of Europe, particularly the British and the Austrians) a unilateral settlement, the abortive Treaty of San Stefano, in which Russian aspirations, especially for the Southern Balkans, were given the widest gratification, but no account was taken of the interests or desiderata of the other Powers. The Turks, for their part, accepted this; but when it became clear that an insistence on the terms of this treaty would be acceptable neither to the British nor to the Austrians, and that either or both of them might oppose it by war, the Russians were obliged to agree, angrily and unhappily, to the submission of the entire problem to a general European Congress, under Bismarck's chairmanship, at Berlin. At this Congress (June 13 to July 13, 1878) the ranking Russian representative was Gorchakov, who, in addition to being old and ill, sulked and evaded responsibility for an arrangement negotiated under what he felt to be a form of humiliating duress. The main burden of negotiation was therefore assumed by his deputy, Count Pyotr Alekseyevich Shuvalov, Russian Ambassador to the Court of St. James, an able and reasonable man. Shuvalov took upon himself in this way, to the lasting detriment of his further career, the onus of extracting from the other Powers the best terms the Russians could have expected, in the circumstances, to get. In this, he was given important help at a number of points by Bismarck, as chairman.

The Russians, all things considered, and particularly in view of their own military and financial exhaustion, did not do badly at the Congress of Berlin. They acquired Bessarabia as well as very considerable, and militarily important, portions of Turkish territory in Asia Minor. They achieved the establishment of a virtually independent Bulgaria, with the tacit consent of the others (gladly given, in Bismarck's case, ungladly in the case of the Austrians) that this new state should be a Russian satellite, if the Russians so insisted. Serbia and Montenegro, both regarded as Russian political clients, received increases of territory. All in all, considering that this had been an unnecessary and seriously bungled venture, beyond their financial means, the Russians could well have accepted the settlement with good grace, considering themselves fortunate that they had been able to avoid war with any of the major Powers.

But this was not to be. Russians seem never to take kindly to the acknowledgment of anything less than a complete success in war. Woe be it to the Russian statesman who negotiates, or signs, a peace settlement that is anything less than blatantly triumphant from the Russian standpoint. He is held personally responsible for the reverse, even though acting under strictest instructions, and his action is never fully forgiven.* No sooner was the Berlin Treaty signed and made known,

---

* One has only to recall, in this connection, Witte's experience as negotiator of the Treaty of Portsmouth, in 1905, or of the indignant voices raised, within the Russian Communist Party, against those unfortunate envoys (Sokolnikov, Karakhan, Chicherin, and Petrovski) who were obliged to sign the Brest-Litovsk Treaty, in 1918.

in any case, than the Russian nationalist press broke out in torrents of bitter incriminations against the Western Powers for depriving Russia of the fruits of her "victory," against Bismarck for having chaired the gathering at which this was done, and, by implication, against Shuvalov for his part in negotiating the agreement. In this outburst of anger and self-pity the fact that the alternative might have been a major war for which Russia, exhausted and nearly bankrupt, would have been wholly unprepared, was allowed to pass unnoted.

The Tsar and his leading advisers had it in their power, had they so wished, to stem this flood of childish, and—for the Germans in particular—offensive, petulance; but this they did not do. It was too useful for them, with its strong antiforeign overtones, as a means of deflecting Panslav discontent away from their own failures of statesmanship. And one senses that it commended itself to them, too, at least subconsciously, as a convenient rationalization for the shortcomings of their own wartime leadership. The press campaign was thus permitted to proceed apace, little heed being paid to its predictable external effects.

It remains to be emphasized to what great extent this entire episode in Russian policy was, if not the direct work of the Panslavs, the product of their influence upon the course of events. It was they who, with their constant intrigues and instigation, fanned the restlessness of the Balkan Slavs with Turkish rule. It was they who encouraged the Serbs to go to war with the Turks and then attempted, unsuccessfully, to take charge of the whole operation. It was their influence that was decisive in moving the Tsar to go to war against Turkey. It was in implementation of their aspirations that Ignatyev made his attempt to steal a march on the other Powers by concluding a unilateral settlement with the Turks. It was they who, when the war was over, insisted on misinterpreting the Berlin settlement and on persuading a great many of their countrymen, including in part the Tsar and the heir apparent, that Russia had been tricked and sold out by the Western Powers, with Bismarck in the lead.

And not only did they have this success but they came out of the whole affair with increased prestige and authority. From this time on, they would continue to be a serious force in the formulation of Russian foreign policy. Neither Alexander II nor his son and successor, Alexander III, was prepared, or even inclined, to put them entirely in their place (partly because both rulers had secret sympathies in that same direction). "It is unfortunately true," observed one of the highest officials of the Russian Foreign Office, in 1879, to the Austro-Hungarian

38

Ambassador in Petersburg (and future foreign minister) Count Kal-nocky,

> that people here are simply *afraid* of the nationalistic press. . . . They do not dare even to apply to it the penalties established by law [for violation of the censorship]. The Tsar, too, notwithstanding the fact that the entire activity of these papers is actually directed against the existing regime, is averse to any attempt to subject them to a strict control. . . . It is the flag of nationalism they have pinned upon themselves that protects them and assures them of powerful support. Ever since the nationalistic tendency has come so prominently to the fore, and particularly since it succeeded in prevailing, against all better advice, in the question of going to war [against Turkey], the so-called "national" party . . . has become a real power, especially because it embraces the entire army. . . . Behind many of these papers stand the military. Everyone knows that the sympathies of the army are with the nationalistic press; and the military entourage of the Tsar takes care to see that it receives excellent and favorable treatment.[2]

It was in this way that there came into existence in Russia a state of opinion, at least in large sections of the educated public, which constituted to some extent a parallel to the bitterness that marked so much of French opinion in the wake of the Franco-Prussian War. The frustrations of the Turkish War came to match, in this sense, the effects in France of the loss of Alsace-Lorraine. There was in each case, rightly or wrongly, a sense of grievance against much of the rest of Europe, and against Bismarck's Germany in particular. There was in each case a sense of national humiliation at foreign hands—and this in an age of an almost pathological intensity of national feeling. Each party was, to some extent, dissatisfied with its position within the *status quo* that Bismarck had created. In each case, domestic opinion was divided; and the sentiments in question were more passionately held by some than by others. But there were few in either country, particularly in the educated classes, who were not touched by these feelings to some degree. And in these circumstances, it was inevitable that people should cast about to see whether means could not be found to combine the efforts and policies of the two countries, to the benefit of both.

Chapter Two

FRANCO-RUSSIAN RELATIONS,
1879-1880

The almost hysterical embitterment against the Western Powers, above all against Germany, that marked educated Russian opinion in the immediate aftermath of the Russo-Turkish War and came so prominently to the fore in the fulminations of the Russian nationalist press of that period, had effects on relations with both Germany and France. These effects proceeded simultaneously, and interacted extensively. The effects on Russo-German relations were the more important of the two in their long-term political consequences; but because they were not unimportantly affected by what was going on at the same time in the contacts between Russia and France, it may be useful to note these latter first. The effects of all this upon German-Russian relations, and indeed on the European situation generally, will be discussed in a further chapter.

At the end of January 1879 elections to the presidency of France replaced Marshal MacMahon, who had occupied that position since 1873, by Jules Grévy, who was to occupy it until 1887. This change completed the period of transition in French political life which ended the curious duumvirate of monarchists and republicans by which France had been governed since 1871; and it set the country on a firmly republican course. One result of this change was that the French Ambassador to Russia, General Le Flô, a monarchist and a close friend of MacMahon, resigned his position at once. He was immediately replaced by another military man: General Antoine Chanzy (1823-1883). Chanzy had a long and distinguished record: as a corps commander in the Franco-Prussian War, as governor of Algeria from 1873 to 1875, then for a time as senator, and finally as unsuccessful candidate for the presidency of France in 1879. Like most higher French officers of his time, he was a strong supporter of the idea of an eventual Franco-Russian alliance, though well aware, as were most French statesmen at that moment, that the time for such an arrangement was not yet at hand.

It may be noted that over the entire period from 1871 to 1886 successive French cabinets made it a habit to be represented diplomatically in Petersburg by senior military or (in one instance) naval figures. This policy was no doubt influenced by the example of the Germans who, on the strength of an arrangement flowing from the close personal bonds that united the two imperial families, had the privilege of stationing in Petersburg, in addition to the regular diplomatic representative, a personal military representative of the Kaiser, who served in the capacity of aide-de-camp to the Tsar. In this capacity, the representative in question had the privilege of being present, as a member of the Tsar's personal military entourage, at many military events—parades, reviews, manoeuvres, and so on—to which a regular civilian ambassador would not normally have been invited. The French, their country being a republic, could not fully match this arrangement; but they did their best by sending as ambassadors men of high military or naval rank, who would at least be more likely to be invited to military functions, and to have relations with senior Russian officers, than would their civilian counterparts. In this last practice, it might be noted, they were also only following a German precedent, for the regular German Ambassador in Petersburg over the period 1876-1892, Lothar von Schweinitz, was a military man of the rank of general who had served in Petersburg in earlier years as military attaché.*

Le Flô, on leaving Russia in early March 1879, was of course given the usual farewell audience with the Tsar, who had a high opinion of him; and Chanzy's subsequent arrival naturally gave him, too, ample opportunity for talks with senior Russian personalities. In all of these encounters it was made evident to the French not only that Russo-German relations had been seriously affected by the bitter antagonism between Gorchakov and Bismarck and by the anti-German tendency of the Russian press but that this had found a perceptible reflection in the Russian attitude towards France. To the departing Le Flô the Tsar expatiated on the desirability of a further rapprochement between the two countries. "Our common interest," he said, "ought to impose upon us the obligation to come together. I know of no question that could divide us, and there are many questions in which it would be desirable for us to move along together. The question of the Orient is among that number."[1] (The reader will bear in mind that the term "Orient" at that

---

* A desire to emulate the German example was, however, not the sole reason for this practice. It was of older origin. Tocqueville, in his *Souvenirs* (p. 319 of the Gallimard edition of 1964) mentions his own action (as French foreign minister in 1849) in sending General Lamoriciere as ambassador to Russia—". . . où il n'y a guère que les généraux, et les généraux célèbres, qui réussissent."

time was used to denote the general area of the Balkans and the Dardanelles.) Gorchakov, too, hinted at the same thing when he told the departing ambassador that it was not in the direction of Germany that the Tsar's eyes were turning at that particular moment, the clear implication being that Paris was a more likely target for their focus.

These were, of course, only straws in the wind; and they were not of lasting importance. France was herself at that point in no position to risk Bismarck's anger by any open flirtations with Russia; and Bismarck, as we shall see in the next chapter, was not lacking in the resources to assure that things did not go too far. The unsubstantiality of these hints and suggestions from the Russian side, which were in reality a reflection of prevailing pique against Germany, were clearly perceived by the counselor of the French Embassy in Petersburg, Count de Vieleustel. In a despatch written during Chanzy's absence (September 23, 1879) Vieleustel commented upon a rather pro-French article that had appeared from the pen of a high official of the Russian Foreign Office, Baron Jomini,* and upon reports of pro-French statements by various senior Russian military officers. France, he wrote, should be on guard against such "banal" expressions of good will. They were not really serious. She should be on guard against them whether they emanated from a cabinet minister (obviously, Gorchakov was meant) who was trying to make use of France to irritate a powerful rival (Bismarck) or whether they came from over-eager personalities in the Tsar's entourage, only too ready to chatter openly about the possibilities of a Franco-Russian alliance.[2]

All this was accepted, no doubt, in the Paris Foreign Office as wise advice with relation to all that might occur on the diplomatic level. But talk of this nature, coming from such high circles, was bound to arouse interest in French military circles, and not just interest but also curiosity as to whether, in the light of this favorable atmosphere, there could not be a useful, if limited, intensification of contacts, quiet and even clandestine, at the military level.

There is, in fact, some question as to whether certain collaborative arrangements between the two military establishments, going beyond anything known to the general public, had not already been in existence for several years before that time. The Soviet historian, A. Z. Manfred, in his work on the origins of the Franco-Russian alliance, makes the interesting statement that there was one particular aspect of the French interest in Russia about which no one ever wrote nor even spoke out

---

* Aleksandr Genrikhovich Jomini (1814-1888), a son of the famous Swiss general of that name, was a senior official of the Russian Foreign Office through the 1870's and most of the 1880's.

loud but which was nevertheless in reality the main one. This, he says, was "a collaboration of sorts, beginning in 1871, in strictly defined areas, between the French and Russian general staffs—a collaboration held in deepest secrecy, quite unknown to the non-initiated, known in fact only to three or four officers."[3] The purpose of this collaboration, Manfred goes on to say, was to facilitate the study of the Russian army by the French. And the French officers initiated into the knowledge of it were (this was presumably in the early 1870's) General Le Flô, Colonel Gaillard (French military attaché in Petersburg 1873-1875), and his assistant military attaché, Barry.[4]

Manfred does not say whence he derived his knowledge of this arrangement; but he had more extensive access to the Russian archives than any Western scholars have had; and it is not to be assumed that he pulled it out of thin air. The suggestion finds a most curious, and evidently unintended, confirmation in his own book. At page 87 there is reproduced, in facsimile, a document, dated the 1st of May 1875, which the author entitles, at the bottom of the page (in translation): "Secret report of an agent in Germany to the Deuxième Bureau of the French General Staff, of May 1875, and decoding." There is writing, in a different hand from that of the original text, between each of the lines; and the reader would suppose that this was the decoding of the original. Actually, the document, closely examined, turns out to be not at all a coded message, and not at all from an agent in Germany, but an internal communication of the French Ministry of War: a memorandum addressed, apparently by the military chef du cabinet of the minister or perhaps by the minister himself, to the Deuxième Bureau; and the writing between the lines was a clearer reproduction of the writing of the original, which was—at least for a foreigner of a different period— difficult to read. Although Manfred himself nowhere mentions it, the text of this message was not uninteresting, particularly when taken in conjunction with what he says in his text about the clandestine collaboration. The text was as follows:

ÉTAT MAJOR GÉNÉRAL.

Il y a lieu de s'occuper dès-à-présent de l'envoi de la mission en Russie. Le Commandant Chanoine pourra y être envoyé mais ce sera indépendamment des spécialistes demandés. Je voudrais envoyer le Commandant Faverot (?) pour la question des haras et des remontes, mais son nom très connu des allemands, peut exciter quelque méfiance. D'ici au 15 juin nous avons le temps d'aviser . . . s'entendre avec les différents services pour la désignation à faire, les officiers prévenus travailleraient à l'État major général jusqu'à leur départ pour se préparer.

G-al [illegible]

The content of this message would seem to confirm Manfred's state-ment that the purpose of this French mission in Russia was primarily to study the Russian army, particularly methods for the breeding and training of cavalry horses.*

Manfred's suggestion raises a number of tantalizing questions, of which the first would be that of the relationship of the Tsar Alexander II to the arrangement. Devoted to his uncle, the German Kaiser, and a great admirer of the German army, it is hard to believe that Alexander would have gone very far in permitting a relationship with the French general staff that was concealed from, and by implication hostile to, the Germans. But he was a complicated and often vacillating man. And control of such matters at the military level in Petersburg was then in the hands of the liberal and pro-French Minister of War Dmitri Aleks-androvich Milyutin (1816-1912), a man held in high suspicion by Bis-marck and viewed by the latter as a major source of anti-German influence at the Russian court. Bismarck's suspicions along this line were no doubt somewhat overdrawn; but of Milyutin's general dislike for the Germans there appears to be no doubt. It is only reasonable to assume, further-more, that Milyutin, in treating of a matter which involved a study of the Russian army, or Russian military doctrine, by foreign officers, would have enlisted the help of his outstanding liberal protégé, General Nikolai Nikolayevich Obruchev (1830-1904), then professor of military statistics at the Nikolayevski General Staff Academy, future chief of the Russian general staff, and a man whose great and persistent interest in the development of the military relationship with France we shall presently have occasion to observe. It is worth noting that in 1872, that is, just at the time when this special relationship mentioned by Manfred was supposedly coming into being, Obruchev was assigned the task of preparing for the Tsar a plan of operation for the Russian army in a hypothetical war with Germany.† This says something, it would seem, both about Obruchev's interests and about the Tsar's preoccupa-tions at that particular moment, in the aftermath of Germany's great victory over France—a time when Germany's hands were free, if they ever were, to take on a conflict with the Russian Empire without having to worry about the possibility of a French attack on her western border; and it lends plausibility to the suggestion that the Tsar might have been disposed, just at that time, to approve a limited and relatively innocuous

* The Chanoine referred to here was to become military attaché in Petersburg some four years later, and, in 1898, minister of war.

† An item to this effect appears in a biographical sketch of Obruchev, contained in the Boisdeffre papers, which I was permitted to examine by courtesy of the Boisdeffre family.

form of Franco-Russian military collaboration. In any case, of all the men in the Russian military establishment of that period, Milyutin and Obruchev would have been the ones most likely to receive with enthusiasm, and to promote, a collaborative arrangement of this nature.

Since the name of Obruchev has already come up, and since it will come up at many points in the remainder of this account, it may be as well to take note, now, of the biography and personality of this very unusual and fascinating man. Son of an army officer but orphaned at the age of eight, he was first sent off to a boarding school for military orphans at Tsarskoe Selo, then to the Page School, after which he entered the Ismailovski Regiment as a corporal. Here, he distinguished himself by developing an interest in historical scholarship and writing a paper on the history of military literature in Russia. This brought him, in 1852, to the War Academy, where again he made his mark as a scholar and advanced in rank. In 1859, after service on the staff of the Guard regiments, he received the rank of colonel and became chief of staff to the Second Infantry Division. Meanwhile, he had pursued his scholarly interests, and become, as indicated above (apparently while still serving in his staff positions), professor of military statistics at the War Academy, a chair previously held by Milyutin. He had founded, in 1858, the monthly military magazine *Voyenny Sbornik*. Here, being himself of a markedly liberal political disposition, he made the mistake of drawing in, as a contributor to the magazine, the revolutionary publicist, critic, and philosopher, N. G. Chernyshevski, whose relations with the Tsarist authorities, destined shortly to culminate in his arrest and imprisonment, were just then moving into their critical period. This was a brief association, and one which Soviet biographers of Chernyshevski are now as happy to forget or ignore as was, no doubt, Obruchev himself in later years. But it was enough to cause Obruchev serious embarrassment and result in him being in effect exiled to France (the mild punishment was surely attributable to Milyutin's friendly intercession) for a year and a half. Here, in Paris, he pursued his scholarly interests. Here, too, he met and married his French wife, who owned a large château and property in the Dordogne. Throughout the remainder of his life, it was customary for the Obruchevs to spend at least a part of the late summer and early fall at this place; so the contacts with France were intensively pursued and developed over the course of the years.

In the 1860's Obruchev became chief of the Committee for Military Education of the Imperial General Staff. He played a prominent part in the Russo-Turkish War, both as a commander and then senior staff officer on the Caucasian front and, as the war came to an end, in a diplomatic capacity in the Balkans. In 1881, upon Milyutin's retirement as minister of war, he became chief of the general staff—a position he was to retain into the late 1890's, in other words, during the entire period of the origins of the Franco-Russian alliance.

Among the foreign observers opinions varied with respect to Obruchev's competence, but there can be no question of his high intellectual distinction; and he was considered by the German military attaché's office in Petersburg to be a tireless worker and a good organizer. It was also alleged by certain of the German military observers that he was "in French pay";[5] but this imputation may safely be dismissed as part of the malicious gossip that was so common to the period.

But, to return to the year 1879: General Chanzy, the new ambassador to Russia, had had on his military staff, both when commanding the Army of the Loire in the Franco-Prussian War and later when serving as governor of Algeria, a young officer for whose personal and professional qualities he had gained high respect: Colonel Raoul le Mouton de Boisdeffre (1839-1919). One may be reasonably sure, therefore, that it was on Chanzy's recommendation that the French minister of war approached his colleague, the foreign minister, on the 13th of March 1879, only a week before Chanzy's arrival in Petersburg, with the request that the Foreign Office ask the Russian government for its agreement to the appointment of Boisdeffre as assistant French military attaché in Petersburg. The reason given for this request was "l'importance des affaires militaires en Russie."[6] The suggestion met with agreement all around; Boisdeffre proceeded to Russia very shortly and served there for several years. The significance of this assignment of a relatively junior officer lay in the fact that Boisdeffre was destined to become in the ensuing years not only the good friend but almost the precise French counterpart of Obruchev as principal architect, negotiator, and signatory of the military convention of 1894, which was the basis of the Franco-Russian alliance, and as chief of the French general staff, as Obruchev was of the Russian one, at the time the convention was finally concluded.

Not long after Boisdeffre's arrival in Russia, the French government requested, and received, the assent of the Russian government to the presence of a French military delegation, headed by an officer of general's rank, at the annual Russian manoeuvres scheduled to take place in that summer (1879) near the suburban imperial residence of Tsarskoye Selo. The delegation duly arrived, was treated (according to Chanzy, who accompanied it to the manoeuvres) with marked cordiality by the Tsar and senior Russian officers, and was even invited to observe further manoeuvres near Moscow and Warsaw. Boisdeffre, it must be assumed, although the record does not so confirm, also accompanied this delegation in its attendance at the manoeuvres.

Boisdeffre summed up the conclusions he had derived from these and other experiences in a long report, submitted in early 1880, on the condition of the Russian army. He ended this report with the following significant observations:

> A war of aggression against Germany lies neither in the desires nor in the means over which Russia alone today disposes; but if she is attacked, she has sufficient resources to defend herself, even alone, and she has no need to fear such an attack, particularly if she feels herself supported by the attitude of France.[7]

While these things were occurring on the French military side, the Russians responded with measures that showed a curious parallel to them. For a Russian military delegation was similarly admitted to attendance at the annual French military maneouvres, held somewhat later that fall; and this delegation was headed by none other than Obruchev. The latter's presence in France in this capacity had the added significance that it appears to have been the touchstone for a whole spate of rumors concerning alleged Russian feelers, at the time in question, for a Russian alliance with France. The German Bismarck biographer, Hermann Robolski, in his *Fürst Bismarck unter drei Kaisern*, claimed that efforts of this nature were made during the aftermath of the war with Turkey, and mentioned in this connection the names of both Obruchev and Milyutin, saying that the latter was also in France at that time. He expressed doubt, however, that the feelers had been advanced on instructions from Petersburg.

A similar allegation can be found in the *Histoire diplomatique de l'alliance franco-russe*, written by Ernest Daudet, journalist, publicist, historian, and elder brother of Alphonse Daudet. Here, it is said that proposals of this nature were made by Obruchev during the manoeuvres and this statement is followed by the tale that the French foreign minister of the day, Waddington, fearful lest reports of these approaches reach Bismarck from other sources, told the latter about them. Waddington, it was said, denied this; but the German Ambassador in Paris, Prince Hohenlohe-Schillingsfürst, was known to have thanked him for the service.[8]

This tale, like many of Daudet's statements, was probably based on rather flimsy hearsay. From the German documents published many years later in the *Grosse Politik der europäischen Kabinette* it is evident that what actually happened was that the German Ambassador in

Vienna, Prince Reuss, reported to Bismarck, in early September 1879, that Andrassy, the Austro-Hungarian foreign minister, claimed to know that Russia was seeking allies in Paris and Rome. Bismarck, greatly concerned at that particular moment to find arguments with which to overcome his Kaiser's reluctance to conclude an alliance with Austria, queried Prince Hohenlohe, in Paris, telegraphically about the substance for this suggestion. Hohenlohe replied that there had been no direct approaches of this nature in Paris, but that hints of this nature had been dropped in discussions between Russian diplomats and Waddington. No mention was made here of Obruchev. It was for this information, presumably, that Waddington was thanked, if he was thanked at all.

Plainly, no one in the Russian service had any authority to make this sort of proposal to the French, and none did so. It would not have been surprising, however, if Obruchev, attending the French manoeuvres and participating in the social occasions by which such exercises are normally accompanied, had enthused, together with some of his French hosts, over the attractive possibilities which a closer association between the French and Russian military establishments might some day present.

The episode is mentioned here simply as evidence of the early currency of thoughts of this nature in both Russian and French circles, and particularly in the military circle that centered around Milyutin and Obruchev.

This was not the only pro-French circle existing in the Russian military establishment. Held in suspicion by many for its reputed liberalism (for Milyutin, like Obruchev, had enjoyed contacts with oppositionist elements in earlier years), the Milyutin-Obruchev milieu was strongly opposed by certain of the older, more strongly monarchistic and more reactionary officers, men whose careers had been mainly in command, rather than in staff positions. One of the most distinguished of these latter was the Grand Duke Nikolai Nikolayevich, brother of the Tsar Alexander II, for the past sixteen years commander of the Imperial Guard, and only recently commander-in-chief of the European front in the war with Turkey. He was a handsome man, resembling his father, the Tsar Nicholas I, but was held by at least one astute observer to be ignorant, self-opinionated, stubborn, and very vindictive.[9]

The grand duke emerged in poor health from his responsibilities as commander-in-chief in the Balkans; and for purposes of convalescence it was thought useful that he should pass the winter of 1879-1880 in France. His visit was officially incognito; but he was accompanied by other members of the family and by several military aides. Attached to his suite, in the capacity of physician or medical adviser, was a most curious individual who was destined to play a certain role—less significant than he himself liked to claim but not entirely negligible— both in the preparation of the Franco-Russian alliance and in the recording, as an historian, of the events leading up to it.* Because his name will appear from time to time in the further reaches of this account, it may be useful to say a few words about him at this point— more words, in fact, than his role might seem to warrant, but ones made necessary by the highly unusual nature of his intellectual and political personality, and by the element of mystery that still surrounds many of his attachments and activities.

This was a man who went, in western Europe, by the name of Élie de Cyon. In actuality, he was a Russian Jew, born in the Jewish pale, somewhere in the neighborhood of Kovno in the year 1843. His Russian name was Ilya Fadeyevich Tsion. He was educated, if his own opaque statements are to be believed, first in Warsaw, then at the university in Kiev, and finally at the University of Berlin, where he studied under the eminent German pathologist Virchow. Within a few years thereafter he had become a distinguished physiologist in his own right, and was given in 1873, when scarcely in his thirties, the chair of physiology at the Medical-Surgical Academy in Petersburg—a quasi-military institution and, at the same time, Russia's leading medical school—the chair, in fact, that had been recently vacated by the famous physiologist Ivan Mikhailovich Sechenov (1829-1905). In receiving this position, Cyon became not only Russia's first Jewish professor but one of the youngest, if not actually the youngest, of persons ever to hold a professorial position in that country.

Of Cyon's distinction as a physiologist there can be no doubt. His name still appears in a number of encyclopedias, including Soviet ones, in this connection. One of the nerves of the heart is named for him. He was the teacher of Pavlov in the field of the physiology of the digestive system; and Pavlov himself was unsparingly generous, in later years, in acknowledging his debt to Cyon in this respect.

But if Cyon's scientific brilliance is beyond question, so is the unfortunate nature of his character and personality. Both the opinions of contemporaries and the implications of the historical record reveal him as a devious, secretive, and cantankerous person—vain, boastful, and vindictive. Of all the contemporaries who had to do with him none,

---

* The reference is to the work published by Cyon in 1895 (Paris: Librairie Charles), entitled *Histoire de l'entente franco-russe 1886-1894. Documents et souvenirs.*

except the well-known editor Katkov (who was not always the best judge of people), had a good word to say for him. The writer, Ivan Turgenev, referred to him as "a great scoundrel." He figures in a history of the French press as "le louche Cyon." One finds, in fact, in the entire record of Cyon's life and activity no evidence of anything resembling a firm and warm friendship—no enduring relationship of confidence with anyone. The record of his life is strewn with conflict, controversy, suspicion, and unpleasantness of every sort. Everyone who had anything to do with him seems eventually to have regretted it. Hated and held in suspicion by many, loved—it would appear—by none, he is said to have died in Paris, in 1912, in utter loneliness. He was, in short, a man as disfavored in personal character as he was favored in intellectual brilliance.

Cyon's sojourn at the Medical-Surgical Academy was characteristically brief and stormy. This was the heyday, in Russian intellectual and student circles, of scientific positivism. The belief that all truth could be revealed and comprehended by scientific means had attained in great parts of the Russian academic community, ironically enough, the status of an unquestioned and unquestionable religious faith. Cyon, however, in contrast to practically every other Russian-Jewish intellectual of his time, was a philosophic conservative, a disbeliever in the absolute powers of scientific thought, and a political reactionary—even a monarchist. He made no effort, as a lecturer on physiology, either to hide his general-philosophic convictions or to temper them to the passionately held contrary views of his students. In his inaugural address at the Academy, in 1873, he shocked his listeners to the core by challenging the materialistic philosophy of the time and insisting that the soul had an existence that was, and would always remain, beyond the reach of natural science.* The following year he introduced thoughts of a similar nature into his initial series of lectures, and even attempted to distribute pamphlets setting forth his views in further detail. Great indignation ensued; the students whistled and protested; the pamphlets were thrown

* Cyon, were he alive today, could—and unquestionably would—claim to have been the inventor of the lie-detector. In this same inaugural address, he described for his listeners the nature of the device known as the cardiograph, just then a medical innovation, and predicted that one would, by examining the cardiograph's findings, be able to tell when people were lying or speaking hypocritically. He was much laughed at for these observations; and the well-known Populist writer, N. K. Mikhailovskii, in a bitterly satirical criticism of this lecture and of Cyon's behavior generally, drew a sarcastic word picture of him, standing there like "a living monument," boasting about his own achievements, while the cardiograph, attached to his chest, wrote the words: "He lies; he lies; he lies." (N. K. Mikhailovskii, *Sochinenija* [St. Petersburg: B. M. Wolf, 1897], V, p. 574.)

back at the professor. The disorders promptly took the characteristic forms of student protest of all ages. Cyon was obliged to ask that gendarmes be stationed outside his laboratory to protect him from student wrath. The unrest spread to other institutions of higher learning in Petersburg, notably to the School of Mines and to the university itself, causing some of them, including the Academy, to be closed for several months.

These events naturally split the faculty of the Academy in the most painful way. Matters were made worse by Cyon's ingratitude and lack of generosity towards his popular predecessor, Sechenov; and the chasm of misunderstanding was deepened by the profound conflict of ideology that separated the two men, Sechenov having been as emphatic in the presentation of his positivist philosophy from the lecture platform as was Cyon in the propagation of its opposite.

Nor was this all. The conflict at the Academy cut into similar differences of outlook within the Russian military establishment as a whole. Sechenov's wife (future wife, actually, at the time of these disorders), née Marya Aleksandrovna Obrucheva, was a cousin of the General Nikolai Obruchev whose personality we have just had occasion to note. She was also the sister of the well-known revolutionary publicist Vladimir Aleksandrovich Obruchev. The latter, like his cousin Nikolai, was originally a military man—even a graduate of the General Staff Academy where Nikolai was later to teach. He, too, like his cousin, had been associated with Chernyshevski (in the editing of Pushkin's erstwhile magazine, the *Sovremennik*); but his ties and attachments to the revolutionary movement were much deeper and more serious than those of Nikolai; and they led, finally, to his arrest and exile in the early years of the 1860's.

To all of this must be added a further curious set of circumstances: (1) that the Medical-Surgical Academy (presumably responding to the liberal influence of Milyutin) was the first institution of higher learning in Russia to admit women as students; and (2) that Marya Aleksandrovna Obrucheva-Sechenova was among the first of these female students.*

* Ninety-six women were accepted into the first female class at the Academy in 1871. They were originally accepted, formally speaking, for midwife training, but this was a ruse employed as a means of getting them in, and they were later permitted to attend other courses and to become physicians. Conservative Petersburg society looked on the innovation with horror, and viewed this female student body as a hotbed of radicalism. In 1881, the admission of women at the Academy was terminated, pursuant to the conservative tendency of the new reign.

One of the women in that first class tells, in her memoirs, of the way Cyon was seen by these women students: a good lecturer but a horrible man. One may

There was thus a close connection between the liberal anti-Cyon faction at the Academy and the Obruchev family, including General Obruchev. On the other hand, there was a similar connection between Cyon and the reactionary, anti-Milyutin, anti-Obruchev element in the Russian officers' corps, and particularly the Grand Duke Nikolai Nikolayevich, who, in addition to appearing as the patron of Cyon, seems to have had an intense personal animosity towards Obruchev.* Plainly, then, the conflict at the Academy only matched and reflected a much more significant division in the Russian military establishment as a whole.

In considering, from here on, the relations between the Russian and French military establishments, and particularly between those elements in each who favored the quest for a Franco-Russian alliance, it will be useful to bear in mind that on the Russian side there was not one faction but two which pursued this end, and that each of them pursued it through its own particular channels. The Milyutin-Obruchev faction proceeded from the milieu of the general staff and the higher institutions of military education and research. Although it had its roots in the more liberal atmosphere of the earlier period of the reign of Alexander II, it was to lose this liberal tinge with the departure from office of Milyutin, in 1881, yet to retain its authority by virtue of the simultaneous advancement of Obruchev, now largely recovered from his earlier liberal leanings and even extensively receptive to nationalist impulses, to the position of chief of the general staff. This faction developed its relations to the French military establishment at the confidential-official level, well concealed from the public view. It wisely avoided association with the private Panslav-chauvinist enthusiasts for a Franco-Russian alliance who agitated public opinion at both ends of the relationship. For this reason, and because it was more mature and serious, it was more effective. It was through this channel that the alliance, as a military arrangement, would eventually be prepared and concluded. It was here that the relatively few initiated French officers,

---

be sure that Obrucheva, the future wife of his intellectual and academic enemy, held no high opinion of him. (See E. K. Pimenova, *Dni minuvshiye* [Leningrad: Kniga, 1929].)

* When, during the Russo-Turkish War, the Tsar wanted to assign Obruchev as chief of staff to his son, the heir apparent, who, as a subordinate of the Grand Duke Nikolai Nikolayevich, commanded one of the three army groups in the Balkans, the grand duke, to the Tsar's intense annoyance, put his oar in and refused to permit it, saying Obruchev was not a suitable person for this position. (See Milyutin's diary: *Dnevnik Milyutina* [Moscow: Manuscript Division of Lenin Library, 1947], item for December 27, 1877.)

Boisdeffre and others, were involved; and if there actually were, from as early as the beginning of the 1870's, special collaborative arrangements between the two armies, it was here that they were hatched and cultivated.

The other faction in the Russian army had its roots among conservative or reactionary officers who, like the Grand Duke Nikolai, occupied command positions, rather than positions on the staffs and in the military colleges; and most prominent within it were those officers, such as the ones mentioned in the last chapter, who had strong, sometimes passionate, Panslav or nationalist leanings. Estranged from the Milyutin-Obruchev circles and as a rule not admitted to those councils, they pursued their contacts with France through such personal attachments as they were able to form, sometimes with like-minded personalities in the French military establishment, sometimes with civilian French figures, often people on the chauvinistic side, who shared their enthusiasm for a Franco-Russian alliance.

It remains now to observe briefly, on the example of Cyon and his activities, how some of these latter contacts proceeded. The Medical-Surgical Academy being, as noted above, a quasi-military institution, the task of coping with the disorders unleashed by Cyon's presence at that institution fell to the military authorities. A commission of investigation was set up; and the man selected to chair it (this was just before the war with Turkey) was the same Grand Duke Nikolai Nikolayevich whose later presence in Paris we have just had occasion to note. The commission, not unsurprisingly, came down on Cyon's side on the questions of principle; but the part his abrasive personality had played in unleashing the disorders could not be ignored, and he was benevolently advised to take a good long leave of absence and to spend it in some place far removed from the Petersburg scene.

This was, as it turned out, a leave of absence from which he was never to return. What he did was to proceed to Paris, to take up residence there, to adopt "Cyon" as the French version of his name, and shortly thereafter to acquire French citizenship. He did all this, it is clear, in the hope of obtaining a chair in physiology at the Collège de France just then being vacated by the French scientist, Paul Bert, who was leaving to become minister of education. Cyon's scientific work having won the attention and admiration of the well-known French scientist, Claude Bernard, Cyon hoped to have the latter's support in his quest for the chair. The effort, however, was not successful. Bert himself, a strong positivist, used the power of his new position to oppose it; and Cyon, whose suspicions were always easily aroused, suspected the Russian Embassy, as well, of putting spokes in his wheel.

This failure was a crucial turning point in Cyon's career. For reasons never fully clarified, he gave up at this point what promised to be, despite this reverse, a distinguished scientific career, and turned, for many years to come, to financial, journalistic, and political pursuits, the nature of some of which we shall have occasion to note as we go along.

The reader will recall that the Grand Duke Nikolai Nikolayevich spent the winter of 1879-1880 in France; and that it was there that Cyon was attached to his suite. And because Cyon's own account of this service to the grand duke, as it appears in his history of the Franco-Russian alliance, suggests that even this was not without political overtones, it will be worth while to take note of the words in which the account was phrased.

> Enlisted as medical consultant to the Grand Duke and living in daily intimacy with him, we thought an excessive isolation to be dangerous for him in view of the state of nervous exhaustion in which he found himself, and for reasons of morale-hygiene, supplemented by certain arrières-pensées of a different nature [auxquelles se joignaient accessoirement certaines arrières-pensées d'un autre ordre], we set about to put him in touch first of all with the French military figures. Propriety obliged us to begin with General Greslay, then Minister of War; others followed; and soon the Grand Duke, who was a soldier from head to foot, felt himself to be— among all these French generals and officers—in his natural element, taking the reviews at Saumur, visiting the French arsenals, inspecting the cavalry regiments, etc.[10]

What is one to make of this curious passage? Aside from the use of the editorial "we," which suggests but does not prove that Cyon was not alone in these efforts, it is evident that he had already formed attachments of some sort in the French military world, and the hint of a political design is unmistakable. Most interesting is the clear impression conveyed by this passage that the inspiration for Cyon's activity in the instance at hand was already proceeding from the French, rather than from the Russian side.

The mystery is compounded by a document that reposes in the files of the French Foreign Office. It is a telegram, intercepted by the French authorities, from the Grand Duke Nicholas to "Docteur Cyon," in Paris, dating from the 29th of May 1880, shortly after the grand duke's tour had been completed. It was sent from Russia, to which country the grand duke had by then returned. The text was as follows:

Confidentiellement je m'empresse de vous remercier pour la dépêche qui m'annonce que le gouvernment m'a fait accorder la médaille militaire. Heureux de partager l'honneur ainsi que la gloire de la grande armée française. ["Confidentially, I hasten to thank you for the despatch informing me that the government has conferred upon me the Military Medal. I am happy to have the honor of thus sharing in the glory of the great French army."]

Why, one is obliged to ask, was it Cyon who was communicating to the grand duke the fact that a French military decoration had been conferred upon him?

This is only the first of the many elements of mystery surrounding Cyon's role in the promotion of the Franco-Russian alliance. This role, as indicated above, was not to be, in the end, a major one. But his involvement in this instance suffices to show that already at that time efforts were being made, in the emotional aftermath of the war with Turkey, to promote close relations between the French and Russian military authorities, obviously with a view to eventual achievement of a greater intimacy between the two armies, and that such efforts were proceeding through channels other than the official level on which Obruchev and Boisdeffre were operating. Although the exact nature of Cyon's personal involvement and motivation is obscure; the conclusion remains almost inescapable, if only by process of elimination, that he was operating under the encouragement of instigation of French principals.

Aside from, or along with, the French military, there was naturally no group of people in France whose enthusiasm for an alliance with Russia was greater, over the entire period from 1871 to 1894, than the chauvinists who lived and worked for the day of revenge against Germany. Of these, the two best known, and presumably most impassioned, were the poet Paul Déroulède and Madame Juliette Adam. Déroulède comes into the pattern of Franco-Russian relations only at a later date. But of Juliette Adam, note must be taken at this point, with due apologies to those who may be already well informed with respect to her biography and her political personality.

The daughter of a good, provincial, bourgeois-intellectual family, not without means, Juliette Adam, née Lambert (1836-1936) was a woman of passionate political temperament, inexhaustible energies, wide interests, and varied tastes. Off and on, over a period of some thirty years, from 1864 to the 1890's, her Opportuniste-Républicain salon was one of the leading literary and political meeting-places of Paris. Beginning in 1879, and for many years into the future, she published her own literary-political journal, *La Nouvelle Revue*, in competition with the long-established *Revue de deux Mondes*. Memoirs and novels poured forth from her untiring pen. But her deepest commitment was to politics. Her second and much beloved husband Edmond Adam, who died in 1877, had been a prominent lawyer and political figure of the Third Republic—prefect of police in Paris, in fact, during the siege of 1870. She shared, as a political ideal, his deep commitment to the Republic; and she combined it with a virulent chauvinism. Of all her enthusiasms and passions, the greatest and most consuming were her hatred of Germany and of Bismarck personally (whom she never met) and her longing for the day of *revanche*. She gloried in the reputation derived from these enthusiasms. Writing in 1911 about a visit she paid to Petersburg in 1882, she referred to herself as "la française connue pour avoir la passion de la 'Revanche.'" The foreign affairs section of her magazine, edited largely by herself, was devoted extensively to this cause. An idea of her notoriety in this respect may be gained from the fact that on the occasion of this visit to Petersburg, the German Ambassador there found himself obliged to let it be known that he could not attend any function at which she was present. Bismarck himself is said to have asked a French visitor on one occasion: "Is there really no one who can silence *cette diablesse de femme?*" When this was reported to the French premier, Jules Ferry, he observed, by way of reply: "Only one person, and he unhappily is dead: her husband, Edmond Adam."

It is said that in 1919, on the occasion of the signature of the Treaty of Versailles, Clemenceau sent his car for this implacable woman, then eighty-three years of age, and had her driven to Versailles, where she was given a place of honor in the Hall of Mirrors from which to witness, in triumph, the humiliation of the unfortunate Germans who were obliged to perform the ceremony of signature. Although she lived to be a hundred, she must, one would think, have died happy if only for this one event.*

Madame Adam's interest in Russia was an obvious extrapolation of her desire for the *revanche*; but it was no doubt stimulated, even before 1879, by certain of her personal connections. After her husband's death she was close to, and seems to have been patronized by, the aging Émile de Girardin, commonly regarded as the founder of the French "boulevard press." His paper, *La France*, was one of two (the other being the *Estafette*) mentioned by the German Ambassador Prince Hohenlohe, in

---

* The Rue Juliette Lambert, in Paris, is named for her.

one of his despatches, as "devoted to Russia."[11] There were close connections between *La France* and *La Nouvelle Revue*.*

Another close friend of Juliette Adam was Princess Yelizaveta (Lisa) Esperovna Trubetskaya (generally known in France as Lison Trubetskoi), a Russian *grande dame* who lived in Paris, kept her own salon there, and endeavored—some said with small success—to emulate the example set in London by her eminent compatriot Olga Novikova, the friend of Gladstone. Princess Trubetskaya, in addition to being excellently connected at the Russian court (she was a daughter of Princess Elena Kochubei, who was shortly to become Mistress of the Imperial Household under the Empress Dagmar), was close to Gorchakov, with whom she maintained a steady correspondence, whose pro-French sentiments she reflected, and for whom she served at one time as a channel of communication with people in France. She, too, was no doubt helpful in bringing Juliette together with some of those highly placed Russians whom Juliette is known to have received and entertained at her home in Paris.†

An interesting illustration of the manner in which Juliette Adam and her activities were connected with efforts to improve Franco-Russian relations in the aftermath of the Russo-Turkish War is to be found in certain of her diary notes from 1879. Early in that year one finds her recording the fact that General Chanzy is being named as ambassador at Petersburg. This pleases her greatly. "Il est, comme moi," she writes, "passioné du désir d'une alliance avec la Russie." But then, more significantly, in June of that year:

> Le Général Chanzy . . . qui s'intéresse à la fondation de ma *Nouvelle Revue*, sachant mes sympathies déjà vieilles pour la Russie, m'écrit que ma revue y aura une sérieuse influence, surtout si la politique extérieure [of the magazine] est dans les mains d'une personne que nul pourra corrompre. Je lui réponds qu'elle sera dans les miennes.[12]

In the spring of 1880, shortly after the grand duke's departure from France, Cyon appeared at Madame Adam's personal and editorial headquarters on the Boulevard Poissonière, bringing with him a lengthy

---

* Émile Masseras, chief editor of *La France* and member of its administrative council, became, in March 1880, secretary of the editorial staff of *La Nouvelle Revue*, and one of its political editors.

† An interesting example of the way these people came together is the mention, in one of Juliette Adam's books, *Après l'abandon de la revanche* (Paris: Alphonse Lemerre, 1910), of a dinner she attended at Girardin's home, in October 1879, at which other guests were the future premiers of England and France: Gladstone and Gambetta; Madame Novikova; and the latter's brother, General Alexandr Alexeyerich Kireyev, aide-de-camp to the Grand Duke Constantine Nikolayevich.

monograph offered for publication in *La Nouvelle Revue*. Anonymous in authorship, this paper purported to be a species of first-hand account of the origins of the Russo-Turkish War and the operations conducted on the European front. It had obviously been written or inspired by some highly placed Russian person who had been present at the events described. Although almost certainly drafted by Cyon, it was clear to any reasonably well-informed reader that the account represented the memories of the Grand Duke Nicholas.

The article duly appeared, in two installments, in two issues of *La Nouvelle Revue* of June 1880. In it were not only poured out many of the resentments and grievances surviving from a confused and frustrating military campaign, but a most cynical and discreditable interpretation was given to the motives of the Tsar's government in launching the war in the first place, and—worse still—the effects, and indeed the very fact, of the Tsar's presence at the front were criticized in the most telling manner.* Even coming from the Tsar's brother, such a reproach was shocking and unprecedented; the Tsar's person was, after all, supposed to be beyond criticism by any Russian.

Just what was the purpose of this act of publication, from the standpoint of Cyon and Madame Adam, is difficult to imagine. Both professed to have at heart the interests of a Franco-Russian alliance; but this action did little to promote it. (It was not the last time that both would show themselves heavy-handed in what purported to be efforts along this line.) The Tsar was furious. The grand duke was privately reprimanded by his brother and stripped, for the time being, of all his senior military positions. It is impossible to believe that Franco-Russian relations were in any way bettered thereby. The episode stands only as another historical oddity, illustrating the curious bonds then coming into existence between chauvinist circles in France, on the one hand, and Russian personalities on the other, upset by the outcome of the war with Turkey and determined to find some means of escape from what they viewed as a humiliating subservience of Russian policy to German authority.

This concludes the account of the brief flurries of Franco-Russian amity that accompanied the tension between Russia and Germany in the aftermath of the Russo-Turkish War. They amounted to very little: mostly hints, rumors, some obscure intrigue, and a few amiable words from

* The future Alexander III, then crown prince, was not criticized in the article, although he, too, had a command at the front; and he does not appear to have experienced the same resentment as did his father over the article's appearance.

the Russian side. The French chargé d'affaires in Petersburg was right in insisting they should be disregarded. At no time did they find any response at the civilian level of government in France; the French premier, Waddington, was, in fact, strongly opposed to all such tendencies. They revealed impulses which were later to lead to the conclusion of the alliance, but they were soon overtaken by events. Relations between France and Russia received a severe jolt when, in early March 1880, as the final act of a long series of bungling mistakes in the matter at hand, the French government released from a French jail the Russian revolutionary Lev Nikolayevich Gartman (Hartman), who had conducted, in late 1879, an unsuccessful *attentat* against the Tsar's train, on its way from Livadiya to Petersburg. So great was the indignation in Petersburg over this French action that the Russian Ambassador in Paris, Prince Orlov, was withdrawn from his post for several weeks.

Beyond that, neither the Tsar, Alexander II, nor the pro-French chancellor, Gorchakov, was in any position, after the beginning of 1880, to pursue personally either this or any other sort of radical departure in Russian policy. The nerves of the Tsar were shattered by the terrible *attentat* of the 2nd of March 1880, which destroyed the dining room of the Winter Palace in which the Tsar and his guests were about to sit down to lunch. Three months later (June 3) occurred the death of the Tsar's unhappy wife, the Empress Maria Aleksandrovna. For the few remaining months of his own life, Alexander was preoccupied not only with the problem of his personal security in the face of the attempts on his life but also by his second (and morganatic) marriage to Ekaterina Dolgorukaya, and with his unsuccessful efforts to obtain social acceptance for this unfortunate lady at the hands of a sullen and hostile Petersburg society. Finally, on the 13th of March 1881, there occurred his own assassination. And just at that time international events took, as we shall presently see, a turn which put an end to most of the speculation about closer Franco-Russian relations for several years to come.

Chapter Three

NEW TSAR—NEW ALLIANCE

When on the 13th of March 1881 the Tsar Alexander II, fearfully maimed by a terrorist bomb thrown at him when he was proceeding by carriage along the banks of the Moika Canal, expired in the Winter Palace, this brought to the throne a man quite different in a number of respects. Thirty-six years old at the time of this assassination, Alexander III was a tall, heavy-set man, of enormous muscular strength. If he lacked his father's imagination, charm, and facility of communication, he also lacked some of his negative qualities as well: notably the irresoluteness, the lack of firmness and persistence in decision, the tendency to an evasive ambivalence, and the suspectibility, as well as promiscuity, in relations with the other sex.

By nature lethargic and in some respects lazy, Alexander III was nevertheless dutiful in the exercise of his responsibilities as the autocratic rule of his great Empire. He was highly conscious of the enormous power that lay in his hands. He tried to exercise that power moderately and decently, albeit with firmness; but he expected his authority to be recognized without question, even by members of his own family, and would tolerate no derogation of it.

Not an intellectual and not particularly drawn to people of that description, Alexander III was nevertheless not at all the stupid "oaf" which his enemies sometimes charged him with being. He was a man of few words, whether written or oral; but those few words were usually clear and to the point; and when addressed, as we shall often have occasion to note, to the problems of foreign policy, they revealed close and intelligent attention to the subject matter. He was a man of strong likes and even stronger dislikes. His policies were by no means always uninfluenced by his emotions, but it cannot be fairly said that he was insensitive to the issues involved.

He had a dislike for all forms of innovation. Slow to form his ideas, he was equally slow to change them, and did so only with the greatest reluctance. His firmness of decision was of a part with the pride he took in his integrity and in the reliability of his word. Nor did he take kindly to the prospect of changes in the faces of those by whom, in the official

60

entourage, he was surrounded. He tended to stick firmly to the appointments he had made, showing much patience with the occasional mistakes and failures of the persons concerned. In general, he relied on his own judgment of their performance rather than on the tenor of outside criticism, for which he had nothing but contempt. But this same immobility of spirit had endowed him with an elephantine memory for any serious displeasure these people might give him. Whoever once earned his ill-graces could not expect to be lightly—if indeed ever—forgiven.

Alexander III was, of course, a profound conservative, who believed that the system of power he had inherited was not to be saved by liberal concessions. This being so, it is not surprising that his ministers should have been, in large part, reactionaries. But his chief fault in this respect lay not in the quality of the highly placed persons who were given the privilege of personal access to him, but rather in the narrowness of the circle. He saw, and consulted with, only an extremely small number of public servants; and his contacts with Russian society at large, beyond the tiny group of family intimates, were almost nonexistent.

Anxious as Alexander III was, particularly in the first years of his reign, not to make hasty changes in the edifice of foreign policy erected by his father, there were nevertheless significant differences in the approaches of the two men to Russia's international problems. Like his father, Alexander III recognized and accepted (if somewhat grudgingly) the tie to Germany that existed in the person of his grand-uncle, the German Kaiser; but it did not mean as much to him as it did to his father. And when it was a question not of this dynastic and personal tie but of the new Germany itself, as a cultural and national phenomenon, he was even more negative. He resented the predominance of German-Balt officers and administrators in high positions in Petersburg. He discouraged the speaking of German in his household and at court. But it must in all fairness be added that he objected to the use of foreign languages generally in high Russian society, and was the first Russian ruler to insist that the internal correspondence of the Russian Foreign Office make the change from French to Russian.

Conversely, and not without relationship to these feelings towards Germany, Alexander III had more sympathy than had his father for Panslav outlooks, and more interest in an ambitious and essentially expansionary policy in the Balkans and at the Straits. It is not clear whence this tendency was derived. His experiences as a divisional commander under the Grand Duke Nicholas in the Russo-Turkish War no doubt had something to do with it. But there was also, one suspects, the influence of his neglected and ill-treated mother, who was decidedly partial to Panslav tendencies. It is obvious that during the final years of the latter's life, and retrospectively after her death, Alexander's sympathies leaned strongly to her side in the painful situation created for her by her husband's passionate and ill-concealed liaison with the Princess Catherine Dolgorukaya (whom, after the Empress' death, he married and attempted to establish as Empress in the face of the violent resentment and opposition of most of Petersburg society). The cleavage in the family created by this situation went deep. It would not have been unnatural that this sympathy for his mother, and resentment of his father's behavior, should have affected Alexander's receptivity to the Panslav influences that prevailed in his mother's entourage.

It should also be noted that together with this greater interest in the Balkans and the region of the Straits there went a strong dislike and suspicion of Austria-Hungary. In this, Alexander III differed little, if at all, from his father. The resentment over Austria's failure to support Russia at the time of the Crimean War, coming as this did on the heels of Russia's intervention in Hungary in support of the Habsburg power there in 1848, had continued to affect Russian feelings and Russian policy ever since. But of comparable importance, in the case of Alexander III, was the influence of his former tutor, Pobyedonostsev, who, as leader of what I have ventured to call the party of the "religious imperialists," had particularly strong anti-Catholic feelings and resented the opposition offered by the Vatican, with Austrian support, to Russian-Orthodox religious interests in Poland and eastern Europe generally.

Whatever the origins of the reservations entertained by the new Tsar with respect to Germany, one thing is certain: those reservations met with no discouragement at the hands of his wife. For the latter—the Empress Dagmar (in Danish usage), Mariya Fyodorovna (in Russian) and Mimi (to her husband)—was a Danish princess, daughter to King Christian IX of Denmark, and sister to the future Queen Alexandra of England. She thus came from a court where bitterness against Bismarck was still strong and deep. Her Mistress of the Imperial Household, Princess Elena Kochubei, was also a good friend of Dagmar's mother, the Danish Queen. So the feminine entourage of the new Tsar tended to reflect, generally, a gentle but perceptibly anti-Bismarckian influence.

Dagmar, like her English-married sister, was a thoroughly admirable person. She managed to combine a fine dignity of position with a simple charm, much gaiety of spirit (sadly needed in the entourage of the heavy Alexander III), and the qualities of a loyal wife and good mother. Her influence on her husband was said to have been more than negligible; but it was an influence confined to narrow subjects and never publicly displayed. While not, in the view of contemporaries, as beautiful as her English sister, she dressed superbly, loved to dance, was consistently kind, sympathetic, and responsive to others, and had, it would seem, few if any enemies. Never, since Catherine the Great, had a foreign-born queen been more happily accepted at the Russian court than was this pleasant, healthy, and unassuming Danish woman.

Alexander III was as steadfast in his marriage as in other features of his conduct. He cherished his Danish wife, and remained a faithful husband to her. This fidelity came more easily to him, one suspects, than to her; for her sunny and pleasure-loving disposition found few outlets in the stuffy and isolated palace existence of the imperial couple. But the firmness of their marriage, contrasting sharply as it did with the example of Alexander's father, won respect both in Russia and abroad. Bismarck, in particular, was impressed by it. Alexander III, he once grudgingly conceded in one of his few approving judgments on that monarch, "geht nicht zu den Weibern" (does not frequent the trollops).

Since Danish attitudes, in addition to being anti-German, were inclined to be strongly pro-French, it is permissible to suppose that some of this, too, may have rubbed off on the new Tsar. He was, of course, thoroughly disgusted throughout his reign with the political and governmental conditions that prevailed in France. Particularly offensive in his eyes was the constant, kaleidoscopic changing of personalities at the head of the French government. He had no confidence in people who remained only a few months in power, or in any government whose policies were buffeted about by constant changes of administrative direction. Yet he was by no means anti-French. He admired French culture (insofar as he had any knowledge of it) and obviously had some sympathy for France in her international position. What he could not stand was simply the confusion and instability of her governmental life. When Waddington, sent as special representative to his coronation, in 1883, pointed out to him that Russia and France "ne sont pas sans avoir quelques intérêts en commun," his reply, most significantly, was: "Oui, oui, je le sais. Ayez de la stabilité, de la stabilité."[1] (If, in other words, you had a more stable sort of governmental system, we could perhaps do business with you.)

One of the first questions that had to be faced by Alexander III, as he became the supreme arbiter of all Russian affairs, was the filling of the position of foreign minister. Gorchakov did not enjoy with relation to the new Tsar the same intimacy he had had with the latter's father.

Beyond that, his unsuitability for retention of the position, in view of his general state of senility and his long absences from Russia, was only too obvious to everyone.

There was no lack of aspirants for the position. Peter Shuvalov, Gorchakov's co-delegate at the Congress of Berlin, was an obvious candidate; and Bismarck was not the only one who would have been pleased to see him get the position. An impressive man, of good judgment, fine presence, and great competence, he was, along with Giers, the best qualified of all the Russian diplomats of the period. But Alexander III was even more sensitive to nationalist opinion, and more timorous in the face of it, than his father; and there was even less prospect now than there had been before the assassination of Shuvalov's being given any senior position. (He was in fact never again to be given any regular post of responsibility.)

Then, too, there was Ignatyev—a man whose career had closely resembled that of Shuvalov (they had started those careers together as young officers in the Imperial Guards) but who stood at the opposite end of the spectrum when it came to views on foreign policy. Ignatyev had left his position as ambassador at Constantinople in consequence of the repudiation by the Congress of Berlin of his handiwork: the Treaty of San Stefano. He had been serving, since that time, as governor general at Nizhni-Novgorod. Alexander III began his reign by dismissing the minister of the interior then in office, Loris-Melikov,* on whose very tentative efforts at liberal reform he tended to blame the state of affairs which had permitted the assassination of his father; and he appointed Ignatyev in his place.† Of his desire to succeed Gorchakov as foreign minister Ignatyev left no doubt; and since the Tsar was at that time well-disposed towards him, one may suppose that he would probably have obtained the position had not the Germans made it known, at the meeting between the German and Russian Emperors at Danzig in September 1881, that this appointment would be by no means agreeable to them.

This left, as the outstanding candidate, Gorchakov's deputy, Giers. Ignatyev is said to have persuaded Gorchakov to delay his own retirement, in order to give him, Ignatyev, more time to intrigue for the position. The Tsar's decision, therefore, was long in coming. But finally, on the 9th of April 1882, a year after the beginning of the new reign, the decision fell in favor of Giers, who lost no time in installing himself and his numerous family in the great residential quarters of the Ministry

---

* Count Mikhail Teryelovich Loris-Melikov (1825-1888), Russian general and statesman, minister of the interior 1881-1882.

† Ignatyev, too, and for reasons similar to those that caused the Tsar to dismiss his predecessor, was not to retain the Interior Ministry for very long.

for Foreign Affairs, at the Pevcheski Most (the Singers' Bridge), which had stood so long, through Gorchakov's prolonged absences, neglected and virtually empty.

The ensuing years, as we shall see, would not be lacking in efforts—including some of great power and violence—by jealous competitors desirous of removing Giers from this seat. But he profited, here, from the Tsar's dislike of new faces and his indolent aversion to new decisions; and though forced to yield progressively, as time went on, in questions of policy, he was able to guard his personal position down to the end of the reign of Alexander III, resigning only in 1895, after Alexander's death and just before his own.

Owing to the non-Russian quality of his name, Giers' national origin and even his linguistic habits and accomplishments were the subject of considerable—and often quite erroneous—speculation on the part of contemporary foreign diplomats and journalists. It was variously alleged that he was Jewish, German, Finnish, and Swedish, that German was his native language, that he did not speak—or scarcely spoke—Russian. The truth is that the family name was of Swedish origin (it came from a distant Swedish ancestor who had moved to Russia at the time of the incursions of the Swedish King Charles XII into Russia in the early eighteenth century). The male members of the family had, to be sure, in a number of instances married women of German-Baltic origin; and the family's religion continued down through Giers' time to be Lutheran. But the family was nonetheless Russianized, as were so many other families of foreign name or origin in nineteenth-century Russia. The suggestion that Giers did not speak Russian is particularly absurd. He was bilingual in Russian and French, but also spoke excellent Polish and an indifferent German.*

Although not one to press himself upon the attentions either of the public of his day or of the historian, Giers stands out, on closer examination, as one of the most interesting and impressive figures in the history of Russian diplomacy. Born neither to wealth nor title, the son,

---

* Giers' linguistic habits and attainments are set forth as follows in the excellent Editors' Introduction, by Charles and Barbara Jelavich, to the English edition of Giers' early memoirs, *The Education of a Russian Statesman. The Memoirs of Nicholas Karlovich Giers* (Berkeley and Los Angeles: University of California Press, 1962): "The linguistic background of Giers was varied. As he reports in his memoirs, he and his brothers and sisters were cared for by Polish-speaking servants. His father, who had been educated in Riga, spoke and wrote German readily and used it in his correspondence with his son. His mother, in contrast, preferred French or Russian. Giers himself used French or Russian interchangeably. His memoirs are in Russian, but his voluminous correspondence with his wife is in French. His style in French was far more lucid and expressive than the writing in these memoirs which is dry and repetitive throughout" (p. 225).

in fact, of a man who held the deceptively modest position of postmaster in a small border town,* Giers nevertheless had the good fortune to be educated at two of Russia's finest educational institutions: the Nobleman's Boarding School of the Petersburg University (from the ages of 8 to 12) and then (for a further six years) the famous Lyceum in the palace at Tsarskoye Selo. Entering the service of the Asiatic Department of the Foreign Office immediately after graduation from the Lyceum, he embarked upon a diplomatic career which included many years of service in what were then called "oriental posts" (which included posts in the Balkans) followed by two assignments (Bern and Stockholm) in western Europe. The later stages of this career were presumably aided by his marriage, in 1849, to a niece of Gorchakov. In 1875, he was brought back to the Foreign Office to serve as Gorchakov's deputy and, for a time, as head of the Asiatic Department.

Over much of his professional life Giers struggled with poverty and the problems presented by his large family of children. One of the attractions, to him, of the ministerial position he received in 1882 was the great apartment it carried with it in the building of the Foreign Office on the Pevcheski Most, and the other emoluments. But even this distinguished place of residence did not make of him a regular member of the Petersburg high society. He kept much to himself: appearing primarily only at official functions. He normally lunched once a week, *en famille*, with his imperial master, the Tsar, when the latter was in or near Petersburg. He often accompanied the Tsar during the latter's long periods of residence at Livadiya, in the Crimea, or at other points away from Petersburg. But he did not participate extensively in the social life of the court or the aristocratic society of Petersburg.

A small, at that time gray-bearded, man, with a shrewd, trouble-lined face and quick penetrating eyes, careful and conventional but not elegant in dress, and walking with a slight stoop, Giers was consistently underrated by the more high-powered figures around the Russian court. In the days of his deputyship under Gorchakov he was often criticized by foreign diplomats and statesmen for colorlessness and timidity; but when he became foreign minister in his own right, he gradually gained among these people what appears to have been an almost universal respect. All seem to have been impressed with his deep experience, his calm judgment, and the reliability of his word. No one ever questioned

---

* Radzivilov, situated in the part of pre-World War II Poland recently acquired by the USSR, was, until the development of the railways, the most important of Russia's western border points, leading as it did into the Austrian Empire. The position of postmaster there was one that had important social and political connotations; and Giers' father had many connections with people well placed at court.

his honesty or integrity. Even Bismarck, not predisposed to uncritical enthusiasm for any foreign statesmen, came gradually to think highly of him, received him gladly in Berlin or at Friedrichsruh, and gave him whatever support he could.

The cynical of that day would have said that Bismarck's favor was the result of the fact that Giers was pro-German. This frequently levied accusation, still sometimes repeated in historical literature, was wide of the mark. Giers was, as a statesman and diplomatist, a seasoned professional. There is no reason to suppose that he was any more naive in his view of Bismarckian Germany than in his view of any other of the phenomena of the international scene. He recognized in the old German Emperor William I a force for peace and stability, well inclined towards Russia. He thought that Russia, assailed with bitter internal problems and in need of a long period of peace after the exhausting war with Turkey, should take advantage of this situation, while it lasted. He had no great confidence that even the *Dreikaiserbund*, negotiated from the Russian side under his direction in 1880-1881, would long survive a change on the German throne; but he was too wise in the way of international life to try to look more than a small number of years into the future, and found the amicable relationship with the Germans not only useful but essential to Russia's security for the period he could foresee.

Though sometimes accused of it, Giers was also not anti-French. He never doubted, in the late 1870's and early 1880's, that the time would come for a closer relationship with France. At times, he even used his influence discreetly to promote such a development. But he hoped that this closer relationship would come as a supplement to continued amicable relations with the Austrians and the Germans, not as a substitute for them.

Giers was at all times very much the servant of his master, the Tsar. He had no other choice. He was well aware that both the retention of his position and the success of his policies were dependent on the preservation of the Tsar's confidence. That meant, at times, a humble deference to the Tsar's prejudices. He studied his master with that shrewd realism of which only a modest and unpretentious man is capable; and no one knew better the weaknesses as well as the strengths of that monarch. But Giers was also completely loyal to him, was discreet where discretion was necessary, participated in none of the court intrigues, remained aloof, largely by virtue of his social obscurity, from the political and personal gossip of the capital, and was steady, consistently well-informed, honest, and reliable as an adviser to the throne. To Alexander III—slow, lazy, puritanical in his standards, averse to sudden changes, and unsure of himself in dealings with the vast complexities of Russian diplomacy—these were uniquely valuable qualities. Even though the two men did not always see eye to eye on the objectives of Russian policy, Giers' authority at the Singers' Bridge assured that the ministerial position in question would not become a center of intrigue and that no major, dangerous errors would be made in the execution of Russian foreign policy. If, as was the case, Alexander III feared to challenge nationalist opinion and often quailed in the face of it, even to the point of undercutting his foreign minister, he also respected Giers' enormous experience and expertise, and realized that he could put himself on thin ice by ignoring it. It was this, and in the end this alone, that enabled Giers to weather the many storms here to be recounted.

Intellectually, and in mastery of the subject matter and methodology of the diplomacy of the time, Giers was not inferior to Bismarck; but he was, of course, incomparably more modest, made no effort to exert authority in internal affairs, neither planned nor conducted any wars, and had no interest in playing anything resembling the role that Bismarck played. Whoever concerns himself extensively, however, with the diplomatic documents of the period, will not be able to escape the conclusion that the record of European diplomacy in the second half of the nineteenth century contains the name of no more competent professional diplomatist and statesman, and of none who was more devoted to the preservation of peace.

The first two years of the reign of Alexander III, representing the interval between his father's death and his own coronation (May-June 1883), were in general quiescent ones in the development of Russian foreign policy. The new Tsar was himself absent from the capital over much of this time. There was, however, one decision of the greatest importance, a decision that would constitute the determining element in foreign policy throughout much of his reign, which had to be taken in the very wake of his father's death. To understand the background and the portent of this decision, we must go back some three years, to the aftermath of the Congress of Berlin in 1878, and trace the development of Russia's relations with Germany and Austria in the final years of the reign of Alexander II.

We have had occasion to note, above (Chapter 1), the differing positions of the two chief Russian delegates at the Congress of Berlin, Gorchakov and Shuvalov:* Gorchakov, ill, senile, bitterly jealous of

* Gorchakov and Shuvalov were not the only Russian delegates at the Congress. There was a third: the Russian Ambassador to Germany, P. P. Oubril (the name was usually written this way in Western usage), a protégé of Gorchakov, whom

Plate 1. N. K. Giers, Russian foreign minister

Nach einer Photographie.   Stich u. Druck v. A. Weger, Leipzig.

Alexander III,
Kaiser von Rußland.

Plate 2. The Tsar Alexander III

Plate 3. The Empress Maria Fyodorovna (Dagmar)

Plate 4. General N. N. Obruchev

Bismarck, acutely conscious of the strength of nationalist opinion at home, sulking and evading responsibility for every concession Russia was obliged to make in order to obtain a settlement; Shuvalov, a man in the prime of life, vigorous, able, and realistic, well aware from his recent experience as Russian Ambassador in London of the dangers with which Russia could be confronted if no settlement was reached, taking upon himself the burden of doing what could be done from the Russian side to bring the Congress to a successful conclusion. Bismarck saw this situation very clearly and made the best of it. He soon learned to look primarily to Shuvalov to give Petersburg a clear picture of what was happening at the Congress and to persuade the Russian government to consent to the necessary compromises. In this way, Shuvalov gained Bismarck's confidence in a degree achieved by few other foreign diplomats, if any. It was clearly Bismarck's hope that when the Congress was over, Gorchakov's health being no longer adequate to the proper performance of his duties as foreign minister, Shuvalov would be selected as his successor.

When the Congress ended, in mid-July 1878, Shuvalov paid a visit to Petersburg, before returning to his post at London; and he was received on that occasion by the Tsar. The audience turned out to be, for him, a distressing experience. The Tsar, already influenced by private denunciations from Gorchakov and others, heaped reproaches upon him. The Congress of Berlin, he charged, had been nothing more than a single anti-Russian coalition. The only one to gain from its decisions had been Austria. Bismarck had wanted it all to end this way; Shuvalov had been duped by Bismarck's cleverness.

Shuvalov did his best to explain what he considered to be the real situation. Throughout the period of the Congress, Bismarck, he maintained, had given quiet but effective support to Russian interests; this was evident in the records of every session. On three specific occasions issues vital to Russian interests—so vital that had they not been settled, a new war might well have ensued between Russia and another of the other Great Powers—had been decided in Russia's favor only in consequence of Bismarck's intercession on her behalf.* The only essential

---

the latter insisted on keeping in Berlin despite the fact that Bismarck both detested and distrusted him. Gorchakov and Oubril appear to have despatched regularly to Petersburg, in violation of a prior understanding with Shuvalov, private reports criticizing Shuvalov's actions at the Congress and undermining his position at home.

* One of these issues was the question of the acquisition by Russia of the Black Sea port of Batum. Here, the British had strenuously objected; and it was only by threatening to resign as chairman of the Congress that Bismarck finally persuaded them to accept the Russian demand.

difference between Ignatyev's original Treaty of San Stefano and the final settlement at Berlin was, Shuvalov argued, the division, and reduced size, of the new semi-independent Bulgaria envisaged by those treaties; but Ignatyev must have known that not only would the greater Bulgaria agreed upon at San Stefano not have been acceptable to the other European Powers but it would have jeopardized in the most serious way the Sultan's position at Constantinople; and this position was something the Russians had no reason to wish to see undermined since the main ones to profit from its destruction would almost certainly be the British.

Shuvalov came away from the interview outwardly professing hope that he had modified the Tsar's outlook in some degree; but actually he was deeply shaken by the realization that the Tsar had been misled into seeing the Berlin settlement as a disaster for Russia, depriving her of the fruits of her hard-earned victory over the Turks; and naturally he was much depressed by being made to feel that he was held personally responsible for this supposedly unhappy result.

On leaving Russia again at the beginning of August 1878, Shuvalov passed through Berlin, where, in Bismarck's absence (the latter was taking the cure at Kissingen), he poured out his heart to Radowitz, whose personality we had occasion to note in connection with the 1875 crisis, and who was, in 1878, serving in senior capacity in the German Foreign Office. Not only did Shuvalov tell Radowitz of the unhappy results of his audience with the Tsar, but he went on to express his concern over the general situation in Russia, and particularly the leniency being shown to the press. In theory, he pointed out, the press was subject to censorship; but actually it was spreading, day by day, the wildest misinformation about foreign affairs, and no one called it to account. "One prefers," he said to Radowitz,

> to leave people with the mad illusion that Russia's interests have been grievously damaged by the action of certain foreign powers, and in this way one gives sustenance to the most pernicious agitation. Everyone wants peace; the condition of the country urgently demands it; but at the same time one tries to divert to the outside world the effects of the discontents produced, in reality, by the mistakes of one's own policies.[2]

Radowitz at once reported all this to Bismarck; and there can be no question of the profundity of the impression it made upon him. Bismarck attached great importance to Shuvalov's future as a Russian statesman, seeing in him the best prospects for a stable relationship between the two countries.* But beyond that, the Russian reaction to the Congress

---

* In later years, Bismarck was to claim that Shuvalov's appointment as ambas-

of Berlin, as reflected in Shuvalov's account and in many other indications that Bismarck was subsequently to receive, seemed to undermine the very foundations of his own foreign policy, based as it was on the preservation of a close and dependable relationship to Russia. It raised at once the spectre of a Franco-Russian alliance, a spectre which was to be given further plausibility over the course of the ensuing months as various rumors were picked up of Russian contacts and feelers in Paris. And above all, it put a final end to his confidence in the Tsar, Alexander II. The latter, to be sure, had never shown any personal warmth for Bismarck; but he was devoted to his elderly uncle, the Kaiser, and up to this time Bismarck had thought he could be depended upon to pursue a policy of friendship with Germany. Bismarck knew that Alexander still wanted no war with Germany. But he now lost all confidence in the Tsar's capacity for effective leadersip. He referred to him, on one occasion, as a prematurely worn-out old man, sick and feeble: "an autocrat without the capacity to rule, a plaything of the armchair generals."[3] He deeply distrusted the influences around the Tsar—particularly the female ones,* but also a number of others that prevailed in the official and political entourage.

Altogether, then, the pattern, as Bismarck saw it, was unsatisfactory and even to some extent dangerous. The Russians, it seemed, were proceeding on the assumption that they could eat their cake and have it, too: permit themselves the luxury of an anti-German press campaign, of strong troop concentrations along the German border, and of a threatening posture towards Austria, and at the same time have recourse to German benevolence whenever they needed it. This, in Bismarck's view, was a dangerous state of mind in which to leave them. As long as it prevailed, there would always be the danger of their allying themselves with some other major European power. It was necessary to force them to choose.

---

sador to London, in 1874, had already been a species of honorable exile, the product of Gorchakov's jealousy, and that when this appointment took place, he, Bismarck, had authorized his banker to sell his Russian securities. His memory may have deceived him, here, about dates (see F. Stern, *Gold and Iron*, New York: Knopf, 1977, p. 288), but of his confidence in Shuvalov, and the importance he attached to the latter's career, there can be no doubt.

* This was, it might be noted, a time when the Tsar's infatuation with the Princess Dolgorukaya, commonly suspected of Panslav sympathies, was being much talked about. And, in general, Bismarck's violent mistrust and resentment of the influence of women in political matters is familiar to everyone who is acquainted with his biography. His feelings with relation to the German Empress at that time, and to the English-born Crown Princess (Queen Victoria's daughter "Vicky"), are an outstanding example of this oddity of the Bismarckian temperament.

Bismarck's policy, in the face of this situation, moved along two lines. One, characteristically, was an effort to make the Russians feel the bite of German displeasure in relatively minor ways. The German press was encouraged to talk back ("but delicately, without offending the person of the Tsar," as Bismarck specified, in an annotation on a diplomatic despatch).[4] Tariffs were raised on the importation of Russian goods. Quarantine restrictions were tightened in a manner quite painful, even humiliating, to the Russians. And in the various international commissions established by the Congress of Berlin to refine certain of its decisions and to assure their execution, the German representatives were instructed to remain passive, to take no initiative, and to support Russian proposals only when these met with the agreement of the Austrians and the other Powers.

This last annoyed the Russians intensely. When Radowitz reported that various Russian figures (up to and including the Tsar) were complaining about the lack of German support in the work of the commissions, he was told, on Bismarck's authority but with an injunction not to quote the chancellor directly, that he should point out to the Russians that the Germans had supported them at the Berlin Congress, even at the expense of their own relations with others; and what had they had for it?—black looks, ingratitude, hostile press campaigns. They could support them no longer.

These, however, were only the minor and relatively public measures. Behind them, and simultaneously with them, there went a move of far more serious importance: the negotiation of a defensive alliance with Austria-Hungary.

If Russia, in the prevailing circumstances, was not dependable as an associate of Germany, then it was essential to make sure of Austria. She could no longer be left on the loose; she might then even ally herself with France. Without the assurance of Austrian friendship and support, Germany ran the risk of isolation. Once that friendship and support were assured to Germany, then it would be Russia who would face the dangers of isolation. She would then be easier to deal with. "Austria," Bismarck wrote in an instruction to his Foreign Office, "is more certain, because her people favor such an alliance. Besides, she brings England along with her, and she becomes vulnerable to hostile influences, if she finds no support with us."[5]

The idea of concluding a defensive alliance with Austria came to a head in September 1879 amid a welter of complications that included an unwise and offensive letter from Alexander II to the German Kaiser, a personal meeting between those two monarchs at Aleksandrovo, on the Russian-German border; a notification of the intention of the Austrian foreign minister, Count Andrassy (whom Bismarck greatly respected) to retire; a meeting between Bismarck and Andrassy at Bad Gastein, in Austria, on the eve of the latter's retirement; and finally, a conflict of epochal dimensions between Bismarck and the German Kaiser over the entire undertaking. Seldom will the diplomatic historian find a more dramatic and politically more revealing series of diplomatic documents than those, particularly the exchanges between Bismarck and the Kaiser, which accompanied this crisis. So intense were the convictions on both sides that each of these historic figures threatened, at one point or another, to give up his position—the Kaiser, to abdicate; Bismarck, to resign the chancellorship—if he did not get his way. The Kaiser, conscious of a bond of loyalty to his Russian nephew, saw no reason for an Austro-German alliance, and was particularly averse to one specifically directed against Russia. Bismarck, not disputing the Tsar's professions of a desire for peace, was nevertheless profoundly suspicious, as we have seen, of the influences then making themselves felt around the Russian throne, and felt it absolutely essential, in the circumstances, that Germany be protected against the possibility of having to face alone an eventual Franco-Russian combination or—even worse—to face a tripartite hostile alliance that would include, in addition to the French and Russians, the Austrians as well. The possibility of negotiating a pact with the Austrians before Andrassy might leave office seemed to him to constitute a unique opportunity, which might never again occur.

In the end, Bismarck had his way, at the cost of much anguished effort and great strain on his nerves and health. The treaty, finally signed in Vienna on the 7th of October 1879, provided for unlimited mutual support in the event either of the parties should be attacked by Russia or by a third Power supported by Russia. In the case of a French attack on Germany, not supported by Russia, the Austrians were bound only to observe a benevolent neutrality; but should the Russians enter on the French side, then Austria was bound to give Germany her support.

Bismarck had not failed to warn the Russians repeatedly that the unsatisfactory state of Russo-German relations would force the Germans to concern themselves for the strengthening of their relations with other Powers; and the fact of Bismarck's presence in Bad Gastein, together with Andrassy, in mid-September made it quite clear to the world that something unusual was going on in Austro-German relations. None of this was lost on the Russian government; and to this has often been attributed the fact that the Russian press, which in August had shown itself particularly violent in its treatment of Germany, suddenly, in September, ceased its attacks, while at the same time the Russian government began to show a distinct interest in the improvement of relations with Germany. This factor—the fear of an Austro-German alliance—no doubt played some part; but the main reasons for this change in the Russian attitude lay elsewhere: first, in the amicable meeting between the two monarchs—the Tsar and the German Kaiser—at Alexandrovo in early September (an encounter which went off extremely well and ended with much good feeling), and secondly, in the activities of one very adroit and skillful Russian diplomat: Pyotr Aleksandrovich Saburov. The latter, at that time Russian minister at Athens, had met and talked with Bismarck at Kissingen in early August, after which he returned to Russia to warn the Tsar of the danger of a change in German foreign policy that could be dangerous to Russia, and to urge, effectively as it turned out, an effort to reach some sort of accommodation with the Germans. Greatly interested in the problems of Russia's relations with Turkey, he was convinced that a bargain could be struck with Germany whereby Russia would give Germany a free hand against France, while Germany would give Russia a free hand at the Straits and would restrain the Austrians from opposing it. Pursuing this dream as he did over the course of years, Saburov seems never to have fully understood that Bismarck had no desire for another war against France and was therefore not greatly interested in a deal on these terms. But his arguments evidently made an impression on the Tsar (who summoned him all the way to the Crimea to hear what he had to say); and Saburov was sent back to Germany to pursue his discussions with Bismarck. Actually, it was while he was on the way to Berlin that the German agreement with the Austrians, uncertain to the very end, was—unbeknownst to him—finally concluded; so the adverse event his mission was supposed to avert had actually taken place before he entered upon his mission and before anyone in Russia knew, or realized, the seriousness of what was afoot. But the conclusion of the treaty with Austria, an action not revealed to the public or to other governments in any case, did not preclude a rapprochement with Russia. On the contrary, the Kaiser, still unhappy over the Austrian treaty which he had been forced, most reluctantly, to accept, was eager to counterbalance it by a friendly action vis-à-vis the Russians, whereas Bismarck, his point now gained and his Austrian flank assured, was only too happy to resume the dialogue with Russia.

Out of these discussions between Bismarck and Saburov there developed, then, further negotiations—at first involving only the Austrians, but later the Russians as well—by virtue of which the Austro-German Treaty, though still held secret from the Russians and retaining its validity only for the two contracting parties, became in effect worked into, or covered by, a tripartite arrangement, the so-called *Dreikaiserbund*.* In this new tripartite agreement, all three Powers assumed obligations to one another similar to those already embodied in the Austro-German Treaty, but directed this time only to the possibility of war by any of the three against other European Powers. The negotiation of this agreement, supervised at the Russian end by Giers (because Gorchakov was now spending most of his time at western European spas), involved many difficulties, principally with the Austrians; and a full year and a half was required to complete it. The agreement was still unsigned at the time of the assassination of Alexander II in March 1881; but the negotiations were by that time far advanced, and Alexander III, while not moved by any great enthusiasm for the enterprise, was in no mood, in those first weeks of his reign, to undertake a complete reversal of his father's foreign policy by questioning its soundness. He therefore signed it, on the 18th of June 1881.

This pact, concluded for a period of three years, bound each of the three parties, in case any other one of them was to find itself at war with a fourth Power, to observe towards the conflict in question a benevolent neutrality (benevolent, that is, with relation to the respective signatory to the pact), and to devote its efforts to a localization of the conflict.

---

* Much confusion has been occasioned by the use of the same names, *Drei-Kaiser-Bündnis* or *Dreikaiserabkommen* in the German, *The League of Three Emperors* in the English, to cover both the curious personal agreement arrived at by the three Emperors in question in 1873, and the formal treaty concluded in 1881. So serious is this confusion that several historians have been misled into describing the second of these agreements as the renewal of the first, although the text of the second clearly states that it is a *replacement*, not a *renewal*, of the earlier one. The difference in content, furthermore, clearly differentiates the two agreements, the first being only a personal arrangement among the three monarchs providing for a species of consultation in the event of a threat to the peace, whereas the second was a full-fledged treaty, binding on governments as well as on monarchs, and having quite different provisions.

Neither of these instruments was given by its authors a title; so the historian is at liberty to choose what he will. The official German *Grosse Politik der europäischen Kabinette*, compounds confusion by using for both the term *Drei-Kaiser-Bündnis*. The English designation *League of Three Emperors* is only a translation. Certain of the diplomatic historians (for example, G. P. Gooch, in his *History of Modern Europe*) have used the German term but shortened it to *Dreikaiserbund*, instead of *Drei-Kaiser-Bündnis*. Since this would appear to be everyman's choice, I have elected to do the same, when speaking of the secret Treaty of 1881, leaving the earlier (and much less important) agreement of 1873 to bear, if one will, the full title of *Drei-Kaiser-Bündnis* (although it was, in reality, hardly that).

This arrangement promised to each of the three Powers an important measure of security. It gave Austria additional assurance against the spectre of a Russian action against her in the Balkans.* To the Russians it gave not only a certain implicit assurance against a common Austrian-German action against them, but, more important still, the assurance that if Russia found herself at war with England over the problems of the Straits or of Central Asia (and this was at that time their most immediate anxiety), England would not be joined by either Germany or Austria. But it was in the case of the Germans that the convention had a significance most important from the standpoint of Franco-Russian relations; for it gave them the assurance that in another Franco-German encounter, regardless of who inaugurated it or who might be held to be the aggressor, Russia was bound to stand aside and observe a neutrality "benevolent" to Germany. This undertaking obviously precluded, for at least three years into the future, the consideration by Russia of anything resembling an alliance with France; since Russia could not simultaneously promise Germany to remain neutral in such an encounter, yet promise France to come to France's aid. The treaty being renewed in 1884, this effectively ruled out any formal approach to such an alliance from the Russian side for a full six years. (The French, of course, remained in ignorance of it.)

In addition to this key provision, the treaty had two other features that deserve notice at this point.

First, there was the extreme secrecy that was maintained with respect not only to the wording but to the very existence of the agreement. Considering that three imperial courts were involved in its negotiation, the discretion successfully observed was positively amazing. It is explicable, in retrospect, only on the hypothesis that very few people in any of the three capitals concerned were admitted to the knowledge of what was being done. Even when knowledge of the existence of the agreement did begin to leak, and when it was finally brought to general attention (by Katkov) in 1887, its exact terms were still not known. It was commonly believed that it had come into existence only in 1884, and then at the meeting of the three emperors in Skiernewice in September of that year (see below). This impression even dominated dip-

---

* Austria was, of course, already protected by the defensive alliance with Germany. But this was operable only in case she was attacked; and the implementation of it was thus dependent upon the usual question of interpretation: who was the aggressor? The convention establishing the *Dreikaiserbund*, while it assured Austria only of the *neutrality* of its two neighbors, said nothing about the question of who might be the aggressor, and therefore inhibited these two Powers from joining with Austria's enemy in any such encounter.

lomatic historiography for many years thereafter.* It appears not to have been until the aftermath of the First World War, when the Germans published the first volumes of their *Grosse Politik der europäischen Kabinette* (1922), that the real circumstances of the origin and existence of the 1881 agreement became widely known.

The second feature of this agreement that deserves to be noted at this point is the accompanying protocol in which mention was made of certain specific Balkan problems. It was agreed here that the Austrians might, at whatever time it might suit them, formally annex the two Turkish provinces of Bosnia and Herzegovina which they had occupied, with grudging Russian acquiescence, during the Russo-Turkish War. On the other hand—and this is of particular importance for the present study—the three Powers agreed not to oppose the eventual reunion of Bulgaria and Eastern Rumelia "if this question should arise by the force of circumstances." This last was, of course, a desideratum advanced by the Russians, who professed at that time ardently to desire such a unification but recognized that it would be in conflict with the provisions of the Treaty of Berlin. They were prepared to see the realization of this union postponed for the immediate future, but were not willing to abandon the project as a long-term aim of Russian policy. We will shortly have occasion to observe the unexpected consequences of the inclusion of this clause.

It should be noted that a number of the difficulties encountered in the ensuing years in Balkan affairs arose partly because of ignorance on the part of lower-level officials of the existence and provisions of this agreement. Much of the indignation, for example, addressed by the Russian Panslavs to the Austrians over questions involving Austrian policy in Bosnia and Herzegovina could have been avoided if the undertaking mentioned above had been publicly known. But Alexander III was persuaded that the obligations undertaken vis-à-vis Austria in this treaty would, if known, have been intensely unpopular in Russia. He was thinking here, no doubt, of the chauvinistic, Panslav wing of educated Russian opinion. For this reason, he was never entirely comfortable about the arrangement and was always fearful that it might leak out. One wonders, in fact, whether even Pobyedonostsev was ever informed of the existence and nature of the treaty, and whether perhaps the Tsar's fear of its being revealed did not reflect his unwillingness to

*Even so nosey a person as Cyon, writing in 1895, was under this impression. So was the well-informed German publicist Heinrich Geffcken, former friend and adviser to the German Crown Prince (and briefly Emperor) Frederick, writing in 1893. The fact that such people were unaware of the 1881 treaty shows how magnificently the secret was kept.

face the angry disapproval which the agreement would have aroused in this formidable paternal figure. However that may be, the *Dreikaiserbund*, as a reality of those initial years of the reign of Alexander III, must be regarded as a very solemn and significant instrument, affecting profoundly the behavior of the three monarchs and their most intimate advisers, but affecting it in ways of which they could give to the wider public no adequate accounting.

While the initial years of the reign of Alexander III were, after the conclusion of the *Dreikaiserbund*, a period of quiescence in Russian foreign relations, the problem of the renewal of that treaty brought about a new flurry of uncertainty and the need for a new crisis of decision—a crisis in which the new Tsar was obliged to shoulder, for the first time, the full burden of responsibility. The treaty, it will be recalled, had been signed on the 18th of June 1881, for a three-year term. It was due, therefore, either for expiration or for renewal in June 1884.

At a very early date—fifteen months before that deadline—Saburov began to agitate for changes in the agreement which would imply German and Austrian sanction for the eventual establishment, at whatever time it might suit the Russian government, of Russian control at the Straits. His basic argument was that whereas the 1881 agreement gave Germany a free hand against France (once again, in this connection, Bismarck was obliged to point out wearily, time after time, that Germany had no intention of attacking France and no interest in doing so), it did not specifically give Russia a free hand against Turkey. This *lapsus*, Saburov insisted, should be corrected when the agreement was renewed.

There can be no doubt that Saburov's agitation in this direction, pursued not just in internal Russian discussions but also in far-reaching discussions with the Germans for which he had no proper authority, was connected with a desire on his part to commend himself to the Tsar and others in Petersburg, and, on the strength of this commendation, to oust Giers from his newly won position and to replace him in it. Since the suggestions in question had considerable appeal to the Panslavs as well as to Russian military circles, the challenge was a dangerous one, and not easy to ward off. Neither the Germans nor the Austrians were interested, however, in changing the treaty along the lines Saburov was urging; and with their help, together with the Tsar's aversion to change in any form, Giers was able to hold his ground, both politically and personally. The treaty was renewed, in 1884, with only a minor modification, thus committing the Russian government for another three years—down to May 1887—to a set of engagements which, while they did not necessarily rule out every sort of improvement in Franco-Russian relations, firmly and definitely precluded anything in the way of an alliance between the two Powers.

With the relationship of the three imperial governments thus secretly defined for at least another three years to come, the world public was given a hint of the continuing relationship when the three Emperors met, at Skiernewice in Russian Poland, later that year.

Both the Austrian and the German Emperors owed, at that time, visits to their much younger Russian counterpart, who had been crowned only the previous year. Alexander III was to be in Poland, in the late summer of 1884, for military manoeuvres; and it was first arranged that he would receive, while there, the visit of the Austrian Emperor, Franz Joseph. Because of strong feelings, both Catholic and Orthodox, over the religious implications of the presence of an Austrian emperor on Russian soil, it had been thought that the Tsar might receive him at Skiernewice, some forty miles southwest of Warsaw, where there was a palace, formerly the seat of the archbishops of Grodno, now used as a Russian imperial château. For a visit to this place, the Austrian Emperor would have to travel only some one hundred and fifty miles into Russian territory, and could avoid appearance in any of the larger cities.

Bismarck, on learning of these plans, became uneasy. He did not trust his two allies to arrive at desirable understandings without the mediating presence of himself and his aged imperial master. He had been involved, just that spring, in a polite, but significant, altercation by correspondence with the Austrian leaders (Kalnocky and the emperor), over Austria's relationship to Bulgaria. He was alarmed by the insistence of the Austrians that although they had no desire at the moment to challenge Russia's predominant interest in that country, and no intention of attempting to support its first prince (see below) against the Tsar, they still had certain interests in Bulgaria—railway matters and others—which made it something less than a matter of total indifference to them what happened there. Aware that he had not been able to overcome these Austrian reservations, and unable to free himself, as he said, from the impression "that Kaiser Franz Joseph attaches to the preservation of peace with Russia less importance than we do and might well shape his conduct accordingly," he skillfully managed to insert his own Kaiser, plus himself and his two foreign-ministerial colleagues, Giers and Kalnocky, into the projected summit meeting, thus making it a tripartite one, and one including governmental personages in addition to the royal ones.

Alexander III had no love for what in another century would be called "summit meetings"—no love, indeed, for formalities of any sort. He had a particular abhorrence of occasions at which he himself might be asked to speak. When, at the end of July 1884, Bülow, the German chargé d'affaires, asked Giers to sound out the Tsar informally and find out whether he would be receptive to the suggestion of a three-Power meeting, the answer came back from Giers, some days later: yes, he would be; but—

> sans enthousiasme! Il ne s'emballe guère. Il ne perd jamais son équilibre, son flegme. Si vous voulez, il accepte, mais à la condition qu'on ne lui demande pas de prononcer un discours. Il a horreur des discours.[6]

And when the German Ambassador, just then returning to Petersburg, found occasion some days later to speak personally to the Tsar about the proposed meeting at a court ball, the latter's response was: "All right. If you like. It is a matter of perfect indifference to me."

The meeting took place from the 15th to the 17th of September 1884, at Skiernewice, in that atmosphere of nervous excitement and intellectual anticlimax that seems to surround all meetings, in every age, of the very great. The presence of so much imperial majesty in one small place was a nightmare to security officers, and there were the usual frantic, tense, confused arrangements.

They were a curious trio, those three Emperors: the old Kaiser William I, thirty-three years older than Franz Joseph; the latter, in turn, fifteen years older than Alexander III. The third of these men was, after all, a grandnephew to the first. But they dutifully did their parts: the first too old to care very greatly; the second skeptical, bored, and politically suspicious; the third averse to all ceremonial occasions, dragged there in fact against his will and anxious only to get it over with. There was no real discussion of political matters—at least not at the imperial level. The Tsar, at the gala dinner, could not even remember the words Giers had composed for his short toasts. For the remainder of the dinner Franz Joseph appeared tired and apathetic, and the Tsar looked as though he could not wait for the moment to get up and leave. When dinner was over, the three Emperors stood and chatted politely together at one end of the dining room; while the Empress Dagmar, who had been taken along in the hopes that an encounter in the flesh would help to reconcile her to the hated Bismarck, stood by the great chancellor at the other end of the room and said amiable things to him about what a pleasure it was to see these three august figures together. Then the Warsaw ballet danced—for what must have been, in the history of that estimable ensemble, the least inspiring of all audiences. And the next day the three foreign ministers had their pictures taken in the park; Kalnocky, bluff and impassive under his heavy black moustaches; Bismarck, towering commandingly in the middle, resplendent in the white uniform he had had designed especially for himself; and at his right, little Giers, in top hat and black overcoat, his hands reposing on a silver-headed cane, endeavoring modestly to efface himself and looking for all the world like an older relative in attendance at an *haute bourgeois* family funeral.

The Skiernewice meeting has been described as the high point of the *Dreikaiserbund*—the high point, in fact, of the diplomacy of Bismarck as imperial chancellor. It made, at the time, a considerable splash in world opinion. As noted above, many people supposed, and continued to suppose for years thereafter, that it was here, on this occasion, that some sort of formal document, uniting the three Empires in a political and military alliance, had been negotiated and concluded. The French chauvinists, like the Russian Panslavs, were angered and discouraged by the event. Certain of the higher Russian officers who had heretofore leaned to strongly Panslav views were given, momentarily, cause for hesitation. By and large the impression was created of a solid political intimacy among the three imperial regimes, precluding for years into the future any such radical and disturbing deviations as the development of a closer relationship between Russia and France.

Giers, of course, knew better. He had sponsored the *Dreikaiserbund*, negotiated the wording of it, defended it against bitter attacks. But he had no illusions about its permanency. For his imperial master it was, he knew, a means only of gaining time, while one recuperated from the damages of the war with Turkey and built up new armed forces—particularly an adequate navy. It was an arrangement that could be depended upon, at the German end, only so long as the old Kaiser lived and Bismarck was still in office. And the Austrian leg of it continued to stand, Skiernewice or no Skiernewice, on the most infirm of foundations; for despite all Bismarck's efforts to coax the Russian and Austrian governments to a recognition of clearly delineated spheres of influence in the Balkans, there was really no complete and dependable agreement between them on these matters. Nor was either of the two imperial governments—the Austro-Hungarian and the Russian—united within itself in relation to the problems involved. The Hungarians were as little reconciled to Austrian policies directed to the cultivation of good relations with Russia as were the Russian Panslavs to Tsarist policies that implied readiness to pay a price for good relations with Austria. And while the breakthrough of these chauvinistic impulses on both sides might be delayed, and while the renewal of the *Dreikaiser-*

bund and the public gesture of the Skiernewice meeting might help to delay it, one could not realistically expect it to be permanently averted. It was idle, Giers confessed to a German representative after the meeting, to suppose that further conflicts over the Balkans could be avoided. "Là-dessus," he said,[7] remembering among other things his recent service as head of the Asiatic Division, "il n'y a aucune illusion à se faire. J'en sais quelque chose; j'ai vécu vingt ans en Orient." ("About this one should have no illusions. I know something about it. I have spent twenty years in the Balkans.")

Chapter Four

A BIT ABOUT PERSONALITIES

Up to the year 1884, the Russian Embassy at Paris remained in the calm and prudent hands of old Prince (and General) Nikolai Alekseyevich Orlov. Aristocrat to the core, a Russian grandee of the old school, distinguished outwardly by the black patch over the socket of an eye lost in the Crimean War, Orlov was liked and greatly respected both by his own staff and by Paris society; but he was well aware of the impediments that stood in the path of any far-reaching development of Franco-Russian relations, and had no emotional commitment to their early improvement. Personally close to Bismarck,* he was a man of the world, with seasoned judgment, skeptical—no doubt—with relation to all, prejudiced—it would appear—against none.

In 1884, however, the failure of Saburov's attack on the original *Dreikaiserbund* resulted in his own removal from the Berlin post; and Orlov, well viewed by Bismarck, was transferred to Berlin as his replacement. This opened the way for a new appointment at the Paris Embassy; and the choice fell on the man who was at that time serving as ambassador to Great Britain: Baron Arthur Pavlovich Mohrenheim. Taking up his duties in Paris in April 1884, Mohrenheim was destined to remain there until the end of the reign of Alexander III and to play a very considerable part in the preparation of the alliance.

Baron Mohrenheim, whose family was said to have come from the neighborhood of Cracow, was evidently a Catholic. (He had, in any case, three daughters who were known as "Catholiques-enragées.") Giers' son Nikolai, then serving as a young secretary in the Paris Embassy, spoke, however, in his recently published memoirs,[1] of Mohrenheim's "intelligent, bemonocled Jewish face." Cyon, who detested him, also described him as Jewish. (He and Cyon likewise reproached each other mutually, at long distance, for improperly appropriating the "de" to their names.)

*For an account of Bismarck's rather moving friendship with both Prince and Princess Orlov, of his devotion to the latter, and his deep sorrow upon her untimely death, see N. Orlov, *Bismarck und die Fürstin Orloff* (Munich: Beck, 1936).

Mohrenheim was an active man, high-powered in manner, and a glib, if long-winded, talker, capable, when it suited his purposes, of displaying a rather fancy adroitness. He was not well liked by his staff—at least not by his Counselor of Embassy and deputy Prince Kochubei, who was the older of the two men, or by young Giers, who suspected him of dipping his hand too frequently into the Embassy till. But he was, at the least, an experienced diplomatist. He had served as minister at Copenhagen, where he had won the good disposition of the Danish court. It was widely believed—and one may suppose it to have been true—that he enjoyed the benevolent patronage of the Empress Dagmar and her pro-Danish Mistress of the Imperial Household, Princess Kochubei, who had known him in Copenhagen, and that this alone accounted for his obtaining the prestigious Paris post. His performance in London had not been satisfactory, at least not in Giers' eyes; and the necessity of his removal from that post had been one of the reasons for his transfer. Giers, in fact, had no love for Mohrenheim at all; but he tolerated his presence and activity in Paris and seems—presumably in view of Mohrenheim's standing with the Empress—never to have pressed for his removal.

It should be added that Mohrenheim, whether as a consequence of his close ties to the Danish court or by virtue of some innate anti-Germanism, seems to have been at all times strongly committed to the idea of a Franco-Russian alliance. From the time of his arrival, therefore, in 1884, the influence of the Russian Embassy at Paris was consistently exerted in that direction. The Embassy, on the other hand, staffed as it was for the most part with Russian noblemen, had no intimacy with Juliette Adam and her republican-chauvinist entourage, and had nothing but suspicion for the shadowy figure of Cyon, for all his grand-ducal connections.

Before leaving the subject of the Russian Embassy at Paris, note should also be taken of the establishment there, in early 1884, of a branch office of the Russian Department of Police, headed initially, and for long into the future, by P. I. Rachkovski. The "Okhrana," as the Russian secret police apparatus was generally termed,* had of course had agents in Paris prior to this time. In the early 1880's, it had been served there (but not satisfactorily, it appears) by one Korvin-Krukovskoi, who continued for some years after Rachkovski's arrival to serve as a subordinate agent. But it was not until 1884 that a regular

*Technically, the term referred to one of the sections of the Department of Police—the so-called Okhrannoye Otdelenie, established in 1881 to handle counter-revolutionary activity.

office of the Okhrana was established, within the structure of the Embassy.

The primary function of this entity was to keep an eye on the activities of the fugitive Russian revolutionaries who resided in Paris, to counteract their influence on French public opinion, and to work in favor of the repression of their activities by the French authorities. But this meant influencing the French press; and the influencing of the press meant involvement, to some extent at least, in the mazes of French politics. It was only natural that since the revolutionaries were at all times concerned to influence French opinion *against* the development of closer ties with Russia, the Paris office of the Okhrana should have been concerned to influence it in the opposite direction; in effect, that is, in the direction of a Franco-Russian alliance.

The activities and connections of this somewhat clandestine bureaucratic entity were extensive. It appears to have made use of the services of a most notorious character: the former Russian diplomat K. G. Katakazi, at one time Russian minister in Washington but recalled from that post in 1872 at the request of the United States government and then dismissed from the Russian diplomatic service.* Another former Russian diplomat, also one who had suffered dismissal but a person of higher personal quality than Katakazi: Sergei Spiridonovich Tatishchev,† seems to have had a similar connection.

Of all of Rachkovski's associates, however, the most interesting, from the standpoint of the history of the Franco-Russian alliance, was the Dane, Jules Hansen, political agent and public relations adviser to both Rachkovski and Mohrenheim, historian (after a fashion) of the alliance, and admiring biographer of Mohrenheim.‡

---

* Seldom does one encounter in the historical record anyone concerning whose general iniquity there was such unanimous agreement as Katakazi. "This," wrote the editor Mikhail Katkov to Pobyedonostsev, in 1887, "is a fellow who will sell out anyone and anything." This view met with agreement in no lower a place than the imperial throne. "That Katakazi was a beast is something I have long known," wrote Alexander III in that same year, "but that he was such a crook and such a scheming scoundrel—this, I must confess, I had not expected." Cited in E. M. Feoktistov, *Vospominaniia E. M. Feoktistova* (Leningrad: Priboi, 1929), p. 288n.

† Tatishchev had been dismissed in 1877, while serving in Vienna, for an indiscretion of which he may or may not have been really guilty. He was close to Katkov and served as Paris correspondent for the latter's *Russki Vestnik*. He was the author of a serious work on Russian diplomatic history: *Iz proshlago russkoi diplomatii. Istoricheskie izsledovaniia i polemicheskie stat'i* (Petersburg: Suvorin, 1890).

‡ Hansen was the author of two books—both of minor, but not negligible, importance—about the background of the Franco-Russian alliance: *L'Alliance*

Having played a considerable role in Danish and European diplomatic affairs in earlier years, Hansen was by this time a fairly well-known figure in Paris. Born in Denmark in 1828, he worked as a journalist and publicist there until 1864. He was then sent by a group of patriotic Danes to Paris, to serve as a press agent for the Danish cause in the conflict with Prussia, then just reaching its climax. This task he seems to have carried out to general satisfaction. But his greatest hankering in life, in addition to his normal profession of journalism, was for the role of the confidential intermediary between governments. He was, though in no invidious sense of the term, a born busybody. He had not been in Paris more than a few months before he found ways of involving himself personally in the exchanges between Denmark and Prussia. Between 1864 and 1870 he was active as an unofficial go-between in the complicated diplomatic manoeuvres surrounding the Schleswig-Holstein question. At the end of this time he had experienced the usual vicissitudes of mediation in high politics: namely, he incurred the displeasure of both parties and found his usefulness largely exhausted. Remaining then in Paris, he appears to have become a confidant, and later an agent of sorts, of both the Russian Embassy and the French Foreign Office.

Hansen's connection with the Embassy began with the appointment as ambassador there of Mohrenheim, whom he had known earlier in Copenhagen. He was in fact for at least two years—in the period between 1885 and 1888—on the payroll of Rachkovski. For the manner in which his services were used we have the testimony of Rachkovski himself, as stated in his report of November 4/16, 1888 to the head of the Department of Police in Petersburg, P. K. Durnovo. Boasting of his achievements in combatting the propaganda put out to the French press by the Russian Socialist-Revolutionary exiles in Paris, Rachkovski wrote:

> Incidentally, thanks to Mr. Hansen, concerning whom I have already had the honor of reporting to Your Excellency, the most brilliant results were achieved. . . . However, considering myself not justified in bothering Your Excellency about Mr. Hansen, I thanked him out of my private funds. But at the same time I became aware of an obvious need of someone who would have access to the various organs of the local press. This need was all the greater because the Foreign Agency [i.e., the Okhrana's foreign apparatus], by its very nature, cannot use those devices which are used without any difficulty in Russia itself. . . . M. Hansen met all

franco-russe (Paris: Ernest Flammarion, 1897) and _Ambassade à Paris du Baron de Mohrenheim_ (Paris: Ernest Flammarion, 1907).

necessary requirements; and I found it best to place him in a relationship of obligation to myself for the accomplishments of those intelligence (*agenturnykh*) purposes which seemed possible of achievement only with the help of the press. Thus, in informing Your Excellency about a delicate financial matter, I may say that I paid M. Hansen over the course of two years 3 or 400 francs per month, taking this out of my own requirements and even going into debt.*

Other passages in Rachkovski's report make it evident that Hansen was also used by Rachkovski as a translator and editor and as a liaison agent with the French police. There is no evidence that he was used as a spy for forward intelligence. His position must, however, have been a most complicated one; for at this time he was also continuing to serve the French Foreign Ministry, which appears to have placed in him a confidence no smaller than that of Mohrenheim and Rachkovski. In April 1887—at a time, that is, when he was almost certainly on Rachkovski's payroll—he became naturalized as a French citizen and (the two events were probably connected) was commissioned in the French diplomatic service with the title of Counselor of Embassy. It seems most improbable that the French Foreign Office would have conferred upon him this status and rank if it had been aware of his relationship to the Russian Embassy.

Hansen, according to the biographical sketch of Fr. de Fontenay in the Danish biographical dictionary, was "a small, unprepossessing, bespectacled man, outwardly shy, who was generally known in Copenhagen under the nickname of 'Spidsmusen' (the Shrew) or 'the President.' " There is no evidence that he was a man of bad character or of sinister designs. His service to Denmark in his earlier years appears to have been patriotic, unselfish, and in no way dishonorable. The same could be said, so far as the available records show, of his relations with the French Foreign Office and the Russian Embassy in Paris. His simultaneous service to two governments was obviously used by him to promote their mutual rapprochement and not to work against the interests of either, as he perceived these interests. But if, as one must assume, one of the two connections was concealed from the other, this must stand as evidence either of a pathetic degree of personal financial distress on Hansen's part, or of a nature devious and secretive beyond the limits of normal acceptability.

*These details concerning Rachkovski's reports are taken from the book by V. K. Agafonov, *Zagranichnaia Okhranka* (Petrograd: *Kniga*, 1918). Agafonov was one of the commission of Russian revolutionaries sent to Paris, after the February Revolution, to open and investigate the premises of the Okhrana office in the Paris Embassy.

It is interesting to note that whereas Rachkovski, prior to coming to Paris, had functioned in Russia as correspondent for the strongly anti-Austrian Petersburg paper, *Novosti*, Hansen, while working for Rachkovski, served as Paris correspondent for the same paper. Considering this connection, considering also Tatishchev's connection with Katkov, and bearing in mind the deep commitment of both Hansen and Tatishchev to the idea of a Franco-Russian alliance, one has here an interesting example of the connection between the Russian Panslavs and chauvinists, on the one hand, and the Paris partisans of the alliance on the other.

———

Meanwhile, in these same years of 1881-1884, there was an almost total quiescence at the official French end of the relationship. Of the numerous individuals who had a share of the responsibility for French foreign policy in those years, either as foreign ministers or as premiers, none had both the inclination and the possibility to undertake any serious move to improve and intensify relations with Russia. The three most important were, of course, Gambetta, Jules Ferry, and Freycinet.

Gambetta, though by no means unreceptive to the thought of a possible *revanche*, was in office too short a time (November 1881 to February 1882) to develop anything in the nature of a personal foreign policy. Fascinated, furthermore, with Bismarck, he was not entirely sure, in the end, that the recovery of at least a portion of Alsace-Lorraine could not eventually be achieved by collaboration with that formidable figure, rather than by a war against Germany. His influence, in any case, was terminated with his sudden death at the end of 1882.

Ferry must be supposed to have shared the general view of the Opportunistes that the idea of closer relations with Russia had attractive implications (despite the fact that the country was, in his eyes, an odious monarchy); but he felt, like many others, that the time had not yet come when it would be possible to take any serious step in this direction: Bismarck, he considered, was too quick and too much on guard: he would immediately spot it; he would launch a preventative war before the arrangement with the Russians could be completed and made workable. Besides, in Ferry's case, he was too extensively preoccupied during his first brief premiership (September 1880 to November 1881) with his educational reforms, and during his second one (February 1883 to March 1885) with colonial affairs, to give concentrated attention to the problems of policy towards Russia.

As for Freycinet: he, like his friend and supporter, Juliette Adam, had, in those initial years of his responsibility for French foreign policy, a singularly heavy and unhappy touch whenever it came to relations with Russia. Originally an engineer, specializing in problems of sanitation, a man of figures and statistics who could analyze with great refinement the complicated play of forces in French domestic life, he appeared unable to master, particularly in those years, the less familiar subtleties of international relations. At a later stage in the development of the Franco-Russian relationship, when the statistics of money and weaponry were to play a great part in the pertinent calculations, he, by this time minister of war, would be on more familiar ground, and his role would be a more positive one. But in the mid-1880's, it was quite the opposite. This was not, certainly, the consequence of any aversion to an improvement of the relationship; it was simply the product of a combination of lack of interest and a tendency to give priority to domestic-political considerations.

When Gambetta came into office, in the autumn of 1881, this was too much for the French Ambassador at Petersburg, Chanzy, just as MacMahon's fall had been too much for his monarchistic predecessor, Le Flô. Chanzy had good republican connections; but the flamboyantly radical figure of Gambetta, bound to be distasteful to the Russians, was more than he could accept. He therefore resigned, much to the disgust of the new Tsar; and Freycinet, as Gambetta's successor in the premiership, was faced with the problem of filling the Petersburg post. His choice fell, with singular infelicity, upon Admiral Constant Jaurès, of the French navy. Seldom, if ever, in the course of French diplomatic history, can there have been a less fortunate appointment. Held in contempt by his own staff, described in fact by Embassy secretary Eugène de Vogüé (the leading Russian expert in the French diplomatic service, later to become a member of the French Academy and to play a major part in introducing Russian literature to the French public) as a "farceur dangereux,"[2] Admiral Jaurès began his career as ambassador most inauspiciously. While marching down the corridors of the Winter Palace to present his credentials and observing on the walls portraits of earlier generations of imperial Romanovs, he inquired of the accompanying Russian chief of protocol: "Qui sont ses magots?" ("Who are these apes?"). This episode appears to have been characteristic of the further course of his ambassadorial career; and for this reason, no doubt, that career was not of long duration. He was withdrawn after little more than a year at the post.

Ferry's choice of a successor to Jaurès was as successful as the earlier one had been unfortunate. The choice fell, this time, on General Félix Antoine Appert, a well-known French officer who had been military governor of Paris at the time of the repression of the Commune. Appert arrived in Petersburg at the end of 1883 and served there until 1886, when he was recalled in circumstances that will be noted below.

There can be no question but that, in choosing Appert for this position, the French government was influenced by the fact that his wife was Danish. The French chargé d'affaires at Petersburg was instructed to point out to the Russians, when requesting agreement for the appointment, that Madame Appert came from "une des meilleures familles de Danemark."[3] It was no doubt thought, and apparently correctly, that this would give her a favorable access to the much younger Empress Dagmar.*

While things were thus quiet on the civilian-official side, there was continued activity, subdued but sustained, at the military level. Only a part of this, one must assume, is now visible in the historical record; but even this part is significant and suggestive. In the summer of 1883, Colonel de Sermet, who had by this time succeeded Chanoine as military attaché in Petersburg, was officially invited to make a long visit to, and journey in, Russian Central Asia, as a guest of the military governor in that region. The latter happened to be none other than the notorious Panslav General Mikhail Grigoryevich Chernyayev (see above, Chapter 1), erstwhile editor of the Petersburg Panslav organ, the *Russki Mir*, and commander (as a volunteer) of the Serbian forces in their unsuccessful war of 1876 against Turkey. The invitation must have been an attractive one for Sermet, because this was a period of growing Anglo-Russian tension over the problems of Afghanistan and adjacent areas, and it was important for the French military authorities, especially from the standpoint of a possible Franco-Russian alliance, to learn something of the real degree and significance of Russian involvement in that region. The Ministry of War in Paris therefore authorized acceptance of the invitation; and Sermet spent most of the autumn of 1883 in Central Asia, in Chernyayev's company. On his return to Petersburg, he recommended to the Ministry the issuance of French decorations to two Russian officers: the order of the Grand Croix to Chernyayev who, he wrote, in addition to being very popular in Russia, "n'a pas caché à notre attaché militaire ses sympathies pour une alliance franco-russe"; and the order of Grand Officier to Prince (General) Ferdinand Wittgenstein, described as "ne perdant jamais occasion de dire du bien de notre nation

* A French biographical reference says that Madame Appert had been a childhood friend of Dagmar. This is unlikely. Madame Appert, daughter of a Danish banker who lived and worked for many years in Algiers, was by seventeen years the older of the two, and had spent much of her youth outside Denmark. It is more likely that it was Princess Kochubei, Mistress of the Russian Imperial Household and close to Dagmar's mother, Queen Louise of Denmark, who had known Madame Appert in the past.

et d'en vanter les qualités."[4] Here, once again, one cannot fail to note the prominence of the Panslavs in the effort to promote a close Franco-Russian relationship, particularly at the military level.

As to the private enthusiasts: Juliette Adam paid a visit to Petersburg in January 1882. The purpose of it is not fully apparent. It was partly, she herself wrote, to see the famous General Mikhail Dmitriyevich Skobelev (see above, Chapter 1), for whom she conceived an intense admiration and about whom, four years later, she was to write a romantically enthusiastic book.* But since he was himself then about to visit Paris, which he did the following month, it would scarcely seem to have been necessary for her to go to Petersburg to see him, unless—and this is also possible—the journey was for the purpose of persuading him to come to Paris. Otherwise her Russian journey, in addition to being quite brief (less than a month), cannot have been a wholly pleasant one. In addition to the rigors of the Petersburg climate in January, there is the curious fact that her friend Chanzy, the ambassador, the enthusiastic backer of her magazine and friend of the Franco-Russian alliance, left Petersburg for good the day after her arrival. There was therefore no one of senior rank in the French Embassy to introduce her to Petersburg society. There is no evidence that she was received at court. She tells, in her account of the trip, of a visit of courtesy paid to her at her hotel by Madame Giers and one of her daughters; and one has the impression that this, a visit by the wife of the acting minister for foreign affairs, was the extent of the attention paid to her by the official Russian establishment on that occasion.† The cautious Giers, just then in the process of consolidating the policy he had inaugurated with the negotiation of the *Dreikaiserbund*, was surely not going to compromise himself in Bismarck's eyes by showering attentions on the great chancellor's most celebrated French enemy.

There is record, in the diary of Eugène de Vogüé, of Madame Adam's

---

* *Le Général Skobeleff* (Paris: La Nouvelle Revue, 1886).

† J. Adam, *Impressions françaises en Russie* (Paris: Hachette, 1912), p. 14. Madame Adam received the two ladies, it is here related, in the yellow ground floor salon of the old Yevropeiskaya Gostinnitsa (in European terms: Hôtel d'Europe), later torn down to make room for the present establishment of the same name. Just prior to receiving les Mesdames Giers, she received General Skobelev; and he, bowing himself backwards out of the room, bumped into the Giers ladies and nearly knocked them down. Madame Giers, after he had left, inquired who the man was. This greatly astounded Juliette, who thought everyone in Petersburg must have known Skobelev. One has the feeling that Madame Adam was very poorly initiated into the mysteries of Russian court politics.

meeting, at dinners arranged for her (one by himself), "les Demidov et les Dournovo."[5] If these are the people one suspects they were, it was very reactionary circles indeed with whom Madame Adam, the hostess of an Opportuniste-Républicain salon in Paris, was coming together. The Demidovs were a well-connected Petersburg family of great wealth; and the Demidov in question was probably Paul, who was nephew and heir to the husband of Princess Mathilda Bonaparte, and was engaged in financing, about this time, the amateur reactionary intelligence service known as the "Svyataya Druzhina." The "Durnovo" was probably General P. P. Durnovo, minister of the Appanages, and also, around this time, president of the Petersburg chapter of the Slavic Benevolent Association. Both couples were connected by marriage with Juliette's Paris friend: Lisa Trubetskaya; and Skobelev's sister was Lisa's sister-in-law. So it is easy to see who arranged Juliette's journey.

The latter left Petersburg on the 30th of January, and returned to Paris. Whether this early departure had been originally planned is also not apparent. Gambetta, the former object of her political adulation, had fallen from power four days earlier; and the reins of government were just then being taken over by her own friend and admirer, Freycinet. In addition to this, she is known to have received, on the very day of her departure, the news that she herself had lost 800,000 francs in the collapse of the banking empire of the French financial adventurer, Bontoux.[6] Obviously, Paris, at that particular moment, demanded her attention. Nor was she slow to take advantage of the new political situation there. De Vogüé disgusted over his own lack of promotion and over the appointment of Jaurès, resigned and went home shortly thereafter; and he tells of being present at her home in Paris, in late March, at a dinner attended by "tout le gouvernement."[7]

Skobelev would appear either to have preceded Madame Adam to Paris, or to have accompanied her; for it was only a fortnight later that he created a sensation by delivering there, to an assembly of Serbian students, a highly inflammatory speech in which he expatiated on the inevitability of a Slav-Teuton conflict. This brought down upon his head a vigorous scolding from the Russian Ambassador, Prince Orlov, and an immediate recall, on the Tsar's orders, to Petersburg. On the 7th of March 1882, he was summoned before the Tsar who, disliking him personally but having a secret sympathy for his political views, gave him, as Skobelev himself described it, a good-humored head-washing.

This, to be sure, did not fully repress Skobelev's political exuberence. He continued, behind the scenes, to pursue with one of the French military attachés (presumably Boisdeffre) vigorous explorations of the possibilities of a common Franco-Russian military collaboration against

Germany, and even invited himself to the French manoeuvres of the coming summer. But his sudden death in Moscow, in July of that year, put an abrupt end to all these undertakings. And his passing (particularly because it appears to have occurred in sordid circumstances) must have been a great blow and disappointment to Juliette Adam, who had fondly seen him not only as the great coming force in Russian governmental affairs, but as the principal architect of the future Franco-Russian alliance.*

By the midsummer of 1882, therefore, with Skobelev dead, Gorchakov shelved, and Giers now triumphantly in control of Russian foreign policy, even Juliette Adam entered upon what must have been a period of deep discouragement. And Paris held no more fervid partisan of a Franco-Russian alliance than herself. The effort to unite France and Russia in an alliance against Germany was now truly in the doldrums.

In leaving, for the moment, the subject of Juliette Adam, it might be well to glance, also at the activities during this period of the other Paris personality already mentioned in connection with her: "Le Docteur" Élie de Cyon. These activities had not at the moment any detectable importance for Franco-Russian relations, but they served, once again, as background for later events of a somewhat larger significance.

Cyon's activities in the period of 1880-1886 are known only in small part. For such of them as *are* known, the motives are, as usual, obscure. He continued to live in Paris. He had by this time become naturalized in France. Failing to obtain the professorship he coveted at the Collège de France, he appears to have abandoned his scientific pursuits.

In February 1881 the venerable editor of *La France*, Émile de Girardin, always a protagonist of close relations with Russia and a faithful patron of Madame Adam, died. Then, within a matter of weeks, Cyon, as mentioned above, became editor, or co-editor, of a Bonapartist boulevard sheet called *Le Gaulois*, which had been founded some thirteen years earlier with Russian money.† Like *La France, Le Gaulois* was pro-Russian. Again like *La France*, it gave flattering attention to Madame Adam and her salon. Cyon's connection with the paper did not last long—only until the middle of 1882. (There were charges that

---

* Skobelev's death, it might further be noted, occurred within a few weeks of that of her other great hero and white hope, Gambetta, which also took place in circumstances that must have been painful to her. Small wonder that the ensuing two or three years found her somewhat subdued.

† The money is said to have come from the head of the Russian Gendarmerie of the time of Alexander II: Nikolai Vladimirovich Mezentsov, who was anxious to obtain Paris press support for a French actress in whom he was interested.

during Cyon's editorship its quality deteriorated.) But the association points in the direction of monarchical connections, especially since Cyon's predecessor and successor in the enterprise was the well-known monarchist figure Arthur Meyer.

Cyon also functioned during these years as the Paris scientific correspondent for the strongly nationalistic and Panslav Moscow paper the *Moskovskie Vyedomosti*, edited by the great Moscow publicist and editor, Katkov. Katkov, like the Grand Duke Nicholas, had defended Cyon—but in this instance publicly—at the time of the latter's difficulties with the students at the Medical-Surgical Academy; and Cyon, over the ensuing years, either retained a gratitude for this service or thought the connection to be worth exploiting. And since it was primarily through his connections with Katkov at the Russian end (the French end is more obscure) that Cyon's activities were to have importance for the development of Franco-Russian relations, this provides a suitable point for a word or two about this famous Russian figure.

The personality of Mikhail Nikoforovich Katkov (1818-1887), and his role in the Russian life of this period, are so well known that one hesitates to expand on the subject. A publicist and journalist of highest capacity, he was also a talented editor, in the great tradition of Russian editorship. He lived and published in Moscow; but his Moscow paper— the *Moskovskie Vyedomosti*—was widely read in Petersburg; and its influence, if the Petersburg *Novoye Vremya* (the organ of the well-known conservative publisher, Boris Suvorin) be excepted, probably outweighed that of all the rest of the Russian press put together. The Tsars—both the Alexanders—read it with respect and sympathy.

In his views on internal affairs Katkov was a strong conservative, and in foreign affairs a nationalist—both of which tendencies commended him handsomely to his imperial sovereigns. Beyond this, he enjoyed the friendship and patronage of probably the two most powerful men in Russia outside the Tsar: the Prokuror of the Holy Synod, Konstantin Petrovich Pobyedonostsev, and the highly reactionary Count Dmitri Aleksandrovich Tolstoi, who became minister of the interior upon the retirement of Ignatyev in 1882.

Remote from the court and the diplomatic corps of Petersburg, Katkov was not often exposed to the cosmopolitan atmosphere and to the limited pro-German influences still to be found in both these quarters. The society in which he moved was rather that of the prosperous merchants of Moscow, provincial, pious, and xenophobic in the old Muscovite tradition, and of the industrialists of central and southern

Russia, strongly resentful of German commercial and industrial competition. Deeply devoted to the conservative monarchical institutions of both Germany and Austria, he was prepared, up to the mid-1880's, to support a close relationship of Russia with the German and Austrian imperial courts, as an arrangement conducive to the preservation of the institution of monarchy. As Russia's troubles and frustrations mounted in the Balkans, however, he tended to attribute her helplessness in the face of these problems to the restraints imposed upon her policy by the ties to the other two Emperors (a form of escapism to which a great many other Russians also succumbed); and this produced, as the years went by, a growing impatience in his mind with those ties, and a desire to see Russia recover what he conceived as her freedom of action.

Katkov was a person of great prominence in Moscow. A portly man, wearing the abundant whiskers of the period, he must have presented a striking figure presiding, as some have described him, at the head of a dinner table around which were usually assembled not only the members of his numerous family (which included eleven children of his own, plus two adopted nephews) but also a considerable troop of the other hangers-on (*prizhivalki*, to the Russians) by whom he was generally surrounded. These latter were not invariably people of high quality. One of Katkov's signal deficiencies appears to have been an inability to distinguish the genuine and the false article in the company of those whom he admitted to his personal entourage. Like many another successful and prominent personality, he could be easily satisfied by a professed agreement with his own views, and often neglected to look carefully at the person behind it. A somewhat greater interest in people might have warned him against the attentions of Cyon, in particular.

Cyon later professed, in his history of the alliance, to have been, at the time of his visit to Katkov in 1883, already partisan of a Franco-Russian alliance, which, he wrote, Katkov was not yet. Cyon confessed, however, that the two men were interested in different things. Katkov was concerned with the Balkans, a part of the world in which Cyon never evinced even a flicker of interest. What the latter's real interests were remains characteristically obscure. He wrote, rather grandly, that what he was concerned to do, at this period, was to "déjouer"—to parry and frustrate—the supposed intrigues of Bismarck against France.

If one were to take this statement at its face value, it would constitute an interesting reflection on Cyon's motivation, suggesting as it does that his loyalties, such as they were, already ran to France rather than to Russia. But it is hard to know what value to attach to it, first of all because there is no evidence of what "intrigues" Cyon had in mind (the writer can think of none of Bismarck's actions of that time that could correctly be so described), but also because of the implications of the following curious incident.

At some time in 1883, Cyon went to Russia, ostensibly to pay a visit to his benefactor, Katkov. It so happened that just at this time (February 1883) the Petersburg liberal daily, *Golos*, an excellent paper edited by the well-known publicist A. A. Krayevski, was closed down (and for good, this time) by the censor. At the moment of its closing the paper stood in a state of feud and polemic with the *Moskovskie Vyedomosti*—a conflict so bitter, in fact, that one is obliged to suspect that Katkov's great influence with the censor, E. M. Feoktistov, had something to do with the closing. In any case, Katkov and Cyon discussed, on the occasion of this visit by Cyon, the possibility of Katkov's acquiring, and Cyon's editing, the now dormant paper. In the end, nothing came of this. But one is astounded to note references, in the correspondence of the German Ambassador at Paris, Prince Chlodwig zu Hohenlohe-Schillingsfürst, to two visits paid to him by Cyon in Paris —one around the end of April 1883—for the purpose of apprising him that he, Cyon, was in a position, through his Petersburg connections, to arrange for the purchase and relegitimation of the *Golos*, and of inviting the German government to take a share in the enterprise, the argument being advanced that this would be useful to Germany. The ambassador, in reporting this to Berlin, expressed doubts as to the reliability of his visitor; and Bismarck refused to have anything to do with the proposed deal, arguing on very sound grounds of principle against the buying-up of foreign newspapers generally.[8]

What is one to make of this extraordinary procedure on the part of one who professed to be opposing the intrigues of Bismarck against France? Cyon speaks at length, in his history of the alliance,[9] of the project for acquiring the *Golos* and describes his discussions with Katkov on this subject, but says nothing, of course, about his approach to the Germans. On the other hand, he hints, in these decidedly cloudy passages, that attitudes towards Germany played a prominent part in his discussions with Katkov, and contrives to convey the impression that it was Katkov, not he, who at that time favored closer relations with Germany, and this in some sort of connection with the problem of the *Golos*.

The historian can only note this episode as one more of the many confusing and contradictory reflections on the motivation of this strange and devious man.

Before one leaves this discussion of personalities, there is one other who was neither French nor Russian but whose part in the tale about to unfold itself was of such importance that his personality also deserves a word or two of comment. This was the commanding figure of the European diplomacy of that epoch, the German Imperial Chancellor Otto von Bismarck.

This writer has no desire to add to the enormous existing volume of biographical and critical Bismarckiana; nor would he consider himself competent to do so if what were involved was the totality of that highly complex personality. But there are certain aspects of this personality which are particularly relevant to the subject at hand and deserve special mention.

Contrary to a widespread popular impression, Bismarck was not, strictly speaking, a German nationalist. He was a loyal servant, albeit a talented and high-powered one, of the crown—at first the crown of Prussia, later that of the new German Empire—under which he was born and to which he conceived himself to owe allegiance. Prussia meant more to him than Germany. When he opposed the views of his monarch, as he occasionally did most vigorously, he did so on behalf of what he believed to be the true interests of the monarchy. The new German Reich was a political arrangement he had found it necessary to create in order to assure what he believed to be Prussia's proper place in the Central European scheme of things. Once created, the Reich had, of course, to be protected; and it was to this protection—against the nightmare of hostile coalitions—that Bismarck's diplomacy of this period was directed. He had no desire to expand the borders of the Reich, as they emerged from the war of 1870-1871. His diplomacy was therefore essentially defensive. He was concerned to prevent a French war of revenge, and thought he could do this successfully so long as France remained devoid of allies. His diplomacy vis-à-vis Russia and Austria-Hungary, including the promotion of the *Dreikaiserbund*, was designed primarily to deprive both of those Powers of all incentive to associate themselves with France in a relationship of alliance. But it was also designed to prevent those same two Powers from going to war against each other; for any war of that nature, whatever form it might take, would be almost sure to disrupt the delicate structure of intra-European relationships which formed the basis of his calculations and in terms of which he *thought* he could see German security assured.

The thesis has been put forward in a number of Soviet historical works that Bismarck was, throughout this period, eager to launch another war against France—a preventive war, this time—but was restrained by the wise and powerful influence of the two Russian Tsars of the period. For this thesis there is not only no evidence but abundant counter-evidence; and this writer considers the suggestion too far-fetched to warrant serious discussion. (Among other things, had Bismarck nurtured such desires,

97

he would surely have taken advantage of the Russo-Turkish War, when Russia was in no position to render any significant assistance to France, as an opportunity to make war on the latter Power.)

Bismarck had no sentimental attachment to Russia. He had served in Petersburg as a diplomat in the 1860's, and was well aware of the various currents and cross-currents, including those dangerous to Germany, that made themselves felt in and around the Tsarist court. It was with a wary and skeptical eye that he watched the development of Russian foreign policy over the 1870's and 1880's.

But at the same time, he was acutely aware of the dangers of becoming involved in a war with Russia. He coveted no Russian territory for Germany. He had to recognize that any eastward expansion of the German Empire would unavoidably mean the incorporation of further portions of Poland; yet his wish was for fewer, not more, Poles in the German Empire. He recognized, as Napoleon had failed to do and as Hitler would fail to do in another century, that the vast territory of the Russian Empire did not lend itself to occupation by an invading force, that even the successful invader would never find a convenient and safe place to stop, and that therefore no such war could find a favorable and decisive ending. And whatever initial successes the Germans might have in such an encounter would serve mainly, as he saw it, to release, on the part of the Austro-Hungarians, imperialistic tendencies with relation to the Balkans—tendencies in which he had no confidence and for which he had no sympathy.

It would have been entirely possible, therefore, for Russia to remain at peace with Germany, and to continue to enjoy Bismarck's diplomatic support, at no greater cost to themselves than a certain amount of restraint in their policy towards the Balkans and Austria-Hungary. It was just this that Bismarck hoped they would do.

Bismarck's mastery and brilliance as a statesman needs no emphasis here; but one of his weaknesses (or what this writer views as weaknesses) ought to be noted in this connection. This was a tendency to exaggerate and overdramatize any incipient dangers to which he saw, or fancied to see, Germany being exposed; to appear to be more alarmed and concerned than he actually was. He hoped by these means to give to those whom he saw as the authors of the threat the impression that Germany was being roused to major, perhaps violent, defensive action; and to encourage them to conclude that they had thus started more than they had bargained for, and had best quickly back down. It was not that he himself, in these circumstances, uttered direct threats against other people; he left this to the German press, and encouraged the editors to make the most of it. But he liked to play the threatened party, even where there was little actual cause for fright, thinking in this way to nip in the bud tendencies which, if allowed to develop, could become truly threatening to Germany's interests. Sometimes this worked; sometimes it redounded to Germany's detriment. Nor did Bismarck invariably correctly calculate the alternatives open to his opponents. Particularly was this true in economic and financial matters, where his touch was less sure than in the military-political ones. And beyond this, there were limitations to his view of contemporary reality. He was in many respects, like the Kaiser William I whom he served so long and so loyally, a man of the eighteenth century. The developing characteristics of the industrial Europe of the late nineteenth century were not always fully visible to him.

But these, in the context of the subject at hand, were incidental failings, not crucial ones. To live side by side with Bismarck was, for French and Russian statesmen, not always easy. There were times when it could arouse feelings of humiliation, of inferiority, of envy, even of anger and hatred. But it may be confidently said that so long as Bismarck remained at the helm of German policy, no alliance between France and Russia was necessary to assure the military-political security of either of them. For policies on their part that led in the direction of such an alliance other explanations, more complex and more emotional, must be found.

With these personalities, all destined to play roles in the further unfolding of this tale, in mind, we are ready to turn to the complications which, in the years 1885-1886, sowed trouble among the members of the *Dreikaiserbund* and opened new prospects for Franco-Russian collaboration.

Part II

THE BULGARIAN "GACHIS"

Chapter Five

COMPLICATIONS IN BULGARIA

The forces that move men and governments to action in the field of international affairs are not always logical ones, nor do they always operate directly. Thus, the impulses that were destined ultimately to play a primary role in the disruption of the pattern of relationships established in the *Dreikaiserbund* and in creating new possibilities for Franco-Russian relations were ones having little or nothing to do with France or Germany, and not even very much to do with Austria: namely, the experiences suffered by Alexander III and the men around him in their relations with the new, autonomous Bulgaria that had been set up by the Treaty of Berlin. For this reason, anyone interested in tracing the real origins of the Franco-Russian alliance has no choice but to examine, as will be done in these next three chapters, the course of events in this Russian-Bulgarian relationship, and the effect this had on the development of Russian policy.

––––––––––

Let us return to the year 1878 and recall, at the risk of a slight repetition, that the Treaty of Berlin had provided for the division of Bulgaria into two parts. The southeastern part, nearest to Constantinople, known as Eastern Rumelia, was to remain in theory a Turkish province, and was to be governed by a governor appointed by the Sultan with the consent of the European Powers. It was stipulated that the governor must be a Christian; also that Turkish troops must not be readmitted to the province without the Powers' consent. The remainder of Bulgaria was to be an autonomous principality, theoretically also under Turkish suzerainty but endowed with its own Constitution and ruled by a prince, as constitutional monarch. The prince was to be selected, initially, by the Russian Tsar; but he was not to be a member of any of the major reigning dynasties of Europe, including the Russian. It was, however, generally envisaged by the Powers that this nominally autonomous principality would be a satellite, if not a protectorate, of the Russian throne.

The Tsar's choice for the first occupant of that throne fell, in April

103

1879, on a young German Prince of the house of Hesse-Darmstadt: Alexander von Battenberg, a nephew of the Russian Empress. This choice was the beginning, for everyone concerned, of a seven-year ordeal of drama, controversy, and angry conflict.

Although the selection of Battenberg for this position was by no means agreeable to Bismarck, who feared it might lead to an undesirable involvement of Germany in Bulgarian affairs, the young man seemed, as he entered on his new duties, to have everything else—to use the American phrase—"going for him."

Battenberg's father, the Grand Duke Alexander of Hesse, being the brother of the Russian Empress, was well known at the Russian court. His standing there had at one time suffered severely, to be sure, by virtue of his morganatic marriage to a woman of Polish origin who was a lady in waiting at that court, a Countess Hauke (Battenberg's mother). By 1879, however, time had softened the resulting asperities, and Alexander of Hesse was once more accepted and *bien vu* in Petersburg. In addition to this, he had served with, and retained his rank in, the Austrian army.

The grand duke's young son, Alexander, to whom the name Battenberg had been given, in addition to being popular with the British royal family, had served, and even seen action, with the Russian forces in the recent war with Turkey. The family was, therefore, an international one, with favorable connections in a number of directions.

Young Battenberg was, at the time of his election to the Bulgarian throne, only twenty-two years old. Although there were conflicting views among his contemporaries, as there have been among historians, with regard to his character, the weight of the evidence reveals him as a healthy, honorable, and courageous young man—the product of a German military education, with all its advantages and drawbacks, full of life, straightforward, manly, and in many ways an attractive character. Tact, on the other hand, though he did his best to muster it on a number of occasions, was not his strongest suit; nor did he ever appear to shrink, when he felt himself in the right, from conflict with older and far more impressive people. Ambitious and intensely rank-conscious, he also showed at times an exaggerated and unwise concern for the outward prerogatives of title and position. His conduct was supported by a stubbornness which was as fortunate when directed to hopeful undertakings as it was calamitous when addressed to unpromising ones. The reader who attempts to pass judgment on his performance in Bulgaria will do well to bear in mind, as many of his contemporary critics failed to do, both his extreme youth and inexperience, and the appalling complexity—in many instances insolubility—of the problems with which he was faced in his new position.

Having chosen, out of courtesy for Alexander II, to receive and accept at the Tsar's summer home in Livadiya (Crimea) the formal invitation of the Bulgarians to assume the throne, Battenberg next made a journey around Europe, paying courtesy calls in the capitals of the various European Powers, and ending with a respectful visit to the Sultan (Abd ul Hamid), whose vassal, however tenuous the pretense, he was theoretically supposed to be. Then, traveling on a Russian warship, he arrived in Bulgaria, at the port of Varna, on the 6th of June 1879.

It was not an auspicious beginning. The young man was still suffering from the intestinal effects of official Turkish hospitality, and had been seasick into the bargain. The Russian military governor, Prince A. M. Dondukov-Korsakov, a much older and grandly pretentious man, very much a Panslav, was hostile to Battenberg from the start, both because of the latter's German nationality and because he himself had had high hopes of becoming the first occupant of the Bulgarian throne. It could hardly be said that he went out of his way to prepare a favorable reception for the young Prince, as the latter entered for the first time on the territory of the principality over which he was to rule.

Worse than all this, however, were the complexities connected with the necessity of attempting to rule, from the start, under the provisions of the Bulgarian Constitution. This amazingly liberal instrument, hastily worked out in the weeks prior to Battenberg's arrival by a Russian commission and a Bulgarian constituent assembly, failed to define clearly the boundaries between legislative and executive authority and gave far more power to the parliament, and less to the reigning prince, than Battenberg could have wished. The politicians who controlled the Bulgarian political parties or came into governmental office under this Constitution were, almost to a man, difficult—many would have said impossible—people to work with: inexperienced, lacking in any sort of understanding of the workings of a parliamentary system, passionate, headstrong, devious, and often corrupt. They divided into two competing political parties: the Liberals, who had by far the greater popular following; and the Conservatives, who were slightly the more responsible of the two.

In addition to this, the young Prince found himself faced, even after withdrawal (August 1879) of the Russian armed forces, with another sort of army: a horde of Russian military and political officials, advisers and administrators, many of them heavy-handed, tactless, and brutal men, who came to Bulgaria with the expectation that the Prince would be a puppet in their hands. There was a local Russian consul general who seldom failed to dabble in the turgid political currents of that distracted country. There were the various diplomatic agents sent out by the Asiatic Department of the Russian Foreign Office. The minister of war in the Prince's cabinet, and sometimes other ministers as well, were normally Russian generals. And then, as though this was not enough, there were the diplomatic representatives of the other European Powers, to whom the provisions of the Treaty of Berlin had assigned certain functions of supervision and control.

By his very position, the Prince found himself almost invariably in the epicenter of all these conflicting interests and strong-willed personalities; and no one—not even a much older and more experienced man—could have reconciled them to general satisfaction. Their sheer numbers provided endless combinations for intrigue and manoeuvre. The Bulgarians played Prince and Russian advisers off against each other. The Russians intrigued exuberantly among themselves. Being usually hostile to the Prince, they also attempted to use first one, then the other, of the Bulgarian political parties against him. The Prince retaliated in kind. The representatives of the other Powers normally stood by, passive and fascinated witnesses to this unending Donnybrook; but occasionally one or the other of them also took a hand.

It would take a larger work than this one to disentangle the skeins of interaction among all these feuding forces, as that interaction ran its course over the ensuing years; and no such effort will be undertaken here. Suffice it to say, at this point, that in the first year or two, up to the death of Alexander II, relations between Battenberg and the Russian government remained tolerable, if not always undisturbed. The first of the Russian diplomatic representatives was a man generally sympathetic to the Prince, even if the minister of war (always a Russian general) was not. When the diplomatic adviser was replaced, as a result of Panslav influence, with one less friendly to Battenberg, the general, on the other hand, yielded place (if only briefly and for the last time) to one who had friendly feelings towards him. And so it went.

Battenberg made an earnest effort, in those first years, to maintain the pleasant relationship with Alexander II which had led to his selection for the position in the first place. Not only did he accept in Livadiya, as noted above, the offer of his crown, but he paid another visit to the Tsar in Petersburg in March 1880. He was in fact among those who would have been destroyed by the bomb placed by revolutionaries in the dining room of the Winter Palace, on the 2nd of March, had not the tardiness of the arriving train of his father, Prince Alexander of Hesse, delayed the movement of the entire company to the imperial luncheon table.

These visits were rendered in the spirit of those journeys which, several centuries earlier, the forefathers of Alexander II—the grand dukes of Moscow—had been accustomed to make to the seats of the Tartar khans on the lower Volga. They were dutiful gestures of respect and submission. But neither Battenberg nor anyone else seems to have realized, during these first two years of his incumbency of the Bulgarian throne, how much of this acceptable relationship between himself and Petersburg rested on the slender thread of confidence which ran from him to his aunt, the Russian Empress, and through her to Alexander II, and how little he would have to depend on at the Petersburg end when, as was very soon to be the case, both of those personalities would no longer be on hand. The development of his relationship with the new Tsar, Alexander III, was a factor destined to have a most profound effect on the entire pattern of Russia's external relations.

When Alexander II was assassinated, in 1881, Battenberg, following the established custom, went to Petersburg once again—this time to attend the funeral. He made an attempt, on this occasion, to discuss his troubles with the new Tsar. One may be permitted to doubt that the latter, distracted by the murder of his father and by the plethora of new burdens now suddenly placed upon him, was able at that moment to give any very detailed attention to the affairs of remote Bulgaria. Battenberg is said by his rather admiring biographer, Corti, to have told the Tsar on this occasion of the difficulties he was experiencing in governing Bulgaria under existing arrangements, and to have intimated that he might soon be obliged to suppress the operation of the Constitution in order to bring things under control.* Corti further relates that the young man came away with the impression that the Tsar had professed readiness to leave the solution of this problem to him but had stipulated that he would have to act on his own responsibility in finding it—he, the Tsar, could not at that time take it upon himself to sponsor any decision.† Whether Battenberg correctly understood the Tsar on

---

* E. C. Corti, *Alexander von Battenberg. Sein Kampf mit dem Zaren und Bismarck* (Vienna: L. W. Seidel & Sohn, 1920), pp. 107-109. E. C. Corti was a nephew, once or twice removed, of Count Luigi Corti, who had represented Italy at the Congress of Berlin and then served as Italian Ambassador at Constantinople over the years of the early 1880's. E. C. Corti had access to Count Corti's papers, which had been bequeathed to his own grandfather. He also had access to Battenberg's own papers—as assembled in the so-called Hartenau Archive. This body of material, unfortunately, was turned over by Battenberg's heirs, in the 1920's, to the Bulgarian National Museum, and is now unavailable.

† It will be recalled that one of the first things Alexander III did, on succeeding to the throne, was to make an abrupt and complete end to the efforts that had been put in hand, in the last weeks and days of his father's life, by the Interior Minister Loris-Melikov, to introduce into the Russian political system the faint beginnings of something resembling parliamentary institutions. Battenberg might well have been forgiven for assuming that a Tsar so averse to any form of constitutionality in Russia would have understanding for his own desire to suspend in

this point is unclear; if he did not, it would by no means be the last time that the two men would fail to understand each other.

Battenberg, as he returned to Bulgaria after the funeral, found himself supported there by the newly appointed Bulgarian war minister: a Finnish-Swedish officer of the Russian armed forces, General Kazimir Gustavovich Ehrnrooth (Ernrut, in Russian transliteration), a straightforward and honorable man with whom Battenberg found it possible to have a relationship of mutual understanding and confidence. With Ehrnrooth's support, Battenberg, on the 9th of May 1881, dismissed the Liberal cabinet then in office, set up one of his own choosing with Ehrnrooth as prime minister, and asked the Assembly to suppress the Constitution and to give him, the Prince, full powers to govern as he might choose for a period of seven years to come. This, on the 13th of July 1881, the Assembly did.

The Panslav faction in Russia was by this time beginning to experience a certain alarm over the manner in which the Bulgarian situation was developing. They had expected Battenberg to be a dutiful Russian puppet and had looked to the newly established principality of Bulgaria not only as a region of Balkan Slavdom in which they could now begin to unfold their own direct influence but also as a staging area for intrigues and political operations farther afield—particularly in Serbia, which had by this time fallen extensively under Austrian influence. But Ehrnrooth was decidedly not their man, nor was the Prince; and the large powers that the Prince was now arrogating to himself in suppressing the Constitution curtailed drastically the possible scope of independent Panslav action. The Russians were also stirred to indignation by tales of Battenberg's iniquities as related by Ehrnrooth's predecessor: the Russian General P. D. Parensov, with whom Battenberg had not got along at all well and who, now back in Russia, was in a good position to make his influence felt.* The result was that even at this early date the influence of the Panslavs, and of ambitious Russian military circles, was beginning to come into play against Battenberg; and this was, for various reasons, an influence not lightly to be trifled with.

Bulgaria a Constitution far more liberal than anything Loris-Melikov had even dreamed of proposing.

* The reader who wishes to hear Parensov's side of the story will find it told in the latter's memoirs: P. D. Parensov, *Iz proshlago. Vospominaniya ofitsera general'nogo shtaba v Bolgarii* (St. Petersburg: B. Berezovski, published in several volumes in the years 1901, 1904, and 1908). Much of this material also appeared in the serial *Russkaya Starina*, particularly in the volumes for 1908: CXXXIII, February, pp. 257-270; CXXXIV, April, pp. 17-47, and May, pp. 257-282; and CXXXVI, November, pp. 435-441.

Among the first effects of this emerging situation were the withdrawal of Ehrnrooth and the appointment, as Russian diplomatic agent in Sofia and adviser to the Prince, of an able but already somewhat notorious Russian diplomat, a dedicated Panslav and an old hand at Balkan intrigue: M. A. Khitrovo. This was a man who had been extensively involved in the affairs of the Balkan Slavs in earlier years as an agent, sometimes of the Asiatic Section of the Russian Foreign Office, sometimes of the Panslav committees, in Montenegro and Serbia.* With this sly and cynical operator Battenberg got along no better than he had with Parensov. They soon developed a number of differences, one of them over an issue which was to cause difficulty between Battenberg and the Russian government for years to come—the question of railway building on Bulgarian territory. The new autonomous Bulgaria was bound by the Treaty of Berlin to respect such international engagements relating to her territory as had been incurred prior to the Congress of Berlin by the Sultan. Among these was a contract with the well-known Austrian financier and railway builder, Baron Hirsch, for the construction through Bulgaria of a projected line from Vienna to Constantinople. This project, however, did not meet with favor in Russia, where competitors of Baron Hirsch, enjoying strong support in Panslav and military circles, entertained plans for the construction of a different line connecting the Russian railway system—again through Bulgaria—with the Turkish capital. The strategic advantages of this, from the Russian standpoint, were obvious; the economic ones were more difficult to perceive. Not only was the estimated cost of the Russian line higher than that of the other, but it was clear that there was far less demand for it economically. The projected Austrian line, on the other hand, connecting Turkey as it would with the industrial heart of Europe, obviously had high economic promise.

Battenberg felt himself legally bound to respect the Sultan's earlier treaty with the Austrians. Khitrovo, not troubled by any such scruples,

---

* It is an ironic fact that Khitrovo's name suggests translation as "the sly one"; for this was precisely the reputation he enjoyed. In a German work written in 1839 (H. F. Geffcken, *Frankreich, Russland, und der Dreibund* [Berlin: Wilhelmini]), Khitrovo, who was later to become Russian minister in Rumania, is quoted as having expressed himself as follows to the French minister there: "Je ne comprends tous les scrupules de la diplomatie de nos temps. Il est malheureux que les diplomats d'aujourd'hui n'aient pas les mains libres comme au bon quinzième siècle, où tout était permis, le poignard et le poison. Quant aux questions d'argent, car après tout on ne peut rien faire sans argent, c'est une préoccupation que je n'ai jamais eue. On va droit devant soi. Si on a besoin d'argent, qu'on en ait ou non, on en dépense, et si, après tout, votre gouvernement vous désavoue et ne paie pas, on se fait sauter le caisson. Du moins on ne s'est pas arrêté en route" (p. 124).

strongly pushed the Russian project. Tension over this and other issues thus developed and grew, as it has a tendency to do, anyway, in small and confined foreign colonies such as that of Sofia; and soon the mails and the telegraphic wires running from Sofia to Petersburg were full of indignant complaints and denunciations of Battenberg and his conduct—denunciations, incidentally, of which he was not normally informed and which he had no opportunity to answer or rebut.

The struggle between the stubborn young Prince and the wily Russian intriguer raged over the first months of 1882, Khitrovo trying to bend the Prince to his will, the Prince trying to achieve Khitrovo's removal from the scene. In May of that year, an exchange of letters with the new Tsar having proved fruitless and the despatch by the Prince of a personal aide to Petersburg having produced no better result, Battenberg proceeded himself to the Russian capital and carried his case to Giers, now just in the process of taking over as foreign minister in his own right.

The removal of Khitrovo was finally conceded (thus adding one more formidable figure to the ranks of Battenberg's enemies at home); but when it came to the question of the selection of a successor to Ehrnrooth at the Bulgarian War Ministry, the cautious Giers, concerned not to offend the powerful Panslav faction at the very outset of his incumbency as foreign minister, packed Battenberg off to Moscow to discuss the matter with the two influential nationalist editors: Ivan Aksakov and Katkov. This action, consigning as it did to these two nongovernmental figures the virtual power of appointment to a senior Russian position in Bulgaria, stands as a revealing measure of the extent to which Russian policy in the Balkans was by this time removed from the effective control of the Foreign Office and shaped by people who had no place in the official governmental process.

The two editors received Battenberg civilly enough (although it was the last occasion on which they would do so); but the result of the consultations was that the Prince, still trying to accommodate himself to Russian wishes, was obliged to receive, as members of his Bulgarian government, not just one new Russian general but two: General Aleksandr Vasilyevich Kaulbars as minister of war, and a younger officer, General Leonid Nikolayevich Sobolev—a very active, intelligent, and nationalistic man—as minister of the interior.

This arrangement turned out to be, from the Prince's standpoint, anything but an improvement. Sobolev's position at the Bulgarian Interior Ministry gave him ample opportunity for political intrigue; and it was not long before the two generals were busy building up an anti-Battenberg faction among the Bulgarian politicians, especially on the

Liberal side, and promoting a movement for the restoration of the Constitution, as a first step towards the reduction of the Prince's authority. On the other hand, a continued heavy-handedness on the part not just of the generals but of Russian officialdom in Bulgaria generally was beginning to arouse antagonism in Bulgarian political circles, sometimes even in the hearts of those politicians who for reasons of opportunism accepted the benefits of an outward collaboration with the Russians. Increasingly, as the measure of Battenberg's conflict with Petersburg became known, the Bulgarians tended to turn to him for support against the local Russian officials; and he, considering his first duty to be to his people (this was in fact the real source of his conflict with the Russians, who considered his first duty to be to the Tsar), tended to give it. The result was that the more unpopular the generals became, the greater became Battenberg's popularity with the Bulgarians. He also enjoyed—surely much to the discontent of the Russians—the sympathy of the crowned heads of the two neighboring Balkan countries: the Hohenzollern Prince Charles of Rumania and King Milan of Serbia, who was himself only half a Serb. Both of these monarchs had had their own unpleasant experiences with the Russians in earlier days; and they could scarcely be other than sympathetic witnesses to Battenberg's difficulties in that quarter. His conflict with the Russians, and particularly the success with which he conducted it, thus began to have negative consequences for Russian policy in the Balkan region generally.

No less galling from the Russian standpoint was the personal sympathy—sometimes overtly manifested, sometimes only partially and unsuccessfully concealed—which the young Prince was beginning to command on the part of the representatives in Sofia of the other European Powers. Enjoying a status laid down and in effect guaranteed by the Treaty of Berlin, Bulgaria remained to a certain extent a responsibility of the community of European Powers. Russian policy, as the Russians had learned to their sorrow at the time of the conclusion of the San Stefano Treaty, had to be kept within bounds generally acceptable to the interests of the other Powers, particularly Britain and Austria, if Russia was to avoid a new and much more serious war than the one she had recently fought. This being the case, Battenberg's relations with the representatives of the other Powers were watched with anxious jealousy from the Russian side.

The English representative, Sir Frank Lascelles, was wholly sympathetic to the Prince and made little effort to conceal it. In this, he was only reflecting the feelings of his sovereign, Queen Victoria, who had at all times a soft spot in her heart for the young man, viewing him as a gallant figure, manfully standing up to the Russian pressures.

The German and Austrian representatives were under injunctions from their governments to show greater reserve; but it was only natural that Battenberg, speaking their language and feeling personally at home with them, should tend to pour out his grievances in their presence; and it was difficult for them to conceal the sympathy they were naturally inclined to feel. Particularly difficult and delicate was the position of the Austrian representative, Freiherr von Biegeleben, whom Battenberg regarded as a good friend. Repeatedly, as the conflict developed, the Austrian Ambassador in Petersburg, Count Wolkenstein, warned Vienna that the slightest evidence of sympathy for the Prince on Biegeleben's part that came to Russian attention could cause serious difficulties in Austro-Russian relations; but Biegeleben could not always avoid the position of confidant; and the ready suspiciousness of the Russian political temperament did the rest.

The coronation of the Tsar Alexander III took place, it will be recalled, in late May 1883. By this time, relations between Battenberg and the generals had become seriously strained. The young man, invited to attend the coronation, left Sofia on the 27th of April, with the intention of visiting certain other countries, including Greece and Turkey, before arriving in Moscow for this purpose.

Taking advantage, evidently, of his absence, the generals brought the railway question to a head shortly after his departure, and attempted to solve it by issuing (presumably on the strength of Sobolev's temporary status as regent) an order in favor of the Russian alternative. Battenberg, learning of this while in Athens, telegraphed a diametrically conflicting order from there. The generals' position was no doubt well explained and fell on sympathetic ears in Petersburg. Battenberg's communication was cryptic and unwelcome. Once again, the wires between Sofia and Petersburg buzzed with indignant protests and denunciations; and one can imagine that the atmosphere for the young man's reception as a visitor to the coronation was anything but favorable.

There were no objective observers—at least none who recorded for posterity their observations—of Battenberg's experience at the coronation. What flows from the memoirs of the persons most intimately involved gives an impression of dreamlike confusion. Plainly, his presence brought to the normal disorder surrounding the preparation of such great functions the added confusion of Balkan intrigue. Prior to departure from Sofia he had selected and appointed a special delegation of Bulgarians to bring the homage of their country to the new Tsar. He accidentally discovered, soon after arrival in Moscow, that the generals, profiting by his absence from Sofia, had appointed an entirely different delegation, made up of Bulgarians hostile to himself, and had, without notification to him, despatched it to Moscow with instructions (so, at least, it was alleged by Battenberg),[1] to beg the Tsar's assent to Battenberg's removal and his replacement by the brother of the Russian Empress, Prince Waldemar of Denmark. To make matters worse, it appeared that the Tsar had agreed to receive this delegation before receiving the Prince himself. Alarmed and infuriated, Battenberg stormed over to the Tsar's quarters and virtually forced himself on the latter's presence—in itself a grievous offense against established protocol. He seems to have gained his point about the delegation; and at some point he seems to have paid his normal official visit to the Tsar. But when the latter came to return the call (both were residing in the Kremlin) Battenberg, whether deliberately misinformed as a result of some intrigue or by dint of his own carelessness, was not there to receive him—a social error, this time, of monstrous dimensions.

Both Battenberg and his father, the grand duke of Hesse, had talks with the Tsar at the time of the coronation about the problems of Bulgaria. What was said on these occasions is wholly unclear. Even Corti, the biographer of both the Prince and his father, gives flatly conflicting accounts, in the two of his books that treat of this episode, of the impressions the two men carried away from their talks with the Tsar.* But of the further development of the Tsar's disposition with relation to Battenberg, there is no uncertainty at all. Either by way of reaction to what was said in these interviews or as a consequence of some ensuing complication unknown to the historian, and by whoever's fault this may have occurred, there was aroused (or perhaps there matured) at this time in the slow and stubborn disposition of Alexander III a hatred and resentment towards Battenberg for which there seems to have been no parallel in the entire history of that monarch's personal relationships. A powerful emotional nerve had been in some way touched and offended—so painfully offended that it would never cease to hurt. From that time on, it would be impossible to reason with Alexander III on the subject of the Prince of Bulgaria. A careless word on the latter's behalf, reaching the Tsar's ears, would suffice to put an end to an otherwise promising career in the Russian governmental service, or to the usefulness of a foreign ambassador at the Russian court. From this time on, hatred of Battenberg would become, for this otherwise lethargic

---

* These books were: Corti, *Alexander von Battenberg*, cited above, which was based on the Prince's papers, as found in the Hartenau Archive; and *The Downfall of Three Dynasties* (translation, Freeport, N. Y.: Books for Libraries Press, 1970 [original German edition published in 1934]), based on the papers of the father.

113

man, an unreasoning and uncontrollable emotional fixation. This disposition on the Tsar's part soon became a matter of common knowledge in all well-informed circles. The Tsar saw in Battenberg, according to the Austrian Ambassador Wolkenstein, "einen schwindelhaft angelegten, verlogenen, und undankbaren Menschen, welcher überdies ihn, den Kaiser—seinen Wohlthäter—in frecher Weise beleidigt hat." ("an untruthful ingrate with a predilection for swindle, who, moreover, has most impudently insulted the Tsar, his benefactor.")[2]

The historian is at a loss to explain the violence of this aversion. There are vague references to words having passed between the two men when they were both at the front, in the Russo-Turkish War. Also, the Tsar seems to have gained an impression that Battenberg had not only lied to him on some occasion but had accused him, the Tsar, of lying. "Zwischen mir und dem Fürsten von Bulgarien," he was reported to have said to the Grand Duchess Maria Pavlovna, in 1885, "liegen die Dinge so, dass entweder ich oder er gelogen hat. Da ich nun in meinem ganzen Leben keine Lüge gesagt habe, so muss Fürst Alexander gelogen haben; zwischen mir und ihm ist also eine Aussöhnung unmöglich." ("The situation between me and the Prince of Bulgaria is this: that either I or he has lied. Since I have never in my whole life told a lie, he must be the one who has lied. No reconciliation is therefore possible between him and me.")[3] It is possible that this impression may have derived from misunderstanding over Ehrnrooth's suggested reappointment to Bulgaria, to be mentioned presently.

Although Battenberg could not long remain unaware of this disposition on the Tsar's part, and although he cordially reciprocated the dislike,* it seems to have taken him a long time to understand the full depth of the Tsar's hatred. Measured against this degree of commitment against him on the Tsar's part, Battenberg's subsequent efforts to restore the relationship appear, for this reason, pathetically unperceptive, naive, and misconceived.

Whatever other impressions Battenberg may have carried away from this, his last personal encounter with Alexander III, there was one en-

---

* Battenberg's resentment of the Tsar comes out strongly in the young man's letters to his father as quoted by Corti in *The Downfall of Three Dynasties* (p. 301): "I *hate* the Tsar and shall never be able to forget what he has done to me . . . ," he wrote in 1884. "You simply have no idea," he wrote in another letter, some months later, "what a fearful hatred I have for the Tsar and his government" (p. 303). And again, in a third letter, in 1886, after his father had protested unsuccessfully to the Tsar about the latter's treatment of the Prince: "Your letter to the Tsar is so forcible that I hardly think he will have shown it to anyone or even preserved it. I don't suppose it will do much good, but it is a satisfaction to think that the thick-headed, narrow-minded oaf should for once have been told the truth" (p. 314).

couraging one: the Tsar, as he understood it, had agreed to reassign Ehrnrooth to Bulgaria, this time in the capacity of aide-de-camp to the Prince, with a view to assuring a more amicable relationship between the two crowned heads. Reassured by this impression, Battenberg thought to take his time returning to Bulgaria, and proceeded first on a visit to Berlin. In the German capital, enjoying as he did the favor of the English-born Crown Princess of Germany, Vicky, he was repeatedly invited to the home of the heir apparent. There he fell heavily in love with the second daughter of the house, Viktoria (sister of the future Kaiser William II), now seventeen years old. The feeling was reciprocated by the young lady, and enthusiastically encouraged by her mother. It aroused, however, an alarmed resistance in a portion of the family, notably on the part of her brother William. More important still, it met with bitter resistance on the part of Bismarck, who suspected Battenberg of an attempt at social climbing, and who saw in the very thought of such a marriage a sure path to German involvement in Bulgarian affairs—something to which he was fiercely opposed. Not only Germany's relations with Russia but in a sense Bismarck's entire European policy seemed to him to be hinged upon the readiness of Germany and Austria to allow Russia a free hand in Bulgaria; and anything that threatened to involve Germany in that quarter was anathema in his eyes.

Battenberg, after his visit to Berlin, proceeded to Austria, where he was courteously and kindly received by the Emperor Franz Joseph and, what was more unusual, by the Empress Elizabeth. (The latter is said even to have let down her beautiful hair for him to see—an almost unheard of gesture on the part of this strange and lovely woman.)

Battenberg was not, however, permitted to enjoy for long this relatively pleasant interlude in a troubled life. Shortly after his arrival at Vienna he became the recipient of a flurry of alarmed warnings from his staff and friends in Bulgaria that things were not going well in Sofia and that his presence was urgently required. He was further surprised and shocked to receive from Giers a message to the effect that Ehrnrooth was not, after all, to be sent to Bulgaria.* Instead, there was to be sent,

---

* Battenberg seems to have regarded this as little less than a betrayal by the Tsar of the understanding at which they had arrived in Moscow. But it is not at all certain that it was meant this way. There is some evidence that Ehrnrooth himself resisted the appointment, believing that it would lead to an impossibly complicated relationship between him and the two Russian generals already on the spot, one of whom was his successor as Bulgarian minister of war. Even as it was, Sobolev attacked Ehrnrooth publicly, three years later, over his earlier pro-Battenberg conduct in Bulgaria; and a polite but unpleasant exchange between the two men was published in the *Russkaya Starina*, August-October 1908.

in the capacity of diplomatic agent, another old hand of the Asiatic Department of the Russian Foreign Office: Aleksandr Semyonovich Ionin. Ionin, the Prince was told, would carry with him detailed instructions as to how things were to be done in the future; meanwhile the Prince was to support the generals and to take no initiative of his own.*

Battenberg returned at once to Sofia, to find the place, as usual, boiling with intrigue. Shortly thereafter, on the 23rd of August 1883, Ionin appeared on the scene.[4] The latter visited the Prince on the day after his arrival; and the initial encounter between the two men was one of such violent and dramatic plain-speaking on both sides that reports and accounts of it, mostly secondhand and none fully reliable, still enliven the annals of the time. Ionin, it is plausibly alleged, brought categoric and severe demands. The Prince was to agree, as the price for a reconciliation with Petersburg, to take no further action and to sign no further papers without his, Ionin's, specific approval. The two generals, meanwhile, were to be confirmed in office, and the handling of all constitutional problems was to be left to their good judgment. This last demand had a menacing note, well understood by all concerned; for the generals' interest in restoring the Constitution was plainly derived from the hope not only of depriving the Prince of his extraordinary powers but also of setting in motion a process that would lead to his removal from the throne.

Battenberg, not unnaturally, was disinclined to accept such terms. This and further meetings between the two men not only led to a deadlock but ushered in a period of extreme conflict, the intensity of which may be judged by the fact that Battenberg at one point felt obliged to leave his palace and to take up residence in the middle of one of the Bulgarian army camps, with a view to protecting himself against a possible Russian-inspired coup against his person. Perceiving the danger of a restoration of the Constitution under the generals' auspices and against his own opposition, however, and having already learned something of the wiles of Bulgarian politics, he now reversed his position and consented, in effect, in secret talks with some of the key Bulgarian politicians, to favor the reinstatement of the Constitution, if only this could be done in such a way as to make it possible for him to dismiss the entire existing government, including the two generals, and to set up

* Opinions among contemporaries about Ionin's character and political style seem to have differed widely. (See reference note 4 to this chapter.) This writer's own impression is that Ionin was an experienced and competent diplomat, no better and no worse than others of this description, who, in his rough treatment of Battenberg, was doing no more than to carry out the stern instructions with which he had been despatched to Bulgaria.

a new one agreeable to the parliamentary assembly—the Sobranje. The result was that on the 6th of September, at a meeting of the Sobranje in the ducal palace, this was suddenly and unexpectedly accomplished, to the amazement of the uninformed public and to the stunned fury of the two Russian generals, who were obliged literally to flee the scene in helpless humiliation, muttering imprecations against those who had betrayed them. In a few days' time they left the country, forever.

Outwardly, of course, Battenberg had won a dramatic victory. But it was questionable whether any victory won in this way—at the cost of the public humiliation of a great neighboring empire, its representatives, and its ruler—should properly have been thought of as a victory at all. The Russians held, over the long run, too many cards. Their initial anger, of course, knew no bounds. The Tsar's feelings must have been beyond expression. Ionin's prestige, at least as Russian political agent in Bulgaria, never fully recovered from the blow. Even Giers was at the end of his tether. In all the forty-five years of his governmental service he had never, he said to Wolkenstein, "been involved in a matter that had disgusted him in the same degree."[5]

The situation created by the expulsion of the generals called, of course, for a new decision of policy on the part of the Russians. It was soon taken, and at once began to find its reflection in the actions of the Russian government and in Giers' statements to foreign diplomats. Russia, it was decided, would insist on her controlling military position in Bulgaria. She would retain her control over the Bulgarian army. The minister of war would continue to be a Russian general. The army would continue to be staffed at higher levels by Russian officers. But beyond this, the Russian government would regard itself as having broken relations with Battenberg and would leave him strictly to his own devices. It washed its hands of him, the foreign representatives in Petersburg were told; it wished to have nothing more to do with him; it no longer knew him. This menacing attitude masked (though very thinly) a decision to work for his removal and replacement at the earliest possible date. But the realization of this objective involved a number of complications, including the discovering of an acceptable successor—acceptable not just to Russia but to the other Powers; and for this reason nothing could be done at the moment.

While his victory no doubt afforded the Prince much momentary satisfaction, and while he would continue to have moments of elation from time to time over the memory of his successful defiance of the Russians, he was aware in the more sober moments that his position was now an extremely exposed and dangerous one. It was plainly unlikely that he could retain his throne indefinitely unless he could either achieve a

117

reconciliation with the Russians or find some strong support among the other Great Powers. A letter addressed to the Tsar in the winter of 1884, pleading for reconciliation, produced only a curt and menacing reply which he should have expected. He turned, therefore, to the other alternative and set forth, in the spring of 1884, on a journey of political exploration in western Europe.

His first visits were, again, to Berlin and Vienna. He could not know, of course, that these visits fell in the very midst of the final phases of the negotiations among the Russian, German, and Austro-Hungarian governments over the renewal of the *Dreikaiserbund*, and that he could not, for this reason, have picked a worse time to attempt to drum up support in the two German-speaking capitals for a policy of resistance to Russian influence in Bulgaria.

His first visit was to the German Kaiser, William I. If he expected to find sympathy in this quarter (which he probably did), he was sorely disappointed. The old ruler, avoiding any mention of the marriage project (although he, too, had been miffed on learning that it was already a matter of common gossip, whereas he had never been consulted about it), took the Prince to task, not unreasonably, for tactlessness and disrespect in his modes of address to his imperial Russian cousin. The Prince, he had heard, had addressed the Tsar in his letters as "Dear Cousin." "Cousin, cousin!" snorted the old gentleman. "An emperor is an emperor. My own son signs himself 'your most obedient servant' when he writes to me."[6] But going on, then, to more important things, the Kaiser made it clear that Battenberg's only course, in his opinion, was to come to terms with the Russians, whatever the cost; Germany could not help him. And when the Prince replied, somewhat dramatically, that in this case he would have no choice but to abdicate and to leave Bulgaria forever, the Emperor's answer was: "All right; go then. It will not disturb me." ("Gut, gehen Sie; mich wird es nicht stören.")[7]

It was left to Bismarck, whom the young man saw two days later, to complete the destruction of his hopes for German support, or even for German sympathy. Like a steamroller, the great chancellor flattened out one after another of young Battenberg's dreams. Mentioning first the marriage project and sweeping aside Battenberg's objection that he had never asked for the girl's hand, he made it clear that such a marriage would simply not be allowed. It would never take place, he said, so long as he was chancellor. And then, turning to Battenberg's political situation: "It is high time," he said

> that you made up your mind whether you are a German or a Bulgarian. You have behaved up to this time like a German, and that can end only with the loss of your throne. . . . If you want to remain in Bulgaria, you must deliver yourself up body and soul to the mercy or the anger of the

Russians. Even adopt, if you must, an anti-German position. In general, I view the entire future existence of Bulgaria as questionable. Some day it will become the object of some sort of a deal [*Compensationsobjekt*] among the Great Powers; and sooner or later you will sit peacefully at the fireside and reminisce about the adventures of your stormy youth.[8]

The visit to Vienna did not produce anything like the brutal frankness of rejection Battenberg had met with in Berlin; there was even considerable sympathy for his position. But here, too, he was given no reason to hope that he would find outside support in his efforts to maintain himself in the face of Russian opposition and Russian anger. Austria had too many other irons in the fire. He returned to Sofia, therefore, greatly downcast, to ponder the question whether he should abdicate voluntarily or should wait for the mighty power of Russia to be brought into action in some decisive way against him.

It was in this unhappy and precarious state that things simmered along in Bulgaria over the remainder of the year 1884 and into the explosive atmosphere of 1885. Outwardly, relations between the Prince and the Russian government were now marked by nothing worse than occasional flickers of a glowing, subsurface hostility. But things in the Balkan regions surrounding Bulgaria were not standing still. The expiration of the five-year term of the first Turkish-Christian governor in neighboring Eastern Rumelia, and his replacement by a quite different personality, revived talk and stirrings with respect to a possible unification of the two territories.

And relations between Bulgarians and Serbs began to deteriorate. In the absence of Russian support for Bulgaria, and possibly not wholly without relation to Russian intrigues, the Serbs now began to make trouble for the Bulgarians over one question or another. The trouble came from the respective native politicians, not from the two crowned heads. The latter remained, for the time being, on good terms, and corresponded from time to time with a view to moderating the existing differences. The Serbian king, Milan, even gave Battenberg friendly advice about his personal position—advice which was the result of long and bitter experience on his own part. Battenberg, he said, should not give way to the Russians and should not abdicate voluntarily. "Remain!" Milan advised him. "I, too, was once the slave of Russia and a vassal of the Sultan. Now I am neither." But he was not impressed with Battenberg's expressions of confidence in the good qualities of the Bulgarians. "Don't put any reliance on your Bulgarians," he wrote, "and don't believe that they are, as you say, good and naive. They are Slavs, and with that, everything is said. My Serbs are not worth much more; and it is against their will that one must do what duty requires, letting then come what will. . . ."[9]

119

Chapter Six

THE UNIFICATION OF BULGARIA

In the diplomacy of nineteenth-century Europe, the late summers tended normally to be the doldrums; but never, it seemed, was there a late summer more languid in this respect than that of 1885. The Anglo-Russian crisis over Central Asia, having reached its culmination in the spring of the year, seemed by early June to be on the way to peaceful resolution. No other major complication was then visible on the horizon. All over Europe, weary statesmen took off from the capitals for their watering-places or their *villégiatures*. Petersburg was no exception. The Tsar, who had already been living relatively inaccessibly at Peterhof, left in the beginning of July for a series of journeys that were to take him, successively, to Finland, to the Moravian town of Kremsier for a meeting with the Emperor Franz Joseph, to southern Russia, and finally, to his great relief, by yacht to Copenhagen, where he could shed the cloying attentions of his Russian bodyguards and courtiers and enjoy the delights of a relative anonymity. Giers, too, liberated by the departure of his imperial master and only too happy to escape from the dust and heat of the capital, the intrigues of his Foreign Office underlings, and the boring interviews with foreign envoys, moved at the end of June to his suburban *dacha* in Oranienbaum. There, in the first days of July, he was obliged to witness (as did how many other people in that century of lung disease?) the lingering death by tuberculosis of a young daughter, Natalie. At the end of the month, he moved his still numerous family to the Bohemian spa of Franzensbad (in Czech, Francuske Lazne), where, with the family installed on an entire floor of the Hotel Stadt Rom, he could take the waters and still be conveniently at hand when the two Emperors would meet, on the 25th-27th of August, at Kremsier, in the neighboring Moravia.

The foreign ambassadors in Petersburg, finding themselves with no one to talk to at the Foreign Office but the colorless Vlangali, who was uninformed, uncommunicative, and only wearily polite, now also fled the summer-bound city for their respective vacation haunts. There remained then, in the chanceries of the embassies and legations, only the chargés d'affaires and the second secretaries. These, if their wives and children were away (as they usually were in summer), were left to open daily the dusty offices, to yawn over the translations from the local papers, to doze in their chairs after the heavy diplomatic luncheons, to grind out the occasional despatch to show that they were still alive, and to go out, perhaps, on the warm evenings, to the islands of the delta or to the park by the Pavlovsk railway station, where in the lingering twilight of the northern summer, the bands played Offenbach from their little drumlike platforms, people strolled on the sandy paths under the heavy chestnut trees, and there were girls to be picked up.

The French Embassy was little different from the others, in this respect; but the chargé, Ternaux-Compans, an alert and experienced man, noted with hopeful interest signs in the Russian press of tension between Russia and Germany over German penetration in Russian Poland, and wrote a long despatch about it. Someone in the Paris Foreign Office, receiving it and noting its significance, drafted an instruction commending him on it, succeeded, despite the summer languor, in getting the instruction signed by the acting foreign minister, and despatched it with the next courier to Petersburg.

In the life of the Prince of Bulgaria, things were never quite that peaceful, summer or no summer. It had been for him, thus far, an agitated year, and matters were growing more crucial. The commitment of the Russian government to his earliest possible removal from the Bulgarian throne was by now a secret to no one. The new Russian political agent, A. I. Koyander, who had relieved the discredited Ionin in the spring of 1884, had thus far devoted most of his time to efforts to persuade the Bulgarian political leaders to take the initiative in getting rid of the Prince. In the pro-Russian Liberal premier, Dragan Tsankov, who served throughout 1884 and who was destined soon to become a regular paid agent of the Russian government, Koyander had found a willing instrument; but Tsankov had not been able to bring his own Bulgarian colleagues to the point of action. Tsankov fell from office at the end of 1884, and was replaced by his Liberal rival, Petko Karavelov.

Karavelov, while still out of office, had lent himself extensively, like his predecessor, to Koyander's influence, visiting the Russian diplomatic agency at frequent intervals, sometimes several times a day. Presumably, he had used his relations with Koyander to promote his own advancement to the premiership. The premiership once attained, however, he began to distance himself from the Russians—a process which made him to some extent an ally of the Prince, but by no means a reliable one.

A third major political figure, Stambulov, though prevented by illness from playing a prominent political role, was at the time (all this was later to change most radically) very much in the Russian good graces— so much so that Koyander considered him the most reasonable of the lot and dreamed fondly of making him dictator, after Battenberg's removal.

It is clear that in these circumstances neither the Russian nor the Bulgarian faces by which Battenberg saw himself surrounded were in the least reassuring. If things were to go on this way, one had to expect it to be only a matter of time before his position was in some way made impossible. But beyond this, he was surely influenced by the realization, brought home to him through the impressions of his recent European travels, that if he was to have any chance at all of getting permission to marry the German Princess, he would have to find some way of composing his differences with the Russians. Both retention of the throne and the possibility of marriage seemed thus to depend on his ability to work a change in the Russian attitude. He had come to feel, by the beginning of 1885, that if such a change could not be achieved, then there was nothing for it—he would have to abdicate of his own accord. But of one thing he was persuaded: whatever the outcome, things simply could not be permitted to drag on as they then were.

With all this in mind, Battenberg set out, in early 1885, to force the issue and bring things to a conclusion. The first step was to test the possibility for accommodation with the Russians and, by the same token, the Germans. He made, therefore, in early winter, an effort to be nice to Koyander—visiting him, talking with him, even asking him for political advice. This undertaking was a source of much embarrassment to the unhappy Russian diplomatic agent, who had no instructions that would permit him to respond favorably to any such overtures, yet thought it premature to confess openly to Battenberg that reconciliation with the Russians was impossible and that they were determined to remove him no matter what he did. Koyander therefore squirmed and equivocated, and Battenberg, by all accounts, soon became discouraged and desisted.*

In addition to this direct approach, Battenberg also wrote, during the winter, to the German Kaiser, William I, begging him to use his influence with his imperial Russian grandnephew, the Tsar, with a view to persuading the latter to listen to what the Prince had to say and to see whether an amicable solution to the conflict could not be worked out.

* The record of these overtures on Battenberg's part, as well as indications of some of Koyander's intrigues with the Bulgarian politicians, will be found in the official Russian documents published in the volume *Avantyury russkogo tsarizma v Bolgarii*, edited by P. Pavlovich (Moscow: Soviet Economic Publishing House, 1935).

The old Kaiser, presumably after prudent consultation with Bismarck, replied to this letter on the 18th of March, demanding, as a price for his intercession, that the young man publicly renounce all intention of asking for the hand of the Princess. Battenberg evidently decided, at this point, to cut his losses, to the extent of postponing, if not abandoning, any hope of marrying the girl. He replied to the Kaiser, on the 26th of April, with a dignified and reasonable letter, setting forth his position. He was prepared to renounce the marriage project. He was also prepared, if this was what was required, to follow the Russian line in foreign policy and to respect Russian interests in Bulgarian internal matters in so far as it lay within his constitutional competence to do so. But he felt obliged to insist (1) that he take his orders directly from the Tsar, not through the latter's underlings; (2) that he have the support of the Russian representatives on the spot—the diplomatic agent and the minister of war—in executing those orders; and (3) that his own recommendations in policy matters be given consideration in Petersburg. What he was *not* prepared to do, he wrote, was to be a puppet, to let his name and position be used as a cover for the actions of others, or to stand by and witness the undermining of his duties and prerogatives as commander-in-chief of the Bulgarian armed forces. This was a not unreasonable position; and one must assume that the elements of it were in some way passed on to the Tsar, although there is no positive evidence of this.

In midsummer, not long after writing to the Kaiser, Battenberg went to England to attend the marriage (July 23, 1885) of his brother Henry to Beatrice, daughter of Queen Victoria.* Passing through Vienna on the return journey at the end of July, he took occasion to renew his effort at reconciliation with Petersburg by speaking to the Russian Ambassador in that city, Prince A. B. Lobanov-Rostovski, and extracting from the latter a promise to put his case to the Tsar. One suspects that by this time there must have been some faintly encouraging reaction from the Russian side. The Austrians, in any case, helpfully invited the Prince to return and to attend their manoeuvres in Bohemia in August. Battenberg welcomed this invitation, as it would give him an opportunity to see not only Lobanov but possibly also Giers, who, it will be recalled, was also in Bohemia, "taking the waters" at Franzensbad, not far from the theater of the Austrian manoeuvres.

* This was not the only connection of the children of Grand Duke Alexander of Hesse with the British royal house. Alexander von Battenberg's other brother, Louis, had married, in 1884, Victoria, a granddaughter of Queen Victoria through her mother, Princess Alice. Had Alexander's marriage project been carried to completion, he would have been the third of the Battenberg brothers to marry into the company of Queen Victoria's children and grandchildren.

A good idea of the Prince's frame of mind at this crucial point in the course of his Bulgarian adventure can be gained from the account submitted to Petersburg by the new Russian-Bulgarian Minister of War Prince Kantakuzin, of what Battenberg said to him during the course of a talk they had in Sofia on the 16th of August, just before Battenberg's return to Austria for the manoeuvres. "In Bulgaria," Kantakuzin quoted the Prince as saying,[1]

> there are only two forces: Russia and myself, and they must work together. If they do, all the local figures such as Karavelov, Tsankov, Stoilov, etc., don't amount to anything. In the absence of collaboration, however, between Russia and the ruling Prince, all the petty egoisms and passions of these figures make their appearance, and they ruin the country. Neither Russia nor I is able to count on a single one of these so-called parties; they only deceive us and exploit our mutual mistrust and our strained relations. I am clear in my mind that this situation cannot be permitted to endure; either you must let me come to Petersburg or I shall have to leave Bulgaria.

Battenberg, upon arrival at Austrian headquarters near Pilsen, requested (August 30) a meeting with Giers and Lobanov together.* Giers agreed; and the meeting took place, at Giers' hotel in the nearby Franzensbad on the afternoon of the 1st of September, shortly after the meeting of the two Emperors at Kremsier.

The discussion went on, we are told, for four solid hours, Battenberg doing most of the talking—more than talking, in fact: pouring out his complaints, trying to explain his position, pleading that Giers use his influence in the direction of a reconciliation, even—according to Giers—embracing the embarrassed statesman two or three times in the exuberance of his emotion. No actual written record of the talk has survived; but a number of secondhand accounts, together with what we already know of Battenberg's state of mind and aspirations at the moment, permit us to arrive at the following as a reasonably accurate summary of what, generally speaking, was said.[2]

1. Battenberg insisted that either there must be some sort of reconciliation, and an agreement on the terms of a *modus vivendi* for the future, or he must abdicate. "You must decide once and for all," he claims to have said to Giers. "If you want me to get out, say so frankly —I should be more than glad to return to Russia the crown of thorns

---

* I am assuming that Lobanov was present. He was in any case in the hotel that day (we know this from the memoirs of Giers' son, Nikolai). It is not to be supposed that the prudent Giers, well aware of the delicacy of the occasion, would have failed to provide himself with so convenient an official witness to the talk.

that I received from her hands. But if you wish me to remain, then make an honourable peace with me."[3]

2. Giers, forewarned, no doubt by Lobanov, of Battenberg's readiness to abdicate, was careful not to reject the offer completely. He said, however, that it was not possible to find a replacement for Battenberg at the moment—he had already made inquiries in this direction. Therefore he, Giers, favored the course of reconciliation; it lay, anyway, along the line of his own tastes. But obviously, he added, the final decision would not lie with him.

3. Giers, probably playing for time, said that before he could say anything more definite, he would also like to talk with Koyander. He inquired whether, in Battenberg's opinion, the situation in Bulgaria was such that Koyander could safely and conveniently absent himself from Sofia for a time, for purposes of such consultation. Battenberg replied that he saw nothing in the political situation there that should prevent this, though it was possible that Koyander might be detained by the present illness of his wife.

4. The question of a possible unification of Eastern Rumelia and Bulgaria was certainly discussed. Both men were well aware that the question, in view of the impending expiration of the term of the Turkish governor, was now once more in the air. It may be confidently assumed that they agreed that unification of the two territories could not be postponed indefinitely. Battenberg, however, expressed the view that things had not gone so far that action in this direction was to be feared for the near future. Giers thought that any spontaneous action in this direction would be opposed by the other Powers. Battenberg suggested that perhaps the Powers might be mollified if it could be agreed that the unified country would be placed under the control of a new governor, selected and appointed by the Powers, or with their consent. Giers, probably sensing in this suggestion a possible means of getting rid of Battenberg himself, indicated a noncommittal interest, but did not discuss it further.

5. Both men came away from the interview slightly encouraged. Battenberg felt that he had made some headway, that his case would be relayed to the Tsar, and that he was distinctly nearer to some sort of resolution of his impossible situation. Giers, to be sure, claimed later to have told the Tsar, after the interview, that he found the talk encouraging only for the short term, and then only if Battenberg's statements were not a ruse, designed to mask preparations for some sort of a coup. But this statement, made to one of the foreign envoys

after his return to Petersburg in October, smacks strongly of a defensive afterthought, designed to relieve the speaker of the suspicion of having been taken in by Battenberg.[4] Actually, Giers, too, for whom the conflict between Battenberg and the Tsar presented many dangers and inconveniences, must have been gratified by the Prince's professed willingness to abdicate if he could not be accepted into the Tsar's good graces, and no less relieved than the Prince to think that the problem might finally be approaching solution.

It was with these feelings, then, that the two men took their respective ways immediately after this interview: Giers, to continue his "cure" at Merano, in the Tyrol; Battenberg, to Bulgaria, to attend the manoeuvres of his own army at Shumla, near the Black Sea port of Varna.

It may be useful at this point, to review briefly, once again, the situation which existed at that moment with relation to the possible unification of the two portions of Bulgaria.

The creation of a unified Bulgaria had been envisaged in the abortive Treaty of San Stefano by which, in 1878, the Russians had attempted to end the war with Turkey. Obliged at the Congress of Berlin, by Austrian and British opposition, to abandon this treaty, and with it the demand for immediate realization of the unification of Bulgaria, the Russians had nevertheless fought strongly for unification as a long-term aim, and had later extracted from the Germans and Austrians, in the *Dreikaiserbund* agreement, the assurance that if unification were to come about spontaneously, "by force of circumstances," at some future date, the Powers would not oppose it. This left the Russians free to intrigue intensively to bring unification about, and they had lost little time in doing so. (Their efforts to organize and to arm a Rumelian faction, designed to work for this purpose, had begun immediately after conclusion of the Treaty of Berlin, Obruchev himself being evidently personally involved.)

But as the conflict with Battenberg developed, Russian enthusiasm for any early realization of the dream of unification cooled. It was clear that such a development, if brought about under the Prince's auspices, would not be in their interests. They could not, of course, renounce their commitment to the idea on principle, for this would only have played into Battenberg's hands. Indeed, they felt obliged to continue to toy with the leaders of the underground unification movement in Eastern Rumelia, lest things get out of hand. But as early as the coro-

126

nation of Alexander III in 1883 they had lost all immediate enthusiasm for the cause; and it was clear that they would not regain it so long as Battenberg occupied the Bulgarian throne. In these circumstances, the promise extracted from the Germans and Austrians in the *Dreikaiserbund* accord threatened to become more of an embarrassment than an aid to Russian policy.

In Vienna and London, on the other hand, exactly the opposite change had taken place. The Austrian and British statesmen had feared such unification so long as there was a likelihood of its occurring under Russian auspices, and as part of the Russian scheme for a greater Bulgaria occupying most of the southern portion of the Balkan peninsula. Now that Russia's influence in Bulgaria had been practically eliminated, however, and Bulgaria was in fact resistant to Russian influence, their anxieties were correspondingly relieved. They had no strong objection to unification, provided only that it came in such a manner that it did not lead to a significant extension of Russian influence or to some other form of instability in the sensitive region of the southern Balkans and the Straits.

Very soon after Battenberg's arrival at his own manoeuvre headquarters near Shumla, in eastern Bulgaria, there appeared there (apparently on September 9*), demanding to see him and succeeding, after some difficulty, in doing so, two curious and not too prepossessing individuals, attired in the uniform of the anti-Turkish insurgents of the Serbian uprising of 1875. They told him that they had come to apprise him of the fact that there was about to occur, in Eastern Rumelia, an uprising against Turkish rule, designed to effect the unification of that territory with the Principality of Bulgaria. They produced an appeal from a so-called Revolutionary Committee in Philippopolis, the capital of Eastern Rumelia, calling on the Prince to espouse the movement and to accept the new province into the existing Bulgarian state.

One of these characters was a Major Mutkurov (apparently of the Rumelian militia) who was indeed a full-fledged member of the conspiracy. The other was a Macedonian exile by the name of Risoff, resident in Philippopolis, where he edited an anti-Turkish Macedonian

---

* There is much confusion surrounding the dates of these various consultations that preceded the Philippopolis putsch, some of the confusion evidently attributable to the dual calendar. The dates used here are drawn from Battenberg's later oral account to Sir Frank Lascelles, as recounted in the latter's report to the Foreign Office. See British State Paper [c. 46127] *Correspondence respecting the affairs of Eastern Rumelia and Bulgaria*, London, 1886, p. 133.

newspaper. (There was a close connection between the Macedonian independence movement and the movement for the unification of Bulgaria.)*

Battenberg, suspicious of the reliability of at least one of the two visitors (not without reason, as it later developed), and noting that the appeal contained no personal signature, put them off with an assurance of sympathy for the general cause, then dismissed them, refusing, despite repeated requests, to receive them further. He did, however, at once despatch an aide to Philippopolis, with instructions to get into touch with the more reliable political figures there and to try to persuade them, if this proved necessary, not to proceed with such an undertaking at that particular moment.

Three days later, on the last day of the manoeuvres, Battenberg received a visit from the Bulgarian premier, Karavelov, who had come ostensibly to congratulate him on his name's day. The Prince told Karavelov of the strange visit he had received, and of his own reaction to it. Karavelov, who almost certainly knew much more of the matter than he was willing to reveal, professed approval of the Prince's reply to the two men, and disappeared again. The following day (the 13th), however, he was back again, at Battenberg's nearby summer residence, to tell the Prince that matters were much more serious than he had supposed, and to advise him to receive one or the other of the two persons again. The next day he appeared once more, this time in company with Risoff. The latter proceeded to give the Prince the names of several better-known personalities of the Philippopolis scene who were involved in the conspiracy, and it was made plain that the undertaking was a serious one, and the proposed action imminent.

Battenberg was filled with consternation at the realization that things were really this way. He found himself in a most awkward position. Not only had he told Giers (and apparently at some point the Austrian Emperor as well) that he did not think such a turn of events was imminent, but Giers had warned him that anything of this sort would not be met with approval by the European Powers. Karavelov must, on the other hand, have impressed upon him that for him to show lack of sympathy for the unification movement, and to try to oppose the planned uprising on principle, could cost him his throne. He found himself, therefore, in a position where, if he encouraged the insurrection, he

* According to the two principal secondary sources (Corti and Golovin), these men actually informed the Prince of the exact date (September 18) on which the unification was to be proclaimed. This seems unlikely. So chaotic and uncertain were the conditions surrounding the preparation of the uprising that any such accurate prediction would have been most remarkable.

risked being deposed by the Powers; if he opposed it, he risked being deposed by his own people.

His only hope, in these circumstances, was to play for time. He begged Risoff to tell his principals in Philippopolis that this was not the moment: that Russia would not approve, nor would the other Powers; that he had only recently told the Austrian Emperor that nothing of this sort was impending. (He did not mention the meeting with Giers.) No one, he said, was ready for such a development. It would sow great confusion. Karavelov, according to Battenberg's account, supported him in this appeal.

Risoff appeared to be convinced, and left crestfallen and dejected. Karavelov also left the same day, giving the Prince the impression that he, too, thought the matter was successfully disposed of.

Whether Risoff made any attempt to persuade his principals to call off the action is not clear. It was probably too late in any case. Only three days after this last meeting, on the 17th of September, there began in Philippopolis and its immediate vicinity a fearfully confused precipitation of events—secret mobilizations, nocturnal marchings, misunderstood or undetected signals, messages, warnings, sudden betrayals and equally sudden reconciliations—all finding their culmination in the early morning of the second day, when the miserable Christian-Turkish governor, Gavriil Pasha, while peacefully eating his breakfast in the upper floor of his *konak* and wondering vaguely about the identity of the somewhat odd company of armed men that appeared to be drawn up in the courtyard below him, was suddenly confronted, and taken into custody, by the leaders of the conspiracy. Too agitated to dress himself, he was clumsily assisted in this process by the equally agitated conspirators, and escorted triumphantly out of the building. Then, in that wonderful mixture of extreme danger and high comedy which the Balkans alone seem able to provide, he ended his morning being paraded through and out of town in an open *fiacre*, under the gaze of the cheering crowds, seated side by side with a virago of a Rumelian schoolmistress, who brandished in one hand, to the peril of everyone else in the vehicle, a naked sword. Surviving, rather miraculously, this unusual excursion, the unhappy governor, continuing feebly to protest that he was just as good a Bulgarian as anyone else, was safely spirited off to Sofia, where he was held in a species of polite house-arrest until the excitement was over. By evening, the unification of Eastern Rumelia with the Principality of Bulgaria was being triumphantly proclaimed, amid high enthusiasm, both locally and throughout the two provinces.

The news of what was happening in Philippopolis reached Battenberg in early afternoon of that same day. Returning from a ride in the countryside, he found awaiting him a sheaf of telegrams, informing him of what was in process and appealing to him to place himself at the head of the action. It was, for him, an intensely lonely moment. Not one of the diplomatic agents of the Powers was there to be consulted; nor, for that matter, was there any member of the Bulgarian government.* It was clear, however, that if he was to act, he must act at once. There was no time for delay. Not only could any hesitation be misinterpreted and cost him his throne, but there was great and real danger that unless he took charge of things without delay, the development could end in a general and bloody conflict between the alarmed Moslem population of Rumelia, who saw themselves being deprived of the Sultan's protection, and the now wildly excited Christians. The "Bulgarian atrocities," which had so agitated English opinion some years before, may well have been exaggerated; but such as they were, they were of recent memory; and unless people were restrained, there was no telling what would happen. The Prince, however, was the only person who could do the restraining. There was now no government of any sort in the liberated province, and no one else who could conceivably bring order into the situation. Against these considerations there remained, of course, the unpreparedness of the Powers, the lack of any indication of Russian policy, the danger that the Russians would in some way exploit the situation to his disadvantage.

Whatever his other faults, however, Battenberg was not lacking in either courage or power of decision. After a bout of anguished reflection in the privacy of his study, where—according to Corti—he paced up and down for an hour with folded arms, he emerged, appeared before the large body who had now gathered to learn of his decision, and announced to them that they could greet in him the Prince of a united Bulgaria. He then proceeded to act, and with great energy and firmness. The entire telegraph system of the country was commandeered. A stream of telegraphic messages at once went forward: to the Philippopolis insurgents, apprising them of his acceptance; to the Bulgarian premier, with similar notification; to the Tsar, informing him of the reasons for his action and requesting his support; to the Turkish Sultan, assuring him of the loyalty of the entire now-united country. Orders were sent

* I recall having read somewhere that one of the diplomatic agents accredited to Sofia subsequently complained bitterly over the inconsiderateness and lack of tact shown by the Rumelian insurgents in staging such an action precisely in late summer, when it was known that all the diplomatists were away on vacation. Putsches were supposed to occur, he felt, only when the diplomatic corps was on hand to react to them. Actually, the absence of these diplomatic agents was said to be one of the factors dictating the choice of this particular moment by the insurgents. G.K.

out for notification of the other Powers, and—in view of the danger of Turkish intervention—for the immediate mobilization of the armed forces.

All this done, the Prince set out at once for Philippopolis. Joined along the route by Karavelov, he arrived there on the 20th. As he approached the city, he was greeted by the two bewildered Russian representatives: the secretary of the Russian consulate general, Count E. B. Igelstrom, and the military representative, Colonel M. M. Chichagov, both in full uniform. Neither had any instructions from Petersburg as to what to do in such a contingency. Both were hesitant about appearing together with Battenberg, knowing the Tsar's hatred of him; but they were equally afraid of being criticized for failing to demonstrate Russia's enthusiasm for the cause of unification. Unhappily, therefore, and full of misgivings, they embraced the young Prince (a gesture they later had cause to regret) but prudently detached themselves from his entourage before he entered the city. His entry was the occasion for wild enthusiasm on the part of the populace.

Once in the center of the city, Battenberg proceeded forthwith to the Orthodox-Christian cathedral, knelt down, and prayed, invoking the blessing of the Almighty, one must suppose, on an event which was all the more likely to require the support of the Divine Power inasmuch as it was most unlikely to receive that of any of the earthly ones. This done, he proceeded to the leading mosque, where, taking off his shoes, kneeling and touching his forehead reverently to the carpet, he did the same to Allah. Emerging from the mosque, he issued a public appeal to both religious groups to observe restraint and avoid further bloodshed— an appeal which, together with an order for the disarming of the Moslems, was crowned with success and may well have averted fearful further misfortunes. All in all, the Prince came out of the ordeal, so far as his relations with the Bulgarian people were concerned, with flying colors, indeed something of a national hero, his internal position greatly strengthened.

Before we leave the episode of the Philippopolis uprising itself and turn to its international repercussions, it might be well to deal with the suspicions, to which it at once gave rise, that there were important figures, outsiders representing one or another of the Great Powers, or Battenberg himself, who had had foreknowledge of what was cooking and had organized, abetted, or encouraged the conspiracy.

For Giers, in particular, this was a painful and burning question. It is obvious that the event came as a great shock to the Russian governmental leaders. The unification of Bulgaria, as noted above, had been *their* great cause. It was the success they had pictured *themselves* as achieving, thereby earning the admiration and gratitude of the Slavic peoples all over southern and eastern Europe. Now it had suddenly come about when they, so to speak, were not looking; and here was this odious young Prince, the Tsar's personal enemy, taking the credit for it, being acclaimed as a hero for espousing it, pre-empting in this way Russian's own trump card in Balkan politics—the last and only fruit of the bloody and exhausting war she had fought with the Turks eight years earlier. Seldom, surely, has a Great Power been required to drink a more bitter cup of gall.

All this being so, how did Giers look, in the eyes of the Tsar and other well-informed people? The event had occurred on the very heels of his long interview with Battenberg. What were people to conclude? That he had sanctioned a development which had turned out to be a triumph for Battenberg and had made Russia the laughing-stock of Europe? Or was it that he, an old and experienced statesman, had been tricked by a snip of a German princeling who had successfully lulled him into a sense of false security while preparing the putsch behind his back? These were the questions that were bound to arise; and so awkward were they, so vulnerable did the episode leave Giers to the attacks of his Panslav and chauvinist critics within Russia, that as much as three months later the Austrian and German envoys in Petersburg were still exchanging gloomy speculations as to whether the episode had not damaged his political situation beyond repair and whether perhaps the entire Three-Emperor relationship was not now in jeopardy. (The first part of this fear turned out to be exaggerated; the second part, unfortunately for them, was well justified.)

The suspicion on the part of outsiders that Giers had been taken in by Battenberg was all the more galling to Giers because he himself was not sure, initially at least, that it was not true. Battenberg, realizing that this was the way things might look, wired Giers within a matter of days after the event, begging him to believe that he had had no knowledge, at the time of their talk, that preparations were under way for an early action of this sort. Giers replied, through Koyander, with an icy rejoinder which clearly betrayed his suspicions in the very course of denying them.[5] "Puisque Votre altesse affirme," the message ran, "qu'Elle a été prise à l'improviste par les événements de Roumélie, je n'ose en douter, mais je déplore l'aventure dangereuse dans laquelle la Bulgarie s'est jetée d'une manière aussi irréfléchie."* It is not impossible that

---

* "Since Your Highness states that the Rumelian events took him by surprise, I would not venture to doubt it, but I deplore the dangerous adventure into which Bulgaria has thrown herself in so ill-considered a manner."

Battenberg, for his part, may have entertained similar doubts with respect to Giers. The latter, after all, had his own sources of information in the Balkans. Could he, too, have been wholly ignorant of what was in the cards?

Let us take first the case of the Prince. We have seen that he was forewarned, on or about the 9th of September, of the imminence of the Philippopolis putsch. Had he had no earlier knowledge, or no suspicion, of what was afoot?

It would seem, at first glance, improbable that he had not. One of his secretaries, a Russian by the name of A. F. Golovin, who later became one of his two biographers,* spent much of the summer of 1885 in Eastern Rumelia, accompanied by his highly political and active wife. The visit of the couple to that province, according to Golovin's own account, was motivated both by a desire to see unification brought about under the Prince's auspices, as a means of strengthening the latter's position, and by curiosity as to what the chances were for the realization of such a project. He was, by his own confession, in close contact with the Rumelian conspirators throughout most of the period of the preparations of the putsch. Returning to Sofia in late July or early August, that is, before the Giers-Battenberg interview, he saw Battenberg there during the latter's brief sojourn in that capital before departure for the Austrian manoeuvres, and discussed with him at least some of the more burning political problems of the moment. Could it be that the Prince remained, through all of this, unaware of what was going on?

Golovin alleges that he omitted, for the Prince's own protection, to inform him either of the reasons for his visit to Eastern Rumelia in the first place, or, on the occasion of their midsummer meeting, of the preparations which he now knew to be in progress. All this seems on the face of it to be implausible; but other circumstances compel us to conclude that it was probably true. Golovin may well have said enough to let the Prince understand that something was stirring; but it is unlikely that he told him any of the details; and it is doubtful that Battenberg, accustomed as he was to the alarms and excursions of Bulgarian politics, took the matter very seriously before he received the visits of the Rumelian leaders in early September. It would simply have made no sense for him, had he known that the putsch was in any way imminent,

---

* Golovin's *Fürst Alexander I von Bulgarien*, a confused, poorly written, but interesting book, appeared in Vienna in 1896 (see Chap. V, n. 4). Golovin was for a time director of Battenberg's Press Bureau, and subsequently a private secretary. He was a great admirer of the Prince; and it is probably not without significance that his book, written in Varna, was published in Vienna, not Russia, and then only in 1896, after the death of Alexander III.

to say to Giers the things he obviously said on the occasion of their meeting. This would only have been to invite unnecessary resentment and trouble. Not only this, but Battenberg met on a number of occasions, while at the Austrian manoeuvres, with a good friend of his, Count Karl von Wedel, then military attaché at the German Embassy at Vienna, and poured his heart out to him just before, and again after, his meeting with Giers. Nothing in his statements or behavior on these occasions suggests any foreknowledge on his part of the impending unification or even any preoccupation with that problem.[6]

An equally puzzling situation presents itself when it comes to the question of what knowledge of these preparations was possessed by the Russian government. That Giers, when talking with Battenberg, was ignorant of what was in the offing seems as implausible, on the face of it, as does the similar ignorance on the part of the Prince. Yet this, too, was probably the case; and if so, it reflected nothing more than great confusion on the spot, in Eastern Rumelia and Bulgaria, and very poor communications, at that point, within the Russian government.

There were at that time only two senior Russian officials stationed in Philippopolis: the secretary of the consulate general, Igelstrom, and the military representative, Lieutenant Colonel Chichagov, both mentioned above. Although the first, in particular, was by all accounts a regular Foreign Office official and a man of considerable dignity of character, the missions of these two men were highly political and by no means excluded the fancier brands of political intrigue. Their standing instructions, one may infer, were to keep the Rumelian unification movement going and to maintain their own contact with it and control over it, but not to bring it to a head so long as Battenberg could profit from it. To this end, they had contact with a group of local characters devoted to the cause of unification, whom they no doubt financed and supported within reason but whom they kept deliberately—to use the modern governmental jargon—"on the back-burner." The action of September 1885 was carried out, however, not by these men but by another group, a number of whom were Macedonians—men whose connections ran not to these local Russian officials but to the Bulgarian premier in Sofia, Karavelov.

Although Golovin, in the hopes that the action would strengthen Battenberg's hand, desired it to proceed, the conspirators themselves, and particularly Karavelov (who was no friend of the Prince), appear to have vacillated right up to the end of August over the question of whether they should couple the action with a forcible removal of the Prince, appealing then (and with very good prospects for success) for Russian support, but perhaps forfeiting some popular support in Bulgaria in the process; or whether they should ask the Prince to associate himself with the action, thus taking advantage of the internal-political prestige of the throne but risking offense to the Russians. The decision fell for the latter alternative—but not by much, and only because the conspirators thought the Russians would be obliged to support the action anyway, once it was a *fait accompli*.

Igelstrom and Chichagov had little excuse for lack of awareness of what was going on with this latter group of conspirators, even if they did not control them. Golovin and his wife stayed at the Igelstroms' home during their visit in Philippopolis; and it is scarcely to be supposed that these highly political guests, operating in the tiny little teacup of the Rumelian capital, successfully concealed from their hosts every trace of the real nature of their activity and interests. Not only did Golovin, if we are to believe his own statements, give to one of the Macedonian conspirators a letter of introduction to Colonel Chichagov,[7] but in early August, in the course of a visit to another part of the province, he wrote a letter to Igelstrom, by agreement with one of the leaders of the conspiracy, warning the Russian official that the administration of the Turkish governor general was becoming increasingly unpopular and that the union of the province with Bulgaria would soon be effected by popular action.[8] Igelstrom either failed to believe this, as Golovin claims to have thought, or—more likely—considered that it would be rash on the part of himself and Chichagov either to oppose the action, on the one hand, or take any responsibility for it, on the other. They therefore appear to have let it ride, but to have been taken off guard, in the end, by the suddenness with which it all came to fruition.*

A greater mystery is why none of this got through to Giers and the Tsar. Here, one can look for explanations only in the general midsummer lethargy of the Russian bureaucratic apparatus, the leisureliness of courier communication between such a place as Philippopolis and Petersburg, the absence of both Giers and the Emperor from the country, and the reluctance of people in the Ministry for Foreign Affairs to burden them with rumors that might or might not turn out to have substance.

An ironic aspect of this insurrection is the fact that the timing of it appears to have been strongly influenced by the repercussions of Batten-

---

* The Austrian representative in Sofia, von Biegeleben, thought the Russian representatives in Philippopolis must have been well aware of the preparations for the action, but let those preparations proceed in the belief that a successful putsch would confront Battenberg with the choice of a conflict with the Powers or a conflict with his own people. See his despatch of October 8, 1885, Austrian Archives, Box XV/91, *Bulgarien*.

berg's own talk, in the winter and spring of 1885, about the impossible position in which he found himself, and about the resulting necessity either of regaining Russian favor or abdicating. It was this that inspired Golovin, a strong supporter of the Prince, to go to Eastern Rumelia and to see what could be done in the way of bringing the unification about under Battenberg's auspices. But when Golovin got there, he found the movement already in progress; and he discovered that one of the main reasons for its activation, particularly on the part of the Macedonians, was the impression gained by the leaders of the conspiracy that major political changes, including a change in the occupancy of the throne, might be in progress in Bulgaria. They, too, had heard rumors of Battenberg's resolve to bring things to a showdown; and they reasoned that the last weeks or months of Battenberg's reign might actually be their last favorable chance for action.*

Noting this fact, the student of the period is obliged to recognize that it was, ironically, the Russians themselves who, by driving Battenberg to desperation in 1884-1885 and bringing him to a point where he contemplated abdication, actually set off, unwittingly, the train of events which ultimately so embarrassed them.

Aside from the question of complicity on Battenberg's side and on that of the Russians, there was one other element of suspicion that can be laid to rest with great definiteness: and that was the suspicion in many Russian minds that in some way or other the Germans or the Austrians were behind the whole affair. In the case of the Germans, not only do the circumstances on the spot provide absolutely no reason to suspect anything of this sort, but any German complicity would have been so utterly contrary to Bismarck's policy that it may safely be ruled out from the start. It was, however, the Austrians upon whom Russian suspicions centered; not, to be sure, the suspicions of the Russian representatives on the spot, who knew only too well what was going on, but rather those of people in Russia proper who had no intimate knowledge of the circumstances but were prone to anti-Austrian reactions from the start. It took the Petersburg *Novosti*, the organ of the Panslavs, for example, only two days to decide, when the news of the putsch came in, that all the other European Powers had had advance knowledge of it, and that the event was not unconnected with the presence at that time of the Austrian Emperor on Bosnian soil. What grounds were there for such assumptions?

* Igelstrom, in a letter to Giers of May 31, 1886, wrote that ". . . it seems more and more probable that the uprising of September 18 was not a well-organized political plot but owed its origin exclusively to rumors about a revival of the dynastic question in the Principality" (*Avantyury*, etc., Document 9).

Again, the answer must be given: none whatsoever. The senior Austrian representative in Bulgaria, Freiherr von Biegeleben, was peacefully enjoying his vacation in another part of Europe during the entire period of the preparation of the action; the haste and obvious consternation with which he rushed back to his post when the news became known is ample evidence of the extent to which this news took him by surprise. The despatches of his deputy, Herr von Steinbach-Hidegkut, who was carrying on in Sofia in his chief's absence, make it wholly evident not only that he, too, was taken completely by surprise but that he had no contact, throughout the entire time of the preparation of the putsch, with any of those who conducted it or knew of its preparation.

Chapter Seven

THE AFTERMATH OF UNIFICATION

It was, of course, not only the Russians who were startled and taken aback by the sudden turn of events in Eastern Rumelia. The *status quo* in the Balkans was regarded as a responsibility of the Great Powers. Its basis was considered to be the Treaty of Berlin. What had occurred in Philippopolis represented a violation of that treaty. True, precisely such an eventuality had been envisaged in the protocol to the secret treaty forming the *Dreikaiserbund*, by virtue of which the Germans and Austrians had undertaken not to oppose unification if it were to come about by the force of circumstances. But this had not been revealed to the other Powers; and besides, it had been predicated on the assumption that unification was something the Russians wanted, whereas it was only too clear that now they did not want it at all. One was left, therefore, with the terms of the Treaty of Berlin itself as the only firm point of reference.

The greatest and most immediate danger visible to the Powers was that if they sanctioned what had now occurred in Eastern Rumelia, or even if they only failed to reverse it, other Balkan countries, seeing that the Bulgarians had been able to get away with a violation of the Treaty of Berlin, would be moved to do likewise. The development immediately produced sharp and excited reactions in both Serbia and Greece. It raised for peoples and governments in both those countries the spectre of a renewed effort by the Bulgarians to achieve the greater Bulgaria which the Russians had tried and failed to achieve by the Treaty of San Stefano. People feared that the Philippopolis uprising was only the first step towards an effort to bring about the incorporation of Macedonia into Bulgaria; and given the prominence among the Rumelian conspirators of Macedonians whose hopes ran in precisely this direction, such fears were not wholly without justification. There was no question but that both Greece and Serbia were ready to go to war rather than to tolerate any such development; indeed, it was not at all certain that these countries could now be restrained from going to war anyway, just over the issue of the unification itself, whether or not it had wider consequences. There was, therefore, a good case to be made, in theory, at least, for reversing the unification by authority of the Powers.

The potentate most intimately affected by the unification, in the formal sense, was of course the unhappy Sultan. He, too, found himself placed by this turn of events in a dreadful dilemma. He had no desire to attempt to reintroduce his troops into Eastern Rumelia, nor did he have any reason to suppose that the Russians, who had fought a war to get him out of there, would wish him to do so. If, on the other hand, he accepted without resistance this most recent of many encroachments upon his crumbling empire, he could scarcely expect that it would be the last one. Macedonia, after all, was still a Turkish province. Battenberg, to be sure, hastened to assure him that Bulgaria's relationship of vassaldom to the Porte would continue to be respected, as applying now to the entire territory of the united Bulgaria; and this gave the Sultan a certain tenuous way out. Still, to accept a violation of the Treaty of Berlin, the only formal protection for what remained of his European empire, was a course replete with danger.

Most excruciating of all was the position of the Russians. They were obliged to bear in mind not only all the complications just recited but also the damage which this development, if allowed to stand, might bring to their own prestige. No wonder that Giers, soon after learning at Merano of the successful completion of the uprising, sent to the Tsar, then in Denmark, an anguished telegraphic message, saying: "Au nom du ciel, pas d'union." The reply which came back from the Tsar was prompt and terse: "Je suis entièrement de votre avis. Venez vite!"[1]

Giers set off at once for Copenhagen. He stopped briefly on the way at Friedrichsruh, to talk once more with Bismarck—presumably with a view to finding out what the Germans knew about the origins of the affair, and what they thought of the situation it had created. At Copenhagen, where he arrived on the 30th of September, he found the Tsar in a state of smoldering fury. Without even awaiting Giers' arrival, he had gone ahead and issued orders for the recall of all the Russian officers in Bulgaria.* Now, Giers discovered, he was determined to in-

* One must suppose that the Tsar, in taking this drastic step, had been influenced by the views of the Russian diplomatic agent in Sofia, Koyander. The latter, in a letter of June 19, 1885, which probably came to the Tsar's attention, had submitted that the best way to handle the Bulgarians would be to bring them to a pass where they would recognize their own helplessness and request Russia's assistance; and he had then pointed out that the entire order of the country rested on the presence of the Russian officers; without them, things would rapidly come to a point of total anarchy. To remove them, he added, would be a risky measure—it might not work; but risky measures were now in order (*Avantyury*, etc., Document 2).

sist not only that the Powers require the rescinding of the entire action and the restoration of the *status quo ante*, but also that they jointly demand the removal of Battenberg. This last intention Giers successfully resisted: it would, he pointed out, only make the Prince a hero, leave the country without a government, and invite foreign intervention. But he was unable to wean the Tsar, if indeed he tried to do so, from the idea of insistence by the Powers on the restoration of the *status quo ante*.

In actuality, the idea of undoing the effects of the uprising and restoring the division of the country was a wholly impractical and even fatuous one. The change had occurred. It had been greeted with enthusiasm by the Bulgarian people, both in the Principality and in Eastern Rumelia. Not all the Tsar's horses and all the Tsar's men could at this point have put this particular Humpty Dumpty together again.

The Tsar's feelings, however, were of the strongest, and he was not, for the moment, to be crossed. The Russian Foreign Office had already sent out, on the 23rd, a circular calling for an informal convening of the ambassadors of the Great Powers at Constantinople, for the purpose of examining the situation flowing from the events in Philippopolis. Giers was now left with the task of framing the instructions by which the Russian Ambassador there, A. I. Nelidov, should be guided in these consultations; and these instructions had to be framed in the spirit of the Tsar's decision.

Giers could not have remained long in ignorance of the impossibility of the task with which the Tsar had charged him. If he did not already know it, he must have become convinced of it after his consultations with the members of a Bulgarian delegation which had been sent to Copenhagen to plead with the Tsar to accept the *fait accompli*, and had arrived there on the same day as himself. The Tsar had received its members most reluctantly (apparently only because they included one high pro-Russian Bulgarian churchman) and had given them small comfort. The unification, he had said to them, was in itself desirable. Russia had once favored it. But he could only disapprove of the manner in which it had been brought about. "I shall do my best," he said, "to save you from the perils into which you have brought yourselves." But he could act, he insisted, only in conjunction with the other Powers.[2]

The visit of the delegation was thus fruitless. But its members no doubt emphasized to Giers the total impracticality of trying now to undo what had been done; and this, coming as it did from people fresh from the Bulgarian scene, must have made a strong impression upon him.

In the face of this realization, the Russian foreign minister found himself faced with a diplomatic task as challenging as any he ever had to face. He was obliged to demand of the other Powers, on the one hand, in deference to the Tsar's imperious wish, that the unification be reversed. On the other hand, he knew very well it could not be, and was obliged to discover some means whereby the Powers, having demanded its reversal, could gracefully accommodate themselves to the fact that this could obviously not be achieved.

Returning to Petersburg after his conferences in Copenhagen, Giers stopped off once more at Friedrichsruh to get Bismarck's help in squaring the circle. He had by this time had opportunity to put his own ingenuity to work; and the line of approach which he suggested to Bismarck was a good example of his great diplomatic skill. Battenberg was to be called upon by the Powers to agree to the formal restoration of the *status quo ante*; but as soon as this was achieved, the Powers would themselves see what could be done to satisfy the aspirations of "the people of Eastern Rumelia." Unification under the authority of Battenberg, in other words, was to be formally annulled; but it was to be followed directly by unification under the authority of the Powers.

Bismarck, who—as the great professional that he was—no doubt admired the ingenuity of this suggestion, was also pleased with it politically. It coincided with his strong feeling that the interrelations among the Balkan peoples, for whom he had no high respect, were something to be arranged by the Great Powers and not by those peoples themselves. "One must give these sheep-stealers plainly to understand," he said shortly thereafter to the French Ambassador (the reference being to the Greeks, Serbs, and Bulgars),[3] "that the European governments have no need to harness themselves to their lusts and their rivalries." But beyond this, being no less aware than Giers that this was a situation to which there was no really satisfactory solution, he saw in the convening of a meeting of the Constantinople ambassadors and in the charging of these helpless figures with the task of squaring the circle, a means—as he later put it to several people—of "drowning the problem in ink."

The ambassadors dutifully met, at the beginning of October, and struggled futilely, as it was intended they should do, with their hopeless task. They succeeded in producing in October the usual useless and high-minded sort of declaration, condemning the violation of the Treaty of Berlin, disapproving the despatch of Bulgarian troops to Eastern Rumelia, and calling upon everyone to preserve the peace. Thereafter, they were asked to constitute themselves a full-fledged Conference of the Powers, with authority to reconcile the existing situa-

141

tion with the provisions of the Treaty of Berlin. To this end, they met several times in the month of November, until their labors were overtaken by other events, presently to be described.

For, in the meantime, things were not standing still. The Tsar, for one thing, insisted on issuing a public Order of the Day (November 7) stripping Battenberg of his rank and membership in the Russian army as well as of all his Russian decorations, and changing the name of the regiment of which he had been the honorary commander. Giers and the minister of war, Vannovski, pleaded with him not to take this petulant step, for which no reason of any sort was offered; but Alexander III was not to be deterred. The personal vindictiveness of the measure was apparent to everyone, and it produced a deplorable impression all over Europe.

Of far greater importance, however, was the steady movement of the Serbs towards the launching of a war against the united Bulgaria. The Serbs were warned from every possible side, and indeed implored, not to proceed with this intention. The Austrians, who had a secret alliance with Serbia which they had not even revealed to the Russians, were particularly embarrassed by it, and exerted every bit of their influence to prevent its realization. Battenberg, too, went to greatest lengths to forestall such a development. He acceded to a whole series of limited Serbian demands, and addressed to the Serbian King Milan a personal appeal couched in the friendliest and warmest of terms. But the Serbs, like the Tsar, now had the bit firmly in their teeth, and were not to be reasoned with. On the 14th of November they declared war and sent their forces across the Bulgarian frontier.

This development not only caused great concern and wringing of hands on the part of the Powers, who now saw the whole *status quo* in the Balkans beginning to disintegrate, but it presented a bitter problem for Battenberg. Most of the Bulgarian army had been moved to the Turkish frontier, to guard against the possibility of a Turkish intervention in view of the challenge to Turkish authority in Eastern Rumelia. Not only this, but the recent departure of all the Russian officers (they had numbered two to three hundred) had left the Bulgarian army stripped of most of its higher officers' corps. Battenberg was forced not only to improvise hastily a new corps of commanders from among the Bulgarian junior officers but also to move most of the units, in forced marches, from the Turkish to the Serbian frontier. But he was, as a person whose education had been largely military, now in his element. Leaving Sofia, he went out to the front, took command, spent the whole period of operations among his troops, sleeping with them on the ground, never even taking his clothes off for twelve days and nights on end, and gave to his forces, as almost everyone was obliged to admit, excellent military leadership.

Initially, the fortunes of battle appeared to favor the Serbs; and the Russian Panslav press, while greatly concerned over the prospect of a Serbian success at the expense of Bulgaria, was full of *Schadenfreude* at the expense of Battenberg. "Now you see," went the general editorial line, "to what a pass Battenberg has brought things through his estrangement of Russia; you see what a catastrophe he has invited upon his country." But on the 19th, the tide of battle began to turn, in operations around the town of Slivnica. The campaign which had begun so favorably for the Serbs now quickly turned into a disastrous defeat for them. Within less than a week, operations had been moved back onto Serbian territory, the Serbian forces were in full retreat, and Battenberg was threatening not only to take Niš but, as was commonly feared, to press on to Belgrade.*

It was now the turn of the Austrians to agonize. Although they had tried to dissuade the Serbs from making war, they could have witnessed with a certain malicious pleasure a limited victory of the Serbs over the Bulgarians. But a Bulgarian victory over Serbia was a different thing. Serbia was a part of *their* sphere of influence. Their secret alliance with Serbia, the existence of which they could not publicly admit, made it awkward for them to stand by and witness a successful invasion by one of her neighbors. Beyond that, there was a strong probability that a further advance by the Bulgarians would lead to the dethronement of King Milan and the replacement of his regime by one that might well turn out to be pro-Russian. The cabinet in Vienna therefore proceeded, in great haste and some desperation, to despatch to the theater of war its minister in Belgrade, Count Rudolf Khevenhüller, who had previously served in Sofia and was well acquainted with Battenberg, with instructions to seek out Battenberg and to see what could be done to bring hostilities to an end.

By dint of an adventurous journey on horseback, Khevenhüller succeeded in crossing the battle-lines and making his way to Battenberg's headquarters. The latter, not at all inclined to let his adversary off thus easily, at first passionately resisted Khevenhüller's demand for an armistice. His resistance, however, was finally overcome when Khevenhüller

---

* Some of the Russian officers, miffed, no doubt, at seeing Battenberg get the credit for victories which they preferred to ascribe solely to the excellent training they had given the Bulgarian army, tended to depreciate Battenberg's leadership as a factor in the Bulgarian victory and to allege that he had simply had good luck: that the decisive turns of events had not been ones directed by him, etc. This may be; but it is hard to believe that had things gone the other way, these same people would not have been the first to charge him with the blame.

143

threatened him with Austrian intervention, telling him that if he would not cease pursuing the Serbian army, he would soon find himself confronting the armies of Austria-Hungary.[4] In the face of this threat, Battenberg yielded, and agreed to an armistice.

Whether in making this threat Khevenhüller was or was not exceeding his instruction has been the subject of some historical controversy. However that may have been, the threat soon became public knowledge, and it added one more bitter blow to the already battered self-esteem of the Russians. They were, actually, as relieved as the Austrians that hostilities had finally been brought to an end. But they could not get over the humiliating recognition that here, in a part of the world they had marked out as the most promising theater of Russian policy, and above all in relations between two of the smaller Slavic peoples for whom Russia was to play the role of the great father and protector, it was the hated Austrians and the even more greatly hated Battenberg who, between them, were making the significant decisions and shaping the course of events. In sullen discomfort, Giers protested to the Austrian Ambassador over the episode, complaining that the Austrians should at least have consulted Petersburg before taking this action.[5] The protest was a feeble one and had no consequences. But it stands as a revelation of the manner in which Russia's embarrassment over the course of events in the Balkans was beginning to make itself felt in an almost pathological sensitivity to any sign of Austrian activity in that part of the world.

The leaders of Panslav and chauvinist opinion in Russia, not to mention the military circles, were by this time beginning to suffer a degree of frustration and humiliation that approached hysteria. The implications for Russian policy of what had now occurred were too painful to be frankly faced. The result was a desperate search for scapegoats.

Characteristic of reactions in this quarter was a leader by Katkov, which appeared in the *Moskovskiya Vyedomosti* on the 2nd of December 1885, three days after completion of the Khevenhüller mission. It was Battenberg, Katkov wrote, who was to blame for the entire situation. But Battenberg was the tool of England. Everything had taken place exactly as England had wished it to take place. Unification in itself was all right; but Battenberg should have "asked Russia" before carrying it out. Europe, generally, wanted unification, but not under Battenberg. England, however, wanted Battenberg, as a citadel against Russian influence. And now, thanks to the Three Emperors relationship, England had got him.[6]

Because the pen from which this statement, and similar ones before and after, issued was the most influential journalistic pen in Russia, it is important to note the high degree of unreality or self-deception by which the statement was informed. England had *not* inspired the unification of Bulgaria; she had in fact had nothing to do with it. Battenberg could not have consulted Russia before staging the event; for he had not staged it. And if the suggestion was that he should, on learning that the uprising was imminent, have consulted Petersburg about the course he should follow with relation to it, it must be noted that he had very good grounds for not doing so. There is every reason to suppose that in this case the Russians, recognizing that for him to oppose the movement would mean the loss of his throne, would have gleefully advised him to do just that; and he, having consulted them, would hardly have been in a position to ignore their advice. As it was, he went to his grave believing, or suspecting, that the Russian representatives in Philippopolis had actually known all along that the conspiracy was in progress but had said nothing about it. They had let things take their course in the confidence that this would eventually confront him with an insoluble dilemma: either to turn for advice to the Russians (who would then artfully advise him to resist the movement), or to sanction the unification without consulting anyone, thus making himself guilty in the eyes of the Powers of a violation of the Treaty of Berlin.

Finally, there was the reference, in this article as in many other statements from this and other Panslav quarters, to the *Dreikaiserbund* as the true source of Russia's miseries—as the factor which, allegedly, hindered her from pursuing her own interests and achieving her historic objectives in the Balkans. This thesis had great importance, for it lay at the heart of the demand which Katkov was soon to make, much more dramatically and effectively, for the recovery by Russia of a "free hand" in foreign policy—a hand, that is, no longer hampered by the ties to Germany and Austria and free to seek an alliance with France.

What truth was there in the suggestion that Russian policy, in the face of the complications just described, was hampered by these ties? What was it that Russia could have done, in this situation, that she was prevented from doing by the terms or implications of the *Dreikaiserbund*? From an historical perspective the answer would appear to be: nothing at all. Throughout the whole course of the Bulgarian crisis, Austria and Germany went faithfully along with every Russian diplomatic initiative. The treaty that formed the basis of this tripartite relationship provided merely that if one of the parties should become involved in a war with an outside power, the others would observe a benevolent neutrality. Nothing resembling this situation was present at all in the Bulgarian crisis. The treaty contained, to be sure, a secret protocol envisaging Bulgarian unification under certain circumstances; but there was nothing there that obliged the Russians to accept it if it came about in circumstances that did not meet their wishes, nor was this clause ever invoked by the others with a view to restricting Russia's freedom of action. One is driven to the conclusion either that Katkov was seriously misinformed concerning the nature of the Three Emperors' relationship, or that it was not really Russian policy towards Bulgaria but much more far-reaching schemes and aspirations on Russia's part, for which Bulgaria stood as a symbol, to which he saw the *Dreikaiserbund* as an impediment.

The line taken by Katkov in the editorial described above had at least the virtue of avoiding the painful question of the Tsar's personal responsibility for the fiasco of Russian policy in the Balkans in this period. But the facts were too obvious to escape notice altogether. For the first time, now, in the wake of Battenberg's victory over the Serbs, voices began to be heard in Russia which were either directly or implicitly critical of the diplomacy of the Tsar. Giers admitted as much in a talk with the French Ambassador, Appert, only one week after the appearance of Katkov's article of the 2nd of December.[7] The Tsar, Giers said, had not changed his mind about Battenberg. But the Panslavs, he went on, were now beginning to agitate. They were beginning to say, "timidly," that the Russian Emperor was sacrificing too much to the Entente of the Three Emperors, and that the moment was ripe for the resumption of a real Panslav policy in the Balkans. People in general regretted, Giers said, to see the Tsar persist in his ill humor towards Prince Alexander. Most of the generals and other officers had forgiven the Prince his "revolutionary escapade" (meaning the unification); they considered that he had atoned for it by his victory over the Serbs. They would now like to see him take the Slavic cause under his personal control.

In general, the press did not dare to bring these criticisms to public attention. An exception was the Moscow journal of the famous Panslav editor, Ivan Aksakov, the *Rus*. In mid-December, this paper came out with a bitter indictment of Russian policy, presumably from the pen of Aksakov himself. "Let us look," wrote Aksakov, "at what we have done. We have provoked the setting up of a Conference in which we have involved all of Europe, without reflecting that not a single one of our allies was really interested in the *status quo ante* in Bulgaria; their interest was rather in its overthrow." These allies, as a result, had fortified Battenberg and given him opportunity to become a hero. His name was now "inseparably connected with the glorious history of Bulgaria." And what, in the face of this, had the Russian representative at the Constantinople Conference done? He had insisted energetically on the Prince's removal. Turning to the recall of the Russian officers from the

Bulgarian army, this measure, the paper said, had only made it possible for Battenberg to boast that he did not need the Russians in order to win victories.

And when it came to stopping the Serbo-Bulgarian War, what had Russia done? She had hidden behind the Austrians. Why had Austria been permitted to act in her own name? Why was it not Russia that took the action? It was argued that Serbia was in the Austrian sphere of influence. But was not Bulgaria in the Russian one? Clearly, there was need for revision of the entire policy pursued since the conclusion of the Treaty of Berlin. "Let us no longer count upon the friendship of the Powers. Let us reflect that Russia is a Slav Power, whose sphere of influence includes all the Slavs of the Balkans and the Bosphorus. Let us expel from the Ministry for Foreign Affairs its old traditions, its routines, its old procedures, and its habit of silence in the face of all of Europe."[8]

This attack, with its scarcely veiled demand for the removal of Giers, aroused the Tsar's keen displeasure. But it was, one must suppose, the appearance of the piece, rather than its content, that was most offensive. Coming precisely from the Panslav circles to whom his secret sympathies strongly inclined, it must have stung his conscience to the quick and heightened his impatience with the situation in which Russia now found herself.

The war between Bulgaria and Serbia made finally and unmistakably apparent the total impracticality of any attempt to restore the *status quo ante* in Bulgaria. Even Giers was compelled to admit it. The time had passed, he said to Appert on the 7th of January 1886, for invoking the Treaty of Berlin. Russia had clung to this position as long as possible; but the events that had taken place between the Serbs and the Bulgars had now rendered it untenable. One had to take account of the *fait accompli*. "And as for the special question of the Prince of Bulgaria," he said, "we will raise no objection if Europe wants to keep him in power; we ourselves will ignore him. The Emperor has not changed his opinion in this respect."[9]

Accordingly, as hostilities came to an end in Serbia, the work of the Constantinople Conference also came to a long halt. Its work had been based on the idea of preserving the integrity of the Treaty of Berlin. The Serbo-Bulgarian War made the unreality of this idea so obvious that one could no longer go on seriously negotiating about it. Beyond this, Battenberg, his hand now greatly strengthened by his military victory, entered, early in 1886, into direct negotiations with his theoretical sovereign, the Sultan, over the situation produced by the unification and the relationship of the united Bulgaria to the Porte. Pending conclusion of these bilateral negotiations as well as of the Serbo-Bulgar peace talks now proceeding in Bucharest, there appeared to be little for the ambassadors to do. The Powers were pleased enough to let Battenberg settle it with the Sultan, if he could contrive to do so.

The peace between Bulgaria and Serbia was signed at the beginning of March; and a month later agreement was finally reached between Battenberg and the Sultan. Battenberg, it was agreed, should be appointed governor general of Eastern Rumelia for a five-year period, with the tacit understanding that this agreement would actually endure indefinitely. The conference of ambassadors, after convening for one final time, ratified this face-saving formula on the 5th of April, and declared its own existence to be at an end.

This action by the ambassadorial conference marked the end of the first phase of the Bulgarian crisis of 1885-1886 as an international problem. It did not, however, mark the end of the painful process of reaction and adjustment, on the part of the Tsar and his leading advisers, to what had occurred.

This process had two facets. The first of these concerned the attitude to be taken towards the person of Battenberg. When Giers told the French Ambassador that there was no forgiveness in the Tsar's heart for the Prince of Bulgaria, he knew whereof he spoke. But there had been a certain ominous change in the Tsar's position. This change was reflected in Giers' further words: "We will ignore him." It also lay at the bottom of the feigned indifference which the Tsar exhibited, in the winter of 1886, with regard to Battenberg's negotiations with the Sultan. The Tsar, quite plainly, had come to the conclusion that if the Powers would not oblige him by insisting, as he had hoped, on Battenberg's removal as a punishment for his alleged infraction of the provisions of the Treaty of Berlin, there were other ways this particular cat could be skinned. Actually, it had been Russian policy ever since 1883 to get rid of Battenberg; there had never, since that time, been any serious thought in Petersburg of accommodation to his permanent occupancy of the Bulgarian throne. But up to the time of the unification, it was understood (this was Giers' view) that one could not proceed seriously to the task of removing him before a suitable candidate for the succession had been found. Now, in the wake of the unification crisis, the Tsar's feelings would no longer tolerate even this precaution. If the Prince could not be removed by fair means, he must be removed by foul ones; there must be

148

no delay or scruple in the effort to bring this about; the question of the succession must be left to take care of itself.

The last of the Russian officers to have dealt amicably with Battenberg, the former Minister of War Prince Kantakuzin, left Bulgaria in early December, as did the last diplomatic agent, Koyander. In Kantakuzin's place, not as minister of war but as military representative, there came a certain Colonel Sakharov; and in place of Koyander, one P. M. Bogdanov, an agent, presumably, of the Asiatic Department of the Foreign Office. The assigned task of these two men was to engineer Battenberg's removal.

At the end of the war with Turkey, the Russians had demanded and obtained from the Bulgarians an indemnity in the amount of several million francs, which they set aside under the name of an "occupation fund." This they now devoted to the purpose of unseating Battenberg. At the turn of the year 1885-1886, three prominent Bulgarian politicians (one, Dragan Tsankov, was a former premier; another, Marco Balabanov, a former foreign minister), all men who for one reason or another professed readiness to serve Russian purposes, were secretly placed on the Russian payroll (to be paid from the occupation fund) and were brought to give solemn pledges, in writing, of their devotion to the Russian cause. They were soon launched on their practical activity, which began with the founding of an opposition newspaper.

All communications dealing with these activities went through the Tsar's hands. He personally determined the sums of money to be allotted and the purposes to which they were to be put. No important decisions were taken, concerning this operation, without his personal approval.* The second facet of the Tsar's reaction to the Bulgarian events concerned the wider objectives of Russian foreign policy; and it is this that has the greatest importance from the standpoint of the future of Franco-Russian relations.

We have already had occasion to note the extraordinary reaction of impatience and even anger with relation to the Austrians and to the *Dreikaiserbund* arrangement in general that took possession of a large section of Russian opinion as the humiliations of the unsuccessful Bulgarian policies made themselves felt. The irrationality of this reaction has already been pointed out. Neither the Austrians nor the Germans had done anything, over the whole course of this crisis, to make trouble for the Russians, to heighten their difficulties, or to obstruct their purposes. But the Russian Panslav and chauvinist press abounded (we have already seen some examples of it) with expressions of suspicion that

* These details are taken from various of the despatches of Koyander and Bogdanov, as reprinted in *Avantyury russkogo tsarizma v Bolgarii.*

Austrian and other foreign influences were behind the Bulgarian events, and there is no reason to doubt that Alexander III, writhing under the pain of his own failures, leaned only too easily to the acceptance of such suggestions. It was simply impossible for him to face and accept the fact that so grievous a series of disasters could really have been the result of his own stupidities; and he searched eagerly for foreign influences to which to attribute a guilt he could not bear to recognize as his own.

The Austrians, hated on religious grounds and appearing—if only geographically—as the nearest visible obstacle to Russian domination of the Balkans, were the most ready target. Beyond that, it had to be assumed that the Germans, who had been in recent years as successful, militarily and politically, as the Russians had been unsuccessful, were really laughing and gloating behind Russia's back—even if the clever Bismarck declined to interfere, professed no opposition to Russia's policies, and left Russia to sweat with her own difficulties. It was easy for the Tsar, in the face of these circumstances, to accept the seductive suggestions of Katkov and his sympathizers, and no doubt of the military leaders as well, that the *Dreikaiserbund* was a drag on Russian diplomacy; that it hindered her freedom of action; that, had he been free of the inhibitions arising from it, he could have done better in coping with the problems of Bulgaria and the Balkans.

But there was, beyond the sheer emotional escapism which made this conclusion attractive, a more serious reason both for hostility towards Austria and for the idea of extracting Russia from the obligations of the *Dreikaiserbund*. Whether Alexander III had ever at any time really abandoned, in the back of his mind, the idea of seizing Constantinople and taking control of the Straits, may be doubted. But there can be little question that the Bulgarian reverses confirmed him in the determination to do just that. The sad lesson of the unification crisis was that the Bulgarian people, once so warmly idolized in Russia, once viewed as the future grateful clients and followers of Russian policy, were really not to be depended upon. Bulgaria was not to be made, of its own volition, into a dependable instrument of Russian policy. In these circumstances, it was concluded, the question of Russia's relations with that country would have to be treated from the standpoint of wider Russian aims, and without regard for the feelings of the Bulgarians themselves. If the national feelings and interests of the people of this small Balkan Slavic country had once been viewed as adjuncts to the expansion of Russian influence in the direction of the Straits, it had now been proven that they could also serve as obstacles to it. Why, in these circumstances, bother about them at all? Why not forget about what Bismarck contemptuously called their "lusts and rivalries," and rely, instead, on Russia's own strong arm? Let the problem of the Balkans be solved, in other words, incidentally, as a by-product of the sweep of Russian power towards the Dardanelles. Russia's armed strength had now recovered greatly with the passage of nearly a decade since the exertions of the Russian-Turkish War. The time was approaching when this power could be again employed.

Nowhere were these thoughts more clearly expressed than in two documents of the time that reflected the Tsar's most private opinions. The first of these was a letter which he appears to have addressed, in the days of greatest agony following the Bulgarian unification (September 24, 1885), to the chief of the general staff, Obruchev. It could not have been more revealing or significant. "In my opinion," the Tsar wrote,

> we must have one main purpose: the taking-possession of Constantinople, in order to establish ourselves once and for all on the Straits and to make sure that they remain permanently in our hands. This is in Russia's interest; and it is to this that our efforts must be directed; everything else that happens on the Balkan peninsula is of secondary significance from our standpoint. We have had enough of seeking popularity at the expense of the interests of Russia. From now on, the Slavs must devote themselves to the service of Russia, not we to theirs.*

The second of the two documents was of slightly later date, but it may well be noted in this connection. It was a despatch from the Russian Ambassador at Constantinople, A. I. Nelidov, dated the 10th of July 1886, setting forth his views on the problems of Russian policy towards Bulgaria. Battenberg, he wrote, had to be mistrusted, even if he should adopt a policy favorable to Russian interests; and he had to be got rid of. The only practicable means of getting rid of him was an internal putsch. For the rest: let the future of Bulgaria flow from "the need that may arise in connection with another Russian-Turkish war." A marginal note showed this despatch to be approved in its entirety by the Tsar.[10]

As this first phase of the Bulgarian crisis of 1885-1886 came to an end there could be no doubt, therefore, of the Tsar's intention to resume at some point the pressure on Turkey which, in his view and in that of the Russian military and Panslav leaders, had been terminated

---

* This letter, which apparently reposes in the *Arkhiv vneshnei politiki* (Archive of Foreign Policy) in Moscow (hereafter referred to as Russian Archives), was cited by A. Bykov in an article entitled "Ot Bosfora k Tikhomu Okeanu" ("From the Bosphorus to the Pacific"), which appeared in the journal *Istorik-Marksist*, No. 3, 1934, p. 3. Although it was not characteristic of Alexander III to express his thoughts in letters of this nature, the writer sees no reason to question the authenticity of this one.

so prematurely and unfortunately by action of the Powers at the Congress of Berlin. But if this advance towards the Straits was to be resumed, then this had implications with relation to the *Dreikaiserbund* and with relation to France—implications, above all from the military standpoint—which, we may be sure, the Russian military authorities did not fail to bring to the Tsar's attention.

It had been, in 1878, pressure primarily from the British and the Austrians which had compelled the Russians to stop short of the seizure of Constantinople. British naval power had threatened the Russian maritime communications with the Russian forces in the region of the Straits, and the Austrians had sat menacingly on the flank of their land communications through the Balkans. The Russian military leaders could, by 1885, see a chance of coping with one of these problems (the naval one), but not simultaneously with both. Some way had to be found to neutralize Austrian power. Alone, the Austrians were not viewed as a great danger; the trouble lay in their alliance with the Germans. Russia could not dream of taking on both those Powers at once.

This problem was rendered even more acute by virtue of the fact that the Russian general staff also had direct design on that portion of Galician Poland that lay to the north of the Carpathians—designs that found strong support, one may be sure, among the religious imperialists. Whether Alexander III shared these aspirations, in the sense of being prepared to contemplate a war against Austria, is unclear; but that they were close to the heart of senior figures in the military establishment is beyond doubt. On the 14th of July 1886 Obruchev wrote to his close friend and patron, the former Minister of War D. A. Milyutin, a letter which included the following passage:

> To me, it seems beyond question that for Russia there are only two basic historical questions for the sake of which it would be worth shedding Russian blood. These are the Polish [Galician] question and that of the Bosphorus. Whether one wishes it or not, these questions will have to be decided by war; and this, precisely, is the war for which we have to prepare.[11]

Similar thoughts are clearly apparent in some of the statements made by Minister of War Vannovski. Altogether, taken in conjunction with the Tsar's determination to gain control of the Straits, they plainly implied at some future point at least the strong risk, if not the certainty, of a war with Austria. And here was where the question of German-Austrian relations came in.

Whether the Russians knew the exact terms of the Austro-German

Alliance of 1879 is not apparent. (They were in any case soon to learn them.) But they were certainly under no illusions with relation to the existence of some tie of this nature. Could one then be sure that in the event of a Russian-Austrian war the Germans would not at some point appear at Austria's side? And how could such an eventuality be averted?

If there was to be a war against Austria, it was important that Russia should choose the time and circumstances of its inauguration. This in itself implied the break-up of the *Dreiskaiserbund*; and it was better, actually, that this should precede the inauguration of hostilities with Austria rather than follow it, for in this case Russia would not be morally bound to give explanations to the Germans and to take into account the lively objections which Bismarck would certainly raise.

But in addition to this, was there not some way in which Germany could be prevented from supporting Austria? There was indeed; and at no time were Russian military minds oblivious to it. It lay in the possibility that German strength and attentions might be diverted, just at the time of a Russian-Austrian war, by new complications with France. If, in other words, a Russian war with Austria could be made to coincide in time with a German war with France, Russia's problem—the great problem of her military strategy in the movement towards control of the Straits—might be solved.

All this was, of course, in 1886, still no more than a gleam in the eye —above all, in the Russian military eye.* The time for it had not yet come. Bitter as was the hostility towards Austria and the suppressed resentment of German military superiority, the *Dreikaiserbund* still existed; there was still the tie to the aged German Kaiser, which the Tsar personally could not conceive of destroying; and Russia was still faced with the dubious quality, as a potential ally, of a country governed by so detestable and unreliable a political system as that of republican France. But these impediments did not preclude a certain cautious movement in the desired direction. Russia could begin to contemplate a nonrenewal of the *Dreikaiserbund*, when the treaty on which it rested came up for renewal in 1887. And she could set about, swallowing so far as possible her distaste for French republicanism, to strengthen on the political level the relations with France which were already progressing so excellently on the military one. It was with such thoughts, seldom

* In early 1887 Polovtsov, the Secretary of the Council of State, recounted in his diary how he was told by a prominent nobleman that the view of the "war party," headed by Obruchev, was that "a war between France and Germany would be advantageous to us because, in taking advantage of it, we could throw ourselves upon Austria and, having smashed her, seize the approaches to the Carpathian Mountains" (*Dnevnik*, January 29/February 11, 1887, II, p. 15).

directly expressed but latent in many minds, including that of the Tsar, that Russia moved from the reverses of 1885 into the trials and problems of the eventful year 1886.

One feature of this line of thought remains, however, to be noted. This was its potential unacceptability to the French. They had no interest in Russia's Balkan ambitions. Russia's aspirations for control of the Dardanelles left them entirely cold. They had no intention of fighting another war with the Germans just to make possible the satisfaction of Russian ambitions in the region of the Straits. A close political and military tie with Russia held interest for them—yes, but only insofar as it might imply the commitment of Russia's entire military strength against Germany, not Austria, and this at a very early stage—if possible, in advance of any outbreak of hostilities between Germany and France.* It was Germany, not Austria, whom they wished Russia to fight. A war with Austria alone, or even primarily with Austria, would represent in their view an undesirable distraction of Russian resources.

This conflict of objectives was one which would run, like a red thread, through the entire history of Franco-Russian relations over the ensuing years. The desire of the French that Russia should fight Germany to assist France to recover Alsace-Lorraine could never be made fully congruous with the desire of the Russians that France should fight Germany in order to facilitate the Russian advance to Constantinople. This incongruity would come to constitute the most serious difficulty to be surmounted in the shaping of a relationship of alliance between the two Powers. In 1885-1886 it was probably a matter of conscious recognition only in the minds of a few military planners on both sides. But the possible advantages of a Franco-Russian military collaboration loomed so large, in these same minds, that hope never faded on either side that the complication in question could eventually be overcome.

* In a despatch sent from Russia in March 1882 to the French Foreign Office and the Ministry of War, Boisdeffre wrote that he considered it a *sine qua non* of an alliance with Russia that the Russians should agree to begin military operations against Germany at least two months before the French; otherwise the war, he maintained, would take place on French soil. (E. Toutain, *Alexandre III et la République Française.* [Paris: Plon, 1929], pp. 20-21). Later, of course, Boisdeffre came to moderate this extreme demand; but the French were never to give up their insistence on immediate mobilization of the Russian armed forces, primarily against Germany (not Austria), in the event of a Franco-German war.

Chapter Eight

THE ESTRANGEMENT OF 1886

Seldom does the calendar year coincide so neatly with a distinct phase of diplomatic history as did the year 1886 and the new stage reached in Franco-Russian relations. It was a year that embraced the life of the third Freycinet ministry in France. It was the bungling of that ministry that was the determining factor, over the course of the year, in the relations between the two countries. The year included, as in the classical love story, first, complications in the development of an intimacy to which both parties inwardly aspired, then an effort at reconciliation, and finally, to all appearances, a relatively happy ending, by which time both parties found themselves the wiser.

We have had occasion to note the effects produced on the mind and spirit of Alexander III by the Bulgarian crisis of 1885: the extreme frustration over developments in Bulgaria herself; the deepened commitment to the establishment of Russian control at the Straits; the suspicion that Germany and Austria had not only been active in engineering Russia's difficulties in Bulgaria but had also profited from them; the final impatience with Austria and acceptance of the thesis that Russia's further advance towards the Straits would probably at some point involve a war with that Power; awareness of the need for distracting Germany's military strength to the west, in order to prevent her coming effectively to Austria's assistance; and finally, in the light of these other reactions, a firm determination to abandon the *Dreikaiserbund*, in the sense of declining to renew the arrangement when this should fall due in 1887.

Such dispositions could not fail to have their implications for the Tsar's attitude towards France. There had been, actually, a certain softening of his position in this respect even before the Bulgarian events —a softening brought about in the first instance, one suspects, by the gentle influence exercised by General Appert and his Danish wife through the feminine entourage of the Tsar. In the winter of 1885 the imperial couple had startled the diplomatic corps by attending a great ball at the French Embassy and encouraging other members of the

155

imperial family to do the same. This was the first time that a Russian monarch had set foot in that building since the establishment of the Republic in France in 1871. The events in Bulgaria, later that year, were bound to give further stimulus to this change, and the signs thereof were not long in making themselves visible. A new note of cordiality crept into the routine diplomatic exchanges between the two governments. On at least two occasions, Giers went out of his way to express to the French government the Tsar's and his own appreciation for the positions taken by the French with relation to the Bulgarian crisis, particularly at the Constantinople negotiations. These gestures were all the more significant for the fact that there is no indication of any similar expression of appreciation being addressed to either the Germans or the Austrians, although actually the positions these latter adopted in the matters at hand conformed more faithfully and consistently to the Russian *desiderata* than did those of the French.

All of this suggests, and there is every reason to believe, that the beginning of the year 1886 found the Tsar in a mood to swallow, at least to a certain extent, his distaste for the French governmental system, and to go along, for the first time, with a significant development of Franco-Russian relations. This disposition should not, of course, be confused with a readiness to seek, at that juncture, anything so drastic as a total change of alliances. The Tsar's skepticism concerning the possibility of a full-fledged alliance between two Powers so differently governed had been by no means wholly overcome. Nor did he wish to abandon entirely the ties of family intimacy and political obligation that bound him to the German court. His aspirations with respect to Germany were primarily to wean that Power from her alliance with Austria, or at least to weaken its practical significance, rather than to turn against Germany altogether. His frame of mind was sensitively and fairly reflected by the counselor of the French Embassy, Ternaux-Compans, who wrote, in a despatch of the 8th of June 1886 (he was by that time chargé d'affaires) that the Tsar needed France as "une force capable d'offrir à la Russie le point d'appui qui lui manque pour se dérober aux nécessités d'une alliance austro-allemande";* and that for this reason he needed in particular a France that was strong and stable.[1] This required, to be sure, a new development of relations with France; it did not require anything as far-reaching as a full-fledged alliance, at least not at that time. The future was another matter.

This last distinction—between present and future—was well brought

* That the Tsar "needed France, as a force capable of offering to Russia the support necessary to make it possible for her to divest herself of the strictures of a German-Austrian alliance."

out in an editorial that appeared on the 19th of May 1886 in the moderately nationalistic Petersburg *Novoye Vremya*—an article so bold in its conclusions, and so close to views expressed by Giers himself, that it may be taken as having some degree of official inspiration.[2] The best course for Russia, it was there stated, would be to preserve a balance in her policies towards Germany and France. The ruin of France would be something Russia would not be able to accept; but it was also necessary for her to preserve and to fortify her relations with Germany. Of course, the German system of government was closer to that of Russia than was the French system. But one should not forget that

> . . . les sympathies du peuple russe se portent plutôt vers la nation française dont les intérêts ne se heurtent nulle part avec les nôtres. . . . En somme, nous pouvons dire que l'Allemagne représente pour nous le présent, la France l'avenir probable. Or, comme il nous est nécessaire de ménager l'avenir aussi que le présent, veillons attentivement à ce que l'un des deux pays n'engloutisse ni même affaiblisse seulement l'autre.*

One had, in this statement, the epitome of the innermost feelings of many highly placed people in Petersburg, to whom the close relationship with Germany had never been really congenial. For these people Germany did indeed represent the present; but France represented the future. Giers, too, had long recognized this, even if it caused him misgivings. The Tsar now felt it, too. This feeling represented a considerable advance, from the standpoint of Franco-Russian relations, over the feelings the latter had entertained prior to the Bulgarian crisis. The stage, therefore, was set for a significant development of Franco-Russian relations, if the French chose to encourage it.

General Appert and the senior officers of his mission—Counselor Ternaux-Compans, the two secretaries of embassy (Edmond Toutain and the young Comte de Voize), and Military Attaché Colonel Sermet— were all well aware of the change that was taking place in the Tsar's disposition. They greatly welcomed this change, took pride in what they viewed as their own part in bringing it about, and saw in it an important —perhaps historic—opportunity for French statesmanship. They must naturally have hoped that this view would find appreciation and sup-

---

* One should not forget that "the sympathies of the Russian people are addressed rather to the French nation, the interests of which nowhere come into conflict with our own. . . . In short, one may say that Germany represents for us the present, France, the probable future, but, since we have to look after our future as well as our present, let us be careful to assure that one of those two countries does not swallow up or even weaken the other."

port at the Paris end. In this hope, they were now to be bitterly disappointed.

The recent French elections, in addition to installing in the presidential office for a second seven-year term the bored and skeptical Grévy, whose interest in the possibility of an alliance with Russia was precisely nil,* had also produced a parliamentary situation in which France could no longer be governed otherwise than with the cooperation of the Radicals, among whom Clemenceau occupied the most conspicuous and influential position. The task of forming a cabinet that could command a parliamentary majority was entrusted, in these circumstances, to that acknowledged wizard of French parliamentary mathematics: the "white mouse," Freycinet, who had been premier twice before. He succeeded in coping with this task, but only at the cost of including in the new ministry four Radical personalities, in addition to accepting as minister of war (because it pleased, momentarily, Clemenceau) the histrionic and undependable Boulanger.

Freycinet, like Grévy, had at that time no particular interest in any further development of relations with Russia. As we have seen, he had in fact exhibited in the past a singularly unfelicitous hand in the direction of France's Russian policy. (It was he who had made the disastrous choice of Admiral Jaurès for ambassador to Petersburg.) Not only was he now uninterested in any extension of Franco-Russian relations but he was engrossed in domestic parliamentary problems, and was quite prepared to sacrifice to political expediency on the domestic scene whatever modest achievements might already have been made in the improvement of these relations.

The new ministry took over on the 7th of January 1886. Its indifference to relations with Russia was not slow in making itself felt. Only a few days after its formation there was proclaimed, as an act of grace on the occasion of the president's renewed assumption of office, an amnesty for all political prisoners. Among those liberated by this action was the well-known Russian anarchist-aristocrat, Prince Peter Kropotkin. He had been confined, for some three years past, in various provincial French prisons, serving out a five-year term for revolutionary-anarchistic activities pursued in France after his escape from Russia.

* Ernest Daudet, in his *Histoire diplomatique de l'alliance franco-russe* (p. 207), cites Grévy's weary and disillusioned response to someone who tried to talk with him about the possibility of a Franco-Russian alliance: "You are not going to have Russia as an ally any more than you are going to have Germany. Nobody wants us—neither England, nor Italy, nor Austria; and it is better that way, because we ourselves have no need of anybody else. Let us resign ourselves to having no more weight than the Swiss. If we stay quietly at home, no one is going to attack us."

The circumstances of Kropotkin's release were normal, and could scarcely be held as a reproach against the French government; but the episode touched Alexander III at an extremely sensitive point. For years, there had been controversy and acrimony between the Russian and French governments over the question of the asylum and freedom of activity extended in France to Russian revolutionaries who had made themselves guilty of acts against the Russian regime regarded by that regime as of a criminal nature. Mention has already been made of the fact that relations between the two countries had been severely shaken in 1880, only a year before the assumption of the throne by Alexander III, when a revolutionary by the name of Hartman (who had been involved, in December 1879, in an attempt to blow up the imperial train on which Alexander II was traveling) was arrested by the French authorities on Russian demand, released again under pressure from the Radicals, and then permitted to make his way to England. On that occasion, too, it had been Freycinet who, as premier, had presided over the badly bungled operation and had received the blame for it in the eyes of the Russian government.

Constantly, over the intervening years, the liberty enjoyed by these Russian revolutionaries in France—their freedom to live there, to associate with radical French circles, to publish their anti-Tsarist literature and to conduct their political activities—had been a thorn in the side of Russian governmental circles. It had contributed importantly to the formation of the negative views of Alexander III about French democracy. Kropotkin's release now came as a renewed rubbing of salt into these sensitive wounds. The French were warned, in a bitter article appearing on the 23rd of January in the semi-official *Journal de Pétersbourg*, that the episode could have repercussions on Franco-Russian relations.

Four days later, Appert, whose conservative sentiments were scarcely less offended than those of the Tsar by the release of Kropotkin, had occasion to report to Freycinet that the Russian government had formally declined to participate in the World's Fair which the French government was just then arranging for the year 1889, in celebration of the centennial anniversary of the French Revolution. The Russians would probably have refused to participate in any case, because at no time was Alexander III in a mood to join in celebrating a revolution which had resulted in the execution of a crowned head. But the close sequence of this decision upon the Kropotkin incident was too conspicuous to avoid notice. One has the feeling, therefore, that it was not without a certain malicious pleasure that Appert submitted to Freycinet the sharp warning of the *Journal de Pétersbourg*, just mentioned, supporting it with his own personal opinion that it would be useless, in the circumstances, to attempt to induce the Tsar to change his mind about the World's Fair.

This despatch of Appert's, together with a telegram reporting the negative result of a discussion he had had with Giers on the same subject, reached Freycinet on the 10th of February 1886. The two messages could scarcely have been agreeable to him. The following day, the premier sat down and penned to Appert a curt note apprising him of his dismissal from his ambassadorial post. The "cruel exigencies of politics," together with "considerations of a general nature," had placed him, Freycinet wrote, under the painful necessity of separating himself from a collaborator—namely Appert—"dont il connaissait les mérites et la valeur des services rendus." The ambassador should be prepared to leave his post within the next few days. Meanwhile, he would be recommended for decoration with the Grand Cross of the Legion of Honor.[3]

Despatched to Petersburg by open mail on the 11th of February (which meant, of course, that the Russian governmental leaders saw it before Appert did), this communication was delivered to Appert on a Sunday evening three days later, as he stood in the Salon Rouge of his Embassy, preparing to greet the guests arriving for a *petit bal* given in honor of the Grand Duchess Catherine. The ambassador was stunned and intensely angered by this abrupt recall. Nothing had prepared him for it. His feelings were further exacerbated when, only one or two days later, and before he could even make formal notification to the Tsar of this development, rumors—leaked by the French Foreign Office to the Paris press—reached Petersburg, apprising the Russian public not only of Appert's recall but of the appointment in his place of another senior French military figure of equal rank: General Jean-Baptiste Billot, who had been minister of war in a previous Freycinet cabinet in 1882.

Infuriated by this entire clumsy procedure, Appert made no reply until he received, on the 19th, a telegram from Freycinet asking whether the letter had reached him. He then replied that he had indeed received it, and was "profondément troublé et affligé" by its content.[4] The episode touched off further exchanges between the two men which, for their combination of smoldering fury with icy politeness, are surpassed by nothing this writer has had occasion to see in any diplomatic records.

Had no more been involved here but the feelings of a poorly treated and offended diplomat, the incident would have no place in this account. But the effect of the incident upon the Tsar was no less explosive than the effect upon Appert. Alexander III, as has already been noted, did not take easily to new faces. The Apperts had won his confidence.

They enjoyed exceptional favor with the Empress Dagmar, as well as with her influential Mistress of the Household, Princess Elena Kochubei. The Tsar's anger was aroused not only by the fact of this abrupt and unexpected intervention by Freycinet into the diplomatic arrangements on which the relations between two heads of state then rested,* but by the fact that the matter had become known to the public, both in Paris and in Petersburg, before anyone had had the courtesy to tell him of it.

The Tsar and Giers did not wait for official notification of the change before taking action. Mohrenheim, in Paris, was at once authorized to inform the French government that the Russian government hoped there was no truth in the rumors which had reached it. Appert, he was told to say, enjoyed the high esteem and complete confidence of the Emperor; the latter would view his replacement "avec beaucoup de peine."[5]

A man more concerned for the state of Franco-Russian relations, or one inclined to allot a higher priority to diplomatic considerations in relation to domestic-political ones, might have taken this warning at its true worth. Freycinet did not do so. He disregarded it and went ahead to request, through formal channels, the usual *agrément* for Billot. When the request was brought to the Tsar by Giers, his reaction was grim and implacable: "Ni Billot, ni un autre. Personne."[6] If this was the way the French government proposed to treat his wishes, then there would be no French Ambassador in Petersburg at all. Mohrenheim, furthermore, was told that when he had transmitted this uncompromising message to Freycinet, he was to leave French territory and to remain outside it until otherwise instructed. There was to be, in other words, a complete break in relations at the ambassadorial level.

On the 26th of March Appert, together with his wife and two children, traveled out to Gatchina to take leave of the imperial couple. The Tsar made no effort to conceal his indignation over what had happened.

"Quel fichu gouvernement vous avez," he is reported by one source as saying to Appert.[7] "Il paraît que c'est un tas de canailles."†

A more restrained, but more authoritative, version of what the Tsar said was recorded in Appert's diary,[8] to wit: "Je n'ai pas de mauvais sentiments pour la France, pour laquelle j'ai toujours eu de la sympathie; mais votre gouvernement n'est plus la Republique; c'est la Commune."‡ And he hinted at one of the main reasons for his displeasure when he observed that he thought Appert's removal could be attributed to the

---

* Note that a foreign ambassador in Petersburg was formally accredited by his own chief of state to the Tsar, personally.

† "What a lousy government you have. They would appear to be a bunch of scoundrels."

‡ "I have never had ill-feelings towards France, for which I have always had sympathy; but your government is no longer the Republic; it is the Commune."

influence of the French Radicals, who, as he understood it, had never forgiven Appert for his part in the suppression of the Paris Commune in 1871.[9]

The observations of the Empress Dagmar, in taking leave of her Danish compatriot, were less severe. She took care to give Madame Appert to understand that the break with France did not reflect any desire to please the Germans nor did it reflect German influence. She would never, she said, forget what the Germans had done to her native Denmark.[10] Appert and his family left Petersburg the following day. Their departure was the occasion for a great and affectionate send-off by the diplomatic corps and other friends.

Shortly thereafter, on the 1st of April, the Tsar and his family left for a stay of some weeks in the Crimea. Giers followed, on the 4th. With these two dignitaries away, it was useless, for the moment, to pursue the matter further. The break between France and Russia at the ambassadorial level was now complete, and of unforeseeable duration.

Before pursuing further the consequences of Freycinet's abrupt and ill-considered action, it might be well to glance briefly at the possible reasons for it. He himself never divulged them. His chef de cabinet, Jules Herbette, wrote, in a memorandum for internal Foreign Office use, that he, in speaking at the time with Mohrenheim, had given to the latter "les vraies raisons du rappel du Gal Appert, raisons ni politiques, ni parlementaires, mais toutes professionnelles."[11] Whatever else may be said about the background of this episode, this statement was certainly not correct. More than this was involved. Freycinet's real reasons for the action appear to have reflected a number of factors, none of them related to Appert's professional competence.

Of these, the one best documented is the influence of Juliette Adam. A good friend of Billot (who appears in turn to have been no friend of Appert), she had herself been influenced, in this instance, by Lisa Trubetskoi, who, now returned to Petersburg, found herself on bad terms with her highly placed mother (Princess Kochubei), and felt herself neglected by her mother's good friends, the Apperts. Frustrated, no doubt, over the loss of the influence she had once enjoyed through Gorchakov, she was evidently sensitive to slights; in any case, she urged that Juliette Adam use her influence with Freycinet to achieve the removal of Appert and his replacement by someone closer to their own circle. Juliette allowed herself to be persuaded (as she later confessed to a friend with much regret), and approached Freycinet along this line.

The approach was clearly not without effect. Juliette Adam, according to Ernest Daudet, who knew a good deal about such things, was a lady to whose influence Freycinet was "not displeased to submit, or at least to appear to submit."[12] But there were other reasons as well for the premier's action. Freycinet was evidently politically indebted to Billot and his parliamentary friends.* He was, furthermore, well aware of Appert's conservative and basically antirepublican sentiments; and he could scarcely have missed the note of malicious satisfaction with which the ambassador reported the unfortunate effects on the Russian government of various concessions made by Freycinet to the Radicals within his cabinet.

There was also a question, at least in Appert's mind, whether the influence of the Rothschilds was not involved. The reason was trivial, but human. A daughter of Alphonse Rothschild, the head of the Paris house, had married an Odessa banker, also Jewish, by the name of Moritz Ephrussi. Madame Ephrussi came to Petersburg, it would seem, for the winter social season of 1884; and on the occasion of the first great ball given by the Apperts, a function attended by the entire elite of Petersburg society, she, towards the end of the evening, appeared unexpectedly among the guests, approached Appert, whom she had never before met, and asked him, then and there, whether he would arrange for her introduction at the Russian court. Appert, after consulting with his career aides the following day, declined to do this, on the grounds that she was now a Russian subject and could not be introduced at court by a foreign ambassador. The reason was valid enough; but she felt herself rebuffed, and never forgave the slight. Appert, on the other hand, when pondering the reasons for his recall, remembered that shortly before that event the *Times* of London had carried two articles predicting his removal from Petrograd because of his alleged poverty. Putting two and two rather boldly together, he suspected the Rothschilds of spreading this report.

Finally, Appert later heard, from sources close to Juliette Adam, that there had also been disloyalty to him on the part of one of his senior aides in the Embassy; and his suspicions fell on the assistant military attaché, Captain Louis Moulin. Whether there was any justification for this suspicion is not evident; but that the suspicion should have run in this direction has interesting implications for relationships within the French army. Appert, for some reason, was not on good terms with his military predecessor, General Chanzy (another good friend, let us recall, of Madame Adam). Moulin was a protégé of Boisdeffre, and Boisdeffre was a protégé of Chanzy.

Moulin, aside from this incident, is an interesting figure in his own

* Appert's Second Secretary of Embassy, Edmond Toutain, in his *Alexandre III*, p. 76, says that Freycinet was "engagé sans doute à fond envers Billot et ses amis parlementaires."

right, from the standpoint of this inquiry. Having been first attached
to the Petersburg Embassy in 1875-1876, under Le Flô, he returned
in 1880, to serve initially as an assistant to Boisdeffre, the latter being
military attaché during Chanzy's ambassadorship. When Chanzy and
Boisdeffre left, Moulin remained in Petersburg and continued to serve
there for many years—at least into the mid-1890's. He learned Russian,
had many Russian contacts, the most important of whom was Katkov,
and eventually took a Russian woman as his second wife. During all
these years he remained in frequent and intimate personal correspondence with Boisdeffre.

If indeed there were, all through the 1870's and 1880's, clandestine
understandings and arrangements between the French and Russian general staffs (and we have seen some evidence that there were), one would
have to assume that Moulin, as Boisdeffre's confidant, was one of the
very few persons, and at times perhaps the only one in the Petersburg
Embassy, who was privy to the knowledge of these arrangements and
was used as a medium of communication with relation to them.

Appert at first thought highly of Moulin. Moulin was, he wrote in a
despatch to the Quai d'Orsay of the 2nd of May 1884, "a very intelligent officer, extremely industrious, having a perfect knowledge of the
Russian language, and excellent contacts in the Russian army and society." Others in the Embassy had an equally high opinion of him. But
it is, of course, possible that Moulin had, laid upon him by the general
staff in Paris, duties and responsibilities of which he was not at liberty
to inform even his own ambassador, and that this had led, as it has and
will in so many other Embassies, to suspicions and antagonisms which,
in this instance, were bound to play a part in the outraged feelings
with which Appert reacted to his sudden recall.

The weight of the available evidence suggests that Freycinet's abrupt
action reflected nothing more than the combination of a desire to appease the Radicals, a disposition to please Juliette Adam by appointing
Billot, displeasure with Appert for his conservative political stance and
his obvious sympathy with the Tsar's disapproval of the French parliamentary system, and, underlying all this, the willingness to accord a far
higher priority to his own domestic-political interests than to the demands of Franco-Russian relations.

On the day (April 4) before Giers' departure for the Crimea, where
he was to join the Tsar, he received the French chargé d'affaires, Ternaux-Compans, and discussed with him the situation resulting from
these unexpected events. He assured Ternaux-Compans that he would

Plate 5. Prince Alexander (Battenberg) of Bulgaria

Plate 6. Prince Alexander renouncing the throne

Plate 7. The removal of Prince Alexander from Sofia

FIGARO ILLUSTRÉ

Mars 1892

EXPOSITION DES AQUARELLISTES. — LE GÉNÉRAL APPERT, par ÉDOUARD DETAILLE.

Plate 8. General and Ambassador Félix Appert

Plate 9.
Count Gustav Kulnocky,
Austro-Hungarian
foreign minister

Plate 10.
Prince Otto von Bismarck,
German chancellor

do his best, while in the Crimea, to mollify the Tsar's outraged feelings. But he left the chargé under no illusion that this would be an easy task.

Ternaux-Compans, returning to his Embassy, pondered Giers' motives in bringing up the subject with him. He set forth his speculations the following day in an illuminating, if somewhat turgidly worded, despatch to the French foreign minister.[13] Giers' main purpose no doubt had been, he wrote,

> to put me in a position to enlighten Your Excellency on his personal views concerning this situation; but I must say that the emphatic tone in which he spoke of the importance he attached to the intimacy beween France and Russia seemed to me to indicate some sort of an ulterior preoccupation on his part. If I might be permitted to pursue this hypothesis, I would be inclined to think that M. de Giers greatly feared the effect on his policy of any sort of cooling-off, even a momentary one, which might occur in the relations between France and Russia and from which Germany might profit. He seemed to feel . . . that this would be a very bad moment for Russia to commit the slightest act of clumsiness. The Bulgarian question is now in a particularly delicate phase, which obliges the imperial government to show itself highly circumspect in order not to alienate sympathies of which it might later find itself in need. There is no question but that at this moment your support would be doubly advantageous for him, whether it be for the immediate solution of a question which he has very much at heart or with a view to complications which might possibly arise and leave him in a position of isolation in the event that the interests of Germany and Austria should no longer be in accord with his own.
>
> I would certainly not wish to claim that M. de Giers, who has been a convinced architect of the entente among the three empires, himself shares the feeling of disillusionment which has taken hold of certain persons and is finding expression in certain of the Russian press organs; but I could imagine that his confidence in Russia's two allies is not so great that he would not consider it a wise policy to keep them aware of the possibility of a rapprochement with us, for the event that they should be inclined to deceive his hopes.

In conclusion, Ternaux-Compans repeated that he was sure Giers would do his best to convince the Tsar that higher interests ought to prevail over personal annoyance; but Giers had emphasized, "with his habitual prudence," that in the meantime any ill-considered approach from the French side could hinder his efforts and compromise their success. He, Ternaux-Compans, had been told by persons close to the Emperor that the episode had already created very serious difficulties for Giers. It was nevertheless possible that certain political considerations which Giers would be able to mention to the Tsar would make it possible for him to surmount these difficulties more rapidly than people at court generally expected.

This strong hint, too, could scarcely have been welcome to Freycinet, and he ignored it. More than that: in early May, he returned to the fray with a further instruction, calling upon the chargé d'affaires to submit a formal request for an *agrément* for Billot. In the absence of both Giers and the Tsar and in the light of Giers' warning this made no sense at all. Ternaux-Compans was able to avoid compliance; but the mere fact of the instruction stands as a further revelation of Freycinet's lack of understanding of the situation.

Giers, meanwhile, was working on the Tsar, as only he knew how to do, to repair the damage. Towards the end of May, just before the return of both men to Petersburg, he thought he had his reluctant monarch on the verge of agreeing to the acceptance of a new French Ambassador—not Billot, to be sure (for this, the Tsar's prestige was now too firmly engaged by his earlier refusal)—but some other acceptable nominee.

At just this time, however, a new complication arose. On the 27th of May, the Freycinet ministry, in further exercise of its perverse talent for annoying the Tsar, proposed to the National Assembly the permanent expulsion from French soil of the heads (and their direct descendants in line of primogeniture) of all families which had at one time or another reigned in France. The Bourbon contender, the Comte de Chambord (who had never lived in the Republic anyway) having died in 1883, this measure affected in the first instance the Napoleonic pretenders, Prince Jérome and his son, and, similarly, the Orléaniste Comte de Paris and his son, the young Prince Victor.

A measure of this nature had long been pressed on the government from the Radical-republican side. Freycinet had first resisted the demand; but a tremendous and spectacular party given by the Comte de Paris on the 14th of May at his Paris residence, the Hôtel Galliera, and attended by some 4,000 people, including the diplomatic corps and the cream of French society, had made a great splash in the Paris papers; and this had come as a red rag to the Radical bull. Freycinet, therefore, always concerned to appease the Radicals, yielded and made the desired proposal to the Assembly. On the 23rd of June, after nearly a month of debate and public discussion, the measure became law.

Alexander III had never harbored in his heart any inordinate fondness for the members of the Orléans family. Like his grandfather, Nicholas I, he had tended to see in them pretenders to the status of constitutional monarchs—and constitutional monarchy was an institution for which he had nothing but distaste. But his feelings had been

166

somewhat assuaged by the marriage, the previous year, of the Empress Dagmar's brother Waldemar to the Orléaniste Princess Marie. And he was disgusted with the rather brutal manner in which this French measure was taken, seeing in it another example of Freycinet's revolting subservience to the Radicals. The effect, therefore, of the news of these happenings was to cause him to back off, once again, from the acceptance of a new French Ambassador.

It was now Ternaux-Compans' time to boil over. Related by family ties to the Orléanistes and disgusted anyway by Freycinet's repeated abuse of the Franco-Russian relationship, he wrote on the 8th of June— even before final passage of the law expelling the princes—a long despatch, the elaborately courteous wording of which could not conceal, and was not designed to conceal, his own great discontent over what the French government was doing. The Orléaniste princes, he wrote, were little known in Russia; there were no partisans of that dynasty there. It was not, therefore, their fate or their future with which people in Russia were preoccupied. It was rather the tendencies revealed by the campaign against those princes, and the possible consequences of an action which, he said, appeared to be ill timed and devoid of adequate reason. Russian opinion was not even greatly concerned about the form of government prevailing in France, provided only that this form could assure to France a domestic stability and an external power sufficient to offer to Russia the alternative which she needed to enable her to free herself from her alliance with Germany and Austria. The expulsion of the princes was disagreeable to people in Russia because they were sure it would further envenom party squabbles in France, and because it would unquestionably have an undesirable effect on the disposition of the Tsar.

The chargé then went on to say the following:

> The national aspirations of Russia, and the obstacles presented to their realization by the two neighboring empires [Germany and Austria], should logically lead any Emperor so penetrated with the sense of his mission as is the Emperor Alexander III to seek an alliance with France. Unfortunately, his conscience as a sovereign speaks louder than his political interests, and his hatred of radicalism is such that it rivets him, so to speak, to Germany. . . .
>
> Under pressure of some national danger the Emperor might, despite his prejudices, incline towards a moderate republican [French] government which could offer him, by means of an *alliance d'occasion*, a way of freeing himself from the German yoke.* But so strong is his monarchical and

* The reader will note the unquestioning acceptance by the French Embassy of the thesis that the relationship with Germany represented an intolerable "yoke" from which it was necessary for Russia to liberate herself if she was to obtain the freedom to pursue her own legitimate objectives.

167

religious faith that he would rather, on the day when he revolts against subjection to German power, take on the resulting struggle alone than to compromise his conscience by entering into a pact with a France governed by a party the doctrines of which are in total conflict with everything that forms, in his eyes, the very foundation of an organized society.
. . .

Prince Bismarck must be too well acquainted with the character of the Emperor not to rejoice in an event [i.e., the expulsion of the princes by the French Government] which so well supports his views and which has the double advantage of exacerbating the intra-party struggles in France and possibly giving permanence to the momentary cooling-off in relations between that country and Russia. The best friends of France [in Russia] understand this extremity and deplore bitterly the influence which parliamentary conditions confer upon the radical element in that country— an influence which seems quite out of accord with that element's numerical importance.[14]

This, coming from a mere chargé d'affaires, was powerful stuff; and Freycinet, fully sensitive to the implied reproaches, did not take kindly to it. The despatch was received in his office on the 14th of June. The next three weeks were taken up with angry exchanges between him and the chargé, exchanges which ended, on the 5th of July, with the acceptance by Freycinet of Ternaux-Compans' resignation—not just from his Petersburg post but from the diplomatic service generally. This resignation was immediately followed by that of one of the two remaining Embassy secretaries, the Comte de Voize. With these resignations, the causes of which were well known and understood in both the diplomatic corps and the Russian government, the French Embassy, already devoid of an ambassador, was reduced to a point where it was led, on the civilian side, by a single diplomatic secretary: Toutain. The break in diplomatic relations was thus nearly complete.

By this time, the measure of the damage done was beginning to become known in Paris and to constitute a source of criticism of the premier in political circles. Stung, for the first time, on his sensitive domestic-political side, Freycinet now realized that he had a problem on his hands to which he must give serious attention. Acting with great despatch, he therefore at once selected—not from the ranks of the career diplomats but from the internal administrative service—a new man, Count Olivier d'Ormesson, to replace Ternaux-Compans, and despatched him post-haste to Petersburg at the beginning of July.

On the 7th of July, with d'Ormesson already on his way, Ternaux-Compans went to the Foreign Office to pay a farewell call on Giers. Giers, bringing up the question of French policy, expressed his unhappiness over the abnormal situation in which the French mission in

Petersburg now found itself. On leaving the Crimea at the end of May, he had thought, he said, that his representations had made a certain impression on the Tsar and that the latter, "satisfait d'avoir marqué son déplaisir," would not long persist in his refusal to reopen full diplomatic relations. Unfortunately, the expulsion of the princes had again spoiled everything. It was now impossible to foresee the time when negotiations might be resumed.[15]

In submitting to Paris, as his last despatch in the French diplomatic service, the account of this cheerless conversation, Ternaux-Compans could not resist accompanying it with the text of an editorial from the strongly nationalistic *Svet*. This organ, he pointed out, was edited by V. V. Komarov, brother of General A. V. Komarov, commander-in-chief in the Transcaucasus, and was widely believed to reflect the views of the Tsar. The article read in part as follows:

> The expulsion of the princes, a measure illegal in itself and detrimental to the cause of peace, has not been without consequences in Petersburg. In all probability, Russia will suspend for a more or less prolonged period her diplomatic relations with France; and she will suspend them not as a result of any hostility or enmity towards that country but because it would be superfluous to try to conduct relations with those lawyers who have seized power there and are degrading France to a level incompatible with the role of a great power.

After referring to the departure of Appert from Petersburg, to that of Mohrenheim from France, and to the resignations of Ternaux-Compans and de Voize, the paper then continued:

> The alliance with France is something dear to Russia. That country would be her best and most natural ally on the European continent. But Russia could not make an alliance with a France fallen into the hands of a group of lawyers who exercise power to the detriment of her interests and exclusively to the benefit of their own—and who, furthermore, are supported by Germany, precisely because [the Germans know that] nothing can so weaken France as the Red Republic.

With this parting shot, well calculated to touch the unhappy Freycinet on the most painful spot, Ternaux-Compans brought to an end both his diplomatic career in Petersburg and his service to the French Foreign Office, leaving relations between France and Russia in a state of complete deadlock.

Chapter Nine

KATKOV'S ATTACK

Serious as were the complications that afflicted Franco-Russian relations at the official diplomatic level in 1886, on neither the French nor the Russian side did the respective chauvinists allow themselves to be significantly discouraged thereby in their hopes for closer ties between the two countries. The Russians now saw favorable possibilities for engineering the removal of Giers, and felt that with his departure all things would become possible. The French also placed their hopes in what they envisaged as an even more momentous change in personalities.

For some time, now, Juliette Adam had been relatively subdued in her advocacy of a Franco-Russian alliance. Already discouraged by the death of Skobelev in 1882, she had found herself obliged since 1884 to exercise restraint in the criticism of French foreign policy because of the presence of her friend, Freycinet, in office. (He had become foreign minister in the Brisson cabinet as early as April 1885.) But her enthusiasm for the cause was finding support in 1886, whether she knew it or not, in the presence at the Ministry of War of General Georges Boulanger, for whom, as a person, she had no regard or sympathy. This intellectually shallow but flamboyant and superficially impressive man, with his great flair for self-dramatization and his formidable powers of demogogic interaction with the masses, had played skillfully both on the existing social discontents and on the national sense of humiliation after 1870. He had succeeded, by mid-1886, in producing a state of sharply enhanced nationalistic and militaristic fervor in broad sections of the French population. The result was new anxiety in Germany and increased tension between that country and France—a situation that did not escape the attention of Russian military leaders and nationalistic circles and could not fail to stimulate their hopes and their activity.

Not only this, but the cause of French chauvinism and *revanchisme* had, by this time, another powerful supporter in the public eye, in the person of the poet and ex-soldier, Paul Déroulède. It was four years, now, since Déroulède had founded his Ligue des Patriotes. Membership in the organization had grown during these years from an original 82,000 to more than half a million. Déroulède himself had become, by mid-1886, a major figure on the French scene.

In April 1886 there appeared in Paris a sensational brochure entitled *Avant la bataille*, from the pen of a friend of Boulanger: Captain Hippolyte Barthélemy, a retired French officer of strongly *revanchiste* views who wrote extensively about military affairs at that period. It was said to have been written with the encouragement and support of Boulanger, and on the basis of materials made available from the files of the French War Ministry. Its thesis was that the French armed forces were now fully equal, if not superior, to those of Germany, and that the day of *revanche* was, or should be, at hand. The foreword to the book was written by Déroulède; and he did not lag behind Barthélemy in his insistence that the Franco-German differences must be resolved by force of arms. "La bataille," he wrote, in defining the theme of the pamphlet, "est inévitable, l'Armée est prête." ("The battle is inevitable; the Army is ready.") And again: "Le rapprochement de la France et de l'Allemagne est necessaire, mais par les armes; oui certes, il sera utile et fécond, mais par la victoire." ("The rapprochement of France with Germany is necessary, but by the force of arms; indeed, it will be useful and productive, but only by virtue of victory.")

Aside from stirring up the Germans and contributing to the growing tension between Germany and France, this brochure did not go unnoticed in Russia. Its appearance was faithfully reported to Katkov by Cyon; and the report of it was published in the *Moskovskie Vyedomosti* on April 19/May 1, 1886.

At just about this time, Déroulède set forth on a leisurely journey that was to take him not only to Athens and Constantinople but thereafter, for the first time in his life, to Russia. What inspired this visit, who initiated it, why the timing, and who made the arrangements and selected the contacts for the Russian portion of it: none of this is apparent. Coming from Constantinople, Déroulède evidently entered Russia at Odessa and proceeded thence to Moscow, which appears to have been the main target of his journey. Only at the end of the journey does he appear to have visited Petersburg. Odessa and Moscow were, of course, leading centers of Panslav and nationalist activity; and it is evident that the respective Russian circles were well aware of Déroulède's approach and anxious to use his presence, to whatever extent possible, for demonstrations of Franco-Russian friendship. Katkov received him and listened attentively to his appeal for an alliance.* Katkov's son served as his companion and interpreter during his stay in the Moscow area.

Giers and d'Ormesson, learning of the preparations for this visit, both

---

* J. and J. Tharaud, *La vie et la mort de Déroulède* (Paris: Plon, 1925), pp. 49-52. The authors thought that Déroulède's *plaidoyer* on this occasion had an influence on Katkov's editorial of July 30 (see below). They related that Bismarck's wife, on being shown the editorial, remarked: "Il y a du Déroulède la-dessous."

took alarm. Déroulède's arrival in Moscow was scheduled for the end of July or the beginning of August. This was just the moment of lowest ebb in the official diplomatic relations between France and Russia, when the task of restoring relations seemed most delicate and difficult. The Tsar, conscious of his personal responsibility for the shaping of Russian foreign policy, was always sensitive to any attempt to force his hand through pressure of public opinion. He was capable of reacting explosively to any demonstrations, whether on behalf of Franco-Russian amity or other cause, that lent themselves to such an interpretation. The likelihood that he would react in this way to any flamboyant demonstrations of Franco-Russian friendship was heightened by the existing diplomatic tension; and it was plain that relations between the two countries could be actually further damaged, rather than benefited, if this should occur.

Efforts to avert the danger, including personal appeals to Déroulède by d'Ormesson and the French consul in Moscow, were therefore put in hand; and they were not without effect. The impetuous poet could not, to be sure, be restrained from journeying to the Sergo-Troitski Monastery (at the present Zagorsk) to attend a funeral mass for the late Ivan Aksakov, bearing with him a wreath decorated with the tricolor and ribbons of Alsace and an inscription reading: "Au grand patriote russe; à l'ami de Scobeleff." But beyond this, demonstrations in the Moscow area did not go; and the ones in Petersburg were even more restrained.

———

While this episode clearly revealed that the possibilities of an open advocacy in Russia of a Franco-Russian alliance were limited at that time, it did not prevent interested persons in the world of Russian journalism and publication from pressing in this direction. There was still the question of a more active Russian Balkan policy, and with it the question of a change in the relationship to Austria and Germany. Here, the Russian press was allowed a liberty that was often the subject of comment on the part of foreign representatives and observers, generally, and of some indignation on the part of the Austrian and German ones, in particular.

Ever since the Rumelian putsch of the previous year, the nationalist Russian press had continued its pressures for a harder and more aggressive Russian policy towards her partners in the *Dreikaiserbund*. Katkov was by no means alone in the effort. The theme was to some extent detectable in the editorials and reportage of almost all the Russian papers. In Petersburg, the conservative *Novoye Vremya* and the strongly anti-Austrian *Novosti* scarcely lagged behind Katkov in their denuncia-

172

tions of Battenberg and demands for the forceful reassertion of Russian authority in Bulgaria. There were others, including the *Svyet*, with its military connections, and the *Peterburgskie Vyedomosti*, organ of the Ministry of Education and its reactionary chief, Delyanov, in which the expression of similar sentiments, albeit sometimes with significant variations of view, could be found. But of all the nationalistic editors, Katkov was the most conspicuous and the most authoritative. It was his views that unquestionably made the greatest impression internationally. It was his views that had the strongest influence on the Tsar.

We have already noted (see above, Chapter 7) the anguished and even neurotic feelings of frustration and resentment with which Katkov reacted to the reverses in Russian policy towards Bulgaria in 1885. Over the ensuing winter he sustained himself, after a fashion, with the faint hope that the other European Powers could be brought into conflict with Battenberg through the Constantinople negotiations, and could thus be induced to join Russia in inflicting upon the latter the punishment and humiliation which Russia, under the influence—as he saw it— of the timid, pro-German Giers, and out of exaggerated respect for her obligations to Germany and Austria, had alone been unwilling to inflict. But when at the beginning of April 1886 it became evident, with the ratification by the Powers of the arrangement finally concluded between Battenberg and the Sultan, that nothing of this sort was to occur, and that Battenberg was to be allowed to retain his position and to bask in the credit for achieving the unification of Bulgaria and defending it against the jealous Serbs, the last trace of Katkov's patience was exhausted. Its disappearance was hastened and made more final, one might add, by the removal, just at that time, of the relatively pro-Russian Ristić cabinet in Serbia and its replacement (under Austrian pressure, as he saw it) by an anti-Russian one under Garashanin; also, by the energetic action of the Powers in restraining the Greeks from undertaking independent military action against Bulgaria along the lines of that recently undertaken by the Serbs.

These developments, coming together in late March and early April 1886, appear to have marked a significant turning point in Katkov's views and positions—a point to which, to be sure, he had long been tending, but which nevertheless did not reach its culmination until that time. That this had its implications for his attitude towards France, in the sense that it was probably at this point that he became persuaded of the necessity of the eventual military collaboration of the two countries against Germany, is something we have no reason to doubt. Cyon relates, in his history of the alliance, how he received just at that time, a prearranged "signal" from Katkov, indicating that the time had come for

173

the launching of a propaganda campaign designed to prepare public opinion in both France and Russia for the conclusion of a Franco-Russian alliance, and giving him the green light for the submission from Paris, for publication in the *Moskovskie Vyedomosti*, of material designed to serve this purpose. Cyon then goes on to list the various stories he submitted, pursuant to this request, over the ensuing weeks, and to suggest that these stories, although Katkov did not use all of them in the columns of the paper, contributed importantly to the celebrated editorial of the 30th of July (about which more will be said presently) and thus to the change in Russian policy that was to take place in the following year.

Here, as in so many other places, Cyon was exaggerating and over-dramatizing his own contribution. He did indeed increase, for a time, the scope and frequency of his stories from Paris, and Katkov printed some of them. But if, as we must assume, it was sentiment for a closer Franco-Russian relationship they were supposed to induce, they were not very useful to Katkov. As a confirmed monarchist, Cyon could not refrain from giving extensive space in his stories to the expulsion of the Orléaniste and Bonapartiste princes; and this material, while Katkov printed it (with a view, presumably, to appealing to the known sentiments of the Tsar), was not precisely suitable for the promotion of friendly feelings towards the existing French government. Only shortly before the appearance of Katkov's famous article of the 30th of July did there appear in Cyon's stories strong signs of the tendency they were supposed, by his claim, to serve.* On the 15th of July, in particular, the paper carried a story from him in which there was mention of the great French military strength and the aggressive spirit which had recently taken possession of the French people; this was followed by an extraordinary passage advising the Russians that they had no further need to take any account of Germany in their Balkan policy, even if it should involve action against Austria—the French would see to it that the Germans remained inactive.† (But one cannot tell whether this passage, which seemed somewhat out of place in the remaining context of the story, really came from Cyon himself or whether it was, in accordance with a practice to which Katkov seems not always to have been averse, inserted at the Moscow end.)

* These stories appeared not over Cyon's own name, but were signed, simply, "K."

† This passage included, for example, the following sentence: "We have no reason to fear Germany; she will not throw herself into any serious action against our plans so long as there is poised behind her back an army of one and a half million men, excellently armed, and prepared to throw themselves upon her with all the genuine *furia Gallica*" (*Moskovskie Vyedomosti*, July 3-15, 1886).

Much more important, over these weeks from April to the end of July 1886, were the materials carried by the *Moskovskie Vyedomosti* on Bulgaria, on the Balkans generally, and on the relationship of Balkan developments to German and Austrian policy. Just who were Katkov's correspondents in Bulgaria (there were probably not more than two, and possibly only one, though four different pseudonyms were involved) is not apparent. Great space was given, in any event, to their lengthy reports, which were carried two or three times weekly, datelined sometimes from Sofia, sometimes from Rushchuk, sometimes from Philippopolis. They exemplified, one is obliged to note with regret, the worst sort of tendentious journalism. They were intensely vituperative and sometimes even viciously mendacious,* in particular, in their treatment of the person of Battenberg. Along with these were published, from time to time, other articles, signed "X. X.," which, while ticketed as coming from Berlin, were concerned primarily with Bulgarian affairs and were strikingly violent in tone. (One is moved to suspect that these last were actually written, or largely written, in Moscow, but were given the Berlin dateline as a means of avoiding editorial responsibility.) All these materials, and those of Cyon, were supported by occasional editorial articles markedly more moderate in tone, which dealt primarily with the major international aspects of Bulgarian and other Balkan events.

It may be useful to summarize the theses which these materials, in their entirety, presented to Katkov's Russian readers, among whom was included, as we know, Alexander III. They were these: Russia had been delicately propelled by the wily Bismarck into an undesirable war with Turkey, after which she had been humiliated by being dragged, like a criminal before the bar of justice, before a tribunal (The Congress of Berlin) composed of her enemies and rivals. More recently, the scheming Battenberg, acting under the instigation of certain outside Powers whose identity it would not be hard for anyone to guess, had mounted a putsch and effected the unification of Bulgaria. Russia had no reason to object

---

* One of these reports, which appeared in the paper on May 29-June 10, 1886, included the allegation, attributed by name to three of Battenberg's Bulgarian friends, that Battenberg had had letters from Bismarck and the German Kaiser, advising him to follow an anti-Russian policy and promising help therein, and one letter, in particular, from Bismarck informing him that Russia was scheming to make Bulgaria into a trans-Danubian Russian province. Not only was this sort of allegation patently untrue, but it was in such total conflict with what is now known about Bismarck's views and policy that one marvels at the readiness of a man so well informed as Katkov to give it a place in his paper. The allegation is of special interest, however, in connection with the false documents which were to appear, and to be fed by the French foreign minister to the Tsar, the following year, advancing similar suggestions with respect to Battenberg's successor: Ferdinand of Coburg.

to this unification as such, but for it to be under Battenberg was unacceptable. The Powers should have put him in his place by refusing to accept it; and when, in their hostility to Russia, they declined to do so, Russia should have taken things into her own hands, and, standing on the dignity of her just claim to leadership of the Balkan peoples, she should have moved independently to put things to rights. But, swayed by her misplaced loyalty to the "concert" of the Powers, she had not done so. Instead, she had sacrificed to a fatuous desire to retain German and Austrian friendship all that should have been hers by right in the Balkans. And the result was that not only had she lost her influence in Bulgaria but she had become the laughing stock of Europe. The others treated her "like a plaintive child," and snickered behind her back. And she had invited this by her own behavior.

In general, in the weeks between April and late July, Katkov, so to speak, lowered his voice at this point and refrained from expatiating further on the implications of this thesis from the standpoint of Russian policy. But at the end of July, he finally abandoned this caution and came out with his celebrated editorial of the 30th of July in the *Moskovskie Vyedomosti* in which he urged, in effect, the abandonment of the *Dreikaiserbund*.

What moved him to do this, and at just this time? It was, unquestionably, the news that there were shortly to be high-level meetings in western Europe: of the German and Austrian Emperors at Bad Gastein;* of Bismarck and Kalnocky, and perhaps Giers as well, at Kissingen; then, the impression that at these meetings the future relations between the three imperial rulers—the source of all the difficulty—would come once more under discussion; and finally, the fear that Giers, unless something was done to warn the Tsar, would somehow trap the well-meaning and unsuspecting Russian monarch into another act of subordination to the policies of his German and Austrian cousins.

How much did Katkov know about the *Dreikaiserbund*? A half year later he was to enrage the Tsar by revealing to the public, in general terms, the existence of an arrangement of this nature. But in 1886, at any rate, his concept of it was decidedly inexact. That some sort of bond between the three Emperors, veiled by the general term the "Concert of the Powers," existed—this he knew. But he then thought, as did Cyon even as late as 1894, that if any treaty existed, it was one that had come into existence at the Skiernewice or Kremsier meetings in 1884-1885. He seems to have known nothing of the true origins of the *Dreikaiserbund*. In his suspicion that a prolongation of the existing treaty

---

* The two Emperors met at Gastein on August 8-9. The meeting was primarily a matter of courtesy, and had no significant political consequences.

relationship would come under discussion at the summer meetings of the various crowned heads and statesmen, too, he was considerably ahead of the game. Another nine months were to elapse before Giers and Bismarck would settle down to a serious exploration of the problems flowing from the forthcoming expiration (June 18, 1887) of the existing three-year term of the *Dreikaiserbund*. But men act on whatever impressions they happen to have; and Katkov's impression was that weighty discussions, possibly committing Russian policy for long into the future, were about to take place. It was this that provoked from him his historic recommendation of the 30th of July for a basic change in Russian foreign policy.

The contents of that editorial are worth reviewing at this point, both because of their lasting influence on Russian opinion, including very probably that of the Tsar, and as a reflection of the political atmosphere of the time.

The piece began with a somewhat bitter and plaintive acknowledgment of the exceptional influence which Bismarck had come to exercise in the affairs of Europe:

> The German Chancellor has acquired, together with his deserved fame, a certain mythological quality. His hand is suspected in all the events of our time; he is viewed as the possessor of the talisman before which all obstacles dissolve and all locks open. Without his agreement, one is given to understand, one may neither lie down nor stand up; he runs the whole world.

But, Katkov went on, was this really true? Was it not simply the Russian belief that it was so that gave it its validity? Was it really Germany's friendship that was necessary to Russia; was it not rather the other way around? Had it not been Russia's friendship that made possible Germany's successes? Had it not been her voluntary service as a stepping stone that had made possible Germany's victory over France? Had Russia's friendship not neutralized the power of Austria and made it impossible for that country to come to France's assistance? Of course Bismarck was clever; of course Count Moltke was a brilliant strategist; but the fact that such plans had been feasible at all was something these men owed to Russia's friendship. It was this that had made it impossible for Austria even to budge, and had thus bound the remainder of Germany to Prussia.

> What would have happened if things had not been this way? Why, even now, Russia would have only to restore the freedom of her own actions—to cease, in other words, to serve as a crutch for Germany— and the phantom of German omnipotence would dissolve in an instant;

Russia would then take her place in the company of other states. We say: all that it would take would be for Russia to restore the freedom of her own actions; by this we by no means wish to say that she should enter into hostile relations with a neighboring Power. On the contrary, it is desirable that our friendly relations with this neighboring Power should be strengthened. But that strengthening is possible only on the condition that there be a complete clarity on both sides as well as mutual independence and mutual respect. It is not natural that a great power such as Russia should remain, under the guise of friendship and alliance, forever or even for long in a state of blind subservience to an external will, as though under hypnotism. Such unnatural relations are bound to give rise to a host of misunderstandings and to create, behind the outward appearance of friendship, all the more profound an inner hostility, which would be bound to come to the surface sooner or later in one way or another.

Having invoked this image of a Russia hopelessly caught in the toils of the clever Bismarck, and choosing to submit blindly to his authority, Katkov went on to question the entire rationale of what he understood to be the Russian relationship to Germany. Why, he asked, did Russia need "these alliances," these "concertations"? True, there had at one time been misunderstandings between Russia and Germany which had needed to be removed. He had himself welcomed their removal. But that had been all that really *was* necessary. What was required was simply the creation of a situation in which neither of the two Powers would conspire against the interests of the other. "Why, then," he repeated, "some sort of alliances, some sort of agreements?" If, he explained,

> . . . what had been envisaged had been some common action, some sort of large-scale, dangerous undertaking, then an agreement would, in view of the common purpose, have been in order. *Do et des.* But, so far as is known, no such common undertaking was envisaged. There has been talk of an agreement on our part with Germany, and through her (by all means, through her) with Austria-Hungary, allegedly for assuring the peace of Europe. But what need do we have to assure the peace of Europe? Are we supposed to be the gendarmes of the European world? And what is the peace of Europe, anyway? It is enough for us to assure the peace of Russia, within the framework of her own interests.

Bismarck, he went on, had talked about a great league of peace. This was what Russia had thought she was entering when she undertook negotiations with the Germans. No sooner had she done this, however, than the phantom of a general league of peace disappeared and Russia found herself enslaved and taken in tow. In the name of the preservation of the peace of Europe, she had been compelled to accept the duty of preserving the security, the peace, and the greatness of Germany, and to place herself completely at the disposition of the policy makers of Berlin. Prince Bismarck, through the agency of this Concert of Powers, had been able to arrange to his satisfaction one after the other of the problems that interested *him*; but Russia, in the meantime, had found herself squeezed out of the Balkan peninsula. Bismarck, having got Russia where he wanted her, was in "a position where he could easily frighten anyone who deigned to oppose his policies. Russia, on the other hand, should she attempt to act outside the Concert of Powers, could always be intimidated by the prospect of a conflict either with England or with European coalitions."

This state of subservience, Katkov took pains to point out, embraced the economic and commercial, as well as the political fields. In the name of friendship, the Russians found themselves obliged to accommodate themselves in economic matters "to the requirements not of our own but of a foreign country." Until Russia liberated herself from this state of dependence she would, Katkov asserted, be a menace to her friends as well as to her enemies. Only as a truly independent country would she be able to be "not the slave, but the real friend of those who are our friends."

> Only by virtue of that independence which is as necessary to the state as air is to the living being will we be able to distinguish enemies from friends and, in the context of moving events and changing circumstances, ascertain with whom it is suitable for us, by the will of Providence, to go together and against whom we should undertake preventative measures.

If the first portion of this editorial was intended primarily as a veiled attack on Giers, the next passage, following these somewhat menacing intimations, was in reality addressed to the Tsar, and was an attempt to wean him from certain of the assumptions that bound him, as Katkov saw it, to the existing relationship with the Germans, particularly his belief that devotion to the monarchical principle required him to go hand in hand with the other emperors. It was not, Katkov wrote, by abstract principles (i.e., the principle of monarchy) that Russia should be guided, ". . . but rather by that which is dear to the heart of everyone, namely, the good of our fatherland." Russia had her own individuality. She was not to be compared with other countries. The Russian monarchistic idea was *sui generis*. Her system was not to be placed on a plane with the monarchical systems of other countries. It could not be made comparable to them by "categories of classification." It was a historic fault of Russia to be led by empty abstractions instead of by her own spirit. Only he could be a true ally who was brought close, by the course of events, to the vital interests of Russia—whether it was the President of the United States or the Bogdykhan of China. One did not have to ask into what category his government was supposed to fit.

(The sense of this last was unmistakable, and could have been lost on no one who was familiar with the basis of Russia's relationships with the other Great European Powers. The Tsar, it was implied, should get over the idea that just because Germany and Austria were imperial monarchies, whereas France was a disorderly democracy, this meant that Germany and Austria were natural allies of Russia and France was not. This was an abstract distinction, which did not accord with the real interests of Russia. There were, particularly in the light of the uniqueness of Russia's monarchical institutions, things more important than the form of government; and it was these that Russia should have in mind as she approached the problems of her foreign policy.)

The final paragraph of the article proceeded to spell out, in cautious terms, the significance of this reasoning from the standpoint of Franco-Russian relations. "We have no doubt," Katkov wrote,

> ... that people will choose to see in our words the hint of a Franco-Russian alliance; but we protest most emphatically against such an interpretation. We would like Russia to be in free, though friendly, relations with Germany, but we would like to see us have similar relations with other Powers, and the same with France, which, whatever one wants to say, is assuming more and more the position that is suitable to her in Europe. Why indeed should we quarrel with her? And what need do we have to mix into her internal affairs? Every country, particularly so important a one as France, has its own fortunes, and we have no reason to involve ourselves in them or to wish to re-shape them according to our desires. But at the same time we do not have any need to contemplate a separate alliance with her. What purpose should such an alliance serve? If indeed there were to take place a conflict between Germany and France, then the most decent, most dignified position for Russia, and the one that would best accord with her interests, would be a strict neutrality. Nothing is worse than to intervene in the quarrel of others; and in an eventuality of this sort what we ought to do would be to take the necessary measures for the assurance of our neutrality and for the defense of our interests, keeping a sharp eye on the march of events. Russia herself does not start anything; everybody knows that; people everywhere are convinced of it. The others, while themselves grabbing everything that is not nailed down, charge Russia with a passion for acquisition. Not being in the habit of starting things, we have no need of allies; but it would be strange on our part not to wish that our opponents had other opponents besides ourselves. We consider it improbable that Germany should ever

wish to pick a quarrel with us. But if, as is possible, England should come into conflict with us in the Near or the Far East, then the present France, which stands in a relationship of scarcely less antagonism with her than with Germany, would probably not remain an idle spectator of the struggle; and in truth, we would have no reason to be discontent with such a situation.

The disclaimer of any intention of advocating an actual alliance with France must be regarded as disingenuous—the product of a very natural prudence, lest the author shock and estrange the Tsar by going too far and too fast. It must be remembered that the article was written precisely at the time of Déroulède's visit to Moscow and his visit to Katkov. That Déroulède was preaching to all who would listen the necessity of a Franco-Russian alliance was no secret to the Tsar or to Giers. It was important for Katkov to avoid giving the impression that he had been unduly influenced from this quarter.

Added to this was the fact that only a few days earlier there had occurred an incident in France, also connected with demands for a Franco-Russian alliance, which was known to have aroused the Tsar's keen displeasure. A ceremony of the unveiling of a monument at Nouart to the former French Ambassador to Russia, General Chanzy, had been taken advantage of by French chauvinists and had turned into a demonstration in favor of an alliance with Russia. The Russian military attaché in Paris, Baron Fredericks, had been in attendance, and had been quoted by the French press in statements which appeared to give support to this particular cause.

The unfortunate Fredericks was not seriously to blame. He had done no more than attempt to respond amiably to an unexpected and embarrassingly fulsome demonstration of friendship for his country. But the affair was blown up by the press. The Tsar was annoyed. The Foreign Ministry saw itself obliged to deny publicly that Fredericks was acting under instructions. And here, too, Katkov had before him a situation with which, in drafting his editorial of the 30th, he had to be careful not to identify himself.

The fact is that Katkov recognized perfectly well that a Franco-Russian alliance could not be, for a variety of reasons, an immediate and avowed goal of Russian policy. Time had to elapse before anything of this nature could be realized in a formal way. He was probably quite sincere in pressing the formula (in essence the same one hinted at by Ternaux-Compans) that what Russia needed, at the moment, was merely a closer relationship with France, as a means of freeing herself from an undue dependence on Bismarck and gaining a greater bargaining power vis-à-vis Germany. But the logic of this view led, as most observers recognized at the time, inexorably to an eventual alliance; because a free hand for Russia vis-à-vis Germany and Austria implied, in the long run, a free hand for those latter Powers vis-à-vis Russia; and this implied in turn for Russia an eventual isolation—a dangerous isolation, the very isolation she had been concerned to escape by entering the *Dreikaiserbund* in the first place—an isolation to which, in the terms of 1886-1887, the only even theoretically feasible alternative was an alliance with France.

It is impossible to take the reasoning of Katkov's article at its face value, because it is remarkable for the unsubstantiality of the factual premises on which it is based. The image of reality put forward there, as a foundation for the argument, was almost wholly false. We have already had occasion to note a number of the distortions. Russia had *not* been innocently pushed by outside Powers into the war with Turkey. The Congress of Berlin had *not* been arranged for the purpose of humiliating her, but rather as a means of saving her from the worst consequences of her own folly. The Powers had *not* instigated the Philippopolis putsch, nor had Battenberg conceived and directed it. Russia was *not* the spineless slave of Bismarck, blindly executing his orders. It was simply absurd to suggest, in particular, that she had subordinated her economic life to that of Germany. (Her tariffs on German goods had been rising steadily ever since 1879, and the balance of trade had developed, in recent years, decidedly in her favor.)

On some of these points, Katkov might have been partially misinformed. However, it is impossible to believe that a man of his connections and experience was misinformed on all, or even most, of them. Generally speaking, the false image of reality on which the article was based has to be put down to that tendency to polemic exaggeration and distortion that seems to be a permanent feature of the Russian political temperament. But the recognition of this fact merely brings us back to the recognition that Katkov's motivation cannot be regarded as adequately clarified just by the terms of the article itself.

There was a tendency among Katkov's critics and opponents to ascribe this change in his editorial line to the influence of the generally anti-German central-Russian industrial and commercial circles by which he was surrounded and with which he was in part connected. These suspicions were carried at times all the way to charges of bribery. Allegations of this nature had in fact long preceded his change of front in 1886. Herbert Bismarck, for example, in writing to his father from Petersburg in 1884, made a reference to Katkov who, he said, "having become very rich through his connections with certain rich Moscow industrialists and merchants, plies his trade as a journalist exclusively in the interests of this little egoistical circle."[1] Two years later Schweinitz, the German Ambassador in Petersburg, quoted Giers as having said to him "some days ago" (the despatch was dated the 30th of July 1886, the very day of the appearance of Katkov's celebrated editorial) that the change in Katkov's editorial line was connected with the fact that he was "personally involved in the enterprises and speculations of the ultra-protectionist industrialists, who are angry at Germany because she refused to put up with any further raising of our duties on iron and coal." Even the Tsar had recently admitted to him, Schweinitz reported, that material reasons and purposes were often decisive in determining Katkov's political line.[2]

There appears also to be, in the German documents,[3] a memorandum written by von Berchem, of the German Foreign Office, on the 14th of August 1886, quoting the landowner and industrialist Count Guido Henkel von Donnersmarck as being of the opinion that Katkov could be "bought up" for a sum of about 50,000 rubles per annum. He, Berchem, the memo continued, had mentioned this to Dr. Rottenburg (economic expert of the Foreign Office), who in turn had spoken to Bismarck about it; but the latter had disapproved of any such attempt.

Finally, the Austrian Ambassador in Petersburg, Wolkenstein, harbored similar suspicions of venality on Katkov's part. On the 24th of October 1886, he cited, among various derelictions which, in his view, had at that time allegedly got Katkov into the Tsar's bad graces, ". . . particularly the proof provided by the Minister of Finance that Katkov is involved in various dirty deals connected with the question of rebates on sugar."[4]

The image of Katkov acting in the interests of commercial circles is one that has naturally commended itself to Marxist historians, accustomed to seek the motivation of historical personages exclusively in their state of subconscious or unscrupulous subordination to their own economic interests and those of the class to which they are seen as belonging.

How much truth was there in these suspicions and insinuations? It is true that the Russian industrialists of the Moscow and Urals regions, being less dependent on German raw materials, less interested in the German market, and more painfully affected by German competition, tended to urge a harder line in policy towards Germany than did the industrial and commercial circles of the Baltic and other Western areas. Particularly was this true of the central-Russian textile manufacturers. It is also true that Katkov had connections in these circles, and that they enjoyed his sympathies. It is entirely possible, even probable, that he

had investments in this direction. It would have been in no way surprising, furthermore, or indeed improper, had financial support for his
paper been forthcoming from this quarter.

But to move from this to the assumption that Katkov, in urging the
abandonment of the political ties to Germany and Austria, was acting
solely or primarily under the influence of these industrial circles is surely
to go too far. Much as he may have appreciated financial support, or
profit, from this direction, he was not, at this stage of his life, dependent
on it; and in general, he was a man too large in stature, too prominent,
too deeply and broadly interested in problems of public policy, and too
conscious of the seriousness of his responsibility as a leader of public
opinion, to act solely on the basis of motives as narrow and petty as
the ones here ascribed to him.

The fact is that Katkov was simply a profoundly committed Russian
patriot and nationalist, not only saturated with the thirst for national
prestige and glory that was a part of the pervasive romantic nationalism
of his century, but bearing with him, as well, the characteristic neuroses
of Russian national feeling, as these had manifested themselves for centuries back into the past: the high sense of national-religious orthodoxy,
the mistrust of the heretical foreigner, the distrust of—and antagonism
to—the sophisticated West, the semi-oriental concern for "face," the
exaggerated sense of prestige. His wish was to see Russia mighty, and
to see her feared, admired, and respected for this might and for all
that it would appear to reflect in the way of superiority of the Russian
spirit, of strength and virtue and cleverness on the part of Russia's
people and their leaders. Above all, he had that strongly competitive
view of Russia's foreign relations which made every Russian success
appear as a blow to others, every foreign success as a blow to Russia.

From this last standpoint, things had not gone at all well in the past
months and years. Bismarck had come to be seen by the world as the
giant and wizard of European politics. Russia, by contrast, had become
(or so it seemed to Katkov) a laughing stock. It was the combination
of these two things—the ignominy of Russia and the success of her
German partner—that was intolerable to him. Possibly he could have
endured Bismarck's successes if Russia had had fewer failures. He
might, conversely, have endured Russia's failures if Bismarck had had
fewer successes. The combination of the two was unendurable.

Katkov was not a Panslav. Insofar as he publicly professed commitment to any particular concept of Russian aims in the Balkans, it
was to the concept of *edinoverstvo*—a concept based on the religious
tie, and implying that all those peoples who shared with Russia the
Eastern-Orthodox faith should look to her for political leadership and

support. But actually, it was really the dream of San Stefano that possessed him—the dream of the wide swath of Russian-dominated territory sweeping across the Balkans from the Black Sea to the Adriatic, cutting off Austria from the Aegean, leaving Russia the master of southeastern Europe and the Straits.

That the realization of this dream was wholly unacceptable to the Austrians was clear. Even those initial steps in this direction which Katkov was known to advocate (although he could not say so openly)— the occupation of Bulgaria and the installation of a Russian commissar as its dictatorial ruler—would probably have set in motion a series of events which would have culminated, sooner or later, in a military conflict between the two rival empires. This, one may be sure, did not frighten him from the standpoint of the prospective bloodshed involved. Like so many others of his time, he still had the romantic conception of warfare as a test of the national virtue—an exercise in which were exhibited the qualities of valor, heroism, and devotion to the national cause, and in which the braver, more inspired side could, granted anything resembling an equality of forces and armaments, be expected to win. He was, one feels, not only ready but even eager to see this put to the test in a war with the Austro-Hungarian Empire alone.

But the problem was with the Germans. And it was to this problem that a close political and military tie with France appeared as the only possible answer.

Chapter Ten

THE END OF BATTENBERG

We left Franco-Russian relations in a sorry state, which it may be useful at this point to recapitulate. There was no French Ambassador to Russia at all, the Tsar having declined to receive any. The Russian Ambassador to France, Mohrenheim, had been instructed to leave that country and to remain outside it until further orders. Afraid of being blamed for not being more effective in averting these complications, Mohrenheim had not returned to Russia; and Giers, who disliked and mistrusted him, had not encouraged him to do so. He had remained therefore in Munich. The chargé d'affaires of the French Embassy in Petersburg, Ternaux-Compans, disgusted with his government's behavior, had resigned his job and abandoned his diplomatic career. A new counselor, Count Olivier d'Ormesson, had been despatched, post-haste, to replace him.

D'Ormesson had been, to that time, serving in the internal administrative service, his last position having been that of préfect of Pau. Unjust as the change may have been to Ternaux-Compans, d'Ormesson turned out to be an excellent man for the task. He had seen some diplomatic service, in the quality of a young attaché, in earlier years. He lacked, of course, his predecessor's familiarity with the Russian scene; but his freedom from emotional involvement with the earlier stages of the diplomatic impasse into which he was propelled was helpful to him in his efforts to overcome it.

The Tsar and his family returned on the 11th of July from a cruise in Finnish waters, and took up residence in Peterhof. Three days later, d'Ormesson arrived. Giers received him courteously, and spoke kindly to him of the departing Ternaux-Compans; but d'Ormesson thought he detected a strong note of reserve in the minister's behavior. Neither man mentioned the subject of diplomatic representation. D'Ormesson correctly sensed that no good would be achieved by attempting to press this painful and delicate question before there was some indication of a change in the Tsar's disposition; it had therefore best be left, for the moment, unmentioned. He communicated this view to Freycinet, who, now at long last taking a serious interest in Russian affairs, accepted

186

it. "Abstenez vous de toutes démarches," he wired d'Ormesson on the 16th. And there, for the time being, the matter rested.

In early August, d'Ormesson was permitted to pay the routine courtesy call on the Tsar. The latter was correct in his behavior, but cold and uncommunicative. It was clear that there had been no improvement, as yet, in his disposition. With Giers' departure for Franzensbad, on the 8th of August, there was, for the time being, no one else of consequence to talk to, and nothing further to be done. Ten days later, Friedrich von Holstein, the future *éminence grise* of the German Foreign Office, confided to his diary the conviction that "our best safeguard now lies in the hatred and contempt felt by the Tsar for the French Republic."[1]

In the diplomatically dull month of August, with Giers away in Bohemia, the Tsar and Tsarina gave their annual *fête* at the suburban palace of Peterhof, on the shores of the Finnish Gulf. The chiefs of the diplomatic missions were invited. The German chargé d'affaires, Bülow, who was present, chanced in this way to fall into conversation with a man whom the diplomats, and particularly the chargés d'affaires, seldom had occasion to meet. This was General Peter Cheryevin, head of the political police, the man who was personally responsible for the security of the Tsar and his family and who therefore customarily resided with the imperial household. Cheryevin, reputedly not averse to liberal use of the bottle, was in an unusually talkative mood; and his statements to Bülow on that occasion are worth noting, by way of interlude, as a picture of the atmosphere prevailing in high official Russian circles at that particular moment, on the eve of the putsch against Battenberg.[2]

Bülow, with Katkov's recent anti-German editorial and similar items from the nationalist press in mind, complained to Cheryevin about the freedom with which the Russian press was permitted to attack Russia's relations with Germany.

For this, Cheryevin said, there were three reasons. The first was simply lack of coordination in the government, owing to the fact that there was no prime minister: each of the ministers dealt separately with the Tsar and followed, so far as he could obtain sanction for it, his own policy. The result was that when one of the ministers was insulted, the others laughed behind his back. "When one attacks Giers, Tolstoi [minister of the interior] shrugs his shoulders."

Secondly, Cheryevin said, the Tsar did not really care. He was indifferent. One had no idea how indifferent he was. "He is just, good, and truly humane. He wishes ill to no one; he has no Caesarian dreams. But he thinks at heart that he has no need to worry about anything, because nothing seems to him important enough to trouble his repose."

Finally, a number of people, he said, thought that in view of the extent of the internal unrest and opposition, it was best to let the press direct its discontents against external targets; it was a means of deflecting the criticisms from the domestic scene.

This policy, Bülow observed in reply, reminded him of the man who jumped into the water to get away from the rain; and he went on to make the prophetic observation that in a conflict with the other two empires, Austria and Germany, Russia would lose in internal stability whatever she might gain in military victory.

"Agreed," was Cheryevin's reply. But Austria was the heart of the problem. Russia had no real conflict with Germany. Her interests, on the other hand, conflicted with those of Austria at every point. The Turkish Empire was rapidly disintegrating. How could the succession to it be arranged without a conflict between Austria and Russia? Austria was not an ally on whom the Germans could count. "Let us arrange our affairs between us, without Austria, and, if you will, at Austria's expense."

Bülow, observing with a certain discomfort that the Austrian Archduke Karl Ludwig* was peacefully eating his supper only a few feet away while this somewhat startling suggestion was being made, argued politely against this thesis. But Cheryevin was not to be moved. If Germany wanted to avoid trouble with Russia, there were three things, he said, which she must do: prevent Austria from supporting Prince Alexander of Battenberg; refrain from interceding on behalf of the German population of the Baltic provinces; and stop sending Germans to establish themselves as farmers in Russian Poland. At the close, they spoke of France. "I have no faith," said Cheryevin, "in the future of the family of Orléans. The Bonapartistes have more courage, but they are too greatly detested; Boulanger has already been devalued. France is a rotting corpse. It would be folly to ally one's self with her. I have no faith in the future of France. She will suffer the same fate as Poland."

The late Russian historian Boris Nolde, to whose admirable and basic work on the history of the Franco-Russian alliance all students of this subject are so extensively indebted, observed, by way of comment on this exchange: "In high Russian circles one was still far from wishing to follow to the letter the advice of Katkov. All that was conceded to him was the hatred of Austria. There was no serious thought of separating one's self from Germany or of orienting one's self towards France."[3]

* Brother of Emperor Franz Joseph, and considered to be a firm friend of Russia.

Formally and officially, this was true. But the Balkan pot was continuing to boil. It was again about to boil over. And the logic of this boiling, for the rather strange psychological reasons that we have had occasion to note, spelled not only the disruption of the *Dreikaiserbund*, but with it also, eventually, the end of Russia's cordial relationship to Germany.

We have already noted (see Chapter 7, above) that the Tsar, after liquidation of the immediate crisis of Bulgarian unification, had committed himself to the early removal of Battenberg by fair means or foul. Clandestine operations, looking to this end, had been put in hand as early as the beginning of 1886. In the ensuing months, while Franco-Russian relations were deteriorating and Katkov,* with Cyon's help, was busy drumming up sentiment for what he viewed as a self-emancipation of Russia from Germany, these plans and preparations were maturing. Through those Russian agents in high Bulgarian political circles whose identity was noted above, contact was established with dissident elements in the Bulgarian officers' corps. Great as was the prestige gained by Battenberg from his victory over Serbia, this armed conflict had also left a legacy of disillusionment and bitterness among some of the Bulgarian officers. The blanketing of Rumelian military personnel into the regular Bulgarian forces had had to be hastily improvised when the Serbs attacked. To assure their loyalty, the Rumelians had had to be given certain positions of rank and command that were coveted by Bulgarians. Feelings had been offended, sensitivities aroused. Most of the army remained strongly loyal to Battenberg, but there were important centers of unrest.

The principal of these centers was the 2nd Infantry Battalion. A point was reached where the conspirators came to the conclusion that this unit could be used for the overthrow of the Prince. But here a difficulty presented itself. This battalion was not normally used for the guarding of the Prince's palace. That task was customarily entrusted to the 1st Battalion, which was loyal to Battenberg and could not be disaffected. To meet this difficulty, a plan was conceived: Battenberg would be fed, through channels to which the conspirators had access, with false information to the effect that the Serbs were hastily and ominously undertaking military preparations along the Bulgarian frontier, and that there was urgent need for countermeasures. He would be

---

* Katkov being in general excellently informed, through both military and Panslav circles, of Russian clandestine activities in Bulgaria, it is probable that he was not unaware, in launching his attack on July 30, that a denouement of some sort was approaching in Bulgaria.

urged to order the 1st Battalion, the one stationed nearest the frontier and most reliable, to the frontier to assure the rapid conclusion of the necessary preparations and to be on hand in case of a Serbian attack. Meanwhile, the guarding of the palace could be taken over, temporarily, by the 2nd Battalion.

This scheme was described, in all its unpleasant detail, in a telegram despatched by the political representative in Sofia, Bogdanov, to the Russian Foreign Office on the 8th of August. The moment for launching the operation, he reported in that message, was imminent. The Prince had been successfully deceived, and the 1st Battalion was expected to arrive at the frontier on the 13th. The moment was considered particularly propitious because almost all of the higher officers loyal to the Prince happened to be away from Sofia. If the putsch was successful, the Russian government should be prepared for new demands for money and munitions to assure the establishment and security of the new regime.[4]

This message was brought at once to the attention of the Tsar. Still smarting from many previous failures, he could not bring himself to muster any great enthusiasm. His doubts related not to the morality of the projected operation but to its chances for success. "I fear," he wrote on the face of the telegram, "that no good will come of this." But he made no effort to stop it.

From his standpoint, this pessimism proved to be unjustified. On the 10th another message went forward from Bogdanov, bringing unexpected good news. Battenberg, Bogdanov reported, had given his consent to the erection of new fortifications along the border, and was preparing to go to Slivnica himself. The only troops remaining in Sofia were ones that were unreliable from Battenberg's standpoint. It was planned to arrest the Prince, either before he left for the frontier, or upon his return. The new regime would then turn to Russia with a request for acceptance of the new situation and for the despatch of a high Russian officer, preferably Ignatyev or Dondukov-Korsakov, to take over the Bulgarian army. The message ended by relaying a request from Colonel Sakharov that the information it contained be passed on to General Obruchev.

The plan was carried out, as devised. The Prince had by this time returned to his residence in Sofia. At 3:30 a.m. on the 21st of August the palace was invaded by the 2nd Battalion, which was supposed to be guarding it. Battenberg, accompanied by his brother, Prince Henry (who was visiting him at the time), and his German pastor, Koch, was arrested and taken to a monastery. There, effectively under threat to his life, he was persuaded to sign an act of abdication. He was then despatched, with his companions, to the Danube where, in company with some 200 armed guards, he was loaded onto his own small yacht and sent downstream to Russia's one Danubian port of Reni, in Bessarabia. There, he was turned over to a wholly unprepared and bewildered set of local Russian officials. The higher Russian authorities (who were anxious to get rid of him) then permitted him to proceed, by rail and under careful escort, through Russian territory to Austrian Poland.

Upon arrival in Poland, Battenberg was thunderstruck to learn that the conspirators who had removed him, in Bulgaria, had in their turn been overthrown by other military and political elements loyal to him, and that he was invited by the latter to return to Bulgaria and resume his throne. This, though sorely shaken by this whole series of events, he consented to do. Traveling via Austria and Rumania, he passed, on the 29th of August, through the Rumanian-Danubian port of Galati. Owing to an understandable failure of signals in this general muddle, among those who came to greet him at Galati was the local Russian consul. This unfortunate official, being wholly without instructions and no less confused than Battenberg himself, joined, in full uniform, the welcoming delegation of Rumanians. Then, after the ceremony of greeting, the consul proceeded to have a long and cordial private conversation with Battenberg, in the course of which he told the latter that Prince Dolgoruki was being sent as the new Russian diplomatic representative to Bulgaria. Battenberg gained from this account the wholly erroneous impression that the appointment of Dolgoruki signified acquiescence by the Russian government in his own resumption of the throne. Thinking that the Tsar would now be in a mood for reconciliation, and that his own triumph over his internal enemies had put him in a good position to make the generous gesture, Battenberg at once sent off a wire to the Tsar (August 29), thanking him for the appointment of Dolgoruki, stating that he viewed the restoration of good relations with Russia as essential to the further prosperity of his own rule, and adding (it was probably meant simply as a politeness) that he could not conceive of himself continuing successfully on the Bulgarian throne unless he had the Tsar's personal confidence.

The Tsar's answer, which reached Battenberg after his arrival in Sofia, was cold and implacable.[5] "J'ai reçu," the Tsar wired,

le télégramme de Votre Altesse. Je ne puis approuver Votre retour en Bulgarie, prévoyant les conséquences sinistres qu'il peut entraîner pour le pays Bulgare, déjà si éprouvé. La mission du général Dolgorucki devient inopportune; je m'abstiendrai d'elle dans le triste état de choses auquel la Bulgarie est réduite tant que Vous y resterez.

Votre Altesse appréciera ce qu'elle a à faire. Je me réserve de juger ce que me commandent la mémoire vénerée de Mon Père, l'intérêt de la Russie et la paix de l'Orient.

Alexandre.*

For Battenberg, this was the last straw. With receipt of this message, he lost all further stomach for the Bulgarian throne. He had misjudged the situation; he had misjudged the Tsar. But the damage was now done. His nerves were shattered by the experiences of the preceding days. He was still heartbroken over the realization that his initial removal had been clandestinely engineered by military officers in whom he had placed his confidence and whom he still considered, as he confessed to one of the foreign representatives in Sofia, to be among the finest of the Bulgarian officers' corps. Against such faithlessness in his own military entourage, and in the face of the Tsar's continued opposition and obvious hatred, he could not face a continuation of the struggle to rule Bulgaria. On Monday the 6th of September, in a moving ceremony of farewell, he gave up his throne—this time, voluntarily and finally— and left the country. But before doing so, he appointed, to exercise the powers of the throne until a new prince might be selected and installed, a regency of three prominent Bulgarian politicians: Karavelov, Stambulov, and Mutkurov. None of them could be viewed by the Russians as entirely reliable. The Russians, in truth, had at that moment no idea how unreliable these people would eventually turn out to be; but they already had no grounds for confidence in them. The circumstances of Battenberg's final departure, attracting to him as they did the sympathies of all of Europe and leaving in power in Bulgaria people who were far from being the pro-Russian figures for whom the Russians had hoped, thus made this event for the Russians at best a Pyrrhic victory.

For Battenberg, incidentally, abdication, while it marked the final end to his official connection with Bulgaria, where he was never again to set foot, did not spell the immediate end either to his significance as a figure in European politics or to tragic personal difficulties. Russian policy through the months following his abdication was colored by a lively apprehension lest he again change his mind and accept a renewed Bulgarian invitation to occupy the throne. Bismarck, too, feared that in

* I have received your Highness' telegram. I cannot approve your return to Bulgaria in view of the foreseeable unfortunate consequences this could have for a country already so sorely tried. The mission of General Dolgoruki has become inopportune; in the sad state of circumstances that will prevail in Bulgaria so long as you remain there, I shall refrain from sending him.

Your Highness will understand what he has to do. I reserve the right to judge what course may be dictated for me by the venerated memory of my father, by the interests of Russia, and by the cause of peace in the Balkan area."

case of any renewed outbreak of war in the Balkans, involving Bulgaria, Battenberg would be enthusiastically urged by the Bulgarians to return and place himself once more at the head of the Bulgarian army. This heightened the chancellor's sensitivity, both to the succession problem in Bulgaria and to the implications of the continued desire of the wife of the German Crown Prince (and of the two persons most concerned) that Battenberg should marry her daughter.

The election of Ferdinand of Coburg as Battenberg's successor on the Bulgarian throne, in the summer of 1887, relieved the first of these anxieties on Bismarck's part; but the marriage problem became, with the successive illnesses and deaths of the old Kaiser and his son, in 1888, the subject of the most intense conflict within the German imperial family—so intense that Bismarck at one point threatened publicly to resign if the marriage came about. With the death, in June 1888, of the second of these two rulers (the former Crown Prince, by then Emperor Frederick III) and the accession to the throne of young William II, this crisis, too, came to an unhappy ending—with the firm decision of the new Kaiser that the match would under no circumstances be permitted. At that point, Battenberg finally and formally renounced his suit for the girl's hand, gave up the Battenberg title, took that of Count von Hartenau (after the name of one of his family's small estates), and, within the space of a few months, married Johanna Loisinger, an actress of the Darmstadt *Hoftheater*, accepted a commission in the Austro-Hungarian army, and settled down to live in Graz. There, five years later (November 1893), at the age of 36, his health still not fully restored after the excitements of his Bulgarian experience, he died.

His body, at the request of the Bulgarian government, was at once taken to Bulgaria and interred with great ceremony, as that of a national hero, in a mausoleum built specially for this purpose in the center of Sofia. His personal papers, which were obviously of very considerable historical interest, remained for some years in Austria, and were used by Corti in the preparation of his biography of Battenberg, in 1920. In the late 1920's, it appears, they were turned over by the Hartenau family to the Bulgarian government at the latter's request, and deposited with the Bulgarian National Museum. The mausoleum is, on latest reports, now neglected and in disrepair. Inquiry of the present Bulgarian authorities (1973) concerning the possibility of consulting the papers elicited only, first, a disclaimer of any knowledge of them, and later, a statement to the effect that they were not available for consultation because the museum was in process of repair.

Against this backdrop of events in Bulgaria, let us glance at what was happening, in just these days, on the Petersburg stage.

A few days before the putsch in Bulgaria, the usual summer manoeuvres had begun at Krasnoye Selo. The Tsar moved to his palace there in order to attend the event. Diplomatic difficulties notwithstanding, the French were invited to be represented. They sent a senior officer, General la Hayrie, specially for the occasion. La Hayrie was treated with signal courtesy by the imperial couple, even being seated several times next to the Empress Dagmar at table. The French were left with the impression that a particular effort was being made to show that the Tsar's impatience with the politicians in Paris had no significance for the course of relations at the military level.

It was during this stay at Krasnoye Selo that the Tsar received the first news of the arrest and removal of Battenberg. That he must have been intensely interested and highly gratified by these initial reports goes without saying. They reached him on the very day (August 21) of the putsch, which had taken place in the early morning; and they included the report of the Prince's initial abdication. The following day, in the absence of Giers (who had now left for Franzensbad), the Tsar locked himself away and saw no one on the civilian side. The probability is that he kept in closest touch with the Bulgarian situation through Obruchev; for it was noted by the British Embassy in Petersburg that when, a day or so later, Battenberg arrived on Russian territory, it was the army who took charge of him and his arrangements—the Foreign Office had nothing to do with it.[6]

D'Ormesson, consumed with curiosity about the effect of these events, made a special trip to Krasnoye Selo on the 24th, to see what he could learn, through the French military delegation, about the Tsar's reaction. The latter, he was told, had reappeared on the 23rd, after his day of seclusion, and had given the impression of being in the very best of humor.

For the rest, the Tsar's reactions to the rapidly developing situation in Bulgaria can only be imagined—there seems to be no record that reflects them. It must have been a series of ups and downs: the putsch; the initial abdication; then Battenberg's triumphant return; his attempt to appease the Tsar; then, Battenberg's final abdication—intensely gratifying, to be sure, but followed in short order by the appointment, in parting, of the anti-Russian regency.

It was in the midst of this bewildering torrent of conflicting events that, on the 30th of August, the Prince's conciliatory message to the Tsar was received in Petersburg. Giers was not there to be consulted.

Vlangali and Jomini, the senior men at the Foreign Office, met with Obruchev, to whom had been assigned (significantly) the leading responsibility in handling the situation created by the action against Battenberg, and drafted a cautious, and relatively mild, reply, which they intended as a private communication, to be sent in code via the Russian consulate in Sofia. This draft was then sent out to the Tsar for his approval and signature. The Tsar, however, after holding it for a day, drafted his own message—the one we have seen above—and had this despatched through the open telegraph channels, thus making it a matter of public knowledge.[7]

Giers, after a visit to Bismarck in Berlin,* returned to Petersburg on Sunday evening, the 5th of September. The Tsar, now back at his usual summer residence of Peterhof, was scheduled to leave the following evening for further manoeuvres, to be held this time in Poland. Giers was to follow him there a day later. On Monday, therefore, the two men conferred at length, at Peterhof. They talked, obviously, about Bulgaria. The news of Battenberg's final abdication had, at that moment, not yet come in. Things still looked black, as usual, in that quarter.

Whether Giers and the Tsar also discussed the state of Franco-Russian relations on that occasion is uncertain. It was their first meeting and their first chance in a month to review the subject. Giers, who received d'Ormesson the following day (September 7), before departing for Poland, denied to d'Ormesson that the subject of Franco-Russian relations had come up for discussion; but this may have been a routine diplomatic evasion, to avoid giving the impression that there had been any significant change in the Tsar's disposition. Indeed, this seems most probable; for Giers went on to say to d'Ormesson that he would be occupying himself with the question in the near future, and that Mohrenheim was now to be ordered home for purposes of consultation, a step which would scarcely have been taken without the Tsar's approval. D'Ormesson, in any case, came away from this interview with an impression that Giers, at least, considered the moment a favorable one for a new approach to the problem of diplomatic relations.[8]

The fact that six more weeks were to elapse before the Russians would profess readiness to consider giving their *agrément* to the appointment of a new French Ambassador suggests that the Tsar, at that time

---

* Giers, on this occasion, had also called on the old German Kaiser, who confessed to having lost all confidence in the good sense of his imperial Russian nephew, and begged Giers not to abandon his position (V. N. Lamsdorff, *Dnevnik, 1886-1890*, ed. F. A. Rothstein [Moscow-Leningrad: Gosizdat, 1926], January 21, 1887, pp. 39-43).

in early August, preoccupied as he was with Bulgarian events, had not committed himself definitely on the question of the renewal of ambassadorial representation, but that Giers had wangled out of him a grudging consent to the recall of Mohrenheim for consultation, had correctly discerned in this concession the beginning of the change in the Tsar's general disposition, and had so hinted to d'Ormesson.

This partial turning point on the Russian side coincided, whether fortuitously or otherwise, with a most curious incident in Paris, the significance of which has never been fully clarified.

The Russian consul general at Marseilles, Aleksei M. Kumani, was a regular Foreign Office official, but one whose career suggests a closer association with the semi-independent Asiatic Department than with the main Chancery of the Ministry. (He had been consul general in Sofia in 1880-1881.) In the summer of 1886 he received a transfer from Marseilles to Peking, where he was to serve as minister. Whether this transfer came when he was in Russia on leave or whether, after receiving these new orders, he went to Petersburg for consultation before taking up his new position, is unclear. He was, in any case, in Petersburg in August. In the last days of that month he was, apparently, received in audience by the Tsar.* He then set out for his new post, traveling by way of Paris and Marseilles, and thence by ship to the Far East.

On arrival in Paris, Kumani asked the Russian chargé there, Prince Kotzebue, to request for him an interview with Freycinet. Though somewhat bewildered by the unusual nature of the request, Kotzebue did so. To Kotzebue's even greater bewilderment, Freycinet agreed to receive Kumani. Kumani seems definitely to have told the prime minister that there was now a disposition in Petersburg to receive a new French Ambassador, and to have recommended that the nominee, if the French were disposed to name one, should be a certain colonel-general whom he had known in Marseilles.[9]

These suggestions, relating to a matter which, as Kotzebue acidly observed, "ne regarde en aucune façon notre Ministre à Pekin,"[10] were startling enough in the circumstances, and led in fact to a new approach

---

* In the postscript to a private letter of August 30 from the acting head of the Foreign Ministry, Vlangali, to Giers, then at Franzensbad, it was said that Kumani had "presented himself" (predstavlyalsya) and had left for Marseilles. The "presented himself" presumably meant "before the Emperor"—i.e., that he had been given the normal audience with the sovereign before taking up duties as the latter's personal representative to a foreign court. It might be noted that at this time, before construction of the Trans-Siberian Railroad, the normal route to the Far East, for Russian diplomats, was by ship from the Mediterranean.

from the French concerning the appointment of an ambassador.* It is hard to believe that they were made without authorization.†

But they were only the less sensational half of the story. For there is also evidence that Kumani did not stop at this point, but went on to make further remarks to Freycinet which the latter took, rightly or wrongly, to be authorized suggestions for something in the nature of a Franco-Russian alliance. This, at any rate, is what Freycinet, as we shall see shortly, was to convey personally to the German Ambassador (albeit without revealing Kumani's identity) at a later date,‡ further indicating that the approach had been seriously considered within the French cabinet, had been discussed with President Grévy, and had been thereupon answered, on the authority of both president and cabinet, in the negative sense.[11]

This story, coming from the lips of the French prime minister, is one of such blatant incongruity that the historian is at a loss to know what to make of it. It simply makes no sense in the known context of the time. Conceivably, the intermediary mentioned by Freycinet might not have been Kumani but someone more highly placed in the Russian hierarchy of power.§ But who could have authorized Kumani, or anyone else, to make suggestions of this nature to the French? Giers? Out

---

* The new French *démarche*, Kotzebue reported, "a été provoqué par une étrange immixtion de M. Koumany, auquel j'avais arrangé, à sa demande, un entrevu avec M. de Freycinet. Notre Ministre en Chine en a profité pour exposer que, après ses observations personelles, la société de Pétersbourg désire beaucoup revoir un ambassadeur français, et il a recommandé . . . un Général Colonel qu'il a connu à Marseilles."

† D'Ormesson, queried telegraphically by Freycinet about the meaning of this visit, replied that he had talked with Kumani in Petersburg, and thought the latter must have been speaking under instructions (telegram, September 7, 1876. French Archives, File: *Russie 1886*, Vol. 274).

‡ The Germans heard substantially the same story from the lips of Clemenceau.

§ Giers, discussing the matter at a later date with Bülow, used language that suggested (although he, too, did not reveal Kumani's identity) a belief on his part that Kumani was the source of confusion. Yet, in asking his own son, Nikolai, to investigate the matter privately in Paris, Giers appears to have made no mention of Kumani's name. It is clear from young Giers' memoirs that he conducted his investigation in total ignorance of Kumani's visit, and under the impression that the approach had been made to the French president, Grévy, and not to Freycinet. This being the case, his suspicions fell on Obruchev, who, being in France for his usual summer vacation, did indeed call on Grévy around the time in question, but later emphatically denied that he had made any such suggestions to the president. The German Ambassador, Münster, furthermore, understood Freycinet to say that the approach had been made personally to him, not to Grévy. The fact that Giers failed to mention the Kumani visit even to his own son, when asking the latter to investigate the affair, suggests that this was a matter of great delicacy, probably involving the Tsar himself.

of the question. Aside from the fact that nothing could conceivably have been farther from his own thoughts, he had been absent from Petersburg since early August, on vacation. His deputy, Vlangali? Equally implausible. Vlangali was a cautious man. So blatant and hostile an intrigue against his chief, not to mention his Emperor, would have been wholly foreign to his nature. Nor does his private correspondence with Giers at this time suggest anything of this sort.

This leaves the Tsar himself. He was, of course, thoroughly disgusted with the French government of the moment and with Freycinet in particular. Diplomatic relations with France had been partly broken off, and no one had as yet even been able to persuade him to accept a new French Ambassador. Nor was he normally given, temperamentally, to personal diplomatic initiatives of this or any other nature, particularly ones that bypassed his foreign minister. Yet he *had* apparently received Kumani just before the latter's departure, at a time when Giers was away and when he, the Tsar, was in a state of great turmoil over the various messages concerning Battenberg's removal. One suspects Kumani's subsequent behavior in Paris to have reflected some sort of misunderstanding of things the Tsar may uncautiously have said to him, plus deliberate encouragement from the Asiatic Department of the Foreign Office, which was now extensively under the influence of Katkov and the military hotheads, and with which Kumani, an old hand of that department and now about to leave for Peking, was in close touch.

On the 6th-7th September, as we have seen, the Tsar and Giers left Petersburg to attend further manoeuvres, to be held this time in Russian Poland, near Brest-Litovsk. The Tsar remained there to the end of the month, returning to the Petersburg area only on the 1st of October. Giers appears to have returned about the 20th of September. Available records yield very little evidence as to what went on at the Tsar's headquarters in the way of discussions and decisions on matters of high policy. Such evidences as exist suggest that the monarch was now entering upon a period of painful struggle and vacillation between conflicting impulses, centering around the rapidly intensifying conflict between Katkov and Giers over the great issues of Russian foreign policy. His known actions and decisions, at this time, reflect these smoldering contradictions.

Less than a week after his arrival at Brest-Litovsk, Alexander III received the visit of the son of the German Crown Prince, the future William II, despatched by the German government (much to the anger of the young man's father, who had not been consulted and who disapproved of the mission) to try to combat Katkov's influence and to put the German-Russian relationship back on what Bismarck had come to view as its normal rails. The Tsar, who had conceived a liking for the young man from earlier acquaintance, received him cordially and talked with him on a number of occasions, in a manner so relaxed and intimate that the attendant courtiers, not accustomed to seeing such affability in their somewhat inscrutable monarch, were most amazed.

The Germans were momentarily encouraged by the results of this visit; and so, presumably, was Giers, although he probably knew his master too well to jump to any firm conclusions. But a few days later (September 18) there was announced, in the official bulletin, the bestowal of the Vladimir Cross on Katkov by the Tsar. The Tsar had signed the order in person at Brest-Litovsk on the 11th of September, one day before the arrival of the German Prince.

The significance of this event is not clear. The honor was bestowed, according to the wording of the order, because of Katkov's academic-educational services and his work of many years in strengthening public understanding for "the real principles of the life of the Russian state." Yet the personal signature by the Tsar, mentioned in the order itself, was unusual; and it is scarcely to be believed that the monarch was unaware of the significance of the timing of the action—almost immediately after the appearance of Katkov's sensational editorial and the reaction it unleashed in Germany and elsewhere. The bestowal of the honor was not, so far as this writer has been able to ascertain, discussed in the Russian press—not even in the *Moskovskie Vyedomosti*, which carried the item without comment. One is obliged to conclude from this that the editors must have been made aware in some way of the extremely sensitive nature of the subject.

Meanwhile, decisions had also to be taken with relation to Bulgaria. The Regents in that country had inaugurated their period of rule by calling for the election of a new national assembly, to decide on the question of a successor to Battenberg. To the Russians, this move was highly disagreeable. The first Prince of Bulgaria had been in effect selected by the Tsar. It was the latter's feeling, and that of his advisers, that the second one should be similarly chosen. Worried lest this mean that things in Bulgaria were again in danger of getting out of hand, the Tsar decided, at some time in the middle of September (the decision was made known on the 18th) to despatch to Bulgaria the Russian military attaché in Vienna, General (Baron) Nikolai Vasilyevich Kaulbars, as a special high-level envoy of the Russian government, with the mission of taking matters in hand and bringing the course of Bulgarian policy into accord with Russian interests. All available evidence suggests that this step was taken on a personal level by the Tsar in Krasnoye Selo, and that it was taken on recommendation from military quarters (possibly with Katkov's support), but either without consultation with Giers or against his advice.[12]

Whoever may have thought that the cup of Russian humiliation over the course of events in Bulgaria was full to the brim at the time of Battenberg's removal and that nothing could add to it, was sorely mistaken. The Kaulbars mission proved to be second to nothing in past experience as a fiasco of Russian policy. The good general arrived in Sofia, on the 25th of September, with instructions to present three demands on the Regents: (1) that they postpone for two months (presumably to give the Russians time to examine the question) the elections to a new national assembly; (2) that they remove at once the state of siege that had been proclaimed at the time of Battenberg's abdication (this was conceived by the Russians as a means of facilitating agitation and activity by the faction favorable to the acceptance of Russian tutelage); and (3) that they liberate, and free from further prosecution, the persons who had engineered the putsch against Battenberg.

What then ensued was an almost fantastic mixture of misguided behavior on the part of the general, and open defiance, to the point of impertinence, on the part of the Bulgarians. A tour around the country by Kaulbars turned into a series of rowdy and humiliating episodes, the Regents having taken care that crowds hostile to Russian authority would meet him and heckle him at every point on his way. His three demands were lightheartedly ignored; the Regents went confidently ahead with their plans, much as though he had not existed. And not only were proceedings against the conspirators of the 21st of August not dropped, but Russian citizens and pro-Russian Bulgarians continued to be the objects of repressive action on the part of the Bulgarian authorities and of harassment, sometimes violent, at the hands of Bulgarian individuals and mobs—actions towards which the authorities, as the Russians saw it, observed only a benevolent detachment. By the 20th of October, the general had been brought to the point where he felt obliged to issue to the Regents a 72-hour ultimatum: either they would take energetic action within that period to halt the excesses against Russian citizens, or he would leave Bulgaria, taking with him the entire Russian official establishment.

Having issued this ultimatum, the least Kaulbars could have done would have been to stick to it. Even this, however, he did not do. It was nearly a month before he finally carried out his threat. On the 20th of

November, under the Tsar's personal instruction, he left Bulgaria in the way that he had threatened, taking all other Russian officials with him and thus producing a final and complete break of relations between the two countries. There was, by this time, nothing left of his own personal prestige in Bulgaria, and very little of that of Russia.

One can easily imagine with what anguish and despair this course of events was followed in Petersburg. Evidences of Kaulbars' failure began to come in at just about the time of the Tsar's return to the Petersburg area, at the beginning of October. It was clear to everyone that the Kaulbars mission represented, in relation to Bulgaria, the last political card in the Russian hand. There were none left now but the military ones.

That the Kaulbars mission was doomed to fail was apparent at a very early date—in a matter of days, in fact—after the general's arrival in that country (i.e., towards the end of September). People in Russia were obliged to reflect, therefore, on the next step. It was not surprising, in these circumstances, that the capital buzzed throughout the month of October with rumors of an impending Russian occupation of Bulgaria. The idea had many supporters. Katkov now openly urged this course.* So did some of the more nationalistically inclined editors and officials. The Russian Ambassador at Berlin, Paul Shuvalov, even urged it strongly upon the embarrassed Giers in the presence of high German officials, on the occasion of Giers' visit to the German capital at the beginning of September.[13]

The military leaders, however, were averse to the idea. They recognized that it would almost certainly lead, sooner or later, to complications with Austria; and while there were probably differences of opinion among them as to the state of readiness of the Russian army to accept war with Austria at that juncture, particularly in view of the uncertainty about Germany's reaction, there seems to have been general agreement that even if war with Austria were to be viewed as a desirable development, it should not begin with the occupation of Bulgaria.

The Tsar, too, came out in the end against occupation. There is no authentic indication of his motivation. Plainly, the disposition of the military carried great weight with him.[14] But there was also the view, often expressed in some official circles, that the wily Bismarck was endeavoring to prod Russia into occupying Bulgaria, with a view to ensnaring her further in the sticky substance of Bulgarian politics. These

---

* "We go on postponing the occupation of Bulgaria, which we might have carried out," Katkov wrote in his issue of October 15, 1886, "in order to free her from the enemies by whom she has been captured; but in the end [if we go on doing this], we shall find ourselves obliged to declare war on her."

suspicions are known to have been brought to the Tsar's ears;* and it would not be surprising if they had appealed strongly to the mistrustful and uncertain frame of mind in which he then found himself.†

The result of these various hesitations was that the Russian government, though feeling itself sorely and almost intolerably provoked by Bulgarian behavior during the Kaulbars mission, abstained from military occupation and confined itself to the mild and not very successful device of the despatch, at the end of October, of two warships to the Bulgarian port of Varna. While intended as a support for Kaulbars, this had little effect outside the town of Varna itself; and with the general's departure, the Russians were obliged to face the painful fact that within seven years of their "liberation" of that country from the Turks by the action of their own arms, their policy with respect to it had ended in a state of total and helpless bankruptcy. In the entire history of Russian diplomacy, one searches in vain for any failure more spectacular, and more searing to the Russian sense of prestige, than this.

---

* Peter Shuvalov said to Schweinitz, in mid-November: "I can assure you that the only reason we did not proceed to the occupation of Bulgaria was that the Emperor thought Bismarck wished to lure him into it" (telegram, Schweinitz to Bismarck, November 16, 1886 [*GP*, V, No. 991, p. 74]).

† There was so little basis for this suspicion that one is obliged to suspect the motives of those (Jomini appears to have been among them) who peddled it in Petersburg. The German position with relation to a possible Russian occupation of Bulgaria was stated to the Russians clearly and unequivocally on a number of occasions. It was summed up in a statement made to the Grand Duke Vladimir Aleksandrovich by Herbert Bismarck, on November 21, 1886. He described the whole idea of Germany trying to provoke Russia into an occupation of Bulgaria as absurd. "We have," he said, "a lively concern lest Austria, in view of the nervousness of the Hungarians and the weakness of the Austrian government, should not sit idly by in the event that Russian troops were to appear in Bulgaria. It has always been the main objective of our policy to avoid a conflict between Austria and Russia. But it is perfectly clear that it would be harder to do this if a Russian army were to be launched against Bulgaria" (*GP*, V, No. 992, p. 82).

Chapter Eleven

THE BREAK REPAIRED

It remains now to note the effect of the events of September and October in Petersburg on the troubled course of Franco-Russian relations.

D'Ormesson, it will be recalled, had gained from his talk with Giers, on the 8th of September, the impression that Mohrenheim was about to be called home for consultation, and that discussions looking to a resumption of ambassadorial relations might then be expected to advance. The impression was erroneous. The Tsar had already left the capital for the manoeuvres in Poland, and Giers followed him the next evening. For a fortnight thereafter, until Giers' return, there was no one to consult; and no sign, either, of the promised Mohrenheim. Towards the end of the month, hints appeared in the Russian press that the latter might soon be coming home; and d'Ormesson queried Giers, who had by that time returned, about the rumors. Giers confirmed that Mohrenheim should soon be arriving, but this was all that could be got out of him. Thereafter, for a further three weeks, there was only the usual enigmatic Russian silence.

In the third week of October, however, the situation changed suddenly and decisively. On Tuesday, the 19th of October, Giers made his weekly journey to Gatchina for consultation with the Tsar. The following day he called in d'Ormesson and told him that the Russian government was prepared to pick things up again at the point where they had been left with Appert's recall, and to receive sympathetically a request from the French for an *agrément* for a new ambassador. He declined to state any Russian preferences with respect to the person of a new nominee or the walk of life from which he should be drawn. This, he said, would be left to the French. They could discuss the matter further, if they wished, with the Russian chargé d'affaires at Paris, Prince Kotzebue.

What had produced this change, and why its timing? Why was the Tsar prepared to authorize on the 19th of October a step which, six weeks earlier, just before his departure for Brest-Litovsk, he had resisted? Others thought at the time (and this writer himself is inclined

203

to believe) that the Tsar's decision to receive another French Ambassador marked a significant watershed of Russian policy: the moment of inner commitment to the eventual abandonment of the agreement with the Austro-Hungarian and German Empires which for five years had constituted the cornerstone of Russia's international position; in its place, embarkation on the long and gradual slope that would lead to the signing, some six years later, of the Franco-Russian alliance. If this is so, then it is worth examining with particular care both the influences to which the Tsar was subject at that specific moment and the frame of mind induced by those influences, superimposed as they were on his previous experience.

Toutain, d'Ormesson's First Assistant in the French Embassy at the time, writing his reminiscences some forty years later with the help of the official French documentation, was still under the impression that the Russian change of heart had come much earlier, at the end of August, and had been signaled to the French government by the itinerant Kumani. Believing this, he took, as did d'Ormesson, the Tsar's decision as simply the product of his concern and despair over the situation in Bulgaria, just then in the turmoil unleashed by the putsch against Battenberg. "J'ai toujours indiqué," he quotes d'Ormesson as writing to Freycinet at that time,[1] "que les circonstances extérieures intéressant spécialement la Russie du côté de la Bulgarie seraient à un moment donné notre meilleur auxiliaire." ("I have always pointed out that ulterior circumstances of interest to Russia in connection with Bulgaria will at a certain point prove to be the best sort of help to us.") If he was correct in this judgment, then the immediate impulses to the Tsar's action would have to be sought partly, no doubt, in the latter's reading of Katkov's recent article of the 30th of July, and partly in his reaction to the dramatic events of late August and early September in Bulgaria.

But, in this judgment, Toutain was only partly right. The Tsar's change of heart actually took place in two stages: (1) towards the end of September, when he authorized Giers, then about to return to Petersburg from Brest-Litovsk, to order Mohrenheim home for consultation; and (2) at some time in the week of the 12th-19th of October, when he finally gave the all-clear signal for reception of a new French Ambassador.

The first of these actions was merely tentative and noncommittal; the monarch retained his liberty of final decision. He had, let us note, at that moment just despatched Kaulbars to Bulgaria, and the success of that venture remained to be clarified. Evidently, the final decision with regard to the French representation was indeed connected, in his mind, with the outcome of the crisis in Bulgaria.

It is interesting, then, to take account, insofar as we know them, of the circumstances of the days immediately preceding the decision made known to Giers on the 19th of October. First of all, the failure of the Kaulbars mission was now clear and irremediable. Greatly depressed, the Tsar and Giers recognized this when they discussed the matter on the 12th of October; and on the 19th, the day before he gave his assent to the receiving of a new French Ambassador, Alexander ordered the withdrawal of Kaulbars and the complete break of all diplomatic and official relations with Bulgaria. This meant that he had played, in effect, his last peaceful card, without success. There now remained no alternative open to him but to proceed to an occupation of the country or to pocket the last and most bitter of a whole series of painful and humiliating rebuffs from the Bulgarians.

It was, as we have seen, for the latter alternative that he opted. The decision was inspired, it would appear, by military considerations: not so much fear of a war with Austria as the view, evidently held by a number of the senior military figures, that even if one wanted a war with Austria, the occupation of Bulgaria at that juncture was neither the place nor the time to begin it, and that such a procedure would only be detrimental rather than helpful, anyway, to the achievement of the ultimate and higher objective, which was control over the Dardanelles. He therefore accepted the situation, as Giers said, "comme un vrai philosophe." But in the ensuing days Europe was rife with rumors of an imminent Russian occupation; and the Tsar himself must have realized that the tense and uncertain situation resulting from the failure of Kaulbars' efforts could not fail to put a further burden on his relations with the Austrians and the Germans. This meant, of course, a heightened need for a close relationship with France, as an anchor to windward.

Secondly, Mohrenheim, summoned home in late September, had now arrived. He had brought with him a long memorandum on Franco-Russian relations—the product of the ruminations of his recent forced exile in Munich. The exact date of his return is not clear; but it was evidently around the 10th of October. According to Toutain, Mohrenheim had long discussions with Giers, and was also received by the Tsar, at Gatchina. He brought his memorandum along on this occasion, and was able, in addition to leaving it for the Tsar's perusal, to show it to the minister of the interior, Dmitri Tolstoi, whom he encountered in the Tsar's anteroom. Hansen relates that Tolstoi praised the document on the spot as the work of a true patriot, and it later became evident that the Tsar, too, was not displeased.[2] Mohrenheim's recommendations, needless to say, were for the immediate resumption of diplomatic relations (other things aside, he was keen to return to Paris), but they appear also to have envisaged a general change in Russia's relations with France.

Finally and more important, surely (for Mohrenheim, though *bien vu* by the Empress, was not a major figure), was influence from another quarter. Just as d'Ormesson was leaving for the Foreign Office, on the 20th of October, to receive from Giers the news of the Tsar's change of heart, there appeared at his office, demanding urgently to see him, none other than Cyon. D'Ormesson was most astonished at this abrupt visit from a man he had never before met, and even more astonished when it developed that Cyon had come to apprise him of exactly the same thing which, though he did not know it, Giers was about to tell him: namely, that the Russians were now willing to receive a new ambassador. Cyon then proceeded to beg him to suggest, as French nominee for this post, the name of General Gaillard.

Cyon had come to Petersburg, obviously at the urging of Katkov, at some time in the first half of October. Katkov had also come to the capital from Moscow, Cyon says, and had been awaiting his arrival there for some days. Cyon arrived—we are following, throughout, his own account[3]—bearing with him from Paris "l'assurance que de son côté le gouvernement français était tout disposé à répondre par un heureux choix au désir du tsar." (". . . the assurance that the French government, for its part, was disposed to meet the Tsar's wish by a suitable choice [of a new ambassador].") He had been meeting and conferring constantly, in the preceding days, with Katkov—even dining with him daily. Now, it appears, he had somehow become aware, even before Giers had had time to communicate the news to d'Ormesson, that the Tsar's opinion had changed; and he also knew that Giers would be informing d'Ormesson of that fact on the same day. Knowing this, he hastened to break in on the chargé d'affaires, to be the first to tell him the good news, and to plant in his ear (even before the chargé could talk with Giers) the suggestion of Gaillard's selection for the vacant post.*

All of these circumstances—Katkov's presence in Petersburg; his summoning of Cyon; the interest shown in the subject by Katkov's friend, Dmitri Tolstoi; and the intimate channel of communication ob-

---

* It may be worthwhile to note the words which Cyon used concerning his meeting with d'Ormesson on the 21st: "J'ai cru de mon devoir de prévenir immédiatement le comte d'Ormesson, etc., comme je savais que Giers devait le même jour lui communiquer la bonne nouvelle, j'ai mis mon amour-propre à l'avertir le premier. J'ai réussi. Mais ne le connaissant pas et l'ayant surpris au moment où il se préparait à sortir, j'ai du lui communiquer tout en quelques mots. Il a sans doute été bien surpris de cette irruption" (Cyon, *Histoire*, 1895, p. 172).

viously enjoyed by Katkov and Cyon to someone in high circles—suggest a line of influence working, quite independently of Giers and probably at odds with him, on the mind of the Tsar at that crucial moment.

The news of the Tsar's willingness to receive a new French Ambassador unleashed at once an intensive flurry of discussion and intrigue over the person of the same. Giers, as we have just seen, wisely stayed out of this discussion and maintained that he had no suggestions to make to the French government on this subject. Others, however, were not so restrained. Cyon, for one, continued to press both Russian officials and d'Ormesson to use their influence to bring about Gaillard's nomination for this post. Gaillard had been French military attaché in Petersburg at the time of the incumbency of General Le Flô as ambassador, in the mid-1870's. He was one of the three French officers said (by the Soviet scholar Manfred) to have been privy to clandestine arrangements set up in the early 1870's for collaboration between the French and Russian armies. (See above, Chapter 2.) He had accompanied the Grand Duke Nikolai Nikolayevich during the latter's service as commander-in-chief of the European front during the Russo-Turkish War. He had been useful in persuading the Rumanians to join the Russians in their military effort against Turkey. He had received in recognition of this service the Russian decoration of the Cross of St. George.

Jomini, on the other hand, while agreeing that the new ambassador should be a man in uniform, expressed a preference for Admiral Jaurequiberry. Cyon, on learning this, accepted Jomini's assurance that the appointment of a naval officer would be most acceptable to the Tsar, and at once changed his own tune. He began now to urge, by order of preference, the names of Jaurequiberry, Gaillard, and Billot.*

Toutain makes it evident in his memoirs that this insistence by Cyon and his friend, Jomini, on the appointment of a military or naval figure was actually intended as a move against Giers. Such a figure, it was reasoned, having direct access to the Tsar at manoeuvres and military ceremonies, would not have to work through Giers and could bypass the latter in his communications with the Russian monarch.

One may be sure that this effort to push Giers aside as a factor in

---

* Jean Bernard Jaurequiberry (1815-1887), was a senior French naval officer. It is interesting to note that he had resigned from the naval service on January 1, 1883, in protest against the decision, taken at that time, to retire officers, notably the Duc d'Aumale, who were in the line of succession of the reigning families of France. The reader will recall that it was Billot, Juliette Adam's friend, whom Freycinet had attempted, unsuccessfully, to appoint as Appert's successor at the Petersburg post.

Franco-Russian relations had the assent of Katkov, if indeed it did not originate with him. Jomini's reasons for pursuing this line, a course of action for which he assuredly did not have either Giers' authority or his blessing and which must have been pursued behind the foreign minister's back, were presumably to be found in the differences of personality and policy that had divided the two men ever since the assumption by Giers of the direction of the Foreign Ministry.

How much of this background was apparent to d'Ormesson is not clear; but on the 23rd of October, only two days after learning of the Tsar's decision, he addressed to Freycinet a personal letter in which he gave his views on the general subject of the desirability of having a military, rather than a civilian, figure at this ambassadorial post. Citing the usual arguments offered for the advantages of having a military personage as ambassador in Petersburg, he then proceeded to present, with great thoughtfulness and perception, certain considerations arguing against this choice—considerations which reflected a high degree of experience and maturity in diplomatic matters. "Given the well-known temperament of Alexander III," he wrote,

> and the brusque manifestations of ill humor to which he is given, one has to ask one's self whether too frequent occasions for contact with him are always desirable. Obviously, if an ambassador succeeds in pleasing him, as Appert did, and before him Le Flô and Chanzy, and if nothing untoward occurs in international relations, all this would work to the benefit of France. But since one has to consider also the opposite case, would one not find it to advantage, in difficult circumstances, to be able to avoid too frequent meetings between our representative and the Tsar? Under such circumstances, would not a prudent, temporizing, and conciliatory Minister for Foreign Affairs, such as the one who today directs the foreign policy of Russia, be all the better an intermediary for the reason that it would be his constant desire to avoid or at least mitigate the sometimes violent outbursts of the Emperor?[4]

D'Ormesson's letter actually arrived in Paris too late to affect the foreign minister's choice. But the choice, happily for him, fell out the way he would have wished it. Freycinet decided to nominate as ambassador Antoine Paul René Lefebre de Laboulaye, a career diplomat just then in the process of taking over an appointment as ambassador to Spain. This latter appointment was canceled in favor of the mission to Petersburg. In making this choice, Freycinet was probably not guided by any motives as sophisticated, in the diplomatic sense, as those that had inspired d'Ormesson's recommendation. His trouble about a military ambassador was probably only the fact that Billot, a powerful political figure, would have been offended if any other uniformed person had been selected in preference to him as the nominee; yet is was clear that Billot, in view of the Tsar's reaction, could not, himself, be nominated.

Laboulaye, then aged 52, had been in the diplomatic career for many years. He, too, had served in Petersburg under General Le Flô, as First Secretary and, at times, as chargé. He had left behind him there, insofar as he was remembered at all after the passage of a decade, a generally favorable impression. A man of quiet and methodical temperament, with the customary reserve of the hard-working career official, he was not initially held in highest regard by all his senior diplomatic colleagues (the Austrian Ambassador even criticized his dinners and his wines—a terrible reproach to a French colleague). Cyon was furious over the appointment, professing to see in it a grievous and irreparable blow to the development of Franco-Russian relations. But Laboulaye soon gained and retained the respect of the Russians, and his mission was to last down to the very conclusion of the alliance, some seven years later. This success stands as a correction, in retrospect, to those who, like Cyon, Jomini, and Katkov, saw in the elimination of Giers, and in the establishment of a direct line of communication between the French general staff and the Tsar, the only possibility of arriving at a satisfactory military and political agreement between the two countries.

————————

Laboulaye arrived in Petersburg on the 19th of November. Credentials were normally presented in Gatchina, but, the Empress' birthday occurring on the 26th, the imperial couple were scheduled to come to Petersburg for that event, and the Tsar chose to receive Laboulaye's credentials in Petersburg that same day. In accordance with normal protocol, the government provided a mounted military escort for the ambassador on his route between his residence on the bank of the Neva and the Anichkov Palace. This afforded an unusual spectacle for the Petersburg populace; and it did not go unnoticed by the press or the other diplomats.[5]

Laboulaye, on this occasion, said the usual polite things about his pleasant memories of previous service in Petersburg, about his desire to contribute to the restoration of good relations, and about his hope that he would have the Emperor's support in this undertaking. The Tsar's reply surprised him with its bluntness. "He gave me to understand," Laboulaye reported to his government,

> that the moment was a difficult one, that it was possible that severe trials lay ahead, and that it might be very necessary that in the course of these trials Russia should be able to count on France and France on Russia.
> "Unhappily," he added, "you French are yourselves going through certain

209

trials which make it impossible for you to have the spirit of consistency in your policies and which scarcely permit us to proceed in agreement with you. This is most regrettable, for we have need of a strong France. We need you and you need us. I hope that France will understand this."*

Whence, one must ask, this language? What "severe trials" did the Tsar see looming ahead? These were strong words, suggesting the imminence of nothing less than a major political, if not military, crisis. And from what was derived the need for a strong France on the part of a Russia already amply protected by a firm political understanding of some years' duration with Germany and Austria?

The answer to this question lay not only in the Tsar's agitated state arising out of the failure of the Kaulbars mission but in a further incident, occurring earlier in November, that had had the effect of rubbing salt in the imperial wounds. It had to do with the Austrian reaction to the situation in Bulgaria.

For some time now, Bismarck, alarmed over developments in the Balkans that threatened the intactness of the existing Three-Emperor relationship and thus of his entire structure of alliances, had been trying to pour oil on the waters by persuading the Austrians that they had nothing to fear from a possible Russian occupation of Bulgaria—they could compensate themselves by increased influence in Serbia and elsewhere. At the same time, he urged the Russians not to take too seriously those occasional voices of alarm over the prospect of such an occupation that were making themselves heard on the Austrian side of the line, particularly in Hungary. Such professions of alarm, he assured the Russians, would be only *pro forma*; they should not be permitted to give rise to anxiety.

This thesis was reiterated on a whole series of occasions. Thus, the chancellor's son, Herbert Bismarck, talking with the Russian chargé d'affaires, Muraviev, on the 20th of September, recognized the possibility that the trend of events might lead to an occupation of Bulgaria by the Russians, and that this would arouse some dissatisfaction in Hungary. "But I can assure you very confidentially," he went on,

* The following is the exact wording of this passage in Laboulaye's report, as it appears in the French Foreign Office Archives, Volume 273: ". . . développant avec brusquerie sa pensée, il m'a donné à entendre que les temps étaient durs, que des épreuves se préparaient peut-être, et qu'il serait bien nécessaire que dans le cours de ces épreuves la Russie pût compter sur la France comme la France sur la Russie. 'Malheureusement, a-t-il ajouté, vous traversez vous-mêmes des épreuves qui vous empêchent d'avoir de l'esprit de suite dans votre politique et qui ne permettent guère de marcher d'accord avec vous. Cela est bien regrettable, car il nous faudrait une France forte. Nous avons besoin de vous et vous avez besoin de nous. J'espère que la France le comprendra.' "

that it would have no further consequences. The Vienna government would confine itself to a platonic protest designed to placate public opinion and the national-Hungarian parliamentarians. That is what Kalnocky thinks; Petersburg should know this. For us, the main thing is to support Kalnocky. With him one can always do business. If he should be replaced by some other Hungarian figure, like Andrassy, things would not go so smoothly.[6]

Five days later Muraviev was told, again by Herbert Bismarck, that Kalnocky had said that the Emperor Franz Joseph considered that the Russians ought to be given a completely free hand in Bulgaria, and that he, Kalnocky, agreed.[7] These urgings were repeated two days later; and on this occasion young Bismarck was reported by Muraviev to have said that "You will have no difficulty making your legitimate influence felt in Bulgaria"—to which passage of the report the Tsar observed, in one of his customary marginalia: "Of course."[8]

As late as the 15th of October, the Russian Ambassador to Germany, Paul Shuvalov, now back in Berlin, reported that Bismarck *père* was of the opinion that while for the moment it was no doubt better for the Russians to abstain from occupation, he, Bismarck, would find such a measure perfectly legitimate, should circumstances later require it, and the Austrians would not go beyond a formal protest.[9]

What, then, in the light of these repeated assurances, must have been the Tsar's feelings when the report reached him, in mid-November, shortly before Laboulaye's arrival, that Kalnocky, speaking (November 12) before the Budgetary Commission of the Hungarian Diet, had made the following statement?

> If Russia had proposed or attempted to send to Bulgaria a commissar who would more or less have assumed the government of the country, or if she had proceeded to a military occupation of the ports or of the country itself, these would have constituted acts that would have obliged us, whatever the reasons for the action, to adopt a resolute posture.

This statement was not only wholly out of accord with all the Germans had been saying; it was at once gratuitous, threatening, and provocative: gratuitous because the situation described was still a hypothetical one—Russia had not, as yet, done the things Kalnocky had described; threatening, because she was very close to doing them—already, in fact, had two warships in the harbor at Varna; provocative, because it placed Russia in a position where she could not now refrain from doing these things without appearing to yield ignominiously to an Austrian threat.

The pill was made still more bitter by the fact that it was Kalnocky, and none other, from whom this statement came; for he was indeed

211

understood to have been ever since the formation of the *Dreikaiserbund* one of the strongest advocates, within the Austro-Hungarian establishment, of a close and peaceable relationship with Russia.

Finally, there was the fact that it was precisely to a Hungarian official body that Kalnocky's statement was made. The demand of the Hungarians, led by the now-retired Andrassy, for a firm and even aggressive policy towards Russia was well known. This pressure lay, as the Russians were well aware, at the bottom of the Austrian ambivalence with respect to Bulgaria—of the unwillingness on the part of the Austrian government to accept unreservedly the Bismarckian demand for a complete division of the Balkans into Austrian and Russian spheres of influence and for a clear renunciation by Austria of all interest in what might occur in Bulgaria. The Hungarians feared, and with them many of the Austrians as well, that a Russian occupation of Bulgaria would render impossible the continued maintenance of an independent stance on the part of the Rumanians; that the latter would be forced back into the Russian orbit; and that with this, the position of Hungary, partially hemmed in as she was between Rumania, Russian Poland, and Bulgaria would become complicated. That Kalnocky should now have been forced to give this reassurance to the Hungarian Diet was clear evidence that even with Bismarck's support he was no longer able to hold the line against the pressures for a defensive reaction which the continuing instability in Bulgaria was beginning to evoke in the Austro-Hungarian governing establishment.

It is difficult to judge just what was the real implication of this Austro-Hungarian threat. It was, precisely because it was gratuitous, more than the empty protest the Germans had been talking about. But the Austrians knew that Bismarck would not support them in any overt attack on Russia or any military encroachment upon the Russian position in Bulgaria. It cannot, therefore, have been this that Kalnocky had in mind. It seems more likely that what he envisaged was the possibility of some sort of occupation of Serbia, or portions thereof, as a counteraction to a possible Russian occupation of Bulgaria. But this in itself would have constituted a serious complication of the Balkan situation. It must, in any case, have been clear to the Tsar, from the reading of this statement, that a Russian occupation of Bulgaria—the only visible alternative to the confession of total Russian helplessness with regard to that country—could not be carried out without producing new tests of strength in the Balkan area, tests for which, at that time, the Russian military establishment was not yet fully prepared. Yet, given the provocative behavior of the Bulgarian Regency, who could tell when a situation would not be created when Russia's prestige would be threatened beyond endurance and an armed action would become necessary?

It was on the horns of this dilemma that Alexander III was writhing, in a veritable agony of frustration and pent-up anger, at the time when he accepted Laboulaye's credentials. He probably felt himself unable to foresee with any precision the further development of Austro-Russian relations in the Balkan area, yet could imagine no way in which the conflict between the two Powers could be peaceably resolved. Hence, perhaps, the prediction of "severe trials" ahead. And hence, no doubt, the cordiality, and the hint of high significance, with which the new French Ambassador was received.

One is moved to recall at this point the description of the state of mind then prevailing in Russian officialdom, as given by Bülow in a letter to a friend on the 15th of November, four days before Laboulaye's arrival, and just at the moment when Kalnocky's statement was becoming known in diplomatic and official circles in Petersburg.[10] It reflects, as do few other documents of the time, the atmosphere in which the Tsar's decision on his relations with the western European Powers had to be taken, in that autumn of 1886.

"For some time, now," Bülow wrote,

> no one has dared any longer to oppose the Emperor in political matters, or even to tell him the truth—Giers even less than those in his immediate entourage. In this way the Emperor sews himself into wholly false imaginings and expectations; when these fancies are destroyed by confrontation with the facts, "une colère sourde" overcomes him, as though someone had done him a great injustice. C'est ainsi qu'à présent il est monté contre l'Allemagne, sans rime ni raison, uniquement parce que les Bulgares ne cèdent pas et que son affreux Kaulbars se couvre de ridicule.
>
> Russia feels that she had disgraced herself without measure in Bulgaria. What has happened there in the last year—the Revolution in Philippopolis, Slivnica, Battenberg's return after the conspiracy of August 21, the manner in which he then abdicated, the behavior of the Regency, etc.,— is viewed here as a series of humiliations. The sense of having produced this fiasco by one's own awkwardness only increases the touchiness. Vorontsov,* on reading in the club an article about Kaulbars in the *Kölnische Zeitung*, remarked, with a bitter face: "Nous sommes comme les chiens qu'on frotte avec le nez dans les ordures qu'ils ont faites." The

---

* This was presumably Count I. I. Vorontsov-Dashkov, minister of the Imperial Household, a strong conservative friend and supporter of Alexander III.

"intelligentsia" is exasperated because the Panslav idea, which for twenty-five years has been regarded as an irreversible dogma, has turned out to be a great humbug. .... The Emperor is embittered because even after the removal of his arch-enemy Battenberg, things are going contrary to his expectations and wishes. Russia and the Tsar, in this mood, ask themselves on whom they should vent their wrath. On Bulgaria? The Panslavs warn against an occupation of Bulgaria, in which they see a mouse trap. On England? They would like to settle their scores with England only after Austria has been disposed of. On us? To be sure, we are hated here, and the Russians are not to be trusted. But this hatred flows more from a vague antipathy to what Germany represents than from political calculation. "C'est plutôt par sentiment que par raisons politiques qu'on est chez nous contre les Allemands," is what they often say. On the other hand the Russians, thank God, fear us greatly. An early attack on us is unlikely. This of course does not exclude spurring the French on behind the scenes. I have already, in August, drawn attention to the intrigues of Zagulyayev, Katakazi,* etc. These semi-official approaches will probably continue. The immediate object of Russian anger is Austria. I hear from every side: "Il faut déplacer la question bulgare." That means that Russia should extract herself from the Bulgarian swamp by a confrontation with Austria.

Bülow went on, then, to dwell on what he believed to be the reasons for the unhappy and disturbed personal state of mind of the Tsar: his abnormal life; the lack of the exercise and activity which so massive a physical frame required, the tradition of psychic eccentricity in the Romanov family; his anxiety about his children—all this added to his unwillingness to listen to unwelcome reports or to go deeply into the questions he had before him. It rendered him vulnerable, as Bülow saw it, to unscrupulous flattery and to backstairs influences, among which, in addition to that of Katkov, the influence of Minister of the Interior Tolstoi was particularly mentioned.

Bülow drew his impressions, of course, from the pro-German, or at least reasonably friendly, circles around the court and the government: from such people, presumably, as the Grand Dukes Vladimir Alek-sandrovich and Mikhail Nikolayevich; the outgoing Finance Minister Bunge; the commander of the Tsar's personal bodyguard, General Cheryevin, and above all, the Shuvalov brothers. Even where these people were well disposed towards Germany and recognized the injustice of the Tsar's growing resentment towards that country, they were for

* Katakazi, an attaché of the Russian Embassy in Paris, has been mentioned above (Chap. 4).

I have been unable to establish the identity of Zagulyayev—probably the Paris correspondent of one of the Russian newspapers.

the most part anti-Austrian, and urged a stiffer Germany policy towards Austria.

It is interesting to note that although people of this political tendency were strongly opposed to the influence of Katkov, they were not particularly well disposed towards the principal target of the latter's political activity—Giers. Both the Shuvalov brothers, for one thing, coveted the position Giers held and resented their exclusion from it. They tended, therefore, to tear him down on every occasion. They viewed him as excessively timid in his relations with the Tsar, and fancied that a bolder and stronger voice, coming from a more high-powered and impressive person, could alter the monarch's disposition. Seeing the power of the various forces—Katkov, other nationalist editors, Tolstoi, and so on—that were being directed against Giers, they predicted his early demise as foreign minister, and speculated freely on his possible successor. But like so many other people in Petersburg, they underestimated both his perspicacity and his tenacity. They failed, in particular, to realize that Giers, in giving the Tsar unwelcome advice, tempered his pressure very sensitively to what he knew to be the limits of the latter's emotional and intellectual patience; also, that when he did give unwelcome advice, he was much too wise a man to boast about this, as many others would have done, to outsiders.

———

Before leaving the subject of the resumption of normal Franco-Russian relations at the end of 1886, it will be engaging, if not conclusively instructive, to take brief note of the background of Cyon's curious appearance in d'Ormesson's office at this particular time.

No sooner had Cyon received, in Paris, the text of Katkov's notable editorial and seen to its circulation in the French press, than he went out to see Juliette Adam, at her suburban home in Gif, and obtained her consent (he claims she herself proposed it) to his assuming, for as long as he might wish to retain it, the directorship of *La Nouvelle Revue*. The purpose of this arrangement was, he claims, to enable him "to possess in Paris a publicity organ with which to support in France the campaign being waged in Russia by the *Moskovskie Vyedomosti*."[11] And indeed, shortly thereafter there appeared, bound between the pages of the next issue of the magazine, a chit announcing that Madame Adam, not being able to devote to the magazine the same burden of effort she had devoted to it in the past, had entrusted its direction to M. de Cyon, with the reservation that the policies of the publication in domestic as well as foreign affairs, would remain in her hands.

A most curious arrangement; for aside from this brief announcement, one searches in vain for the slightest evidence that this change had any effect on the magazine throughout the year that Cyon was its director. He was absent from Paris much of that year; and it is clear that he had nothing to do either with the general editing or with the office administration of the journal. One is reduced to the conclusion that this was purely a *pro forma* arrangement, to which Madame Adam was probably brought to agree by the argument that it would be useful to the present political purposes of Katkov. Actually, the appointment brought her criticism and ridicule from portions of the Paris press. "In what sort of an epoch do we live," asked the editors of the good bourgeois Paris *Siècle*,[12] "that a *diffamateur* of the *Moskovskie Vyedomosti* should be directing one of the great magazines of France?" And in an article carried the following day in the same paper, its Petersburg correspondent made the biting comment with relation to Cyon: "Trop réactionnaire pour un ministre du tsar, et juste à point pour prendre la direction d'une revue républicaine." ("Too reactionary for a minister of the Tsar, and just the man to assume the directorship of one of the great republican magazines of France.")

It was against this background of activity that Cyon proceeded to Petersburg in October 1886. Katkov had summoned him there, it appears, at some time towards the end of September, that is, at just the time when the first rumors were heard concerning the probable recall of Mohrenheim to Petersburg. In doing this, Katkov had forewarned him (if we may believe Cyon) that this summons had to do with a forthcoming renewal of ambassadorial relations (". . . qu'il s'agissait de travailler à la reprise des relations diplomatiques normales entre la Russie et la France."[13]) It was for this, presumably, that Cyon's presence was desired.

Before leaving Paris, Cyon, thus forewarned by Katkov, busied himself with the question as to who the new French Ambassador to Russia should be, and he himself claims to have proposed *to the French government* (these are his own words) the candidacy of General Gaillard. (This he did, no doubt, through the agency of Madame Adam, who represented his by far most promising, if indeed not his only, avenue of approach to the French prime minister.)

What prompted Cyon to advance this candidacy—even weeks before Alexander III had actually signaled his consent to the renewal of normal relations? The suggestion did not come from Juliette Adam. Her favored candidate, after all, was Billot; and it was evidently to her, and through her, that Cyon's suggestion was being made. Conceivably, as Cyon implies, it might have been the product of his own enlightened judgment: his appreciation for Gaillard's superior qualities, his certainty that Gaillard would be acceptable at the Russian "Court" (meaning probably to the Grand Duke Nikolai Nikolayevich), and his belief in the desirability of having a uniformed figure in this position. But could he, one wonders, have taken such a step, recommending to both the French, and later the Russian, governments an appointment of such importance, unless he had satisfied himself in some way that the appointment would be acceptable to the man in question and (since Gaillard was, after all, a senior military officer) to responsible circles in the French War Ministry and the general staff?

Once in Petersburg, Cyon, during the days from the 21st to the 24th of October, while this question of a new ambassador was being decided, sent a rapid series of reports—four letters and several telegrams—to Madame Adam. The tenor of such of these communications as he publishes in his book makes it evident that he viewed her primarily as a channel of communication to the French premier. She herself does not appear to have been greatly interested: she did not reply; and he was shocked to learn, in the middle of all this, that she had actually gone off to Bordeaux to attend the wedding of Pierre Loti. She was not, therefore, the one who was prompting him.

What, then, was Cyon's motivation? He shared none of the preoccupations with Balkan problems that impelled both Katkov and the Tsar to move towards a change in Russian policy. He himself admits this. And his claim that all this activity on his part on behalf of a Franco-Russian alliance was inspired by a desire to "déjouer les intrigues de Bismarck contre la France" does not ring true. There is nothing in his previous career to explain his professed hatred of Bismarck; and we have noted (Chapter 4, above) his curious effort to sell to the German government the control of the Petersburg *Golos* in 1883. Nor were genuine political passions of this sort, as distinct from considerations of self-interest, exactly in his nature. There must, then, have been some other impulse.

One is led irresistibly, by a long string of circumstantial evidence, towards the conclusion that Cyon had special connections of some sort, if not with the French military establishment as such, then with certain highly placed figures in that establishment, and that his activity on behalf of a Franco-Russian alliance reflected in some way influence or instigation from this quarter. In order to recognize the force of this suspicion, one need only recall the several suggestive circumstances that point in this direction; his long-standing personal connections in that quarter, particularly with General Saussier; his service to the Grand Duke Nikolai Nikolayevich in 1879-1880, and his equivocal explanations of its reasons; his repeated praise in his book for those French officers who were known to favor the alliance; his significant claim that Bismarck suspected him of being an intermediary between Katkov and the French general staff; and now the assiduousness with which he agitated for a military appointment to the Petersburg ambassadorship and pressed the choice of General Gaillard.

There is already powerful evidence that the Russian Panslavs, and probably the Russian military as well, had an important hand, through the agency of Katkov, in the pressures which brought the Tsar by the end of October 1886 to a point where he was prepared to change his European policy and to direct it towards an alliance with France. Proof is of course lacking, as it usually is when it comes to questions concerning the motives of the intensely devious and secretive Cyon; but if there is any substance at all to the evidence of some sort of connection between him and the French general staff; then one must note that the hand of the French military was also not uninvolved in the concealed pressures which, carefully circumventing the more cautious and peaceable Giers, impelled the Tsar to this momentous change of course.

On the 3rd of December, one week after Laboulaye's presentation of credentials, the Freycinet cabinet, the parliamentary support for which had for some time been becoming increasingly fragile, fell from office. The reasons lay solely in the complexities of French domestic politics. No one in the Assemblée Nationale seems to have given even as much as a thought to whatever foreign political effects such a change of government might have. Indeed, taking note of the total primacy conceded to domestic political considerations by the French legislators, and of their pervasive indifference to the external effects of their own political actions, the historian can do no less than recognize that Alexander III had substantial grounds for his doubts as to the steadiness and reliability of the various rapidly changing French governments as possible partners in an international alliance.

Since no questions of external policy were at issue in the events leading to Freycinet's fall, this development had no significance from the standpoint of the views of the French public and its parliamentary representatives on Franco-Russian relations. It did, however, mean a change of personalities at the head of the conduct of foreign affairs in Paris; and this was by no means without significance.

The fall of Freycinet brought to an end a stage in the Franco-Russian relationship which may be said to have coincided roughly with the year 1886; and it opened the door for a new phase. This phase was marked, first, by a greater readiness on the part of Alexander III to contemplate a strengthened relationship with France, and, secondly, by the presence at the head of the French Embassy at Petersburg of a man who, while no more popular with the Tsar personally than his predecessor had been, was less controversial in the light of French parliamentary opinion and more skilled in those patient arts of professional diplomacy by which, and by which alone, in the circumstances of that day, a further development of Franco-Russian relations could be successfully pursued.

Part III

THE REINSURANCE TREATY: GIERS VS. KATKOV

Chapter Twelve

FRANCE IN THE SPECTRUM OF
RUSSIAN FINANCE

Up to the point at which this narrative has now arrived the incentives as well as the impediments to a closer Franco-Russian relationship lay overwhelmingly, in fact almost exclusively, in the political-military field. They were destined to continue to remain primarily there, down to the fall of Tsardom. But beginning with the year 1887 financial and economic considerations began to be a more than negligible factor in this relationship and to affect the behavior of at least some of the persons most prominently involved.

Down to the middle of the nineteenth century Russia was, despite her great size and relative populousness, what would today be called a less developed country. Her economy was based predominantly on agriculture, and on a patriarchically ordered system of agriculture at that. Industry was only rudimentarily developed. Production of consumer goods was still largely in the handicraft stage. Such heavy industry as existed had for the most part been created by the state, for military purposes.

If, despite these circumstances, Russia had contrived throughout the eighteenth and early nineteenth centuries to play the role of a major European Power and to be accepted as such, this was because in these respects she differed only moderately from her western European counterparts, and her greater manpower made up for the relative backwardness of her technology.

All this was significantly changed by the advance of the Industrial Revolution in England and western Europe during the first decades of the nineteenth century. This development, which very drastically transformed certain Western countries, particularly England and Germany, affected Russia, in that first half-century, scarcely at all. The result was the sudden emergence of a much more marked disparity between the Russian and Western economies than that which had prevailed in the past—a disparity, in particular, in just those facets of economic growth which helped to determine military power.

It was the painful experience of the Crimean War that first brought this situation to the general attention of the members of the Russian governing elite. To be sure, except in the field of naval operations, the Crimean War was not a contest in which it was possible for the Western allies to bring fully to bear all those advantages which their superior industrial development would normally have brought them. But the naval superiority alone was partly the product of a superior industrial development, and it made a deep impression on the Russians. The difficulty they experienced in moving troops, arms, and supplies from the central Russian bastion to the shores of the Crimea also brought home to them in the most painful way what severe handicaps were placed on their ability to defend their far-flung frontiers by their lack of modern communications.

For this and other reasons, during the reign of Alexander II that followed the Crimean War they mounted a significant effort at industrialization and an even more intensive program of railway construction—both undertakings carried forward under the encouragement of the state and with its financial help. The industrial development was moderate in scale, especially when compared with that which would later be put in hand by Witte. Adequate statistics are not at hand; but it would probably be safe to say that the industrial plant of the country was roughly doubled over this quarter-century from 1856 to 1881. This was not an inordinate rate of growth by the standards of a later age, but it was not negligible. The rate of railway construction was more impressive. The 750 miles of track that Russia possessed before the Crimean War grew, by the end of Alexander II's reign, to something close to 15,000.

For all of this, of course, capital was required; and this was a requirement not easily met in a country whose indigenous sources of accumulation were few and where there was only the slenderest tradition of private industrial initiative and investment. The major part of the burden of raising this capital came thus to be shouldered, one way or another, by the state. It was a burden that had to be piled on top of the other abnormal burdens the state Treasury was already bearing: notably, the costs of the military efforts of the Crimean and Russo-Turkish Wars as well as the suppression of the Polish uprising of 1863, and also the costs of absorbing and developing the new territories then being opened up on the Central Asian and Far Eastern frontiers of the great and expanding empire.*

* The Crimean War was estimated to have cost Russia 800 million rubles, and the war with Turkey 1,000 million. As will presently be seen, the cost of the two wars alone thus accounted for approximately 30% of the Russian state debt as of the 1880's, and for nearly the entire Russian foreign debt of that time.

The result, not unsurprisingly, was the accumulation of a heavy state debt, partly internal but partly in the form of obligations to foreign creditors. By 1881, this debt amounted to just over 6,000 million rubles, and 6,488 million by 1886.[1] To the servicing of this debt the state was obliged to devote, in 1886, some 264 million rubles, a figure that represented 28 percent of the budgetary expenditures and constituted in fact the largest single item among them, even slightly exceeding the military expenditures, which ran to 257 million rubles. This was a burden of debt payment higher, relatively, at that time than that of any other major country except France. Of this total state indebtedness, approximately 30 percent, a figure somewhere around 2,000 million rubles, was owed to foreigners.*

The forms in which this foreign indebtedness were clothed presented, in their entirety, a pattern of great and bewildering variety. Part of the debt was composed of direct borrowings by the state. Another great part was made up of bonds of private or semi-private Russian companies, which had been guaranteed or bought up by the Russian government, had then been sold abroad, and were now held by foreigners. Of the first of these—the state loans—47 were outstanding as of the 1st of January 1887; of the bond issues—57. The total number of such loans thus ran to over 100. Their terms varied so widely as to constitute a veritable crazy-quilt of external obligation. Interest rates were stipulated at various levels, running from 3 to 6 percent. Some of the loans included lottery features; some did not. Some called for interest and amortization payments in paper rubles, others in silver rubles, still others in foreign currencies, sometimes even in currencies without fixed parities. Similar divergencies existed in the agreed modalities (time and place) for interest payment, for amortization, and for redemption. For some, security had been required; for others, not.

For the Russian Treasury such a hodge-podge of commitments un-

* German holdings of Russian paper at the end of 1886 were generally believed to be worth about 1,200,000 rubles; and René Girault, in his admirable study of French investments in Russia in the subsequent period (*Emprunts et investissements français en Russie, 1887-1914* [Paris: Librairie Armand Colin, 1973], p. 140) cites Élie de Cyon (*Histoire*) as his source for the statement that these German holdings comprised three-fifths of the total. Cyon was not always a reliable authority; but on such matters he was likely to be well informed. Other fragmentary evidence, furthermore, would seem to support the conclusion that the foreign debt amounted, by 1886, to somewhere between 1,500 and 2,200 million rubles, of which (this is Bismarck's own figure) the Germans held some 1,200 million.

Eugène Calschi, in his doctoral thesis (1963) on *Les relations financières entre la France et la Russie de 1886 à 1892* (available in the Bibliothèque de la Sorbonne), gave the figure of the external indebtedness for 1886 as 2,210 million rubles.

avoidably presented great inconvenience and considerable unnecessary expense. It was difficult to calculate the real amount of existing indebtedness or to anticipate future requirements. Even the experts found difficulty in gauging the totality of the demands with which the Treasury might expect to be faced at any given time. In addition to this, many of the outstanding issues carried relatively high interest rates, either because this was so stipulated in the respective instruments of indebtedness or by consequence of the rates at which the obligations were discounted in foreign markets.

It was only natural, in these circumstances, that the thoughts of Nicolas Bunge, who from 1881 to 1886 held the office of minister of finance, should have turned to the possibility of one or more large operations of conversion, whereby the heterogeneity of small loans with varying terms could be converted into a much smaller number of large loans with uniform terms, longer periods of amortization or repayment, and, accordingly, lower rates of interest. It was estimated that in this way a saving of something upwards of 10 million rubles could be effected in the annual cost of the debt servicing. The reduction in the number of loans outstanding could be expected, furthermore, to ease the administrative and accounting burdens of the Treasury and to facilitate fiscal planning for the future.

Exploration of these possibilities in official Russian circles began as early as 1885 and was even more seriously pursued in 1886, as a consequence of the depression of the prices for Russian securities on the Berlin and other west European exchanges which took place in that year. On the 23rd of February, 1886, the Council of State formally charged the minister of finance with the task of endeavoring to work out agreements with foreign banking circles along this line. Talks were at once put in hand with Adolf von Hansemann, head of the Berlin Discontogesellschaft—a house which had taken a prominent part in arranging early Russian state loans, notably that of 1883. Hansemann visited Petersburg in early 1886, and the matter was evidently discussed with him at that time. It was hoped that he might be able to form a consortium, to include not just the major German banks but also certain of the French *établissements de crédit*, for the arrangement of conversion of Russian securities on a major scale.* For reasons the exact nature of which is not apparent but which probably included political hesitations

---

* The French chargé d'affaires at Petersburg reported (April 24, 1886) that while the London Rothschilds were unwilling to participate in this proposed conversion, they would, in view of certain modifications recently introduced by the Russian government in its treatment of the Jews, not oppose the undertaking (French Archives. File: *Russie, 1886*, Vol. 273).

on Bismarck's part as well as the competing issuance of a major French state loan at just that time, nothing came of these consultations; and their failure, followed as it was by a further sharp decline in the prices for Russian securities on the Berlin exchange, was seized on by Bunge's enemies, who included Katkov and others of the nationalist, high-tariff lobby, as one more ground (there were already several others) for criticism of his handling of the Finance Ministry.

The chosen candidate of Katkov and his friends for the replacing of Bunge at the Finance Ministry was Ivan Alekseyevich Vyshnegradski. A strong conservative and nationalist, former university professor, stockholder and board member of a number of prominent Russian companies, Vyshnegradski was reputed to be a high protectionist. At the beginning of 1886 he had been appointed (apparently in response to pressures from Katkov and the minister of the interior, Dmitri Tolstoi) a member of the State Council; and throughout the remainder of the year rumors of his forthcoming appointment as finance minister were rampant in the Russian capital.

It was claimed by Cyon, who professed to have it directly from Hansemann, that in the final weeks of 1886 Vyshnegradski, already privately assured of his appointment, spent some weeks in Berlin in the offices of the Discontogesellschaft, familiarizing himself with the modalities of international finance in that city.* One could think it more likely, if he did indeed visit Berlin at that time, that the purpose of his visit was to see, in anticipation of the responsibilities he was about to assume, whether the impediments that had caused the failure of the earlier effort to arrange a conversion through the Discontogesellschaft could not be overcome. However that may be, his appointment as finance minister took effect on the 1st of January 1887, and was generally regarded as a triumph for the high-tariff lobby and the nationalist cause. It took its place, therefore, among the series of blows that were falling just at that time, as will presently be seen, on the shoulders of the hard-pressed Giers.

The opening of the year 1887 thus found Russia with a new finance minister, charged—like his predecessor—with the task of seeking the large-scale conversion of Russia's foreign indebtedness, but uncertain as to how and where he should approach this task and evidently far, as yet, from any thought of turning to the Paris financial marts as the

---

* Cyon, *Histoire*, p. 237. Cyon was by the time he wrote his book, a bitter enemy of Vyshnegradski; and his purpose in relaying this tale was evidently to throw suspicion on the latter as a person closely connected with the Germans; but, open as he was to correction by Hansemann and Vyshnegradski, he is hardly likely to have taken the tale out of thin air.

solution to his problem. Conclusive evidences of his thinking at that time are lacking; but the skimpy available evidence suggests two aspects of it, both of which militated against any early and serious consideration of the possibility of arranging such conversions primarily through the French. The first was his belief that the Rothschilds, offended by the treatment of Russia's Jewish population at the hands of the Russian authorities, were not to be had for such an undertaking, whereas without their active collaboration and participation no operation of this nature could be successfully carried through in Paris at all. The second, less clearly documented but suggested by much of his behavior, was the recognition that the prevailing low prices for Russian securities made that particular moment a bad one for the arrangement of their conversion, and that it was therefore first necessary to get on with fiscal measures designed both to strengthen the Russian currency and to bolster the quoted prices for the securities. Both of these considerations appear to have rendered him, as we shall shortly see, somewhat resistant to the suggestion that the process of conversion should be pushed energetically forward at that juncture, and quite skeptical of the chances for arriving at any satisfactory arrangement with the Paris bankers, in particular.

In the pattern of Russia's commercial and financial relations with the outside world during the reign of Alexander II and through the first half of the 1880's, it was Germany that took overwhelmingly the first place. In the late 1870's imports from Germany made up around 44 percent of total Russian imports. The corresponding figure for Russian exports to Germany was 34 percent.[2] These exports, including as they did about one-fifth of the total Russian grain production, assumed a very prominent place in the Russian economy. In addition to this, the German market had by 1886 absorbed, as we have seen, somewhere between 60 and 80 percent of Russian foreign borrowing. Berlin, in particular, had been the source of the most recent large-scale Russian state loans: one in 1877 and another in 1883. Finally, the economies of the two countries were somewhat intertwined by virtue of their respective possession of parts of the divided Poland: by the prominence, that is, in the Russian part of it, of numbers of German landowners and industrialists, and by the presence, in the German part, of large numbers of workers and small farmers, mostly Polish or Jewish in ethnic origin but Russian in citizenship. In the period up to the mid-1870's the economic activities of these groups had proceeded without placing any great strain on relations between the two governments. But in subsequent years, probably largely as a consequence of the Russification policies of the Russian government, this had begun to change.

Of the three main areas of involvement just mentioned, it was the border problems that were the least important from the standpoint of relations between the governments. But they were not negligible. Out of the 1,191 industrial enterprises in Russian Poland 296 were owned by foreigners, mostly Germans, as was some 2.2 percent of the agricultural acreage. Altogether, there were some 450,000 Germans living on the Russian side of the line. Not only did their presence there conflict with the policy of Russification of the area, but it was evidently the cause of some anxiety to Russian military and police authorities charged with the security of a border region constantly agitated by military espionage efforts of one sort or another. It also presented a natural target for demonstrations of chauvinistic fervor on the part of the anti-German Panslavs and other nationalists.

Friction over these problems increased significantly in the mid-1880's. The French Embassy at Petersburg found it serious enough to warrant calling the attention of the French government to it in mid-1885. And as the year 1887 began, it found the Russian government preparing to take sharp measures (the first of a series of *Ukazy* (imperial decrees) along this line would be issued on the 24th of May 1887) to restrict German activity, notably the ownership and use of industrial or agricultural property, in the border region. Alone, these frictions over Poland would not have been enough to trouble significantly the relations between the two governments. Combined, however, with other sources of trouble, they played a perceptible part in the general pattern of deteriorating German-Russian economic relations that marked the mid-1880's.

Among these other sources of trouble, the most serious was the perennial problem of import tariffs. Over roughly the first twenty years of the rule of Alexander II both Russian and German governments pursued low-tariff policies, and such small duties as were levied on each other's exports presented no serious problem. Among the many unhappy consequences of the war with Turkey, however, was the beginning of a change in this fortunate situation. As the possibility of Russia's involving herself in such a venture began, in 1876, to loom seriously on the horizon, the Russian finance minister of the day, M. Kh. Reutern, did his best to warn the Tsar of the deplorable consequences which this could be expected to have on Russia's finances. Finding his warnings ignored and the attack on Turkey now (in early 1877) a virtual certainty, he then proceeded to protect the interests of the Russian Treasury as best he could: by insisting that customs duties should be collected from that time on in gold. This had the effect of increasing, by a factor of something between 30 and 50 percent, the prevailing Russian duties—a change which, in view of the prominence of Germany in Russian import trade, fell heavily on the Germans.

This move was followed shortly by Reutern's own resignation, and by the general deterioration of Russo-German relations that occurred in the aftermath of the war with Turkey; and these developments, combined with certain internal-political changes in Germany, caused the Germans, in their turn, to go over to a new and more aggressive tariff policy. In 1879 there began a series of increases in German customs duties which served, ultimately, to affect Russian interests quite severely. Most onerous were the successive increases in the duties levied on imports of Russian grain—increases totaling 400 percent in the years from 1879 to 1885 alone (from 1 mark to 5 marks a hundredweight). These increases, designed to protect German landlords from Russian competition, served finally to produce a 50 percent drop in grain imports from Russia in the year 1886 alone.

Russian duties on German goods, conversely, continued to rise throughout this same period. The demands for these increases came primarily from the textile manufacturers of the central Russian region and from the mining and machine-building entrepreneurs of the Urals and south Russia. With strong support from Katkov and the other nationalist editors, these circles came to constitute a powerful and effective high-tariff lobby, operating in large measure through the respective trade and professional associations.

In 1885-1886, pressures from these quarters rose to a point where they finally produced a small crisis of decision for the Russian government. The association of the leaders of the Russian metallurgical industry, convening in November 1885, demanded further increases in duties on imports of pig iron and heavy machinery—both of them items imported largely from Germany. The German government, made aware of these demands, responded in the spring of 1886 by warning the Russian authorities that Germany would retaliate with further increases in her own duties if this demand of the Russian industrialists was acceded to. The Russian moderates—Giers, Bunge, and Peter Shuvalov, among others—threw the weight of their influence into the scales against any yielding to the demands of the industrialists. They succeeded in forestalling action along this line by insisting that the question be submitted for decision to the Council of State, which was not scheduled to reconvene before the autumn. To the anger and disgust of Katkov and his associates, the matter thus lay dormant over the summer and was not taken up by the Council of State before the final weeks of the year 1886. But then, the Council's deliberations on this subject were interrupted by the change at the Finance Ministry. Vyshnegradski, taking over at the Ministry on the 1st of January 1887, was evidently given time to study the matter and formulate his own recommendations. And there, as the new year began, the matter rested.

From the standpoint of the German government, none of this was reassuring. It was generally taken for granted that Vyshnegradski's influence would come down (as indeed it soon did) on the side of further tariff increases. German exports to Russia, meanwhile, were continuing to fall rapidly. Russian exports to Germany, on the other hand, despite the decline in grain shipments, were holding up very well.* In the face of these developments sharp differences began to arise in the German Foreign Office over the question as to whether German interests could best be served by conciliatory policies towards Russia in the economic field or by an outright trade war in which the full weight of Germany's formidable economic power would be mobilized to teach the Russians the dangers of challenging Germany on this level.

These various sources of friction began, by 1886, to have their effect on German policies in the financial field as well. It is clear that Bismarck had by this time entertained serious doubts about the desirability of continuing to give official German support to the maintenance of Russian credit on the Berlin exchange. Only recently, in 1883, he had exerted his own personal influence, through his banker, Baron Bleichröder, and the Seehandlung (the Prussian state bank), to ensure the successful floating on the Berlin market of the last of the Russian state loans to be placed there—a loan of 300 million marks, at a stipulated rate of 5 percent.† The operation had left a bad taste in everyone's mouth. Bleichröder had fallen under suspicion of having taken a secret and illicit personal commission on it; and the Russian nationalists, arguing that the terms were too favorable to the Germans, made it the subject of further attacks on Bunge.

In the period between then and 1886, an interval marked by the Bulgarian crisis and the obviously growing power of the anti-Austrian and anti-German faction in Russia, Bismarck had been unable to detect any signs of appreciation on the official Russian side for the trouble he had given himself in connection with the recent loan. In addition, he

* In the period from 1880 to 1890, Russian exports to Germany rose from 331.4 to 542 million marks (Kumpf-Korfes, *Bismarcks "Draht nach Russland,"* p. 128).

† This loan was placed largely but not exclusively in Berlin. One of the participants in the consortium that handled it was the Paris house of the Danish banker, Hoskier, who was to play a considerable role, some five years later, in opening up the Paris market to Russian borrowing. (See below, Chapter 21.)

had keenly in mind the fact that nationalist pressures in Russia were beginning to undermine prospects for renewal of the *Dreikaiserbund* upon its forthcoming expiration in 1887; and he had very little confidence in the future of any German-Russian relationship that would be devoid of this, or an equivalent, political basis. In the face of these circumstances, he was beginning to wonder whether the large German holdings of Russian paper did not already constitute a serious overcommitment, which it would be wise to reduce rather than to expand. The amount of these holdings, as he pointed out, was roughly equivalent to the entire savings-bank deposits of the state of Prussia. Finally, he was compelled to ask himself whether, the steady expansion of German credit to Russia having evidently failed to make the Russian government aware of its stake in good relations with Germany, a partial denial, or retraction, of this credit might not have a more favorable political effect.

There were two ways in which such doubts and misgivings on the part of Bismarck and his associates at the Foreign Office could find practical expression. One was the withdrawal of their behind-the-scenes support for the prices of Russian securities already being traded on the Berlin exchange. The other was the denial of further credit to Russia. The first of these devices was somewhat hesitantly tried, with the result that these securities, as well as the Russian ruble, began to decline in value from about March 1886, the securities suffering a loss of approximately 7 percent during the remainder of the year, despite vigorous efforts from the banking side to support their prices.

As for the extension of further credit: the Russians, as we have just seen, were at this time more interested in converting old debts than in incurring new ones; and the question of further credit arose, therefore, really only in connection with the proposals for aid in conversions. But even here, the Germans were no longer prepared to go very far out of their way to be helpful. We have already had occasion to note the failure of the effort undertaken in the spring of 1886 to arrange a major conversion through the agency of Hansemann and the Discontogesellschaft. There can be no question but that this failure was heavily influenced by Bismarck's reluctance to support the enterprise. A second effort appears also to have been made towards the close of the year—presumably by Vyshnegradski, this time, on the occasion of his visit to Berlin—but this, too, if it occurred at all, was obviously unsuccessful.*

The beginning of the year 1887 thus found the Russians frustrated in

* It should be noted that this denial of further German lending to Russia was only a part of a general curtailment of German foreign lending in progress at that time. The proportion of foreign investment with relation to total German investment declined from 86% in 1886 to 61% in 1887.

their effort to make further use of the German market as a source of credit, and seriously worried over the fall in the values there both of their securities and their currency. The depressed prices for their securities even damaged the chances for their borrowing on favorable terms anywhere else but in Germany; for new issues would, in the face of this depressed market for the old ones, have been heavily discounted. It was in the face of this situation that the new finance minister, Vyshnegradski, evidently felt, as noted above, that the task of first priority was to build up the Russian government's holdings of gold or its equivalent in foreign exchange, and only then to proceed in all seriousness to see what could be done to effect the necessary conversions.

It is important, before leaving the subject of these economic and financial difficulties, to recognize that while they might be to some extent the products of political tension between the two governments, they were only in small degree, if at all, the sources of it.

One searches in vain through the entire diplomatic correspondence of the years from the Russo-Turkish War to 1887 for any signs that economic or financial problems played an appreciable part in shaping the political relationship between Russia and Germany. Bismarck occasionally encouraged German economic measures moderately irritating to the Russians, as a means of making the latter aware of the inconvenience of incurring German displeasure. But he was always ready to abandon these pinpricks in return for even a mild improvement of the political atmosphere. His public position on the relationship of economic and financial problems to political issues was clearly set forth in the opening passages of the memorandum of guidance which he prepared for the Kaiser in preparation for the latter's meeting with the Tsar on the 18th of November 1887 (see Chapter 19, below).[3] "Nous sommes loin de nous plaindre," Bismarck wrote, on that occasion,

des mesures douanières et legislatives qui portent atteinte aux intérêts materiels des Allemands. Ce sont des questions de politique intérieure que chaque Gouvernement doit regler selon sa convenance. Ces différends de douane et autres ont toujours existé, depuis 60 et 70 ans, sans infirmer notre intimité politique et personelle. ["We are far from complaining of the tariff and legislative measures affecting the material interests of Germans. They are questions of domestic policy which every government has to regulate in accordance with its own convenience. These differences over customs and other such matters have always existed—as much as 60 or 70 years back—without disturbing our political or personal intimacy."]

Had the behavior of the Russian government in the political field been reassuring at that particular time, which it was not, Bismarck would not have attached such importance as he did to the economic and financial difficulties in question and would have continued to use his influence, as he had used it in earlier years, to alleviate such sources of tension. It was the fact of their superimposition upon political anxieties of the most serious nature that gave these questions the importance which, as of the beginning of 1887, they appeared to have.

While relations between Germany and Russia in the economic and financial fields were being thus troubled, France was—figuratively speaking—standing by with a pattern of conditions singularly favorable to the prospects for her replacing Germany, if she should ever wish to, as the principal center for Russian borrowing.

There was, first of all, the volume and nature of French private savings. In comparison with other European countries, wealth, in France, was widely distributed. Great landed fortunes were rare; and so were great private accumulations of capital. By and large, on the other hand, the French were a frugal people; and the accumulation of small savings in the hands of individuals was favored both by custom and by certain of the social institutions governing French life. The result was the existence, in the France of that day, of a host of small savers, whose savings represented, potentially, a major source of investment capital. Something of this capability had been revealed by the success of the state loans issued to cover the indemnity payments to the Germans after the Franco-Prussian War. The French bankers had not failed to note the implications of this success from the standpoint of the French capacity for foreign investment generally; and by the 1880's this source had in fact already been extensively tapped, but only in small degree for Russia.

To support this abundance of investment capital, actual and potential, there was a relative dearth of opportunities for investment within France itself. The French economy was one marked by a relatively slow growth of industry and a small domestic capital market. Much of industry was still operated out of family resources, often on a semi-handicraft technological base. Communes and municipalities tended to borrow directly, where necessary, from the state-controlled credit institutions rather than to put out bonds of their own. Domestic prime rates of interest, furthermore, were extremely low, averaging little over 3 percent and never rising as high as 4 percent during the entire period from 1870 to 1914.[4] French securities sold, to be sure, at somewhat higher interest rates, averaging 4.5 percent in 1873; but foreign securities paid still better—5.5 percent on the average; and this difference was sufficient to give them a distinct advantage in the eyes of the French investor.

Finally, France was by this time equipped with a banking system singularly well designed to arrange the tapping of these private savings for investment purposes. The most celebrated of the French banking institutions were, of course, the great family houses known by such names as Rothschild, Hottinguer, and Vernes, forming collectively what was generally called *la haute banque*. They operated in considerable measure with their own capital, did not generally provide banking facilities for the small depositor, particularly outside Paris, and were not given, as a rule, to the floating of loans on the domestic market. They had been, in earlier decades, the dominant figures in the world of international finance. But there had now grown up side by side with them, particularly in the period of the Second Empire, other institutions, known collectively as *les établissements de crédit*, which were well constituted to perform the task of eliciting investment capital from the small saver. These latter, of which the Crédit Lyonnais and the Comptoir National d'Escompte were only two of the most prominent, were in a favorable position to provide working capital, to act as intermediaries between smaller French banks and major foreign borrowers, to advise the smaller investor, and, finally, to get securities into his hands.

These circumstances had combined to produce a situation in which, by 1886, the purchase of foreign securities had become for the French something like a national habit. Russia had not been wholly neglected in the indulgence of this habit. Up to the mid-1870's such participation as had been forthcoming from Paris in the international lending to Russia had come almost exclusively from *la haute banque*, above all, the Rothschilds; but by that time the *établissements de crédit* were eager to break this monopoly, and the events of the late 1870's—notably the Anglo-Russian political tensions over relations with Turkey, which estranged the London Rothschilds from dealings with Russia, and the problem presented by the growing problem of the treatment of the Jews in Russia—favored this purpose. When, in 1877, the Mendelssohn Bank, of Berlin, acting in conjunction with certain Dutch banks and one French one (the Comptoir d'Escompte) arranged a major loan of 300,000,000 marks to the Russian Treasury, several other French banks participated (at handsome profit) in the marketing of the Russian obligations by which the loan was secured. In addition to this, there was a certain amount of direct French investment in Russian mining and industrial enterprises.

The success of the prominent French participation in the 1877 loan (the French actually put up two-thirds of the initial "advance") whetted the appetites of the *établissements de crédit*, and stimulated the Crédit Lyonnais to open in Petersburg in 1878 the first, and for many years the only, branch of a foreign bank in Russia.[5] The undertaking, for which there was no precedent, fell victim to the usual vicissitudes that attend pioneer ventures, and was brought to completion only after overcoming (partly by the judicious greasing of a number of expectant palms) the numerous obstacles imposed by Russian custom and by the habitual obstructions of the Petersburg bureaucracy.* The possibilities for usefulness of the establishment were severely limited, furthermore, by the insistence of the imperious master of the Crédit Lyonnais, Henri Germain, that the branch should not engage in the normal functions of commercial banking, such as loans to Russian industrial enterprises, but should serve primarily just as an observation post, cultivating local contacts and watching vigilantly for an opportunity for the bank to take the lead in what he envisaged as *un gros affaire*: a major loan to the Russian government. Thus, the little office was forced to lead, for years to come, a dim and largely inactive existence, from which more than one of its early directors retired, voluntarily, in frustration. The frustration must have been particularly severe in 1884 when the Germans, acting with Bismarck's blessing and presumably with that of the Rothschilds as well, walked off with the only major external Russian loan of the early 1880's, leaving the Petersburg representatives of the Crédit Lyonnais to further years of inactivity. But Germain stuck to his guns, and the office was retained, to live on into the changed situation which the end of the decade was finally to produce.

Thus, the French involvement in Russian governmental finance remained, down through 1886, at a relatively subdued level. The total French investment in Russia as of that year, including industrial investment as well as holdings of Russian obligations, has been estimated at 1,500,000 francs, or approximately 9.4 percent of total French foreign

* Bouvier (*Crédit Lyonnais*, p. 757, n. 1) gives a colorful description of the opening of this branch office, marked by a ceremonial dinner at which the French Ambassador, General Le Flô, and a number of Russian financial dignitaries were in attendance. The local French-Protestant pastor, Crottier (himself a wealthy man), toasted *le commerce de Saint Pétersbourg* and invoked God's blessing on the activities of the new establishment. But a Russian clerical dignitary, also duly invited, arrived accompanied by two uninvited deacons who evidently perceived in the proffered refreshments the first of the divine blessings, insisted on being seated at table, ate and drank for ten, and then proceeded to store away in the ample pockets of their clerical robes what they had been unable to consume on the spot. This must have been the first of many reminders to the first director of the office, Cellérier, that Petersburg, despite its great palaces and avenues, was not Paris.

investment of that day.[6] Of the total foreign borrowing by the Russian state, the French participation could not have exceeded 15 percent as compared with the 60 percent share of the Germans.

It is also important to recognize that such interest as was taken by the French banks in Russian business, up to 1887, flowed solely from commercial, not from political, motives. Even in the case of the Crédit Lyonnais, one searches in vain for any evidence that Germain's unfailing interest in seeing his bank become a major financier for the Russian government reflected any motives other than purely pecuniary ones. The same was true of the other French bankers. A Franco-Russian alliance was not, in those years, a serious prospect. What the bankers were interested in was the making of money, not the weaning of Russia from her ties to Germany. It was left to the diplomats and the generals to dream of warping Russia to France's side some day by the creation of a web of financial obligations.

And the diplomats and generals did so dream. Even as early as 1880 we find Eugène-Melchoir de Vogüé, future translator and introducer of Russian literature to the French public and at that time secretary of the French Embassy at Petersburg, chatting with his chief, General Chanzy, on this subject, and afterwards attributing to the general, in his diary notes,[7]

> . . . vues assez justes sur l'intérêt qu'il y a à rattacher ce pays [i.e., Russia]
> au nôtre, avant tout essai d'accord, par les seuls liens qui comptent
> aujourd'hui, des liens financiers. Pour cela, émission d'emprunts russes en
> France, substituée a l'Angleterre comme banquier de la Russie; puis
> expansion des capitaux français dans les entreprises russes. On ne se
> connaîtra, on ne se liera qu'à ce prix. [". . . fairly sound views about the
> advantage for us of attaching that country to our own, even in advance
> of any political understanding, by the only bonds that count, these days:
> namely the financial ones. For this purpose: placing of Russian loans
> in France, the latter taking England's place as Russia's banker. Only at
> this price will the two countries learn to know each other and to become
> connected."]

De Vogüé's impression that the English were then the bankers of Russia was, of course, erroneous. They had been, prior to the Crimean War, but were no longer. This, let it be repeated, was early in the game—1880. Obviously, discussion of such possibilities languished during the doldrums that followed Gambetta's fall—the years 1882-1885. But by 1886 things were changing: Cyon, on May 17 of that year, included among his reports for the *Moskovskie Vyedomosti* one vaunting the great success of the French internal state loan just issued, and pointing to this success as evidence of the availability in France of great amounts of capital for which, at the moment, there was no adequate outlet.* And if the French Embassy in Petersburg did not specifically mention, in its reports on Russian plans for debt conversion, the possibility of France's becoming the major source of support for such operations, one may be sure that the thought was never wholly absent from the minds of its senior officials.

We see then, altogether, that the circumstances of the turn of the year 1886-1887 were in several respects favorable to a major change in Russia's financial relationships with western Europe. The Germans were disillusioned in their earlier efforts to bind Russia tightly to their side by indulging her and helping her in the economic-financial field. They were finding in their own domestic market safer and more advantageous opportunities for investment than those that presented themselves abroad. The future of their own relationship with Russia was beginning to appear increasingly uncertain; and the incentives to reduction of their financial commitment to the Russians were beginning to loom larger in their eyes than any conceivable advantages of its increase. France, on the other hand, was waiting in the wings, armed with abundant potential reserves of investment capital, equipped with a banking system excellently designed to discover this capital and make it available to Russian borrowers, and increasingly vulnerable, as her own military power increased, to the insidious suggestion that if only Russia's political ties to Germany could be loosened, and the freedom of Russia's hand restored, the power of French finance could be used to assure Russia's support for France in a future Franco-German war.

* Cyon claimed, in his *M. Witte et les finances russes* (Paris: [Chamerot & Renouard, 1895], pp. XXI-XXII) to have been the first to perceive of the possibility of switching the market for French securities to Paris. The claim was, of course, as we have just seen, inaccurate.

Chapter Thirteen

BISMARCK'S ANXIETIES

The preceding chapters have afforded numerous examples of the fact that throughout the period under review the Franco-Russian relationship was in large measure a function of the relationship between Russia and Germany. Only to the extent that the latter relationship might be weakened could the former be strengthened—strengthened, at least, beyond a certain point. For Russian statesmanship, Germany was of outstanding importance, not only because of her geographical position and her dominant role in Russian trade but also because her diplomacy was a crucial factor in Russia's relationship to Austria; and Austria was at that time, in the eyes of the Tsar and of a great many other Russians as well, including outstandingly the military and the Panslavs, Russia's greatest problem.

The weeks following Laboulaye's presentation of credentials in late November 1886 were a period of uncertainty, nervousness, and barely concealed crisis in Russo-German relations. The Tsar, as we have seen, was now in a state of great bewilderment and frustration over Bulgaria. Aware that the Kaulbars mission had been his last political card, he could see no further solution to the problem other than a military occupation of the country, to which for various reasons he was averse, or another clandestine operation, aimed this time at the removal of the Regency, along the lines of that successfully mounted against Battenberg. For this last, he authorized the undertaking of preparations (we shall see at a later point with what results); but he did so with little confidence of success. He recalled, no doubt, that it was not really the action resulting in Battenberg's initial expulsion that had caused his final departure from Bulgaria—rather, only shattered nerves and a tactical error on the Prince's part at a later stage; nor had this outcome worked any great improvement, from the Russian standpoint, in the Bulgarian situation.

Again, as in the past, the Tsar found it impossible to believe that the failure of the Kaulbars mission could really have occurred had not Bismarck wished it to occur. Much of Europe was now swayed by the belief that not a sparrow could fall in the forest of European diplomacy but that Bismarck had willed it so. This thesis had a particular appeal to the Tsar because it relieved him of the sole responsibility for the deplorable consequences of his own blunders. Surely, he reasoned, Bismarck could have done more than he did to prevent the recent trend of events: he could have put more pressure on the Austrians; with Austrian help he could have intimidated the Bulgarian Regency into accepting Kaulbars' demands and shaping its conduct accordingly; he could have compelled the Austrians to agree to accept an eventual Russian occupation of Bulgaria, instead of making unpleasant noises about it. Well, if Bismarck was unwilling to bring the Austrians into line, perhaps Russia would have to do this herself. And perhaps, as Katkov was arguing, she would have better chances for doing this if she could exploit the ever-present phenomenon of Franco-German tension, with a view to diverting German military attention and effort to the west, so that Austria would be effectively deprived of her only real ally, and would stand alone in the face of Russian pressure. But would not Russia be in a better position to do this if, as Katkov was also arguing, she first freed herself from the entanglements of the *Dreikaiserbund* and recovered what Katkov described, so enticingly, as a "free hand"?

There were limits, of course, as Giers was constantly pointing out, to the distance you could go along this path. Of course, Alexander would have agreed, one must not court war prematurely with a Germany still headed by the loyal and chivalrous old Kaiser, the uncle of one's own father (a Germany that was too strong for Russia anyway, unless Russia had France with her); and of course one could not ally oneself formally with the kaleidoscopic procession of political mountebanks that marched across the face of French political life in the guise of foreign ministers and premiers. But Katkov was demanding neither of these things—he was demanding only that one free oneself from the humiliating and restricting "friendship" of Bismarck. At the very least (and this had been clear ever since the failure of the Kaulbars mission) one could decline to renew the *Dreikaiserbund*, as a tripartite arrangement, when it came up for renewal the following June.

It was with such thoughts, coupled with a real fear that by cultivating the tie to Germany he might offend nationalist sentiment in the Russian official and journalistic establishments, and not least in the opinions of the formidable Ober-Prokuror Pobedonostsev, that Alexander struggled through the autumn of 1886, not fully committing himself either way but leaning increasingly to the Katkov view as the poison of frustration and humiliation over Bulgaria ate its way into his opaque and not uncomplicated psyche.

Natural as all this was, it was equally natural that the increasing evidences of it should be highly disturbing to Bismarck. Far from being conscious of any failure to bring sufficient pressure to bear on the Austrians, he felt that he had already brought all of such pressure that the German-Austrian relationship would stand, and more than was really justified. The urgings he had given to the Austrians to respect Russian interests in Bulgaria were too numerous to count. The failure of the Austrians to give full acceptance to these urgings was a source of annoyance to him, but he could not jeopardize the entire Austro-German relationship by pressing the issue further. It meant too much for him. An estranged Austria would be a natural ally for the French. With such an estrangement his whole system of alliances would collapse, and Germany would find herself effectively in isolation. He would do what was in his power to influence the Austrians behind the scenes; but he could not be expected, as he repeatedly explained to Russian representatives, to be more Russian than the Russians, to make good *all* their blunders, to put himself wholly at their service, and to sacrifice Germany's relationship with Austria for their benefit. He had made it clear to the Russians that he, for his part, would not object to a Russian occupation of Bulgaria, though he hoped it would not occur. What more did they want? That he should make war on Austria and serve Bulgaria up to them on a silver platter? Let them fight their own battles. Bismarck was unable to see how the Russians could fail to understand this. And yet he was obliged, from the midsummer of 1886 on, to witness a whole series of disturbing developments in what was—or appeared to be—Russian policy.

First of all, there were Katkov's editorial of the 30th of July and the series of similar pronouncements, echoed in large part by the remainder of the Russian nationalist press, that followed it. What disturbed Bismarck here was not so much that the respective editors held such views as the fact that the Tsar was so obviously unwilling to forbid the publication of them. He knew that the Tsar, in occasional conversations with Giers or with German representatives, pooh-poohed the importance of these press opinions: it was not these irresponsible scribblers but himself, Alexander claimed, who made Russian policy. But Bismarck was not reassured. If the Tsar really did not approve of these attacks, he could have stopped them.

Then there was the Nouart incident (see above, Chapter 9). Bismarck could not forget that not only had the Russian military attaché, Baron Fredericks, made a speech on this occasion about Franco-Russian brotherhood, but he had done so before a monument (to General

Chanzy) to which was affixed a plaque declaring that it was across the Rhine—that is, in a war against Germany—that French officers were to win their Marshal's batons.

Then, too, there was Déroulède, and his recent journey to the various centers of nationalist and anti-German sentiment in Russia. This last, in particular, stuck in Bismarck's craw. How could the Russians have permitted it? Repeatedly, he caused the question to be put to Russian representatives: how would you have felt—how would your government have reacted—if we had received a known and committed enemy of Russia, Battenberg for instance, and had permitted him to travel around Germany making inflammatory anti-Russian speeches and calling in effect for a German war against Russia?

In themselves, these phenomena were disturbing enough. But they acquired a new level of seriousness with the arrival in Berlin, in the course of that same autumn of 1886, of a flurry of reports concerning alleged Russian feelers in Paris for a Franco-Russian alliance. It may be instructive to note how these reports reached, and affected, the German government. The first of them came from the German Ambassador at Paris, Count Georg Herbert zu Münster, in early October, and was based purely on hearsay. Bismarck, though disquieted and placed on his guard, was inclined to attribute it to the wide-ranging imagination of the well-known and colorful correspondent of *The Times*, Blowitz.* But Münster assured him, in a private letter of the 7th of October,[1] that he was convinced there was some substance in the story. And the whole question was raised to a new order of importance when, at the beginning of November, Münster relayed to the Berlin Chancery a tale, just poured out to him by Freycinet, which, as a source of muddiness in the international exchanges, can rarely have been excelled. After first voicing doubts as to the Tsar's emotional stability and citing, as evidence for this, the latter's reaction to Appert's recall and to the expulsion of the French princes, Freycinet went on to confirm that at the beginning of September 1886, a person in the Tsar's confidence had made to him "proposals which I shall not describe to you in detail, but the nature of which you will easily guess, and which went very far."[2] These proposals, Freycinet added, had been courteously rejected, because he, President Grévy, and the majority of the cabinet, wanted no *politique d'aventures*.

Coming from the lips of none other than the French premier himself, these allegations had to be taken seriously. Bismarck passed them on at

* The reference was to Henri Blowitz (real name: Oppert), a French citizen who functioned as *Times* correspondent in Paris and had, in addition to a wide acquaintanceship in European official circles, a reputation for being privy to many diplomatic secrets.

once to Schweinitz, in Petersburg, with a query as to whether he had any confirmation. Schweinitz replied with an eloquent despatch, expressing his unwillingness to believe that the report could be true. Of course, he wrote, one could not expect from Alexander III the same sort of loyalty and attachment to things German as had marked his father. No reliance could be placed on his emotional reactions, and still less on the disposition of the Empress. But he, Schweinitz, could not believe that the Tsar was putting out feelers to France. This was too contrary to his known interests, aspirations, and instinctive reactions. Alexander III, he wrote,

> ... who is not lacking in the normal talents of a strong character, who has musical talent and a feeling for beauty and more book-learning and knowledge than he shows on the surface, is not rich in ideas, but he holds tightly to those that he has, and does not take the trouble to think them through to their wider consequences.[3]

The Tsar, Schweinitz went on, was interested primarily in the establishment of a Russian position at the door to the Black Sea, that is, the Straits. He had not made up his mind whether it was a key or only a bolt that he wanted to that door—whether only the denial to others of the right of naval entrance or the freedom for Russian warships to move through it to the Mediterranean. For the realization of the first of these aims the French might be helpful. In the case of the second one, they were unlikely to be, since they, too, feared the appearance of a Russian fleet in the Mediterranean. From the standpoint of the improvement of Russia's position at the Straits, Germany was still the most promising source of support. The Tsar, he thought, would not forget that. Bismarck and the old Kaiser both read this despatch from Schweinitz with great attention and accepted it so far as it went, but remained puzzled and not greatly reassured.

Schweinitz took occasion to talk to Giers about the matter on several subsequent occasions. In mid-December he showed to Giers an instruction he had received from Bismarck (on which more will be said later) in which a passing reference was made to the fact that the Germans had learned from Freycinet that Russian approaches had been made in Paris for "a joint anti-German policy." Giers, with whom a copy of the instruction was left, took it to the Tsar and discussed it with him. A few days later, Schweinitz having in the meantime left on a short trip to Germany, Giers received von Bülow, now German chargé d'affaires, and veritably exploded over the allegation. He himself, he said, had been utterly flabbergasted by this report. And the Tsar had been simply unable to understand how the French could put out such a story about him.

Giers was naturally stung by the suggestion, implicit in Freycinet's allegations, that either he had himself been deceiving the Germans or that foreign policy was being made in Petersburg over his head and without his knowledge; and he reacted with a vehemence normally foreign to his character. He returned to the subject more than once in his talks with German representatives over the ensuing weeks and months. Not only did he totally reject even the possibility of anything of this sort ("I will let my head be cut off," he said to Bülow on the 22nd, "if the Emperor has ever made advances to the French"), but he voiced the sharpest resentment of Freycinet's peddling of this cock-and-bull story, and this at a time when Russia, under French pressure, had just resumed regular diplomatic relations with France. "These accursed French," he observed to Bülow, "are a bunch of swindlers; they have no idea how to do business; they mistake every itinerant Russian for a confidential agent of the Emperor and erect a mountain of hopes and dreams on every phrase he utters." Giers was particularly indignant over the suggestion that he was minister in name only. "I do not know," he said, "how long I shall remain in office. But as long as I am the Minister, I know what the Emperor wants."[4]

Once again, one stands helpless before this extraordinary affair. That the Tsar could knowingly have authorized such an approach seems, in the circumstances, incredible. But that someone told the French that he *had* authorized it, or that the French so understood something someone said, seems equally clear. Most probably, the source of the confusion was the itinerant Kumani.* (See above, Chapter 10.) But how Kumani came to perpetrate this confusion—whether by inadvertence or by misunderstanding, or as the working of one of those intrigues now so common in the practice of Russian diplomacy—will probably never be known.

The Germans, in any case, were seriously disturbed by the whole affair. While they evidently allowed themselves to be somewhat reassured by Giers's denials, they remained—particularly Bismarck personally—mystified and mistrustful. The history of Russian diplomacy contained too many examples, as Bismarck was well aware, of double-dealing, of the simultaneous pursuit of conflicting policies by different entities in the Russian structure of power, of the right hand's not knowing what the left was doing, for him to dismiss the episode as being wholly without significance.†

---

* The reader will note Giers' reference, just cited, to "every itinerant Russian." This strongly suggests Kumani.

† "The Russian diplomatic service," Holstein observed in a diary entry of January 26, 1884, "moves about as independently as the maggots in the cheese."

244

All this, together with the other disturbing symptoms in Russian behavior, produced in Bismarck a new distrust of Russian policy which he was never to overcome. From now on he would see in Russia only an unreliable partner, to be closely watched at every turn. But things were made worse by the fact that Russia was not, at that moment, his only problem. He had others—very serious ones—with which the Russian wavering had to be taken in conjunction.

First, there was the obstreperousness of the Austrians in insisting that they had an interest in Bulgaria and in reserving their position with relation to a possible Russian occupation. The effort to avoid complications in Austro-Russian relations had lain at the heart of Bismarck's policy ever since the formation of the German Reich. The present Austrian behavior was jeopardizing this policy. Particularly galling, and even menacing, was the evidence that the Austrians, caught between the anti-Russian pressures of the Hungarians and Bismarck's pro-Russian policies, were choosing for the former, and were thus straining the Austro-German Alliance itself. If the *Dreikaiserbund* was one cornerstone of the Bismarckian policy, the alliance with Austria was the other. The Tsar's vacillations were undermining the first. Vienna's subservience to the Hungarians was now undermining the second; and this appears to have been, for Bismarck, a source of no smaller concern than the unfavorable phenomena on the Russian side.*

Finally, there was the situation that confronted Bismarck on Germany's western border; for it was precisely at this time that the so-called war scare of 1887 was ripening and beginning to play a dominant role in European life.

It is not easy to trace the origins and development of this general state of anticipation and apprehension of a new war between France and Germany which swept over Europe in the final weeks of 1886 and the first months of 1887. It must be recalled that by 1885-1886 the French armed establishment had been essentially restored to what might be called its normal peacetime strength. The effects of the war of 1870 had now been fully overcome. Numerically, the French army alone was now slightly more than the equal of the German. It had in fact only recently received a certain increase in strength by virtue of the return to the French mainland, after the collapse of certain of Ferry's colonial involvements, of units previously stationed overseas, particularly in Indo-China.

---

* Bismarck observed to Peter Shuvalov, in early January, that when he concluded the alliance with Austria, in 1879, he had thought he had to do with a mighty Emperor. He had now to recognize that what he had really done was to ally himself with a Hungarian parliament (F. von Holstein, *Die geheimen Papiere* II, p. 374).

Since the beginning of 1886, furthermore, the flamboyant Boulanger had been in office as French minister of war; and his conduct had left no doubt in anyone's mind of the depth of his commitment both to the general cause of *revanche* and to the idea of a Franco-Russian alliance. Throughout 1886, the German military attaché at Paris, Lt. Col. von Villaume, had been plying Berlin with alarmist reports of Boulanger's aspirations and activities, citing the general's inflammatory speeches, his close relations with Déroulède and other French chauvinists, and the various measures he was putting in hand for the strengthening of the French army. Villaume professed to see in this a serious danger of French action against Germany within the relatively near future.*

The tone of Villaume's reports was strongly contradicted, to be sure, on the civilian side of the German Embassy at Paris. Ambassador Münster correctly pointed out that Boulanger did not represent the French government as a whole; that any warlike plans the general might entertain would be supported neither by the French Parliament, nor by his cabinet colleagues, nor by President Grévy; that his program for development of the French army was one that would take years to complete. Even Count Waldersee, Quartermaster General and Acting Chief of the German General Staff, hot-headed militarist that he was, was disinclined to take Boulanger as seriously as did Villaume, and saw in the French military preparations nothing to justify fears of an early attack.

Bismarck, while not disagreeing with Waldersee's conclusion, took a somewhat different view, flowing partly from his objective judgment, partly from his situation of the moment. Conceding that neither the government then in power in France nor the Parliament wanted war at that time, he nevertheless viewed France as essentially *revanchiste* in spirit; and he considered that the chauvinists, while admittedly a minority, could easily at any time be brought into a position to exercise a decisive influence on events. Germany, he felt, could deal with a French attack if she could concentrate her entire force on the repulsion of it. The French, he had no doubt, must know this. But he was not at all certain of what the French would do in case Germany were to become involved in serious complications on her eastern border. It was largely for this reason that he was so anxious to avoid a conflict between Russia and Austria-Hungary. For while he was determined to do all in his power to avoid German involvement in such a conflict, he was well aware that this would not be easy—that a war of this nature would set up strains for German policy which he might not be able to overcome. In such a contingency no one, he was sure, would be able to restrain

* Villaume, it might be noted, was shortly to be transferred to the German Embassy at Petersburg.

the militaristic and *revanchiste* element in France from carrying the day and leading France into an effort to take advantage of the situation by force of arms.

This was, however, not Bismarck's only reason for reacting sharply, as he did, to the activities of Boulanger and his associates and supporters. While it might well be, as Münster and others claimed, that the measures being put in hand by Boulanger for the strengthening of the French armed establishment were not of such a nature as to presage any early attack, they were still of such dimensions as to call, in Bismarck's eyes and those of the German military leaders, for reciprocal measures of preparation on the German side. This consideration was particularly compelling at a time when the relationship with Russia seemed to be in jeopardy; for it must be remembered that if the French forces were at then only moderately larger than the German ones, the Russian ones were considerably larger than either of them. Just the number of men Russia was maintaining on her western border was about three-fourths that of the entire German army. Together, the French and the Russians had well over double the number of German men under arms and nearly double the German and Austro-Hungarian forces combined.*

In the face of this situation, and with rumors of a Franco-Russian alliance being freely bandied about both in Petersburg and in Paris, one could not afford, as Bismarck saw it, to permit the French alone to

---

* See the article by Michael Howard, "The Armed Forces," Chapter VIII of Volume XI of the *New Cambridge Modern History*.

Exact figures on force levels for any given period are hard to come by; but the following totals of men under arms, distilled from approximately twelve different sources, would not be very wide of the mark:

In standing ground forces, as of 1886

Germany	435,000	France	524,000
Austria-Hungary	285,000	Russia	850,000
	720,000		1,374,000

Potential wartime strength (including reserves)

Germany	2,250,000	France	2,633,000
Austria-Hungary	2,050,000	Russia	2,835,000
	4,300,000		5,468,000

It will be seen from these figures that the French and Russians had nearly double the number of men under arms that the Germans and Austrians had. The situation with respect to reserves also favored the Franco-Russian combination, but less so.

The Russian excuse for keeping so many men under arms, and so large a proportion of them (nearly half) on the western border, was of course the limited nature of Russia's facilities, far inferior to those of the Germans, for rapid mobilization of reserves.

establish even a small margin of real military superiority. Countermeasures were therefore called for.

But this, of course, meant new parliamentary appropriations for the German army; and it was essential, in Bismarck's view, that these be valid for a sufficient span of time to make possible a long-term program of military preparation, running over several years. A corresponding bill, based on the principle of the so-called *Septennat*—that is, to run over seven years—was therefore laid before the German Reichstag on the 26th of November 1886.* But it soon encountered serious opposition on the liberal side of the house; and as of the end of the year 1886 its passage still looked dubious.

In these circumstances, as the crisis over the appropriations bill came to a head at the turn of the year, Bismarck was not averse to permitting the danger of a French attack to appear to the German public, and with it to the Reichstag, as somewhat more real and urgent than it actually appeared to himself and the German military leaders. Hence his tendency—if not to exaggerate in his public statements the danger of a French attack, then at least not to correct the exaggerations appearing in the German press—entered once again, as in 1875, into the shaping of German policy.

In accordance with that law of reciprocal momentum that seems to govern, at all times and in all places, such things as competitive military preparations and professed military fears, these German exaggerations were gleefully received and portrayed on the French-nationalist side as signs that the Germans were themselves planning to launch an attack at an early date, and were only looking for a pretext. And so it went, in the spirit of nationalism and sensationalism that dominated most of the press of that day in both countries. A rousing polemic, each side accusing the other of hostile intent, soon dominated the newspapers on both sides of the line. It was easy, then, for official circles throughout Europe, in a day when wars broke out much more easily than they do in our time, to jump to the conclusion that war was imminent. And again, as in 1875, the fact that neither of the two governments involved wanted war or had any plans whatsoever for initiating it, was neither here nor there.

This was the situation—in Russia, in Austria, and in France—that Bismarck faced, as the year 1886 came to an end; and it is easy to understand that he must have seen in it a real danger not only to his policies of the moment, in the narrower sense, but to the entire system

* The appropriations called for by this bill envisaged an increase of some 7.4% —to 470,000 men—in the standing army.

of international relations which he had created in Europe and on which, as he (with good reason) saw it, the peace of the continent depended. Such a conclusion called for preventive action; and he was not slow to take it.

To the Austrians, in the first place, he made it brutally clear that while Germany was prepared, in loyalty to the Austro-German Alliance of 1879, to defend them against a direct Russian attack or a Russian attempt to move into Balkan territory west of Bulgaria, it would not support them in any resistance they might mount to anything the Russians might do in Bulgaria. If they were to initiate action against Russia merely by way of reaction to nothing more than a Russian occupation of Bulgaria, they would have to do so on their own, and at their own risk.

In addition to this, Bismarck set about, quietly and with great skill, to create a situation in which, even if the Russians and the French were to combine against Germany, they would not find support anywhere else. Bearing in mind his principle that in a company of five great European Powers, it was essential always to be one of a grouping of at least three, he skillfully manipulated international events in such a way as to assure that the French and Russians remained, at the most, two. He proceeded to negotiate the renewal of the so-called *Triplice*—the Triple Alliance among Germany, Austria-Hungary, and Italy that had been concluded in 1882, thus depriving the Russians of all hope of Italian support in case of the war with Austria, and making it clear to the French that in the event of a war with Germany, they would also have Italy, such as she was, to deal with. In addition to this, he used his influence effectively to promote a closer *entente* between the British, on the one hand, and the Italians and Austrians, on the other, particularly in Mediterranean problems, thus assuring that in the event of a Russo-Austrian conflict the Russians would be faced, once again, with the threat of hostile action of British naval power in the Aegean and at the Straits, and that Russia would have to face this threat alone—without allies other than, possibly, the French.

As for Russia: shaken as he was, Bismarck pursued a policy of great prudence and reserve, not making an official issue over the various disturbing phenomena, professing continued confidence in the treaty relationship, leaving it to the Russians to say so if they had objections to its renewal, but watching sharply and mistrustfully each evidence of Russian policy.

It was by these principles that the German chancellor's conduct was guided in the rather intensive exchanges of the views between the German and Russian governments that marked the weeks around the turn of the year, and to which we must now briefly turn.

Chapter Fourteen

THE TSAR'S CRISIS OF DECISION

On the 23rd of November 1886, at the end of General Kaulbars' disastrous mission to Bulgaria, Giers sent to the Russian Ambassador at Berlin, Paul Shuvalov, and to other Russian chiefs of mission, an instruction for their guidance, giving the official Russian interpretation of the failure of that mission, affirming the Russian intention to continue efforts to create a more satisfactory situation in Bulgaria, and assuring the other Powers of Russia's "desire" to achieve this goal by peaceful means, if at all possible. Shuvalov was instructed to show this document to the appropriate officials of the German government, but not as a direct communication to them—only as an internal Russian communication they were permitted to see.

Bismarck reacted, in a similarly indirect manner, with an instruction to Schweinitz (December 2) which the latter was likewise authorized to show to Giers. It was a conciliatory statement, recalling the respect Germany had always shown for Russia's special position in Bulgaria, repeating the assurance of Germany's lack of interest in Bulgarian affairs, but pointing out that Germany, in the light of her relations of the moment with France, would not be in a position to take any active steps in support of Russian policies or purposes in Bulgaria.

Giers took this communication and showed it to the Tsar. The latter was generally pleased with it, but authorized a reply in which, although expressing appreciation for Bismarck's position, he once more requested the latter to use his personal influence with the other European Powers (this was a euphemism for Austria) to induce them to give their support to Russia's efforts to create a more satisfactory state of affairs in Bulgaria.[1]

Bismarck was much irritated by this request, the last of many similar ones. He felt he had put all the pressure he could on the Austrians. If he were really to try to please the Tsar, he once observed, nothing would suffice short of Germany's going to war with Austria.

On the day before the despatch of this last message, the Tsar took Schweinitz aside, at a palace ceremony, and spoke to him with much frankness and earnestness about the state of German-Russian relations.

He was obliged to see in the old German Kaiser, he said, Russia's only ally and friend. The Emperor Franz Joseph was all right; personally, he was loyal and reliable; but one could not say the same thing for his government. He, Alexander, would not break the peace. What the Russian papers were writing about Germany was all stupidities; that would soon change. But what they were writing about Austria: that was justified.

Twice during this interview, Schweinitz reported, the Tsar had emphasized that "so long as Kaiser William is alive, we will have no war," but he had made it clear that he had no such confidence in what might happen in the wake of a change in the occupancy of the throne.* Schweinitz tried, of course, to reassure him as to the disposition of the German Crown Prince, but felt that his words did not have any appreciable effect.

What the Tsar said on this occasion about the forthcoming improvement in the treatment of Germany in the Russian press found a certain confirmation, a few days later, when the Russian Foreign Office issued (December 15) a most unusual communiqué, calling the press to order for its treatment of Germany. "Certain papers," it was said, instead of reporting facts, were resorting to guesses and assumptions, deviating from objectivity, and placing themselves in contradiction to the facts. Particularly was this true with respect to the allegations that "the difficulties which hinder a satisfactory solution of the Bulgarian question must be attributed primarily to the clandestine influence of Germany." There followed a strong paragraph about the importance of German-Russian relations and the Russian government's desire for the maintenance of good relations with Germany, as well as its confidence that Germany would "refrain from any measures that could affect either the dignity of Russia or those interests which have grown up as a result of our historic relationship to our co-believers in the East." The communiqué ended with a summons to prudence and coolness of judgment, particularly on the part of "certain press organs whose voice is by no means devoid of importance in international affairs."[2]

The background of this curious document, the only plainly pro-German statement to come from the Russian government in the course of several years and one obviously aimed at Katkov, remains an interesting mystery. Prepared between the 9th of December and the 13th (on which day it went to the printers), just when the Tsar was under the influence of Bismarck's conciliatory reply to his communication about the failure

* Kaiser William was by this time 89 years old. His son, and heir-apparent, the future Frederick III, was generally understood to be strongly anti-Russian, and his wife, Queen Victoria's daughter, even more so.

251

of Kaulbars' mission, it might, on the face of it, be construed as the work of Giers, taking advantage of this momentary improvement in the Tsar's disposition towards Germany. The fall of the French government, together with the Tsar's irritation over Freycinet's allegations about Russian feelers for an alliance in Paris, may also have had something to do with it. In any case, the language went too far—so far that one almost suspects a deliberate act of sabotage, directed against Giers.*

The communiqué infuriated influential Russian opinion. "We have prostrated ourselves before you" and "I hope you're satisfied" were the sort of remarks Schweinitz was obliged to listen to in the ensuing days. Katkov, in particular, refused to publish the document in the *Moskovskie Vyedomosti*. The Tsar was annoyed at this and had his displeasure made known to Katkov through the minister of the interior; but there was (to the indignation of at least one of the grand dukes) no public reprimand.[3] In fact, the communiqué proved, if anything, to be an isolated phenomenon. There was decidedly no follow-up in other manifestations of Russian policy. This was to remain the last halfway friendly statement towards Germany from the Russian side for months and years into the future.

It will be noticed, however, that striking as the document was in its affirmation of a desire for good relations with Germany, it was equally remarkable for its studied omission of any similar sentiments with relation to Austria. Many of the contemporaries saw in this feature its greatest significance. Certain of those who had some knowledge of the existence of the *Dreikaiserbund* even interpreted it, not incorrectly, as the decisive public warning that Russia would not be willing to continue this relationship.

While the above-mentioned exchanges were taking place, Bismarck was working, in his spare moments, on an historical résumé, intended for the eyes of the Tsar. The idea had originated (although the Tsar himself was not aware of the fact) with Count Peter Shuvalov who, meeting Schweinitz at a hunting party in mid-November, had voiced the view that a lot that was unfortunate in the Tsar's attitude towards Germany was the result of his ignorance of the real events of the 1870's, and particularly of the background of the Austro-German Alliance of 1879. "Une remémoration historique," Shuvalov had said, "lui serait très utile."[4]

---

* The evidence suggests, but does not prove, that Giers had obtained the Tsar's consent to the issuance of something along this line but turned the drafting of the document over to someone else (probably Jomini), failed to clear the final text with the Tsar, and let it go out without giving it his own careful consideration.

Bismarck, to whom this conversation was of course reported, was impressed with the suggestion. In early December he drew up, in the privacy of his country home at Friedrichsruh, a long historical résumé, designed to meet this need, and sent it to the German Embassy at Petersburg. Schweinitz showed it to Giers on the 22nd of December. The latter, while conceding its historical accuracy, advised against its submission to the Tsar in the existing form. He recommended certain changes, designed to make it less offensive to the Tsar's known sensibilities. These suggestions, relayed to Berlin, met with Bismarck's agreement. The document was revised accordingly. On the 5th of January it was finally shown to the Tsar by Giers.

Alexander's reaction was curt and ill-humored. "What is said in this document about the past," the monarch grumbled, "is too one-sided." ("He has shared too extensively," Giers later reported to Schweinitz, "the errors of our public opinion to be able to admit without difficulty that these were actually errors.")

To be sure, the monarch, according to Giers, had reaffirmed, in reacting to the document, his commitment to a good relationship with Germany. He had shown understanding, in particular, for the fact that "it was stupid to suppose that by flirting with France we could render Germany better disposed to make concessions to us, as Katkov and his friends believed."[5] But Schweinitz was surely on solid ground when he gave it to his government as his own opinion that Alexander had been exposed to too many falsehoods about German policy since 1878, and was of too slow an intelligence, to be capable of perceiving the correctness of all the points made in the historical résumé. The Tsar's opinions and prejudices, once formed, were not easy to shake.

The question of the renewal of the *Dreikaiserbund* lay, meanwhile, very much on Giers' mind. Six months remained, now, until the expiration of the pact. The war scare in the West, stimulating the French to new hopes of Russian assistance, seemed to Giers to heighten the urgency for clarification of the future of the treaty. Doubts about the fate of the German-Russian relationship were already in the air, and were spreading. The failure to mention Austria in the communiqué of December 15th was leading to a widespread impression that the relationship with the Austrians was damaged beyond repair. A letter had already been received from the ambassador in Berlin, Paul Shuvalov, based on the assumption that the existing tripartite pact could not be renewed, and presenting ideas for a bilateral Russo-German agreement to replace it. It was dangerous to let things go on this way.

Early discussions were therefore, as Giers saw it, in order—with both the Germans and the Austrians. But the difficulty, here, was obviously the Tsar's continuing preoccupation with the situation in Bulgaria. Plainly, Alexander could not be brought to make up his mind about the renewal of the treaty until he could see more clearly some path of exit from the Bulgarian morass. Worried, and finding himself at the end of his own rope, Giers could think of nothing better than to turn to the Germans and Austrians for help. Nothing could be done about the treaty, he told Schweinitz on the 30th of December, so long as the existing Bulgarian "gâchis" endured. Could they not do something about it? A similar communication was made to Wolkenstein, the Austrian Ambassador.

Giers must have known, in his heart, how little promise there was in this effort. It was a confession of helplessness and despair. But it was his last card, and he saw no choice but to play it. A letter was despatched, meanwhile, to Paul Shuvalov (the text of it is not available), obviously telling him to hold his horses—that the time for discussion of a separate pact with the Germans had not yet come.

Two or three days later, reports were received in Petersburg of re- newed agitation, in England and in Bulgaria itself, for a return of Battenberg to the Bulgarian throne. The reports were wholly without substance. There is no evidence where they came from—very possibly it was from the Bulgarian officer-exiles, still hanging about in Petersburg and intriguing wildly for official Russian support. In any case, Giers, while disinclined to credit them, correctly sensed trouble in the fact that such reports were again circulating.

On the 3rd of January, the imperial couple entertained with an eve- ning dramatic performance in the theater of the palace at Gatchina. The cream of Petersburg court society was there. Giers, very unwillingly (because he was in ill health) but having no choice, was obliged to at- tend. While there, he met Peter Shuvalov, brother of the ambassador. Shuvalov happened to mention that he was leaving the next day for Berlin to spend the Russian New Year's holiday (the 12th of January, Western Style) with his brother and other members of the family.

A few moments later, the Grand Duke Vladimir took Giers aside and told him that the members of the imperial family, worried about the rumors of Battenberg's possible return to Bulgaria, had convened in family council and had decided that the Emperor should write both to the German Kaiser and to the head of the family of Hesse-Darmstadt, asking them both to forbid the young man to return.

Giers, expressing skepticism as to the reality behind the rumors, con- veyed to the grand duke the impression that he thought the Tsar's pro- posed letters unnecessary. But the grand duke warned that for him to remain inactive in the matter, in the face of the Tsar's strong feelings, could well cost him his position. Startled by this, Giers agreed with alacrity to collaborate in the enterprise: but he suggested, very sensibly, that (1) informal soundings first be taken to assure that a useful answer would be forthcoming from the German Emperor, and (2) that Bismarck be forewarned of the approach. To this, the grand duke agreed. Bethinking himself then of Peter Shuvalov's forthcoming visit to Berlin, Giers suggested that Shuvalov be charged with the task of taking the matter to his ambassadorial brother and, if necessary, personally carrying out the soundings in question. To this, the grand duke also gave his assent.*

Peter Shuvalov, a man deeply concerned for the successful progress of Russo-German relations, was immensely pleased to find himself again being used for a diplomatic task after years of inactivity in the political doghouse (as a result of the Tsar's impression that he had sold out the Russian case at the Congress of Berlin). Departing the following day on his mission, he arrived in Berlin on the morning of the 6th of January. He had a long talk that same day with Herbert Bismarck, at the Foreign Office. The talk first turned, of course, on Battenberg and the question of the Tsar's request to the Kaiser that the young man be forbidden to return to Bulgaria. Young Bismarck undertook to promote the necessary soundings with the Kaiser.

This question exhausted, Shuvalov then proceeded to launch himself —in a manner which, considering that he had no instructions along this line from either Giers or the Tsar, can only be called astounding—on a discussion of the delicate question of a possible bilateral pact between Russia and Germany to replace the expiring *Dreikaiserbund*. Nothing, he told young Bismarck, could be simpler than the negotiation of such a pact. He was convinced that he could persuade the Tsar within twenty-four hours to set his signature to a formal promise of Russia's benevolent neutrality in the event of a Franco-German war, if only Germany would promise a similar neutrality in the face of a Russian action to assure to Russia "la fermeture des détroits." If Austria, then, could help a bit to find a way out of the Bulgarian mess, all three of the great Empires could live in peace and freedom. Germany could then do what she liked with France, even if this meant, it was facetiously added, defeating France in a new war, levying reparations to the amount of 14 million francs, and appointing a Prussian general as governor of Paris.[6]

* This account of the exchanges at Gatchina is reconstructed primarily from the invaluable diary of Count V. N. Lamsdorf, at that time senior counselor of the Russian Foreign Ministry and chief confidant of Giers. Without this record, our knowledge of the background of Russian policy at this time would be far poorer. (See V. N. Lamsdorf, *Dnevnik, 1886-1890*).

The boldness of this approach was, as noted above, wholly astonishing. These ideas about the treaty were presumably substantially those which Shuvalov's brother had recently laid before Giers in his letter. It is plain that these views had not received, to that point, either Giers' approval or that of the Tsar; these latter had not even authorized any discussion at all of this delicate question with the Germans. One is constrained to suspect that Peter Shuvalov saw in this approach a gambit which, if successful, would restore him to the Tsar's good graces and install either him or his brother at the Pevcheski Most as the successor to Giers. Shuvalov was not ill-inclined towards Giers, but considered him too cautious. Like many others in Petersburg, he no doubt assumed that Giers' days as minister were numbered in any case, in view of the intensity of Katkov's attacks upon him; and he must have been well aware that rumors had been circulating in Petersburg for some time to the effect that he, Shuvalov, was a prominent candidate for the succession.*

Herbert Bismarck, somewhat taken aback by Shuvalov's statements, avoided comment at the moment, but of course reported the whole conversation at once to his father, then still in the country at Friedrichsruh. He added that Shuvalov was prepared to go to Friedrichsruh to see the chancellor in person, if the chancellor so desired. The reply came back that Shuvalov should stay in Berlin; the chancellor was returning to the city in order to address the Reichstag, in the matter of the military appropriations, on the 11th of January; the Shuvalov brothers were invited to dine with him on the 10th—that is, on the eve of the Reichstag speech.

This, of course, the brothers did. Whether Paul remained for the more political part of the conversation, after dinner, is not fully apparent— probably not. But Peter then proceeded to go even farther with the chancellor than he had gone with the latter's son. He presented to the German statesman the actual draft (we must suppose: the same one that his brother had submitted to Giers) of a basis for a possible German-Russian treaty, and he solicited Bismarck's comments on, and amendments to, its wording. The draft, predicated on the assumption that the tripartite German-Russian-Austrian arrangement could not be renewed and would be replaced by a bilateral German-Russian one, proposed the following bases for a new treaty:

---

* Earlier in December, according to Lamsdorf's diary, the Russians had intercepted messages from the Italian Embassy in Petersburg, reporting a rumor that Shuvalov was to replace Giers. The Tsar had written, in the margin of the respective report: "This is news to me. I never heard of it and am glad to be informed" (*Dnevnik, 1886-1890*, entry for December 1, 1886, Old Style, p. 4).

Germany would recognize Russia's exclusive right to exercise her influence in Bulgaria and Rumelia.

Russia, furthermore, could count on Germany's friendly neutrality if the Tsar found himself obliged to assure the closing of the Straits and to retain in his hands the keys to the Black Sea.

Germany, on the other hand, could count on the same friendly neutrality on Russia's part in the face of any conflict that might arise between Germany and France.

Both Powers recognized the existence of the Austro-Hungarian Empire as necessary to the maintenance of the European equilibrium and, except in the case of aggression on Austria's part, agreed not to take any action against that Empire's integrity.

Both recognized the necessity of maintaining the independence of the Kingdom of Serbia.[7]

Aside from adding a phrase to limit the operation of the last point, Bismarck appears to have indicated his general acceptance of these points as a basis for the drafting of a new bilateral treaty.

It was with this document in his pocket that Peter Shuvalov left Berlin, the following day, for Petersburg, to report to the Tsar. Bismarck, meanwhile, the impressions of the discussion of the preceding evening still fresh upon him, was delivering that same day (January 11) his famous speech in the Reichstag in support of the military appropriations.[8] The speech has come down in history as one of his greatest political-oratorical efforts and acts of statesmanship. Space does not permit a complete summary of it, which is a pity, because his entire outlook and policy of that agitated winter were reflected in it.

For the Austrians, he had brutal words of warning: they could expect no German support if they went to war with Russia over Bulgaria. With relation to France, Bismarck's statements were long and detailed. They even roamed back over history, and included the recollections of his own reluctance to go along with the acquisition of all of Alsace-Lorraine. He reiterated, time after time, that Germany would not attack France. Nor did he suspect any comparable intentions towards Germany on the part of the French governmental leaders of the moment. "Messrs. Goblet and Flourens are not the men to wish for a war with us; and it was the same with the governments of Freycinet and Ferry." If anyone could guarantee him the continuance of such governments in office, he would say: "Let us save our money." But France had always been governed by minorities. Who could say what minority would come into power tomorrow? There were elements in France who wanted revenge— who wanted war.

257

When he turned to Russia, the chancellor showed great caution. He did not want to do anything to spoil the atmosphere for the success of the project he had discussed with Shuvalov the night before. Only in the most veiled form, therefore, did he permit his words to reflect the heavy doubts about Russian policy that had plagued him in recent weeks. (He admitted later, to his official aides, that he had presented the picture, in these passages of the speech, in much rosier colors than he himself saw it.)

Whether or not there had been, at an earlier date, considerations connected with relations with Russia that supported the need for increased German armaments, this, Bismarck said to the Reichstag, was no longer the case.

> We stand in the same friendly relations with Russia as under the late Emperor (Alexander II); and under no circumstances will these relations be disturbed by us. What interest could we have in seeking trouble with Russia? . . . Peace with Russia will not be disturbed from our side; and I do not believe that Russia will attack us. I also do not believe that the Russians are looking around for alliances in order to attack us in company with others, or that they would be inclined to take advantage of difficulties that we might encounter on another side, in order to attack us with ease. The Emperor Alexander of Russia has always had the courage of his own convictions; and if he intended to enter into unfriendly relations with Germany he would have been the first to say so and to let this be recognized. Anyone who has had the honor to know him closely can have confidence in this. Any arguments in favor of our appropriations bill, therefore, deriving from the assumption that we would have to face a coalition of France and Russia, are ones I cannot accept. Our strength is not to be reckoned by this measure. . . . We will have no trouble with Russia, unless we go to Bulgaria to look for it.[9]

But it was not, Bismarck hastened to add, a question of any German alliance with Russia against France, either.

> I had the honor as recently as yesterday of dining with the Russian Ambassador. He said nothing to suggest that he was proposing an alliance. I expressed my confidence that Russia would not attack us nor conspire (against us) with any other countries—that she was not seeking an alliance against us. And we have no alliance to fall back on, if we have to fight with France.[10]

One can only admire the skill with which these passages were drafted. Avoiding any direct expression of suspicion of the Tsar's intentions with respect to Germany, Bismarck placed delicately upon him the onus of saying so frankly if he wished any sort of change in the relationship. Otherwise, it was inferred, the Germans would expect things to go on as they had before. By this delicate approach, the chancellor passed the initiative to the Russians and left his own hands free to deal with any position they might adopt.

———————

Both Bismarck and Peter Shuvalov would probably have had quite different feelings, and would have handled themselves somewhat differently when they met in Berlin on that evening of the 10th of January, had they known that while they were talking, the Tsar was just receiving, or had just received, a document of a wholly different tenor which was destined to produce upon him an impression deeper than anything Shuvalov would be able, on the basis of his talk with Bismarck, to report. For if the author, or authors, of the official Russian communiqué of the 15th of December, so friendly to Germany, had meant thereby to improve the prospects for the favorable progress of Russo-German relations, the most important effect of their effort was a highly ironic one. The appearance of the communiqué stung Katkov into what was now to be his greatest and most effective effort. Instead of replying publicly to the document in the editorial columns of his paper, where he would have been obliged, in view of the censorship, to moderate his statements, he retired into seclusion and composed a personal communication to the Tsar, a weighty monograph of almost book length, in which he poured out the full measure of his aroused feelings and opinions. The writing and editing of it took him some time. It did not reach the Tsar until sometime around the 9th and 11th of January, some days after Giers brought in Bismarck's historical résumé. There can be no question as to which of the two documents affected him most deeply. For nearly three months to come, the monarch's behavior would reflect the deep impression made upon him by Katkov's lengthy and impressive private communication.

First published nearly a half-century later, in the *Krasny Arkhiv*,[11] Katkov's letter of the 8th of January 1887 ranks among the basic political documents of the period. Katkov reveals himself here as much better informed about the secrets of the Russian government than he had been when he wrote his editorial of the 30th of July 1886. One suspects that he was even aware of the preparation of Bismarck's historical résumé, for he goes to great lengths to expound his own view of the events of the 1870's and early 1880's. Beyond this, he speaks openly of the "treaty of 1881" and the question of its renewal, indicating that he had by this time been generally informed of the existence and origin of the *Dreikaiserbund*.

The first pages of the document were personally defensive: he told

259

why he had disapproved of the December communiqué; why he had at one time urged the occupation of Bulgaria; why he had then dropped that subject and had taken, instead, a position in favor of assisting the Bulgarian exiled officers to unseat the Regency by a putsch.

He then dealt freely and extensively with various Russian personalities. Vannovski, the war minister, was all right—a true servant of the Tsar and "Russian in feeling"; but of certain of the higher officers he could not speak so favorably. With Giers, he said, he could never be intimate. Their casts of mind would never be compatible. He had had better relations with Zinoviev, head of the Asiatic Department, but even with him there had been certain differences. The Foreign Office, he complained, had not kept him sufficiently informed; many of the things he wanted to know he had been obliged to learn "through other channels."

As for his positive views and recommendations: He favored conspiratorial action against the Bulgarian Regency; but the Foreign Office, endeavoring to please Bismarck, had been half-hearted about it. Bismarck, he charged, did not wish to see Russia escape from her Balkan difficulties; but even if he did, who, except of course the Russian Foreign Office, would wish to see this happen with German sympathy and support? He was unwilling to believe that the Tsar had of his own volition agreed in 1884 to the renewal of the *Dreikaiserbund*—a treaty which was actually the product of the period of diplomacy preceding his assumption of the throne. The diplomats, surely, must have pushed him into its renewal "to please our friends." He predicted (showing a very intimate understanding of the governmental exchanges of the moment) that Bismarck would now urge, in place of the *Dreikaiserbund*, a separate pact with Germany. The Tsar, he said, had declined to enter into such a pact three years ago, because Russia was not yet ready to act against Austria. But was she ready now? And even if she were, what good would come of such a pact? Germany would not dare to come to Austria's assistance in any event, in view of the danger from a rearmed France. Therefore, no pact was needed to assure Germany's neutrality in case of a Russian war with Austria. It was France, actually, whose help would then be needed; for she alone could deter England from coming in on Austria's side. And if Russia did not wish to proceed to an "active policy" (a euphemism for launching a war with Austria) in the near future, then what good was a pact with the Germans, anyway? Chained to Germany, Russia would merely remain isolated.

Again, as in the July article, Katkov avoided the pitfall of urging an actual alliance with France. It would be enough, he wrote, to establish an equal relationship with France and Germany. (He reckoned, ob-

Plate 11. Alexander III and Giers (contemporary German caricature)

Plate 12. The young Juliette Adam

Plate 13. Paul Déroulède, poet and chauvinist

Plate 14. The central arch of the General Staff-Foreign Office building on the Palace Square, Petersburg

Plate 15. The Anichkov Palace on the Nevski Prospect, where Alexander III and Dagmar usually stayed when in Petersburg

viously, that the tie to Germany once broken, the alliance with France would become an inescapable alternative. No need, therefore, to press for it now.)

As noted above, this letter, dated the 8th of January, presumably reached the Tsar some time between the 9th and 11th. It is doubtful that he had time to read it before his move from Gatchina to Petersburg on the 12th and the strenuous diplomatic reception and other protocol activities that followed on that day in connection with the Russian New Year. He presumably read and studied it in the ensuing days—probably over the weekend of the 15th-16th. Obviously, not everything in it pleased him. Opposite the passage alleging that the Foreign Office had taken a lukewarm attitude towards the conspiracy against the Bulgarian Regency "in order not to irritate Bismarck," he wrote in the margin: "All this is entirely untrue. Lies!" Furthermore: E. M. Feoktistov, the official censor, who was well informed with regard to the whole affair, wrote in his memoirs that the Tsar was probably unfavorably affected by many of the criticisms of what Katkov took to be Giers' policies, recognizing that the policies in question were really his own. Nevertheless, according to Feoktistov, the Tsar, after reading the document, ordered someone (presumably Feoktistov himself) to express to Katkov "my thanks, and tell him I have no doubt of his devotion and his desire to serve the interests of the fatherland, as he understands them, to the best of his ability."[12]

Not only that, but when, some days later, Katkov, greatly heartened and excited by the Tsar's encouraging note, appeared in Petersburg and asked for an audience, his request was at once granted. Unbeknownst to Giers, he was received by the Tsar on the 22nd of January, on which occasion he may be presumed to have pressed his case even more forcefully than in his paper. He came out of the audience, in any event, boasting to his friends that he had the Tsar's assurance that no treaty with Germany would be signed before the two men had again had opportunity to meet and consult.[13]

It is clear from all available evidence that Katkov's paper, not to mention the subsequent interview, made a profound impression upon Alexander III. Even more important than the force of the substantive arguments themselves seems to have been the fact that the Tsar came away from the reading of it persuaded that Katkov's view reflected the passionate feelings of great and influential portions of Russian society—feelings of such importance that they deserved deference regardless of how well or ill founded they were. This was, as Lamsdorf observed in his diary, a new note in the psychology of the Russian throne.[14] Seldom if ever before had a Russian Tsar confessed to reckoning with such a thing as public opinion. The opinion of the monarch himself had normally been what counted. So true had this been of Alexander III in earlier years that one has to recognize the possibility that this professed concern for public opinion, which the monarch mentioned to Giers on several occasions, may actually have been a rationalization designed to cover the monarch's embarrassment before Giers for his yielding to Katkov's blandishments, so congenial to his own emotional impulses.

However that may be, the effect of Katkov's letter upon Alexander III was not only profound but, for the moment, politically decisive. Without the knowledge of this background factor, Alexander's behavior over the ensuing two-and-a-half months is not wholly intelligible. To explain Russian policy during that period it is necessary to bear in mind that the Tsar was now acting primarily under the influence of a document of which, at the time (and for many years thereafter) neither the general public nor the diplomatic corps had, occasional rumors notwithstanding, any accurate knowledge.

It was the unsuspecting Giers on whom, in consequence of Katkov's secret victory, the first blow fell. Ordered to the palace by telephone for an audience with the Tsar on the afternoon of Monday, the 17th of January, he left his office rested, now, and in the best of spirits, after the fatigues of the New Year's celebrations, to resume with the monarch the exploration of the possible paths of exit from Russia's diplomatic difficulties. He returned, an hour or two later, crushed and distressed. Of the fact that Katkov had written to the Tsar personally and at length, and that the monarch was acting under the fresh influence of this document, Giers had of course no knowledge. That being the case, he had no possibility of replying to Katkov's arguments. He could only guess at the cause of the complete change in the Tsar's attitude and behavior. But never, he later confessed, had he had a less satisfactory audience. The tenor of the interview is perhaps best represented by what Lamsdorf wrote in his diary, that evening, after listening to what the foreign minister had to tell about it. "Evidently," Lamsdorf wrote,

> the intrigues of Katkov or certain other nefarious influences have once
> again knocked our ruler off the track. His Majesty is not only now
> talking against the *Dreikaiserbund* but is even against a bilateral pact
> with Germany. He claims to have reason to know that such an alliance
> would be unpopular and contrary to the national feelings of all of Russia.
> He confesses that he fears the consequences of a failure on his part to
> reckon with those feelings, and does not wish to destroy the confidence
> of the country in his foreign policy. All this stands in such open contra-
> diction with everything that he has recently been saying and writing that

one doesn't understand anything any more. . . . . He even hints at the possibility of an occupation [of Bulgaria] in case of an attempt by Battenberg to return—"I will send a brigade," he says—and he denies that an occupation would present any danger at all.[15]

Two days before this audience with Giers, the Tsar had received Peter Shuvalov, just returned from Berlin, full of the importance of his discussion with Bismarck. Of what passed on that occasion, we have no knowledge. Obviously, the monarch was at best noncommittal with respect to the document Shuvalov brought back with him, and demanded time for reflection. But by the time Giers arrived for his unhappy audience on the 17th of January, the imperial mind was made up. The first thing the foreign minister was obliged to do, on returning from this interview, was to sit down and write to Paul Shuvalov, saying that he regarded the proposals made to Prince Bismarck by the ambassador's brother as representing simply statements made in the course of a private conversation between two friends, which could not have any official character.* At the same time, Giers, acting again obviously under the Tsar's orders, instructed the ambassador to refrain, until further notice, from all discussion of a renewal of the *Dreikaiserbund*, in view of the uncertainty surrounding the future of this arrangement.[16]

The Germans, as a consequence of these decisions, received no reply of any sort from the Russians concerning the document Peter Shuvalov had taken to Petersburg—a document, to which, after all, Bismarck had given his reactions and to which, therefore, a reply of some sort was certainly to be expected. For the moment, and for weeks to come, a total and mysterious silence settled over the Russian side of this relationship.

To the Germans this behavior was unintelligible. They found it difficult to believe that Peter Shuvalov, escorted to the Imperial Chancery—after all—by his brother, the Russian Ambassador to Germany, had not been speaking under instructions. The silence that followed his visit could be taken, in the circumstances, only as the indication of some change, and one of a far from reassuring nature, in Russian policy.

The effect on the Germans can best be judged from two highly

---

* There is no reason to suppose that Giers himself was in any way enthusiastic about Peter Shuvalov's proposals. It is clear from the Lamsdorf diary that the minister regarded Shuvalov's memorandum for the Tsar, reporting his talk with Bismarck, as ill-informed, weak, and even absurd. But the Tsar's injunction against any further discussion with the Germans about the renewal of the *Dreikaiserbund* was of course a serious blow to Giers' policies; and it can only have been with a heavy heart that he passed this injunction on to the ambassador at Berlin.

significant instructions that went out from Bismarck to Schweinitz in the course of the ensuing winter. On the 17th of February, more than a month having now elapsed since Peter Shuvalov's visit and nothing further having been heard of the matter, Bismarck told Schweinitz that the German government could only assume that Shuvalov's *démarche* had had no success, and that one could not reckon with any inclination on Russia's side to pursue it further. He advised Schweinitz to say nothing further about it "since this would create the impression that our need for such agreements was greater than that of Russia, and it would thus be misunderstood." But Giers would surely know without being told, the instruction continued, that the Germans would be obliged, in the prevailing uncertain circumstances (i.e., the war scare), to take into account, in designing their own policies, the possibility that a French attack on Germany would receive Russia's diplomatic or military support.

A further instruction went forward ten days later on the same subject. In the light of the Russian silence, the anti-German press campaign in the Russian papers would, the Chancellor said, now have to be credited with serious significance. No answer was, after all, also an answer. Again, Schweinitz was admonished not to bring up the subject, and to avoid any and every sort of initiative with respect either to the renewal of the *Dreikaiserbund* or to the negotiation of a bilateral German-Russian agreement.[17]

It was on this dead center that German-Russian relations stuck, over the winter of 1887.

To understand the importance of the Tsar's unwillingness, as of the 17th of January 1887, to pursue further discussions with the Germans about the expiring treaty, it is necessary to bear in mind that it was not just Giers' policies but also his position that was now very much at stake. The sensitive Lamsdorf, the minister's sole confidant, who, as a bachelor, lived on the lower floor of the Ministry and came daily upstairs (even outside of office hours) to see his chief, was quick to perceive this. On noting, in the letter Giers was writing to Shuvalov after the audience of the 17th of January, the Tsar's injunction against further discussions with the Germans about the treaty, Lamsdorf was overcome, as he recorded in his diary, with heavy foreboding: "It occurred to me that this presaged the removal of my dear Minister, and that people had probably succeeded in persuading the Tsar that he was too unpopular in Russia."

Lamsdorf's instincts did not deceive him. Among the things that

Katkov's friend, Tatishchev, reported to Polovtsov, when they met some days later (see note 13 above), was that Katkov was now more than ever determined to hound Giers out of office and had commissioned Tatishchev to write articles against him in the *Russki Vestnik*. After which he, Tatishchev, had gone ahead to discuss the question of a possible replacement for Giers. He mentioned, in this connection, the names of Paul Shuvalov, Peter Saburov, and the ever-ambitious Nikolai Ignatyev. Each of these, he indicated, believing that Katkov's opinion would be decisive in determining that of the Tsar, was trying hard to obtain Katkov's support for his particular candidacy.

Thus, by the end of January 1887 the battle was fairly joined—not only for the dominant influence over the formation of Russian foreign policy but also for the office of Russian foreign minister.

Chapter Fifteen

FRANCE AND THE RUSSO-GERMAN CRISIS

As was noted above, the change of government that took place in France at the beginning of December 1886, was not occasioned by any considerations of foreign policy. The new government of René Goblet had no intentions, as it came to power, of making any significant departures in this field. The new foreign minister, M. Émile-Léopold Flourens, described by Nolde in his history of the alliance[1] as a "personnalité inconnue de tous et n'ayant aucune espèce de compétence," was an attorney who had for some years been Directeur Général des Cultes at the Conseil d'État and, more recently, chairman of the Section de Législation de la Justice et des Affaires Étrangères of that same body, as well as chairman of the Comité consultatif des Protectorats at the Foreign Ministry. He was not, at that time, a parliamentary deputy, and he played no significant domestic political role. While he was alleged, by his admirers, to have an exceptional knowledge of international law, he had had no previous diplomatic experience. His knowledge of diplomatic procedure as well as of the international situation of the moment was obviously slight. His interest in Russia does not appear to have been, at the time of his entry into office, appreciably greater than that of his predecessor, Freycinet. But it was an interest which, as we shall see, would be greatly stimulated by his early experiences in office as well as by certain of his personal contacts; and he was shortly to become, despite sharp and enduring differences with Boulanger, no less sanguine a partisan of the idea of a Franco-Russian alliance than that individual himself.

The first weeks of Flourens' incumbency as foreign minister coincided, of course, with the similar period in Laboulaye's service as ambassador at Petersburg. The latter, by nature a cautious and prudent man, was well content, in these first weeks of his new mission, to confine himself to renewing his acquaintance with the Russian capital and taking the measure of the current situation. It was not to be expected, however, that in an atmosphere buzzing with rumors of a possible Franco-Russian alliance, and with a war scare brewing up in the West, his duties and interests could long remain detached from the political excitements of the moment. It was indeed not long before these excitements began to demand his official attention.

The first occasion was the appearance of the official communiqué of the 15th of December, warning the Russian press against an excessive anti-German fervor. Noting in the communiqué the phrase: "Having the firm intention to continue as in the past to give due attention to Germany's particular interests . . . ," and viewing this with the characteristic sharp French sensitivity to anything that might conceivably affect French interests adversely, Laboulaye took occasion, at his next weekly meeting with Giers, to draw the latter's attention to this passage and to inquire, archly, whether the wording was not susceptible to more than one interpretation. Giers, in reassuring him on this point, got in a delicate little dig. "You have no need at all," he said,

> to take umbrage. These words have no more than a momentary significance. We had all the more reason to give Germany this small satisfaction because the German government, acting on the basis of erroneous information, claimed to have at hand proof that some sort of an agreement had been arrived at between Paris and Petersburg.

Having said this much, Giers evidently concluded that he had better now go further and lay this subject of a Franco-Russian alliance to rest in no uncertain way. "Ardent spirits," he went on,

> (and you have them in Paris just as we have them here) do not content themselves with reproaching me for pro-German tendencies I do not have; they go to the point of desiring of me that I should break with Germany entirely in order to conclude an alliance with France. (Pause). Very well, Mr. Ambassador, if I were to propose to you today an alliance of this sort, what would be your reply? You would tell me no doubt that France is no more inclined than is Russia to tempt her fortunes in a war— that she, too, has her financial embarrassments and her internal difficulties, less than Russia, perhaps, but has them nevertheless.

Confronted with this attack, Laboulaye had no choice but to retire. "I would reply," he said glumly (and nothing could have been more true) "that I was without instructions."[2]

On this meager but useful understanding matters were to rest for another month, insofar as the official exchanges between the two governments were concerned. But meanwhile, a situation was developing that was to have, simultaneously and together with Katkov's memorandum, a sharp effect on the Tsar's disposition. In the wake of Kaulbars' departure from Bulgaria and the effective diplomatic break between that country and Russia, the members of the Bulgarian Regency, feeling it important to the security of their position that they should now move rapidly to find a successor to the Bulgarian throne, and anxious to enlist the sympathy and support of the other Powers in this effort in view of the violent hostility they were now encountering on the Russian side, despatched a delegation to various European capitals. Its mission was to apprise the various Great Power governments of the Regency's point of view and to solicit their advice in the question of the filling of the vacant throne. The delegation's instructions called for it to visit Petersburg in the initial stage of its journey; but when it was learned in the Russian capital (to the Tsar's intense displeasure) that the Russian Ambassador at Vienna had received the delegation briefly as it passed through that city, Russian envoys all over Europe were advised that it would not be received if it came to Petersburg, and they were instructed to have nothing to do with it. This instruction was deliberately publicized. In these circumstances, none of the other governments, knowing the Russian government's attitude, was inclined to receive the delegation officially; but everywhere, its members were received by the respective Foreign Office officials *en titre privé*.

After Vienna, the first of the capitals visited was Berlin. Here, the delegates were received by Herbert Bismarck, who gave them the coolest of receptions. We have a verbatim account of the beginning of this reception, as told to Peter Shuvalov by young Bismarck himself:[3]

Enter the spokesman, a little fellow with white tie and black tail-coat. He comes in holding out his hand. Count Herbert puts *his* hand behind his back. The Bulgarian, already flustered, begins

"Your Excellency! Allow me to present my colleagues . . ."

"Certainly not. By what right do you present them? Each can come separately and speak for himself."

"But they are here to . . ."

"Here to what? Let them wait. All you have to do is to seek a reconciliation with Russia."

"But how can we, when the Tsar has cut off all communication with us?"

"Well, you know his candidate.* Elect him! Then perhaps his Majesty will graciously condescend to acknowledge your existence."

The other deputies were let in and treated after the same fashion.

Thus rebuffed, the members of the delegation went on to London. The atmosphere there was naturally much more friendly and sympathetic,

---

* Herbert Bismarck evidently thought he knew who was the Tsar's candidate for the throne of Bulgaria. (There had been talk both of the Prince of Mingrelia and of Prince Waldemar of Denmark.) The historian is not aware that the Tsar had ever committed himself to any particular candidacy.

but once again they got little advice as to prospective candidates for the throne. Finally, then, on the 8th of January, they arrived in Paris.

Flourens, long forewarned of their approach and aware that he was now for the first time about to be thrust, as a participant, into the dangerous arena of Balkan politics, had taken pains to inform himself in much detail, both in advance and afterwards, of the reception given to the Bulgarian delegation by the Germans, in order that he might be guided by it. Except for the fact that he received the members of the delegation collectively rather than individually, he then followed faithfully the German precedent, both in form and in the content of what he said. Pointing out, precisely as had Herbert Bismarck, the limitations that rested on Bulgarian sovereignty, and the responsibility of the Powers, particularly the Sultan, for the development of Bulgaria's international relationships, he went on to say: "Personnellement, je ne peux donc que vous engager à vous entendre avec la Russie, puisqu'elle a déjà tant fait pour votre pays et que c'est à elle que celui-ci doit son existence."[4] ("Personally, I can do no other than to urge you to come to an understanding with Russia, since Russia has already done so much for your country and since it is to her that your country owes its existence.")

Considering that this procedure was modeled strictly on that of the Germans, one might have thought that the effect on the Tsar would have been no more than a restrained satisfaction. This, however, was not the case. At his New Year's reception for the diplomatic corps, on the 13th of January, the Tsar, on coming to Laboulaye (the latest arrival), at the end of the line of ambassadors, uttered first the usual protocolaire phrases and then, raising his voice so that others could hear it, said:

> Je suis particulièrement content de vous dire combien j'apprécie l'attitude de votre pays et le langage tenu par M. Flourens aux délégués bulgares. Ce langage net et droit, d'une correction parfaite, est vraiment digne de la France. Aussi ai'je le ferme espoir qu'il contribuera grandement à prévenir les difficultés et à arranger les choses. Malheureusement, je ne pourrais en dire autant de tous les autres cabinets d'Europe.[5] ["I am particularly happy to tell you how much I appreciate the attitude of your country and what M. Flourens said to the Bulgarian delegates. This direct and sincere statement, of a faultless propriety, is really worthy of France. And I confidently hope that it will contribute importantly to the avoidance of difficulties and to the straightening out of things. Unfortunately, I cannot say the same of all the other European governments."]

All this was said within hearing distance of the English Ambassador, to whom the Tsar had made only the most perfunctory remarks. The episode was, of course, a minor one; but these words, spoken so ostentatiously by the Tsar on such an occasion and in such an atmosphere, went the rounds and produced no small sensation. The French never forgot them. They appear in all the accounts of the diplomacy of the period.

Schweinitz, a few days later, complained to Giers, quite correctly, that the Tsar had exaggerated the significance of Flourens' reception of the Bulgarians; Flourens, after all, had only followed the German example. Giers, in his weekly audience with the Tsar on the 25th of January, mentioned Schweinitz' complaint. "Yes," replied the Tsar, "but Bismarck after all was just being sly; Flourens and Goblet spoke simply and frankly."[6] Plainly, in the Tsar's book of that moment, the Germans could do no right.

———

At a soirée given by the British Ambassador on the day following the New Year's reception, First Secretary of the French Embassy Edmond Toutain found himself approached by an acquaintance (whom he described as the delegate in Petersburg of "the Moscow Panslav committees," a man by the name of Tolstoi),* who then proceeded to deliver himself of a most startling series of political confidences. The long and short of these revelations was that the Panslavs, led by Katkov, were about to triumph over Giers. Katkov, Tolstoi said, had recently been summoned to Gatchina by the Emperor and had delivered to him, at the latter's request, a forty-page memorandum, "longuement et soigneusement élaboré." After describing the contents of this document in some detail (Toutain quotes so extensively from them as to suggest that Tolstoi must have given him at least excerpts from the original, probably in French translation), Tolstoi went ahead to claim (this was actually an exaggeration) that the Tsar had not only thanked Katkov most warmly for the document but had professed complete agreement with the views there set forth and had congratulated Katkov "dans les termes les plus élogieux de l'élévation de ses sentiments et de ses idées." In the wake of this success, Katkov's influence, M. Tolstoi said, was "at its apogee." This being the case, the French should not allow themselves to be deceived into thinking that the language used by the Foreign Office represented the real "sentiments" of Russia. It was to the Moscow press that the foreigners should now turn for their understanding of Russian policy. The French should know all this, because "it will now be necessary for us to work together." Tolstoi added

* I have been unable to ascertain the identity of this Tolstoi.

that "their" next task (i.e., the task of Katkov and his associates) would be to arrange to have Giers replaced by Count N. P. Ignatyev.

Toutain, bubbling with excitement, reported all this to Laboulaye the following morning. The ambassador encouraged him to cultivate the contact with Tolstoi, but wisely said he would prefer not to talk personally with the gentleman, because he was obliged to guard his fences with Giers.[7]

A curious gloss is placed on this situation by a further feature of Toutain's account. Just as he was finishing his report to the ambassador on this matter, they were joined by the assistant military attaché, Captain Moulin. Moulin, who, as we have already noted, had close contacts with Katkov as well as in Russian military circles, was astounded to learn that all this had happened and that he, Moulin, had not been told of it. It disconcerted him slightly. He had been to Moscow to see Katkov only a month before, he remarked, and the latter had said nothing of all this. Even if the events described by Tolstoi had occurred in the interval since their meeting, he felt that their mutual relations were such that Katkov should have summoned him and told him all that Tolstoi had told to Toutain.[8]

This was, as will be seen shortly, not the only evidence of close connections between the French military authorities and the Russian nationalists; but this alone would have sufficed to demonstrate that lines of communication of this nature existed, and were being carefully cultivated, over the heads of the regular Russian authorities.

Moulin asked the ambassador to give him time to check up on Tolstoi's statements. This Laboulaye agreed to do. For this reason, he did not report the incident to Paris at once. He waited until the 22nd of January, by which time Moulin had confirmed Tolstoi's account. Even then, in reporting the matter, Laboulaye refrained from identifying the source.

Even prior to Toutain's talk with Tolstoi, the French Ambassador had begun to feel a certain uneasiness over his own lack of instruction in the face of the obviously growing importance of Panslav influence. He had exposed this uneasiness to Flourens on the very eve of the New Year's reception. In a telegram of the 12th of January,[9] he pointed to the possible danger of continuing to turn a deaf ear—as he then felt obliged, for lack of instructions, to do—to advances from the Panslav side. He realized, of course, that France's relations with Germany made it incumbent upon him to observe great prudence in this respect. But there was, he considered, a no smaller danger to which he

271

was obliged to call attention: ". . . ce serait de glacer par notre accueil la source du courant qui se dessine ici en notre faveur." (". . . this would be to freeze up, by our attitude, the sources of the stream which is now beginning to run in our direction.")

Flourens did not at once react to this apt phrase, but it struck home and he was not insensitive to the implied reproach. He, too, was now becoming increasingly worried over the possibility of an early outbreak of hostilities with Germany, and his thoughts began to turn increasingly to the cherished French image of a Russian Tsar saving France from a German attack, as one such Tsar was conceived to have done in 1875. He began, accordingly, to cultivate assiduously his relations with Mohrenheim. In this, he was enthusiastically aided by Jules Hansen (see Chapter 4, above), who, enjoying the confidence of both men and always welcoming a chance to indulge his passion for the role of unofficial mediator, ran incessantly from one to the other over that entire winter of 1887, feeding each of them at every turn with the prejudices and misimpressions of the other, not to mention his own.

At some time around the 18th of January, Flourens appears to have sent Hansen to Mohrenheim with the query: what, in the latter's opinion, would be Russia's reaction if Germany were to threaten France openly. Mohrenheim at once passed this question along to Giers. "The rumor has reached me," he wired (somewhat disingenuously) "that the French government would like to know whether, in case it were to receive from Berlin a demand that it disarm, it could count on a certain moral support from the imperial (Russian) government." Giers sent Mohrenheim's message to the Tsar. The latter, after pondering it, wrote in the margin, opposite the passage in question: "Oui, certainement."

Giers was now in a quandary. It was only three days after his alarming interview with the Tsar. He did not know what now to expect from his aroused monarch. If he were to pass the Tsar's reaction back to the French, it would excite some of them beyond measure. Given the tendency to febrile imagination and to sweeping exaggeration that dominated the atmosphere of Paris at that moment, it would be taken and portrayed as a virtual promise of Russian support. God alone knew what then would follow. Very wisely, therefore, he decided that before making any reply to Mohrenheim's rather opaque query he would ask the Russian Ambassador at Berlin for an assessment of the seriousness of the danger on which the query was predicated. This was done. The reply, not unsurprisingly, came back to the effect that the danger was being greatly exaggerated: there was no evidence that the Germans were planning any sort of ultimatum of this nature.

Giers had had some difficulty in getting his own master to accept at face value these reports from Berlin, and to sanction this attempt to calm the French. "How can we reassure the French?" the Tsar had asked him. "We know nothing about Prince Bismarck's intentions." Of Bismarck, the Tsar went on, anything was to be expected. He did not suspect the Germans of preparing to attack Russia; but when it came to their attacking France—who could say?

Giers, nevertheless, appears to have wired the reassuring information from Berlin to Mohrenheim, as a means of calming down the French and avoiding the necessity of a reply to their awkward inquiry. But he also took occasion, on the 26th of January, to speak along the same lines to Laboulaye, who as yet knew nothing of Flourens' feeler. They had received, Giers told the ambassador, "des dépêches très sombres" from Mohrenheim, but they felt that the French were exaggerating the danger: the reports from Berlin were entirely reassuring.[10]

Laboulaye, intrigued by Giers' vague reference to Mohrenheim's reports, decided then that he would himself take the bull by the horns. Would Russia, he asked the minister, have full freedom of action—would her hands be free—in the event France were to be subjected to a German invasion?[11] The implied meaning of the question was, of course: was Russia, or was she not, bound by any formal obligations to Germany that would limit her ability to give support to France in such a contingency?

The cautious Giers, remembering 1875, was not easily to be caught on this most treacherous of hooks. In such a contingency, he replied, Russia, conscious of her interests, would have her word to say. His advice to France, meanwhile,[12] was: do not be the aggressors.*

One sees, surprisingly, no evidence that the French understood the obvious hint in Giers' words. What he was clearly meaning to convey was that "We have no formal obligation vis-à-vis the Germans that would limit our freedom of action in the event *they* were to attack *you*; but if *you* were to attack *them*, our hands would not be free to assist you."

Actually, this was not strictly correct. The terms of the *Dreikaiser-*

---

* It should be noted that Nolde, without citing his source, gives quite a different version of Giers' reply (*L'Alliance*, p. 414). In this version, Giers, in reply to the query as to whether Russia still had freedom of action, said: "Permit me to preserve that freedom precisely by not accepting an engagement vis-à-vis *you*," reminding the ambassador pointedly, in addition, that Germany, in the event of war, would not be without allies. (In other words: "We could not come to your assistance without having to fight the Austrians, and perhaps others, as well.") Nolde's version is confirmed by Lamsdorf (in his diary for January 26, 1887), who adds that Giers told Laboulaye that he was not going to repeat Gorchakov's mistake and send off a telegram, as had that well-known figure, to the effect that "From this moment, peace is assured."

bund, still formally in effect, did not distinguish between offensive and defensive wars in stipulating the benevolent neutrality Russia was bound to observe. What Giers was hinting at, here, must have been his understanding of Russian *policy* of the moment, not Russia's formal obligations as set forth in the *Dreikaiserbund*, these latter being about to lapse and not destined, as Giers well knew, to be renewed.

Laboulaye at once reported to Paris his casual inquiry and Giers' response. Instead of being welcomed there, the report drew upon the ambassador's head a sharp reprimand from Flourens. Referring, in a telegram of the 29th of January, to both of Laboulaye's recent messages (that of January 12 and the other of the 27th, reporting his talk with Giers), he admonished the ambassador to observe greater caution. He appreciated, he said, the pro-French sympathies prevailing in Russia; but:

> I must nevertheless warn you against the inconvenience that would be
> involved in appealing to these sympathies with a view to any immediate
> arrangements. I cannot urge you too strongly not to take the initiative
> in suggesting such arrangements, and not to encourage such an initiative
> on the part of those with whom you talk. If Giers makes direct overtures to
> you, you will say that you have no instructions and will refer the matter
> to me. I only half regret the reply he gave you; had it been more
> categorical, it could have embarrassed us. Any exchange of views on so
> delicate a subject is for the moment premature.[13]

All that the French wanted, Flourens continued, was that Russia should retain her complete freedom of action. This alone would suffice to bring the two governments together "in certain contingencies." Certainly, he added, we should not "glacer par notre accueil la source du courant qui se dessine en notre faveur"; but one should also not stimulate that current, the direction of which "could easily get away from us." Again, he wrote, he would only recommend prudence:

> It is important that we should remain on a good footing with Petersburg;
> but if Germany gets the impression that we are anxious to estrange her
> from Russia and to take her place in the future alliances of that country,
> I would have to fear that this attitude would attract precisely the danger
> it was designed to avert.

Thus was poor Laboulaye squelched for making what was essentially the same inquiry his chief had just made—as to whether, that is, the Russians would have freedom of action in the face of an eventual Franco-German war.

Exactly a fortnight later, however, Flourens' view changed—completely and dramatically. On the 13th of February, he fired off to the bewildered ambassador a telegram with instructions directly contrary to the ones he had just given him. Gone, now, were all the fears of provoking a hostile German reaction. The Germans, he told the ambassador, were now making great efforts to draw Russia into a new *entente* —an alliance, in effect, against France.* "You must do everything possible," he went on,

> ... to frustrate these efforts.
> Keep me informed of all the information you can gather and of all the symptoms you note. The most precious interests of France are at stake.

Two days later, he followed up this instruction with a private letter, phrased in the most agitated and exalted of terms. "It is you," he wrote,

> who at this moment have the fate of France in your hands. It is evident today, in effect, that if Russia falls into the trap that is being prepared at this moment for her and for us—if she allows herself to be drawn into a great war in the West—we shall immediately be attacked on our Eastern frontier.†

Going on to say that in such an event France, in the absence of Russian support, could be destroyed even before she was able to place herself on the defensive, he continued with his instruction to Laboulaye:

> The soul of the Emperor of Russia, so great and so loyal, cannot permit such an infamy as is now being prepared against us. He cannot thus permit France to be wiped out. Tell him, or let him be told if you cannot approach him, that we are not demanding of him an alliance—we are not asking him to involve himself in a war. We ask only that he should remain with his hands free; so long as they [the Germans] have not succeeded in paralyzing his action they will not dare to carry out under his eyes the Machiavellian plot which has been hatched with a view to simultaneous complication in East and West. You will see it for yourself: the situation is becoming more and more grave. But one must not despair so long as Russia's hands remain free. This is the only hope we have of avoiding an unequal struggle . . . [etc.]

Thus, Laboulaye, who only a fortnight earlier had been severely taken to task simply for inquiring casually whether Russia's hands were or

---

* The reader who calls the account of German-Russian relations of this period given in the last chapter will not fail to note that this statement of Flourens was wholly erroneous. At the moment these words were being written, German representatives were under strict orders not even to raise, in their contacts with Russian officials, the subject of Russia's treaty relationships with Germany.

† What Flourens obviously had in mind, in referring to "the trap" being prepared for Russia, was the rumor that the Germans were urging Russia to attack Austria, while they themselves disposed of the French.

were not free, now found himself charged in the most emotional way with beseeching the Tsar to keep them free, and was told that the fate of France hung by the success or failure of his effort.

What had occurred to produce this sudden and remarkable change of heart on the part of the French foreign minister? Motives are, of course, almost never wholly scrutable, and the full spectrum of Flourens' calculations cannot be recovered. But there are certain suggestive circumstances which might be worth noting.

Flourens' messages to Laboulaye of those days of early February 1887 suggest a mind dominated, in particular, by three impressions: (1) that a German attack was, if not actually imminent, very likely to occur in the future; (2) that the Germans, with a view to placing the Russians in a position where they would not be able to come to French assistance, were encouraging Russia to attack Austria-Hungary; and (3) that if war did develop at that time between Germany and France, the latter, in the absence of Russian assistance, was likely to suffer a disastrous defeat just in the first days of hostilities (". . . nous pouvons être écrasés avant même de nous être mis sur la défensive" were the words Flourens used in his letter to Laboulaye).

The first two of these impressions were wholly inaccurate. The third, considering the known strength of the French armed forces, was startling, to say the least. Where had Flourens got these ideas?

The first of the three impressions, namely, that a German attack was imminent, was one Flourens appears to have received around the 10th of February. In a message of the 12th to the French Ambassador at Berlin, he recounted a whole series of developments taking place in various parts of Europe which he interpreted as pointing in the direction of an early German attack on France. Among these, he mentioned specifically an intercepted communication of some sort from Bleichröder (he did not say to whom this was supposed to have been addressed), in which the banker had said that war had been decided upon by the German government and that the declaration of war was being held up only until the promise of Russian neutrality should be received.

Where, one wonders, could Flourens have learned of such an intercepted message? Not from his ambassador at Berlin, obviously, because it was he, Flourens, who in this telegram was informing the ambassador about it, not vice versa. Presumably, then, it came from the French military intelligence service—the organization normally charged with interceptions of this sort. This service was at that time under the control of Boulanger.* Subsequent events were to show, as will be seen at a later point in this account, that Boulanger's agents and spies were by no means above planting false information on their own government when they thought it might be useful to their own purposes.

It is clear, in any case, that the report about Bleichröder's message was some sort of a falsification. The alleged statement was wholly untrue. Yet Bleichröder was too well-informed a man not to have known that it was untrue. And he had nothing to gain by planting in the French mind an impression, certain to do much damage, which was directly contrary to the assurances Bismarck had only recently given in his January speech.

As for the second of Flourens' delusions: the notion that Germany was endeavoring to provoke a war between Russia and Austria was one that was circulating, just at that time, in Russian Panslav and nationalist circles, and which even received some credence among Russian military figures. What has been recounted above about Bismarck's views and policies would suffice, no doubt, to show that the rumor had very little relation to the truth. But it might be useful at just this point, when the rumor attained such currency and had so strong an effect upon the French, to have a sharper look at the views and policies of the great German statesman in this particular respect.

Bismarck's entire European policy was predicated on the preservation of a reasonable balance of power between Austria and Russia and the avoidance of any major conflict between those two Powers. It was of the utmost importance in his eyes—indeed, he viewed it as the basic requirement of Germany's security—that the Austro-Hungarian Empire not be broken up or destroyed and that Austria retain its status as one of the Great Powers of Europe. The disappearance of Austria, as he clearly perceived, would not only be profoundly unsettling in its effect upon internal conditions within the new and as yet not fully consolidated German Reich but it would leave Germany isolated in the face of a Franco-Russian combination. On the other hand, he had no inordinate confidence in the strength of the Austro-Hungarian armed forces. It was essential to his policy, therefore, that peace be maintained between that country and Russia.

With this in mind, Bismarck did all in his power, over the course of many years, to reconcile the policies of those two countries, and to in-

---

* It might be worth noting that the French Ambassador at Berlin was complaining, at just this time, that his military attachés were sending secret despatches to Paris, the contents of which they were unwilling to reveal to him (*DDF*, VI, No. 435, p. 451).

duce them, in particular, to accept a division of spheres of influence in the Balkans whereby Bulgaria would fall into the Russian sphere, Serbia into the Austrian. He was determined not to let the Austrians wheedle him into sponsoring any challenge by them to Russian interests in Bulgaria; and he told the Austrians, many times, that if they insisted on challenging the Russian position with relation to that country, they could not count on German support. Similarly, he told the Russians that while Germany would not oppose a Russian occupation of Bulgaria, it would also not support it unless it proceeded by agreement with the Austrian government. It was probably statements of his along this line which, relayed and distorted through the gossip channels of Europe, became misinterpreted as assurances to the Russians that they might have a free hand in the Balkans, and thus as encouragement to them to start a war in that part of the world.*

To suggest, in the light of these facts, that Bismarck was preparing deliberately to provoke hostilities between Russia and Austria in the Balkans was to distort the real facts so fantastically as to indicate either great ignorance or a real desire to make mischief.† Flourens, however, appears to have accepted this suggestion without question.

---

* The manner in which the German position on this question became misinterpreted is well illustrated by a passage from Lamsdorf's diary for January 22, 1887. The Russian minister of war, Vannovski, had urged upon Giers, Lamsdorf relates, the desirability of a Russian attack on Austria, citing in justification for this suggestion Bismarck's alleged position that Russia and Austria should settle Balkan affairs between them. Vannovski had spoken along this line to the Tsar. The latter, unconvinced, had replied (very correctly): "Yes, but the Germans would not let us get to Vienna." Vannovski then explained that what he really had in mind was only the conquest of Galicia. Giers, at that point, found it necessary to remind the sanguine war minister of the existence of the Austro-German Treaty of Alliance (V. N. Lamzdorf, *Dnevnik, 1886-1890*, pp. 43-46, entry for January 10/22).

In mid-October 1886, Bismarck said to the Russian Ambassador, Paul Shuvalov: "It is in Germany's interest that the number of Great Powers should not decrease. If the two Powers, Russia and Austria, which are on terms of friendship with us, were to engage in war, we could at best calmly look on and see a battle lost by one or the other. But we could not tolerate that one of them, no matter which, should be dismembered or otherwise so greatly weakened that it ceased to be a Great Power. Such an event we should have to prevent" (Letter, Holstein to Hatzfeldt, October 26, 1886 [*Holstein Papers*, III, pp. 193-194]).

† The possibility should also be noted that rumors to the effect that Bismarck was encouraging Russia to pursue an aggressive policy in the Balkans may have been stimulated by the extreme statements of certain of the members of Bismarck's own Foreign Office entourage who were discontented with his policy of patience and restraint towards Russia and distorted his position—in this case, maliciously, one must conclude—in this direction. This was true, at any rate, of the leader of this faction: Holstein, who intrigued outrageously against the Rus-

Where one must ask, could he have derived the misimpression? There are two interesting possibilities. We have already seen (note 6 of this chapter), that on the 29th of January, according to Toutain, "certain highly placed Russians" conveyed to Flourens, in Paris, the same information that had been conveyed to Toutain on Katkov's behalf earlier in the month by a certain Tolstoi. Who these "highly placed Russians" were is not stated. But there is a very strong probability that one of them, if not the only one, was General Evgenii Vasilyevich Bogdanovich, a busybody and intriguer, nominally an official of the Russian Ministry of the Interior, who served, actually, as an emissary of Katkov, and who was almost certainly in Paris at that time.* If so, one may be reasonably sure that he would not have failed to convey to Flourens any thesis of this nature that Katkov was anxious to communicate.

An even more tantalizing possibility is to be found, as so often happens, in the somewhat elliptical statements of Cyon. He cites in his history of the alliance the major passages of an editorial from Katkov's pen which appeared in the *Moskovskie Vyedomosti* on the 3rd of February 1887, and of the contents of which, he says, he was apprised by telegram from Moscow on the 4th. He attached great importance to it. The final paragraph, as it appeared in Cyon's condensation of the editorial,[14] read as follows:

> Berlin is just now in the process of stirring up things in Southeastern
> Europe with a view to involving Russia there and thus distracting her

---

sian policy of his chief and did not hesitate to distort the latter's position for this purpose. He accused the two Bismarcks, father and son, of first irresponsibly encouraging the Russians to occupy Bulgaria and then telling them that they could not expect German support in such a venture (*Die geheimen Papiere*, II, p. 353).

* According to the Soviet historian, P. A. Zaionchkovski, Katkov, in 1886, sent to France "for unofficial negotiations with the French Government, his creation, a parvenu in the full sense of that word, General E. V. Bogdanovich" (P. A. Zaionchkovski, *Rossiiskoye Samoderzhavie v Kontse XIX Stoletiya*, [Moscow: Mysl, 1970], p. 278). This same mission is referred to in a despatch from Laboulaye of January 12, 1887 (French Archives, *Russie, 1887*). There is also a reference in the memoirs of the Russian censor, E. M. Feoktistov, to the German Emperor's having protested personally, in a letter to the Tsar, over Bogdanovich's activities in Paris, where he was said to have visited a number of highly placed persons and made suggestions to them about a Franco-Russian alliance (*Vospominiya*, p. 263). That he was in contact with Flourens is evident from an instruction of April 14, 1887 (French Archives, *Russie, 1887*) from the latter to Laboulaye, in which he sends his regards to the general, and sees no reason why Laboulaye should not enter into relations with Katkov through the intermediary of that individual.

Feoktistov described Bogdanovich as "one of the petty agents of the court camarilla, author and publisher of clerical-patriotic pamphlets, liberally financed by the Treasury" (*Vospominaya*, p. 287).

attention. But none of these plans will succeed. Russia desires first to see what happens in the West, knowing very well that Southeastern Europe will not escape her. The troubles in Southeastern Europe have their origins elsewhere; they are symptoms and not causes. It could happen that Russia would prefer to occupy herself with the causes rather than with the symptons. . . . Anything is possible. . . .*

This editorial was wired to Cyon, it may be safely assumed, with a view to his making good use of it at the French end. Otherwise, Katkov would scarcely have gone to this trouble and expense. As we shall see presently, Cyon was in touch with—and visited on the day following his receipt of this telegram—General F. G. Saussier (see below). The latter, in turn, was in close touch with President Jules Grévy and with Boulanger in just those days, and would not have failed to relay to them anything of this nature coming, as did this, directly from Katkov.

Finally, we may note that *Le Figaro*, reporting (February 10, 1887) the arrival in Paris of a certain General Martinov, whom it described as the youngest and most brilliant of the *aides de camp* of the Tsar, said that his visit was connected with the Bulgarian question, and claimed that he was to be received by Flourens the following day, the 11th of February. This was, of course, simply one more possibility of the sources from which the impressionable and gullible Flourens could have derived the impression that Bismarck was trying to involve Russia in war with Austria in order to obtain a free hand against France.

As to the third of these impressions—that if war did break out, France was in imminent danger of being crushed overnight, before she could even organize her defenses—there is, again, an interesting background. For reasons having nothing to do with this particular episode— reasons we shall have occasion to note in the next chapter—Cyon was preparing to leave Paris for Russia on the 6th of February. On the eve of his departure, by his own account,[15] he was spoken to by "un personnage occupant une très haute situation dans l'armée française," who asked him to take a message of much importance to "the proper persons" in Russia.

---

* It is a curious fact that this particular passage, which according to Cyon produced a greater sensation in Paris than even the famous editorial of the previous summer, does not appear in the text of the article in question included, in the original Russian, in the respective volume of Katkov's editorials published some years later by his widow (*Sobranie peredovykh statei Moskovskikh Vyedomostei*, 1887, pp. 42-44). This Russian version, to judge from the ellipsis with which it concludes, was also a condensation. On the other hand, it is odd that precisely this final paragraph, to which Cyon attached such great importance (it was this, he said, which convinced him of the change in Russian policy), should have been omitted from Madame Katkov's version of the original document.

It is clear from the context of Cyon's account that the "personnage" in question could have been none other than his close acquaintance and well-wisher of many years' standing: General Felix Gustave Saussier. Saussier, who had been serving since 1884 as military governor of Paris, had—it appears—come into conflict with Boulanger, as a consequence of which he had now lost his position as military governor and was functioning as vice president of the Conseil Supérieur de la Guerre. The substance of the message he wanted Cyon to convey to "the proper persons" in Russia was that the French were at that moment quite unprepared to cope with a German attack; they would require a breathing space of two or three months before they could hope to do so. Why? Because the inept Boulanger had recently scrapped the entire existing mobilization plan, worked out with immense care over the course of years, and had substituted for it a plan of his own, designed to shorten the mobilization period by two days. It had developed, however, that a dreadful error, relating to the movements of railway rolling stock, had been made in the new plan; and all was now confusion. Disregarding— evidently—their recent differences, Boulanger had appealed to Saussier (and others, presumably) for assistance in correcting the error and putting the arrangements back in order. Saussier had undertaken to assist him. But it would take some weeks, he explained to Cyon, to straighten things out. Meanwhile, France would be, in effect, at the mercy of the Germans.*

While Cyon was not always the most reliable of narrators, there is no reason to doubt the existence of some factual basis for this particular tale. This would explain, of course, the exceptional agitation of mind that obviously inspired Flourens' communications to Laboulaye in the ensuing days, and particularly his statement, in the letter of the 15th of February, that in the absence of Russian help "nous pouvons être écrasés

---

* That something unusual must have occurred to cause this panicky reaction on Flourens' part seems evident. The French army, while numerically more than equal, was inferior to the German in a number of respects and would probably have suffered eventual defeat in a war at that particular time. Such, at any rate, was the view of most serious students of military affairs at the time. (See, for example, the discussion of this question in J. F. Maurice, *The Balance of Military Power in Europe* [Edinburgh and London: Wm. Blackwood & Sons, 1888]. But no one supposed that the French military establishment, which included formidable fortifications all along the German frontier, was so inferior as to be susceptible of complete destruction before it had even begun to fight. Its peacetime fighting strength was, after all, numerically more than equal to the German; and the number of men who could have been mobilized for immediate service on the German frontier was presumably even greater than the comparable German figure, since the Germans would have been obliged to keep a considerable portion of their forces on their eastern border.

avant même de nous être mis sur la défensive." And this is not all that it would explain.

For on the 4th of February, just at the time when Saussier was approaching Cyon, Boulanger invited to his office none other than the French military attaché at Petersburg, Captain Moulin, who, in the immediate wake of his recent contacts with the entourage of Katkov, had now come to Paris, presumably to report personally to his superiors in the Ministry of War, and was now about to return to his post.[16] Boulanger asked Moulin to take a private letter from himself to the Tsar. It is plain that the purpose of the manoeuvre was to bypass both of the Foreign Ministries concerned.

Moulin at once recognized the danger which such a procedure could involve for himself. It was one thing to relay, with the authorization of his superiors, the views of Katkov to the French minister of war; it was another thing to serve, behind the backs of his own military and diplomatic superiors, as an intermediary between the war minister and the Russian monarch. He therefore told Flourens of the request. Flourens, infuriated by this attempt of a cabinet colleague to invade his province without his knowledge, took the matter up at a stormy cabinet meeting on the 6th or 7th of February, demanded Boulanger's resignation, and threatened to resign himself if the letter went forward. In this way, the general was brought to desist. Flourens, however, still fearful that the Germans might learn of Boulanger's attempt through other channels and that it would touch off the attack he now so feared, took the unusual step of apprising the Germans of it through what might be called a calculated leak: namely, by authorizing Madame Flourens (or so we must assume) to tell the whole tale to the daughter of the German Ambassador, Count Münster. This, in any case, is what she did, to the great edification, no doubt, of the German Foreign Office, and also, incidentally, of the Russian one, which intercepted the message in which the Germans informed their ambassador at Petersburg of the affair.[17]

To return, however, to Flourens' dramatic instructions to Laboulaye: the latter, upon receipt of the minister's letter, dutifully sought an appointment with Giers and was received on the 20th. Groaning inwardly, no doubt, over the strange ways of inexperienced foreign ministers, the ambassador exposed Flourens' view of the dangers with which France was confronted, expressed the hope that his compatriots would find in Russia at this critical time "a loyal and sympathetic witness to their conduct," and evidently stressed the great importance to France of Russia's not permitting herself to be led at this particular moment into a war in the Balkans.

Giers once more took refuge in the reassuring reports from Shuvalov.

The latter, he pointed out, was a discriminating and well-informed man. If anything was really stirring in German plans, it would be hard to conceal it from himself and his Foreign Office. In such a situation, the French would be at once informed.[18]

On the 21st of February 1887, new elections in Germany gave Bismarck the majority he wanted in the Reichstag, assured the passage of the *Septennat*, and deprived the chancellor of whatever incentive he might have had for prolonging the high state of tension between Germany and France. From this time on, with the exception of the brief period of the Schnaebele episode in April 1887, fears of a new Franco-German war would be somewhat moderated, at least insofar as press and public were concerned, though they would be in part replaced, as the year ran its course, by increased anxiety over the possibility of an armed conflict between Russia and Germany.

None of this appears, however, to have had any great effect on Flourens. He had now become, and was to remain to his death, a passionate advocate of a Franco-Russian alliance; and the conclusion of such an arrangement could not, one feels, have come too soon to suit him. In this respect, he was scarcely less sanguine than his colleague at the Ministry of War. His objection to Boulanger's effort to communicate directly with the Tsar was evidently of a procedural rather than a political nature: what he objected to was not the approach *per se* but the fact that it was Boulanger and not himself who had undertaken it. He therefore now proceeded to attempt to establish on his own initiative, and under his own control, the contact with the Tsar which he had objected to Boulanger's establishing independently.

The means chosen, however, were different. There had been an obvious formal impropriety involved in the effort of a mere cabinet minister to communicate personally and directly by letter with a foreign crowned head and chief of state. In the formal sense, the impropriety would have been no smaller had Flourens himself sent a letter of this nature. He came, therefore, upon the idea of obtaining the assistance, as an intermediary, of Eugène Melchior de Vogüé, former member of the French Embassy at Petersburg, now a well-known authority on Russian literature and contributor to the *Revue de deux Mondes*. De Vogüé, married to a daughter of the prominent General N. N. Annenkov, builder of the trans-Caucasian Railway and former adjutant general to Alexander II, was known to speak Russian and to be excellently connected in high circles of the Russian capital.

On the 25th of February, Flourens called de Vogüé in, asked him to undertake a private and unofficial mission to Russia, and, when de Vogüé agreed, armed him with a personal letter of recommendation to Giers. It is plain that the purpose of the projected mission was to explore informally, at as high a level as possible, the possibilities for a closer relationship, if not an alliance, between the two countries.[19]

Nothing came, however, of this initiative. Mohrenheim, who was kept informed by Hansen, thought it necessary to sound out Petersburg, telegraphically, in advance. Giers (this we know from the Lamsdorf diary) sent the telegram on to the Tsar, with the observation that a visit of this nature seemed to him untimely and not justified by circumstances. "I am deeply convinced," he wrote, "that such a mission would do more harm than good, and that it would scarcely be possible to keep it secret." To this the Tsar replied: "It would be well to have more details. What is it, specifically, that the French government wants? For the moment, all we have are rumors, and very unclear ones at that. Let Mohrenheim report in greater detail."

This was all Giers wanted. He despatched at once a corresponding message to Mohrenheim. It happened that the Germans, just at this time, were reported to be despatching a special emissary, Prince Hohenlohe, to Paris (where he had once been ambassador). "In view of the lack of clarity about Hohenlohe's mission to Paris," Giers wired to Mohrenheim, "we see no reason to enter into negotiations about undefined questions, particularly through the mediation of secret agents. If you receive more precise information, kindly let us have it."[20]

With this, not only was the Vogüé mission laid to rest, but Giers' victory over Katkov was partly won. For Flourens' impetuousness had run full tilt, at this point, up against the Tsar's more lethargic temperament. Alexander III, all Katkov's pressure notwithstanding, had not yet made up his mind; and he intensely disliked having his hand forced.

———————

To complete the recital of the various French attempts of the winter of 1887 to enter into contact with the Russian government at a high level and to assure themselves of Russian support in the face of the danger of war with Germany, one must take note of the strong evidence that French President Jules Grévy himself addressed a personal and highly confidential letter to the Tsar at just this time, and that this letter reached its destination. The evidence for this rests, to be sure, exclusively on Cyon's statements to this effect: first, in an obituary article written for *Le Gaulois* just after Grévy's death in 1891, and later in his book about the alliance.[21] But Cyon also claims to have been involved in determining the channel through which this letter should be sent, with a view to its bypassing Giers; and there is no reason to doubt the general veracity of his report, which seems nowhere to have been challenged or questioned.

On the face of it, it might seem surprising that Grévy should have taken this step. Now eighty years of age, he was known for his phlegmatic, skeptical temperament, and was never considered to be an enthusiast for the alliance. He was decidedly unreceptive to Flourens' excited reports and appeals for action. "Mon cher Flourens," he is reported to have said to the minister on the occasion of one of the latter's frequent visits at this time, ". . . vos visites me sont ordinairement agréables, mais, dans les circonstances actuelles, non. Il me semble toujours que vous allez m'apporter de mauvaises nouvelles. Venez moins souvent. J'aime mieux ne pas vous voir."[22] ("My dear Flourens, ordinarily your visits are agreeable to me, but in the present circumstances—no. It always seems to me that you come bringing bad news. Come less often. I prefer not to see you.")

But it is not wholly implausible that Grévy should have wished, in the circumstances, to address a personal letter to the Russian monarch. He was the only person in France whose position entitled him to do this with propriety. It would have been in no way surprising if, in rejecting Boulanger's initiative, the members of the cabinet had appealed to the president to take just this step. Cyon says that the letter was written and sent without the knowledge of the members of the cabinet—also quite plausible, since Grévy could not wholly depend upon their discretion. Finally, one may be sure that the letter, if it was indeed written, was drawn up in much more prudent and calm tones than anything that would have emanated from either Boulanger or Flourens. It probably consisted primarily of a stressing of France's peaceful intentions and the expression of a hope that if war, contrary to France's desires and in spite of her best efforts to avert it, did break out, she would have the sympathy and moral support of the Tsar.

Just how this letter was finally transmitted is not apparent. Cyon indicates that he was first asked, not directly by Grévy (whom he never met) but by Saussier, to arrange for its delivery through Katkov, and that he considered this possibility, but that he then thought it would be better if the editor were not to be involved in such an undertaking, and therefore suggested another channel, "not less sure and more official," through which the communication was then despatched.

What was this channel? We do not know. Cyon was himself just leaving, at that time, for Petersburg. Presumably he took the letter with him. It could then well have been transmitted, with the help of Cyon's military contacts, through the minister of the interior, Dmitri Tolstoi.

It will be seen from the above that there were five attempts by highly placed French figures, during the winter of 1887, to get into touch with the Russian Tsar or his leading advisers with a view to assuring the Tsar's support for France in the light of what was believed to be the great danger of another Franco-German war, and to persuading the Tsar, if possible, to threaten the Germans with Russia's intervention on France's behalf, after the pattern of his father's supposed intervention in 1875. Three of these attempts proceeded from Flourens, one from Boulanger, and one from Grévy. Two—Boulanger's projected letter and Flourens' attempt to despatch de Vogüé as an emissary—were abortive. Two others were skillfully deflected by Giers, who succeeded in proving to the Tsar's satisfaction that the danger was greatly exaggerated. We do not know the effect of Grévy's letter. Perhaps the Tsar never even told Giers about it.

It will also be seen that the highly placed French figures who initiated these approaches were acting, in large part, on the basis of erroneous or misleading information: an exaggerated image of German aggressive intentions, probably influenced by Boulangiste intrigues and propaganda; a very poor understanding of the existing state of Russia's obligations vis-à-vis Germany; and a wildly inaccurate picture of Bismarck's policy with relation to Russia and Austria. Both of these last two misimpressions they owed in considerable measure to Katkov and the Russian Panslavs. The inadequacy of this background of information is historically evident from the fact that neither did the dangers thus envisaged actually mature, nor could the Russian Tsar be induced to move in the direction they desired—this last, despite the fact that this was a moment at which the prestige of Katkov was at its height, and the position of Giers precarious as never before.

How was this failure to be explained? The answer lies, surely, in the amateurism, the ignorance, and the emotional erraticism of the forces agitating for a new Franco-Russian alliance on both sides—the anguished French patriots, on the one hand, and the exalted, emotional Panslavs with their Russian-nationalist followers, on the other.

In France, the active center of enthusiasm for the alliance had passed, by this time, from the impassioned but genteel republican-intellectual salon of Juliette Adam to the crude dilettantism of Boulanger and his associates, reinforced by the bewildered and agitated Flourens, with

Jules Hansen and the rest of the intelligence section of the Russian Paris Embassy at his elbow. Only people of such limitations could have indulged themselves in the illusion that the Russian Tsar could be induced to forget thus suddenly all his family ties to the German court, to accept the situation of dangerous isolation in which a total break with Germany would leave him, and to risk war against a coalition that included Germany, England, and Italy as well as Austria—and all this just for the sake of helping republican France to recover Alsace-Lorraine.

On the Russian Panslav-nationalist side there was a similar lack of realism. Here, people plainly pictured a Franco-German war which would tie up German forces on the west and prevent Germany from coming to Austria's assistance while they, thus relieved of the necessity of coping with Germany, would settle their scores with the hated Austrians. To suppose that such a scenario could hold any attraction for the French, and this at a time when French military leaders were actually demanding of their Russian counterparts, as part of the price for an alliance, that Russia agree to enter into any war with Germany three months before the French would do so, was the height of unrealism. In addition to which, these people seem cheerfully to have disregarded the possibility that in the general European war which all this implied, they might well be faced with the hostility of England as well as Austria. They seem, finally, to have been wholly incognizant of the fact that Boulanger and Flourens did not have the support of the French political and governmental establishment as a whole either in their apprehensions as to the danger of war or in their desire to seek an immediate alliance with Russia.

Giers, hard pressed as he was, was hampered by none of these illusions. He knew very well that Flourens and Boulanger could not speak for the entirety of the French political establishment. This was the basis for the sharp challenge which he flung at Laboulaye when the latter, in their interview of the 26th of January, tried to sound him out on Russia's reaction to a Franco-German war: "Eh bien, Monsieur l'Ambassadeur, what would you say if I were to offer you, here and now, an alliance between our two countries against Germany?" It is no less significant that it was Giers who, on the same occasion, felt it necessary to point out to Laboulaye, delicately but in a phrase full of meaning, that Germany, in the event of a war with France, would not be without allies.

The fact is that in each case the partisans of the alliance had their eyes riveted on the local situations with which they were preoccupied: Flourens and the Boulangistes on Alsace-Lorraine and France's eastern border, the Russian nationalists on Austrian Galicia or the Dardanelles. Bismarck and Giers, on the other hand, acted from a knowledge and an awareness of the European situation as a whole, as well as from long experience and well-trained powers of calm analysis. It was these elements of superiority that enabled them, at the time in question, to carry the day.

Chapter Sixteen

RUSSIAN WINTER, 1887

It is not normally within the province of the historian to occupy himself with hypothetical questions. But it is not exceeding the bounds of the permissible, surely, to point out that had Katkov's influence prevailed in the winter of 1887, the course of history would have been significantly changed. Giers, unquestionably, would have been removed. There would have been no attempt, on the Russian side, to arrive at any bilateral pact with Germany to replace the expiring *Dreikaiserbund*. Bismarck, we may be sure, would not have left the further initiative to the Russians. The departure of Giers would have been warning enough to him. Even as it was, he was busy by the beginning of 1887, as we have seen, hedging his bets and taking precautions for the possibility that the worm might turn in such a direction. Had Giers been removed, these efforts would have gone into high gear, impelled by all the resourcefulness, the experience, the prestige, and the mastery of diplomatic art which the old chancellor possessed. In these circumstances, there can be no doubt that the political map of Europe would have been decisively changed. New impetus would have been given to the project of a Franco-Russian alliance. On the other hand, new forces, enlisted and marshaled by Bismarck's skillful hand, would have been introduced for the purpose of its frustration.

The month of February 1887 represented substantially the high point of Katkov's success in his struggle for the reversal of Russian foreign policy—the period when he was closest to the realization of his dreams. The conflict with Giers was at this time at its height; and all of politically sophisticated Russia was aware of it. The bare-boned structure of the diplomatic documents does not reveal more than the smallest part of the human emotions and stresses which this conflict—a conflict of outlook and political philosophy as well as personality—engendered. Yet without an awareness of these emotions and stresses, the documents themselves lose much of their meaning.

This, in the writer's eyes, is the justification for interrupting, at this point, the strictly diplomatic narrative and pausing to take a more

289

intimate day-by-day view of what was occurring at that time in the lives of certain of the major participants at the Russian end of the struggle, as reflected particularly in the experiences of one minor actor.

————————

When Ilya Fadeyevich Tsion, alias Élie de Cyon, boarded the train for Berlin and Petersburg at the Gare du Nord on the 6th of February 1887, he must have been greatly excited with the consciousness of his own importance. He was presumably the bearer of an oral message of great importance from the French high command to their Russian counterparts concerning the state of French defenses in the light of the supposed great danger of war. He also presumably had in his pocket, or somewhere on his person, a highly confidential letter from the French president to the Tsar of Russia, of which not even the members of the French cabinet were aware, and which, he must have supposed, could well be crucial for the peace of Europe. Never mind that the war scare was exaggerated. Never mind that the president's letter was probably much less dramatic than Cyon himself pictured it. Cyon had no means of knowing all this; and political imaginations, in those days of romantic nationalism, were nothing if not feverish. One can imagine with what smug contempt he must have viewed his ordinary fellow passengers on that long train journey, and with what glowing self-satisfaction he—a talented and ambitious but frustrated man, with a passion for conspiratorial secrecy—must have said to himself, as he brushed past those fellow passengers in the corridors or confronted them in the dining cars: "Ah—if they only knew."

There was, in the long train journeys of those days, a sense of mystery and concealed meaning which another generation will never know. From Paris to Moscow via Petersburg is a distance of some 2,200 miles. If one performed it in the winter, as did Cyon, one's sleeping car pulled out of Paris in the early darkness of the northern-European winter afternoon. In the afternoon of the following day one was in Berlin, where the make-up of the train was rearranged. The second night was passed droning over flat, frozen fields of West and East Prussia, with a long halt at Königsberg in early morning. It was afternoon before one reached the German-Russian border at Eidkuhnen-Virballen. Here, there was another long wait while the Russian officials, impressive in their greatcoats, went through the ceremonies of customs and passport inspection, and one changed from the standard-gauge *wagon-lits* of western Europe to the commodious broad-gauge Russian cars, with the icicles hanging from their roofs and the charcoal smoke floating up from the little samovar-chimneys into the still, frosty air.

One was in Petersburg the following morning; and if, like Cyon, one was going on to Moscow, there was plenty of time for the ride across town in a hired sleigh through the drifted streets, their extraordinary silence (on which so many foreign visitors commented) broken only by the jingling of the harnesses, the cries of the bundled coachmen, and the squeaking of the runners over the icy patches.

It was dark, once more, when the train pulled out of the Nikolayevsk Station onto the celebrated arrow-straight 400-mile stretch of track that led to Moscow (so constructed, legend has it, because this was the way the Tsar Nicolas I had once drawn it on a map with a ruler). It was an overnight journey, and a quiet one, because the deep snow muffled the rattling of the wheels. And if at any time one cared to scratch the frost off the window and peer through into the night (which Cyon probably did not, for he had little interest in such things), one could see only the still, snow-covered fields, the shadowy lines of distant forests, and the half-buried log cabins of the villages, all gliding past in the moonlight. It was mid-morning, then, on the fourth day out, when one arrived in Moscow and emerged into the raucous chaos of the snow-covered square before the station, to struggle and bargain for another sleigh.

Cyon claims, in those portions of his diary that were published many years later in his history of the alliance,* to have passed through Petersburg, on this occasion, "without stopping." This was surely an exaggeration. He had ample time, while there, to deliver Grévy's letter into the proper hands, and to pass on to "the proper persons" the information Saussier had given him about the state of the French armed forces; and there is no reason to doubt that he did so.

He arrived in Moscow, in any case, on the morning of Thursday, the 10th of February, and was very shortly lunching alone with Katkov at the latter's home and office on the Strastnoi Boulevard. Both men were bursting with news. What Cyon had to tell, we already know. Katkov, for his part, confirmed (and Cyon never doubted his authority for the statement) that the Tsar was determined to guard Russia's freedom of action; that he had decided not to undertake any new obligations to the Germans; that he would not permit France to be attacked. Cyon, after lunch, rushed off to send telegrams, in prearranged code, to Patinot, editor of *Le Journal des Débats*, to F. Magnard, in similar position at *Le Figaro*, to Juliette Adam, "et à plusieurs autres personnes." (The

---

* *Histoire.* Where not otherwise indicated, the data recounted below concerning Cyon's activities in Russia in February-March 1887 are taken from his own narrative, studded with passages from his diary, as they appear on pp. 233-253 of Chapter VIII of the *Histoire.*

despatch of these telegrams, he recorded in his diary, became known in circles around the Moscow bourse, where the news led to considerable speculation.)

The two men then resumed their talk, and continued it until late into the evening. Katkov told of his memorandum for the Tsar. It had unfortunately become known, he said, through an indiscretion of Feoktistov, the censor. The latter, learning of it from the minister of the interior, Dmitri Tolstoi (who had told him of the immense impression made by the memorandum on the Tsar), had not been able to keep the news to himself.

Katkov went on to tell of "offers" by Bismarck to the Russians of a Russo-German treaty directed against Austria, and of how a similar offer had been made by the Germans in 1883, but how Giers had rejected it because he was afraid that the acceptance would bolster the prestige of Saburov, his rival for the office of foreign minister. (Katkov was, of course, wholly wrong, on both points; but the purpose of this chapter is partly to show how faulty and erratic was the understanding of events even among the most interested of outsiders at this particular period; what vales of error they were all traversing; by what clouds of misleading gossip the real transactions of governments were surrounded and obscured.)

The following day, the 11th of February, was spent in similar conferences between the two men, after which Cyon, once again, sent off a confidential communication—a letter, presumably, this time—to Magnard. The talks went on over the entire weekend of the 12th-13th of February, sometimes uninterruptedly for many hours on end. Cyon took all his meals at Katkov's home. Like Cyon, Katkov was convinced that the election of an anti-Bismarckian majority, or at least of one that would not support Bismarck's demand for the *Septennat*, in the forthcoming German elections (February 21), would mean war. The Germans would no doubt then attack France; and the Austrians, upon expiration of the "treaty of Skiernevice," would invade Podolia;* whereupon the Germans would also march into Poland. It was obvious that Katkov had his information from Russian military circles; for he was also able to tell Cyon of energetic measures just then being put in hand

---

* In mid-December 1886, at a meeting of the Council of State, Vannovski, the war minister, had put out the same tale, to the effect that Austria was preparing to attack Russia, citing it in support of his demand for larger military appropriations (Lamsdorf diary, December 17, 1886). The tale was of course wholly untrue, and mischievous in the highest degree. Giers had been greatly indignant, and had demanded an explanation. One sees here, once more, the evidence of close and confidential contact between Katkov and the high military command.

by the Russian Ministry of War, including the transfer of troops from the Caucasus to Poland, to reinforce the western frontier.

Much of the talk concerned the possibility of shifting the Russian borrowing from Berlin to Paris. Cyon told of the talks he had had, before leaving France, with various representatives of the French *haute banque*, including one of the Rothschild brothers. The latter had assured him that his house was "toujours à la disposition de notre [i.e. the Russian] Ministre des Finances" with a view to resuming the relations which it had been necessary to interrupt, some twelve years earlier, when France had found it necessary to employ her capital for domestic needs.* Katkov, greatly impressed, urged him to proceed at once to Petersburg and to see the new finance minister Vyshnegradski. So Cyon, armed with a letter to that dignitary, and no doubt similar letters to others as well, set off for Petersburg on the night train. By noon the next day, the 14th of February, he was on hand there, primed for what he viewed as the most momentous of business.

The situation of Giers, meanwhile, had remained precarious. Katkov had been in Petersburg in late January. He had been received in audience by the Tsar on the 22nd of January. He had also visited extensively with the head of the Asiatic Department of the Foreign Office, Zinoviev—of that department which, it will be recalled, had traditionally enjoyed a wide margin of independence and had been closely connected, at all times, with the Moscow Panslavs. The editor had made no bones, in his talks with Zinoviev and others, of his intention to unseat Giers; and it was generally thought by informed people in the capital that he would succeed. The talk of the town revolved mainly around the question of who would be the successor: whether it would be Ignatyev or Zinoviev, the latter's candidacy being increasingly favored as the news of Katkov's conferences with him got about.

Giers himself thought, for a time, that he had small chance of surviving. Katkov, he observed to Lamsdorf on the day before Katkov's audience with the Tsar (January 22), would unquestionably persuade the monarch to drop him. "I am thinking," he said, "only about some dignified way of departing." He repeated this view two days later, after

* In the draft of an instruction from the German Foreign Office to Schweinitz of April 11, 1887, a copy of which was kindly brought to my attention by Professor Fritz Stern, of Columbia University, it is stated, among other things, that Cyon had a brother in Paris, who was an official of the Banque Parisienne. It was perhaps through this brother that Cyon had his access to French banking circles.

the Katkov audience had taken place. He was glad, he said to Lamsdorf, not to be responsible for the confusion into which Russia was being drawn. A policy that encouraged French hopes and at the same time talked peace with Bismarck was not for him.[1]

In the last days of January and the first days of February things looked, to be sure, slightly better. The indecisive monarch, always reluctant to admit new and untried faces to his entourage, was obviously finding it easier to change a policy than to change a minister—particularly a minister in whose integrity and ability he had learned to have confidence. His reactions, furthermore, were made somewhat less edgy when, at the beginning of February, he received the German Kaiser's reply to his appeal for support against a possible return of Battenberg to the Bulgarian throne. The reply was satisfactory and reassuring. It lessened the emotional appeal of a demonstratively anti-German policy, and eased Giers' position. At audiences that took place on the 22nd of January and the 1st of February, the Tsar received Giers, to the latter's great relief, not unkindly.

In these circumstances considerable importance came to be attached, in Giers' mind, to the response the imperial couple might make to an invitation which Giers and his wife had extended to them: to attend a great evening function, on the 22nd of February, in the Foreign Office premises on the Singers' Bridge. It had been impossible not to include the Emperor and Empress in the invitation; but Giers sensed that the suggestion was personally disagreeable to them, particularly to the Empress, and perhaps politically embarrassing to the Tsar. He thus awaited with bated breath their reaction, which he thought would be an important straw in the wind. At his weekly audience on the 8th of February, the Tsar, to his surprise (because the audience was in other respects an unpleasant one), indicated acceptance.

In these circumstances Giers took heart and did what he could to defend his position. On the evening of the 6th he and Madame Giers, braving the curious looks and over-the-shoulder whisperings of the diplomats and courtiers, who had come to regard them as already politically dead, attended an imperial ball at the Anichkov Palace. A day or two later, Giers caused to be inserted in the semi-official organ of the Foreign Office, the Brussels Le Nord, a biting item rejecting the extravagant interpretations being placed on Katkov's editorial of the 3rd (see above, pp. 279-280), challenging the picture of the Russian government's position which that article conveyed, and emphasizing that in Russia it was the Tsar alone (ergo, by implication, not nationalistic editors) who made foreign policy. The Tsar's position, it was pointedly observed, was too elevated to permit of his having any "amis" or "confidantes."

The battle was thus still joined; but the outcome, despite these encouraging signs, was still far from secure. At the Foreign Office, where the probability of Katkov's success was now given wide credence, intrigue and betrayal swirled around the heard of the hard-pressed minister. Lamsdorf alone, the neurotic bachelor and co-inhabitant of the Foreign Office premises, remained faithful, following his chief's comings and goings as well as the ups and downs of his fortunes with anxious devotion. The other senior officials—Vlangali, Jomini, Zinoviev, and the rest—were for the most part hedging their bets, extending elaborate courtesy, when opportunity presented itself, to Katkov and his various envoys, taking at least in part what they believed to be the great editor's line, striving in this way to ingratiate themselves and protect their positions for the future.

On the other hand, Katkov's conduct was now beginning to arouse uneasiness in certain of the higher court and official circles, where it was coming to be seen as detrimental to the prestige of the Russian government as a whole. When, on the 2nd of March, Polovtsov, the secretary of the State Council, took his daily walk in company with the Grand Duke Vladimir Aleksandrovich, the latter said to him:

> I made up my mind to have a frank talk with the Tsar and, taking advantage of the first week of Lent, I unburdened myself of all that I had long wanted to say about Katkov—what we have talked about more than once, namely: that it was wrong to create outside the framework of government some sort of special independent force; that this force had recently become especially conspicuous; that rumors had reached me to the effect that Katkov had boasted that it was he who had replaced Nabokov, he who had replaced Bunge, and that now he intended to replace Giers; that all this weakened the Government and was particularly impermissible with relation to foreign policy. Foreign policy had always been the policy of the ruling emperor, and to permit it to be adversely criticized as the *Moskovskie Vyedomosti* had been doing was to disrupt confidence in the supreme power.

To which Polovtsov replied: "You have performed a great service to the state."[3]

Cyon arrived in Petersburg on Monday, the 14th of February, and passed the remainder of the week waiting for his appointment with Vyshnegradski. He was, however, anything but idle during the interval. He spent the first day despatching further letters and other communications to his friends in Paris—"avec renseignements et conseils." The following day he called on the highly conservative Minister of Education Delyanov, a good friend of Juliette Adam as well as of Katkov, and was shaken to be told by Delyanov that he and other friends of Katkov, worried over the increasing signs of fatigue in the editor under the strains of making frequent visits to Petersburg as well as editing and publishing the paper, were urging him to move to Petersburg completely; and that when he did so, they hoped Cyon would consent to take over in his place the editorship of the *Moskovskie Vyedomosti*. Delyanov further advised Cyon to make courtesy calls on the two most powerful men in Russia after the Tsar: Pobyedonostsev and Minister of the Interior Dmitri Tolstoi.

Among the numerous visits paid during that week by Cyon, one was to a certain Monsieur V———, a person whom he had not previously known but who had invited him to a *soirée* at his own home.* This gentleman, who was an intimate friend of Ignatyev, urged Cyon, as Katkov had already done, to make Ignatyev's acquaintance. Cyon was hesitant, remembering that the articles of the Grand Duke Nikolai Nikolayevich, which he himself had ghost-written and then published in Madame Adam's *Nouvelle Revue* in 1880, had included bitter criticisms of Ignatyev. But Katkov had told him that the latter was too large a man to be put off by such trifles; so Cyon paid his visit, talked for three and a half hours with the former statesman, and came away wholly charmed. Ignatyev, who at that time had high hopes of shortly taking Giers' place, was, needless to say, a firm supporter of Katkov, in whose policies alone he professed to see the salvation of Russia.

This, actually, was a good day for Cyon. He went, that evening, from his hotel to the nearby "Circus" (the same building that continues today to house that function), and was moved to tears when there appeared on stage, to the accompaniment of the strains of the Marseillaise, some little boys dressed in the uniform of the French *zouaves*, who evoked from the crowd an ovation that lasted a full ten minutes.

On the following day, Sunday the 20th, Cyon finally had his appointment with Vyshnegradski. This was not, evidently, a wholly satisfactory encounter. Cyon outlined to the minister his proposals "for our economic emancipation from Germany and for the transfer of the market for our securities to Paris." He told of the talks he had had with

---

* Other than by the initial, Cyon does not indicate the identity of this previously unknown gentleman who invited him to a *soirée* and then put him into touch with Ignatyev. The man was, obviously, of Katkov's party. He had evidently been advised in advance of Cyon's arrival. One is tempted to suppose, from the initial and the circumstances, that it was Prince A. I. Vasil'chikov, prominent member and vice president of the Petersburg branch of the Slavonic Benevolent Association.

the Paris bankers, submitting in this connection a memorandum on the French banking system. He confessed that he had made similar proposals the previous autumn to Vyshnegradski's predecessor, Bunge, who had not been impressed.

Vyshnegradski showed little more enthusiasm for these ideas than had Bunge, pleading as the basis for his skepticism, as Bunge had done, the difficulty of obtaining the cooperation of the Rothschilds. Cyon professed confidence that he could obtain the collaboration of that house— "on ne peut [être] mieux disposée"; no French bank, he was sure, would deny to Russia its collaboration in the existing circumstances.

But Vyshnegradski was not to be moved very far in that direction. The best Cyon could get out of him was a grudging admission that they might sound out the ground, in a smaller way, by an attempt to get the collaboration of the Rothchilds in the conversion of a single and very minor component of Russia's foreign indebtedness: namely, the shares of the Mutual Land Credit Bank (Crédit Foncier Mutuel, in French; Vzaimni Pozemel'ny Kredit, in Russian), an institution in which the Russian large landowners, known partisans of close trading relations with Germany, were most intimately interested. This would not have commended itself greatly to Katkov; and it commended itself no better to Cyon. The Rothschilds, he argued, would be more inclined to interest themselves in converting obligations of the Russian Treasury, over which Vyshnegradski presided, than the shares of this quasi-private institution. But the minister was not to be persuaded. The Tsar, he said, was personally interested in this particular conversion, and it had been approved in principle by the Council of State. Cyon, swallowing his disappointment, departed, bearing with him the entire official file on the bank, which he had undertaken to study with a view to drawing up, and presenting to Vyshnegradski, a plan for arrangement of the conversion.

On the following days there were visits to Pobyedonostsev and to Minister of the Interior Tolstoi. The latter was extremely amiable, encouraged Cyon to remain in Russia, and complimented him on his attacks on liberalism which had appeared the preceding summer in Katkov's *Russki Vestnik*. These, the minister said, he and members of his family had read aloud to each other at their country *dacha* during a recent vacation.

Later that day, Cyon's new-found friend, Mr. V——, appeared again, bringing with him, this time, S. S. Tatishchev, a well-known publicist and historian. Like Cyon, Tatishchev was an occasional contributor to Katkov's *Russki Vestnik*. It will be recalled that he had previously been in the Russian diplomatic service, but had been forced to leave it in 1877 over an incident (an alleged indiscretion) occurring in Vienna. Closely connected with Katkov, he had recently been following the latter's lead in attacking the official policy in his articles. He now exhibited a marked and persistent interest in learning what, if any, were Cyon's connections with the Boulangistes.* Cyon assured him that he had none, that he had never met the general. But the questioning aroused his own ready suspicions, and set the tone of their relationship for the remainder of their lives.

Petersburg, one might mention, was rocked in just those days, as was much of western Europe, by the appearance in rapid succession in the Petersburg *Novoye Vremya*, which until recently had been considered reasonably close to the Foreign Office, and in the Brussel's *Le Nord*, which was its own *officieuse* organ, of articles reflecting in overwhelming degree the Katkov line on Russian foreign policy, rather than that with which the Foreign Office had generally been associated. It was the article in *Le Nord* which, in view of the known quality of that sheet as a Russian Foreign Office mouthpiece, caused the greatest stir, especially in western Europe, where the paper was widely read in diplomatic and journalistic circles. The article began with two paragraphs of summary of Katkov's well-known editorial of the 3rd of February (which it attributed simply to "une feuille russe"), and then went ahead to develop precisely Katkov's view: Russia, in view of the danger of a Franco-German war, should not allow herself to get bogged down in Bulgaria; Bulgaria could wait; Russia's gaze should now be directed to the Rhine; she needed no alliance with France; but she had every reason to retain her full freedom of action, which meant no agreement with the Germans, either; in this way, both parties in western Europe could be kept guessing as to Russia's ultimate decisions, and she would become the arbiter of Europe.† Naturally, the close accordance of these views with those of

* Cyon's disclaimers were, at that particular time, perhaps not too misleading. Initially, upon Boulanger's accession to the War Ministry, Cyon, knowing of Boulanger's recent conflict with Saussier, viewed him with sharp disfavor. Later, however, he changed his opinion and became well acquainted with Boulanger, whom he entertained as a guest at his home on at least one occasion, and also with the latter's follower, Lucien Millevoye.

† Copies of *Le Nord* seem to be difficult to come by. Even the *Bibliothèque Nationale* has them only beginning with the year 1892, by which time the journal had moved to Paris; and even these are incomplete and in very bad shape. But a curious volume published in 1888 (*L'Année politique 1887*. Paris: Charpentier), edited by men who had no knowledge of the later Reinsurance Treaty and who still took the editorial as a solemn *Manifeste* of Russian foreign policy, carried what were either long extracts or the entirety of the article of February 19 as well

Katkov was widely noted; and the conclusion was drawn that this was evidence of the complete and final triumph of the editor's policy recommendations not only in the mind of the Tsar but also in the very apparatus of the Foreign Office.

Actually, the articles had been written by a language teacher by the name of Giaccone, who, in addition to being in the pay of the Foreign Office, was a regular correspondent of *Le Nord* and of several Petersburg papers. It was the general opinion of the Petersburg diplomats that Giaccone was, to use Laboulaye's words, "usually inspired by Jomini." The latter therefore at once fell under suspicion; and Giers was soon besieged by diplomatic visitors demanding to know whether it was true that the article had emanated from one of his leading subordinates. Jomini, called to account, defended himself by claiming that he had only advised Giaccone to take his cue from the *Novoye Vremya* article. This may have been true, but few believed it; and it only led to the further question: who had inspired the *Novoye Vremya* in the first place? Giers had no choice but to pretend to believe Jomini's story; but he suspected, he said to the Austrian Ambassador, that the "imprudent chattering" to which Jomini was given might well have had something to do with it—Jomini was, after all, a "bavard," who changed his views ten times a day.[3]

In addition to severely reprimanding Giaccone and the editors of *Le Nord* and *Die politische Korrespondenz* (the Vienna counterpart of *Le Nord*, which had also carried the piece), Giers at once issued and caused to be published in the Foreign Office's local organ, *Le Journal de Pétersbourg*, as well as in *Le Nord*, a sharp denial of the Foreign Office's paternity and of the authoritative quality of the article.[4] People were warned against attaching any importance to it. Serious editors ought to know, it was said in this communiqué, that relations among empires bound to one another by the bonds of centuries did not depend on a few more or less fantastic press reports ("que les rapports entre les empires attachés par les liens séculaires ne dépendent pas de quelques correspondances plus ou moins fantaisistes").

The incident gradually died down, as all such incidents do, but not before it had made a deep impression on public opinion. The repercussions of it will be found in most of the relevant diplomatic and journalist correspondence of the period. The Germans, in particular, were sharply affected. To Bismarck, the article was one more bit of evidence of the undermining of Giers' position and of the growing

---

as of another and similar one that followed a week later. It is from these reprintings that the description of the article, above, is derived.

unreliability of Russia as a partner in international affairs. Taken alone, he wired to Schweinitz on the 28th of February, the article might have been disregarded; but coming on top of the Russian silence concerning Shuvalov's earlier proposal, it could not be ignored. Schweinitz was admonished, once again, not to bring up the subject of the bilateral pact Shuvalov had once proposed, but he was encouraged to enter a sharp protest over the *Le Nord* article, and did so.

———

On the 23rd of February, after working all night over the files of the Land Credit Bank, Cyon read in the papers, with consuming interest, of the vote in the German Reichstag which assured to Bismarck the eventual passage of his *Septennat*. "Ahah," he will have said to himself, "no immediate outbreak of war between France and Germany." Everything would now depend on the preservation by Russia of her freedom of action. This was the time to get on with the strengthening of Franco-Russian relations. But what would Bismarck do now?

Cyon met later that day with the most mysterious, and probably the most significant, of his Petersburg contacts; a certain General X——. (Whereas in other instances, Cyon usually hinted at the identity of his contacts by using their true last initial or its French counterpart, he was careful in this instance to use an initial which had no counterpart in the Russian language.) There is no evidence that this was the first time the two men had met. One is obliged to suspect that it was probably General X—— who was the immediate recipient of Cyon's information about the state of the French armed forces.* General X——, as it turned out, was scheduled to attend that same evening a *soirée* at the German Embassy; and Cyon, who was most decidedly *not* invited to this function,† appears to have had no difficulty in persuading the general to act as his eyes and ears on that occasion.

* This general was obviously a Russian. He must have been in close relation with Katkov, but was probably not too well known as such, or he would not have been invited to the German Embassy and permitted to talk high policy with Schweinitz. He could not possibly have been either Ignatyev or Bogdanovich—the two other generals Cyon mentions seeing in Petersburg at this time—because neither of them were at all likely to have been invited to the German Embassy, and Bogdanovich is specifically distinguished from General X—— in another passage of Cyon's diary.

† The German Embassy's views on Cyon can be described only as "wild and wonderful." A telegram from the German chargé d'affaires at Petersburg, von Bülow, of April 13, 1887, described Cyon, in response to a query from Berlin, as a "mendacious and venal Jew with revolutionary tendencies." The references to Katkov in this message were no less wide of the mark. A facsimile of this telegram was kindly made available to me by Professor Fritz Stern. The original

The next day (February 24) was largely taken up with a long talk with Jomini, Cyon's last remaining contact at the Foreign Office. They talked first of the article in *Le Nord*. Jomini blamed its appearance on his own "subordinates," but was careful to add, knowing Cyon's relations with Katkov, that he personally was entirely in agreement with Katkov's policies. There followed, then, a long discussion of the origins of the "treaty of Skiernevice." (Could Jomini, one wonders, Giers' number three at the Foreign Office, really have been ignorant of the true nature and origins of the *Dreikaiserbund*? The answer is probably "yes"; otherwise the secret would never have been so well kept.) The discussion ended with a plea by Jomini that Cyon induce Katkov to moderate his attacks on Giers. The triumph of Katkov's policies, he argued, was now assured—the attacks were superfluous.

That afternoon, Cyon took to Vyshnegradski his completed plan for the conversion of the Land Credit Bank obligations. The minister professed himself pleased with the work. They discussed, for some two hours, the possible modalities of its realization. Cyon departed (or so he claims) with a promise by Vyshnegradski that if he should succeed in reestablishing acceptable relations between the Rothschilds and the Russian Ministry of Finance, Vyshnegradski would report this achievement to the Tsar and would see to it that Cyon was given a senior post in the Ministry.

The following day, the 25th, was Cyon's last in Petersburg. He paid a farewell visit to Delyanov. He then received, himself, the visit of General X——, who came to report the content of a conversation he had had with Schweinitz at the German *soirée*. The general had expressed to the ambassador on that occasion the hope that Bismarck, having now obtained his *Septennat*, would be content to leave France alone, and that peace would thus be assured. That, the ambassador replied, would depend on France. Who could guarantee Germany against a French attack? "If the Tsar," Schweinitz went on (this is still General X——'s report)[5]

> . . . is really intent on the preservation of peace, and we do not doubt
> that he is, there is a very simple means by which he can assure it, and
> that is to state to France that he is ready to guarantee her against any
> aggression from the German side, but that he would not intervene in any
> way, should the declaration of war proceed from the French.*

reposes in the German Foreign Office files, at the Politisches Archiv, Bonn, in the folder entitled: "Französische Journalisten, vom 15 April, 1886 bis 31 Dezember, 1887."

* It is not likely that these were Schweinitz's actual words. A seasoned diplomatist, with long experience in Petersburg, he would scarcely have made such a

General X——, obviously himself the strong partisan of a Franco-Russian alliance, was convinced that Bismarck would advance proposals along this line with a view to restoring Germany's alliance with Russia or to compromising Russia in the eyes of France. He thought that this line, cleverly conceived as it was with an eye to the peaceful inclinations of the Tsar, had dangerously good chances of success, and that "a warning" should therefore be issued. He begged Cyon to proceed at once to Moscow and to alert Katkov to the danger. Greatly impressed with all this, and having now completed his business with Vyshnegradski, Cyon cut short his stay in Petersburg, caught the night train to Moscow, and was back in Katkov's office on the morning of the 26th.

There then ensued four long days of agitated and intense discussion—such discussion as only Russians can conduct and endure—between Cyon and Katkov. To these talks Cyon devotes over 4,000 words in his diary. They are not uninteresting, particularly with relation to the intimate ideas of the great publicist in these final months of his life. He was now a very ill man. Cyon, brilliant physician that he was, could not help but perceive this; and he must have known that it was to this that much of Katkov's overwrought psychic state—his unnatural excitability and choleric oversensitivity—had to be attributed. His condition was aggravated, in just these days, by the beginning of the Russian Lent, in response to which he began the seven-week "great fast," restricting his diet to a mushroom dish of curious aspect which Cyon, once again the doctor, viewed with dark suspicion and dismay. It was under these conditions that the talks proceeded, sometimes uninterruptedly for as much as thirteen hours on end.

The first subject was the warning of General X——about Schweinitz' statement. It is revealing for the true aspirations of both men that they found this suggestion—that Russia should guarantee Germany against French aggression as well as vice versa—extremely dangerous. It would amount, Cyon pointed out, to a guaranty by Russia of the terms of the Treaty of Frankfurt, with which the war of 1870 had been ended. Yes, said Katkov, and Bismarck would have only to provoke France into initiating action in order to establish a claim on Russian neutrality. Plainly, neither Katkov nor Cyon wished to contemplate a situation in which France would be unable to attack Germany without forfeiting Russian support.

---

suggestion to a casual inquirer among his party guests. What he probably did was to turn General X—— off by saying that Germany had no aggressive intentions and therefore no need to seek Russian support for any aggressive undertakings. If, then, the Tsar wished to assure peace, he needed only to make it clear to the French that they, too, could not expect his support in an attack on Germany.

The future of the *Moskovskie Vyedomosti* came next. Katkov confirmed that he had thought of asking Cyon to replace him as its editor. If he did not succeed in bringing about Giers' removal, then, he said, he would go abroad for a long time and nurse his health. In any case, he would require a long vacation, and would need a replacement.

Cyon, already taken aback at hearing this suggestion from Delyanov, was shattered to hear it confirmed by Katkov himself. Ambitious, to be sure, but always a man of the shadows, he recoiled at the prospect of overt responsibility for the editing of Russia's oldest and most celebrated daily newspaper. He pleaded, in addition, his existing involvement with Vyshnegradski, and his age. "Nonsense," replied Katkov, "I was exactly your age when I took over the *Moskovskie Vyedomosti*, twenty-five years ago; and our careers are similar. Like myself, you started by teaching in a university; and like myself, you gave it up at the age of twenty-two to enter the profession of journalism." Cyon fails to tell us what was their final decision.*

On the afternoon of that second day, Katkov, pacing up and down like a caged lion in his little office, poured out to Cyon, "avec une vivacité singulière," his innermost thoughts on Russia's foreign policy. Cyon had the impression that he sensed his impending death, and that this long and passionate monologue represented a species of political testament. It amounted to this: Russia should remain deaf to any and all approaches from Berlin. She should do all in her power to preserve the peace for at least several years. If necessary, she should conclude a purely defensive alliance with France, in order to deprive Bismarck of his possibilities of manoeuvre. In this way she should prolong the *status quo* until the expiration of the Austro-German treaty of alliance. Then, and then only, should she proceed to "an active policy."

At this intriguing point, Cyon, alarmed—presumably—at the depth to which he was descending, broke off his account, explaining in a footnote that he had thought it better not to pursue these views further, but pointing out simply that the lapse of the "treaty of Skiernivice" would leave Russia without restrictive obligations concerning Bosnia and the Sandjak of Novy Pazar.

(The reader will note how closely this line of thought corresponds

* Feoktistov, who was a member of the governmental commission charged, after Katkov's death, with the selection of a successor to him at the *Moskovskie Vyedomosti*, expressed skepticism as to the veracity of this tale of Cyon's. Why was it, in this case, he asked in his memoirs (*Vospominaniya*, pp. 269-70), that Katkov never mentioned the candidacy to other friends? The conflict of assertion is indeed a flat one; for Delyanov, with whom Cyon claims to have first discussed the matter, was also a member of this commission, as well as a friend of Katkov. Therefore Katkov *did* mention the candidacy to at least one of his friends.

to the analysis of nationalist-Panslav-military policy given above, in Chapter 9. The idea, obviously, was to prepare the way for a Russian war with Austria by (1) depriving Germany of any formal pretext for intervention on Austria's behalf, and (2) making it impossible for her so to intervene without being obliged simultaneously to fight a war with France. It is strange that Katkov and like-minded Russians failed to see that the disruption of Germany's ties with Russia, and the conclusion of a Franco-Russian alliance, would leave Germany no alternative but to stick with Austria through thick and thin.)

On the evening of that second day, while the two men were still conferring, news arrived of the denial concerning the article in *Le Nord* which Giers had caused to appear in the *Journal de Saint-Pétersbourg*. There was also a telegram from a certain Mr. P——, former official of the Foreign Office, asking to be received by Katkov and hinting that the purpose of his visit would be to try to set up a meeting where the differences between the editor and the Foreign Office could be resolved.

Katkov was furious over the first of these developments, and wholly unreceptive with regard to the other. So aroused was he by the denial of the article in *Le Nord* that he wanted to leave for Petersburg the next day, with a view to taking the matter up with the Tsar and crushing, at long last, his recalcitrant opponent. Giers, he said, was a traitor to his sovereign. He was following a personal policy. In a democracy, that might be permissible; in an autocracy it was different. Under an autocratic system, refusal to carry out the orders of the Tsar (Katkov never doubted that the Tsar had now been won entirely over to his point of view) was to betray both the monarch and the country. Never would he consent to deal with Giers or to seek agreement with him.

The 28th of February was Cyon's last day in Moscow. Upon arrival in the morning at the editorial office, he found Katkov still fuming over the communiqué that had appeared in the *Journal de Saint-Pétersbourg*. He charged Cyon with drafting a telegram to Havas, in Paris, for publication by that agency, informing the French public that Giers' denial did not reflect Russia's real policy. Cyon was somewhat startled to discover in this way that the editor had a regular arrangement, of which he, Cyon, had been quite unaware, for direct communication with Havas—the purpose of which was, as Katkov explained it, to combat material appearing in *Le Nord*. A suspicious man in any case, Cyon thought it strange that he, Katkov's representative in Paris, had not been told of this. "Curieuse situation," he observed, drily, in his diary.

Katkov then asked Cyon to write an editorial, for the paper, on the *Le Nord* incident. This Cyon did, producing the finished piece in some two hours—much to Katkov's admiration for the speed of the accomplishment. There followed a late dinner, after which Cyon, who had already sent his luggage to the train, was due to leave for the station. To his acute distress, Katkov detained him, at that point, with further long monologues on the subject of the "treaty of Skiernevice" as well as with fond and prolonged parting embraces. With some difficulty, Cyon detached himself at long last from these attentions on the part of a patron he was never to see again, tore for the station, and arrived just in time to leap onto the moving train and rejoin his nearly lost baggage.

Disembarking at the Nikolayevsk Station the following morning, Cyon found awaiting him there a friend who had come to tell him that General X—— had an important communication to entrust to him, for which purpose the general begged that in leaving for Paris later that day, Cyon should take care to arrive a half hour early at the station, where the message would be imparted to him; and this was agreed.

Lunch was taken, in the interval, with General Bogdanovich. Bogdanovich told Cyon how he had recently succeeded in disabusing the Grand Duke Vladimir Aleksandrovich of the impression, then rather widespread, that Cyon was the author of the celebrated articles, signed with the pseudonym "Count Vassili" and entitled "La Société de Saint-Pétersbourg," which had recently appeared in Madame Adam's *La Nouvelle Revue.** Bogdanovich had also denied to the grand duke that he himself was the author of a rather violent pamphlet advocating a Franco-Russian alliance that had appeared in Paris in January over the signature of "a Russian general."†

Appearing a half hour early at the Warsaw Station that afternoon, Cyon encountered the intermediary from General X——, who told him that the Tsar had perceived "the trap" that lay behind Schweinitz's recent words, and that there was now nothing to be feared from that

---

* The pseudonym "Count Vassili" was used by Madame Adam for a number of works published anonymously in *La Nouvelle Revue* in the mid-1880's. Certain of these, though apparently not all, were actually written by Princess Catherine Raewuska Radziwill (later, by a second marriage, Madame Charles Kolb-Danvin); and *La Société de Saint-Pétersbourg* appears to have been one of these. Much of its substance was probably carried over into her later work: *Behind the Veil at the Russian Court* (New York: John Lane, 1914), which also appeared under the pseudonym of Count Paul Vassili. These were valuable works, filled with vivid and shrewd pen-portraits of many contemporary figures.

† This pamphlet, according to Cyon, was entitled *L'Alliance franco-russe.* Laboulaye, in a despatch of January 12, 1887 (French Archives. *Russie,* 1887), reported the appearance, in both French and Russian editions, of an anonymous phamphlet entitled *Quelques mots sur le Général Skobeleff par an officier russe,* the purpose of which, he said, was the advocacy of a Franco-Russian alliance. I have been unable to ascertain whether these two anonymous pamphlets, which seem to have appeared simultaneously, were identical or in any way connected.

quarter. There was also communicated to Cyon, as coming from the general, information concerning Austrian military dispositions in Galicia, from which it was clearly discernible that the Austrians were planning to invade Russia towards the end of March. And the Germans, Cyon was told, were carrying out similar preparations along their section of the western border of Russia.

Armed with this extravagant, erroneous, and highly mischievous misinformation, Cyon concluded his visit to Russia, and started off for Paris, to report to General Saussier and his other friends at that end of the line.

By way of completing this account of Cyon's midwinter journey, it will be well to take brief note of what was in the minds of the leading actors on both sides, as this crisis of Russian policy of the late 1880's approached its *dénouement*.

In France, we find a highly erratic and unscrupulous minister of war, dizzy from the great popular acclaim now falling to his lot, deriving his information, and misinformation, from a military intelligence establishment the undependability and corruption of which was to be demonstrated, some seven years later, in the Dreyfus case. This minister of war is literally pining for a war of revenge against Germany but very uncertain of the adequacy of the French army itself to face such a contest, greatly overrates the likelihood of a German preventative attack on France, and is almost hysterically possessed with the idea that only an immediate alliance with Russia can save France from catastrophe. At the French Ministry of Foreign Affairs there is a wholly inexperienced and incompetent minister who, much as he dislikes his colleague at the Ministry of War, is vulnerable to much of the same misinformation, is equally unfitted to make any balanced and sensible judgment of German policy, is similarly persuaded both of the momentary worthlessness of the French army and of imminent danger of a German attack, and is no less obsessed than his colleague with the conviction that France's safety now lies in the hands of the Russian Tsar.

In Russia, we have a slow, indecisive, and not very communicative Tsar, torn between the influences of a moderate and experienced foreign minister, who tells him things he does not particularly want to hear, and a great Moscow editor, a commanding figure in the world of Russian journalism and public opinion, who feeds him information that greatly appeals to his nationalistic prejudices, his envy and resentment of Bismarck, and his suspicious dislike of foreigners generally. The editor's behavior, like his communications—public and private—to the Tsar, is informed by a whole series of grievous and remarkable misconceptions: that Bismarck has been encouraging Russia to attack Austria; that Bismarck is promising Germany's neutrality in the face of such a conflict, in return for Russia's agreement to stand aside while Germany attacks France; that this nefarious plot has been frustrated by his, Katkov's, timely intervention with the Tsar; and that the wily Bismarck is now resorting to a much more dangerous and insidious tactic, which is to concede to Russia her freedom of action in the event Germany were to attack France, but to bind her to inaction in the case France were to attack Germany. Katkov is also evidently inclined to believe that the Austrians, presumably determined to anticipate a German-Russian deal against them, are preparing to attack Podolia. Finally, and as his most serious aberration, Katkov is firmly convinced that his interventions of recent weeks with the Tsar—his long memorandum of the turn of the year and his subsequent personal visit—have converted the monarch completely to his own way of thinking, converted him to a point where he has wholly adopted as his own the Katkovian line of policy: that is, the termination of all bonds with Germany and the preservation of a free hand for Russia so that France will be encouraged to take a bold line towards Germany in the West, and Germany will be obliged, eventually, to abandon Austria to Russia's good graces.

As for Katkov's opponent, Giers: he, seeing the international situation more clearly than any of these others, perceiving the high unlikelihood of any German attack on France or Austrian attack on Russia, and knowing that no good could come of any Russian-Austrian war, not only sees no reason why the tie with Germany, on which the peace of Europe has successfully rested for some six years, should now be abandoned but clearly perceives the great danger of such a course for the position of Russia herself; for he realizes that the French political establishment as a whole is at present in no position to conclude an alliance with Russia, so that a Russia deprived of her German tie would face nothing other than complete isolation—Germany, Austria, Italy and England all being against her. And even if the French should eventually conclude such an alliance, its only effect, he reasons, would be to lock Russia into a war with Germany from which she has nothing to gain and a great deal to lose, to the intense gratification of her opponents in southeastern Europe, the British and the Austrians, who would now be able to pursue with impunity and at Russian expense whatever aspirations they might have for gains in that part of the world.

Giers was too astute a man not to detect the signs of continued uncertainty in the mind of his imperial master. He knew that the Tsar's anxieties had been relieved by the unreserved quality of German support in the matter of Battenberg's possible return to the Bulgarian throne. He knew that the hesitant monarch, who so acutely disliked having his arm joggled, had been rendered uneasy by the importunate nature of the attempts by Boulanger and Flourens to get into touch with him. He knew, furthermore, that, strong as was the emotional appeal of some of his urgings, Katkov was beginning to tread on very thin ice with his criticisms, explicit or otherwise, of Russian policies of recent years; for Giers had been careful to assure himself of the Tsar's support at every turn, and attacks against him that took the form of attacks against Russian policy could therefore easily be deflected in the direction of the Tsar himself.

Giers knew, finally, particularly on the strength of the recent incident concerning Appert's replacement, that the Tsar's occasional balkiness and periods of recalcitrance, as now in his refusal to discuss the renewal of the *Dreikaiserbund*, often represented a species of emotional rebellion against courses he knew he would eventually have to follow but was not yet ready to pursue—a means of documenting his discontent and warning others that there were limits to his patience; but that once this had been amply documented, and the passions of the moment given time to subside, reasonableness tended once again to reappear; and that then, if he were approached tactfully, business could again be done with him.

So Giers, though hard pressed and conscious of enduring the hardest of all his winters, bided his time, held his tongue, professed to agree with the Tsar that the time for talking with the Germans had not yet come, and waited, wisely, to see which way the cat would jump.

Chapter Seventeen

THE CRISIS SURVIVED

While the diplomatic, bureaucratic, and journalistic communities of Petersburg were being thus rocked by the various agitations of the mid-winter of 1887, the question of the renewal of the *Dreikaiserbund* was hanging fire. It had by this time become reasonably clear to all initiated parties that there could be no question, in the existing circumstances, of the renewal of that treaty as a tripartite arrangement. The Tsar's reluctance to contemplate a prolongation of the treaty arrangements with Austria was no longer a secret to well-informed people in Berlin and Vienna. Any meeting of the minds between the Russians and the Austrians over Balkan problems seemed now more remote than ever. What was really at stake, then, was the question of a possible bilateral Russo-German pact, to replace the expiring tripartite one. It was this which Bismarck thought he had been discussing with Peter Shuvalov on the eve of his Reichstag speech in early January. But since then the Russians, as we have seen, had lapsed into a cryptic and ominous silence. It was impossible to get a word out of them.

The disturbing implications of this situation, as we have also seen, were not lost on Bismarck. By mid-February he was forced to conclude that the Shuvalov proposal was dead, and he had now to ponder the implications of the Russian failure to follow it up with any further proposals, or even any efforts to discuss the subject. We have already noted (see above, Chapter 13) his message of the 17th of February to Schweinitz, admonishing the latter not to initiate any discussion of the matter with the Russians, lest the erroneous impression be created that Germany had greater need of a new pact than did the Russians themselves.

We have also noted his further message of the 28th of February (i.e., after the appearance of the disturbing article in *Le Nord*) in which he told Schweinitz that whereas in normal circumstances the anti-German fulminations of the Russian press could be ignored, serious significance would have to be attached to them in this instance in the light of the continued Russian silence about the renewal of the treaty relationship. Once again, in this message, Bismarck warned the ambassador not to initiate any discussion of the treaty.

309

Giers, meanwhile, well aware of the dangerous effect this was producing on the Germans, saw nothing to do but to remain silent, hoping that some new turn of the situation would, before it was too late, bring his imperial master to a more reasonable frame of mind.

As it turned out, he did not have long to wait. On the 18th of March 1887, the *Moskovskie Vyedomosti* came out with an editorial which began as follows:

> In order fully to understand the present state of affairs it is necessary to know that just in this month of March there is expiring that "tripartite alliance," so pernicious for Russia, into which she was lured, for a period of three years, at the time of her national humiliation, and which was then secretly renewed, again for three years, in 1884. The existence of this treaty was held in darkest secrecy. For long it was not even known whether a written instrument existed. Only recently did its content become known and did it become clear why Russia's importance has declined and why, losing progressively the character of an independent country, she has been pushed, step by step, out of the Orient [i.e., the Balkans].

There followed, then, passages informing the reader that Russia, "as it seemed," had finally decided to free herself from the cloying restrictions of this treaty and to recover her freedom of action in European affairs, but that this, of course, was leading to feverish efforts on the part of her ill-wishers to entice her back into their treacherous nets, and so on, and so forth.

This editorial struck the Tsar with the force of a thunderbolt, and for several reasons. The treaty establishing the *Dreikaiserbund*, in the first place, had indeed been held in strictest secrecy. It had been the intention of the Tsar that it should remain that way. The mere revelation of its existence, not to mention the dates of its original signature and later renewal and supposed time of expiration, was in his eyes evidence of grievous and impardonable breach of governmental security somewhere along the line.

Worse still, this revelation hit the monarch personally on a most sensitive spot—on a spot to the sensitiveness of which Katkov, ironically, had made a major contribution. For years, now, Katkov had labored to persuade the Tsar that the close tie with Germany was unacceptable in the eyes of Russian public opinion. Plainly, his efforts along this line, particularly in recent weeks, had had considerable effect. On the 5th/17th of January, for example, Lamsdorf, after talking with Giers upon the latter's return from his very unpleasant audience with the Tsar, noted in his diary that:

> ... His Majesty is talking not only against a tripartite treaty but also against a treaty with Germany. He seems to have obtained the impression

that such a treaty would be unpopular—that it would be in conflict with the national susceptibilities of all Russia. He confesses that he fears the effects of a failure to take account of these feelings—that he does not want to destroy the faith of the country in his foreign policy.

Just what Alexander III envisaged as "public opinion" is hard to determine. He could scarcely have had in mind the feelings of the peasant masses who made up 80 percent of the population. He is more likely to have had in mind the higher military commands, the nationalistic editors themselves, Pobyedonostsev and the clerical hierarchy, and critical members of the imperial family and court camarilla (including his own wife)—people who were, for the most part, xenophobic, anti-Austrian, enviously discontented with Bismarck and the Germans, greatly concerned for Russia's prestige, always on the lookout for failures on the part of Russia's policy makers to hold high the banner of Russia's power and glory in the face of what they viewed as the wily contumacy of an heretical outside world. Alexander III, lacking serious analytical powers and at heart very uncertain of himself, hoped to retain the confidence of these circles by a public posture that avoided any hint of friendliness towards Germany, while at the same time reinsuring against real trouble by secret arrangements with the German court. The Germans were well aware of this. They often complained that, while the Tsar was willing to deal with them and to say nice things about them in private, he would not say a word on their behalf publicly, nor would he make any serious effort to restrain the anti-German excesses of the nationalistic Russian editors.

By revealing the existence of the *Dreikaiserbund*, and particularly by revealing the fact that it was now expiring and that the Russian government was confronted with a difficult and delicate decision of policy towards Germany, Katkov cut mercilessly into this cherished habit of prevarication on the Emperor's part. He placed the monarch in a position where he was virtually forced either to abandon a tie which was a matter of personal loyalty as between himself and the German Kaiser and on which he knew, in his heart, that Russia's security depended, or to espouse that tie openly and thus offend precisely those segments of the Russian official establishment whose confidence he most wanted to retain. This spoiled his own private little game; and nothing could have infuriated him more.

Finally, how could Alexander III take Katkov's savage criticisms of the *Dreikaiserbund* other than as criticisms of himself and his policies? The arrows had been aimed, of course, at Giers; but Katkov, blinded by his resentment of Giers and his habitual exaggerations of the latter's failings, failed to realize that Giers' position was such that these arrows

311

were bound to fly past him and strike the Emperor. Had not the treaty of 1881 been a treaty concluded among the three imperial courts and not the foreign ministries? Had it not been signed by Saburov, Russian Ambassador at Berlin, on behalf of the Tsar, personally? Giers, after all, had not even been foreign minister at that time. Who, if not the Tsar, bore the primary responsibility for the acceptance of this treaty, and for its renewal in 1884—ratified, as that renewal was, by the Tsar in person at Skiernevice? And at whom, then, were these criticisms aimed? Was it not unheard of, and intolerable, that the actions of a Russian Tsar should be held to public contempt in this manner?

Katkov's editorial was included in the news summary, prepared by the Ministry of the Interior, that lay on the Tsar's desk on the morning of the 19th of March. From the Tsar's marginal comments on the news summary, as quoted by Nolde,* it is clear that there were two points in the editorial that particularly annoyed him. Opposite the passage revealing the existence of the treaty, he wrote: "If he learned that, he learned it only from a traitor."[1] Then, there was another passage in which Katkov scoffed at the presence in Petersburg of a German military delegation, which he described as having come there to open an exhibit of new German weapons and to impress France with the intimacy of German-Russian military ties. The mission in question seems actually to have been one of courtesy, sent as a gesture of friendship to his Russian nephew by the old German Kaiser in connection with the forthcoming celebration (March 22) of his own ninetieth birthday; and this bandying of malevolent gossip about it by Katkov, bound as it was to be picked up by the Germans, also aroused the Tsar's anger. Opposite this passage he wrote: "Amabilité personnelle du vieil empereur; sortie inconvenante et grossière."

The Tsar's immediate reaction, upon reading the news summary with the account of Katkov's article, was to return it at once to the acting minister of the interior, V. K. Plehve, with the following comment:[2]

> This is a highly disreputable article. In general, Katkov forgets himself and tries to play the part of some sort of dictator, forgetting that foreign policy is my business—it is I who answer for the consequences, not Mr. Katkov. I *order* you to give Katkov an initial warning for this editorial and for the recent line of the paper generally, in order to temper his madness. There is a limit to everything.†

* Nolde does not name his source for these marginal notes, but he was so meticulous and responsible an historian that his quotations of them may confidently be relied upon.

† For journals appearing in the two capital cities, Petersburg and Moscow, as distinct from those appearing in the provinces, there was at that time no pre-censor-

The Tsar's order threw instant consternation into the camp of Katkov's high-level supporters at the Russian court. Pobyedonostsev at once submitted a letter of protest. The text of that letter is missing from the published record of Pobyedonostsev's correspondence; but the Tsar's reply is there, and it shows how squarely and effectively the letter of the Ober-Prokuror had hit the mark. "Having read your letter about Katkov's article, and having reflected on all that you write me," the Tsar wrote (March 24, 1887),

> ... I have become convinced that you are right and that I, in the heat of the moment, acted inconsiderately in giving the order for the issuance of a warning to the *Moskovskie Vyedomosti.*
>
> I have directed Feoktistov [the chief censor] to read to Katkov the observations I made about his article, and to give him, in addition, an oral reprimand; and I am sure that that will be enough.
>
> Sincerely, your
Alexander.[3]

The Tsar, it further appears, had coupled his orders to Feoktistov with authorization to tell Katkov that he would be given an audience if he cared to come to Petersburg for this purpose. Feoktistov at once proceeded to Moscow, carried out his orders, and returned the following day, bringing with him the aroused editor. An audience with the Tsar was then arranged for him by Pobyedonostsev.

Before the audience took place, Pobyedonostsev sent to the Tsar a letter he had received from Feoktistov, telling of the great indignation that prevailed in certain court and governmental circles over the extraordinary leniency shown in the withdrawal of the warning. Plehve, the police chief, was quoted, in this letter, as saying that he could recall no instance of such extreme agitation in higher governmental circles. The matter had been discussed in the State Council. Abaza, the former minister of finance, had raised his voice in protest. The Grand Duke Mikhail Aleksandrovich had summoned Plehve to his office and had talked at length about the damage this would do to Russo-German relations. Giers, Feoktistov reported, had decided to resign, and was about to leave for Gatchina with a request to be relieved of his duties.[4]

All this, as indicated above, was made known to the Tsar before he received Katkov; but it had, to all appearances, no great effect. The editor had little difficulty in appeasing the vacillating monarch, softened

---

ship. But warnings could be issued for items that gave offense; and upon the third warning, the paper could be suspended or made subject to pre-censorship. A warning of this nature was thus, especially when issued on the Tsar's personal orders, a serious matter.

as he already was by Pobyedonostsev's intercession. The Tsar did, however, speak to Katkov, on that occasion, in defense of Giers. The latter, he said, was needed. Russia was not yet ready for war. Giers was cautious; he would know how to gain time. Alexander urged Katkov to make his peace with the minister, and even directed him to call on Giers and to let the latter explain to him the rationale of Russian foreign policy.

Katkov, swallowing his pride, proceeded at once to Giers' office with a view to carrying out this order. Giers, correctly sensing that he was being asked in effect to make his views acceptable to Katkov in order that they should be made fully acceptable to the Tsar, drew the line, declined, for once in his life, to defer to the Tsar's instructions, and declined to receive the editor. To receive Katkov in the prevailing circumstances, he explained to the Tsar, would be to accept such a diminution of his personal dignity as would render him no longer an effective servant of the throne. The Tsar, at a loss to know how to cope with the situation that would be created by Giers' departure, accepted this, but not gladly, and not without reproach to the minister for his recalcitrance.

To understand the tensions of those days one must remember that they were the closing days of the long and wearing Russian winter. Slush and dampness enveloped the city. In the first days of April the ice on the river began to break up, pushing slowly down, with thunderous groaning and cracking, towards the Gulf of Finland, thrusting great piles of ice slabs up against the buttresses of the Neva bridges. This was, of course, the first harbinger of spring; but the late winter illnesses and the long Lenten fasting had taken their toll of people's patience and buoyancy. Tempers were short, emotions were sensitive.

On the 12th of April, five days before Easter, the Russian secret service intercepted, and sent to the Tsar, an instruction of the Berlin Foreign Office to the German Embassy at Petersburg, relaying a report received from Paris about Cyon. The Tsar sent it on to Giers. The report was sheer nonsense: Cyon, portrayed here as a dangerous Radical-revolutionary, was supposed to have said, in French parliamentary circles, that he was pressing for a German war with Russia because he knew that Russia would be defeated and the Tsar would then be forced to grant a Constitution. Von Bülow's reply (he was at that time chargé d'affaires), similarly intercepted the next day, was even sillier. Cyon, Bülow reported, was "a mendacious and venal Jew with revolutionary tendencies," close to Katkov (see above); but this only showed that Katkov was either crazy or himself a concealed revolutionary. It was rumored that Cyon was scheduled to join the editorial staff of the *Moskovskie Vyedomosti*; but this, Bülow added, was not surprising, because Katkov had a habit of surrounding himself with dubious characters. (In this last connection Tatishchev was mentioned particularly.)

What the Tsar thought about all this is not apparent. His only marginal notation on the intercepted documents was the amused observation: "The Germans really hate Katkov, don't they? Actually, this is understandable."

Lamsdorf thought these intercepted messages would redound to Giers' advantage. But Giers, scarred by long and bitter experience, remained to be convinced.

On the 15th of April the Tsar sent to Giers another long polemic paper which Katkov had submitted to him immediately after, and under the fresh impression of, Giers' refusal to receive him. It was, as Giers described it to Lamsdorf, a lengthy and violent "denunciation." In it, Katkov raked over those episodes—the unification of Bulgaria, the circumstances of Battenberg's removal, and the failure of the Kaulbars mission—which he knew to have left the most painful impressions on the mind of the Tsar. He attempted to prove that in each instance it was none other than the faithless Giers who had sabotaged the monarch's policies. There then followed an eloquent plea (reflecting Cyon's influence) for abandonment of the tie to Germany and conclusion of a defensive alliance with France. In the concluding passages, claims that Russia had only the most peaceful of purposes were coupled, significantly and somewhat incongruously, with hints that failure to renew the *Dreikaiserbund* would free Russia's hands to challenge Austria's position in Bosnia-Herzogovina and in the Sandjak of Novy Pazar.[5]

In the fact that the Tsar had passed this paper on to him without comment, Giers prudently professed to see a mark of confidence in himself. He acknowledged it with a note thanking the Tsar for the courtesy and pointing out, in a single sentence, that the assertions of fact contained in the paper were seriously distorted. But actually, he was not reassured by the episode. One could depend upon it, he observed to Lamsdorf: the memorandum had left some sort of a mark on the Tsar's disposition.

One did not have to wait long for the confirmation of Giers' judgment. The following day, the 16th, was the day before Easter. There was to be, that evening, the customary conferring of Easter decorations. On several recent occasions, the last being the New Year's ceremonies, Giers had been passed up when decorations were conferred upon other members of the government. The omission had been widely noted by the diplomats; and it was generally expected that the *lapsus* would be made good on Easter Day, when tradition called for another distribution of decorations. So sure were the diplomats that this would be done that Flourens wired to Laboulaye, three days in advance, authorizing him to extend to Giers the congratulations of the French government if, as expected, he received the *Cordon de Vladimir*.

It was the custom that the Easter decorations were sent to the recipients early on Easter Eve, by special messenger, just before the great midnight services that marked the end of Lent and the real climax of the Russian year. On the afternoon of that day, Giers' senior assistants assembled in Lamsdorf's rooms to drink tea and to speculate on the sort of decoration Giers would be given. Vlangali professed to know from reliable sources that it would be the Vladimir Cross, First Class, and that it would be accompanied by a brief but flattering inscription.

The hours passed. The early evening came and went, but no messenger. Poor Giers, around 9:30 p.m., went out for a lonely walk; one can imagine with what feelings. Returning about 10:00 p.m., he summoned Lamsdorf and said to him, "Well, was I not right?" Lamsdorf still refused to abandon hope.

Two packages arrived later in the evening—both, as it happened, from the Imperial Chancery. Neither contained the decoration. It was later learned that the imperial rescript conferring the decoration had been prepared, with the blessing of the Tsar himself, and lay ready for signature on his table, but a last-minute intervention of Pobyedonostsev had sufficed to dissuade the monarch from signing it.[6]

Towards midnight there began the great Easter service in the chapel of the Winter Palace. The imperial couple arrived in late evening, from Gatchina, to be present. Lamsdorf had been invited to attend. Giers, being a Protestant, had not. But Lamsdorf, in the circumstances, could not face it. Heartbroken and embittered, he stayed, like his chief, at home in the great deserted Ministry on the Palace Square.

Some hours later, Easter Sunday dawned, gray and raw. The streets and squares were deserted, as the people of the capital slept off the elaborate celebrations of the night. Similarly deserted, in view of the Easter holiday, was the building of the General Staff and the Foreign Office on the Palace Square. In mid-morning Lamsdorf, overcoming a reluctance to break in on his chief at a moment of such humiliation, mounted the great stone staircase, his footsteps resounding in the cavernous stillness of the empty building, and knocked at the door of the minister's *cabinet* to see whether there was anything he could do for him. He found Giers sitting there, in solitary splendor, in his great office, surrounded by that forest of small articles that was thought to give dignity to such premises in the Victorian age. Lamsdorf hesitated to bring up the events of the night before, but Giers did so himself; and it appeared to Lamsdorf that he was taking the blow quietly and with dignity. What pained him, Giers said, was mostly his impression that this would diminish his authority and undermine his usefulness as a point of contact with the foreign diplomats.

While all this was happening, another kind of ice—the ice that had for so long frozen all discussion of the situation created by the forthcoming expiration of the *Dreikaiserbund*—was also beginning to break up.

The event that set this process in motion was the ninety-first (and last) birthday of the German Kaiser, William I, on the 22nd of March. As a mark of his respect for the old gentleman, the Tsar had sent his brother, Grand Duke Vladimir Aleksandrovich, to Berlin, to represent him at the birthday ceremonies. The grand duke, always *bien vu* in Berlin, had taken occasion to speak at length with Bismarck, as well as with the Kaiser, about the possible renewal of the treaty discussions. Bismarck had accepted only with great reluctance the idea of a bilateral pact instead of a trilateral one including the Austrians; but in the end he had done so; and he had defined his own position with customary bluntness. The Russians could do what they wanted with Bulgaria; they could take the Dardenelles, if they wished to, with or without permission of the Sultan; but they must not try to destroy the Austrian Empire; and they must agree, in any bilateral pact with Germany, not to support the French in any aggressive action against Germany, but rather to observe a benevolent neutrality.[7] He would gladly leave to the Tsar's judgment the question of who, in the event of such a conflict, was the aggressor.

This was the message which the Grand Duke Vladimir carried back to his imperial brother; and it evidently sufficed, this time, to induce the latter to consent to a reopening of the talks with the Germans. (Whether it would have sufficed had not the shadow of Katkov, still so intimidating in mid-January, now lost something of its minatory power, is, of course, another matter.)

Giers had already mentioned the subject in the course of a routine *tour d'horizon* with Schweinitz on the 19th of March, the very day the Tsar was boiling over upon the reading of Katkov's article. A new treaty including Austria was, Giers had told Schweinitz, impossible. Somehow or other, one would have to negotiate a bilateral one. But there would be, he warned the ambassador, one condition from which the Russians would not depart: absolute secrecy.

Schweinitz, still bound by Bismarck's injunction not to show eagerness, did not respond to this sounding (which was probably only the result of Giers' somewhat despairing personal initiative); but in reporting it to Berlin, he showed himself well aware of the reasons for the Russian requirement of secrecy. "The Emperor Alexander believes," he explained, "that while an alliance with us would be advantageous for his foreign policy, a show of hatred for Germany is nevertheless necessary for his domestic popularity and security."[8]

Now, in April, with the Tsar's confidence in Katkov severely shaken, and the influence of the Grand Duke Vladimir being brought to bear in the right direction, Giers took the matter up once more with the Tsar (April 23) and succeeded in getting the monarch's unenthusiastic assent to a formal inauguration of negotiations. He was authorized to tell the German Embassy that Paul Shuvalov, Russian Ambassador at Berlin, who had recently been on vacation in Russia, would shortly be returning to his post; when he did, he would be empowered to explore with the Germans the possibilities for a bilateral agreement.

All this, Giers promptly conveyed to von Bülow, now German chargé d'affaires; but in doing so he confessed that he had certain misgivings about the choice of Shuvalov as a negotiator. Shuvalov, he said (prophetically enough) was too unruly, too much given to independent initiatives. But Giers hoped to restrain him. He had already admonished him:

... qu'il ne fallait pas demander à l'Allemagne la lune. Je l'ai prié
d'imiter ma manière de procéder, qui est prudente, lente et modeste, mais
à mon avis la plus sûre.[9]

Giers, it may be noted, had more than one reason to be mistrustful of Shuvalov. The latter, before returning to his post at Berlin, revealed to Schweinitz (now once again in Petersburg) in a private conversation that his personal interest in concluding the treaty with Germany flowed from the fact that he wished to shape German-Russian relations during the period of his ambassadorship in such a way that they would require no further development when, as he confidently expected, he would return to Petersburg and take Giers' place. To this point the intrigues, as one sees, had by no means ceased to swirl around the minister's head.

On the 5th of May Shuvalov, back in Petersburg after his Easter vacation, had a long personal audience with the Tsar. Immediately thereafter he returned to Berlin, bringing with him the draft of a possible German-Russian treaty. An initial article provided that if one of the two Powers

318

should find itself at war with a third Great Power, the other would observe a benevolent neutrality and attempt to localize the conflict. A second article confirmed German recognition of Russia's historic rights in the Balkans, and bound both parties not to accept without opposition, except by previous mutual agreement, any disturbance or modification of the *status quo* in that part of the world. A third article reaffirmed the attachment of the two Powers to the "European and mutually obligatory character" of the principle of the closure of the Straits,* and spelled out the measures they would take to prevent Turkey from infringing on this principle or vacillating in her attachment to it.

Shuvalov met with Bismarck on the 11th of May (the talks were continued on the 13th, 14th, 17th, and 18th) and submitted the draft treaty for his consideration. Most of the language Bismarck accepted without significant alteration. But he was concerned lest the obligation to maintain a benevolent neutrality in the face of a Russian war with Austria be interpreted by the Russians in a manner that would be in conflict with the Austro-German Treaty of Alliance of 1879. He proposed, therefore (and this was accepted by the Russians), to add a clause to the first article making it clear that this obligation to maintain a benevolent neutrality would not apply in case the war in question resulted from a direct attack by either of the two parties on another Power: it would not apply, that is, in case of an aggressive war by Russia against Austria.

It should be noted that this article, as supplemented by the proposed extra clause, had precisely the effect that Katkov and Cyon so abhorred and so violently opposed. It bound Russia, by implication, not to come to France's assistance in any Franco-German war in which France could be held to be the aggressor. It thus meant the continued renunciation by Russia of precisely that "free hand" which Katkov had been so insistently demanding.

Even this language, however, did not wholly relieve Bismarck's anxieties. He was haunted by the fear that his consent to the abandonment of the *Dreikaiserbund* would be taken by the Russians as giving *them* something in the nature of a free hand against Austria. He had been assuring them ever since 1876 that Germany would not and could not accept a complete destruction of the Austro-Hungarian Empire. The Russians had no excuse for ignorance at this point. But he was not sure that they wholly understood that Germany would be obliged to come to Austria's defense in *any* war aggressively undertaken against her by Russia, whether or not that war led, or threatened to lead, to the actual

---

* This was the algebraic expression of an agreement not to recognize any unilateral English arrangement with the Porte, detrimental to Russian interests.

destruction of the Austro-Hungarian state. He therefore solicited and received the consent of the Austrian government to his revealing to Shuvalov, in the course of the negotiations, the provisions of the Austro-German Alliance of 1879. Although it was widely assumed in informed quarters that some arrangement of this nature existed, the actual terms of that treaty had never been revealed. So he showed Shuvalov the text of the document; but he deliberately kept the Russian in the dark about the period of its validity. This was, one may suppose, his response to the repeated hints in Katkov's editorials that the day would come when the German-Austrian treaty would expire, and when Russia could then take after the Austrians with impunity.

The treaty, finally signed in Berlin on the 13th of June, came generally to be known (when its existence was revealed) as the Reinsurance Treaty (*Rückversicherungsvertrag*). It had a period of validity of three years. The signature did not occur, however, before Shuvalov, by way of vindicating Giers' prophecy, had muddied the waters by introducing into the negotiations at the last minute new demands which (on all available evidence) represented nothing more than his own idea and for the advancing of which he had no authority at all from his own government. These demands would have required the Germans to bind themselves, in effect, to assume the burden of throwing out the Bulgarian Regency for Russia's benefit, and thereafter to accept as ruler of that country whomsoever the Tsar might decide to appoint for this purpose. Bismarck found this demand childish and outrageous, and unhesitatingly refused to accept it. Shuvalov then backed down, let the demand fall, and agreed to sign the treaty without it. But this whole performance, obviously conceived by him in the hope of demonstrating to the Tsar that he had succeeded in obtaining from the Germans more than Giers had ever asked for, produced the most deplorable effect on Bismarck. It aroused his most lively suspicions (even, for a time, about Giers, too), and caused him, actually, to agree to the extension for another five years of Germany's treaty of alliance with Austria, whereas he would otherwise have renewed it only for three.

In general, the circumstances surrounding the negotiation of the Reinsurance Treaty—the long interruption of the talks over the winter, the many evidences of Katkov's ascendancy over Giers, and finally Shuvalov's reckless free-wheeling and last-minute introduction of new and far-reaching proposals—were such that by the time it was finally signed, it had been deprived of much of its value in Bismarck's eyes. It was, to be sure, as he saw it, better than nothing. It served to gain time. It gave Germany at least a talking point in case the Russians should begin to go too far in their relations with the French. But Bismarck's confidence in the Tsar's commitment to a close German-Russian relationship had by this time been sorely shaken, and he was constrained to wonder whether even the solemnly accepted engagements of this treaty would really restrain the Russians from entering the conflict on France's side if another Franco-German war were to occur, regardless of who began it.

While all this was happening (unbeknownst to the French) on the plane of Russo-German relations, the lines of communication between France and Russia were relatively quiescent. This was in part because of the decline, after late February, of the intensity of the war scare. Even the week-long Schnaebele crisis, occurring at the end of April,* did not disturb the atmosphere sufficiently to prevent the gradual subsidence of press exchanges and feelings of tension and anxiety. But in addition to this was the fact that French President Grévy, and Premier Freycinet, both alarmed by Boulanger's adventurism and Flourens' jitteriness of the past winter, exerted their influence with a view to tempering the climate of Franco-Russian relations; and came out, in this connection, against the idea—so agreeable to the Boulangistes and certain of the French military figures—of playing the card of Katkov and his associates against Giers. Instead, they made what appears to have been a deliberate decision, with Laboulaye's prudent approval, to continue to work through Giers and to make the most both of his superior access to the Tsar and of his known disposition, which was, after all, despite all his cautiousness and unwillingness to contemplate an immediate change of alliances, not unfriendly to France. This decision was not interpreted to mean that all French contacts with the Katkov faction were barred; on the contrary, Flourens rather unwisely authorized Laboulaye (April 14) to maintain contact with Katkov through Bogdanovich; but the ambassador was warned not to get himself mixed up in Katkov's conflict with Giers, which conflict, Flourens said, the French government regretted.[10]

The Russians, it may be noted, exercised a comparable restraint in the face of the fulsome approaches of the French chauvinists. The Russians, Giers told d'Ormesson, were not at all pleased by the violent demonstrations of French sympathy for Russia that were forthcoming

---

* This was a crisis in Franco-German relations occasioned by the arrest by the Germans, in the frontier zone adjoining Lorraine, of a French border official, a police commissar by the name of Schnaebele, suspected by the Germans of being a major French intelligence commander. Schnaebele was released, and the episode thereby settled, on April 28.

from this quarter. They preferred, he said, to deal with the French government,

> ... tel qu'il est actuellement constitué, c'est à dire, composé de partisans de la république ouverte et moderée, qui travaillent dignement et pacifiquement à maintenir la France au rang qu'elle doit occuper dans l'équilibre Européen.

Russia could not give her support, Giers went on, to those who, "dans la lutte des partis, sont les ennémis acharnés du ministère Rouvier-Flourens et cherchent à le renverser." They wished to see this ministry remain in power; but they would not intervene in French affairs by opposing any other cabinet that had parliamentary support.[11]

Thus, potential sources of difficulty between the two governments were deliberately played down, at this period, by both sides. The Russian government's refusal to participate in the forthcoming Paris World's Fair was taken calmly and without remonstrance by the French. An attempt on the part of a group of Moscow Panslavs to send through General Bogdanovich to General Saussier a sword with the inscription: "Qui vive? La France. Dieu favorize les audacieux. Au plus digne. La Russie, février 1887" was discovered and aborted in good time by the Russian authorities. The French continued to cultivate Russian favor by supporting the Russian position against the British in the Egyptian question, just then in one of its periodic states of crisis. And Flourens pleased the Tsar most mightily by forwarding to him, through Laboulaye and Giers, despatches from the French representative in Sofia, Monsieur Flesch, who was, as it happened, very pro-Russian and stood in a state of smoldering feud both with the Bulgarian Regency and with his Western diplomatic colleagues at that post. These despatches told, with indignation, of the treatment of pro-Russian opposition figures at the hands of the Bulgarian authorities; and nothing could have pleased the Tsar more. "Extremely interesting. Exactly as though it were a report of our own representative," he wrote on the margin of Mohrenheim's covering note. "What nasty things are going on in Sofia; and [scornfully] what lovely sort of conduct on the part of the European representatives! ... It was extremely courteous of the French government to transmit these reports to us."[12]

On the 7th of May Grévy invited Mohrenheim to a private and confidential interview at the Elysée Palace. Mohrenheim's flowery and wordy report of this conversation, replete with flattery for the Tsar (to whom he knew it would be transmitted), reposes in the Russian diplomatic archives.[13] Grévy's alleged statements are set forth verbatim at such length that one is obliged to conclude either that he gave Mohrenheim an *aide mémoire* of what he had to say or that Mohrenheim was pretending to a memory such as no one actually possesses. Grévy, according to this account, dwelt, not unnaturally, on France's precarious position and on her peaceful intentions, defended the French government in the face of the charges of aggressive intentions towards Germany, and expressed gratitude for what he took to be Russian support. He professed to believe in Bismarck when the latter said that he wanted peace; he had to want it, Grévy said, because if he did not observe it he ran the danger of losing his allies, who, as Grévy professed to suppose, were bound to him only by *defensive* agreements. In this connection, he counted on Russia's moral support; for Germany, in the event of an aggression by her against France, would be placed by France in such a situation that the moral feeling of the entire world would be aroused against her. France, Grévy went on, would fight only to defend herself. He did not believe in the inevitability of war; but France was preparing for it as though it were going to come tomorrow. As for Alsace-Lorraine: they had lost it

> par suite d'une guerre aussi malheureuse que coupable et inepte de notre part. Nous en portons l'expiation, mais non le remords. La France—ou, pour être dans le vrai, une partie de la France—en conserve le régret, mais ne croyez pas que ce régret aille jamais jusqu'à l'envie d'entreprendre une nouvelle guerre pour les reconquérir. Nous nous y sommes résignés!

The Russians (this about Boulanger) should not attach any importance to ideas about *revanche*. There were hotheads in every country. So long as he was president, the French hotheads would not run things. He left his ministers wide latitude in domestic affairs, not in foreign ones.

To all of this, Mohrenheim replied by speaking of the Tsar's determination to preserve his complete freedom of action—not to commit himself to anyone.

This despatch was read by the Tsar, who expressed, in the margin, his complete approval and gratification for Grévy's sentiments.

What lay behind these words, on Grévy's part, and his summoning of Mohrenheim to listen to them, was no doubt the fact that plans were already then under way for reforming the French government in such a way as to get rid of Boulanger. While the reasons it had come to this were primarily of a domestic-political nature, the move could plainly be expected to have strong external repercussions and to lead to much speculation in the foreign press regarding its possible international significance. It was presumably with a view to assuring that the Russians should see the move in its proper light and not misinterpret it that Grévy spoke to Mohrenheim as he did. Within a few days, in any case, Mohrenheim was able to report to Petersburg that the change was in the wind. At the end of May, the entire Goblet cabinet, including Boulanger, was dismissed, and a new one formed by the Opportuniste politician and friend of Freycinet, Maurice Rouvier. The only member of the old cabinet to retain his previous position was Flourens, who was permitted to continue as minister for foreign affairs.

This change was greeted with relief, in Russia as elsewhere. It reduced still further the danger of another Franco-German war. Welcome as such a war would have been to the Panslavs and to certain of the Russian military, Giers and even the Tsar must fervently have hoped, particularly in the light of their secret relationship with Germany, that they might be spared the strains of decision to which such a war would have subjected them. But aside from this, the formation of the new cabinet was the occasion for a most curious incident within the Russian diplomatic community, which was not without a certain effect on the position of Giers and thus on the future of Franco-Russian relations.

Some months earlier, when the Freycinet government fell from office, there had been talk of choosing as the new foreign minister, in place of Flourens, the Radical leader, Charles Thomas Floquet, then president of the Assemblé Nationale. From the standpoint of his attitudes and behavior of the moment, there would have been no objection to Floquet from the Russian side; but Russian memories were long, and one of them, in this case, was greatly troublesome. In 1867, on the occasion of a state visit by the Tsar Alexander II to Paris, when the latter was just in process of mounting the steps of the Palais de Justice, Floquet, attired in his lawyer's robes (which caused the Tsar to mistake him for a priest), had approached the visiting monarch, saluted him with his hat, and had said, in a welcoming tone of voice: "Vive la Pologne, Monsieur." The bewildered and offended monarch had immediately retreated, regained his carriage, and caused himself to be driven away. Since that time, the name of Floquet had been, for obvious reasons, *non grata* at the Russian court.

Now, twenty years later, President Grévy, who knew that the Russians would not have forgotten the episode, took the matter up with Mohrenheim through an intermediary, and was startled to hear Mohrenheim talk of being obliged to resign his ambassadorial position if Floquet became foreign minister. Floquet's candidacy was therefore withdrawn (although the question was to arise again, and to be solved in a different way, several months later); and Rouvier was appointed in his place. But when the cabinet was reformed, as just noted, at the end of May

1887, there was talk, once more, of Floquet's candidacy, this time for the position of premier.

Meanwhile, at just this time (the end of May 1887) Katkov had come to Petersburg once more, on the last of many visits. He came this time in connection with questions concerning the school reform—a subject in which he had always taken the most lively interest. He was by this time a seriously ill man, suffering already from the effects of the cancer which was soon to carry him away. On the 29th of May, while still in Petersburg, he was urgently summoned to the suburban *dacha* of the minister of the interior, Dmitri Tolstoi, where the latter produced for him, with the demand for an immediate explanation, a telegram just received from Mohrenheim in Paris concerning the French governmental crisis. It read as follows:

> Freycinet écarté. Floquet fait tout sorte de tentatives pour devenir ministre.—A produit à Grévy lettre de Katkov, dans laquelle Katkov dit que son ministère sera bien vu en Russie et que gouvernement russe ne manquera pas faire dans ce sens déclaration à Laboulaye. Le fait et sûr. Intermédiare entre Katkov et Floquet Cyon.[14]

Translated both from the French and from the "cablese," this amounted, of course, to substantially the following: As a candidate for the premiership Freycinet had been, for some reason, eliminated. Floquet was now trying in every way to get the position. With this in mind, Floquet had shown to President Grévy a letter from Katkov in which the latter said that a Ministry headed by Floquet would be viewed with approval in Russia and that the Russian government would not fail to give official notice to this effect through Laboulaye. There could be no doubt, it was said, about the accuracy of these facts. The intermediary between Katkov and Floquet had been Cyon.

These allegations, if confirmed (and here was Mohrenheim testifying in the most categorical terms to their accuracy), were obviously damaging in the extreme to Katkov, for they showed him interfering in the most impermissible way, behind the backs of the Tsar and Giers, in the conduct of Russian foreign policy. Tolstoi, in showing the communication to Katkov, told him that the Tsar was highly displeased, had suspected Ignatyev of complicity in the matter, and had instructed Tolstoi to take energetic measures with a view to putting an immediate stop to this sort of thing.

Katkov, who in the earlier episode of the revelation of the existence and terms of the *Dreikaiserbund* had had only himself to blame, was in this instance blameless. Indignantly denouncing the alleged letter as a forgery and denying all complicity and all knowledge of the matter, he came away from his interview with Tolstoi immensely upset, inclined even to believe (this was surely a sign of his advancing illness) that the Tsar himself had found it necessary "to have a shadow cast over me"[15] and was thus involved in the intrigue. He at once wrote to Cyon, now in Paris, asking him to investigate the matter and to obtain proof of their common innocence. (This Cyon did, with characteristic fury and energy, devoting much of the months of June and July to the effort. The convincing results were reported privately by him, later that summer, to Pobyedonostsev, and through him to the Tsar.)

Three people, it appeared, were prominently involved in the mystification. One was the redoubtable Katakazi, who seems to have been the moving spirit. The second was a Paris journalist by the name of A. M. Sivinis, presumably of Greek extraction, who had at one time been the Athens correspondent of the *Moskovskie Vyedomosti* and was now connected with the Havas agency.* The third was young Nicholas Giers, eldest son of the foreign minister, who was at that time a secretary of the Russian Embassy at Paris.†

Mohrenheim's message reached the Tsar, seemingly by coincidence, just at a time when the latter was receiving from other quarters unfavorable information about Cyon and two other associates of the editor: Bogdanovich and Tatishchev; and the Tsar's wrath was poured out not just on Katkov for the Paris incident but on all three of the others as well, and on Katkov, once again, for surrounding himself with such "scoundrels" as these.[16] Bogdanovich, who had the status of a major general in the service of the Ministry of the Interior, was at once cashiered.‡ Tatishchev, active as a publicist and historian, was forced to lie low for a time. Cyon, who had been quite unjustly denounced to the Tsar as the author of *La Société de Pétersbourg*, was able to retain

---

* Cyon also described Sivinis as "one-time publisher of the Russophobe *Le Danube* in Vienna." (*Pobyedonostsev*, pp. 797-800.) Sivinis himself wrote to Cyon that he had been at that time working for a year and a half, both at Havas and with other Paris papers, in support of Russian interests. (*Ibid.*, pp. 812-15.)

† The same story as that relayed in Mohrenheim's telegram seems to have appeared, in essence, in the Paris *Voltaire* on May 29. Cyon accused Katakazi of having fed it to that journal; Sivinis accused young Giers of the same thing. It is most charitable to assume, as does this writer, that both young Giers and his chief, Mohrenheim, were genuinely taken in by Katakazi and believed in the authenticity of the report, and that Giers unwisely lent himself to its circulation.

‡ Bogdanovich was reinstated the following year; but the reinstatement was conceived by both Tolstoi and the Tsar as an act of charity, designed to relieve him of the abject poverty into which he had fallen; and he seems never to have played any significant role after that time.

his tenuous title as an official of the Ministry of Finance only because the Tsar was not aware that he had it.

While Cyon was eventually able to clear both himself and Katkov of complicity in this curious affair,* it was, of course, for the moment a blow to Katkov and his faction and a reinforcement—perhaps even a decisive one—to the position of Giers. Katkov, in any case, did not survive to enjoy his own vindication. Overwrought and seriously ill, he took to his bed soon after his return to Moscow, suffered a stroke, and died on the 1st of August 1887.

With Katkov's death, Russia lost one of her greatest publicists—a man of outstanding literary and editorial talent as well as intellectual capacity, passionately patriotic and wholly sincere in his defense of Russian national interests as he saw them, but not always well informed about the international affairs he undertook to discuss, easily imposed upon by persons unworthy of his confidence, and often misguided by the intensity of his own political passions. His judgment had suffered, in those final years, from his sense of humiliation over Russia's numerous failures, and his consuming jealousy of Bismarck; a jealousy reflecting the sense of inferiority of the nineteenth century in the face of the eighteenth, and of the classless urban intellectual of the Victorian period in the face of the eighteenth-century rural landowner that Bismarck, by temperament, really was. But in the totality of his life's work Katkov remained, for all of that, a great man. It is not without a certain sadness that the writer of these lines has seen himself obliged, by the nature of his subject matter, to occupy himself mainly with the aberrations in matters of foreign policy that marred the final months of the activity of this formidable and talented personality, and to leave aside the great services he rendered to Russia at other times and in other fields.

---

* That Cyon, and Katkov too, in the main were innocent of any direct complicity in this affair, and that the story of the letter, in particular, was apocryphal, cannot be doubted. But a number of the accompanying circumstances—Katkov's connection with Havas (for long concealed even from Cyon); Sivinis' connection with that same agency, as well as his former connection with Katkov's paper; finally, Sivinis' own confession that he had long been working in Russian interests—all these facts leave one wondering whether there was not some small shred of substance behind all the confusion: whether Katkov had not indeed said something that invited distortion at the hands of Katakazi.

Part IV

THE DEMISE OF THE BISMARCKIAN SYSTEM

Chapter Eighteen

THE AFTERMATH OF THE REINSURANCE TREATY

While there is no direct evidence of the attitude of Alexander III to the Reinsurance Treaty, there is every reason to believe that it was only with sullen reluctance, and because he saw no better alternative, that he gave his assent to the signing of it by Shuvalov. Giers had no doubt pointed out to him, not once but many times, that the French were not at that time prepared for an alliance with Russia, nor was the Russian army prepared to face Austria and Germany together without the assurance of French help; therefore, a failure to obtain some further guaranty of German neutrality in the case of an armed conflict between Austria and Russia would leave Russia in a dangerously isolated position. While it could be, and had no doubt been, argued by others in the Tsar's entourage that in the event of a Russian-German conflict the French would be bound to come in on the Russian side, alliance or no alliance—that they would not be able to afford to stay out—this had to be recognized as at best a possibility, not a certainty, particularly in the light of the confusion brought into French military affairs, first, by Boulanger's bungling activity as minister for war, and now by his sudden departure from that position.

Giers' advice therefore carried the day—but barely. The Tsar studiously avoided associating himself personally with the conclusion of the new arrangement: he sent no message to his imperial German granduncle on the occasion of its signature; he made no word of direct comment on it for transmission to Bismarck; he left it to Giers to take responsibility for the whole procedure. The best the latter was able to say to the Germans about the Tsar's relationship to the affair (and even this was straining the point) was that the Tsar was "entirely satisfied" with the successful conclusion of the talks. Whoever cares to search for the reasons for this lack of enthusiasm will not have far to go. If he has read the earlier chapters of this account, he will turn at once, and be safe in doing so, to the situation in Bulgaria.

It was mentioned above (Chapter 13) that in the light of the failure of the Kaulbars mission the Tsar gave a rather skeptical assent to the mounting of another clandestine military-political operation, along the lines of that which had played a part in Battenberg's removal, but directed this time, of course, to the removal of the Bulgarian Regency. There can be no question but that Giers viewed this project with sharpest skepticism and did all that he could to keep the Foreign Office aloof from it. But the plans for it evidently went ahead in those dark and mysterious pockets of the Russian governmental establishment where matters of this nature were normally handled. On the 20th of December 1886, General Bogdanovich came to see Giers, ostensibly on behalf of Katkov, to complain over the lack of support in the Foreign Office for the undertaking. At his request, Giers received the two prominent Bulgarian emigré oppositionists, Gruyev and Benderev, both of whom had been leading organizers of the putsch against Battenberg and had been obliged to flee Bulgaria in consequence thereof. Giers found them reasonable men, themselves skeptical of the wisdom of undertaking another operation of this nature at the given moment. But it is evident that other forces were at work behind the Russian official scene; for within a month the two men had been won over by the hotter heads, at least to the point of accepting the responsibility of leadership of the undertaking. At the middle of January 1887, they petitioned the Tsar for a grant of 3,000 rubles, to be transmitted through the Legation at Bucharest, and for permission to move 2,000 rifles through Russian customs—apparently to Rumania.

Giers, who thought the proposal quite silly, was obliged, on the Tsar's orders, to consult with Minister of War Vannovski about the matter. (He was appalled to hear Vannovski advocate, on this occasion, a Russian attack on Austria with a view to acquiring Polish Galicia for Russia.) Despite all Vannovski's arguments, Giers remained unconvinced of the soundness of the proposed Bulgarian operation, and even privately warned the minister at Bucharest, Khitrovo (who became charged with supervision of it), of the dangers of an unsuccessful effort.

But the Tsar had by now been persuaded that this was the best alternative, and could not be deterred. Over the opposition of the Foreign Office, the request for money and arms was granted. On a despatch from the Russian Ambassador at Constantinople, Nelidov, who had also talked with one of the Russian-supported Bulgarian conspirators (the former premier, Dragan Tsankov), the Tsar wrote (January 27): "All this convinces me more and more that we have to support the military movement with money and supplies, and that this alone will be helpful. All other agreements and negotiations with the parties are empty nonsense and will change nothing." And when Nelidov, too, urged caution, lest the Russian government lay itself open to the charge of promoting revolution in Bulgaria, the Tsar wrote angrily, on the despatch: "This is not revolution. This is the establishment of order, and Nelidov ought to know it."[1]

With the Tsar's personal commitment thus established, the operation was launched, primarily in the border regions of Silistria, in the first days of March 1887. It ended within a matter of hours, as Giers had feared it would, in total failure, and in bloody catastrophe for those of the insurgents who fell into the hands of the Bulgarian authorities. (Some sixteen of them were executed.)

Once again, Alexander III was obliged to turn away, in anger and frustration, from the result of a blunder in his Bulargian policy for which he had primarily himself to blame. And once again, he was obliged to ask himself, no doubt, whether all this would have occurred had not the Austrians and the Germans, snickering behind his back, given at least some sort of moral support to the Bulgarian Regency.

Giers, well aware of this situation, pondered, over the spring, the problem of how the strong-willed monarch could be rescued from his helplessness, and the Bulgarian question (the root, as Giers well knew, of most of his own difficulties) brought to some sort of agreed settlement. In early June, he fancied for a time that he had the answer. Bismarck, snickering or no, must also have an interest, he reasoned, in finding a solution to this wretched Bulgarian question which lay like a thorn to both parties at the sensitive point of contact between Russia and Germany. Let Russia nominate for the position of temporary governor of Bulgaria, in place of the Regency, a moderate Russian figure acceptable to the Western Powers (i.e., not a Panslav intriguer); let Bismarck solicit the support of the other Western Powers and of the Sultan for this appointment; then let all the interested Powers join in insisting that the Regency make way for the new provisional governor, with the understanding that the election of a new prince for that country would take place under the latter's supervision.

This suggestion was put to Bismarck in early June, in a letter from Giers, together with the proposal that the man to be selected for this purpose should be the former Bulgarian war minister, General K. G. Ehrnrooth, who, as we have seen, was a highly honorable and universally respected officer, of Swedish-Finnish origin, in the Russian military service. Personally, the name of Ehrnrooth was entirely acceptable to Bismarck, as it probably would have been to the statesmen of all the other Powers. Ehrnrooth was known as a moderate and reasonable man, capable of firmness when needed, though conciliatory in disposition.

Giers' idea had, therefore, much to be said for it. But Bismarck was infuriated by the suggestion that Germany should be looked to once again, as in 1878, to pull Russian chestnuts out of the fire. He was finally induced to take soundings, grudgingly, of the Austrians. But Austrian acceptance was not to be gained. Again, the objection was not the personality of Ehrnrooth; what worried the Austrians was the prospect of an outright Russian-controlled government in Bulgaria.

But the sounding-out of the Austrians took time; and by early September, the situation in Bulgaria had changed in such a manner as to obviate the proposal entirely.[2] For while all these exchanges were taking place, the Bulgarian Regency, quite unmoved, had continued its quiet search for a new prince; and in the first days of July it became known, to the astonished incredulity of most of Europe, that it had found one in the person of the young Prince Ferdinand of Saxe-Coburg-Gotha, then 26 years old, son of an Austrian general and a French mother of regal birth: Princess Clementine, daughter of King Louis Philippe of France.

The origins of this candidacy remain shrouded in obscurity. The Germans certainly did not advance it; and there is no evidence that the Austrians did, although they had no negative feelings about Ferdinand. The strongest evidence points to Italian circles, and to the quiet initiatives of Ferdinand's high-powered mother, as the original sources of the suggestion that Ferdinand should become Prince of Bulgaria.

Official Russia received the news of this selection at first with disbelief, then with scorn and indignation. The Russian government never dreamed of accepting him as Prince. In the eyes of the Tsar, he was the creature of the Bulgarian Regency, the legitimacy of which the Russian government had never conceded. That made him *ipso facto* unacceptable.

As for the other Powers: they, too, not wishing to lock themselves unnecessarily into a conflict with the Tsar, held off and waited to see what would happen. Their hesitation was supported by the fact that Ferdinand—soft, rotund, aesthetic rather than martial in taste—was an unprepossessing figure in the eyes of the European society of that day: a mother's boy, effeminate in manner, given (it was often said) primarily to the pursuit of butterflies, and a poor horseman—in every way the opposite of the manly Battenberg. Few believed, when the fact of his selection by the Regency became known, that he would accept; and fewer still believed that if he did accept, he could last more than a few weeks in the face of Russian hostility and nonrecognition by the Powers. It remained for time to show, as it did, that under this somewhat unimpressive exterior there were resources of shrewdness, slyness, and—

when need be—even ruthlessness, which, combined with personal wealth and an excellent knowledge of how money could be used to good effect, gave Ferdinand superior qualities for survival among the wild political currents of Balkan and Bulgarian politics. Ferdinand himself was aware of all this; and he commented with amusement, in later years, on the fact that his task was easier than that of Battenberg because he, like the Bulgarians, had "oriental" blood in his veins (through an Hungarian grandmother) and could be no less devious, when occasion demanded it, than his Bulgarian subjects.

For some time after the offer of the Bulgarian throne to him became known, Ferdinand, then living in Austria, wisely let his reaction remain a mystery. But at the end of July he suddenly announced that he was accepting, and left instantly for his new country, arriving there on the 11th of August. He was crowned at Trnovo on the 14th, and took up residence at Sofia on the 22nd. In this way, he took the sleepy chanceries of the summer-bound European capitals quite by surprise, and left them no chance to concert any action with a view to forestalling his action.

In Petersburg there was initially only helpless incredulity, and then renewed anguish, over this course of events. It did nothing to relieve the Tsar's feelings. On the contrary, it left him with new grounds for suspicion of the Austrians and the Germans; for the Russian nationalist papers were replete with suggestions that none of this could have happened without the tacit approval and connivance of those two Powers. While the main burden of this suspicion was directed against the Austrians, Bismarck, too, naturally came in for his share.

In the face of these deplorable and infuriating developments in Bulgaria, coming on top of Bismarck's strongly stated refusal to make himself the agent of the Russian government in an attempt to find a solution to the Bulgarian problem, it was only natural that the Tsar did nothing, even in the aftermath of the conclusion of the Reinsurance Treaty, to restrain the anti-German fulminations of the nationalist Russian press. Instead, locking his frustrations away into his uncommunicative and outwardly phlegmatic but actually highly emotional psyche, he set forth on the usual round of summer manoeuvres and holiday journeys, culminating in departure, with his entire family, at the end of August, for a long visit to his Danish in-laws at Copenhagen.

The result was, of course, that the nationalistic faction in the Russian press and officialdom (and not least among the senior military officials), aware of the Tsar's passivity and unaware of the conclusion of the Reinsurance Treaty, continued, unabated, its fulminations and intrigues against closer Russo-German relations as well as the pursuit of its contacts with the French chauvinists. There was indeed, in the light of the Tsar's reticence and absence, no one to stop them.

Even the mortal illness of Katkov, which incapacitated him from the beginning of June, placed no perceptible restraint on such activities. On the contrary, the editor's death (August 1) was the occasion for further demonstrations of enthusiasm over the glorious future of Franco-Russian relations. Déroulède, on hearing the sad news, set off at once for Moscow, accompanied by the secretary of the Ligue des Patriotes, Gupille, with a view to attending the funeral. The two men were held up for twenty-four hours at the border (the evidence does not indicate just how or why, though one suspects the hand of Giers), and were thus unable to arrive in time for the funeral. But they proceeded to Moscow anyway, attended some of the endless requiem services that followed the burial, and went out, in company with Madame Katkov, to lay a wreath on the grave. At the burial itself, a wreath was presented from Lockroy, until recently French minister of commerce and industry and now head of the French journalist association. And there was another one, rather pathetically, from "le Professeur Cyon," who had arrived in Moscow at the very hour of the great editor's death, and for whom, whether he realized it or not, this event spelled the end of many a glorious dream.

Déroulède and Gupille, anxious to make the most of their presence in Russia, followed their appearance in Moscow by pursuing their journey to other places in that country, including Nizhni-Novgorod, where they were given an impressive and well-publicized banquet by the governor, General N. M. Baranov. On this occasion, both Baranov and the vice-governor and district military commander, Neklyudov, delivered inflammatory pro-French speeches, which found their way into the newspapers both in Russia and in western Europe and occasioned much comment. And the press did not fail to note that Neklyudov, shortly thereafter, was given a decoration, by order of the Tsar.

Before leaving Russia, Déroulède also visited Petersburg. There was the usual anxiety in the French Embassy and the Russian Foreign Office as to what he, and his Panslav friends, might do on this occasion. Actually, the visit passed off with little excitement or publicity. The poet attempted to pay a call on Giers, at the latter's Finnish *dacha*; but Giers declined to receive him. Déroulède did, however, have the pleasure of being the guest of honor at a dinner given for him, rather significantly, by none other than V. V. Komarov, editor of the Petersburg *Svyet*, the paper closest to the Russian High Command—a dinner which took place in the home of Komarov's brother, Alexander, Russian military commander in the Caucasus.

It must be stressed once more that the senior officials of the French Embassy at Petersburg, no less patriotic but considerably more discerning than their chauvinistic compatriots, were in no way deceived as to the real motives of the Russian military and Panslav figures who conducted or promoted these close contacts with the Boulangistes and other French nationalists. D'Ormesson, in particular, was quick to recognize that behind these manifestations there lay primarily a desire to embroil France with Germany in order that Russia might have the opportunity to satisfy her Balkan ambitions without German interference. "Si nos amis sincères ici," he wrote to Flourens in a personal letter of the 22nd of October 1887,

> ... craignent de nous voir courir ces aventures, sachant bien qu'il ne nous faut pas faire trop fond sur les sympathies et sur le concours de la Russie, d'autres, plus bruyants mais moins francs, ne seraient pas fâchés de nous voir tirer les marrons du feu pour eux. Ils envisagent bien la possibilité d'un échec de la France, mais celui-ci ne les atteignant pas directement, ils s'en consoleraient plus aisément.[3]

None of this Franco-Russian agitation was lost, of course, on the Germans, least of all on Bismarck personally. The chancellor, as we have seen, had conducted the negotiations for the Reinsurance Treaty in a spirit of deep and ill-concealed suspicion of his Russian counterparts. He had no illusions that the treaty was a final solution to his problems with the Russians. The latter, he suspected, saw in it only a means of gaining time—either for the completion of the French and Russian programs of armament expansion or for the reestablishment of the monarchy in France and the conclusion of a Franco-Russian alliance.[4] Well, if it was a means of gaining time for the Russians, it could be the same for Germany. The value of the treaty for Germany, he indicated in a memorandum dictated to his personal political aide, Count Rantzau, on the 28th of July 1887, lay only in the fact that it forestalled for three years the conclusion of the alliance between the Russians and the French.[5] His son Herbert had an even dimmer view of the treaty's significance. "The secret treaty," he wrote, on the day after the signing of that document,

> ... is fairly anodyne; it binds us to neutrality in the face of an Austrian attack on Russia (which is practically unthinkable) and by the same token binds Russia to neutrality in the face of a French attack on us. It has a term of three years, and is entirely secret. It gives us a certain means of pressure on the Tsar, and in the event of serious complications it keeps

the Russians off our necks some six or eight weeks longer than would otherwise be the case. So it has some value, after all.

It is obvious that Herbert Bismarck, and presumably his father as well, thought—like many other people—that in the event of a Franco-German war it would be impossible, treaty or no treaty, to prevent the Russians from coming in against the Germans in a short space of time; but it is clear also that he felt the existence of this Russian-German pact would make impossible a sufficient intimacy of advance planning, as between Russians and French, to assure an immediate entrance of Russian forces into the fray, and would thus give the Germans a short space of time in which to concentrate their forces on the defeat of the French. In this respect, the German calculations were very similar to those of some of the senior French military figures, who foresaw—with corresponding anxiety—exactly the same contingency and therefore considered that no confidence could be placed in the possibility of Russian military help against Germany in the absence of a formal Franco-Russian alliance and military convention.

Nothing that occurred in the weeks following the signing of the treaty served in any way to reassure Bismarck about the meaning of the document. He noted carefully the continued failure of the Tsar to place any restraint on the nationalist segment of the Russian press, and viewed this with great seriousness. He followed with a suspicious eye the progress of Déroulède's journey throughout Russia, and took note, darkly, of the subsequent conferring of decorations—not just on Neklyudov but also on the official censor, E. M. Feoktistov, whom the Germans tended to regard as the mainstay of the Pobyedonostsev-Katkov faction.

Bismarck's suspicion and concern over Russian behavior came to expression partly in a series of long and rather useless lectures and warnings delivered by Herbert Bismarck to Shuvalov in Berlin, and by Schweinitz to the unhappy and helpless Giers, in Petersburg. But the main thrust of Bismarck's reaction was, of course, his effort to make the Russians feel the bite of German displeasure by punishing them in their commercial and financial relations with Germany. And to take the measure of this, we must go back slightly in time and pursue a bit further the questions surrounding Russia's external borrowings and the efforts of the new finance minister to place her external indebtedness on a sounder basis.

———

We left the devious and mysterious Élie de Cyon, it will be recalled (Chapter 16, above), embarking, at the end of February 1887, on his return journey to western Europe, charged by the new Russian finance minister, Vyshnegradski, with the task of arranging for the conversion (to a longer maturity period and a lower rate of interest) of the obligations of the Russian Mutual Land Credit Bank (the Vzaimni Posemel'ny Kredit) which had been sold in western Europe in the 1870's.

In the light of Cyon's close connections with the most violently anti-German of the French and Russian monarchistic and military circles, and of his own claim to be motivated in all his activity primarily by a desire to "frustrate the intrigues" of the German chancellor, it is somewhat surprising to note that his first point of call in western Europe was not Paris but Berlin, and this, specifically, for the purpose of calling upon Bismarck's banker and intimate financial advisor: Baron Gerson Bleichröder.[6] The reasons why he turned first to Bleichröder for help in the task with which Vyshnegradski had charged him are not fully clear; they presumably had something to do with the fact that Bleichröder's bank was the majority underwriter of the obligations of the Land Bank and a member of the Rothschild syndicate which had originally issued them. The two men, furthermore, appear to have had an acquaintance from earlier years.[7] But one is also constrained to wonder whether the wise and prudent Rothschilds, well aware of certain of Cyon's less reassuring characteristics,[8] had not preferred to deal with him, in the first instance, at one step removed, and whether they had not deliberately referred him to Bleichröder, insisting that he should arrange matters, initially at least, through the latter.

However that may be, the contact with Bleichröder was established, after which Cyon went on to Paris and had further discussions with the Rothschilds. On April 5, he was able to wire to Vyshnegradski that the discussions were going well. He appears then to have returned to Petersburg in mid-April (seeing Bleichröder again in Berlin, on the way), to have obtained Vyshnegradski's final consent to the terms of the deal, and to have received, accordingly, the coveted appointment as a species of unsalaried official-at-large for the Finance Ministry. At the end of May, now back in Paris, he was able to report to Bleichröder that the deal had received the Tsar's approval and was thus presumably consummated. Further correspondence with Bleichröder involved the personal cuts both men were to receive on the transaction—a matter which was later to lead to bitter differences between Cyon and the Russian Ministry of Finance.

This conversion of the shares of the Mutual Land Credit Bank was not a major transaction. The amount converted was variously reported at the time, but it appears to have been in the neighborhood of 108 million marks (about 32 million rubles), or only 5-6 percent of the

Russian paper left at that time in Germany.* But Cyon did, after all, bring the deal to a successful conclusion; and one might have supposed that he, in these circumstances, would have continued to play a major role in the development of Franco-Russian financial relations. He himself obviously expected to do so; for one finds him in the summer of 1887 making various ambitious, and possibly very imaginative, proposals to Vyshnegradski: for the purchase of Baron Hirsch's railway holdings in the Balkans, for the establishment of a "metals bank" in Petersburg, for the organization of a French syndicate to buy up Russian securities on the Berlin market, and so forth. In August, furthermore, he gave up his directorship of *La Nouvelle Revue* for the reason, he claimed, that it conflicted with his duties to the Russian Treasury.

But of all of this, nothing seems to have come. Increasingly, as the summer and autumn of 1887 wore on, there would be contacts and dealings between the Russian Treasury and Russian concerns, on the one hand, and Paris bankers, on the other; but it would not be Cyon who stood at the center of them. Just when he lost his status as a species of representative-at-large of the Russian Treasury is not apparent. There are no indications of his functioning in this capacity later than 1887. The reasons for this are not clear. Whatever they may have been, the fact remains that from the time of Katkov's death this curious man, so favorably endowed by Nature in some respects, so poorly in others, largely fades from the spectrum of this particularly study.

Cyon's further career, however, was far from uninteresting, and deserves a word. Following Katkov's death, he was among those seriously considered as successor to Katkov in the editorship of the *Moskovskie Vyedomosti*, but failed to get the job. He soon became a great enemy of both Vyshnegradski and his successor, Witte, and directed against the latter, in the 1890's, a whole series of bitter books and articles attacking his financial policies.†

In 1895, having been summoned by the Russian authorities to return to Russia, and having declined to do so, he was deprived of his Russian citizenship. In 1896 his villa on the shores of the Lake of Geneva was raided, apparently by agents of the Russian secret police, and many of his papers were stolen. From this point on, he appears to have ceased his

---

* *The Moskovskie Vyedomosti* quoted (July 29, 1887) the *Journal de Pétersbourg* as saying that 97 out of 108 million marks' worth of the shares (at least the statement appears to refer to marks) had by that time been offered for conversion.

† Among these were: *Les Finances russes et l'Épargne française. Réponse à M. Witte* (Paris: Charles, 1895); *Où la Dictature de M. Witte conduit la Russie* (Paris: Eichler, 1897); *M. Witte et ses Projets de Faillité devant le Conseil de l'Empire* (Paris: Eichler, 1897).

attacks on Witte, at least the direct ones, a circumstance that has led to the occasional suggestion that prior to the disappearance of the papers, he had held Witte under some form of blackmail. Henri Rollin, in his *L'Apocalypse de notre temps*, published in Paris (Gallimard) in 1939 (and now a very rare book indeed), adduced serious evidence to suggest that Cyon was the author of the famous anti-Semitic forgery: *The Protocols of Zion* (the reader will note the play on his name), and that this was intended by him as a veiled attack on Witte and his policies.

One encounters Cyon once again, in Witte's memoirs, trying pathetically to see Witte as the latter passed through Paris on his way back to Russia from the Portsmouth Conference in 1905. One notes an equally pathetic effort on Cyon's part, in the early years of the twentieth century, to return to science, the love of his youth, in which he once did so well. One finds, in the Library of the Académie des Sciences in Paris, some of his correspondence with other scientists from the years 1901-1911, and one letter from him to Katkov's son, in 1907. One reads of his death in Paris, in loneliness and poverty, in 1912; and one hears, through the scholars' grapevine, that somewhere in France (no one knows where) there is supposed to be a trunk full of his papers. But from the summer of 1887 he recedes from the story of the Franco-Russian alliance as enigmatically as he entered it—mysterious to the end, the tragic example of a major scientific mind in a seriously twisted soul. The tale, from this point, must go on without him.

Cyon's apparent eclipse from the field of activity he so ardently desired to enter was probably in part a consequence of the fact that knowledge of his dealings with Vyshnegradski and of the latter's interest in large-scale conversions was now spreading through both Russian and French banking circles, and people more important than Cyon in Vyshnegradski's eyes, and capable of acting not as intermediaries but as principals, were now getting into the act. A. I. Sack, director of the Petersburg Discount Bank, and probably Laski, of the International Bank, as well, visited both Berlin and Paris in June, consulting in the first of those places with Bleichröder, and then receiving various proposals from Paris bankers for a major loan to Russia. Other contacts took place in the ensuing months.* And at the end of the year, Kleinmann, the high-

* Available evidence suggests that talks were held with Rothschild representatives as well as with some of the *établissements de crédit*. The Rothschilds were said to be demanding concessions in the treatment of Russian Jews, which the Russian authorities were unwilling to make, but without which the Paris house of the Rothschilds could not obtain the support of the other houses of the family.

powered Directeur des Agences Étrangères at the Crédit Lyonnais, came to Petersburg and called on the Russian finance minister for similar soundings.

But Vyshnegradski, at that time, would not hear of a new loan, particularly a relatively small one (and this was all that the Crédit Lyonnais was able, from its own resources, to offer), or even of any further large-scale conversions. For the reasons why he would not entertain such suggestions, we must return to the restrictive and punitive measures against the prices of Russian securities and the rate of the ruble on the Berlin market which were being taken, at Bismarck's instigation, over the summer and fall of the year 1887. These measures, it should be noted, were not solely a reflection of Bismarck's discontent with the political situation in Russia. They were also a reaction to an Imperial Russian *Ukaz* of the 24th of May 1887, which imposed heavy burdens and restrictions (leading even to eventual forced liquidation) on foreign owners of property in Russian Poland, both agrarian and industrial, as well as forbidding the employment of German managers on Polish estates. The persons most seriously affected by this *Ukaz* were Germans; and among these were some of the richest and most influential families of Germany: the Henkel von Donnersmarks, the Radziwills, the Ratibors, and the Hohenlohes. Bismarck was pressed from these quarters to make the Russians feel the bite of German displeasure; and this influence was sufficient to override the contrary pressures of the Berlin private banking world, which by and large disapproved of economic and financial reprisals against the Russians.

The upshot of all this was that there was waged in the German press, over the summer of 1887, a sharp campaign against Russian securities, as a consequence of which their quotations on the German exchange, already seriously depressed by similar pressures in 1886, suffered a further decline, as did the rate of the ruble. These pressures against Russian securities reached their climax in the fall of the year with the issuance (November 10) of the so-called *Lombardverbot*—an order prohibiting the acceptance by the German State Bank (the Reichsbank) of Russian securities as collateral for loans.

The *Lombardverbot* has achieved a certain historical notoriety, being frequently depicted as the main reason for the subsequent switch of Russian borrowing from Berlin to Paris and hence for the Franco-Russian alliance. For this reason it is often cited as a major blunder on Bismarck's part. The real circumstances do not bear out this rather overdramatized judgment. The measure was neither as unusual, nor as abrupt, nor as drastic, as the legend would have it appear. The desire

342

to damage Russian interests was not the sole reason for it; nor did Bismarck fail to foresee—or even to desire—its consequences.

The practice of the acceptance of foreign securities as collateral for loans by state banking institutions was not common in the Europe of that day; the Reichsbank was in fact the only one that did it at all. The burden that was placed upon Russian securities by the Reichsbank's refusal, after November 1887, to continue this practice was therefore no greater than that to which these same securities were subjected in other capitals, including Paris. The Reichsbank's holdings of such collateral had never been great: in midsummer they amounted only to some 37 million marks (roughly 11.2 million gold rubles), a tiny proportion of the total of Russian paper traded at that time on the German market. In general, the terms for the discounting of these securities were better, anyway, at the private Berlin banks than at the Reichsbank. Thus, the measure was not of great financial significance.

Nor was it abrupt or unexpected. Pressures by the government on the Reichsbank to restrict this sort of lending had been exerted ever since the early summer of 1887. In midsummer, the Reichstag was already debating the issue; and the *Kölnische Zeitung* was reported as saying, at that time, that: "Even today there can be no doubt that the German Reichsbank will no longer accept Russian paper as collateral. . . ."[9]

Nor, as noted above, was the measure taken solely with a view to its effect on Russian securities alone. The tendency of the German public to invest in issues of foreign securities, many of dubious soundness, had by this time reached such proportions as to be a source of serious concern to the German government and to cause the latter to use its influence (which it did with considerable effect) to bring about a movement away from foreign investment in favor of investment within Germany. This was specifically mentioned in the recommendations of both Count Berchem and Herbert Bismarck (of July 14 and October 11, 1887, respectively) that led to the issuance of the *Lombardverbot*. That the measure was greatly stimulated by the Russian *Ukaz* of the 24th of May and by the political tensions of the moment, is beyond question; but these were not the only reasons for it. It fell in with other and wider undertakings of policy on the part of the German government.*

---

* An interesting exposé of the motives of both the press campaign and the *Lombardverbot* is to be found in the memoirs of L. Raschdau, *Unter Bismarck und Caprivi* (Berlin: S. E. Miller & Sohn, 1939), p. 18. Raschdau, who in 1887 was responsible for the Overseas Desk of the Commercial-Political Department of the German Foreign Ministry and claimed to have been charged with the inspiring of the press campaign against Russian securities, wrote:

Nevertheless, the psychological effect of the *Lombardverbot* was great. The Russians exploited it to their own advantage, overdramatizing its significance and using it to excuse their own excesses, both past and future. Scathing references to it run through the utterances of Russian statesmen down through the ensuing years. But the most immediate effect, not just of the *Lombardverbot* but of the campaign against the Russian securities generally, was twofold. It resulted, in the first place, in a very extensive movement of Russian securities away from Germany. In part, the securities were repatriated to Russia, where bankers and others took advantage of the low prices, no doubt with the blessing of the Russian Ministry of Finance, to buy them up. But a very considerable portion also went to other European capitals, and notably to Paris.

The exact dimensions of this movement of Russian paper are not apparent.* The outward movement had begun in 1886; considerable amounts must have been removed before the beginning of 1887. Austrian and Russian despatches (diplomatic and journalistic, respectively) estimated the total of such paper remaining in Germany as of midsummer, 1887, at something in the neighborhood of 577-666 million rubles. This would suggest that by this time approximately half of the original holdings had been removed from the German market. One may be sure that by 1888 the total had sunk still further.

But a second effect of the bear market for Russian securities in Germany was to cause Vyshnegradski to approach only with the most extreme circumspection all suggestions for further foreign loans or operations of conversion at that particular time. He had little interest in conversions that would be based on the existing depressed prices for the Russian bonds, because the rates at which they would be converted

---

The battle was by this time being deliberately waged from our side, although the readers did not entirely grasp its real meaning. They supposed it signified only a temporary disturbance of relations, whereas the real purpose was to deprive a hostile government of the means for the development of armaments directed against us. . . . We wished, by our refusal to cooperate, to render this adversary less belligerent. Let the Russians, we thought, get money, if they had to, from their friends, the French. We believed, furthermore, that the soundness of the loans already contracted in Germany would be improved by this spreading of the risks.

* The Austrian Embassy at Petersburg estimated that by late August, 1887, some 100-125 million rubles' (300-375 million marks') worth of these securities had been in one way or another repatriated to Russia. (Austrian Archives, despatch from Beust to Foreign Office, August 24, 1887.) The *Moskovskie Vyedomosti* gave the figure on August 10, 1887, of "several tens of millions'" (evidently rubles') worth of such securities as having already gone to other capitals.

would reflect this depression, and the real interest rates to be paid by the Russian Treasury for the converted issues would be proportionately higher. At the same time he was unresponsive to suggestions of loans from individual French bankers, because the latter were demanding that the amount to be yielded for the Russian Treasury by these loans should be governed by the prices which the new securities could be expected to bring on the European exchanges. Above all, he had in mind the need for strengthening the ruble as an essential preliminary for conversions of this nature; and for this reason he was interested only in a very large loan which would increase substantially the gold holdings of the Russian Treasury. But none of the proposals made to him by the French bankers in 1887 met this requirement.

So Vyshnegradski held back, over the whole year 1887, claiming that Russia had no great need of any further foreign borrowing at that moment, and deliberately placed his terms for further loans at a level which he knew the European bankers were unlikely to meet. The year 1887 thus ended with French investors acquiring considerable quantities of Russian securities previously held in Berlin, and with the Paris bankers now seriously interested, for the first time, in major financial transactions with the Russian Treasury but unable to achieve any positive results along this line because of the depressed market for Russian securities which Bismarck and his associates had succeeded in creating. In this respect the Paris bankers found themselves, in fact, in a dilemma, for whereas the depressed market for Russian securities helped them to acquire these securities and thus to move them from Berlin to Paris, they also diminished the chances for the large-scale conversions and further loans to the Russian Treasury that they were anxious to make.

All this was painful and disagreeable to certain Russians, including outstandingly Vyshnegradski; but Bismarck miscalculated in his belief that this sort of punishment would have an appreciable effect in softening Russian policies towards Germany in the political field. The Tsar, to whose processes of thought financial and economic considerations were largely foreign, was content to leave such matters to the minister of finance; and he was little concerned for the problems that the latter might encounter in the handling of them. The same was true of Giers. The very absence of any cabinet or other means of coordination among the various Russian ministries operated to distance the foreign minister from the effect of such pressures. The various ministers often failed to see one another for months at a time. ("Nous avons," Giers said to Bülow on the 27th of October 1887, "trois Gouvernements en Russie, moi, les ressorts intérieurs, et puis, depuis Katkow, l'Empereur forme un Gouvernement à Lui tout seul.")[10] In these circumstances, discomfort experienced by the Ministry of Finance was felt only dimly, if at all, by the Foreign Office, and then only as a rule after long delay. And by the Tsar it was scarcely felt at all, especially when he was off in Copenhagen, which, as we shall see presently, was the case in the late summer and autumn of 1887.

Chapter Nineteen

THE FERDINAND DOCUMENTS

During the four months following the signing of the Reinsurance Treaty in June 1887, the Tsar Alexander III gave little attention to official affairs. Much of July was taken up with a cruise in Finnish waters on the imperial yacht. In August there were the traditional manoeuvres at Tsarskoye Selo. These last were completed on the 19th of August. A week later the whole imperial family left for what was intended as a good long visit to the Empress' parents in Denmark, after the fashion of that day. The visit, actually, turned out to be even longer than planned, by reason of the illness of some of the Tsar's children, who came down with the measles shortly after their arrival in Denmark. The family's return to Petersburg had thus to be postponed until well into November.

A few days after the Tsar's arrival at the Fredensborg Palace, near Copenhagen, which was to be his place of residence throughout this visit, the former French Ambassador to Petersburg, General Appert, and his Danish wife arrived from Paris on a visit to Copenhagen, and were asked to dine at the palace. There is strong reason to believe that Appert brought from Paris, on this occasion (August 31), a batch of documents which he had been asked by Flourens, the French foreign minister, to transmit, in strictest confidence, to the Tsar. These included a further series of despatches from the French representative in Sofia, Monsieur Flesch. The reader will recall (see above, Chapter 17) that several of Flesch's despatches had been privately sent by Flourens to the Tsar at an earlier date, the latter being enormously pleased with them and appreciative of Flourens' courtesy in making them available. Now, just recently in fact, Flesch, much to his own discontent, had been re-called by Flourens from his post at Sofia and had arrived in Paris, bringing with him, no doubt, a number of his final reports. These were presumably the ones that Flourens sent to the Tsar; and there can be no doubt but that the monarch was predisposed to receive them benevolently and to give them extensive credence.

But these reports from the French mission in Sofia were not all that was included in the batch of materials Flourens now sent. There were two other documents, ones which had come into Flourens' hands by less regular means, which he now hastened to send on to the Tsar as well. One of these purported to be the copy of a letter written by the German Ambassador in Vienna, Prince Reuss, to Prince Ferdinand of Bulgaria, undated but (if genuine) clearly written shortly before Ferdinand's departure for Bulgaria (i.e., some time in late July 1887). In this communication, the German government was depicted as secretly favoring Ferdinand's assumption of the Bulgarian throne and as promising him eventual German support. The second document was the copy of a letter purporting to have been written by Ferdinand on the 27th of August 1887 (that is, a few days after his arrival in Sofia) to his aunt, the Countess of Flanders, sister-in-law to the Belgian King, and herself a resident of Brussels. In this letter, Ferdinand described his situation, boasted of the clandestine support of Bismarck, and enclosed, as confirmation for this claim, the communication from Prince Reuss. He asked the countess to intercede with her brother, the King of Rumania, and through him with the Tsar, on Ferdinand's behalf. There could, of course, have been nothing better calculated than this to aggravate the Tsar's already aroused suspicions of, and hostility towards, Bismarck than documents of this tenor; and this was (of this there can be no doubt) the reason why Flourens thought it desirable to see that the material reached the Tsar's hands.

Some time later, during the Tsar's stay at Fredensborg, another emissary arrived from Flourens on a similar mission. The emissary, this time, was almost certainly Jules Hansen, who, as we have seen, was an agent both of the French Foreign Office and of the chief of the intelligence section of the Russian Embassy at Paris, P. I. Rachkovski. Hansen brought with him two more documents of similar character, which he probably transmitted to the Tsar through the agency of the latter's personal aide-de-camp, Prince Vladimir S. Obolenski, a good friend of Rachkovski. One of these documents purported to be a copy of another such letter from Ferdinand to his aunt, confirming his previous claim to secret German support. The other was a description, from an unknown third hand, of a third and similar letter. Assuming their authenticity (and after all, Flourens' action in sending them implied his sponsorship of this), these documents constituted damning evidence of Bismarck's bad faith in precisely the question which most engaged the Tsar's emotions and which, more than anything else, had inspired his already existing suspicions of the German chancellor.

The Tsar, at some time during his stay in Denmark, sent these com-

348

munications (or copies of them—one does not know) by courier to Giers, with the annotation: "Kuriosnye dokumenty" ("Curious documents"). But Giers, meanwhile, had himself received certain of them directly from the Russian Embassy at Paris.

It was the middle of November before the Tsar's children were well enough to undertake the return journey to Russia. It being too late in the season to risk a sea passage in the yacht, there was nothing for it but to return by rail, which meant, in terms of the facilities of that day, via Berlin. This was a necessity to which the Tsar yielded only with the utmost reluctance, for he had no desire to visit the German capital. But there appeared to be no alternative. He could not, of course, pass through that city without greeting his imperial German grand-uncle; but he determined to limit his stay there to a single day; and the 18th of November was fixed for this purpose.

Just before his departure on this return journey, the Tsar's already aroused feelings received a new and severe jolt when the news came in of another speech which Kalnocky had delivered, in the first days of November, before the Austro-Hungarian "Delegations." The reader will recall that the Tsar had reacted violently when, just a year before, Kalnocky had spoken before a similar gathering and had indicated that the Austrians would not have been able to accept a Russian occupation of Bulgaria, had the Russians endeavored to take such a step. Now, in 1887, Kalnocky rubbed salt in the wound. Any unilateral intervention in the Bulgarian question, he said, would be absolutely unacceptable. Up to that time, it had proven possible to avoid the intervention of any foreign Power in Bulgaria. It was to be hoped that things would continue this way; this, alone, would represent a considerable success. He continued to hope, he said, that Russia would eventually move, farther than she had done to date, towards the peaceful and conservative attitude adopted by the Central Powers.*

Some idea of the fury with which these statements were received on the Russian side may be gained from the report of the British Ambas-

---

* The French-language text of this passage, as reported by the British Ambassador at Petersburg, read as follows:

... toute intervention isolée dans la question bulgare doit être absolument exclue. L'immixtion d'une Puissance etrangère a été conjurée jusqu'ici et l'on peut espérer qu'elle le sera pour toujours, ce qu'on doit considérer comme un important succès. ... Je ne renonce pas à l'espoir d'aboutir à ce que j'ai toujours cherché, c'est à dire à ce que la Russie se rapproche davantage que ce n'est pas le cas aujourd'hui des tendances pacifiques et conservatoire des Puissances Centrales. ....[1]

sador in Petersburg, Morier, to the effect that one highly placed Russian, closely acquainted with Bismarck (the reference was probably to the Grand Duke Vladimir or one of the Shuvalov brothers), had termed Kalnocky's statements "equivalent to a declaration of war." And indeed, nothing could have been better calculated to arouse the Russian monarch than this reiteration of the Austrian refusal to recognize a special Russian position in Bulgaria which the Russians conceived themselves to have won by their successful war against Turkey, and which they thought had been in effect recognized by the other Powers in the Berlin settlement of 1878.

What between the documents purveyed to him by Flourens, on the one hand, and Kalnocky's provocative statements, on the other, Alexander III may be safely assumed to have contemplated his return journey in a state of high dudgeon against both of his recent allies—the Austrians and the Germans. It is not surprising, therefore, that shortly before his arrival the German government received an informal tip from the Russian Embassy to the effect that while the Tsar of course wished to call upon the old Emperor during his passage through Berlin, he had no desire to see the German chancellor.[2] Stung by this rebuff, Bismarck, then at his country home, expressed reluctance to come to Berlin at all for the occasion. But the old Kaiser would not have it. Some days before the event, it was officially and publicly announced, with extraordinary bluntness, that Bismarck would indeed be coming to Berlin "on the Kaiser's orders." Not only that, but shortly thereafter the Russian Embassy at Berlin received from the Germans a formal request that the German chancellor be received by the Tsar during the latter's presence in the German capital.

In the face of these inauspicious omens, the Tsar's passage through Berlin took place as scheduled, on the 18th of November. It was one of those cold autumn days, gray but bracing, to which the Berlin climate so often inclines. The Tsar's special train arrived at the Lehrter Bahnhof in mid-morning. A heavily guarded cortège of carriages, moving at a brisk trot, then carried the imperial party to the palace. There, the old Kaiser was waiting to receive his illustrious guest; and the two monarchs had a preliminary talk that lasted half an hour.

We might pause, for a moment, to note that Bismarck had taken pains to brief the Kaiser as thoroughly as he could in preparation for this encounter; and the memo with which he provided his august master for this purpose (he even drew it up in French, knowing that this would be the language the two crowned heads would use) not only gives a good idea of the atmosphere of the moment but constitutes one of the major revelations of the chancellor's views on the problems of relations both with Russia and with France.[3]

He began with a bitter complaint over the failure of the Tsar to curb the anti-German fulminations of the Russian nationalist press. Anyone in Russia, he wrote, was apparently free to press with impunity for war and to encourage France to resort to it. A hatred of Germany was thus being fostered which some day, if things continued this way, would get beyond the Russian government's power of control. It was, furthermore, a contagious hatred; and it would not fail to become, sooner or later, reciprocal.

> The hatred that exists between French and Germans has long been mutual; history explains it. That of the Russians against us has no reasons, or even any historical pretexts. We have done nothing to deserve it. It is unjust. We have done what we could to win the friendship of the Russian people. ["La haine entre Français et Allemands est mutuelle depuis longtemps; l'histoire l'explique. Celle des Russes contre nous manque de raisons et même de prétextes historiques. Nous n'avons rien fait pour la mériter; elle est injuste: nous avons fait ce que nous avons pu pour gagner l'amitié de la nation russe."]

Of course, Bismarck continued, there was the Reinsurance Treaty. But this was secret. The public had no knowledge of it. And under the umbrella of it, people were arming with a view to a break at a later date. It could only be concluded that the treaty was, in Russian eyes, no more than a means of gaining time until both Russians and French could complete their military preparations or until the monarchy might be reestablished in France, thus making possible a Franco-Russian alliance.

Nobody believed, Bismarck wrote, that Germany or Austria or Italy or England (the four countries, incidentally, that he was then attempting to mobilize in opposition to Russian policies) were disposed to unleash the scourge of war. It was only from France that one expected, sooner or later, a warlike explosion. And it was only Russia that seemed to want this explosion to take place; for it was Russia alone that was encouraging the militant party in France by dangling before it the vision of a Franco-Russian alliance.

In Russia, Bismarck went on, it seemed that the Tsar and Giers were the only persons who exhibited towards the Germans sentiments other than hatred,

> but their pacific disposition remains unknown to the world at large, and above all to the nations most interested—the Russians, Germans and French; whereas the hatred of all the other Russians against us is osten-

tatiously proclaimed in all quarters. [". . . mais leurs dispositions pacifiques restent inconnues au monde, surtout aux nations intéressées, Russe, Allemande, Française, tandis que la haine de tous les autres Russes contre nous se proclame partout et avec ostentation."]

In these circumstances, Germany had no choice but to look around for allies against a probable Franco-Russian alliance. Nor could she be expected to sacrifice the friendships she now had (the reference was of course to the Austrians) just in order to please the Russians.

> We have lost the confidence we were once accustomed to place, up to 1879, in the intimacy and firmness of the mutual friendship between Russia and Germany. The cooling off experienced since 1879 obliges us to envisage the moment when we may have need for the help of other Powers in order to defend ourselves against a Russian-French coalition. ["Nous avons perdu l'assurance qu'autrefois, jusqu'en 1879, nous étions habitués à placer dans l'intimité et la solidité de l'amitié mutuelle entre la Russie et l'Allemagne. Le refroidissement survenu depuis 1879 nous oblige a prévoir le moment ou nous pouvons avoir besoin de l'assistance d'autres puissances pour nous défendre contre la coalition russo-française."]

Never before, Bismarck concluded, had the great monarchies of Europe had greater interest in avoiding war. Someone, after all, had to lose a war; and peoples were now in the habit of holding their governments responsible for such reverses. Even in Germany the democratic and republican forces would gain considerably from a German defeat. The next great war would have less the quality of a war of government against government than that of a struggle conducted, under the red flag, against the forces of order and conservatism.

———

It was with these powerful and prophetic words, in which one clearly detects the presentiment of the events of 1917-1918 in Russia and Germany, that Bismarck attempted to arm the frail old Kaiser for his encounter with his robust and towering Russian counterpart. How much of it the Kaiser really understood, and how much of it the old gentleman, courtly and tactful to the end, succeeded in conveying to his Russian visitor, we shall never know—probably not much.

In early afternoon Bismarck himself called at the Russian Embassy on Unter den Linden, ostensibly for the purpose of performing the customary courtesy of signing the guest book; and he was then, by prearrangement, told that the Tsar, made aware of his presence in the building, would like him to come upstairs and have a talk.

That these two men should meet and talk was regarded as a sensation.

It attracted the eager attention and speculation of most of the European press. There is, however, no detailed or reliable record of the ensuing conversation. Bismarck's memorandum for the Kaiser, mentioned above, may be taken as a fairly accurate indication of what he himself attempted to convey. The Tsar was obviously nervous and ill at ease in this encounter with a man towards whom he had for so long nurtured such intense ill-feeling but for whose intellectual ascendancy and mastery as a statesman he had a respect approaching sheer awe; and, according to Bismarck, he chain-smoked furiously throughout the interview. In general, the encounter appears to have had a positive result, in the sense that the Tsar returned to Petersburg less incensed with the Germans than he had been before. Giers, who had initially been offended and uneasy over the fact that the Tsar had not invited him to come to Berlin for the occasion, told several of the Petersburg diplomats, apparently quite sincerely, that the visit had in general gone well and been useful, and that he was glad, in retrospect, that he had not been there, because he thought it was useful for the Tsar to experience things for himself and to learn at first hand—not just from Giers—that the Germans were not as unreasonable as he had supposed. And indeed, one of the results of the encounter was that the Tsar, on his return, did take pains to restrain some of the more violent anti-German tendencies in the Russian press— an effort which was, however, destined soon to be overtaken by other events and was thus of short duration.

On that same evening, after a state dinner given by the Kaiser, the Tsar again boarded his special train and was off to Petersburg.

During the Tsar's interview with Bismarck, the painful question of Bulgaria had, of course, come up. It was apparently Bismarck who raised the subject by asking permission to speak about it, to which the Tsar responded (this Bismarck later told his intimates) with "a yellow smile" and a summons to the chancellor to "allez, allez." Bismarck then protested over what he held to be the unfounded suspicions of the Russians with relation to Germany's policy towards Bulgaria. He pointed to the scrupulousness with which the Germans had refrained from interfering there and to their unceasing efforts to persuade the Austrians to leave the Russians a free hand in that country. This, then, provoked from the Tsar the statement that he had evidence that things were not exactly as Bismarck had described them; and in support of this assertion he either showed to Bismarck the documents that had come into his hands in Copenhagen, or described them (probably the first), taking good care not to reveal the sources from which he had

353

them. Bismarck at once pronounced the documents forgeries, and asked the Tsar to provide him with copies, in order that he might investigate them more carefully. This request was acceded to; the Tsar, upon arrival in Petersburg a day or so later, at once sent copies back with a special courier. Immediately upon their receipt, Bismarck, without revealing the texts of the documents themselves, leaked the general circumstances of the episode to the *Kölnische Zeitung*, which published on the 23rd of November a news story and a long editorial article on the subject. In this way there was brought to the attention of the European public generally, in a rather sensational form, the fact that the Tsar had received from some unknown source documents designed to undermine his confidence in Bismarck; and the appetite of the journalistic world in general was whetted for a look at the texts of the documents themselves.

Bismarck, meanwhile, had begun to conduct ("with rage," as Giers later put it) an investigation into the sources of the intrigue. Here, he was handicapped by two circumstances. The first was his own violent and not wholly rational suspicion of ultramontane influences in Europe, and his initial assumption, amounting almost to an *idée fixe*, that the Orléanistes had been the sources of the intrigue.* In leaking the story to the *Kölnische Zeitung*, he even purveyed his suspicion of the Orléanistes to its editors, who reflected it in their story, thereby putting their readers and many others in Europe off the trail.

The second impediment to Bismarck's inquiry into the origins of the documents was the extraordinary reluctance of the Russians to be in any way helpful. Giers, questioned repeatedly by Bülow and Schweinitz about the matter, professed not to know (it is quite possible that the Tsar had indeed concealed this from him) who had purveyed the documents to the Tsar. In any case, he produced only smoke clouds of professed suspicions of his own as to where the culprits might be found—suspicions which, actually, were for the most part quite wide of the mark.

As the remaining weeks of 1887 went by, it became increasingly clear that the Russians had no desire to see the mystery dispelled. Towards the end of December, they began to put out, through their own press, rumors that the documents were known to have been fabricated in

---

* He had in mind here, presumably, the connections of the Danish royal family with the Orléanistes, Dagmar's brother Waldemar having married a Princess Marie of Orléans. But he may also have had in mind Dagmar's sister Thyra, who was married to Prince Ernest August of Cumberland; for he referred on one occasion to the documents having emanated "from Guelphic circles"—a veiled reference, apparently, to the House of Hanover. Actually, the Danish royal family did not particularly favor the Orléaniste dynasty: the predilection seems rather to have been for the Buonapartes.

Vienna by persons interested only in the monetary price they might command—thus conveying the impression that the affair had no political significance.

At just this time, as it happened, Bismarck requested, through Giers, the Tsar's permission to make public the actual texts of the documents, arguing that nothing less than this would be fair to the people whose names had been improperly used in them. To this the Tsar, despite Giers' disapproval, assented. But in conveying this assent, Giers supplemented his oral statement to Schweinitz with a curious handwritten note, on paper without letterhead, addressed to Bismarck and sent by special courier to Berlin. Here it was stated that the matter was a very delicate one, and that the Tsar thought it undesirable that the affair should be permitted to give new fodder to the impassioned speculations of the press. It was further pointed out that the Germans had knowledge of the documents only through the courtesy of the Tsar himself and that this implicitly bound them to respect the Tsar's feelings about how the matter was to be handled vis-à-vis the public. It is highly likely, in fact to be assumed, that the same courier, a high-ranking one, brought a similar personal note from the Tsar to the German Kaiser, with a similar request.[4]

The upshot of all this was that on the last day of December 1887 the full texts of the documents were made public by the German government in the official *Reichsanzeiger*, with an accompanying note identifying them as forgeries but pointing out the seriousness of the unfounded suspicions which someone, through the agency of the documents, had attempted to throw on the authors of German diplomacy. The matter was a one week's sensation for the European press, which speculated richly but inconclusively on the source of the documents. The Russian press, having remained largely silent about the matter from the outset, was now permitted to publish the texts of the documents, but was not permitted to comment extensively on them. And within a matter of days after their publication, the semi-official Petersburg *Novoye Vremya* carried an obviously inspired statement to the effect that, the fraudulent nature of the documents having now been established, the question of their provenance was no longer of any interest—the matter, therefore, should be considered closed.

With this, the question of the origins of the so-called Ferdinand or Bulgarian documents may be said to have passed, generally speaking, from the attention both of contemporaries and, to this point, of historians. One of the reasons for this lack of interest on the part of contemporaries was, of course, the fact that the latter had no knowledge of Flourens' involvement. This became known (and then primarily just in the sense of being available to interested scholars) only some years later, after Flourens had passed from the scene. But in view of that involvement, and in view of the curious disinclination of the Russian governmental leaders either to conduct any public investigation themselves or to have others do so, a few words on the background of this curious episode may be in order.*

There is no reason to doubt that Flourens himself, an inexperienced and gullible man and an easy target for false information of all sorts, believed these documents to be genuine and sent them on to the Tsar in good faith. (Even so, the dates of the documents and of their delivery to Denmark make it evident that he could have conducted no serious investigation into their authenticity before sending them—an omission for which, alone, he could be seriously faulted.) On the other hand, it is equally clear that the documents themselves were spurious from beginning to end. None of the persons in question had written or received any such communications as the forgeries suggested. Nor was there any basis in fact for the general thesis they were meant to convey. Bismarck had never favored Ferdinand's candidacy. He had several very good reasons for doing nothing of the sort. Nor had he made any effort to communicate with Ferdinand, directly or indirectly. Who, then, lay back of this intrigue?

The man who produced the documents for Flourens, and who unquestionably had played a major part in forging them, was a colorful character, ostensibly a Paris journalist and presumably a French citizen (though he might have been Belgian), by the name of Foucault de Mondion. A professional swindler, blackmailer, forger, and purveyor of allegedly stolen diplomatic documents, Mondion had for some years been a Russian spy—an agent, presumably, of Russian military intelligence. In this capacity, he had operated a clandestine espionage center in Berlin from 1884 to 1886. With the usual proclivity of such persons for serving—and deriving revenues from—more than one master, he had also become, by the time these documents were concocted, a well-paid secret agent of General Boulanger.

* A detailed monograph on this subject, entitled *The Mystery of the Ferdinand Documents*, from the same pen as this volume, will be published in the *Jahrbücher für Geschichte Osteuropas*, N.F., XXVI, 1978, pp. 321ff. In view of the fact that the complexities of this matter, in so far as they are known, are set forth and documented in considerable detail in that paper, I shall spare the reader the documentary references for the summary of the circumstances of the episode that appears in this chapter. The curious reader will find them in the article in question.

Formerly a resident of Brussels, Mondion had served at one time as personal secretary for, and tutor to the children of, the Prince de Chimay, who was now, in 1887, Belgian foreign minister. Together with an associate by the name of Nieter, who had had a somewhat similar position with relation to the Belgian minister of the interior, Mondion was operating in Brussels, just at the time when this episode occurred, a species of factory for the production of false documents, by means of which the two men endeavored—apparently with partial initial success— to blackmail their former benefactors: the two ministerial figures. Not long after the peddling of these particular documents to Flourens, their activities along this line were to come to light and to produce (1889- 1890) a major political crisis in Belgium. In addition to this, Mondion's name was also destined to come up (1889) in the trial of Boulanger, who was charged, among other things, with having turned over to Mondion, at the time when he himself was minister of war, 30,000 francs to be used for clandestine skullduggery of one sort or another. (This transfer of funds would have had to be made, of course, shortly before the "Ferdinand documents" appeared.)*

As to how Mondion got his documents into Flourens' hands: there are three published versions, one by Mondion himself, one by a close friend and supporter, and one published anonymously but probably written (after Mondion's death) by the same friend and supporter. All differ, and all are demonstrably at least in part apocryphal. But the weight of evidence suggests, as the most plausible hypothesis, that Mondion availed himself for this purpose of the help of Étienne Lockroy, head of the French journalists' association, who, as we have noted, had been minister of commerce and industry in the Goblet ministry (see above, Chapter 18), was a passionate advocate of a Franco-Russian alliance, and had just recently sent a wreath to Katkov's funeral on behalf of the French journalists. Lockroy appears to have enlisted and received the support, in the undertaking, of his recent cabinet colleague, Boulanger. The money (allegedly 50,000 francs) was apparently put up, on the urging of Lockroy and Boulanger, by the head of the Comptoir d'Escompte de Paris, Edouard Hentsch (who in the following year was to stand trial for the mismanagement of the funds of that institution). Just where the intelligence section of the Paris Russian Embassy came

---

* He who lives by the sword perishes by the sword; and the reputed circumstances of Mondions' death, in the mid-1890's, were an illustration of this maxim. Fallen on evil days, and preparing to revenge himself on society by the publication of memoirs that would presumably have embarrassed many a high personage, Mondion, it is reported, died in his home, poisoned, evidently, by a meal prepared by his own cook, after which the cook was found to have absconded with all his papers—neither cook nor papers ever to be seen again.

into this picture, is not apparent; but it was probably through Jules Hansen, who had extensive connections in the Paris journalistic world, who must surely have known Lockroy, and who probably knew Mondion as well.

Aside, perhaps, from the revelation that the man who was thus feeding false and highly mischievous information to the French foreign minister and through him to the Russian Tsar was an agent of Russian military intelligence, all this would not have been greatly surprising. The manufacturing and exploiting of false documents was, as the Dreyfus case was shortly to show, not an uncommon thing in the Europe of that day, particularly in the intimate entourage of the military intelligence services. But this is not quite all that was involved in the background of the Ferdinand documents; and the remainder, too, has a bearing on the present inquiry.

Mondion's hand, while the leading and most active one, and the one from which the documents seem to have passed directly to the intermediaries mentioned above, does not appear to have been the only one involved in the actual authorship of the material. One gains the impression from a close study of their contents that large parts, and perhaps even the larger part, of the three letters purporting to emanate from Ferdinand were written by someone primarily interested in Balkan affairs, particularly in the person of the King of Rumania, and anxious to portray the King, for some reason, as extensively involved with Ferdinand.* This would not seem to fit Mondion, whose stock in trade was the blackening of the image of Bismarck and who is not known to have had any special interest in Balkan affairs. The material in the letters depicting Bismarck as Ferdinand's secret protector seems in fact to have been grafted onto some sort of original text dealing exclusively with the Rumanian King.

The identity of this Balkan hand is not, and probably never will be, reliably known. The false letter of Prince Reuss evidently had a somewhat different origin from the others. It was separately published in the Paris Boulangiste organ, the *Agence Libre*, at the end of November 1887, Mondion later taking credit for being the person who placed it there. But there is some evidence to suggest that this letter had been

---

* The preoccupation of the author or authors with the person of the King of Rumania is evident from the choice of the King's sister, the Countess of Flanders, as the ostensible recipient of the letters. Actually, Ferdinand never corresponded with her. He *did*, very occasionally, correspond with her husband, who, like himself, was of the House of Saxe-Coburg. If the concern of the author had been only with the plausibility of the letters, the husband would thus have been a more credible target. The only apparent reason for the choice of the Countess, instead, was to work in the Rumanian angle.

produced by a French resident of Bucharest, a journalist, translator, and author of a Franco-Rumanian dictionary, by the name of Frédéric Damé. Damé had previously been editor-in-chief of a pro-Russian French-language paper published in Bucharest, the *Indépendence Roumaine*, obviously a subsidized organ of the Russian Legation in that city. Mondion had made a tour of the Balkans in the later summer of 1887, presumably as a spy for the Boulangistes, visiting Vienna just when Ferdinand was making his decision to accept the Bulgarian throne, arriving in Sofia just in time for Ferdinand's arrival there, and in all probability visiting Bucharest on the way back. In Bucharest, incidentally, his path would have crossed, or nearly crossed, with that of Déroulède, now returning from Russia. In Bucharest, Mondion would probably also have seen Damé, and he may well have brought the document back to Paris with him.

But the other three false documents treat of subjects, and contain suggestions, of which there is no hint in the Prince Reuss letter. They seem to have come to Brussels through other channels. There is some evidence to suggest that these may have been the channels of Russian military intelligence. The Russian military attaché in Brussels, Colonel M. M. Chichagov, was a very political sort of military attaché, whom we have already encountered as one of the Russian officials serving in Bulgaria at the time of the unification of that country in 1885. It is evident that he had some sort of connection or involvement with Mondion. And we must note, as another suggestive circumstance surrounding this episode, that the two Russian diplomatic missions in Bucharest and Brussels, serving as intelligence centers for the Balkans and for French-speaking Europe, respectively, were closely connected. Prince Lev Pavlovich Urusov, Russian minister at Brussels, had recently come there directly from Bucharest, where he had been serving in similar capacity, carrying with him the reputation of being a bitter enemy of the Rumanian King. There appear to have been other close connections between the two missions, as well, particularly in the intelligence field.

All in all, the available evidence points to what might be called the paid journalistic entourage of the Russian military intelligence network, in Bucharest and in Brussels, as the most likely source of the Balkan component of the Ferdinand documents—the component onto which Mondion then grafted his anti-Bismarckian material. This, together with knowledge of Mondion's part in the affair and of his previous relationship to the Russian government, would have sufficed to explain Giers' obvious embarrassment in the face of the whole episode, and his eagerness to see the matter hushed up as soon as possible. The Tsar's motives, however, were somewhat different: they seem to have included, primarily, a desire not to bring embarrassment to his Danish relatives, whose guest he had been when the documents came into his hands, and some of whom may even have been instrumental in getting them there, but also a reluctance on his part to betray the confidence of those French officials, notably Flourens, who had, between them, supplied him with this material.

A year before all this happened (i.e., in June 1886), there had been a very similar effort, reflected in the Russian press (and specifically in Katkov's *Moskovskie Vyedomosti*), to portray Battenberg, then still in Sofia, as the secret agent of Bismarck; and here, too, there were false allegations of secret communications having passed from one to the other. It was precisely from Bucharest, too, that these reports emerged. Six months after the surfacing of the Ferdinand documents (i.e., in June 1888), furthermore, another representative of General Boulanger, the Boulangiste parliamentary deputy and editor, Lucien Millevoye, would show up in Petersburg with another batch of documents, which he would describe as a "supplement" to the Ferdinand documents, and which he would try frantically to transmit into the hands of the Tsar.

Déroulède, too, is reported to have endeavored, after his return from Russia in the late summer of 1887, to get certain documents into the Tsar's hands, and even to have visited Copenhagen, in vain, for this purpose. Boulanger himself, immediately after leaving office in 1888, attempted to pay a visit to Petersburg (the venture was frustrated by the combined efforts of the French and Russian Foreign Offices); and it was presumably because of his inability to carry out this purpose that Millevoye was sent in his place. It is clear, then, that the Ferdinand documents were only one part of an intensive campaign waged by the Boulangistes and other French chauvinists, in all probability with help from circles connected with Russian military intelligence, with a view to fanning, by the use of spurious rumors and documents, the Tsar's known suspicions of Bismarck in connection with the Bulgarian problem.

That the Tsar was aware that such a campaign was being conducted is clear. There is no evidence that he had any very favorable view of its presumed supporters. (He is said to have referred to Boulanger, in his talk with Bismarck on the 18th of November, as "cet animal.") But on the other hand one sees no signs of any particular resentment on his part over the deception which people were trying, in this instance, to work upon him. It is not apparent that he ever seriously held the matter against Flourens (who later wrote a highly flattering book about him), although he did decline to receive the latter when, several years later, he visited Petersburg as a private person.

Of particular interest, in just this connection, are the observations made about this episode by one of the shrewdest and best-informed of observers of life at the Russian court in the period of Alexander III: Catherine Radziwill. In her descriptive book, published under the pen-name of Count Vassili (and sometimes attributed by contemporaries to Cyon), about the life and personages of that court, Princess Radziwill wrote that Alexander III "never quite believed that the documents were not genuine."[5] Nor did he ever fully abandon his suspicions of Bismarck in this connection. With the words: "Tout mauvais cas est niable," he dismissed, she says, Bismarck's professions of innocence and of ignorance of the source of the documents. "Perhaps," she continues, "this conviction proceeded from his knowledge of the person from whom he had received them, and whom he probably considered as one who would not have stooped to such a means of revenge as helping to impose upon him such a gross fabrication."

This episode stands, then, as a vivid example not only of the intensity of the efforts put forward by both Russian and French chauvinists, in 1887, to disrupt relations between Petersburg and Berlin and to deflect the Tsar's policies into a direction favorable to an eventual alliance with France, but also of the considerable impact these efforts had on a mind so predisposed to credit their tendency as was that of Alexander III.

It should be added, to avoid misunderstanding, that there is no evidence that either Flourens' cabinet colleagues—with the exception of Boulanger and Lockroy—or indeed President Grévy, had at the time any knowledge of Flourens' action or would for a moment have approved it, had they known of it. But it is hardly to be supposed that they could long remain unaware that it had happened. It is interesting to note that not long after the appearance of the documents, and as soon as the immediate wave of public discussion and speculation to which they gave rise began to subside, Flourens was dropped from the cabinet (April 3, 1888), never again to have a ministerial post—and this despite the fact that his activity in the office of foreign minister was generally held to have been creditable and successful. No reason was ever given, so far as this writer is aware, for his removal at that time; but the historian must be allowed to entertain the suspicion that when the day of his departure from office arrived, with the European public still ignorant of his part in purveying the false documents to Alexander III, there were great sighs of relief on the part of a number of French politicians and officials who by that time knew rather more than they had known in the late summer of 1887 about the true circumstances of the episode.

Chapter Twenty

THE DETERIORATING
THREE-EMPEROR RELATIONSHIP

While the conclusion of the Reinsurance Treaty was held, at the Tsar's insistence, in deepest secrecy, the change marked by the lapse of the earlier *Dreikaiserbund* was something of which informed circles throughout Europe were generally, if somewhat dimly, aware. It was, in particular, no secret to the other European Chanceries that this development marked a significant deterioration—or at least the recognition of an existing deterioration—in Austro-Russian relations. And it was this situation that was the background, if not the cause, of the Russo-Austrian war scare that arose with much suddenness in the final weeks of 1887 and continued into the first weeks of 1888.

The war scare in question, which had little more in the way of substance behind it than the Franco-German one by which it was preceded, seems to have taken its departure primarily from two developments in Russian policy. The first of these consisted of certain military measures put in hand by the Russians at that time, primarily the transfer of the 13th Cavalry Division from the Moscow to the Warsaw military district, where it was deployed near the Austro-Galician border. In vain did the man on the spot, in this case the Austrian military attaché in Petersburg, Lt. Col. Klepsch, endeavor to persuade his superiors in Vienna that the move was no proper source of alarm—that it had been long planned and had nothing particular to do with the situation of the moment. The War Ministry in Vienna, as well as the Western press, insisted on interpreting it, together with certain other minor measures for the strengthening of Russia's western garrisons, as a sign that Russia was preparing to launch an attack on Austria-Hungary. There was, accordingly, a certain ruffling of the feathers in the Austro-Hungarian general staff; the press picked up the smell of it, and the scare was on.

Accompanying these military changes was the fact that a good deal of anti-Austrian talk was now beginning to be heard in the civilian echelons of the higher Russian bureaucracy—even from the lips of a person normally so conciliatory as Giers, and in such quantity that it seemed to indicate some sort of authoritative official inspiration. There was some speculation in German and Austrian diplomatic circles about the causes of this development. It seems to have begun just prior to the return of the Tsar from Denmark to Russia, at the end of November; so if it reflected any changes in his own outlook, these must have been ones that had their origin during his stay in Denmark. One will not be far wrong, surely, in attributing it to an explosive reaction on the Tsar's part to Kalnocky's publicly reiterated refusal to accept a special Russian interest in Bulgaria—a reaction which did not fail to become known, in some way, to the Foreign and the War Offices in Petersburg.

One could interpret as one liked this new access of anti-Austrian talk in the Russian capital. Some of the Germans professed to see in it a desire on the part of the Russians to provoke the Austrians into some sort of hostile action against Russia—a desire inspired, supposedly, by the knowledge in Petersburg that the Austro-German Alliance obliged the Germans to come to Austria's defense only if Austria were herself the victim of Russian aggression, and by the hope, accordingly, that in the event of a Russo-Austrian war in which the Austrians could be made to appear as the aggressors, the Germans, suitably buttered-up, could perhaps be induced to stand aside and to await the French attack on Germany which (everyone was convinced of this) would then most certainly ensue. In this way, it was argued, there was at least the possibility of realizing the fondest Russian dream—that of a war with Austria from which the Germans would have justification for remaining aloof, and reason for doing so.

These and other speculations connected with the Austro-Russian war scare sufficed, in any case, to unleash between the Germans and Austrians, around the turn of the years 1887-1888, a whole series of tense and agitated exchanges over the interpretation of the Austro-German Alliance of 1879, particularly the exact nature of the *casus belli* therein envisaged. The Austrian generals were anxious to get the Germans to agree that the *casus belli* should arise not only in the face of an *actual Russian attack* but also in case it should appear certain that the Russians *were preparing to attack*. They pressed the Germans, accordingly, to enter into staff talks envisaging a preventive attack by the Austrian and German forces on Russia—an attack designed to anticipate a supposed Russian move and to assure to the Central Powers the advantages of surprise. These pressures aroused the violent opposition of Bismarck, not only because such an undertaking would be in conflict with the Reinsurance Treaty (about which the Austrians knew nothing), but because he was determined, as a matter of principle, not to permit Germany to become involved in a war with Russia in defense of Austrian interests in the Balkans.

Bismarck realized clearly the great danger that would be created for Germany by a complete destruction of the Austro-Hungarian Empire. He was prepared, for that reason, to defend that Empire against an outright Russian attack. But he was adamant in his insistence that Germany should not be made a party to Austria's Balkan involvements and aspirations. He feared that if Germany agreed to participate in anything resembling a preventive atttack on Russia, the Austrians would be encouraged to provoke the very situation—that is, a further strengthening of Russian forces on the German-Austrian border—to which such an attack would be a response. In this way Germany, if she had entered into staff talks of this nature, could easily be carried into an offensive war against Russia in the service of interests other than her own. He was determined this should not occur. He therefore fought this suggestion, tooth and nail, to the great discontent of his own generals, most of whom were longing for the adventure of a good war with Russia, and of the Austrian military leaders, who claimed to see themselves condemned in this way to await passively a Russian attack they had come to view as inevitable, thus forfeiting the advantages of surprise. The bitterness of the Austrians was all the greater because Bismarck, while refusing to assure them of German support for preventive action, constantly pressed them to increase the strength and readiness of their own armed forces. This, for reasons of economy, they were reluctant to do. Obviously, they would much have preferred to have the Germans fight their battles for them than to go to the trouble and expense of preparing to fight them alone. However, this was precisely what Bismarck was determined not to permit.

The struggle was not just one between the German and Austrian governments; it was also one between Bismarck and his own military leaders, for it involved the wider question of the general desirability, or inevitability, of a Russo-German war. The old German Field Marshal Count Moltke and the Quartermaster General Count Waldersee both professed to interpret the strengthening of the Russian military position along Russia's western border as a clear sign that Russia had decided to attack Austria and was preparing to do so. They therefore associated themselves strongly with the pressures of the Austrian military leaders for a preventive attack on Russia, and specifically for an early one—during the forthcoming winter, in fact, when the roads and rivers would be frozen, and military mobility would be greater than at other seasons. This view was formally put before Bismarck and the Kaiser in a memorandum submitted by Moltke at the end of November 1887.[1] And not only was this the view of these senior military figures but it found the support (this was particularly disquieting to Bismarck in view of the failing health of both the Kaiser and the Crown Prince) of the young Prince William, destined so soon to inherit the throne.

Bismarck thus found himself under the necessity of defending his position not only before Germany's Austrian ally but before powerful elements in his own military and civilian structure of power. And the result was a series of written communications, some to the German Ambassador in Vienna, some to persons in Berlin, which may well be said to have constituted the old chancellor's last great effort of statesmanship—an effort on which the peace of Europe unquestionably depended and by which that peace was in fact saved, at least for the period in question.

Never, surely, was the issue more clearly drawn than here between the duty of the statesman to avoid, if possible, the horrors of war in the modern industrial age, and the perennial tendency of military leaders to see as inevitable any war for which they are asked to plan and prepare, and to wish to begin that war at the time, and in the circumstances, most favorable to their side.

Bismarck argued, first of all, that he was unconvinced that war with Russia really was inevitable. But he could also not be brought to concede that, even if it should appear inevitable, this would necessarily mean that one should initiate it at any particular juncture—even one that appeared favorable from a military standpoint. The course that appeared most favorable from the purely military standpoint was not always, he maintained, the most favorable one from the political standpoint.

Beyond this, Bismarck was not willing to concede that even a war against Russia that could be expected to end successfully in the military sense was necessarily desirable. What would be Germany's objectives in such a war? The conquest of new territory? But the Germans wanted no Russian territory. The destruction of the Russian armed forces? But a total destruction of them was not possible. Nor would any such destruction be permanent. A military humiliation of Russia would merely produce on Germany's eastern border, Bismarck argued, another irreconcilable opponent, to join the one Germany already had to the west of her, across the Rhine. And the Russian armed forces would not long remain destroyed, or prostrate, in any case. They would soon be restored. It had taken the French only four years to rebuild their own after the recent war of 1870-1871. For what, then, would the Germans be fighting? For what would they be prepared to settle? It was always easier to start a war, he pointed out, than to end one.

A military victory over Russia, Bismarck went on, would not solve any of Germany's problems—or those of Europe. It would only be the seed of future troubles. And these future troubles would be more serious than any the war had been intended to remove. A war with Russia would inevitably lead at once to war with France as well. Such a war, regardless of its military outcome, could only be, in its consequences, a calamity for all Europe. Its consequences would present the most serious dangers for the survival of the three imperial monarchies themselves.

These were, of course, farseeing views. But they found little echo, anywhere, either in Austrian or German circles, or in Petersburg itself. The military view—the view which assumed war to be inevitable and sought only the most favorable moment to unleash it—was being put forward in all three capitals; and it seemed easier for most people to understand.

On the 26th of January 1888, the German Ambassador in Petersburg, Schweinitz, tried to make clear to the Tsar, in a talk they had at a palace function, the nature of Bismarck's anxieties over the militarization of German-Russian relations.[2] But the talk, to Schweinitz's despair, soon degenerated into the shopworn argument as to whose military preparations were the most menacing to the other, and why they were necessary at all. Schweinitz, at this point, observed that it was incredible, after all, that the two of them should be sitting there talking about the respective preparations for a war for which no one had been able to cite the slightest plausible political reason—a war which would most likely lead only to revolution throughout Europe. The best the Russians could hope from the favorable outcome of such a war, he argued, would be the destruction of Austria-Hungary. But this in turn could lead only to the appearance along Russia's western frontier of a lot of small anarchical republics which could be an even greater problem to her than the existing Empire. Why, then, all this talk about war? Why all these military preparations? Why not drop the subject and abandon the fears it engendered?

Yes, replied the Tsar, uncertainly—Bismarck had said much the same thing to him. But then, after a puzzled pause, he returned at once to complaining about Austrian military behavior. Within a few moments, to Schweinitz' despair, the two men were right back at the question of the Russian reinforcements along the western border, and the Tsar was explaining why these were necessary to match the military capabilities on the other side. It was plain that the lack of any plausible political rationale for a war was not to be permitted to interfere with the belief that it was inevitable or with the determination to win it militarily. In the struggle between reason, on the one hand, and the momentum of military competition, on the other, reason proved a poor competitor.

Questions of this nature, as noted above, preoccupied both the

German and the Austrian Chanceries throughout the final weeks of 1887 and the month of January 1888. They appear to have come to a rather abrupt end, however, with the publication, on the 8th of February 1888, of the terms of the Austro-German Alliance of 1879. The wording of their treaty, as we have seen, had been revealed privately to the Russians during the negotiations leading to the Reinsurance Treaty; but it had not been made public. Bismarck's insistence on publication of the document in the winter of 1888 was a move aimed at both the German and Austrian higher military commands, not all the members of which had previously known the actual terms of the treaty. It was designed to bring home to all these people the limited and defensive nature of Germany's obligations to Austria under the terms of the treaty—to force the Austrians to recognize that they could not expect Russian help in any war they might themselves initiate, and to impress it upon the consciousness of the German military leaders that Germany's obligations to Austria were only of a strictly defensive nature and afforded no basis for German assistance to Austria in a conflict the latter might herself inaugurate. And this, coming as it did on the heels of Bismarck's many and energetic statements of his position behind the scenes, seems to have been successful. The war scare, in any case, died as abruptly as it had arisen. As a preoccupation for the senior German statesmen, in particular, its place was about to be taken by sadder and even more fateful events.

On the 9th of March 1888, only a few days short of his 92nd birthday, the old German Kaiser, William I, surrounded by his family and a small group of senior officials, passed quietly away in his palace in Berlin. His son, who then became Kaiser Frederick III, was already at that time, and had been for many months, mortally ill with cancer of the throat. Unable to take any significant part in the ruling of the country during the brief weeks of his nominal reign, he too then died, on the 15th of June, whereupon the throne passed to his own vigorous, not greatly aggrieved, but also not greatly beloved, 29-year-old son William, who became, and was destined to remain until the end of the German Empire, Kaiser William II.

If the death of Frederick III was significant primarily as an event in the domestic-political life of the new Germany (for it was around him that many of the hopes of the German liberals had centered, and with his death that many of those hopes died), it was the death of his father, William I, that was of greatest importance from the standpoint of Germany's international position. Mention has already been made of the great affection and respect in which the old Kaiser was held by the Tsars Alexander II and Alexander III—less, to be sure, in the case of the latter, but even in his case enough to constitute a serious, and in the view of many a decisive, impediment to any complete deterioration of Russo-German relations. Giers, for example, who saw these things more clearly than anyone else, was always convinced that so long as the old Kaiser remained alive, there would be no war between Russia and Germany.

William II, to whom, in the circumstances, the prestige and to some extent the influence of the throne had virtually passed upon his grandfather's death in March, was like neither his father nor his grandfather. In contrast to both the old Kaiser and Bismarck, who were in many respects eighteenth-century personalities, he was very much a product of the late nineteenth century, with all its inner uncertainties and extravagant pretentions. Not unintelligent nor even devoid of occasional brilliant insights, he was nevertheless intellectually mercurial and undependable, seemingly incapable of sustained and disciplined attention to any given problem, and neither profound nor steady in his broader conclusions. There was lacking in his intellect some sort of an inner balance-wheel of serious reflectiveness. Though not incapable of impulses of real human warmth, he was often childish and vulgar in his personal conduct. In his official and public appearances, he was histrionic rather than serious, more concerned with appearances than with realities, given to the enjoyment of what he was pretending to be (the clever, superior, self-confident military leader) rather than what he really was. His everlasting posing tended to offend foreign rulers and statesmen, sometimes even to alarm them; in any case it caused them to react more skeptically and adversely than they otherwise would have done to his statesmanship. Lacking the outstanding personal qualities— the charm and integrity—of his grandfather, he was incapable of inspiring elsewhere in Europe anything resembling the confidence the old monarch had inspired.

Not surprisingly (for it was a deficiency he shared with many other highly placed people), William II was quite incapable of grasping the subtle logic of the principles of statesmanship by which Bismarck was guided. This came clearly to light even before his assumption of the throne, during the brief nominal reign of his father. Impressed with the use made by Bismarck and other senior German figures of marginalia on despatches as a means of stating their own views, he at once adopted the same practice, but in a style that was peculiarly his own: arrogant, supercilious, and scornful, designed to suggest great cleverness, omniscience, and incisiveness of judgment on the part of the writer. For him, these comments were simply another way of posing before those who would supposedly read them.

Now it happened that the German Ambassador at Vienna, in a despatch of the 28th of April 1888, quoted Austrian Foreign Minister Kalnocky as observing that perhaps the general staff officers in Berlin and Vienna had been right, after all, the previous autumn in their repeatedly expressed desire to mount an effort to destroy Russia's military power before it could become too dangerous. Opposite this passage in the despatch William, then still Crown Prince, wrote in the margin: "Ja."

Bismarck, acutely aware that the young man was bound shortly to become Kaiser, was stung to the quick. The note indicated flat opposition to his own policy. He at once wrote a short letter to the Crown Prince, summing up those of his views on a possible war with Russia that were described earlier in this chapter. On this communication, too, William again had the temerity to affix marginalia indicating disagreement. This, in turn, provoked from Bismarck a longer letter, obviously written in very considerable agitation of the spirit—an agitation only too understandable in the light of what might well be involved for Germany, for Europe, and for his own position, in this difference of opinion. In all probability, Bismarck pointed out, the power of decision in questions of war and peace would soon lie in the young man's hands. He professed himself unable to hope that the differences of opinion between the two of them that had been brought to light could be overcome by further argument on his part. He nevertheless felt called upon, he wrote, to draw attention to certain of the implications of the Crown Prince's view. Noting that a destruction of Russia's armed power would leave Germany in a position of helpless dependence on Austria for her security, he went ahead to point out that if one were to accept the view to which the Crown Prince subscribed, then the whole direction of German policy since the recent death of the old Kaiser had been wrong. Then one should have permitted the Battenberg marriage (a telling point with young William, who detested Battenberg), and should have tried to place him once more on the Bulgarian throne—a move which would certainly have provoked the war the Crown Prince apparently wished to bring about. But even then, if one were going to unleash a two-front war (and this after all, would have been the effect of the attack on Russia which the young man seemed to want), then it would have been better, for various reasons, to provoke first a conflict with France. In any case, Bismarck concluded, he would now have to lock up all the papers upon which the Crown Prince had entered his marginalia; for if this difference of opinion were ever to become known to outsiders, all confidence in Germany's peaceful intentions, in Germany as well as elsewhere, would disappear. Not even he himself would be able, then, to keep up the pretense of peaceful purposes; because for the policies of the German Empire, he wrote, the reputation of insincerity was "more dangerous even than the most determined tendency to resort to war, provided that such tendency proceeds from real political conviction."

Confronted with this attack, and acting on the advice of his senior military friends, young William backed down with a rather unconvincing reply; and the matter was allowed to rest. But one sees clearly in this incident, as one does in the other evidences of thinking in the immediate military and diplomatic entourage of Bismarck at this point, how extensively the understanding and support for the latter's policies, the main pillar of the political relationship between Russia and Germany that had existed since 1870, was now beginning to be undermined, with the old Kaiser no longer there to support it.

On his earlier visits to Russia, before he became Crown Prince, William II had made a good impression on Alexander III. Now, on assuming the throne, the young man insisted, with supreme tactlessness, in embarking —within a few weeks of his father's death and long before the traditional period of mourning had expired—on a series of visits to foreign capitals, beginning with Petersburg. This precedence accorded to Petersburg was of course offensive to the Austrians, whose Emperor was by far the senior of the three, and who, as Germany's principal ally, had a reasonable claim on the young monarch's first visit. The British, too, were none too pleased. The young Kaiser was, after all, Queen Victoria's grandson. Generally, this unseemly haste made a bad impression.

The Kaiser made the journey to Petersburg in the imperial yacht, accompanied by an impressive naval squadron; and the visit, which lasted for five days, was one exhausting round of displays, parades, dinners, and sight-seeing appearances. Bismarck *père* did not join the Kaiser's party; but his son, Herbert, went along, was well received, and was accorded interviews both by the Tsar and by Giers. The interview with the Tsar was highly satisfactory, young Bismarck being in a position to supply much gossip about the abundant intrigues that had agitated the Berlin court during the 99-day interval between the deaths of the two Emperors—a subject about which the Tsar showed himself poorly informed but very curious. With Giers, Herbert Bismarck had a desultory political talk, from the records of which one gains the impression that neither side had much to say to the other: both were tired of the old subjects of argument and well aware that little good would come of any effort to pursue them further. The Germans were determined not to let the Russians feel that they had any great need of Russian favor at that point, and were therefore careful to ask for nothing and to show no inordinate interest in explaining their position. Giers attempted to impress upon young Bismarck how unfortunate it would be if the Austrians were to attempt to take advantage of Russia's momentary helplessness in the Balkans. Herbert Bismarck pointed out that the Austrians were most unlikely to do anything of the sort. Beyond that, there was not much to say. The talk, as young Bismarck put it, simply "fizzled out" at the end.

By and large, the effect of the Kaiser's visit was, for the moment, mildly favorable in its effect on Russian opinion; but it changed little in the basic fabric of the relationship between the two countries. Aside from the fact that the Tsar and his family were less favorably impressed with young William than on previous occasions, the dispositions of the Russian nationalist press remained only slightly and momentarily affected. The grim embitterment against Austria which pervaded all influential Russian society, official and journalistic, and which constituted the most serious source of potential conflict in German-Russian relations, remained substantially unaffected.

Several of the events of the year 1887 and the first half of 1888, just recounted, had the effect of exercising a decisive change upon Russia's relationship to the other great continental powers, particularly Germany and France.

First, there was the revelation to senior Russian officials, and later to the general public, of the terms of the Austro-German Alliance of 1879. Then there were the differences of view that were brought to light in the negotiations for the Reinsurance Treaty. Beyond this, there was the general deterioration of Russo-German relations caused by the unrestrained anti-German fulminations of the Russian nationalist press. These developments all served to destroy whatever lingering hopes might have existed in Petersburg that there could be a war against the Austrians from which Germany could in some way be brought to remain aloof. From this time on the Russian general staff was compelled to proceed, in its plans and preparations, on the assumption that any war it might initiate against Austria would also mean a war against Germany. And from this it was only a step to the recognition that in a war against Germany it would be the behavior of the French that would probably make the decisive difference between success or failure of the Russian effort. But the behavior of the French, as one was also compelled to recognize in Petersburg, was something that would depend at least to some degree on the state of Franco-Russian relations at the given moment, and particularly on the nature of the understandings, or lack of understandings, that might then prevail between the two governments and their general staffs.

Secondly, there was the death of the old Kaiser. Up to 1888 there had been, in the form of his presence at the head of the new German Empire, a certain floor beneath which Russo-German relations could not sink, and, by the same token, a ceiling above which Franco-Russian relations could not rise. Now, with the death of the old gentleman, this last but very effective barrier to any basic change in the Russo-German relationship was removed.

Thus, the latter part of the year 1888 found the Tsar faced not only with a new incentive to the development of a closer political and military relationship with France (implicit in the recognized necessity of finding a powerful ally against Germany if he was to have any chance of defeating the hated Austrians) but also a new freedom, such as he had never before enjoyed, to pursue the building of that relationship, undeterred by any feelings of personal loyalty to the crowned head of imperial Germany. For if the visit of William II had gone off pleasantly enough on the surface of appearances, the young Kaiser's deficiencies were evident to anyone who cared to look. Not by the remotest flight of the imagination could the young man have taken the place in the Tsar's affections and respect that had previously been occupied by his grandfather.

It might have been thought, and no doubt was thought in some quarters, that so significant a change in the situation of Alexander III, weakening his attachment to the tie with Germany and freeing his hands for the development of a closer one with France, would have reflected adversely on the position of Giers, so long attacked for his allegedly pro-German tendencies. Actually, it was not this way at all. The personal attacks on Giers had been largely the doing of Katkov. With the great editor out of the way, the nationalist press was content to continue its attacks on the German tie without making Giers the butt of them; in addition to which Giers himself, no longer on the defensive, was able to apply his delicate skills to the improvement of Franco-Russian relations without appearing to yield ground to clamorous and vindictive enemies. There is no reason to doubt, furthermore, that the influence of the French Embassy at Petersburg, whose senior officials had correctly seen in the use of Giers as an intermediary with the Tsar the best prospects for strengthening the French position in that capital, had a perceptible effect in dissuading the Russian nationalists from attacking his person. Finally, with the cessation of the personal vendetta against Giers from the nationalist side, the Tsar, too, found his position relieved; for he could now lend his support to Giers without having to fear that this would place him in opposition to Pobyedonostsev and the whole nationalistic wing of Russian opinion—a situation which he wanted, above all things, to avoid.

The upshot of all this was that there was celebrated in Petersburg on the 13th-14th of October 1888, with a pomp and ceremony that clearly reflected the personal approval of the Tsar, the 50-year anniversary of Giers' entry into the Russian diplomatic service. The celebrations went on for two days. They included not only dinners by the senior officials at the Ministry and by the Petersburg diplomatic corps but a seemingly endless series of congratulatory messages, including one from the Tsar (not yet returned from the Crimea); courtesy visits by hundreds of people, including several of the grand dukes; and the presentation of a wealth of gifts—a massive inkwell with miniature statuary, after the fashion of the time, from the diplomats; an ornate album with pictures of all the scenes of his official service from his Foreign Office subordinates, and so on. And some days later, after the Tsar's return, there came, at long last, the Order of St. Vladimir which the unhappy Easter evening a year and a half before had failed to bring.

Thus was Giers finally rewarded for the patience and fortitude with which he had endured the pressures against him in the difficult winter of 1887; and thus was vindicated, at least in the eyes of the foreign governments, his long and faithful adherence to the principles of restraint and conciliation in his dealings with the representatives of the other Powers. From now on, his personal position was secure to the end of the life and reign of Alexander III—an end which coincided so closely with the fading, and finally, the collapse, of his own strength.

On the other hand, the policy which Giers had at one time, in 1887, fought so hard to defend was by now irremediably undermined. The Reinsurance Treaty notwithstanding, it would be, in essence, the policy of his opponents that would eventually triumph—but under his leadership, this time, not theirs, and not immediately. It is one of the supreme ironies of this tale that Giers' personal triumph and vindication should have coincided so closely with the weakening of the arrangements he had so long sought to preserve.

And what, then, of the French, and their reaction to all this? It can only be said that their reaction, at least on the formal diplomatic-political level, was almost negligible. There were several reasons for this. Of these, the most prominent, from the autumn of 1887 until late in 1888, was an extensive preoccupation (characteristic of turbulent democracies) with France's own internal political affairs. But personnel changes also entered in.

First, there was the disaster that overtook, in the late summer and autumn of 1887, the elderly French President Jules Grévy. Finding himself most outrageously and tragically compromised by the conduct of his son-in-law, Daniel Wilson (who was found to be selling honorific decorations as a means of escape from his own financial embarrassments), Grévy resigned the presidency on December 2, 1887. He was 80 years old at the time of his retirement, and would presumably not have had much longer to go, in any case, as an active force in French foreign policy. But his departure marked, as did so many other things that occurred in that crucial year of 1887, the end of an epoch. His services to France in the field of foreign policy had been great. From his presidential position he had constituted almost the only steadying influence in a time of great instability at the parliamentary and cabinet levels of French public life. It was to his imperturbable temperament and disillusioned skepticism more than to any other factor that France owed her survival of the dangers presented, in Franco-German relations, by the military demagoguery of Boulanger, and in Franco-Russian relations, by the political impetuosity of Flourens. Grévy, seeing the underlying divergence of aims between France and Russia and the inherent weakness of Russia as an ally, had not been a partisan of a Franco-Russian alliance; but at the same time he did not conceive of himself as an enemy of Russia, nor did he oppose the effort to achieve a quiet strengthening of Franco-Russian relations. His approach to the problems of the relationship was similar to that of Giers in that it was aimed at the stabilization of relations among the European Great Powers generally, and at the avoidance of abrupt alterations in the existing balance of power. One cannot resist the impression that had it been possible for Grévy's influence to endure, if not in his own personal effort then in the attitudes of his successors, France—and with her the rest of northern Europe—might well have avoided the fateful path that carried them all to the disasters of the First World War.

Grévy's successor in the presidency, elected the day after his retirement, was the republican politician and former cabinet member, Sadi Carnot. The scion of a distinguished republican family, a grandson of "le grand Carnot," like Freycinet an engineer by training but a politician by taste, Carnot was destined to serve in the presidency from 1887 until his assassination in June 1894. His encumbency thus embraced the entire period of the negotiation and conclusion of the Franco-Russian alliance.

Although he was to show himself in the course of time a strong partisan of the alliance, and was to go down in history as such,* Carnot observed, during the initial months of his presidency, a circumspection second to that of none of the others when it came to Franco-Russian relations. This was, among other things, exactly the time when Boulanger, now no longer in the government, was mounting his bid for power through electoral and parliamentary success; and it is permissible to suppose that Carnot, standing his ground manfully against the Boulangiste intimidation, was not anxious to call attention to the delicate question of a possible alliance with Russia, so dear to Boulanger's heart.

Boulanger himself had been obliged to give up the War Ministry, in May 1887, in the reformation of the cabinet that accompanied the change in the presidency. His place was taken there by Freycinet—a man deeply interested in military affairs and who rather fancied himself as an expert in them. Freycinet was anxious to set the development of France's armed forces back on an even keel after the stormy and not always helpful vicissitudes they had suffered at Boulanger's hands. Here, in the military field, his contribution to the formation of the alliance was destined to be more constructive and effective than anything he had accomplished in his previous capacity as premier. But like his colleagues in the cabinet and at the Foreign Ministry, he was not anxious to see France become involved in the intimate discussion of military relations with Russia until the post-Boulangiste reordering and development of the French armed forces was further advanced than was the case in the first months of 1888; and for this reason he, too, in 1888, was not inclined to force the pace.

In early April 1888, the Tirard cabinet, which had followed briefly on the change in the presidency, fell from office and was replaced by one headed, as premier, by Floquet. It will be recalled that the mere suggestion of Floquet's becoming premier had been sufficient, less than a year before, to cause Mohrenheim to threaten his own retirement because of the insult once offered by Floquet to the Tsar Alexander II. For Floquet, now president of the Chamber of Deputies, this Russian cold shoulder, well known to the public, had become a major political embarrassment. One of the sensations of the Paris season, therefore, in the winter of 1888, was a public reconciliation brought about between Floquet and the Russian Embassy after extensive discussions between Flourens and Mohrenheim. This reconciliation obviously had the Tsar's

---

* One notes that Madame Carnot's salon, even after her husband's death, was faithfully patronized by just those military and civilian figures, including Boisdeffre, Saussier, and Hanotaux, who had the deepest interest in the alliance.

specific approval; and the fact that this approval was forthcoming may stand as one more evidence of the slow but steady change in the monarch's disposition towards France. No sooner had the reconciliation taken place than Floquet was at once elevated (April 1888) to the premiership.

This was all very well; and in one sense, of course, it removed one of the obstacles to a better Franco-Russian understanding. But it was obvious that Floquet could not be thought of, in the light of his past, as a particularly warm friend of Russian autocracy; and his advance to the premiership, while tacitly accepted by the Russians, could not have been expected to be initially welcomed in Petersburg with anything other than a considerable measure of caution and reservation.

With Floquet's appointment as premier, Flourens was dropped as foreign minister, his place being taken by former Premier René Goblet. The reasons for dropping Flourens were never publicly revealed. It seems highly probable, as suggested above (Chapter 19), that the move was not unconnected with the affair of the Ferdinand documents. Flourens had served for several months in Goblet's cabinet, in the first months of 1887; and there is no evidence that relations between those two men were in any way strained. Now, however, in early 1888, the Ferdinand Documents had just been published; and some, at least, of Flourens' cabinet colleagues must have been aware of his part in the matter and of the embarrassment that could be caused to the French government if his complicity became publicly known.* There was apparently no desire among these colleagues to see a French foreign minister venturing out for a second time on such thin ice.

But Goblet's appointment represented a clear setback from the standpoint of any interest or enthusiasm for the development of Franco-Russian relations. His attitude in this respect was one of pronounced reserve, skepticism, and caution. To judge from the pages of the official *Documents diplomatiques français*, it was a full six weeks after Goblet's assumption of office before Laboulaye received any evidence that his new foreign minister was interesting himself in any way in Russian affairs; and a full eight months were to elapse before Goblet provided his ambassador at Petersburg with anything in the nature of guidance in this respect.

---

* Boulanger certainly knew of the matter, as did, supposedly, Lockroy, formerly minister of trade and industry. Flourens himself continued his political life as a deputy, but was never (much to his embitterment, it was rumored) to return to the Foreign Office. He later involved himself in business affairs, having to do with Russia, and made a trip to that country in the 1890's. The Tsar, on that occasion, declined to receive him; but this did not prevent him from writing and publishing, in 1894, a rather strange, wildly hagiographic, and historically valueless, book about Alexander III, the motive for which remains to this day obscure.

In September 1888, Goblet, evidently not satisfied that the ambassador's reports were giving him the whole story, sent to Russia his chef de cabinet, Monsieur Robert, with a view to getting a first-hand picture of the situation there. The moment was poorly chosen, as anyone in Petersburg could have told him. Both the Tsar and Giers were then away, as was their custom at that time of year. The best that d'Ormesson, then chargé d'affaires (and himself just on the point of terminating his service there in order to become chief of protocol in Paris), was able to do for the visitor was to get him an interview with the uncommunicative Vlangali. Robert was depressed by this encounter with the languid, late-summer Russia; and he returned to pour cold water on any hopes for an early improvement in Franco-Russian relations. Russia, he reported to Goblet, had much more need of France than vice versa. The attitude, "à la fois amicale et réservée," which Goblet had already adopted towards Russia was just the right one, Robert wrote, for the coming period.

Goblet accepted the advice. One should try to live on the best possible terms with Russia, he felt, but without attempting to establish more intimate bonds. This last, he recorded in his memoirs, "the Russians themselves would no doubt have repulsed, and [it] could have proved compromising for us. However one looked at it, there was nothing for us to do but to wait."[3]

Thus Goblet continued, throughout those first eight months of his encumbency at the Foreign Ministry, to take the line in his private discussions that ". . . for the moment, my lips were sealed, but that later, when we should have put fairly in hand the reconstruction of our [armed] forces, I would open my ears very wide indeed in order to receive any communications which one might wish to make to us." ("Je disais volontiers dans mes conversations familières que, pour le moment, j'avais bouche close mais que plus tard, et quand nous aurions activé la reconstitution de nos forces, j'ouvrirais les oreilles tout grandes pour reçevoir les communications qu'on pourrait avoir à nous faire.")

Relations between Russia and France at the public and formal diplomatic level remained, therefore, throughout the latter half of 1887 and all of 1888 in a state of complete quiescence. There were no major frictions. There were also no major excitements. The Tsar, secretly bound by the Reinsurance Treaty and probably somewhat intimidated by Bismarck's formidable Reichstag speech of January 1888, evinced no desire to stir up the quiet waters of European diplomacy. He spent long periods, in the summer and fall of 1888, away from Petersburg. And those who were at that time the architects of French diplomacy had, as we have just seen, little interest in Russia—only a firm resolve not to become involved at that time in anything resembling the rash and adventurous approaches to Russia which Flourens and Boulanger had vied with each other in attempting in the agitated winter of 1887.

But behind the scenes, in areas of international affairs less susceptible to public scrutiny and less immediately sensitive from the standpoint of European opinion generally than were the formal diplomatic exchanges, possibilities were beginning to open up and to be exploited—possibilities which would be of great, indeed decisive importance for the future of Franco-Russian relations. It is to these that we must turn in the next of these chapters.

Chapter Twenty-One

FINANCIAL AND MILITARY
STIRRINGS

The late summer and early autumn of 1888, like that of 1886, seems to have been a period of partially concealed but highly significant change in the dispositions of the Tsar and his leading advisers with relation to foreign affairs. The similar period of 1886 brought the decision not to renew the *Dreikaiserbund*; but it did not include any immediate and far-reaching development of relations with France—relations only recently so troubled by the Appert episode. Two years later this, too, changed; and one can easily see, in the record of events over the late summer and autumn of 1888, the emergence of a decision to permit the formation of intimate relations, at least on the financial and military levels, on a scale which only two or three years before would have been unthinkable. The Reinsurance Treaty ruled out, of course, any comparable advance on the political-diplomatic level; but such an advance was by no means essential from the standpoint of those who were interested in closer financial and military relations; and it is clear that certain of the latter succeeded at some time or times during this period in obtaining the Tsar's consent to the significant new undertakings in their respective fields. Just when the crucial discussions took place is not apparent; but one would think it must have been in August 1888, shortly after the young Kaiser's visit to Petersburg; for from the 26th of that month to November 4 the Tsar was away from Petersburg, and yet by this time moves in Russian policy reflecting the decisions in question were well under way.

Let us first examine the happenings on the financial scene.

———

We have already had occasion to note (see Chapter 18) that sporadic but inconclusive soundings were taken from the French side at various times during 1887, and particularly in the autumn of that year, to see whether there were possibilities for French loans or financial assistance of one sort or another to the Russian government. These soundings were obscured at the time, and remain so to some extent even today, by the secrecy with which the bankers habitually surrounded them. They seem to have been made, at various times, both by the *banques de dépôt*, notably the Crédit Lyonnais, who would have liked to have arranged for a relatively small private operation of conversion, recouping their advances by selling the new bonds to the public through their branch offices, and by some of the members of *la haute banque* (possibly including, indirectly, the Rothschilds), who seem to have been more interested in a curious proposal for establishment of a large French bank in Russia. This was the proposal in which Cyon[1] professed so strong an interest, and of which he claims to have made himself, albeit without success, the spokesman in Petersburg.* None of these suggestions, however, appealed to Vyshnegradski, pressed as he was by the disastrously low rate of the ruble and the poor market for Russian securities. Thus, the year 1887 ended with virtually no progress having been made along these lines beyond Cyon's small achievement in arranging for the conversion of the Russian Land Bank shares.

The Germans were generally aware of this situation, and some of them, including the Reichschancellor, rejoiced in it, supposing that it would soften the Russians up and make them more responsive to German pressures. "The Reichschancellor wishes . . ." (thus read an instruction going forward on March 4, 1888 from Friedrichsruh to the Foreign Office in Berlin)

> that the failure of the attempts to arrange a Russian loan should be treated in the *Kölnische Zeitung*, the point being made that Russia is in the position of a spendthrift in need of a guardianship—that only a court decision is lacking for the declaration of incompetence. Russia, it should be said, has lost its credit because it lives an improvident life and has no control over its expenditures.[2]

Bismarck was no expert in financial matters; and on this particular occasion, his smugness was seriously misplaced. For at the very time when this order was being transmitted, another and more serious effort was being put in hand to arrange a French loan to Russia—more serious, because in this case not just the bankers but both governments were benevolently involved: the Russian government as ostensible initiator of the exchanges, the French government as explicit supporter of the French banking spokesman. On the 28th of February 1888, Mohrenheim got into touch with Isaac Denfert-Rochereau, director of the Comptoir d'Escompte, one of the leading *banques de dépôt* and one

---

* Cyon alleged that the plan was aborted by Giers and Mohrenheim, but offers no evidence, nor any very plausible explanation, for this thesis.

which had particularly close relations with the French government, and asked to see him at once. The interview took place the following day. Mohrenheim showed his visitor two highly confidential letters he had recently received from Giers. From the first of these it emerged that the Tsar had called together a special *ad hoc* council, consisting of the three former ministers of finance, Reutern, Bunge, and Abaza, together with Siemens (director of the State Bank) and Vyshnegradski, to consider some sort of project envisaging the establishment of a consortium under the leadership of the Comptoir; and that it had been decided on this occasion that the Russian government would be prepared to enter into contact with the Comptoir on this subject, but only "sans aucun intermédiaire." In the second letter, which Mohrenheim said he had just received, Giers inquired whether it would be possible for Denfert-Rochereau to come to Petersburg for the discussion of the project, armed with full powers to conclude a deal on the spot and without reference to Paris.[3]

What lay behind this, on the Russian side, is not readily apparent. The meeting of this special council must have taken place, one would think, in early February. It was evidently responsive to some sort of suggestions already made from the French side, and specifically from the Comptoir, and these, one may suppose, were made some time in January.[4] There must, however, have been special reasons for the alacrity, and for the extremely high-level attention, with which the suggestion was considered in Petersburg. The nature of these reasons must remain a matter of conjecture; but it is permissible to suppose that they were not unconnected with the anxiety then being felt in governmental and financial circles in Petersburg over the extremely awkward position into which certain of the Russian financial houses had got themselves through their efforts to buy up, and then to resell, Russian obligations previously offered on the Berlin market. The purchases had been made, as a speculation, on three months credit, in the confidence that by the end of that time it would be possible to sell the bonds at a profit. Actually, their prices, in the meantime, had been further depressed; and this had led not only to the bankruptcy of at least one private Petersburg house (that of Baron Fehleisen) but to serious difficulties for the Russian Foreign Trade Bank, which had particularly close Berlin connections and which had often served as an agency for foreign transactions of the Russian Treasury. All this must have been a source of extreme anxiety for Vyshnegradski; and there may well have been, at the beginning of February, something approaching a moment of panic on his part, arising from the fear that without major outside help neither the bonds of the Russian government nor the Russian currency would be able to withstand the pressures the Germans had been putting upon them.

What is most interesting here is that it seems never even to have occurred to Alexander III to alleviate the distress of his finance minister, as he could easily have done, by entering into new political talks with the Germans and attempting to dispel some of the differences that had given rise to these German financial pressures. Instead, his mind seems to have turned instantly to the possibility of French assistance. And it is clear that the motives by which he was inspired at this point were by no means only financial. For Mohrenheim, in talking with Denfert on the 29th of February, made to him certain statements of a political nature which could have been stimulated only by instructions he had had from Giers; and these, in turn, could only have reflected recent exchanges Giers had had with the Tsar.

The Tsar, Mohrenheim divulged to Denfert, was determined to keep the peace. He would not waste a cartridge on Bulgaria. Even Bismarck was sincere in wishing "this time" for a peaceful settlement of the Bulgarian question. Austria, too, wanted a solution. And it would be another two years before Russia herself would be in a position to consider with any degree of confidence a conflict with any of her neighbors. The French, therefore, need not worry that Russia was likely to become involved in a war in the near future. "Your papers can say various things." Mohrenheim asserted. "Your statesmen can give speeches. Even in Russia there may be violent polemics. Peace will not be troubled at the present juncture."

In these observations, clearly inspired at the Russian end by a desire to offset any anxieties that might have been aroused in France by the Austro-Russian war scare, and containing the clear hint that whereas Russia was not then prepared to contemplate military involvements, within two years (i.e., upon expiration of the Reinsurance Treaty) she might well be so prepared, one had an important intimation of the political *arrières-pensées* with which the Tsar had now authorized his senior subordinates to turn to France for the solution of their most pressing financial problems.

Actually, Denfert's journey to Petersburg, which took place at the beginning of April, was not successful. This was certainly not for lack of support from the French government, which instructed Laboulaye to facilitate Denfert's mission in every way, even to the extent of placing at his disposal the facilities of the French diplomatic cipher. Nor was the failure a consequence of any lack of high-level attention at the Petersburg end; for Denfert was given opportunity to meet and talk not just with Vyshnegradski but with Giers and the war minister, Vannovski, and with all the distinguished members of the Tsar's special council, in addition to which the matter was treated, during his visit, by the State Council itself.

For the reasons why Denfert's mission did not succeed, it will be most instructive to follow his own account of the course of his visit. Arriving in Petersburg on Sunday, the 8th of April, Denfert called on Vyshnegradski the same afternoon. Vyshnegradski explained to him that the exceptional abundance of investment capital in France had encouraged the Russian government to hope that it might be able to find there sizable quantities of gold to augment its existing holdings and thus to reduce the anxieties that were affecting the exchange rates for its paper currency. It was not correct (this with some vehemence) that the Russian Treasury was itself in need of money; whoever said that was dealing in false pretenses and talking maliciously.

Denfert was a bit taken aback by this statement, which seemed to make what he had come to offer seem naive and impertinent; but he pursued the conversation, and it was agreed, finally, that he should put his proposals in writing, and let Vyshnegradski have them the following day.

This Denfert did in a long memorandum, the full text of which is now available in the French archives. He began by pointing out that only the Rothschilds (who plainly were not associated with his present visit and proposals) were in a position to make a major loan out of their own resources; the other French banks could do so only by passing on a large portion of the Russian obligations to the French public. But if a consortium of French banks was to make a loan to the Russian government at a fixed price, then when they came to market the bonds, they would still be at the mercy of the Germans, who could depress still further the prices for Russian securities generally, and create a panic in Paris. He therefore proposed a bond issue, on option, to the nominal amount of 125 million rubles, on which the French bankers would pay, initially, only an agreed advance, leaving the final amount payable to the Russian government to be determined by whatever the bonds might bring on the French market. Under such an arrangement, he argued, the French bankers, being protected against serious losses, would be less inclined to panicky selling and would find it in their interest to hold out for good prices.

It is interesting to note that this proposal, as outlined by Denfert-Rochereau, follows almost to the letter the concept put forward just ten years earlier by the president of the Crédit Lyonnais, Henri Germain, in discussing with the Russian railway magnate, Polyakov, the question as to how the French banks could help in the restoration of Russia's finances after the war with Turkey.* What it amounted to was, of course, simply that the French *établissements de crédit*, lacking the great independent capital of the Rothschilds, were prepared to act only as brokers for a Russian bond issue, limiting severely the possible risk to themselves.

Denfert's memorandum was sent to Vyshnegradski on Monday morning. That evening Denfert was summoned away from a dinner at the French Embassy to meet privately with the elderly Abaza, who, as a member of the Council of State, had attended the afternoon's meeting of that body and was obviously authorized to communicate its decision to the French banker.† It was clear from this meeting, and from a long talk Denfert had with Vyshnegradski on the following day, that the Russians were quite unwilling to accept any proposal of this nature. It would, they said, damage their credit. It would mean at best a long delay in the transfer of the proceeds of the loan.

Vyshnegradski, maintaining that he was interested only in a loan of 125 million gold rubles at a firm price, fixed in advance,‡ went so far as to intimate that even for this he did not find the moment particularly favorable—the autumn would be better; he hoped that by that time a good harvest, making possible an increase in Russia's grain exports, would put him in a position to assure without difficulty the service of a firm loan. Denfert was thus obliged to return to Paris empty-handed.

The reasons for this sharp rebuff by the Russians to an approach they had themselves encouraged probably had to do with two phenomena, visible in early April, which had not been visible to the Russian statesmen in early February. One of these was to be found in the anticipated

---

* Jean Bouvier, in his *Les Rothschild* (Paris: Fayard, 1967), p. 271, quotes as follows from a letter sent by the director of the Crédit Lyonnais to the head of the bank's Petersburg branch, describing Germain's remarks to Polyakov: "M. Germain est d'avis que nous devons nous mettre sur les rangs, et que le terrain à choisir est tout indiqué par le précédent de l'affaire Mendelssohn. Ce serait une avance de fonds, gagée par un emprunt à émettre, avec une option sur cet emprunt."

Compare this language with that of Denfert's memorandum, where mention was made of a French syndicate's being entrusted with a loan, on option, with the understanding "qu'une avance d'un montant à convenir garantié par l'emprunt lui-même soit accepté par le gouvernement impériale à titre d'arrhes purement et simplement et comme prélude des opérations qui doivent découler de l'emprunt . . ." (French Archives, File: *Russie. Finances. Mars-Avril 1888. Voyage de M. Denfert-Rochereau*).

† Denfert reported to his principals in Paris that of all the men he met in Petersburg, Abaza was the most impressive; and he appeared to be treated as the senior figure.

‡ His words, as quoted by Denfert, were emphatic and eloquent: "C'est du ferme et rien que du ferme qui sera la base."

good grain harvest in the forthcoming agricultural season. The other (admittedly a matter of conjecture rather than proof) may well have been signs that the low point was shortly to be reached in the prices for Russian securities abroad. Not only was there increasing resistance in Germany to further sales at the low prices now prevailing but the volume of these securities now transferred out of Germany to other markets was beginning to make itself felt in an increasing resistance outside Germany to any further depressing of the prices. Denfert, while in Petersburg, was permitted by Vyshnegradski to see the Russian figures on the extent of these movements. According to these figures, the Russians themselves had by that time bought back a total of some 166 million rubles' worth of this paper; and another 30-40 million, they thought, had gone to Paris or Amsterdam. (This last was probably a very considerable underestimation.)[5] Both of these considerations would have argued for an unwillingness on the part of the Russians to make any deal at all at that particular moment. But in addition to this, there was the fact that Denfert's offer, affording no certainty at all as to what the Russians would eventually get out of the deal and assuring only that whatever they did get would be long delayed, clearly failed to meet Vyshnegradski's requirements; and it would have been difficult for him or for the members of the State Council to defend it against possible critics within the Russian governmental establishment.

So much for the tale of the first abortive effort, in early 1888, to arrange for a major French loan to Russia. It tells us much; but much also remains unclear. The strong interest of the French government, or at least of the French Foreign Office, in the matter is plain.* But whence came the initial impetus? As noted above, the terms of Giers' letter to Mohrenheim clearly suggest that the Russian government, in taking its initial action on the matter, was acting in response to some sort of suggestion from the French side—and presumably from the French bankers. But from whom, and when? The Comptoir, one would suppose, was almost certainly involved at that stage. M. René Girault, author of the most exhaustive and authoritative work on Franco-Russian financial relations of the period,[6] saw reason to suggest that the Banque de Paris et de Pays Bas (Paribas) was also associated with the Comptoir in the whole venture, and that the two banks were possibly influenced by

* The telegram which Flourens sent to d'Ormesson, directing him to facilitate Denfert's mission, was dated March 31, four days before Flourens' own retirement. Could it have been just an expression of Flourens' personal enthusiasm? By the time Denfert reached Petersburg, on the 8th, a new French foreign minister, decidedly less interested in Franco-Russian relations, had taken over. Could this, too, have had anything to do with the Russian change of heart?

the fact that they both had interest in certain existing investments, and projects for new ones, in private Russian industrial concerns. But other banks, one would think, must have been involved as well. Flourens, in instructing d'Ormesson to facilitate Denfert's mission, described the latter as prepared to speak "in the name of the Comptoir d'Escompte *and of a consortium of French bankers.*" The Russians, in inviting him to Petersburg, specifically demanded that he come prepared to conclude a deal, without further reference to Paris, thus implying that they expected him to have completed all arrangements with whatever French banks were involved in his proposals, and to come with full powers to deal on their behalf. Yet in the statement he submitted to Vyshnegradski Denfert implied that the composition of the consortium was something still to be determined in agreement with the Russian government.* Could it be that he came to Petersburg prepared to speak only for the Comptoir and Paribas? And could this have had something to do with the Russian government's hesitation?

Finally, there is a welter of unresolved questions concerning the personal involvement of Denfert-Rochereau and that of the leadership of the Comptoir, generally, in Russian affairs. First, there is the strong evidence that it was the president of the Comptoir, Edouard Hentsch, who, some months earlier, had put up the money for the acquisition by the French government of the Ferdinand documents. Secondly, there was the fact that some months later the Comptoir got into serious difficulties through its involvement with the Société des Métaux (which appears to have speculated unsuccessfully on the price of copper.) Hentsch was made the defendant in a sensational trial of the Comptoir for financial mismanagement. Denfert-Rochereau, on the other hand, committed suicide on the 5th of March 1889. Presumably the suicide was connected with the difficulties of the Comptoir, of which he was director (though it might also be noted that Denfert had taken a personal share in the Panama Canal syndicate of 1883, the difficulties of which were now also beginning to become acute). But Cyon, in a private letter to Bleichröder written shortly after Denfert's death, said that he had it on the best of authority that the suicide was the result of demands placed upon Denfert by the Russian government.[7]

While at least the motives and nature of the Russian government's behavior in connection with this abortive effort are reasonably easy to discern, considerable further research will have to be accomplished before those of the French government and banking world become

---

* Denfert mentions, as an hypothesis, that the deal might be entrusted "à un groupe français dont le Gouvernement Impériale aurait préalablement apprécié la loyauté, la compétence et les moyens d'action."

entirely clear. But it will be well to bear in mind, particularly, the connection of the Comptoir, and of its chief, Hentsch, with this first attempt to arrange a French loan; for Hentsch's part in the purchase of the Ferdinand documents was, as will be seen shortly, not his only connection with circles in the Paris business and military world interested in France's financial relations with Russia.

If it is indeed true, as suggested above, that hopes for a good grain harvest and for a revival of the strength of the ruble and of Russian bonds on the European markets played a prominent part in the calculations that led Vyshnegradski and his associates to decline Denfert's offer in the spring of 1888, then the months that followed vindicated this foresight in generous degree. The Russian harvest of the year 1888 was excellent beyond even the more optimistic hopes; and its value on the world markets was enchanced by crop failures in several other main grain-growing regions of the world. Exports of Russian grain to France, in particular, increased greatly during that year, thus affording heightened assurance, as Vyshnegradski had hoped it would, of the Russian ability to meet the service of an expanded foreign indebtedness. In addition to this, the prices of Russian securities began to pick up markedly in June, and above all on the crucial German market.

The reasons for this last phenomenon are complex and must also remain in part a matter of conjecture. It will be noted that Denfert's proposals were remarkable for the fact that they made no mention of anything in the nature of a conversion of earlier Russian loans, although for two years this had obviously been a primary objective of the Russian Ministry of Finance. The reason for this was probably a desire on the part of those who supported Denfert's mission on the French side to avoid involvement with the German banks, which had taken so prominent a part in the earlier loans (although the Comptoir had also had a share in that of 1877), and the collaboration of which would obviously have facilitated the conversion. Now, however, in the summer of 1888, the view seems to have gained currency in Paris that a conversion loan would have more prospects for Russian acceptance than any other, and that for this reason a certain measure of German participation could not be avoided. In any case, the strong support which began to be given to the prices of Russian bonds in the summer of the year, by Bleichröder among others, suggests that by that time the German bankers had strong hopes of participation in another major Russian loan and were concerned to correct a bear market for Russian securities which could affect unfavorably the prices at which a new issue could be sold.

All this may serve as a background to the main event of the year 1888 in Franco-Russian financial relations, which was a new attempt on the part of Paris bankers in the late fall of the year to arrange a major loan to Russia. Again, the preliminaries are shrouded in obscurity. Even of the process of negotiation much less is known than in the case of Denfert's attempt. German bankers, as well as French ones, appear to have participated in some fashion; and there were rumors of sharp conflict between the two.

It was not, this time, the Comptoir which appeared as the spokesman for French banking circles, but rather Charles Sautter, director of the Banque de Paris et Pays Bas, and, even more prominently, another man whose name has not previously appeared in this account but who took a significant part, from this time on, in the development of Franco-Russian relations. This was the Danish-French private banker Emil Hoskier.

Born in Norway of a Danish father (also a banker), Hoskier had founded, many years earlier, his own bank in Paris on the Boulevard Haussmann, and had conducted its affairs with outstanding prudence and success. At the time of his death, in 1915, he had been for many years Danish consul general in Paris. (Whether he occupied this position as early as 1888 is not apparent.) He thus appears to have had very good connections in Copenhagen, although he was not popular with the Danish colony in Paris, and one Danish necrologist referred to him after his death as "more Norwegian than Danish, and more French than Norwegian."

Outstanding, among Hoskier's characteristics, were his interest in Russia and his close connections with that country. His sister, Ellinör, was the wife of General Appert, who, it will be recalled, served as French Ambassador at Petersburg from 1883 to 1886 (see above, Chapters 4 and 8), and was particularly *bien vu* by Alexander III and his Danish consort. Two of Hoskier's nieces, daughters of another sister, married into the Hentsch family—to sons, apparently, of the Edouard Hentsch who was head of the Comptoir. In which connection it might be again recalled that it was apparently the elder Hentsch who put up the money for the purchase of the Ferdinand documents, and Appert who, at Flourens' request, took them to the Tsar. It will be seen, therefore, that Hoskier was connected through his two sisters both with the Comptoir d'Escompte, through the pro-Russian Hentsch family, and with Appert, and through him with the Russian court as well. Small wonder, in these circumstances, that he stood at the center of the first efforts to arrange the first major French loans to Russia.

Hoskier, in any case, proceeded to Petersburg, together with Sautter, around the end of October 1888, and the negotiations took up a good

Plate 16. Prince Ferdinand of Bulgaria

Plate 17. Jules Grévy, President of France

Plate 18. The French-Danish banker, Emil Hoskier

Plate 19. The Presidential Crisis of 1887. From left to right: Floquet, Brisson, Clemenceau, De Freycinet, Grévy, and Goblet

part of the month of November. On the 8th of November, in the midst of the negotiations, an imperial *Ukaz* was issued authorizing large-scale conversion of the existing debt; and the agreement with the bankers was finally signed on the 17th of November by Hoskier and Sautter for the French banks, by one Herr Fischel (of the Warschauer Bank) for the Germans, and by Sack and Laski, directors of the Petersburg Discount Bank and the Petersburg International Bank, respectively, for the Russians. What was envisaged was an international loan for a nominal value of 500 million francs, of which the Russian government was actually to receive 417.5 million, the remainder being the margin left to the bankers. This would actually yield for the Russian government approximately 160 million gold rubles, of which some 108 million would be used for the retirement of the 5 percent loan of 1877 (in the floating of which, during the Russo-Turkish War, the German bank of Mendelssohn had taken the leading part), and its replacement by a new one at 4 percent, to mature in 81 years instead of the previous 37. The loan was, as Vyshnegradski had insisted earlier in the year in his talks with Denfert-Rochereau, in effect for the "prix ferme," in the sense that the members of the banking consortium guaranteed, among them, the amount to be realized by the Russian government. Of the total amount, slightly over one-half was put up by a group of French banks, of which the Pays Bas, the Banque d'Escompte de Paris, and the Comptoir took up the largest shares, four others, including the Crédit Lyonnais and Hoskier & Co., dividing the remainder. The two Russian banks came in for 100 million, and three Anglo-Dutch banks (Baring, Hambro, and Hope & Co.) for 50 million. Two German banks, Mendelssohn and the Berliner Handelsgesellschaft, were also involved.

While this loan did not, of course, appreciably diminish the total amount of the foreign indebtedness of the Russian state (on the contrary), it did in effect add some 60 million rubles to its gold holdings of the moment; it resulted in a further sizable shift in the outstanding indebtedness from Berlin to Paris; it put an end to the bear market for Russian securities; and it gave, in fact, a much-needed fillip to Russian credit the world over. The issue of new 4 percent bonds, 86 percent of which were eventually placed in France, was handsomely oversubscribed. The price on the French market rose so substantially, in the months following issuance, that the original subscribers were able to realize, by the end of the following year, a profit of 14.7 percent.* M.

---

* The bonds, purchased by the bankers at approximately 85% of par, were quoted in January 1889, i.e., within a few weeks of their issuance, at 93; and by April of that year the figure had risen to 95.5 (Nolde, *L'Alliance*, p. 511). The French bankers thus profited enormously—a fact which the bitter Cyon never allowed Vyshnegradski to forget.

Girault recounts that within a short time after their issuance these securities were described in the French financial journals as "des placements de père de famille." The general impression of the public, he writes, was: ". . . ces fonds russes, quelle belle affaire!"[8]

And the success did not cease at that point. Within a matter of weeks, as will be explained below, talk began of further and even greater transactions of this nature. What was now envisaged was the conversion of railway bonds, of various categories, to a nominal value of nearly two billion francs. These bonds had been originally issued through the facilities of the Rothschilds; and the Paris house of that family, impressed no doubt with the success of the 1888 loan, now inserted itself very skillfully and effectively into the picture.

A conflict ensued in the negotiations because of the insistence of the Russian authorities that Hoskier be granted a share in the transaction. It seems evident that Hoskier, who was received in audience by the Tsar after the conclusion of the 1888 deal, continued to enjoy the favor of the Russian imperial couple, but was not on terms of confidence with the Rothschilds. (Cyon, too, whom he edged out of the negotiating process, must have viewed him with intense resentment.)* The Rothschilds were unwilling to yield to the demand for Hoskier's participation; but the difficulty appears to have been avoided by the device of conceding to Vyshnegradski himself a personal share, which he was then at liberty to sell (and apparently did so sell) to Hoskier—an arrangement which, seriously misunderstood, figured heavily in the bitter charges Cyon was later to levy against the finance minister.

This impediment having been overcome, and the Tsar's hesitations presumably having been relieved by Hoskier's involvement in the transaction, two further conversion loans, encompassing between them the conversion of the entire sum mentioned above (about 640 million gold rubles, or well over half the remaining outstanding Russian indebtedness), were arranged through the Rothschilds in the winter and spring of 1889.

With these transactions, it is evident that the transfer of Russian borrowing from Berlin to Paris was effectively achieved. The groundwork had now been laid for the further great loans—no longer conver-

---

* While the other Paris bankers were evidently inspired in this instance primarily by financial motives, there can be no question of the high political significance which Hoskier himself attributed to the operation. In a letter of January 16, 1889, to Laboulaye, complaining of the failure of the French government to give adequate recognition to his services, he referred to the operation as "cette grande affaire qui au point de vue des relations entre la France et la Russie est destinée à avoir les conséquences les plus heureuses" (French Archives, File: *Russie, 1889. Finances, Emprunts*).

sion ones, but direct loans to the Russian Treasury—which were to mark, with irregular intermissions, the entire period down to 1914, and to make the Russian debt to France, by that time, the greatest body of indebtedness of one country to another that the world had ever known.

————————

If the exchanges which led to the major French loans to Russia in 1888 and 1889 are in part obscure, an even greater obscurity surrounds the exchanges which, in those same years, were occurring between senior officials of the two countries at the military level. Yet, their results, to judge from the meager evidences available, were no less significant. For here, too, the stagnation that prevailed at the political-diplomatic level was not seen as a necessary impediment to a highly significant consolidation of relations behind the scenes. It was a consolidation explainable, no doubt, by ignorance on the part of most of those involved of the existence and nature of the German-Russian Reinsurance Treaty. (Here, as elsewhere in the history of this relationship, one is reminded of the limited value, and sometimes even the unfortunate and counterproductive results, of political understandings held secret—concealed, that is, not just from the public but from the overwhelming majority of the officials who had to continue, at their lower level, to conduct what they supposed to be "policy.") But it was also a consolidation that could not have occurred without the assent of those few people, and outstandingly the Tsar himself, to whom the existence of the Reinsurance Treaty was known.

Let us review briefly the state at which, by mid-1888, the relations between the two military establishments had already arrived. Ever since the aftermath of the Russo-Turkish War there had been close personal relations between senior military figures in the respective countries. We have seen the unusual attention paid by senior figures in Petersburg to French officers throughout the earlier years of the 1880's. This attention flowed primarily from military colleagues; but the Tsar, too, made it clear on several occasions that his aversion to the French political system did not extend to the French military establishment. Above all, the two men who for fifteen years stood at the heart of the efforts towards rapprochement, and eventually alliance, between the two armies—Boisdeffre and Obruchev—had not flagged in their enthusiasm for progress in this direction. Both were now rapidly advancing to positions of influence and authority which made it possible for them to act more effectively to this end. Obruchev had been chief of the Russian general staff since 1881. With the help of the minister of war, Vannovski, who strongly and steadily supported him, he was slowly but clearly overcoming the suspicion with which the Tsar had originally viewed him. Boisdeffre, on the other hand, had been made a brigadier general in 1887; and one of his strongest patrons, General Miribel, a man who had also served in Russia as military attaché in earlier years and whose enthusiasm for a Franco-Russian alliance was in no way inferior to his own, had now just become chief of the French general staff. (Boisdeffre was to become his first deputy in that capacity in 1890 and finally, in 1893, to succeed him in it.)

Obruchev and Boisdeffre had pursued down through the 1880's the close and cordial personal relations they had developed in the period of Chanzy's ambassadorship, when Boisdeffre was serving in Petersburg. Obruchev regularly spent the late summers and early autumns at his wife's fine château in the Dordogne, near Bergerac; and it is to be assumed that Boisdeffre was his guest there on more than one occasion in these earlier years of the 1880's. The two men remained, in any case, indirectly in correspondence over all those years through the agency of Madame Obruchev, who appears to have conducted this correspondence on behalf of her husband—possibly because of his insufficient knowledge of French, but also, possibly, for reasons of political security. The tone of these letters was cordial but not intimate, and affords no substance to the gossip which at times connected Boisdeffre's name with hers.

The vital lines of contact had thus been consistently maintained, throughout the mid-1880's, between the two general staffs; but circumstances had continued to place, throughout those years, narrow limits to the progress that could be made. Now, by 1887, the worm had begun to turn. On the French side the strength of the armed forces, partly despite but partly also because of Boulanger's efforts, was being brought to a level fully equal, on paper at least, to that of their German rivals—a circumstance which could not fail to increase France's value in Russian eyes as a potential ally. The French, furthermore, had by this time been weaned from the hope they had previously entertained that they would be allowed to stand aside, in the event of a German-Russian war, and wait with impunity until the Russians had had time to go through their relatively slow process of mobilization and bring their entire great military weight to bear against the Germans. It was doubtful that French opinion would itself permit this. The French were thus now obliged to recognize the possibility that they might be obliged to enter at an early stage into any war that might develop between Germany and Russia. This, however, involved a need for coordination of operations with the Russians in those initial stages of hostilities. And this, in turn, made it almost imperative that the two general staffs should know what was expected of them, and what they might expect of the other, in those initial, and

392

possibly crucial, days of a war. For this, staff talks, at the very least, were indicated. There is even reason to believe that in 1887, in the winter of high alarm over the assumed possibility of a German attack, the French general staff, acting no doubt under Boulanger's urging and probably without the knowledge of the full cabinet, had made an unsuccessful effort to initiate precisely talks of this nature.*

The Russians, on the other hand, recognizing both the increased strength of the French army and the high probability of German participation on Austria's behalf in any war they might undertake against Austria-Hungary, were now coming to view a prearranged collaboration with France as essential to their success in any such conflict. Beyond which there was the highly significant factor of the death of the old German Emperor and consequent removal of a sense of personal obligation which, more perhaps than anything else, had previously restrained the Tsar from encouraging any specific steps in the direction of significant military arrangements or involvements with the French.

It is interesting to note, then, with particular relation to this last circumstance, that within a matter of months after the old Kaiser's death significant collaborative arrangements came, for the first time, under discussion between the military authorities of the two countries—and this time at Russian initiative. Freycinet relates in his memoirs[9] that in the first days of November 1888, he received word that the Grand Duke Vladimir, then in Paris, would like to see him; that he therefore called upon the grand duke at the latter's apartments in the Hotel du Louvre; and that Vladimir then approached him with the astonishing request that he be supplied with a specimen of the new Lebel repeating rifle with which, at that time, the French infantry was being equipped.† Frey-

---

* In a confidential memorandum drawn up in 1891 by General (Baron) Fredericks, Russian military attaché in Paris, on the subject "de l'opportunité d'une entente préalable à établir entre les deux États Majors russe et français, en vue d'une coopération éventuelle," it is related that in 1887 General Haillot, Miribel's predecessor as chief of the French general staff, made overtures to Fredericks looking to arrangements of this nature; that Fredericks reported this to Vannovski (the Russian minister of war); and that the latter responded by sending him a special code in which he was to conduct any further communication relating to the matter. Fredericks, however, does not mention any further consequences of the approach; and one is obliged to suppose that higher authority on one side or the other, or both, found the suggestion premature and quashed it (Boisdeffre papers).

† The Lebel rifle, which the Frnch were then in the process of introducing into their infantry units, did not prove to be the best of guns, but it had the virtue of being one of the first, if not the first (the Germans were already working on a rival one), to allow for the use of smokeless power, which of course offered enormous advantages from the standpoint of concealment of the unit employing it, as also

393

cinet said that he would have to consult his cabinet colleagues. This he then did (November 6); and the decision of the cabinet was that this was a request they could not evade. A presidential decree, necessary to permit an item of military equipment to be alienated in this way, was procured. A general officer, General Mathieu, was then charged with presenting the rifle to the grand duke, reminding him at the same time of the strict secrecy with which the French government would expect the entire matter to be surrounded.

Freycinet, in his memoirs, gives the impression that the grand duke's request was made in personal terms—that he claimed to want the rifle simply to satisfy his personal curiosity about its qualities. This suggestion deserves no serious credence. The grand duke was the commander of the Imperial Guard. It is absurd to suppose that he would have held secret from his own government and his own military colleagues the results of any examination to which he might have subjected the weapon. That the French government fully understood the significance of the request was evident from the high-level consideration they accorded to it. The official character of the approach is also evident from the Russian side; for some two months later Baron Fredericks, Russian military attaché in Paris, came to tell Freycinet that the Russian government was interested in placing orders in France for the manufacture of a rifle very similar to that of the Lebel model and wished to know whether French experts would join with Russian officers in giving a final study to the model they were proposing to buy. Once again, the matter was taken up in the cabinet. Freycinet pointed out to his colleagues that if they were to accept this request and to proceed further along this line, it could unquestionably be expected to provide occasion for more intimate contacts with the Russian government. The cabinet took his point, and granted this second request also, with the result that a delegation of Russian artillery generals soon arrived to participate in the study,

---

from the standpoint of their own vision of the terrain before them. The Russians, getting wind of what the French were doing, and fully aware of its significance, were anxious to develop a weapon with similar characteristics to replace the old Model 2 Berdan, which had been in use in the Russian army ever since 1872 and had constituted the mainstay of the attacking power of the Russian infantry in the Russo-Turkish War. The Berdan was a good gun, dependable and effective within its technical limits, but heavy and not capable of being used with smokeless powder.

It may also be noted, at the risk of jumping a bit ahead of the story, that the Russians, on receiving this specimen of the Lebel, did not just copy it but studied it together with a large number of other weapons and proposed alternatives, and produced, three years later, a 30-calibre rifle of their own, designed by S. I. Mosin, which, officially adopted in April 1891, proved to be an excellent gun and served the Russian and Soviet armies down to, and including, the Second World War.

General Mathieu serving as their liaison officer. And this arrangement was followed shortly by a similar one, involving the study by a group of Russian military engineers of French processes for the production of gunpowder.

When the request was made by Fredericks for French governmental approval of the placing of the first Russian order for these new rifles (a batch of 5,000, to be produced at the Chatellerault works), Freycinet, in agreeing to support such a decision, observed to Fredericks—with a smile, yet by no means facetiously—that the French would like to feel assured that these rifles would never be fired against Frenchmen. Fredericks replied that this was the Russian understanding—they could in fact guarantee that this would be the case. Some days later (apparently), Mohrenheim observed to Freycinet that he approved entirely the reply that Fredericks had given, and asked whether this satisfied the French. "Yes," said Freycinet, "but I would be even more satisfied if this were to be confirmed to our foreign minister." This, then, occurred. Mohrenheim, some days later, repeated his statement to Spuller, who had by that time (February 1889) replaced Goblet at the Foreign Ministry. One may be sure, from this evidence, that the deal had the knowledge and concurrence not only of Vannovski but also of Giers.

It would be wrong, in the opinion of this writer, to underestimate the significance of this episode. It marked a turning point in the military relationship, initiating a train of events that led to the final negotiation of the alliance some years later.

That the French should have been willing to turn this corner was not greatly surprising. A military arrangement with the Russians was a natural objective of French military and political policy—an attractive objective to which they had, in fact, scarcely any remotely comparable alternative.

More significant was the Russian decision to proceed to this step. The assurance to the French that the rifles would never be used against them was equivalent to an assurance that Russian troops would not be found fighting alongside those of Germany in any Franco-German war. This was, of course, not formally in conflict with the Russo-German Reinsurance Treaty, which provided only that Russia would observe neutrality in case such a war should result from a French attack. The assurance to the French that these weapons would not be used against them was not yet a pledge that the Russians would enter a Franco-German war on the French side. But it did establish a relationship in which the Russians would not only be under a certain moral obligation to the French but would be dependent in a small way on French sources for military equipment, as well as for the financial credit necessary to make possible the necessary purchases. Furthermore, it involved secret arrangements of a military nature from the knowledge of which the Germans were carefully and strictly excluded. This was a far-reaching change. It had serious political connotations.

Did these decisions really reflect a fundamental change in Russian foreign policy, conceived as such and deliberately taken in full consciousness of its significance? There is no evidence that this was the case.

Insofar as the loan was concerned, the weight of the evidence suggests that all through that period—not just in the autumn but in the preceding spring, at the time of Denfert-Rochereau's negotiations, as well—the Tsar was content to leave such questions to the discretion of Vyshnegradski, on the understanding that the latter would act with the advice of the high-level *ad hoc* group headed by Abaza, which obviously had the controlling voice in determining the Russian response to Denfert's proposals.

As for the approach to the French concerning the Lebel rifle: it must be remembered that the Tsar was absent from Petersburg, and obviously taking little part in governmental affairs, from the 26th of August to the 4th of November. This absence included, in the order named, a visit to his brother, the Grand Duke Sergei Aleksandrovich, governor general of Moscow; more manoeuvres in Poland; then, a long stay in the Crimea; and, finally, the terrible train accident at Borki (October 29) on the return journey to Petersburg, which left him a sorely shaken man, able for some time into the future to give only a distracted attention to public affairs. He had, it appears, had conferences with Giers and the military leaders in the middle of August, before leaving on these peregrinations; and he could have given on that occasion the authorization for the approach to the French. Or he could have given it, informally and orally, to the Grand Duke Vladimir at the time of the manoeuvres in Poland shortly afterwards. But it is doubtful that he exercised any close supervision over policy in the military field at any time later than September. Soon after his return in early November, Vannovski tried to talk to him about what were termed, in Polovtsov's diary, "important measures in the military field" (a phrase which may be assumed to have had reference, probably among other things, to the results of the approach to the French), but he found the Tsar still so distracted over the Borki disaster that he could not be brought to give his attention to anything else.[10]

Altogether, one has the impression that the incentives to the two new

396

and important involvements with the French flowed very largely from the impulses of those high-ranking people who had immediate responsibility for determining Russian policy in the financial and military fields; and that Alexander III, no longer seriously concerned for his relations with Berlin, was content to let those persons explore as they liked the possibility for collaboration with the French in their respective fields. The conclusion seems inescapable that the death of the old Kaiser marked the end of his interest in the tie with Germany. If, in these circumstances, his subordinates could work out suitable arrangements with the French, publicly in the financial field and secretly in the field of military collaboration, so much—in his view—the better.

Chapter Twenty-Two

1889. THE RUSSIAN BREAK
WITH GERMANY

At the beginning of 1889 relations between Berlin and Petersburg were already seriously, in fact almost fatally, undermined. The damage that had occurred could now be felt on both levels of the relationship—the dynastic and the governmental.

That the young Kaiser's visit to Petersburg, in the summer of 1888, did not enhance his stature in the eyes of Alexander III and the men around him has already been mentioned. How serious the estrangement was, on that particular occasion, is not apparent from the evidence now available. But at the end of January 1889, people in the Tsar's entourage noted, and were somewhat puzzled by, signs of an enhanced antipathy on the Tsar's part for his young German cousin. The feeling against Bismarck on the Tsar's part was not new, and occasioned little surprise. But the sharpness against young William seemed to reflect some recent unpleasant experience.* The Tsar was heard to refer to him on one occasion as "a rascally young fop, who throws his weight around, thinks too much of himself and fancies that others worship him."[1] And when Alexander was pressed by his advisers to return the Kaiser's visit, it being suggested to him that his failure to show any interest in doing so was causing offense in Berlin, the reply was an explosive declaration that he was not going to permit this young "pipsqueak" to interfere with his plans. Such outbursts on the part of Alexander III were not common, and usually reflected strong feelings. In the face of them there could no longer be any doubt that of the close ties which only a decade earlier had united the two imperial houses, nothing—literally nothing—now remained.

The Tsar rubbed this in to the Germans when, in May 1889, in offering a toast to the visiting Prince Nicholas of Montenegro at a state dinner, he hailed this visitor as Russia's only sincere and true friend. This rather strange statement struck hardest, of course, in Berlin, though it also

---

* One suspects here the effect of gossip in the special grapevine of the royal courts of Europe, perhaps connected with the Kaiser's recent and rather unsuccessful visit to Vienna.

caused raised eyebrows in several other European capitals, including Paris and Copenhagen.* It was, however, enthusiastically hailed by much of the Russian press.

Alexander was finally prevailed upon to pay, on his return to Russia from his Danish holiday in the fall of 1889, a grudging and belated visit to his German cousin in Berlin; but this was a protocol gesture of the most perfunctory nature, and one may be sure that it was only with a sense of profound relief, and a feeling of "that is that," that he mounted his train, at the end of the visit, and pursued the journey to Petersburg.

As for the young Kaiser: he was now being intensively belabored by Waldersee, who had become chief of the general staff in October, with alarming (and surely exaggerated) data about Russian military preparations and their allegedly menacing implications. Waldersee himself later denied in his memoirs that he was trying to drive the young monarch into a war with Russia, as Bismarck so strongly suspected. For this, he wrote, he did not consider the circumstances opportune; the golden moment (1888) had been lost. But that he thought such a war inevitable; that he ardently wished for it to take place at the earliest favorable opportunity; and that he did his best to bring the young Kaiser to a similar persuasion, cannot be doubted.

Bismarck, of course, was under no illusions about the state of affairs that prevailed in Petersburg; and he was anything but insensitive to its implications for German policy. He was fully aware of the Tsar's *ressentiments* against Germany, of Giers' helplessness in the face of them. The anti-German tone of the Russian press was now no longer confined to those papers that customarily pursued the Panslav-Germanophobic line: it pervaded the entire spectrum of Russian journalism. And the Tsar's failure to curb these manifestations continued to loom higher in Bismarck's eyes than any of the other symptoms of Russian hostility.

But Bismarck did not, like Waldersee, see war as the answer. His highly prophetic views about the senselessness of such a war (that it would bring no conclusive victory; that Germany would not know what she was after and would find no suitable place to stop, etc.) remained unchanged. He also had the Reinsurance Treaty in the back of his mind. And he knew the Russians too well to suppose that they could, or would, launch such a war out of the blue.

It was, as usual, to the political plane that Bismarck's thoughts con-

---

* When the German military representative at the Russian court, commenting in one of his reports on this toast, observed that in his opinion the Tsar was quite sincere in believing that except for Prince Nicholas, Russia had no friend of this description, the disillusioned Bismarck noted in the margin of the report, opposite this observation: "Wer hat denn einen?" ("Who, then, has one?")[2]

tinued to turn. He had, as we have seen, gently nudged the British into something resembling an entente, or an understanding, not publicly declared but privately agreed, with the Italians and Austrians, directed to the preservation of the *status quo* in the Mediterranean and in the Balkans. He saw this as a way of reminding the Russians (for some of it was bound to leak out, and did) that aggressive behavior could bring in against them not only the Austro-German Alliance and the Triple Alliance of Germany-Austria and Italy, but the British as well. (This arrangement had found its final confirmation in notes exchanged among the participating Powers at the end of 1888.) Then, in early 1889, he attempted to strengthen this arrangement of European international relationships by urging the British to conclude a genuine secret defensive alliance with Germany, along the lines of the earlier Austro-German one. Such an arrangement, he argued, would assure both Germany and England against the danger of a French attack. The proposal was evaded, though in no unfriendly way, by. the Salisbury cabinet; no British government, as Bismarck might have known, could conclude that sort of a pact behind the back of Parliament. But the fact that something was going on in German-English relations could not be wholly concealed from outside opinion; and it no doubt made its mark on the Russians, as Bismarck had intended that it should. Not only that, but out of the attendant discussion there did arise the origins of the agreement, to be concluded the following year, for cession to Germany of the previously British island of Helgoland, off the mouth of the Elbe River, in exchange for German recognition of the British claim to a protectorate over Zanzibar.

It was in these attempts to assure, in accordance with his own established principle, that Germany remained at all times one of a group of at least three within a concert of five Great Powers, that Bismarck responded to what was now an unmistakable and far-reaching Russian rebuff. But at the same time he was most reluctant to sacrifice anything that could possibly be retained of the Russian tie. His reasons for this were logical and obvious. He wanted, if at all possible, to avoid a war with Russia. He wanted to retain any and all levers that would permit him to obstruct the conclusion of a Franco-Russian alliance. He wanted to retain some possibility of mediating between the Russians and the Austrians. Pursuant to these considerations, he was anxious to avoid unnecessary anti-Russian agitation and to keep tensions to a minimum.

It was amazing to note how total was the failure of the young Kaiser and Waldersee to understand this rationale of Bismarck's policy. In their simple-minded acceptance of the inevitability (even in Waldersee's case the desirability) of a war with Russia, they saw in Bismarck's behavior only the evidences of a fatuous and suspect pro-Russianism, and comforted each other (neither of them knowing remotely as much about Russia as did the chancellor) with mutual assurances that Bismarck was naive; that it was useless to try to appease the Russians; that the latter understood nothing but brute force; and so on. This lack of understanding was not for failure on Bismarck's part to explain his policy: he had set it all forth in writing and in great detail in letters to the Kaiser the previous year. The cause lay rather in a total inability of the two men to grasp the subtleties of a policy that aimed to handle the Russian problem by means short of war.

Meanwhile, the development of Franco-Russian financial relations was proceeding apace. The loan arranged by Hoskier in 1888 had opened the door; and into this door there now walked, as mentioned above, to everyone's surprise and with startling promptness, none other than the greatest competitor of the Hoskier group: the Paris Rothschilds. In the first months of 1889, two loans, both of them for the conversion of considerably larger amounts than the earlier Hoskier loan, were negotiated with a group led by the Rothschilds. Exact and fully comparable figures are not available; but, according to data compiled by the French consul in Petersburg, Pingaud, the two operations amounted to 1,941,929,000 francs, or approximately 747 million gold rubles, of which the Russian government received, net, some 654 million. Although these loans were officially negotiated with the Rothschilds, it appears that various of the French *établissements de crédit* served as exchange and sales outlets for the new bonds.

The background of these two Rothschild loans has never been revealed.* They were the last which that firm was ever to make to the Tsar's government, the problem of the treatment of the Jews in Russia becoming thereafter too formidable an obstacle to permit further financing from that quarter. But in 1889 the way was still clear, from this standpoint; and Vyshnegradski's disposition to turn to the Rothschilds may safely be attributed both to the obvious fact of their great independent resources, together with his own reluctance to commit himself entirely, if he could help it, to either of the two rival groups, preferring to retain the possibility of playing them off against each other.

* Lamsdorf's diary (February 15/27, 1889) suggests that these loans were actually negotiated, on behalf of the Rothschilds, by Bleichröder, in Berlin. Although the Rothschilds would not have permitted anyone to negotiate on their behalf except under closest supervision and control, it is not at all impossible that Berlin was the locus of the negotiations. This would explain why so little information about the subject can be found in Paris.

While there can be no doubt that encouragement from the French government, out of political motives, played an important part in the case of the loan from the Hoskier-Sautter consortium in 1888, it does not appear to have been a factor of any significance in the two later Rothschild loans. M. Pingaud, to be sure, discussing the motivation for these loans from the French side,[3] made perfunctory mention of the fact that Russian policy was considered in France to be a policy of peace; but he laid greater stress on the disillusionment of French investors with Italian investments just at that time; on the disposition of British and German investors to get rid of their Russian holdings for political reasons; and on the effects of the Panama and Comptoir disasters, which caused French investors to shy away from private promotional or speculative schemes and to seek security in governmental loans, especially when the latter offered, as did these Russian ones, the relatively favorable interest rate of about 4.5 percent. We may be permitted to conclude, then, that while the 1888 loan had at least a part of its origin in the political enthusiasms of Flourens and Hoskier and those around them, the Rothschild loans of 1889 reflected simply the response of a formidably able and sophisticated banking concern to the market realities of the moment.

The two Rothschild loans of 1889 were supplemented, it might be noted, by another and smaller one negotiated simultaneously by Bleichröder and Hansemann (head of the German Disconto-Gesellschaft) in Berlin. The circumstances of the origin of this loan, and of the relationship to it of the Paris Rothschilds, are also obscure, and have little importance from the standpoint of the Franco-Russian relationship. Although Professor Fritz Stern, in his recent account of the Bleichröder-Bismarck relationship,[4] says that the two German bankers signed the contract on behalf of the Rothschild consortium, and although it is clear that Bleichröder was in close touch with the Paris Rothschilds during the negotiation, 52 percent of the loan was taken up by the Germans, and the Rothschilds had only a small participation. It was a small conversion loan, for only 75 million gold rubles (250 million marks); and, like the two Rothschild loans of the same period, it was the last the Germans were ever to make to the Russian government. It was, however, the source of bitter controversy in Germany, where the Kaiser and the anti-Russian and antisemitic faction around him charged that the Jewish bankers, with Bismarck's support, were financing Russian preparations for war against Germany, bitterly attacked the whole operation, and did succeed in diminishing, if not wholly preventing, its financial success. In view of the fact that what was involved was only a conversion, that the new obligations were to be marketed largely outside

Germany, and that the amount was trivial in comparison with similar deals being made in Paris, the charge was absurd, but it was none the less effective.

It is clear that with the completion of the four conversion loans of 1888-1889, bringing to the Russian Treasury, as they did, something upwards of 800 million gold rubles, the Russian government had pretty well cleaned up the hodge-podge of old debts at high interest rates which they had had on their hands in 1887, and had replaced them with a very small number of new issues at a considerably lower rate of interest and for much longer periods of maturity. With this, the credit of the Russian government, sorely tried in 1887, had been reasonably well restored; and that government was now in a position to borrow further money—not, this time, for the conversion of old debts but for purposes of that military expansion which it strongly wished to carry out and which the French had every reason to encourage.

This, then, was the background—deteriorating Russo-German relations and an improving Russian financial situation, in the improvement of which the French were taking the major part—against which Franco-Russian political and military relations took their course in 1889.

The year 1889 opened with Franco-Russian diplomatic relations on the best of footings—nothing but cordiality on both sides. But the winter then brought a minor disturbance of a tragi-comic nature, embarrassing to both sides. The full story of the episode has yet to find its historian.[5] A certain individual by the name of Achinov, evidently a former merchant, but claiming to be a Cossack ataman, had for some reason paid a visit earlier in the decade to Ethiopia, had returned full of the discovery that the Coptic-Christian Abyssians were in effect (by virtue of doctrinal similarities) co-religionists with the Russians, and had conceived a scheme for the establishment of a semi-ecclesiastical Russian colony on the shores of the Red Sea. Having talked his way into the confidence of Katkov (Cyon tells of having met him in Katkov's office in 1887) and of the minister of the navy, Admiral Shestyakov, and having in this way won the predisposition of Pobyedonostsev and the support of a number of pious Moscow merchants, Achinov organized for this purpose a curious expedition, consisting of a hundred or so "Cossacks" together with a number of priests, these latter headed by a monk from Mount Athos named Paissi. With this motley group, accompanied by some of their womenfolk, he proceeded (apparently without the knowledge of the Russian Foreign Office) to the Red Sea, where the members of the expedition first proceeded to squander, in the dives of Port Said, a good deal of the money they had collected from their trusting Russian patrons, and then to the port of Obock, in what has been known in recent years as French Somaliland. The territory had at that time only recently been taken under French control—a fact of which Achinov appears to have been ignorant before his landing, and which, upon being apprised of it, he declined to recognize. The company installed themselves on shore, and resisted efforts by the French governor to get them to move on into the interior. In early February, the French government protested to the Russian chargé d'affaires in Paris over this unwanted intrusion, and the matter was reported by him to Petersburg. Giers, presumably after checking with the Tsar, immediately authorized the chargé to tell the French that the Russian government knew nothing about the expedition; that Achinov was acting wholly on his own; and that if, as appeared to be the case, he was on territory which was under French protection, it was up to him to respect French law and authority.

Meanwhile, however, unbeknownst to all of them, an admiral, despatched by the French government to take charge of the situation, had undertaken an armed action to bring the company to submission and had killed several of them in the process. The Russian government, in view of the position it had taken before this news came in, was now in no position to protest; and it submitted with good grace to the situation, despatching in its turn a naval officer to arrange for the evacuation of Achinov and his company. But soon, of course, the matter came to the attention of clerical circles in Moscow and Petersburg, as well as of the Russian press. Angry voices then began to be heard, protesting the violence of the French action; and for some time a certain cloud hung over the Franco-Russian relationship, particularly because Achinov and Paissi enjoyed considerable sympathy among the Panslavs and religious circles. Even Giers was obliged to make it clear to the French, with some embarrassment, that he thought they had gone too far. But the Tsar, fortunately, had been greatly annoyed by Achinov's action, and was not disposed to let an incident be made out of it.* In May, therefore, not long before the Tsar's celebrated toast to Prince Nicholas, the Russian press campaign over the French action was abruptly terminated on orders from above; and Giers was left secretly rejoicing over the fact that the Tsar had now got a good taste of the more unpleasant manifestations of Panslav-religious nationalism.

* In February, the Tsar had given orders, in a marginal note on a communication, that "this animal" (referring to Achinov) should be removed from Abyssinia at once; and that even Paissi should not be given too much support—"He will only compromise us, and we will be ashamed of his activity."[6]

Simultaneously with the termination of this press campaign, the semi-official *Novoye Vremya* was moved to run two obviously officially inspired articles, one dealing with the Achinov affair, the other with the recent visit of Italian Foreign Minister Crispi to Berlin (a visit highly displeasing to the Tsar, who was still sulking and refusing to make a similar one). Here, the Franco-Russian relationship was referred to in startlingly fulsome terms. Praising the success of the Paris centennial exposition (in which Russia had refused to participate), the paper emphasized the great respect this had won for France, and expressed Russia's pleasure over this fact. It was of high value to Russia, the paper said, that France, who so constantly manifested her sympathies for Russia, should regain her former political importance—an importance indispensable to the equilibrium of Europe. Russian opinion applauded this return of French prestige, because it was irresistibly drawn to see in France "the most desirable ally of Russia." France and Russia, having no conflicting interests, could march hand in hand down the avenues of civilization, of commerce, of art, and of science, assisting each other whenever foreign undertakings menaced the existence of the one or the other. "It is an alliance without treaty or written instrument," the paper concluded, "but one founded in a mutual necessity; perhaps this sort of an alliance is, of all the possible varieties, the most solid."[7] These were far-reaching words; and Giers, in authorizing their use, must have assured himself in some way of the Tsar's approval.

Later in the year (early October), to be sure, a certain modification was introduced into this concept, by the same newspaper. Russia, it was explained, would not go to war just to achieve the restoration of Alsace-Lorraine to France, but she could not allow the quality of France as an essential component of European equilibrium to be diminished. Should there be aggression from the German side, such as would be certain to ensue if the Waldersee faction should come to predominate in Berlin, then the alliance would indeed have to be concluded.[8]

This formula also no doubt had its origin with Giers, who, bearing in mind the existence of the Reinsurance Treaty and remembering that it was shortly to come up for renewal, wished it to be made clear that Russian support could be assured to France only if the aggression, in a Franco-German war, did not come from her side. The article appeared just at the time of the visit to Berlin which the Tsar was finally prevailed upon to make; and Giers did not want the Germans alleging that the Russians were already making promises to the French that were by implication in conflict with the treaty.

On the diplomatic level, and from the French political side, there was now nothing but the most total inactivity. The shadow of Boulanger still caused the French politicians in power to wish to avoid all unnecessary talk about Franco-Russian relations. The Quai d'Orsay, from April 1889 down into 1890, was in the hands of Eugène Spuller, former friend of Gambetta, and a routine republican politician of the most pedestrian sort. Devoid of diplomatic experience, and having no greater an interest in relations with Russia than did his predecessor Goblet, he, too, was content to let sleeping dogs lie, particularly since things were going very much France's way: the Russo-German relationship was obviously deteriorating, and almost nothing but pleasant noises were emanating from Petersburg. Like most French statesmen he was firmly convinced that an open flirtation with Russia would carry the risk of a new war with Germany. And nothing could have been farther from his thoughts than the idea of negotiating a political-military alliance with Russia and being obliged, then, to submit it to the French Parliament.

On the military side in Paris the situation was, of course, quite different. We have seen the curious Russian assurances that developed out of the Russian request for a specimen of the new French rifle. That there were now in operation forms of collaboration between the two military establishments as obscure to the eyes of contemporaries then as they are to the eyes of the historian today, cannot be doubted. The French military leaders, fully convinced that France would have to enter at once any war that might develop between Germany and Russia, must also by this time have been reasonably convinced that Russia, even in the absence of any formal alliance, would be similarly unable to resist participation in any war that might develop between France and Germany. (They were, of course, unaware, as were most of the Russian military, of the partially contrary provisions of the Reinsurance Treaty.)

But they were not greatly comforted, and certainly not fully satisfied, by this supposition. For while the Russian high command had been working hard, with the Tsar's blessing and support, to improve the arrangements for mobilization in the event of war with Germany, these arrangements still lagged far behind those of the French and Germans in point of speed of completion; and there was the usual fear in Paris that Germany would profit by the resulting delay to dispose of France first, leaving the Russians to be taken care of after the French collapse. So powerful still were the trauma of the war of 1870-1871 that this nightmare—of being obliged to fight the Germans alone—haunted French strategists despite the fact that in many respects the French army was now the equal of, if not superior to, that of Germany. (In Berlin, Waldersee and the Kaiser were talking, at that time, for example, of a

French superiority of 500 in the number of artillery pieces.) And all this in the face of the fact that while Germany might adopt, during the initial conflict with France, a defensive and inactive posture on the Russian frontier, she would still be obliged to keep a large portion of her forces there to contain a Russian army that was, even in peacetime and without mobilization, numerically far superior to her own.

For the French military leaders, therefore, the breakdown of the Russo-German relationship was only the beginning, not the end, of the problem of collaboration with Russia.

———————

The tale of the complications that led to Bismarck's retirement, on the 20th of March 1890, has been told too often to require recapitulation here. The political reasons were domestic as well as foreign. They included his natural incompatibility with the new Kaiser, the urgings and intrigues of Waldersee, as well as the weariness, excitability, and loss of firmness of touch in the aging chancellor himself.

The fall of the great statesman was in itself, of course, by far the most important, and even fateful, of the events of that spring of 1890, from the standpoint of Russo-German and Franco-Russian relations; for with it there passed from the active scene the only person of any consequence in Germany (aside from Bismarck's son, Herbert, who left very shortly thereafter) who had understanding for the policies on which the peace of Europe had been maintained since the early 1880's or who cared seriously about their preservation. But the great change was unexpectedly made; and the nail of Bismarck's failure was driven deeper by the refusal of the German government, in the days immediately following his departure, to renew the Reinsurance Treaty, due to expire in June of the same year.

Here, too, the tale has been often told. It would not add much to the story of the background of the Franco-Russian alliance to go over it all once more in detail. It is a tragic story of overstrained nerves, of bureaucratic disloyalties, of reversals of opinions, of shortsightedness and secret longings for war on the part of lesser figures now at last relieved of the imposing presence and authority of the great statesman. Initially, the young Kaiser was quite prepared to renew the treaty; but Holstein, his genius for intrigue now given free reign, succeeded in leaking the knowledge of the treaty to several of his associates who, like himself, could be counted upon to oppose its renewal, and then mobilized their presumed expertise to persuade the Kaiser, the new chancellor (General Caprivi), and for a time even Schweinitz, that it would be unwise to renew it. The two principal arguments used to support this recommendation were (1) that the Reinsurance Treaty was in conflict with the Austro-Russian Alliance of 1879, and even more so with the German treaty of alliance with Rumania signed in 1883; and (2) that the Germans, by renewing it, would place themselves in the hands of the Russians, who could at any time, by revealing its existence, destroy the confidence of others in Germany's good faith. Particularly shocked, it was thought, would be the Austrians; such a revelation would weaken their loyalty to Germany and affect their performance in any future war. Underlying this view was the conviction, so common to the thinking of the time and so prevalent in the entourages of both Giers and Bismarck, that war was inevitable and that the aim of statesmanship should be not to avoid it (this, in most instances, they did not even *want* to do) but to place themselves in the best position to conduct it successfully.

There was something in both these arguments, but not much. The first, relating to the alleged conflict between the provisions of the Reinsurance Treaty and the obligations to Austria and Rumania, represented a rather far-fetched legalistic quibble which Bismarck, his eye always on the essentials rather than on secondary factors, would have dismissed with contempt. And as for the second: there was no one who more greatly feared public revelation of the existence of this treaty than Alexander III, who was persuaded that it would be intensely unpopular in Russian opinion. The last thing to be feared was that he would intentionally betray the secret himself.

It was also argued that while the maintenance of a structure of treaties so complicated and fragile as this one lay within the competence of a master like Bismarck, it was too much for the simpler, more direct, and (it was implied) less devious men that his successors held themselves to be; for the latter, the only recourse was to a more open, less intricate set of relationships. This argument appealed particularly to Caprivi, who was highly conscious of the grave domestic problems he faced, as Bismarck's immediate successor, and wanted no unnecessary complications of foreign policy.

Actually, there was a deeper justification than any of these for the abandonment of the treaty. The truth is that the psychological foundation for it had been extensively undermined at both ends, in official as well as in public opinion. Whether or not Giers or the Bismarcks understood this, the hour was now too late; the damage had been done; the last effective supports for such a relationship as the treaty implied had been swept away—in Russia with the excitements of 1886-1887, in Germany with the death of the old Kaiser in 1888. A Reinsurance Treaty renewed in these circumstances would have hovered precariously in the air, without firm support at either end.

Giers, nevertheless, saw in its disappearance the wreckage of the efforts and achievements of a decade, and took it hard. It was not that he feared or deplored the strengthening of relations with France that was bound to flow from it; but he feared that without the established tie to Germany an improved relationship with France would lack the necessary counterweight and would fall under the control of those—the chauvinists and military adventurers on both sides—who wished to use it for the purposes of war rather than peace. So for weeks after the initial German decision he struggled desperately to find some way of reversing it or getting around it, proposing one expedient after the other, hoping to save something from the wreckage and to tide things over until a new German leadership could get a better understanding of the situation and come to appreciate what he believed to be the rationale of the old policy.

But the effort was a vain one. The Germans were not to be shaken in their decision. It was all the easier for them to adhere to it because they knew that Giers stood no less alone in Russia, in his attachment to the treaty, than did the Bismarcks in Germany. An effort to preserve good relations with Germany found support at that time neither in Russian public opinion, nor in the military High Command, nor in the higher Foreign Office officials by whom Giers was surrounded. Least of all did it find support with the Tsar. He had never liked the treaty in the first place. Had the Germans wished, at this point, to renew it, he would have gone sullenly along—to please Giers, and to avoid raising new problems. But he was relieved that they did not so wish. No longer, he must have reflected, would he be plagued by those pangs of conscience vis-à-vis Pobyedonostsev and the Panslavs which the existence of the treaty had occasioned. No longer would he have to worry about the possibility of its existence becoming known. No longer would Giers be coming to him with questions of its possible renewal or modification. On Giers' report of his final interview with Schweinitz on the subject, the Tsar wrote: "I am personally content that Germany was the first to indicate a desire not to renew the Treaty, and I do not particularly regret that it no longer exists. . . . It seems to me that Bismarck was right when he said that the Kaiser's policy would change after his own departure."[9]

Giers was thus left pitifully alone with his doubts and anxieties: the only one to regret the collapse of a structure of relationships on which the peace of Europe had reposed for a decade; the only one to sense in this development the preparation of the eventual German-Russian war from which no good *could* come—from which, as it turned out, no good *would* come, only the destruction of both Empires.

Of those who have studied and pondered the course of the Franco-

Russian relationship in those years, none has examined it more scrupulously, judged it more dispassionately, or done more to help others understand it, than Boris Nolde, a friend both of France and of the old Russia. It may be fitting, therefore, that this discussion of the demise of the Reinsurance Treaty should conclude with the final words of Nolde's account of this historic turning point:

> Giers understood better than did the Tsar the importance of the change
> which had come about. Men of superficial and limited intelligence had just
> destroyed the balance of a structure which he had erected with such pains
> and at the cost of so many efforts. He was justifiably proud of it, because it
> met Russia's needs as he understood them. Now, everything had to be
> begun all over again, and this, in conditions at least as difficult as those of
> 1879. One will understand that he had done all he could to save this, his
> creation. It was not his fault that he had not succeeded. But his spirit
> continued to work, and his energies were not diminished. We shall see this
> oldster of seventy years take up with vigor the search for new diplomatic
> combinations to make secure the future of his country.[10]

The events just recounted—Bismarck's retirement and the ensuing lapse of the Reinsurance Treaty—form, in combination, a suitable point for the termination of this examination of the background of the Franco-Russian alliance. For Bismarck's retirement, marking as it did the end of an era in European diplomacy, removed from the scene the last great personal opponent of a closer military-political relationship between Russia and France; and with the lapse of the Reinsurance Treaty there disappeared the last serious formal impediment to such a development.

What followed, in the years immediately ahead—the actual negotiation of a military convention between the two Powers and the effects which this would have on the situations, and the behavior, of both parties—will make suitable material for a further volume of this study, always assuming that those common hazards of personal life that attend the completion of most large undertakings of historical scholarship will permit, by the grace of Providence, the accomplishment of this one.

CONCLUSIONS

The reader who has had the patience to follow this account from end to end, if such there be, will by now be so far from its beginning, in both time and space, that he might like to be reminded of the purpose for which it was undertaken. This purpose was to identify, if possible, the motives and calculations by which the most influential figures on both French and Russian sides were inspired as they moved, over the span of the 1870's and 1880's, towards the readiness to conclude a military alliance, and to see how their expectations related to the results to which, in the terrible crucible of 1914-1918, the alliance finally led. It was the author's hope that light might be thrown, in this way, not only on the nature of their miscalculations but through them on those general workings of the human spirit that cause statesmen to make great errors in the effort to assess the probable effects of their official actions.

What, then, does the study reveal?

Let us look first at France.

The impulses which moved not only the senior French military circles and the civilian chauvinists but also a considerable portion of the remaining French population to look hopefully towards the possibility of an alliance with Russia are obvious. The movement was outstandingly a reaction to the Franco-Prussian War and its aftermath. The successive humiliations of 1871, falling upon a people unaccustomed to such experiences, and the galling nature of the isolation and helplessness which Bismarck forced upon France in the ensuing two decades, were bound to draw the hopes and aspirations of the French towards the possibility of an association with the one great continental military power conceivably capable of breaking Bismarck's domination of the diplomacy of the time and of forcing a division of German military attention between east and west.

In the face of this situation it is easy to say (and there were many who said it) that the Germans brought the alliance on themselves—that the French reaction was inevitable and predictable—that things could not have been otherwise. There is much to be said for this view; but things were, as is usual in international affairs, not quite that simple.

411

If one takes under scrutiny only the Franco-Prussian War itself and the French military defeat, as distinct from the uses the Germans made of their victory, there is, as this writer sees it, little to choose between the responsibility of the two sides. The French were unwilling to accept the unification of Germany which Bismarck was in process of bringing about, and were quite prepared to fight a war to prevent its completion. Their part in unleashing hostilities in 1871 was fully as great as was that of the Germans. The main issue over which the war ostensibly developed —namely, the question of the Hohenzollern candidacy for the occupancy of the Spanish throne—had, after all, been settled, generally to French satisfaction and not without a certain humiliation of the Germans, some time before the war began. And as for the allegations, still occasionally heard, that France was "invaded" by the Germans three times in the course of seventy-five years: this was, in the case of the conflict of 1870-1871, purely a question of military superiority—of who, to use the familiar military phrase, "got there firstest with the mostest." Had the French forces been stronger, more alert, better led, and better armed than they were, the hostilities might just as well have taken place on German rather than on French soil, in which case the Germans would have just as much right, and just as little, to complain in later decades that they had been "invaded" by the French.

The behavior of the Germans in the exploitation of their military victory was, however, a different matter. The choosing of the Hall of Mirrors at Versailles as the place to proclaim the establishment of the new German Reich was a tactlessness of gigantic dimensions: a gratuitous affront to a defeated people, not even warranted from the German standpoint, and bound to burden further a relationship already grievously encumbered with bitter memories and resentments. The heavy financial indemnities imposed upon the French were unwarranted and unnecessarily humiliating. They even redounded in the end to German disadvantage insofar as they made the French political establishment aware, for the first time, of the true magnitude of private savings in France and of the ease with which these could be mobilized for governmental purposes. And then there was, of course, Alsace-Lorraine.

Here again, in the case of the "lost provinces," the situation was less simple than the subsequent Allied propaganda, particularly of the First World War period, has been at pains to suggest. With the exception of a portion of the population of Lorraine, there was not much nostalgia in these places for the earlier tie with France. The interests of their inhabitants ran in the main along social-economic rather than national lines, so that they could well have accepted the tutelage of whichever of the two Powers was willing to treat them best in this respect. The tearful sentimentality about the loss of the provinces, as symbolized by the black-draping of the respective symbols on the Place de la Concorde, was something for the Parisian chauvinists, not for the Alsace-Lorrainers themselves. One cannot, even today, read without sympathy the devastating words of the polemic addressed to this subject in 1891 by the unfortunate Rémy de Gourmont (for which, incidentally, he lost his job at the Bibliothèque Nationale and ruined a budding literary career):

> Have they, in truth, become so unhappy, these corners of territory beyond the Vosges? Has one by chance made them change their language, their customs, their pleasures? . . .
> It seems to me that this has lasted long enough: this ridiculous image of the two little enslaved sisters, dressed in mourning and sunk to their knees before the frontier-post, weeping like heifers instead of tending their own cows. You may be sure that now, as before, they are gobbling their roasts with current jelly, nibbling their salt pretzels, and guzzling their mugs of lager beer. Have no illusions: they are also making love and creating children. This new Babylonian captivity leaves me entirely cold.[1]

All this was to the point and well deserved. But if the inhabitants of the two provinces had less to weep about than the Parisian sentimentalists pretended, the Germans also had less to boast about when it came to their part in the whole affair. The taking of the territory in the first instance was a great folly: a needless concession to the appetites of the German military leaders, and one which Bismarck only partially approved at the time, and greatly regretted in later years. And the subsequent treatment of the inhabitants at the hands of the German authorities was one long series of neglected opportunities and mistakes. The government in Berlin was for years unable to make up its mind about the proper relationship of the territory to the remainder of the German Reich, and its policies were in part paralyzed by the resulting vacillation. The German military leaders persisted in viewing the administration of the territory solely from the standpoint of German military advantage, with the result that the Berlin bureaucrats, under military influence, persistently overruled the more constructive proposals and efforts of the respective governors general.

It was true that the peasants and the good burghers of Alsace and Lorraine continued to eat their roasts, to drink their beer, and to make love—that they were as comfortable physically, in other words, as they had ever been; but it was also true that the German government, by the mistakes and inconsistencies of its policies, gradually forfeited a good part of whatever respect it might originally have enjoyed on the part of these people, with the result that the population it was forced to deliver up to the French in 1918 was one much less well inclined to Germany than the one for which it had assumed responsibility in 1871. And if all this did not justify the mawkish effusions of such people as Déroulède and Juliette Adam, it did play into their hands as nothing else could have done. It provided a symbolic rallying-point for French *revanchisme* which established it for a large part of French opinion as an undying cause. It went far to preclude that accommodation between the French and German peoples which Bismarck himself would have been glad to see and which alone could have averted, so far as northern Europe was concerned, the disasters of 1914-1918.

The German occupation of Alsace-Lorraine, in short, came to constitute a heavy mortgage, and an unremovable one, on Bismarck's policies of the 1880's, making impossible any complete realization of his purposes, and putting a constant premium on the achievement of precisely that Franco-Russian alliance he was concerned to avoid.

In the face of this situation, it must be recognized that the French statesmen responsible for the policy of the 1870-1890 period observed, for the most part, a remarkable restraint in relations with Russia. There were of course notable exceptions: the Duc Decazes at the time of the 1875 crisis, Flourens and Boulanger in 1887. But in the case of the others one looks in vain for any sign of their pressing the cause of a Franco-Russian alliance; they seem rather to have waited for the Russians to come to them. The reasons for this were several. For one thing, most of these men held office only briefly and were extensively occupied, during their respective incumbencies, with the hazards and intricacies of French parliamentary politics. They had little opportunity to design and execute long-term military-political policies; and their parliamentary situation did not normally permit them to contemplate bold, far-reaching approaches that would have involved ultimate parliamentary approval. But beyond that, and more important still, they generally feared that any initiative they might take in the direction of an alliance with Russia would become known to the Germans and would draw down upon France's head a German preventive attack for which France would be ill prepared. They all had vividly in mind the disaster of 1870-1871, and wanted no part of responsibility for anything resembling its repetition.

These fears were no doubt strongly influenced by such information and advice as the civilian political leaders were able to get from the military side. The French general staff was at all times aware of the potential importance of the Russian army from the French standpoint, pursued every opportunity to learn about it, and studied most intently all that it could learn. There was a general feeling that some day that army would be of vital importance to France. But down to the end of the 1880's the French general staff officers could never be satisfied on the subject of the possible speed of Russian mobilization. They, like their civilian counterparts, feared that the attempt to conclude a formal alliance with Russia might serve to provoke a German attack, whereas the prospective speed of Russian mobilization, even in the best of circumstances, was so unsatisfactory (a minimum of three months was the usual estimate in the early 1880's) that France would be left to fight Germany alone in the initial stages of the war, and the struggle might be settled and ended to her disadvantage before the Russians could make their strength seriously felt. In addition to which, the French must have been made wary by the abundant evidence that the interests of many influential Russians ran primarily to southeastern Europe and to a conflict with the Austrians, rather than with Germany; and that indeed many Russians looked to a Franco-German war precisely as a development which, they hoped, would free Russia's hands for a concentration of her military power against Austria, the French being left to handle the Germans. All this argued against any attempt to force the pace of the movement towards an alliance, and favored a policy of prudent restraint until such time as the Russians could prove a capacity for rapid mobilization on their western border and could give adequate assurance that the concentration would be directed primarily against Germany and not against Austria.

It was not until the end of the 1880's that a number of situations came into being which served to override these hesitations on the part of the French military. These included:

the greatly improved strength and readiness of the French forces themselves, which meant that they had a better chance than was previously the case to hold up a German attack until the Russian strength could be brought into play;

the clear signs of a deterioration of the Russian-German relationship, in the face of which the Russians, now confronting the dangers of isolation, could be expected to be more amenable to French pressures for a planned concentration of their forces against Germany rather than Austria;

similar signs that the Russians had come to recognize, especially in the light of the public revelation of the terms of the Austro-German Alliance of 1879, that the Germans were not likely to remain aloof in the face of any serious Russian-Austrian conflict, and particularly of one which threatened the integrity of the Austro-Hungarian Empire; and that therefore they had to accept the necessity of concentrating against

Germany, the stronger enemy, in any future armed conflict in eastern Europe; and finally,

that the Russians had not only improved materially (if not decisively) their facilities for rapid mobilization, but had also strengthened their forces stationed along the western frontier to a point where the Germans would in any case be obliged to keep strong forces of their own along that frontier and even to fight certain defensive actions there in the early stages of a Franco-German war, and would thus not be able to concentrate all their forces against France.

With these developments, many of the hesitations of the French military leaders were overcome, and they became inclined, for the first time, to explore the possibilities for a formal military convention with the Russians.

––––––––––

It was, of course, the Russians, not the French, who took the leading part in breaking up the Russian-German-Austrian relationship of the early 1880's and thus bringing themselves to the point where an alliance with France became, for them, virtually the only alternative to a total isolation. And their reasons for doing this present an interesting historical problem; for their situation was wholly different from that of France. They shared almost none of the French grievances against Germany. Bismarck had inflicted no isolation on them; on the contrary, he had done all in his power to prevent them from falling into such a position. He had fought no wars against them—had in fact stoutly resisted all the efforts of his military leaders and foreign office associates to promote one. And if the Russians came away from their war with Turkey with sour feelings, it was, as we have seen, not German intrigue but their own bungling they had to blame. One must look elsewhere than to German stupidities for the mainsprings of Russian behavior in the case at hand.

The problem is all the more intriguing because the Russian statesmanship of this period was so obviously misguided and self-destructive. The Russian Empire of the final decades of the nineteenth century had no need of wars, of external adventures, of the acquisition of satellites. On the contrary, no country ever had a more urgent need for a long period of peace. Russian society was at that time caught up in a tremendous, inescapable, highly delicate, and dangerous process of social and political change. Having experienced no Renaissance, no Reformation, and no more than a superficial touch of eighteenth-century enlightenment, and only beginning to experience the Industrial Revolution, Russia faced the task of moving a sullen, embittered, and brutal-

416

ized peasantry, constituting 80 percent of its population, directly out of its own peculiar form of feudalism into a modern age for which no previous experience had prepared it. This task, with its multitudinous attendant social and political strains, was one that would have taxed the resources of Russian society to the utmost even in the total absence of external efforts and involvements. In these circumstances, it was sheer folly, as some of the wiser Russian statesmen understood, to pursue the will-of-the-wisp of a control at the Straits, to try to create a zone of influence in the Balkans, to launch a war on Turkey in 1877, and to promote a break-up of the Turkish Empire. All these ventures were bound to divert attention and resources urgently needed for the tasks at home. The pursuit of power and glory externally was, in short, the enemy of the successful accomplishment of the vast process of change and adaptation in Russian society, without which the dynasty itself had little chance of surviving.

These external undertakings would have been invidious from the standpoint of their internal effects, even had they succeeded. But they had the added disadvantage of unbalancing, psychologically, the designing of Russian foreign policy, particularly policy towards the major Western Powers: of causing a desperate search for scapegoats on whom the respective Russian failures in the Balkans could be blamed; of poisoning, in particular, the relationship to the two neighboring Empires, Austria-Hungary and Germany, on the preservation of peaceful relations with which Russian security, in the long run, was bound to depend; and finally, of adding significantly to a financial stringency and dependence which would eventually deprive Russian diplomacy of much of its autonomy.

To what must be attributed so disastrous a series of mistakes? The answer is clear: primarily to the spirit of nationalism that overtook so much of the educated portion of Russian society in the aftermath of the Crimean War. Nationalism was not a new force in Russian educated opinion; but the forms it assumed in the late nineteenth century were complex and violent; and they deserve a special word of comment.

In its traditional form, running back into the Muscovite period, Russian nationalism had a religious base in the Eastern-Orthodox faith and was the property of all classes of the population. This kind of nationalism had survived into the nineteenth century, but only as a feeling experienced by the Orthodox-Russian portion of the population in what was now a multilingual and multicultural Empire. The same feeling was not, and could not be, experienced by the Protestant and Catholic peoples of the Baltic states and Poland, by the Jews of the Pale, or by the Moslem peoples now being brought under Russian authority in Central

Asia. Yet this feeling still operated to inspire, in one part of the population, the peculiar sort of religious imperialism we have had occasion to note, centered in the person of Pobyedonostsev, and directed particularly towards those Christian peoples of the Balkans whose religious affiliations had Byzantine, rather than Roman, origins.

Now, in the late nineteenth century, this deep-seated Russian feeling was joined—sometimes displaced, sometimes supplemented—by a new form of nationalism, this time of Western origin, secular and romantic in spirit, intimately linked to linguistic identity. Precisely because of its great linguistic emphasis, this form of nationalism, like the religious one, carried with it the seeds of danger for the multilingual Russian Empire, as it did for the Austro-Hungarian one. The Tsars would have been well advised to be wary of it; for it was bound, in the end, to inflame the centrifugal tendencies within the Empire. But it appealed mightily to new intelligentsia of the Russian portions of the Empire. It served as the impetus to the Panslav movement. It had a powerful appeal to large portions of the bureaucracy. The new bourgeois press, frustrated in the effort to play any significant critical role with regard to internal developments, embraced it with enthusiasm. It contrived, despite the deep philosophic differences that divided the two movements, to combine effectively, in many instances, with the older religious nationalism. And between them both, these tendencies had a powerful influence not only on the new bourgeois intelligentsia but also on people in the higher ranks of military establishment, where they fused all too easily with professional pride, arrogance, ambition, and—with relation to the militarily successful Germans—envy.

All in all, the heady nationalism of the latter part of the nineteenth century seriously distorted Russian foreign policy, causing it to serve irrational, costly, and ultimately self-destructive purposes instead of those which a sober consideration of the highest interests of the Empire would have indicated.

Where, then, was the fault? When one person makes a bad decision or allows himself to be inexcusably misled, one can speak of moral responsibility. When millions of people succumb to a given hysteria (and what was this heady exaltation of nationalism, with its self-adulation, its extravagant claims to virtue, its professions of an innate superiority, but an hysteria?), then one has to seek for objective causes.

The analysis of collective psychology—national psychology—is a neglected subject, and one in which this particular writer can claim no expertise. But it appears to him reasonably clear that in essence the nationalism in question was the expression of a crisis of identity on the part of great masses of people displaced by the over-rapid social and economic changes of the nineteenth century—displaced from those positions in the structure of society to which they and their families had long been accustomed. It was from these traditional vantage points that they had learned to relate themselves to the national community—to establish their rights, their duties, their claims to respect. The Russia of the decades with which this book deals held millions of people for whom, sometimes because of upward social movement, sometimes because of downward, sometimes because of educational experience, sometimes because of the change from country to city, these familiar and reassuring points of orientation had been lost. Yet the great mobility of wealth, and the prevailing love for ostentation wherever wealth existed, raised false standards, set up painful contrasts, heightened differences, inflamed sensitivities, and created artificial sources of snobbery. Particularly among those who had a little education (but not quite enough) and a little money (but again, not quite enough), there were great underlying uncertainties. And these uncertainties could be relieved, if not removed, by identification with one's people as a whole, identification with them on the basis of the most obvious—and probably the most primitive—of criteria: that of speech. In the cultivation of the myth of collective glory—the glory of the national society to which one belonged —one could lend to the individual experience a meaning, or an appearance of meaning, that the artificiality and insecurity of the individual predicament was unable to supply. Thus, millions of people, not only in Russia but almost everywhere else in Europe as well, found in the flag-waving, the brave rhetoric, the sentimentalities and exaltations of nationalistic fervor, the impressive image of themselves which individual experience could not convincingly provide.

If there is any appreciable substance to this view, then it is primarily to the over-rapid pace of social change in nineteenth-century Russia that we must attribute the surge of nationalism which so distorted the external relations of the Empire. From which reflection one could well derive the lesson that if a society is to adjust successfully to great changes in the underlying conditions of its life, whether by virtue of technological discovery, of revolutions in public health and population growth, or by whatever other causes, these changes must not take place at a pace which exceeds the human capacity for controlled and equable adjustment.

The Tsar Alexander III, poorly educated in the first place, indolent and unsociable by temperament, and physically isolated by the necessity of protection against the constant danger of assassination, had few contacts with the Russian society over which he presided, and only the narrowest conception of its needs. At heart unsure of himself, unaccustomed to thinking things through independently, and disinclined to any personal initiative, he found it hard to resolve the conflict between, on the one hand, the ties to Germany which he had inherited from his father, and the value of which Giers continued to stress, and, on the other hand, the essentially anti-German tendencies supported by such impressive figures as Katkov, Pobyedonostsev, and Dmitri Tolstoi. Unable or unwilling to commit himself to either alternative, he tried to sneak through somewhere in the middle, without losing his options in either direction. Taking advantage of the lack of any such thing as cabinet responsibility in the Russian governmental system, he tried to pursue both policies simultaneously out of different bureaucratic pockets: permitting Giers to pursue close diplomatic and treaty arrangements with the Germans out of the Foreign Office Chancery (but secretly, so that no one should know about it), while at the same time encouraging the nationalists of the Panslav committees, the police establishment, the Asiatic Division of the Foreign Office, and the military High Command, to pursue their various intrigues and enterprises in the Balkans. Meanwhile the press was allowed to criticize Germany, and by implication Giers as well, with general impunity. In this way, Alexander hoped to appease publicly the nationalist sentiments he could not bring himself to oppose, while secretly (and without enthusiasm) preserving the tie to Germany which, as Giers frequently reminded him, alone protected him against the possibility of a hostile German-Austrian-British coalition.

None of this, of course, was lost on Bismarck. He was well aware, as early as the autumn of 1886, of the Tsar's vacillations, of the seriousness of the challenge being raised to the previous Russo-German relationship, of the tenuousness of the ties he had so long cultivated between the two countries. And no one could have been better aware than he was of the dangers of the emerging situation. To a Russian-Austrian war (and it was to this that the nationalist impulses in Russia were tending) there could be only one of two outcomes: either Germany would be dragged in and would find herself fighting for the Balkan aims of the Hungarians—for interests, that is, other than her own—with the further result that the French would be invited to attack from the other side and Germany would be caught in a two-front war; or the Austrians would be defeated, in which case the very existence of the fragile Austro-Hungarian Empire would be threatened. But there was nothing Bismarck feared more than precisely this break-up of the old Habsburg Empire. His great life's work had been the unification of Germany; but this had required the extrusion of the German-speaking Austrians from the framework of the new German Reich. Included in that Reich, they, together with the Bavarians, would overbalance Prussia, just as the ultramontane Roman Catholic population of the Reich would then overbalance the Protestant one. A situation would thus be created in which Bismarck, and his Emperor, would be in real danger of losing control. It was in fact doubtful whether German unification could survive at all the reinsertion of the Austrians into the existing German scheme of things. Yet it was clear that in the event of a break-up of the Habsburg Empire, the German-speaking population of Austria would have nowhere else to go but to Germany. The whole great problem of German unification, which it had cost Bismarck three wars and the exertions of two decades to solve, would again be thrown open, and his life's work endangered.

In this situation, the old statesman manoeuvred desperately to save what could be saved. He did what he could to stimulate, quietly and behind the scenes, a Mediterranean coalition—of Britain, Italy, and Austria—which could hold the Russians in check in the Balkans and at the Straits. At the same time he insisted on clinging, as long as this could possibly be done, to the treaty tie with Russia. Of course, this tie was tenuous. He did not need his critics within the German governmental establishment—Holstein and the military leaders—to tell him this. He understood it better than anyone else. But it served to gain time. It stood as a certain impediment to formal Franco-Russian military understandings. It gave him grounds on which to press for Russian neutrality in the case of a Franco-German conflict. So he held his ground, effectively though with increasing difficulty, to the end of his tenure as German chancellor. Then the whole structure collapsed, and the road to a Franco-Russian alliance was open.

Bismarck has often been reproached for cultivating a system of alliances too complex and intricate to be useful—a system that no one but himself could understand or manage. The reproach is hard for this writer to accept. Bismarck's treaty structure of the 1880's was designed to keep peace between the Austrians and the Russians, to make it clear that neither could expect German help in an effort to attack the other, but also to assure that neither of them would become the ally of the French in an aggressive war or war of revenge against Germany. These were simple and logical aims; and the provisions of the respective treaties served them as long as Bismarck was in a position to preserve their structure. The thrust of the respective treaty provisions was essentially defensive: to prevent wars of aggression either among Germany's neighbors or by any of those neighbors against Germany—wars that could have threatened directly Germany's security or undermined the structure of relationships (including the integrity of the Austro-

Hungarian Empire) which alone could assure the stability of the new, and in some respects still fragile, German Reich.

The weakness of this concept (and this was Bismarck's own tragedy) was that the *status quo* to the preservation of which it was directed was a flawed one from the start, not indefinitely tenable no matter what genius of statesmanship was applied to its maintenance. It rested on the permanent political-military isolation of France, in semi-humiliating conditions, and on the continued suppression of every trace of Polish independence. Both of these purposes were in conflict with the developing forces of the epoch. The concept further assumed the indefinite endurance of the multilingual Austro-Hungarian Empire in the face of all the romantic nationalism of the time. It envisaged a Russia in which the authority of the Tsars would suffice indefinitely to hold in check both the nationalistic and the revolutionary tendencies of the age. It envisaged a succession of Tsars wise enough to hold to a treaty relationship which was bound to limit Russia's freedom of action in European affairs—a treaty relationship, the humiliating effects of which could not fail to be visible to the influential public but the rationale of which (because the exact nature of the treaties could not be revealed) could never be fully explained.

It was not, then, because Bismarck's treaty structure was illogical or overelaborate that it could not be indefinitely successful. It was that the European *status quo* it was designed to serve did too much violence both to the feelings of the French and to the underlying forces for change in European society generally. The Bismarck of 1886-1890, in other words, found himself hung up, in his efforts to maintain a stable Europe, by the Bismarck of 1871. He was now the victim of the mistakes of the Prussian military leaders whom he had used, in earlier years, as instruments to the attainment of his political ends. Through such indirect ways, and thus belatedly, are the mistakes and excesses of one generation of statesmanship sometimes visited upon the generation that succeeds it.

It could well be argued that the Bismarckian *status quo* of the 1870's and 1880's was better, despite these flaws, than the disasters that flowed, as Bismarck clearly saw they would, from its break-up. The isolation of France did not prevent the complete autonomy of her political life, nor a great flowering of French culture, nor impressive economic and social advances. The situation of the Alsace-Lorrainers was only politically, not physically, uncomfortable; and a longer patience might well have seen the Germans advance to a more mature understanding of the problems of the association of these provinces with the

422

Reich. The Austro-Hungarian Empire still looks better, as a solution to the tangled problems of that part of the world, than anything that has succeeded it. And no real pain was caused to Russia—quite the contrary—by her inability to dominate several Balkan countries or her failure to acquire bases at the Straits. None of the fruits of the break-up of this *status quo* could possibly make good, furthermore, for any of the peoples involved, the sacrifice of some eight million of Europe's best sons on the altar of sentimental nationalism during the long years of agony known as the First World War. But none of this was visible (with very rare exceptions) to the statesmen of the time, or to the journalists and others who provided the critical reaction to their decisions. And the reason why it was not visible is one that deserves special mention, as the final reflection induced by this account.

No one who, in the aftermath of the two world wars of the twentieth century, has pursued the evolution of European diplomacy over the two decades treated in this volume can have failed to be struck by the wide currency at that time of the impression that further wars among European Powers were inevitable, and by the lightheartedness with which people contemplated this prospect. People appear to have viewed war solely as a possible *instrument* of national policy, advantageous or deleterious only insofar as it was successful or unsuccessful. There was no suggestion of an understanding that war, as an exercise for highly industrialized societies in the modern age, would have subjective, as well as objective consequences, quite aside from its ostensible military outcome, that is, aside from the question of military victory or defeat. It was not understood that there could be genetic losses of such seriousness that they could not be made good by any conceivable fruits of victory—impermanent, shifting, steadily yielding to the sands of time, as all these fruits were bound to be. It was not understood that the anguish of modern war could weaken even the ostensibly victorious society, breaking the rhythm of the generations, loosening social bonds, brutalizing sensibilities, sowing sadness, bewilderment, and skepticism where once the opposites of those qualities had prevailed, laying the groundwork for even greater emotional instability and extremisms in future years, as maimed generations grew to maturity. It was not understood, in other words, that all-out war between great industrialized nations in the modern age had become a senseless undertaking, a self-destructive exercise, a game at which no one could really win, and therefore no longer a suitable instrument of national policy.

The reason why these things were not understood was, of course, the survival into those decades of the romantic-chivalric concept of military conflict: the notion that whether you won or lost depended only on your bravery, your determination, your sense of righteousness, and your skill. In this view, warfare became a test of young manhood, a demonstration of courage and virility, a proving-ground for virtue, for love of country, for national quality. It was not understood that changes were taking place, even then, in the technology of warfare which would come close to eliminating whatever reality these concepts had ever had—that forms of butchery were in process of development before which such things as individual valor and patriotic inspiration would have very little meaning. The common soldier of the future First World War might endure with great stoicism his wretched existence in the muddy trenches, he might be brave as a lion, and delirious with patriotic fervor; these qualities would do him no good under a direct hit by enemy artillery, nor could they save him if he was ordered to try to attack through barbed-wire entanglements under enemy machine-gun fire. And meanwhile, so long as he remained alive, things were being done to him, psychologically, and to the society he conceived himself to be defending, which were in any case depriving his sacrifice of a great deal of its meaning.

The people who influenced decisions in those decades—the statesmen, journalists, parliamentarians, and generals—had more reason than we have today to be oblivious to these realities, but insufficient reason for ignoring them entirely. The Crimean War and the American Civil War, not to mention the Russo-Turkish War, had all revealed situations which should have given pause for thought to even the most sanguine military chauvinist of subsequent years. (Before the fateful dividing point of 1914 was to be reached, there would be other, and even more eloquent, demonstrations of this nature, particularly in the war between Russia and Japan at the outset of this century.) That such lessons were not more frequently and generally perceived than was the case in the 1880's must be attributed in part to the same euphoria of nationalism that has played so large a part in the tale unfolded in this work. Today, in the face of the abundant weapons of mass destruction, when war between great nations has become not only suicidal with relation to themselves but apocalyptically destructive even with relation to millions of innocent bystanders, and to the entire civilization of which they form a part, there is no excuse for denying them recognition. If this truth alone can be reinforced by the examination of the mistakes and bewilderments of political leaders acting nearly a hundred years ago, then even the length and detail of this portion of a study of the Franco-Russian alliance will not have lacked their justification.

424

NOTES

INTRODUCTION

1. A. Leroy-Beaulieu, *La France, la Russie et l'Europe* (Paris: Calmann-Lévy, 1888), p. 47.

PROLOGUE

1. For the translation of this letter I have availed myself of the English edition of the work by the Duc de Broglie, French premier at the time of this episode: *An Ambassador of the Vanquished* (London: William Heinemann, 1896), p. 196. The French original is available in other sources.

CHAPTER 1. RUSSIAN OPINION AND THE WAR WITH TURKEY

1. *Russia and the Balkans 1870-1880* (Oxford: University Press, 1937).
2. Haus-, Hof-, und Staatsarchiv, Vienna (to be referred to hereafter as Austrian Archives). Foreign Office files, Box 73. PA-X. *Russland, Berichte, 1879*. Despatch of November 5, 1879, from Kalnocky to the Austro-Hungarian foreign minister, Haymerle.

CHAPTER 2. FRANCO-RUSSIAN RELATIONS, 1879-1880

1. *Documents diplomatiques français*, First Series (1871-1900), II, No. 392, p. 452. Despatch from Le Flô of March 11, 1879. (This source will hereafter be referred to by the initials *DDF*. Unless otherwise specified, subsequent references are to the First Series.)
2. Archives des Affaires Étrangères, Paris. Volume of correspondence between the Foreign Office and the Embassy at Petersburg, entitled *Russie, 1879*.

    These archives of original communications, most of them, like this despatch of Vieleustel, not published in the *DDF*, will be referred to hereafter as French Archives.
3. A. Z. Manfred, *Obrazovanie russko-frantsuskogo soyuza* (Moscow: Nauka, 1975), p. 36.
4. Ibid., p. 37.

5. Count Herbert von Bismarck, in a letter to his father, the chancellor, of February 1, 1884, written during a visit to Petersburg, attributed this allegation to the German military attaché there, Liegnitz (*Die Grosse Politik der Europäischen Kabinette*, III, No. 621, p. 324. This source will hereafter be referred to by the initials *GP*).

6. French Archives. *Russie, 1879*. Aff. Div. Attachés militaires.

7. French Archives. *Russie, 1880*. Despatch of Boisdeffre to foreign minister, of March 20, 1880.

8. E. Daudet, *Histoire diplomatique de l'alliance franco-russe* (Paris: Allendorf, 1894), pp. 128-129.

9. P. Vassili (pseudonym for Princess C. Radziwill), *Behind the Veil at the Russian Court* (New York: John Lane Co., 1914), p. 33.

10. Élie de Cyon, *Histoire de l'entente franco-russe 1886-1894. Documents et souvenirs*. Paris: Librairie Charles, 1895, p. 35.

11. *GP*, III, No. 477, p. 81, footnote.

12. In English: "General Chanzy, who is taking an interest in my founding of *La Nouvelle Revue*, knowing my long-standing sympathy for Russia, writes to me that my journal will have a serious influence in Russia, above all in case its editorial line on foreign policy is in the hands of someone whom nothing could corrupt. I replied that it would be in mine." (Adam, *Après l'abandon de la revanche,* diary note from June 1879. Exact page number not available.)

CHAPTER 3. NEW TSAR—NEW ALLIANCE

1. B. Nolde, *L'Alliance franco-russe* (Paris: Droz, 1936), p. 317.

2. *GP*, III, No. 440, pp. 5-6.

3. H. Plehn, *Bismarcks auswärtige Politik nach der Reichsgründung* (Berlin & Munich: R. Oldenbourg, 1920), p. 153.

4. *GP*, III, No. 440, p. 6. Marginal note by Bismarck.

5. Ibid., No. 453, p. 25.

6. *Mémoires du Chancelier Prince de Bülow* (Paris: Plon, 1931), Chap. XL.

7. *GP*, III, No. 647, p. 374.

CHAPTER 4. A BIT ABOUT PERSONALITIES

1. "L'Ambassade russe à Paris, 1881-1898: les mémoires de Nicolas Giers," ed. B. Jelavich, *Canadian Slavic Studies*, I, 2 (1967).

2. *Journal du Vicomte E.-M. de Vogüé, Paris-Saint Pétersbourg, 1877-1883* (Paris: B. Grasset, 1932).

3. French Archives. Personal file on Appert.

4. French Archives. *Russie, 1883. Voyage de Colonel de Sermet, Attaché Militaire.*

5. De Vogüé, *Journal*, entries for January 8 and January 15, 1882.

6. Ibid., entry for January 30, 1882.

7. Ibid., entries for late March 1882.

8. This episode is recounted in W. Windelband, *Bismarck und die euro-päischen Grossmächte* (Essen: Essener Verlagsanstalt, 1940), pp. 472-473.

9. Cyon, *Histoire*, pp. 125-127.

CHAPTER 5. COMPLICATIONS IN BULGARIA

1. E. C. Corti, *Alexander von Battenberg. Sein Kampf mit dem Zaren und Bismarck* (Vienna: L. W. Seidel & Sohn, 1920), pp. 132-133.

2. Austrian Archives. Personal letter of Wolkenstein to "Mein sehr verehrter Gönner" of October 2, 1885.

3. Ibid.

4. Battenberg himself referred to him as "einen der berüchtigtsten russischen Diplomaten" ("one of the most notorious Russian diplomats" [Corti, *Alexander von Battenberg*, pp. 140-144]). W. Kirby Green, at one time British representative in the Montenegrin capital of Scutari where Ionin was his Russian colleague, described the latter as "one of the cleverest of the Slavophile band" (C. Jelavich, *Tsarist Russia and Balkan National-ism* [Berkeley and Los Angeles: University of California Press, 1958], p. 124). One of Battenberg's private secretaries, Golovin, also had the impression that he was "ein eifriger Anhänger des Panslawismus" ("a zealous Panslav partisan" [A. F. Golovin, *Fürst Alexander I von Bul-garien* (Vienna: Carl Fromme, 1896), p. 240]). Giers, on the other hand, who knew him well, thought him "prudent and well-balanced"; and the Austrian Ambassador Wolkenstein described him as "an intelli-gent and useful agent who, though a warm patriot, was not a Panslav agitator" (Jelavich, *Tsarist Russia*, p. 124). The reader may take his choice.

5. Corti, *Alexander von Battenberg*, p. 147.

6. Corti, *Downfall of Three Dynasties*, p. 296.

7. Corti, *Alexander von Battenberg*, p. 164.

8. From a memo written by Battenberg in his own hand, found by Corti in the Hartenau Archive (*Alexander von Battenberg*, p. 166).

9. Ibid., pp. 177-178.

CHAPTER 6. THE UNIFICATION OF BULGARIA

1. *Avantyury*, etc., Document 3. Letter from Koyander to Vlangali, August 16, 1885.

2. By way of evidence for the tenor of this discussion, we have excerpts, as unearthed from Battenberg's papers and published by Corti, from the

handwritten memorandum about the talk drawn up by Battenberg at the time, as well as two or three sentences from a letter written by him to his father shortly thereafter. We also have a brief summary from the pen of a competent and reliable German journalist (A. von Huhn, *The Struggle of the Bulgarians for National Independence under Prince Alexander* [London: John Murray, 1886]) of what the Prince said to him about it after he returned to Bulgaria. Finally, we have skimpy evidences, in the French and Austrian diplomatic documents, of what Giers, after his return to Petersburg, said about the interview in his talks with the respective foreign envoys. Battenberg's remarks to Kantakuzin, quoted above, also give us some idea of the line he was prepared to take with Giers.

3. Corti, *Downfall of Three Dynasties*, p. 308.

4. French Archives. *Russie, 1885.* Personal note from Appert to Freycinet, October 22, 1885.

5. Austrian Archives, Box XV/91, *Bulgarien.* Telegram of October 6, 1885, from the Austrian representative in Sofia, von Biegeleben, to the Foreign Office in Vienna. The text of Giers' reply was cited in full in the message.

6. See letter of Septembr 2, Wedel to Holstein, *The Holstein Papers*, ed. N. Rich and M. H. Fisher, III: *Correspondence, 1861-1896* (Cambridge: University Press, 1961), pp. 149-154. The Holstein papers have been published both in English and in German (see Bibliographical Note). The author has used both editions, according to which was available.

7. Golovin, *Fürst Alexander I von Bulgarien*, p. 289.

8. Ibid.

CHAPTER 7. THE AFTERMATH OF UNIFICATION

1. Austrian Archives. Telegram of October 14, 1885, from Wolkenstein to Foreign Office.

2. Ibid. Despatch of October 8, 1885, from Biegeleben, in Sofia, to Foreign Office.

3. Letter of October 22, 1885, of de Courcel to Freycinet (*DDF*, VI, No. 103, pp. 123-131).

4. F. von Holstein, *Die geheimen Papiere Friedrich von Holsteins*, ed. N. Rich, M. H. Fisher, and W. Frauendienst (Göttingen: Musterschmidt, 1957), II, p. 296.

5. Austrian Archives, Box XV/89, *Bulgarien.* Telegram, November 29, 1885, Giers to Lobanov, Russian Ambassador at Vienna.

6. *Sobranje peredovykh statei Moskovskikh Veidomostei.* Vol. for 1885. Item No. 334, December 2, 1885.

7. French Archives. *Russie 1885.* Despatch of December 8, 1885, Appert to Freycinet.

8. Ibid. Despatch of December 22, Appert to Freycinet.

9. Ibid. Despatch of January 7, 1886, Appert to Freycinet.

10. *Avantyury*, etc., Document 9.

11. This passage is cited in footnote 76, for the year 1888, on p. 484, of the second volume of Polovtsov's diary (*Dnevnik gosudarstvennogo sekretarya A. A. Polovtsova* [Moscow: Nauka, 1966]). The source for it is given as the Milyutin papers on deposit with the Manuscript Division of the Lenin Library in Moscow.

CHAPTER 8. THE ESTRANGEMENT OF 1886

1. *DDF*, VI, No. 256, p. 259.

2. Toutain, *Alexandre III*, p. 88.

3. The full text of Freycinet's letter, which does not appear in the *Documents diplomatiques français*, is included in Appert's personal file in the French Archives. Toutain, in *Alexandre III*, cites some of the phrases from it.

4. Toutain, *Alexandre III*, p. 76.

5. Ibid.

6. Ibid.

7. Geffcken, 1893, p. 112.

8. By kind permission of the Appert family, I was permitted to see this passage.

9. Toutain, *Alexandre III*, p. 80.

10. Ibid.

11. French Archives. Personal file on Appert.

12. Daudet, *Histoire diplomatique*, p. 181.

13. French Archives. *Russie, 1886*. Despatch, Ternaux-Compans to Freycinet, April 5, 1886.

14. *DDF*, VI, No. 256, p. 260. Despatch of Ternaux-Compans, June 8, 1886.

15. French Archives. Despatch of Ternaux-Compans, July 7, 1886.

CHAPTER 9. KATKOV'S ATTACK

1. *GP*, III, No. 634, p. 342.

2. Ibid., No. 977, p. 45.

3. See M. Katz, *Mikhail N. Katkov. A Political Biography* (The Hague: Mouton & Co., 1966), pp. 116-117. Katz cites, as the source for this information, the following document from the microfilmed German archives: *Auswärtiges Amt, Akten, Russland 82 No. 4, Sect. Russische Journalisten (Katkov)*. Microfilm: CU 1:264, Frames 28-30.

4. Austrian Archives. Telegram, Wolkenstein to Kalnocky, October 24, 1886.

Notes

CHAPTER 10. THE END OF BATTENBERG

1. *The Holstein Papers*, ed. N. Rich and M. H. Fisher, II: *Diaries* (Cambridge: University Press, 1957), August 18, 1886 (p. 298).
2. *GP*, V, No. 980, pp. 51-54.
3. Nolde, *L'Alliance*, p. 350.
4. *Avantyury*, etc., Document 3.
5. A. Koch, *Fürst Alexander von Bulgarien* (Darmstadt: A. Bergsträsser, 1887), pp. 279-280.
6. Despatches of September 8 and 15 from Sir Robert Morier, British Ambassador at Petersburg, to the Foreign Office. Public Record Office, London. Vol. *F.O. 65, Russia*, 1299.
7. An account of this episode will be found in the diary of the Russian State Counselor Polovtsov (*Dnevnik*, I, p. 443).
8. *DDF*, VI, No. 307, pp. 308-309.
9. Personal letter, Kotsebue to Giers, September 9, 1886 (Russian Archives. Delo 70).
10. Ibid.
11. See Chap. XXXIX, *Rüssisch-Französische Allianzfühler 1886-1890*, in *GP*, VI, pp. 91-124.
12. See, in this connection, the statements made by the Grand Duke Vladimir Aleksandrovich to Herbert Bismarck (*GP*, V, No. 992, p. 80) and Katkov's later complaint to the Tsar (his letter of March 31/April 12, 1887 [*Krasnyi Arkhiv*, LVIII (Vol. III of the 1933 series), p. 81]) to the effect that the Foreign Office had disclaimed responsibility for the Kaulbars mission and had criticized it in terms identical with those used by the foreign press.
13. Memo of August 10, 1886, by German Foreign Office official, von Berchem (*GP*, V, No. 879, p. 49).
14. See the telegram of Schweinitz to Bismarck, November 23, 1886 (*GP*, V, No. 993, p. 84).

CHAPTER 11. THE BREAK REPAIRED

1. Toutain, *Alexandre III*, p. 131.
2. J. Hansen, *Ambassade à Paris du Baron de Mohrenheim* (Paris: Flammarion, 1907), pp. 20-21.
3. Cyon, *Histoire*, pp. 169-170.
4. Toutain, *Alexandre III*, p. 135.
5. See despatch of Austrian Ambassador Wolkenstein, November 30, 1886 (Austrian Archives, Box 83. PA-X. *Russland, Berichte, 1886*).
6. Russian Archives. File: *Kantselyariya, 1886*. Delo 18. (My translation, from the French.) Despatch, Muraviev to Foreign Office, September 8/20, 1886.

7. Ibid. Despatch, Muraviev to Foreign Office, September 13/25, 1886.

8. Ibid. Despatch, Muraviev to Foreign Office, September 15/27, 1886.

9. Ibid. Personal letter, Shuvalov to Giers, October 3/15, 1886.

10. *GP*, V, No. 990, p. 69. In translating these passages, I have left in French those portions which were written in that language, translating only the German passages.

11. Cyon, *Histoire*, p. 163.

12. *Le Siècle*, December 9, 1886.

13. Cyon, *Histoire*, p. 166.

CHAPTER 12. FRANCE IN THE SPECTRUM OF RUSSIAN FINANCE

1. M. T. Florinsky, *Russia. A History and Interpretation* (New York: Macmillan, 1953), pp. 945, 1107.

2. S. Kumpf-Korfes, *Bismarcks "Draht nach Russland"* (Berlin: Akademie Verlag, 1968), pp. 7-8.

3. *GP*, V, No. 1127, p. 320.

4. For these statistics, as well as for most of this portrayal of the potential advantages of France as a center for Russian borrowing, I am indebted to the work of my late colleague at the Institute for Advanced Study, Herbert Feis: *Europe, the World's Banker* (New Haven: Yale University Press, 1930), Chaps. II and IX.

5. These details about the Petersburg branch of the Crédit Lyonnais are taken exclusively from the valuable work of Jean Bouvier: *Le Crédit Lyonnais de 1863 à 1882* (Paris: S.E.V.P.E.N., 1961), II, pt. 4, Chap. IX.

6. The figure is taken from H. D. White, *The French International Account 1880-1913* (Cambridge, Mass.: Harvard University Press, 1933), Table 25, p. 123.

7. *Journal*, p. 167.

CHAPTER 13. BISMARCK'S ANXIETIES

1. *GP*, VI, No. 1201, p. 95.

2. Ibid., No. 1203, pp. 96-98.

3. Ibid., No. 1206, p. 100.

4. Ibid., No. 1210, pp. 105-108.

CHAPTER 14. THE TSAR'S CRISIS OF DECISION

1. These communications will be found in *GP*, V, Nos. 994-999, pp. 85-94.

2. The full text of this communiqué, as originally published in the *Pravitel'-stvuiushchii vestnik*, December 3/15, 1886, is reproduced in "M. N.

Katkov i Aleksandr III v 1886-1887 gg.," *Krasny Arkhiv*, LVIII (Vol. III of the 1933 series), note on pp. 61-62.

3. Polovtsov, *Dnevnik*, II, February 18/March 2, 1887.

4. *GP*, V, No. 991, p. 74.

5. Ibid., No. 1005, p. 116.

6. Ibid., No. 1062, p. 212.

7. The exact French text of this document will be found in Ibid., No. 1063, pp. 214-215. Bismarck had added, in pencil, to the last clause the words: "tant qu'elle reste telle qu'elle est et sous le sceptre du roi Milan." The *GP* refers to this document, in a footnote, as "im wesentlichen akzeptiert"—i.e., "accepted in its main points"—by Bismarck.

8. The full text of this speech will be found in Vol. XII (entitled *Die Reden des Ministerpräsidenten und Reichskanzlers Fürsten von Bismarck im Preussichen Landtage und im Deutschen Reichstage 1886-1890*) of the series, *Die politischen Reden des Fürsten Bismarck*, ed. H. Kohl (Stuttgart: Cotta'schen Buchhandlung, 1894), pp. 175-210. The translations are my own.

9. Ibid., p. 180.

10. Ibid., p. 218.

11. LVIII (Vol. III of the 1933 series), pp. 58-85.

12. Feoktistov, *Vospominaniya*, p. 252.

13. This was related to A. A. Polovtsov, the influential Secretary of the State Council, by Katkov's friend and journalistic collaborator, S. S. Tatishchev, who had just seen Katkov in Petersburg. (See Polovtsov, *Dnevnik*, II, entry for January 14/26, 1887.)

14. Lamsdorf, *Dnevnik, 1886-1890*, January 6/18, 1887. "There was a time," Lamsdorf wrote, "when the Russian autocrat held himself above the gossip of the press; he personally gave the desired direction to policy, and compelled public opinion to accept it. Only recently His Majesty wrote the following in connection with the attacks on our press: 'But is newspaper gossip really the same as public opinion?' Now he submits to the influence of Katkov and Meshcherski and others like them."

15. Ibid., January 5/17, 1887.

16. Ibid.

17. *GP*, V, Nos. 1068-1070, pp. 218-220.

CHAPTER 15. FRANCE AND THE RUSSO-GERMAN CRISIS

1. *L'Alliance*, p. 395.

2. Toutain, *Alexandre III*, pp. 153-154.

3. J. F. Baddeley, *Russia in the "Eighties"* (London: Longmans, Green & Co., 1921), p. 169. In the interests of greater clarity, I have taken the

liberty of indenting the individual statements in this passage; in Mr. Baddeley's book they were run together in a single paragraph.

4. Toutain, *Alexandre III*, p. 160.

5. Ibid.

6. Lamsdorf, *Dnevnik, 1886-1890*, entry of January 13/25, 1887. According to Nolde (*L'Alliance*, p. 396), the Tsar's exact words were: "Oui, mais Bismarck a finassé, tandis que Flourens et Goblet se sont prononcés avec simplicité et franchise." Nolde does not give the source. My translation is taken from the Lamsdorf diary version, which was itself, of course, a translation from the French.

7. Toutain, *Alexandre III*, pp. 164-170. Toutain indicates that the same information was conveyed to Flourens personally on January 29 by certain highly placed Russians. He does not reveal the identity of these persons. The most likely possibility is General Bogdanovich.

8. Ibid.

9. French Archives. *Russie, 1887*.

10. It may be added that the available evidence for this feeler by Flourens is so tangled and complex that one hesitates to burden the reader with the citation of it, even in a footnote. The *Documents diplomatiques français* contain no reference to it, other than Giers' veiled statement to Laboulaye (*DDF*, VI, No. 410, pp. 421 f.); nor is there any other note of it in the official correspondence between the Quai d'Orsay and the French Embassy in Petersburg, as contained in the French Archives. Toutain, too, does not mention it. Hansen, in his *Ambassade à Paris du Baron de Mohrenheim* (pp. 28ff.), does indeed mention it, gives the wrong dates, and exaggerates the importance of the episode beyond all measure, proudly recounting his part in it and ascribing to the Tsar's reaction the final abandonment by Bismarck of the idea of attacking France. Solid evidence that the query was made, under Flourens' inspiration, is to be found only in Lamsdorf, *Dnevnik, 1886-1890* (entry of January 10/22. 1887). But Nolde, who evidently saw more in the French Archives than he cared to cite specifically, gives further details, including the textual quotation of the Tsar's reaction (pp. 412f.), but without citation of source.

11. *DDF*, VI, No. 410, pp. 421-422.

12. Ibid.

13. This and the immediately following citations from Flourens' messages are taken from *DDF*, VI, No. 414, pp. 424-425; No. 438, p. 454; and No. 441, p. 457.

14. *Histoire*, pp. 229-231.

15. Ibid., pp. 233-234.

16. The facts of this episode, as revealed in the Russian documents, were recounted and made public for the first time in 1935 (in the *Krasny*

Arkhiv, LXXII [Vol. V of the series for 1935], pp. 56-57) in an article entitled *Bulanzhism i tsarskaya diplomatiya* (pp. 51-109). The episode was mentioned, however, in Lamsdorf's diary, under the date of February 6, 1887.

17. Lamsdorf, *Dnevnik, 1886-1890*, February 6, 1887.

18. *DDF*, VI, No. 447, p. 461.

19. Our knowledge of this initiative rests primarily on Hansen's account, in his *Ambassade à Paris du Baron de Mohrenheim* (pp. 34-36); but it is generally confirmed both by Lamsdorf's diary and by Nolde. It is not mentioned either in the *Documents diplomatiques français* or in Toutain's account.

20. These details of the Russian correspondence pertaining to this matter are taken from Lamsdorf, *Dnevnik, 1886-1890*, February 13/25, 1887.

21. *Histoire*, p. 223.

22. Daudet, *Histoire diplomatique*, p. 208.

CHAPTER 16. RUSSIAN WINTER, 1887

1. Lamsdorf, *Dnevnik, 1886-1890*, January 23, 1887.

2. Polovtsov, *Dnevnik*, II, February 18/March 2, 1887.

3. Austrian Archives. Despatch of Wolkenstein to Foreign Office, March 2, 1887.

4. The text of this announcement will be found in Cyon's *Histoire*, p. 239.

5. Ibid., p. 240.

CHAPTER 17. THE CRISIS SURVIVED

1. Surprised and shocked as the Tsar apparently was at the fact that Katkov brought the existence of the *Dreikaiserbund* to public knowledge, it is difficult to understand his professed indignation at learning, at this late date, that Katkov himself knew of it. Katkov, as we have seen (see above, Chapter 13), had mentioned, in the secret monograph he presented to the Tsar in January 1887, the "treaty of 1881," as well as the fact that this treaty was now up for renewal. And the Tsar himself had suggested to Giers, on January 25, only three days after his own meeting with Katkov, that it might be a good idea to inform the editor more explicitly of the terms of the treaty. Both Giers and the Tsar were aware that Katkov had met with Zinoviev, head of the Asiatic Department of the Foreign Office, on January 12, and had revealed on that occasion a general knowledge of the existence of some sort of treaty.

   The person on whom there fell the heaviest burden of guilt, in the Tsar's eyes, for revealing the terms of the treaty to Katkov was the former ambassador at Berlin, Peter Saburov. Whether or not Katkov obtained his knowledge exclusively from this source, Saburov was indeed far from innocent. He had been in touch with Katkov throughout the winter of 1887. Writing to Katkov on January 18 about Bismarck's famous speech of the 13th, Saburov had referred specifically to "the tripartite agreement now in existence" (Katkov papers, Manuscript Section, Lenin Library, Moscow). He had seen Katkov in Petersburg, a few days later. On the 26th, Polovtsov was told by Tatischev that both Ignatyev and Saburov, in their anxiety to obtain Katkov's support in their quest for Giers' position, had gone to see Katkov and presented to him "not only their personal reminiscences but also papers from their private files" (Polovtsov, *Dnevnik*, II, p. 10).

Saburov and Katkov would meet again in April, after the appearance of Katkov's article, but before it was known that Saburov was under suspicion. Finally, on May 16, under similar circumstances, Saburov would write to Katkov, enclosing a detailed memo about the treaty, in which certain of its provisions were not only discussed *in extenso* but also cited verbatim (Katkov papers, Manuscript Department, Lenin Library, Moscow).

That memo must have just "slipped in under the wire"; for either later that day, or on the following one, the blow fell on Saburov in the form of a notification from Minister of Justice N. A. Manaseyin, to the effect that he was charged with revealing state secrets to Katkov. Obliged to face a judicial proceeding, he defended himself on the grounds that in his discussion with Katkov he had found the latter already well aware of the treaty's existence and of the date of its original signature. All this, he charged, Katkov had learned from leaks in the press and from Zinoviev. (See *K. P. Pobyedonostsev i ego korrespondenty* [Moscow/Petrograd: State Publishing Co., 1923], I, p. 691.)

Saburov managed to escape judicial penalties, but he never recovered from the disfavor in the eyes of the Tsar which this episode had brought upon him.

2. Feoktistov, *Vospominaniya*, p. 253.

3. The text of this note is reproduced in *Pobyedonostsev*, I, pp. 644-645.

4. Ibid., pp. 793-794. This is confirmed by the Austrian despatches. Giers told the Austrian Ambassador, Wolkenstein, on March 30, that he had offered his resignation to the Tsar the previous day, but that it had not been accepted (Austrian Archives, Box 84, *Russland, Berichte*. Telegram, Wolkenstein to Foreign Office, March 31, 1887).

5. *Krasny Arkhiv*, LVIII (Vol. III of the 1933 series), pp. 79-85.

6. Austrian Archives, Box 84, *Russland, Berichte*. Telegram of April 18, 1887, from Wolkenstein to Foreign Office.

7. Polovtsov, *Dnevnik*, II, March 15/27, 1887.

8. *GP*, V, No. 1071, pp. 220-221.

9. Ibid., No. 1073, p. 223.

10. French Archives. *Russie, 1887.* Telegram, Flourens to Laboulaye, April 14, 1887.

11. Ibid. Despatch from d'Ormesson, September 23, 1887.

12. Russian Archives. *Sekretny Arkhiv, 1887.* Despatch, Mohrenheim to Foreign Office, February 26/March 10, 1887.

13. Ibid. Despatch, Mohrenheim to Foreign Office, April 25/May 7, 1887.

14. Feoktistov, *Vospominaniya*, p. 260. This account of the incident in question has been reconstructed from Feoktistov's memoirs and from various communications reproduced in *Pobyedonostsev*, notably nos. 690-693, 738, 742, 744-748, and 753.

15. *Pobyedonostsev*, p. 117.

16. Feoktistov, *Vospominaniya*, p. 262.

CHAPTER 18. THE AFTERMATH OF
THE REINSURANCE TREATY

1. These data about the Tsar's role in the preparation of the Silistria fiasco are all taken from the respective passages of Lamsdorf's diary; but they are confirmed by the documents published in the *Avantyury russkogo tsarizma v Bolgarii*. The full text of Giers' letter to Khitrovo will also be found on pp. 38-40 of *Avantyury*.

2. The exchanges with Austria are set forth in detail in *GP*, V, Chap. XXXIII, *Fortwirkung der bulgarischen Krise 1887*. See also the biography of Ehrnrooth by M. Ehrnrooth, *Casimir Ehrnrooth. Trogen Tvenne tsarer och en furste Alexander* (Helsinki: Svenska Litteratur sällskupet i Finland, 1965), pp. 284-293.

3. *DDF*, VI, No. 628, pp. 626-629.

4. See the briefing memorandum prepared by Bismarck for the old Kaiser in preparation for the latter's interview with the Tsar on November 18, 1887 (*GP*, V, No. 1127, p. 321).

5. Quoted by P. Jakobs, *Das Werden des französisch-russischen Zweibundes 1890-1894* (Wiesbaden: Otto Harrassowitz, 1968), p. 12, from a letter of Herbert Bismarck to his brother William of June 19, 1887, as found in the Bismarck family papers at Friedrichsruh.

6. In the following account of Cyon's relations with Bleichröder, as well as of his activities generally in the period 1887-1890, I have drawn heavily, and with much gratitude, on the copies of 21 letters addressed by Cyon to Bleichröder in those years, made available to me through the kindness of Bleichröder's biographer, Professor Fritz Stern of Columbia University.

7. A document from the German Foreign Office files (despatch, September 10, 1886, from the German Embassy at Paris; German Archives, File: *Französische Journalisten*), also kindly made available to me by Profes-

sor Stern, speaks of Cyon as having vainly tried to enlist Bleichröder's help in 1883 in buying up the shares of the expiring Petersburg *Golos.*

8. In the doctoral dissertation of Eugène Calschi, entitled *Les relations, financières entre la France et la Russie de 1886 à 1892,* 1963, which is held in the Bibliothèque universitaire de la Sorbonne, there is cited a paper from the archives of Rothschild Frères, in which Cyon is described as "un homme d'une honorabilité douteuse, et rien ne prouve qu'il n'a pas commencé par se présenter là-bas en notre nom comme il se présente ici au nom du ministre, en vertue d'un double mandat volontaire qu'il se serait octroyé à lui-même"—not, all in all, a bad description of the person in question.

9. *Moskovskie Vyedomosti,* July 17/29, 1887.

10. *GP,* V, No. 1122, p. 308.

CHAPTER 19. THE FERDINAND DOCUMENTS

1. Public Record Office, London. Vol. *F.O. 65, Russia,* 1299. Despatch, Morier to Foreign Office, November 11, 1887.

2. See Holstein, *Die geheimen Papiere,* II, diary note for November 18, 1887.

3. The full text of Bismarck's memorandum, dated November 10, 1887, will be found in *GP,* V, No. 1127, pp. 320-323.

4. The original of Giers' note is in the files of the Politisches Archiv of the German Foreign Office (hereafter referred to as German Archives), V, *Bulgarien,* No. 20.

5. *Behind the Veil at the Russian Court* (see above, Chap. II, note 9), p. 169.

CHAPTER 20. THE DETERIORATING THREE-EMPEROR RELATIONSHIP

1. The text of this memorandum will be found in Graf Moltke, *Die deutschen Aufmarschpläne* (Forschungen und Darstellungen aus dem Reichsarchiv, VII [Berlin: E. S. Mittler & Sohn, 1929]), pp. 137-143.

2. *GP,* VI, No. 1176, pp. 46-50.

3. R. Goblet, "Souvenirs de ma vie politique," *Revue politique et parlementaire,* CXXXVII, No. 410, January 10, 1929. The above is Goblet's summary of Robert's conclusions.

CHAPTER 21. FINANCIAL AND MILITARY STIRRINGS

1. *Histoire,* pp. 341-342.

2. German Archives, VI, *Russland 71.* Memo, Rothenburg to von Berchem.

3. These and other data concerning this matter are taken primarily from the

file entitled *Russie. Finances. Mars-Avril, 1888. Voyage de M. Denfert-Rochereau,* in the French Archives.

4. Note *DDF,* VII, No. 20 (telegram of January 31 from Herbette).

5. See Girault, *Emprunts,* p. 148.

6. Ibid., p. 153.

7. The text of the letter, along with others, was made available to me from the Bleichröder papers by the kindness of Bleichröder's biographer, Professor Fritz Stern, of Columbia University.

8. *Emprunts,* p. 167.

9. C. de Freycinet, *Souvenirs 1878-1893* (Paris: C. Delagrave, 1913), Chap. XIII.

10. Polovtsov, *Dnevnik,* II, November 12/24, 1888.

CHAPTER 22. 1889. THE RUSSIAN BREAK WITH GERMANY

1. Lamsdorf, *Dnevnik, 1886-1890,* January 30/February 11, 1889.

2. *GP,* VI, No. 1356, pp. 354-355.

3. French Archives. *Russie, 1889.* Despatch, Laboulaye to Foreign Office, June 8, 1889.

4. *Gold and Iron,* p. 446.

5. This summary of the events of the Achinov affair has been compiled from a variety of sources, among which the documents in the French Archives figure most prominently.

6. See Lamsdorf, *Dnevnik, 1886-1890,* February 7/19, 1889, for the Tsar's reference to Achinov as "this animal" and also for the reference to Paissi.

7. French Archives. *Russie, 1889.* Despatch of May 23, 1889, from Laboulaye to Foreign Office.

8. Ibid. Despatch, October 11, 1899, Vauvineux (chargé) to Foreign Office.

9. Nolde, *L'Alliance,* p. 575.

10. Ibid., pp. 575-576.

CONCLUSIONS

1. R. de Gourmont, *Le Joujou patriotisme* J. J. Pauvert (1967), pp. 59-60.

Date _____ Mar 23, 19 8

M _____

No. _____

Reg. No.	Clerk	ACCOUNT FORWARDED		
1				85
2			13	50
3			3	00
4				
5			27	0
6			1	3
7				
8			6	00
9			3	25
10				
11				
12				
13				
14				
15				

001499-29

Your account stated to date. If error is found return at once

BIBLIOGRAPHICAL ESSAY

1. *Archival Resources*

Among the primary sources used in the preparation of this volume, the excellent official series of French Foreign Office correspondence entitled *Documents diplomatiques français* naturally took a leading place. This series is made up primarily of a careful selection, from the standpoint of political and historical importance, of the official communications—instructions, despatches, and telegrams—exchanged between the Quai d'Orsay and the French diplomatic missions abroad; to which are added, most usefully, a considerable number of private letters (*lettres particulaires*) addressed by chiefs of these various diplomatic missions to senior officials in the Foreign Office. It does not appear to contain communications exchanged directly with other governments, except insofar as these are reproduced in the internal governmental correspondence just described. The selection of documents is generous and discriminating; and while the arrangement is strictly chronological, without breakdown by country or subject, the indexing is so complete that use of the series for such a study as the present one presents few problems.

Comprehensive as is this collection for the purposes of the student of the general diplomacy of the period, there are many documents which its editors felt obliged to omit but which are nevertheless of interest from the standpoint of a highly focused study such as the one presented here. The use of the published series was therefore supplemented, in the preparation of this volume, by many weeks of work in the original files of communications from the French Embassy at Petersburg, now available in the Archives des Affaires Etrangères at the Quai d'Orsay. Of outstanding value, among these last, were the extensive reports on the Russian press submitted at regular intervals (usually twice a month) by that Embassy. These included (normally in French translation but sometimes, in the case of French-language items, in clipping form) the texts—or excerpts thereof—of editorials and articles on diplomatic matters from the leading Russian newspapers of the day; and since the periodicals in question are today difficult, if not impossible, to find, and

439

for various reasons not easy to scan when found, this summary record of their pertinent contents is of exceptional historical value.

The comparable documents of the Russian Foreign Office for the period in question have never been published, but they have been well preserved and are available to scholars, or at least to some scholars, in the Archive of Foreign Policy (Arkhiv vneshnei politiki) in Moscow. While one finds references to them in the works of Soviet authors, very few Western scholars appear to have used them. Whether this was due to denial of permission, to lack of interest in this particular period, to the difficulty and expense of visiting Moscow for the long periods required for their study, or to the fact that the Soviet archivists normally require the visiting scholar to name in advance the particular documents he wishes to see, whereas no catalogue from which such a selection could be made appears to be available, I cannot say. I, at any rate, was courteously received, was promptly shown, and was permitted to examine at leisure (sometimes even permitted to photograph) any document I asked for. I regret only my inability to remain longer in Moscow and to study a larger part of this valuable material, which struck me as in no wise inferior to the comparable French documents in point of historical importance and excellence of preservation.

Franco-Russian relations for the period in question being in so high degree an obverse reflection of those that prevailed between Petersburg and Berlin, the similar documents of the Imperial German Foreign Office, now in custody of the Politisches Archiv in Bonn, are of an importance, for the subject in question, scarcely smaller than that of their French and Russian counterparts. Of these, too, the more important ones have, of course, been published—in the valuable series entitled *Die grosse Politik der europäischen Kabinette*, compiled and published in the years after the First World War by way of indirect rebuttal to the war guilt clause of the Treaty of Versailles. While this series has occasionally been treated with severity by French and British historians, I must say that I found those of the respective documents that dealt with Russo-German and Franco-German relations also to be in no wise inferior in historical value to those published by the French, and could discern no signs of tendentious editing or of any tendency to conceal significant portions of the record. The system of organization (by subject and period) of this material is different from that employed in the French series. Both systems have their merits and their drawbacks.

Here again, as in Paris, it is possible for the interested scholar to supplement the use of the published series by recourse to the original files of diplomatic correspondence available at the Politisches Archiv. Although unable to make as extensive use of this privilege as I should have

440

liked to do, I was able to consult these files on several occasions for clarification of specific points of inquiry.

Of the archival holdings of the former Austro-Hungarian Foreign Office there is no published series, but the originals are readily available to serious scholars at the Haus-, Hof-, und Staatsarchiv in Vienna; and of these, too, I was able to make extensive use. I found them, giving as they do a relatively detached view of Franco-Russian relations, not to mention their importance for relations between Vienna and Petersburg, of high value for purposes of this study.

The British Foreign Office correspondence for this particular period has unfortunately not been included in the excellent series of diplomatic documents which have been published for other periods of time,* but here, again, the original files are available to scholars at the Public Record Office in London. The manner in which these latter are catalogued and made available seems somewhat cumbersome in comparison with continental practices, but with patience and persistence most inquiries eventually yield their fruits.

Here, again, circumstances restricted my own use of these materials to the clarification of specific questions. But it is questionable how valuable a more comprehensive coverage of them would have been. Britain's interests at that time were naturally more closely related to Russia's policies at the Straits and in Central Asia than to her relations with Paris and Berlin. On this latter subject, the British Embassy at Petersburg was not generally very well informed; and the picture purveyed in its reports cannot compare in point of authority and detail to that which emanated from the despatches of the Embassies of the major continental Powers.

In addition to these major archival resources, the author occasionally had recourse to the official Belgian and Danish archives.

It might also be mentioned that while the Russian diplomatic correspondence for this period has not been published by the Tsarist-Russian or Soviet governments, a number of official or semi-official Russian documents have seen publication in Russian historical-documentary series (particularly the *Krasny Arkhiv*), in secondary treatises of one sort or another, or in special published collections. Of these latter, particular mention must be made of the two rare and curious volumes of documents on Russian policy in the Balkans from the period in question: the one entitled *Avantyury russkogo tsarizma v Bolgarii. Sbornik dokumentov,*† prepared in 1935 on the basis of the holdings of the Arkhiv

---

* The reference is to the series of *Documents on British Foreign Policy 1919-1939*, published in London, in various years, by His Majesty's Stationery Office.

† Prepared by P. Pavlovich. Moscow: State Social-Economic Publishing House, 1935.

Vneshnei Politiki, and containing the texts of some 182 documents, or excerpts therefrom, presumably to be found in the holdings of that Archive; the other, a similar set of documents stolen (apparently) from the files of the Russian Consulate at Rushchuk or the Legation at Bucarest by the former Dragoman of the Rushchuk Consulate, Jakobsohn, and published by him in Berlin, in 1893.* (These latter are, of course, of something less than impeccable reliability; but some of them appear to be identical with the ones produced in the volume entitled *Avantyury*, etc., mentioned above.)

In addition to the official archival documents, mention should also be made of two fine collections of manuscripts and personal papers to be found in the Manuscript Division (Rukopisny Otdel) of the Lenin Library in Moscow, and of the literary museum-library, the Pushkinski Dom, in Leningrad. These contain a number of personal papers that might well have bearing on the events recounted in this volume. Except for a brief glance into a small portion of the Katkov Papers at the Lenin Library, I was unfortunately not in a position to explore these sources.

2. *Memoirs, Diaries and Published Correspondence of the Time*

There is a marked dearth of memoir literature emanating from persons on the Russian side who were professionally concerned with problems of Franco-Russian relations.

We owe to Professors Charles and Barbara Jelavich, of the University of Indiana, the valuable historical service of microfilming, and arranging for the preservation at the Library of the University of California, of the family papers of Nikolai Karlovich Giers, the statesman, as well as the publication both of his uncompleted memoirs and those of his son, Nikolai Nikolayovich Giers, who was, in the 1880's and 1890's, a diplomatic secretary serving in the Russian Embassy at Paris.† The father's memoirs cover unfortunately only the early period of his life (into the 1840's) and are interesting, from the standpoint of this study, primarily as a reflection of his literary style and personality. Those of the son, while indifferently written and based on memories that were

---

* Under the title: *Documents secrets de la politique Russe en Orient.*

† For the father's memoirs, see: Jelavich, Barbara and Charles, eds. *The Education of a Russian Statesman. The Memoirs of Nicholas Karlovich Giers.* Berkeley: University of California Press, 1962.

Those of the son were published serially in various issues of *Revue canadienne d'etudes slaves*, beginning in the spring of 1967 and continuing into 1969.

All of these materials were made available from the papers of M. Serge Giers, grandson of the statesman, to whose generosity we are also indebted in this connection.

not always entirely accurate, throw a vivid light on the activities of the Russian Embassy at Paris and its entourage in Mohrenheim's time, and constitute a valuable addition to the available source material on this subject.

Of occasional interest for this study, especially in connection with the activities of M. N. Katkov, were the memoirs of his good friend, the man who was chief censor for the Russian government throughout the entire reign of Alexander III (from the beginning of 1883), E. M. Feoktistov.*

The most valuable of the diaries are unquestionably those of the future Russian foreign minister, in the 1880's director of the Chancery of the Foreign Ministry and Giers' most intimate aide and collaborator, Count V. N. Lamsdorf (Lamzdorf, in Russian transliteration). Lamsdorf, like Giers, resided in the building of the Foreign Ministry and saw his ministerial superior daily. His diary, of which only isolated portions seem to have survived, was unearthed and published (in the Russian language) in Moscow in the early Soviet period.† It is now a very rare item, available only in a few major libraries; and the paper (particularly that of the first volume) is rapidly disintegrating. It has the further drawback of being only a translation into Russian (how faithful and complete we do not know) from the original French. Nevertheless, what has survived in this form gives a uniquely intimate view of the motives and background of Russian foreign policy for the periods in question— particularly for the agitated winter of 1887.

There are several other published diaries which, while not addressed primarily to foreign affairs, throw occasional light on the diplomatic problems of the day. Most important, among these, are the diaries of Alexander II's liberal war minister, D. A. Milyutin;‡ of the State Secretary and Secretary of the Council of State, A. A. Polovtsov;§ and of the well-known editor and publicist, A. S. Suvorin.¶ Of particular importance is the published correspondence of the famous and highly influential Ober-Prokuror of the Holy Synod of the Russian Orthodox

---

* Feoktistov, E. M. *Vospominaniya E. M. Feoktistova. Za kulisami politiki i literatury.* 1848-1896. Leningrad: Priboi, 1929.

† This material was published in two volumes, both entitled Lamzdorf, V. N. Dnevnik: the first by Gosizdat (Moscow) in 1926 and containing the entries for the years 1886-1890; the second by Akademia (Moscow) in 1934, and containing those from 1891-1892.

‡ *Dnevnik Milyutina.* Moscow: Lenin Library, Manuscript Division, 1947. Edited by P. A. Zaionchkovski. (In four volumes.)

§ *Dnevnik gosudarstvennogo sekretarya A. A. Polovtsova.* Moscow: Nauka, 1966. Edited by P. A. Zaionchkovski. (In two volumes.)

¶ *Dnevnik A. S. Suvorina.* Moscow/Petrograd: L. D. Frenkel, 1923.

Church, Konstantin Pavlovich Pobyedonostev.* Very poorly arranged and indexed, hence not easy to use, but copiously and usefully annotated, this great volume of material contains a number of items, available from no other source, that throw light on Franco-Russian relations.

On the French side, again, there seems to be only one book of published memoirs that deals directly with the subject of this study: those of Edmond Toutain, who was Second Secretary of the French Embassy at Petersburg under the Ambassadors Appert and Laboulaye.† Written long after the event, and having the nature of a treatise on Franco-Russian relations of the period as well as a memoir, this book is unique in its quality as a picture of that relationship, as seen from the French Embassy in the Russian capital.

Of other French memoirs, there seem to be very few that contain anything of significance from the standpoint of this study. A minor exception may be made for those of the politician and inveterate cabinet member, Charles de Freycinet,‡ which throw light on at least one significant episode, and, similarly, of those of another French premier of the time, René Goblet.§

Finally, while we are on the subject of memoirs, diaries, and correspondence, mention must be made of the various volumes of the papers of Friedrich von Holstein, the well-known *eminence grise* of the German Foreign Office, which embrace all three of those categories. Holstein was increasingly out of sympathy with Bismarck's Russian policy as the decade of the 1880's neared its end, and his intimacy with this subject declined for that reason; but his papers contain numbers of passages on this subject which are either directly revealing or symptomatic of what was being thought and said in Bismarck's entourage.¶

3. Books

When it comes to the secondary literature in book form, first mention must go, unhesitatingly, to the fine work published in 1936 by Baron

* *Pobedonostsev, K. P. i ego korrespondenty*. Moscow-Petrograd: Gosizdat, 1923.

† Toutain, Edmond. *Alexandre III et la République Française*. Paris: Plon, 1929.

‡ Freycinet, Charles de. *Souvenirs 1848-18*. Paris: Ch. Delagrave, 1912.

§ Goblet's memoirs entitled *Souvenirs de ma vie politique*, appeared serially in the *Revue politique et parlementaire*, in the years 1928-1931.

¶ For the English version see: *The Holstein Papers*, edited by Norman Rich and M. H. Fisher. (Four volumes.) Cambridge: At the University Press, 1955-1963. The original German texts of much of this material were published, in part subsequently to the appearance of the English edition, under the title of *Die geheimen Papiere Friedrich von Holsteins*, by the Musterschmidt Verlag, in Göttingen, in 1956-1957.

Boris Nolde, entitled: *L'Alliance franco-russe*, etc.* Nolde, once a professor of jurisprudence in Petersburg and legal adviser to the Tsarist Foreign Office, wrote this book in Paris, in the emigration—primarily, one supposes, on the basis of the then recently published *Documents diplomatiques français*; but he appears to have supplemented the study by the consultation of French officials who had had personal experience or knowledge of the subject. The work embraced the period covered by this volume, plus the ensuing years down to the signature of the alliance in 1893-1894. So superior is this treatise in authority, objectivity, and penetration that I was repeatedly obliged to ask myself whether an attempt to go over this same ground in the 1970's was really warranted. Several reflections, however, gave me reassurance. A number of materials, not available when Nolde wrote his book, were available now. There was no translation of his book into English; and it would have been a pity to make a translation without use of the later materials. His account, finally, was a strictly diplomatic one, concerned mainly with the exchanges among governmental chanceries, whereas the focus of my own curiosity was rather on the motivation of the various statesmen and other actors of the drama. So I chose the path of an entirely new study. But in presenting this study, I cannot refrain from acknowledging my deep debt—a debt shared, I am sure, by all others who have interested themselves in this subject—to Nolde for his pioneering work.

There are, of course, a number of studies addressed to the conclusion and the effects of the alliance which took, as the point of departure, the fall of Bismarck and the beginning of the negotiations for the military convention, in 1890-1891.† I am omitting mention of these, as not directly relevant to the period covered in this volume.

Of the others—those that treated of the 1880's—none compares with that of Nolde in importance. A unique place is occupied, however, by Élie de Cyon's *Histoire de l'alliance franco-russe*, written in 1895-1896.‡ A work reflecting many of the oddities of this most curious of men, this account moved uncertainly along the borderline between history and memoirs and represented primarily an attempt to claim for Katkov and for Cyon himself credit for having given the decisive im-

---

* Nolde, Baron Boris. *L'Alliance franco-russe. Les origines du systeme diplomatique d'avant guerre.* Paris: Librairie Droz, 1936.

† Notable among these were: Langer, William Leonard, *The Franco-Russian Alliance 1890-1894.* New York: Octagon Books, 1967, and Georges Michon, *L'Alliance franco-russe 1891-1917.* Paris: Andre Delpeuch, 1927.

‡ Élie de Cyon, *Histoire de l'entente franco-russe. 1886-1894. Documents et souvenirs.* Paris: Librairie Charles, 1895.

petus to the Russian break with Germany and embarkation on the path that led to the alliance. While perhaps more significant as a memoir than as history, and certainly to be taken with caution (for Cyon was anything but a dispassionate observer), this book deserves a place among the major secondary works on the subject.

Similar to Cyon's work in point of the author's eagerness to claim credit for promoting the alliance, but far inferior to it in point of intellectual depth and historical interest, are the two skimpy but pretentious little volumes written by the Danish go-between and intriguer, Jules Hansen.* One of these was a hagiographic essay addressed to the person and activity of his chief at the Russian Embassy in Paris, the Ambassador Arthur Mohrenheim, with whom he was so intimate; the other was addressed to the preparation of the alliance itself. These books, too, like that of Cyon, confused history with memoirs and are quite unreliable; but they were written by a man who at one time stood close to events, particularly at the Paris end, and contain occasional useful hints of what actually occurred.

Not much better, in this last respect, but more serious and more strictly historical is the work of Ernest Daudet, entitled: *Histoire diplomatique de l'alliance franco-russe. 1873-1893.*† It is a strongly anti-German *apologia* for the French policy of the period; but since Daudet had good connections with a number of those who had taken active part in French diplomacy of the 1880's, it contains interesting and significant passages.

An excellent recent work which, while not specifically addressed to the origins of the Franco-Russian alliance, sheds considerable light on this subject, is that entitled: *Das Werden des französisch-russischen Zweibundes, 1890-1894*, written by the contemporary German scholar Peter Jakobs.‡ This book is of particular importance for the military history of the period, a subject on which there is a great need for further research.

Two works of Soviet historians deserve mention here. The first is that of Professor V. M. Khvostov (editor of the well-known Soviet *History of Diplomacy*), entitled: *Franko-russki soyuz i ego istoricheskoye znachenie.*§ The second is the work of the late Professor A. Z. Man-

---

* Hansen, Jules. *Ambassade à Paris du Baron de Mohrenheim. 1884-1898.* Paris: Flammarion, 1907; and *L'Alliance franco-russe.* Paris: Flammarion, 1897.

† Paris: Ollendorf, 1894.

‡ Osteuropastudien der Hochschulen des Landes Hessen, Reihe II. Marburger Abhandlungen zur Geschichte und Kultur Osteuropas, Band 8. Wiesbaden: Otto Harrassowitz, 1968.

§ Khvostov's treatise, an article rather than a book, represented his contribution

fred, entitled *Stanovlenie russko-franzozskogo soyuza.** In a manner characteristic of the Soviet historiography of the late-Stalin period, both these works appear to have been designed to serve primarily a contemporary political purpose: namely, establishment of the thesis that it was Russia that saved France from further German aggression in the 1870's and 1880's, with the implication that it was again Russia, and only Russia, who could do the same in a later epoch. Viewed as contributions to the history of the period, therefore, these works do not do justice to the erudition of their authors. They do draw, however, on a large and in some respects unusual body of source materials, not all of which are readily available to Western scholars. That of Manfred, in particular, adds significantly, through the detailed attention given to social and political developments in France during the period in question, to the available historical record.

There are two peripheral fields with relation to which the existing secondary literature was of importance for this study. One of these is the tangled question of Russian policy towards Bulgaria in the 1880's. Not all of the secondary works addressed to the difficulties and adventures of Alexander of Battenberg as Prince of Bulgaria deserve mention here; but special note must be made of Egon Corti's two semi-popular books: *Alexander von Battenberg. Sein Kampf mit dem Zaren und Bismarck*† and *The Downfall of Three Dynasties.*‡ The first of these is of particular value, based as it was on the so-called Hartenau Archive (Battenberg's personal papers), which seems now to have disappeared into the mysteries of Bulgarian archival custody and is (or was, at least, when this present study was prepared) unavailable to Western scholars.

The other of the two fields just mentioned is that of the financial and economic relations between Russia and Germany, and Russia and France, in the late 1880's. Here, mention must be made of the relatively recent doctoral dissertation by René Girault, published under the title of *Emprunts russes et investissements français en Russie. 1887-1914.*§ While focused primarily on developments of a somewhat later date, this

---

to the Tenth International Congress of Historians, at Rome, in September, 1955, and was published in the proceedings of that gathering.

* Moscow: Publishing House "Nauka," 1975.

† Vienna: L. W. Seidel, 1920.

‡ Freeport, N.Y.: Books for Libraries Press, 1970. (This is described as a translation from the German: but I know of no evidence that the German original was ever published. It does not figure, in any event, in the 106 titles of works by Count Corti listed on the cards of the Library of Congress.)

§ Paris: Armand Colin, 1973.

volume contains valuable information on events of the late 1880's. Of further importance are the various books, written for a wider and less specialized public, of Jean Bouvier, a specialist on the French financial history of the period—notably his useful study of the early efforts of the Crédit Lyonnais to break the German near-monopoly on credits to Russia.* And special mention must be made in this connection of the work of the East German scholar, Professor Sigrid Kumpf-Korfes, entitled *Bismarck's Draht nach Russland*.† While concentrating on German-Russian economic and financial relations, this book brings considerable rare and interesting material (the author worked in the Russian, as well as the German, archives) and constitutes a valuable contribution to the history of Russian financial and commercial policies of the day.

I must pass over, at this point, the abundant German secondary literature on the period, including the vast accumulation of Bismarckiana. Some of this sheds occasional minor flickers of light on Franco-Russian relations. I made use of bits and pieces of it, as the reference notes will show.

4. Periodical Literature

On the borderline between these primary materials and the secondary ones stand the files of the daily press and other periodicals of the period, as well as those of the later historical magazines.

When it comes to the newspapers and magazines of the period, the historian, particularly one working in loneliness, finds himself confronted with a serious and discouraging problem. The body of available material is immense; and in many instances the ore is of such low grade, from the standpoint of a study such as this one, that it scarcely pays to attempt to identify and separate the true metal from the dross. Literally years of effort would be required to examine carefully the files of the leading papers of Paris, Petersburg, Moscow, Berlin, and Vienna for the period in question.

Certain of the Russian newspapers being, for various reasons, particularly revealing, I made such use as I could of them, notably Katkov's *Moskovskiye Vyedomosti* and its bitter rival, the Petersburg *Golos*, availing myself for this purpose of the remarkable and unique holdings of the Library of the University at Helsinki. Still others could no doubt have been profitably examined. But the bulk of this material was, as just noted, tremendous, the type small, and the paper often faded. Eye strain and lack of time placed limitations on what could be done. Who-

---

* Bouvier, Jean. *Le Crédit Lyonnais de 1863 a 1882*. Paris: S.E.V.P.E.N., 1961.
† Berlin: Akademie-Verlag, 1968.

ever could overcome these handicaps would find a good deal, I am sure, to enrich and refine the account presented above.

As for the leading Paris papers, as well as the British and German ones, they were used, like certain of the archival collections, primarily for the clarification of questions left unanswered by other sources. Scanned in their entirety, I have no doubt that they, too, would yield a number of items bearing on the subjects of this inquiry. But this, too, would be the work of years. And the same applies to the magazines. Just the perusal of Katkov's monthly *Russki Vestnik* and of Juliette Adam's fortnightly *La Nouvelle Revue* over the years in question proved to be a long and exacting task.

The files of the leading historical magazines, Russian, French, British, German and American, over subsequent decades, also contain occasional items of interest from the standpoint of this study. I did what I could to discover these items and to make use of them. I cannot claim that the search was always exhaustive.

INDEX

Abaza, A. A., Russian Finance Minister, 313, 381, 384, 396

Abd ul Hamid II, Sultan of Turkey, 105, 109, 130, 139, 148, 269, 317

Académie des Sciences, French, 341

Achinov, Russian adventurer, 403-404

Adam, Edmond, lawyer and political figure, 56

Adam, Juliette (Madame Edmond), *revanchiste* publicist: personalia and interest in Russia, 55-58; publishes Grand Duke Nicholas' war memoir, 57-58; 84, 88; journey to Russia, 91-92; 93, 162, 170, 207n; appoints Cyon to *La Nouvelle Revue*, 215-216; 286, 291, 296, 305n, 414

Afghanistan, 90

Agafonov, V. K., lawyer and writer, 87n

Agence Libre, Paris newspaper, 358

Aksakov, I. S., Panslav journalist, 33, 110, 146-147, 172

Alexander, (Grand Duke) of Hesse, 104, 106, 113, 114n, 123n

Alexander, (Prince) of Bulgaria. *See* Battenberg, Alexander

Alexander II, Tsar (1855-1881): and war scare of 1875, 12, 16, 18-22; influences on political attitude, 32-33, 38; and the Russian press, 39; attitude towards military cooperation with France 41-45; criticized by his brother, 58; attempts on his life, 59, 159; death, 60, 75; and German-Austrian Alliance, 71-74; chooses Alexander Battenberg for Bulgarian throne, 103-107; Russian economy during reign, 224, 228-230; and Floquet, 324

Alexander III, Tsar (1881-1894): suspicions against Germany and

Austria, 9-10; and Panslavs, 38; 58; personalia and political attitudes, 60-65, 155, 419-420; and Giers, 64-68, 307-308; interview with Shuvalov after Berlin Treaty, 69-70; and *Dreikaiserbund*, 75, 77-78, 150, 155, 262-264, 308-309, 317; at Skiernewice, 79-80; 85n, 89, 92, 120; Battenberg, and Katkov's influence on, 94, 173-183, 199, 206-207, 240, 259-262, 267, 270, 284, 293-295, 304, 306-308, 315, 317-318; Battenberg, and Russian-Bulgarian relations, 103, 107, 110-118, 122-123, 125-126, 131-132, 139-142, 144, 146-149; effort to remove Battenberg, 148-154, 189-192; opinion on the Straits, 150-152, 155, 243; 153, 155-157; and Appert, 155, 160-167; response to release of Russian anarchists in Paris, 159; 187; and Kumani incident, 196-198; and possible occupation of Bulgaria, 199-202, 205, 210-214, 239; and Kaulbars mission, 199-202, 240; willingness to receive a new French ambassador, 203-213, 218-219; 241-243; crisis of decision over relations with Germany and France, 250-265; 268; comment to French ambassador at 1887 reception, 269-270; and alliance feelers from France, 272-276, 284-287, 308; 297, 301-302; and Katkov's disclosure of the *Dreikaiserbund*, 310-314, 434n1 (Chap. 17); and Reinsurance Treaty, 317-320, 331, 337, 408-410; 322-324; and clandestine operation in Bulgaria, 1887, 332-333; and Ferdinand of Bulgaria, 334-335; and the Land Credit Bank

451

Index

German minority in Russian Poland
and Baltic States, 188
German-Austrian Treaty of 1879,
72-75
German-Rumanian Treaty of 1883, 408
Germany: armed forces, 281; elections
of 1887, 292; Foreign Office, 231-
232, 282; Petersburg embassy of,
238, 300, 318; policy towards Bulgaria, 104, 112, 115, 118-119,
122-123, 136, 145, 202-203, 277-
278; proclamation of German Reich
at Versailles, 412; state bank
(Reichsbank), 342-343; tariff policy,
72; unification of, 7, 42
Giaccone, M., Russian Foreign Office
agent, 299
Giers, Nikolai Karlovich, Russian Foreign Minister, 28, personalia and
political attitudes, 64-67; relationship with Alexander III, 64-68, 213,
306-308; linguistic habits, 65n; and
the *Dreikaiserbund*, 75, 79-82, 91;
attempts to remove, 78, 170, 265,
270-271; at Skiernewice, 79-82; 84,
93, 120; Battenberg, and Bulgarian
situation, 110, 117, 124-126, 128,
131-135, 139-142, 144, 146-148,
195; and estrangement of Franco-
Russian relations, 156-157, 160-162,
164-169, 194-196; 171; Katkov
attacks, 173, 176-179, 181, 183, 215,
251-252, 260-262, 270-271, 284,
289, 299-301, 314-315, 320-321,
372; 186-187; and Kumani incident,
196-198; 199, 201; and acceptance
of new French ambassador, 203-207;
his political detractors, 215; 218,
227, 230, 240; and alleged joint
policy with France against Germany,
243-244; 250; and renewal of
Dreikaiserbund, 253-256, 263; 267;
and alliance feelers from France,
272-274, 282, 284-288; 292n, 293-
295; diplomatic reception, 294; fails
to receive Vladimir Cross, 316-317;
and the Reinsurance Treaty, 317-320,
408-410; 322, 324, 326-327; and
clandestine operations in Bulgaria,
331-334; declines to receive Déroulède, 336; 345; and the "Ferdi-

nand documents," 348, 359; 351,
353, 362, 368; receives Herbert
Bismarck, 370-371; his fifty-year
anniversary jubilee, 372-373; and
French loan negotiations, 381-382,
385; 396; and Achinov affair, 404-
405; 420
Giers, Nikolai Nikolayevich, son of
Nikolai Karlovich, 83-84, 124n,
197n; and Floquet affair, 326;
memoirs, 442
Giers, (Madame) Olga Mikhailovna,
visits Juliette Adam, 91; 294
Girardin, Émile de, French publicist,
and Juliette Adam, 56-57; 93
Girault, René, historian of Franco-
Russian financial relations, 225n, 385,
390, 447
Gladstone, William, British Prime
Minister, 57n
Goblet, René, French Premier, later
Foreign Minister, 257, 266, 270; as
foreign minister, attitude to relations
with Russia, 376-377; 406
Goblet cabinet, 324, 357
Golos, Petersburg newspaper, 96, 217
Golovin, A. F., secretary to and
biographer of Alexander Battenberg,
128n, 133-136
Gontaut-Biron, (Viscount) Elie de,
French Ambassador to Germany,
17-18
Gooch, G. P., historian, 75n
Gorchakov, (Prince) A. D., Russian
Chancellor and Foreign Minister:
and war scare of 1875, 12-22; 32,
42, 57; replaced by Giers, 63-65;
and Berlin Treaty, 68-69; 71, 75,
93, 273n
Gourmont, Remy de, pamphleteer, 413
Great Britain: and Russo-Turkish War,
36-37; and unification of Bulgaria,
144-145
Greece, 138, 173
Greslay, (General), French Minister
of War, 54
Grévy, Jules, French President, 40,
158, 197, 242, 246, 280; letter
to Tsar, 284-286, 290-291; explains
French policy to Mohrenheim, 322-

Library of Congress Cataloging in Publication Data

Kennan, George Frost, 1904-
   The decline of Bismarck's European order

   Bibliography: p.
   Includes index.
     1. Russia—Foreign relations—France.   2. France—
Foreign relations—Russia.   I. Title.
DK67.5.F8K36   327.47'044   79-83997
ISBN 0-691-05282-4